C0-ATC-742

THEATRE ARTS ANTHOLOGY

THEATRE ARTS ANTHOLOGY

A RECORD AND A PROPHECY

Edited by

ROSAMOND GILDER

HERMINE RICH ISAACS

ROBERT M. MacGREGOR

EDWARD REED

New York

THEATRE ARTS BOOKS : ROBERT M. MacGREGOR

GRATEFUL ACKNOWLEDGMENT is here made to all contributors to this anthology, or their heirs, executors or agents, for permission to reprint their articles; to the League of American Authors for advice on a plan whereby all contributors will share in the royalties of this volume; to Theatre Arts, Inc. and Edith J. R. Isaacs for the reprint permission of the copyright owners. Acknowledgment with thanks is also made to the following publishers for their consent to the reprinting of the indicated articles which have appeared in the listed books:

Alfred A. Knopf, Inc. for "The Magic Theatre of Bali" from *Island of Bali* by Miguel Covarrubias, Copyright 1936, 1937, by Alfred A. Knopf, Inc.

W. W. Norton & Co., Inc. for "Tragedy" from *The Greek Way* by Edith Hamilton, Copyright 1930, by W. W. Norton & Co., Inc.; and for "The Four Georges" from *Broadway in Review* by John Mason Brown, Copyright 1940.

University of North Carolina Press for "Drama and the Weather" from *The Hawthorn Tree* by Paul Green, Copyright 1943.

NOTE: As in *Theatre Arts* magazine the editors of this anthology have allowed contributors their individualities in spelling and punctuation.

DESIGNED BY MAURICE SERLE KAPLAN

MANUFACTURED IN THE UNITED STATES OF AMERICA

THIS BOOK IS OFFERED
AS A TRIBUTE OF AFFECTION
AND ADMIRATION BY ITS
EDITORS TO THE EDITOR
EDITH J. R. ISAACS

TABLE OF CONTENTS

IV. MUSIC AND THE DANCE

V. ACTORS AND ACTING

VI. THE FILM

VII. SCENE AND COSTUME DESIGN

VIII. ARCHITECTURE

IX. RADIO AND TELEVISION

X. TRIBUTARY THEATRE

XI. DIRECTING AND PRODUCING

XII. THE FILMS IN REVIEW

XIII. BROADWAY IN REVIEW

FOREWORD

RELIVING the life of *Theatre Arts* magazine, which extended from 1916 to February 1948, the editors of this book have been impressed by two things: the validity of the basis on which *Theatre Arts* was founded and the integrity with which its ideals were maintained through the shifting scenes of theatre life and the cataclysmic events of world history.

Theatre Arts had an extraordinarily long life for a theatre magazine. It survived two world wars and a major depression. It fell at last in 1948, a victim of economic necessity, and though its name continues it should be stated here that the present magazine bears no organic editorial connection with the original *Theatre Arts*. February 1948 was the last issue of the *Theatre Arts* from which this anthology is drawn.

The reason for *Theatre Arts'* long life and for the high standard maintained from 1916 to 1948 is not hard to discern. The magazine reflected a completely homogeneous editorial policy. Established by Sheldon Cheney in the first issues published in Detroit by the Arts and Crafts Theatre, it was maintained, developed and enlarged by Edith J. R. Isaacs during the years when, as editor and publisher, she guided its destinies in New York.

Theatre Arts was founded in the year of Shakespeare's Tercentenary, but its motivation was forward-looking rather than historical. It raised the banner of the "new movement in the theatre," it was the mouthpiece, the forum of the young artist in revolt against the stale, the conventional, the stereotyped. It flaunted the word "art" in the face of "show business" and proclaimed in its first issue the intention to "conserve and develop the creative impulse in the American theatre; to provide a permanent record of American dramatic art . . . to hasten the day when the speculator will step out of the established playhouse and let the artist come in."

The first stepping was done by *Theatre Arts,* itself, perhaps somewhat to its surprise. Its publication during the first World War of a photograph of a German theatre building agitated Detroit and, in answer, Sheldon Cheney took the slim quarterly to New York. Here *Theatre Arts* found the warm support of the young men and women who, putting their war experiences behind them, wanted to build a living theatre in the cause of better international understanding and world peace.

By 1919 Sheldon Cheney, Edith J. R. Isaacs, Kenneth Macgowan and Marion Tucker were the editorial board. From 1924 on Mrs. Isaacs as editor expanded the scope and influence of the magazine, developing it from a quarterly into a monthly and later increasing its size and bulk to include a review of the English theatre, with Ashley Dukes as English editor, and more articles on European theatre by European authorities. *Theatre Arts* became truly international and its contributors and its subscribers circled the globe.

As it grew, other associate editors joined the staff, replacing those who went on to farther fields. The roster includes Stark Young, John Mason Brown, John K. Hutchens, Carl Carmer, Morton Eustis, Edward Reed, Rosamond Gilder, Hermine Rich Isaacs, George Beiswanger, Norris Houghton, Robert M. MacGregor, Cecil Smith. Most of these were dramatic critics as well, and their appraisals of the Broadway stage month by month over the years were the focal point of a magazine that concerned itself with the American theatre as a whole. For, though *Theatre Arts* started as the medium of a group of ardent young revolutionaries in the "art theatres," it grew with them and with the theatre they represented. As they made their way into the citadel of the commercial theatre, *Theatre Arts* was there to welcome them while constantly reminding them of their origins. So, too, did *Theatre Arts* cover the theatre in education and in the community, for it recognized that the American theatre embraces all of these as parts of its mainstream. And so with the films, which were subject to the same calibre of evaluation and, in fact, found nowhere else the over-all critical and pictorial record which *Theatre Arts* made for them.

"A Record and a Prophecy": This was *Theatre Arts'* slogan; this, surely, its achievement.

The "record" is there in the fifty-five bound volumes in which, month by month, the contemporary scene is reported in word and picture, document, criticism and comment. The record of the past is also there—in the special articles and issues which brought to bear on particular subjects the resources of historical research, artistic expression and editorial skill, making these special projects of permanent historic value—the issue on Adolphe Appia, for example, which is still the best study in English of that great pioneer of modern stage design; the issue devoted to the Negro in the American theatre, as another example, which needed little extension to become the definitive book it now is; the issues on Lope de Vega, on musical comedy, on "The World in the Mirror of the Theatre," on Shakespeare and the modern stage, and on the English, French, Swedish and Soviet national theatres—all these remain extraordinarily informative and pictorially captivating.

The "prophecy" is there in *Theatre Arts* too—in the words and deeds of the young men and women of the theatre who received their first recognition in its pages, and in the new ideas, the new impulses, the new paths which were advanced and explored in *Theatre Arts'* constant search for ways in which the theatre might spread to wider fields through wiser methods.

It was this well-nigh inexhaustible treasury of record and of prophecy which made the task of the editors of this anthology surely as difficult as any the editors of *Theatre Arts* itself faced during the magazine's thirty-two years. The first selection of articles for this anthology would have filled half a dozen volumes of this size. And when the "final" selection was made and all the kind consents for reprinting had been received, the number was still great enough to fill at least two books. The last elimination was no more and no less difficult than the first.

What is here, therefore, is an honest indication of the calibre of *Theatre Arts'* contributors and contributions, but only a small fraction of "the best of *Theatre Arts*." Whole categories have had to be cast aside. There are none of the one-act plays—the early works of such playwrights as Eugene O'Neill, Pirandello, Paul Green. There is no poetry, the very core of drama, such as Edwin Arlington Robinson's "Demos and Dionysus," Hallie Flanagan's "Chorus for the Delian Apollo," Langston Hughes' translations of Lorca. And, greatest omission of all, there is none of that visual record—the reproductions of stage designs, one of *Theatre Arts'* chief concerns.

But for all its sins of omission, the editors hope this anthology will give at least an indication of the *Theatre Arts* which Barrett Clark described as "part and parcel of the growing up of the modern American theatre."

"Every month for nearly a third of a century," Mr. Clark wrote, "*Theatre Arts* proclaimed the importance and dignity of the theatre, and was a rallying cry for all of us who helped, or thought we helped. We drew a good part of our inspiration from its pages, and somehow it gave us courage and faith when the going was hard."

"Every month." This was one secret of Mrs. Isaac's success as editor of *Theatre Arts*. She was a brilliant editor, clear and firm in judgment. She had the journalist's sense of the immediate values, the critic's sense of the permanent values. She wrote easily and often for the magazine but she was willing to devote endless time to discovering and developing talent in others, disciplining the exuberant, encouraging the timid and finding in the artist and the technician the unexpected gift of words.

Mrs. Isaacs' range of taste and knowledge—stretching from the written word through the fields of painting, music, dance, poetry, architecture—combined with a generosity of spirit which rejoiced in other people's triumphs rather than in personal recognition, made her influence unique. She balanced this with an able and practical business head, an important part of her editorial equipment, enabling her to see things in concrete terms, to manage all the business affairs of the magazine herself and to recognize the importance of the economic aspects of the theatre. Under her, *Theatre Arts* pioneered along practical as well as aesthetic lines, waging an unflagging campaign for better building laws, reform in ticket speculation, new theatre architecture and cooperation among the many theatre groups. Testimony to this practical interest lies in such special issues as the one called "Stop, Look and Listen!", a series of warnings addressed to architects by theatre artists and technicians, and the one devoted to "What's Wrong With the Theatre?", to which a large group of theatre leaders contributed, as well as in the momentous series of articles by Morton Eustis which became the book *B'way, Inc.*

Despite its limitations, the editors believe the pages that follow will bring the reader the pleasure of discovery as well as the delight of recognition. They offer this anthology in appreciation and gratitude to those friends (Dorothy Whitney Elmhirst, in particular) who contributed through their moral and financial support to the development of *Theatre Arts*. They offer it as well to the artists, playwrights, critics, poets, directors, actors, musicians and dancers of three decades who found *Theatre Arts* hospitable to their dreams and made it what it is—a record of that which it prophesied, a golden book of the Golden Age of the American theatre.

THE EDITORS

I · THE DWELLING PLACE OF WONDER

* * *

ROBERT E. SHERWOOD

*

The Dwelling Place of Wonder

WHEN I CONTEMPLATE the present state of the theatre I am deeply moved to ask myself, "Why am I in it?"

When I look at the prospect of Broadway, and at the Broadway barons and the Broadway critics, I cannot avoid the conclusion that I am in a lousy business and I feel unclean.

I dislike to work in the theatre and I dislike to go to the theatre. The theatre is too expensive, too unrewarding and, above all, too damned uncomfortable. If I want stimulation, I greatly prefer to read. If I want diversion, I prefer the movies (Garbo, Chaplin, Disney, Lubitsch, Capra, Korda, René Clair, Alfred Hitchcock, and so forth).

And yet—I am now itching all over with a desire to write a new play. I want desperately to say something and, whether I like it or not, I know that the theatre is still the best possible place in which to express my most profound convictions.

Give me a newspaper column with a circulation equal to Dorothy Thompson's added to Walter Winchell's—give me a nation-wide hook-up of all the combined networks—give me the same distribution as *Gone with the Wind* (both as published by Macmillan and as filmed by Dave Selznick)—and I still would rather speak my piece to a few hundred people eight times weekly in the Alvin or the Nixon or the Curran.

Is this because I am stage-struck? Perhaps like many another playwright, past and present, I am just a frustrated actor, exercising vicariously an exhibition complex?

Perhaps that's it—but I prefer to believe otherwise.

I prefer to give another explanation of my devotion to a medium in which, by nature and temperament, I can never seem to feel at ease. The explanation is as follows:

The theatre is the spiritual home of one who is barred from the church by distaste for dogma but who still requires and demands expression of great faith.

Does that sound a bit pretentious?

All right.

But I persist in thinking of the theatre as the workshop of Sophocles and Shakespeare rather than a mere testing ground for the movies. I still persist in believing that although the fate of any play that I may write will be decided by the verdict of the most frivolous and inattentive of juries, the New York first-night audience, I must go on trying to say what I want to say in the one way that is best for me to speak.

Sophocles wrote:

> Never to have been born is much the best;
> And the next best, by far,
> To return thence, by the way speediest,
> Where our beginnings are.

Which is certainly a confession of abysmal despair. But Sophocles also wrote:

> *Wonders are many and none is more wonderful than man.*

The theatre is the dwelling place of wonder.

The essence of Shakespeare's philosophy is in Hamlet and the essence of Hamlet is in the speech:

> What a piece of work is man! How noble in reason! how infinite in faculty! in form and moving how express and admirable! in action how like an angel! in apprehension how like a god! the beauty of the world! the paragon of animals! And yet, to me, what is this quintessence of dust? man delights not me; no, nor woman neither.

Was there ever a more magnificent summing up of all human hopes and misgivings? "How like an angel"—and—"this quintessence of dust." And when you read those lines you know that they were written to be spoken from a stage by an actor—preferably an actor not averse to hamming it up a bit.

That is writing for the theatre—bitterness and confidence—exaggerating both, but not illegitimately. Actors and actresses are in themselves fabulous beings and therefore qualified to express that which print can never adequately convey.

What Shakespeare said—what all the great dramatists have said—is that man is frail, man is vain, man is mortal but that he is still capable of reaching, as did Prometheus, into the highest heaven and snatching the very fire from the hand of God.

That is what the theatre has been for, from its very beginning—to make credible the incredible, to awaken the king that dwells in every humble man, the hero in every coward. The Athenian dramatists first attempted and achieved this at a time when men trod warily in a tiny world which was completely surrounded and beset by the supernatural, the divine, the inexplicable. The sun had not then been measured and analyzed chemically. It was a god in a chariot. The wind that blew over Hymettus and the sea that beat against Sunium were dread beings. And yet, in the midst of this fearful bewilderment, in the face of a generally hostile and entirely incalculable Nature, the Athenian dramatists managed to assert for the first time on earth the dignity of man.

"We easily believe that which we wish," said Corneille.

The dramatist cannot be dismissed as merely a successful merchant of wish fulfillment. For there is historical proof that every age which has produced great dramatists—in Greece, in England and Germany and France—has presaged an age of renewed, vigorous assertion of human rights.

For it is in his wishes that man becomes like an angel, like a god. And the assurance that his wishes can and will be fulfilled is the supreme source of inspiration to man.

A great play, then, is a great inspiration, and its performance is a kind of revivalist meeting. The great dramatist is one who knows that in the tragedy of blindness Oedipus discovered the inward power to see the ultimate truth.

Yet I have heard many young dramatists explain their present inactivity by saying that in this, the most tremendous moment in the history of the world, "there is nothing for me to write about."

The American dramatist today can know that he has immeasurably more to write about than Sophocles had, or Shakespeare, and he is far freer to say what he pleases. He does not have to look into legend to find assurance of the essential heroism and nobility of man; he has only to look into this morning's newspaper. And the American dramatist can know also that he has available more good actors and directors and scene designers to interpret and present his works.

Even the speculators and the critics aren't so bad as I often think they are.

February 1941

* *

LOUIS JOUVET

*

Success

THE THEATRE'S ONLY PROBLEM

THERE ARE NO PROBLEMS for the theatre, there is only one problem: success. Without success there is no theatre. It is the only law of our profession. The acquiescence and applause of the public are, when all is said, the sole end of that art called by Molière *"le grand art,"* which is the art of pleasing. *The art of pleasing, in the theatre, is the art of writing plays; it is furthermore, to a somewhat less degree, the art of mounting and acting them.*

Every time the sea-serpent disappears into the South Seas, or there is a lull in crime or scandal at home, the newspapers become concerned over the problems of the theatre and attempt to wring our hearts or fill us with alarm about some particular aspect of theatrical activity. They reveal the unemployment of actors and their misery, or consider the decay of subsidized theatres; they try to disentangle the threads which unite theatre and cinema, or study radio plays or measures for protecting youth and for security against fire-hazard; they debate the wearing of hats in the orchestra, or hold forth on the decadence of stage settings, on transparent scenery, the revolving stage, on theatre architecture or on intermissions. They call attention to the decrease in production or in revenue from taxes; they discuss repertories, or the suppression of cut-rate tickets; they organize for the extermination of ticket-brokers or of tipping in the cloakroom. All of these evils have belonged to our profession forever. Attaching importance to them is a sure symptom of myopia. These conundrums swell and fester through newspapers and idle conversation, and, while they preoccupy the public, one may be sure that there is a graver underlying illness.

One of these false problems, for example, has at last been solved after two centuries of effort: the question of having spectators on the stage. On the improvised structures where theatrical shows were given in the Middle Ages, influential spectators formed the habit of watching the play standing or sitting at the sides of the trestle-stage on which the actors moved. Shakespeare, Corneille, Molière and Racine were, as everyone knows, played under these conditions. For two hundred years this false problem occupied the intellectuals and enlivened chronicles and conversation. To some, it represented the poverty or indignity of the art; to others, a sign of decadence; in everyone's opinion, this infirmity of the stage prevented real progress in the theatre.

Finally the eighteenth century came and a gallant knight set out on a crusade. Louis-Félicité de Brancas, Comte de Lauraguais, succeeded after many attempts in dislodging the spectators and paid a large sum for the privilege, for it was one that had been comfortably established by usage. The spectators gave up the stage, or at least that part of the wings where they had enjoyed the company of the actresses and a view of the house at the same time, and took refuge in the boxes—called since then stage-boxes—which are still to be seen in certain theatres, hollowed out at each side of the proscenium or built into the actual framework. Their intimate position remained the prerogative of the patrons of dramatic art, just as in our day the place where the prompter crouches is reserved for those close to the profession.

It must be admitted that these spectators standing or seated in the wings, these personages of quality who coughed or blew their noses noisily, according to the degree of nobility, conversing freely during dull moments in the play, staring at the rest of the house, sometimes even accosting the audience, entering and leaving at will and mingling with the action in a quite Pirandellian intimacy, enhanced neither the playing of the actors nor the illusion of the setting. However, with some reflection, and in spite of the disquieting effect of this idea on our mental habits, I scarcely see how the suppression of this awkwardness has caused any great gain in dramatic art or hastened its progress. I readily admit that the scene shifters have secured some space, that scene painters have been pleased, that discipline in the wings has been facilitated, and that the actor, whose entrance has been cleared, can now go into action without resembling a gentleman loaded with parcels trying to grab the last free place in a bus.

These are evident advantages, but dramatic art has, strictly speaking, gained nothing from them. It is not the presence or absence of spectators on the stage which matters, *it is the written work, it is the imagination and the voice of the dramatic poet.* What matters is *the direct, intimate connection between the man who speaks—the author—and those who listen—the audience, the public.* And there is no other problem than that, if one wants to define what I have just now called success under its true aspect and in its final truth.

In musing on the aspect and arrangement of our modern auditoriums and the continual attempts at further modernization, I wonder whether even that inconvenience which formerly worried people of the theatre was not, on the whole, preferable to the so-called liberties gained by the reform, and whether the inundation and debaucheries of technical inventions that we have witnessed since this liberation of the stage have been as beneficial as we have been led to think.

In that intimacy and familiarity with the spectator, *theatrical convention* appears to me to have been more pure, and the *sense of ceremony* more fundamental. The rules of that noble game, the theatre, seem to me *more strict* on a stage that remains a platform, where the real illusion, that of the play, defies the false illusion of the scene painter; where, in short, the work and the genius of the playwright are obliged to appeal more to the understanding in an exercise where the actor's talent has scarcely any support beyond the text.

If I had to choose, I should prefer those working conditions to the ones many modern stages offer, with their majestic contrivances and fancy tricks where, amid a debauch of decoration, rather doubtful performances are sometimes perpetrated. Moreover, now that we are rid of that friendliness of the spectator which used to seem such a nuisance, we prove how dear it was to us, and how much we miss it, by the efforts we are making to regain it and by our constant preoccupation with it.

The free stage, guarded at all points—even by State ordinances that say, "No person not officially connected with the company may pass through the stage door"—this free stage is seeking in every way to return to the bosom of its public, and to place its play and its players back in the bath of humanity where they find a more effectual radiation. It may be experiments in giving comedies or tragedies in a circus ring; the joining of stage and hall by a bridge suspended over the audience; the entrance of actors from the aisles; the innovations called "scenes in the audience" where you suddenly see pseudo-spectators rise up and take part in the playing of the actors; it may be the scenic devices invented in Russia or in America, where the audience surrounds curious areas marked out for the performance; it may be attempts to decorate the whole hall as a part of the setting—where the designer, breaking loose from the stage, amplifies his role. Every day, in our time, there is proof in one form or another of the desire of the theatre man to push himself toward the audience, to retrieve by any possible means that intimacy of other times, the necessity for which is one of the laws of dramatic art; that intimate penetration of two elements, audience and performance, whose magnetic powers of attraction are in inverse proportion to their distance.

In spite of all the shocking or distressing implications such an assertion may entail, there is in the theatre just one problem, if one may so designate what will always be an enigma—that is, success.

Obviously one can speak of the dramatic question from a more noble or more abstract point of departure. But this quest for success, this obligation, this compulsion toward the art of pleasing is what seems most evident and most necessary to those who practice our profession.

Success, to be a success, to have a success—the layman does not know, as we do, what that is. He gets an intimation of it when he sees the box-office besieged and has to buy tickets elsewhere at a higher price, and at no profit to us, from speculators. But he does not know the warm emotion, the inward radiance, felt by the actor, the playwright or the director, at that noise like a bag of nuts being shaken or a basket of crabs in commotion that the impatient, chattering audience makes, so that the *régisseur,* the stagehands and the actors come to marvel, through the hole in the curtain, at those hundreds of faces irradiated with impatience and interest. He does not know the voluptuous quiver caused by the sight of a theatre brimming over with humanity, that widening of response, that emotion which you cannot recognize either as tenderness or horror, when the curtain finally rises in silence . . . and there suddenly appears that human monster with a thousand eyes and ears, lurking in the shadow.

If it does seem necessary to seek a problem in the theatre, it may be found in the inexplicable mystery that is exercised every night, in the magic that acts on both audience and actor and is recognized by even the least experienced among us, in that sorcery which a performance evokes, the ordinary and familiar practice of which is a mystery deeper than that hidden in the films or in the wireless. Let me, in explaining this mystery but without dwelling on it too much, propose a few questions whose insolubility allows them, for once, to justify the name of problem.

Why does a theatre with 700 seats, which one night scores an overwhelming success, then have regularly an average of 700 spectators turning their steps toward those 700 places? Why are there not 1400 persons one day, and none at all the next? Railroad stations, beaches, resort hotels, drill fields and even race tracks have not the same characteristic and mathematical constants. They have not the same unanimous life, as Jules Romains would say, nor the same soul as theatres. Because the theatre has a soul!—a soul which is formed little by little from successive accretions of the plays it has housed. A sort of dramatic sediment is deposited, a perfume is released. There are, for example, in any theatre, acoustics not to be altered by specialists, that have a kind of life according to the hour, the setting, the play, its actors and its audience (and it may be said of a theatre that it has the acoustics that it deserves). A theatre has, too, an individual nature, and a definite state of health, also according to its actors, its director, its playwright and its audience, the success or unsuccess of its repertory.

Another question: why, exactly at the fifteenth cue in *Doctor Knock,* when Bouquet-Parpalaid's chauffeur, pointing uneasily at the rickety old automobile, approaches to ask, "Shall I start the car?" and Bouquet-Parpalaid, with false assurance, replies in his suave voice, "Yes, yes, start it going, my friend"—why, if the audience laughs at this fifteenth cue, should Bouquet be reassured, and wink at me stealthily? It is because he is sure the house will be good that evening. And why, if the audience does not laugh at that line, are we completely unable to make them unbend? Do not try to say that this test is not infallible. I have seen Bouquet's beaming or disappointed face more than six or seven hundred times, and in his name I venture to formulate this irrefutable law warranted by his observations. Again, how can you always foretell, on the stage, two seconds before it happens, the resonant silence that your partner's lapse of memory or slip of tongue is going to create?

Why did Pierre Renoir, who was in the garden (stage right) while I was in the court (stage left), feel just as I did, at the same second, after the first few lines of Alfred Savoir's *Margrave*—that the game was lost and the play was not going to go? At that moment I was in the wings, waiting for my entrance cue, and I remember the dismay I felt in listening to my comrades and feeling, like a current of cold air, the disfavor of the entire house. I tried to explain it, blaming the possibility that I had set the stage wrong, or that the audience perhaps was not yet in the right mood, that the beginning of the play might be wrong and the action should possibly start from a point further on. But when, summoning all my courage, I made my entrance onto the stage with the energy of despair, why was it that I definitely understood, from that mute hostility, that glacial cold, that the play had no hope of audience-response?

Why and how can a person, in the theatre, without possibility of error, estimate the meaning of a silence? Why does one never confuse indifference with emotion? The silence of the *dramatic stasis* induced in a human mass hypnotized by pity or terror is no different *to the ear* from the silence arising from boredom or disapproval.

Nor can laughter be mistaken. Why is the laughter directed in ridicule at an actor whose wig has just fallen off or who persists in trying to open a door in the wrong direction always so quickly and so instinctively identified, even by those in the wings, who guess instantly that something abnormal has occurred?

Turning to the matter of plays, to what do Pirandello's works owe their success? To the fact that Pirandello touches—directly and uniquely—what I call dramatic magic; to the fact that he dares, perhaps sacrilegiously, to remagnetize old formulas and transmute long-rejected dramatic values. This remagnetization, this transmutation, borrow from the very mysteries of dramatic art. The six characters who come onto the stage in search of an author, for example, live only because they have picked apart, or divulged, the secret of plot in the theatre—I nearly said they had profaned it, for in all of Pirandello we find a sort of violation of dramatic secrets and formulas; the character, disemboweled by a cruel hand, walks onto the stage trailing his springs and gears after him, and attempts to awaken in the spectator an abnormal curiosity.

To what, on the other hand, do Jean Giraudoux's plays owe their success? The answer is of an entirely different nature. It has also to do, it is true, with dramatic magic, but with a dramatic magic of good alloy and of grand tradition, the only one there is: that of the Word. For we deal here not with a sorcerer who works through necromancy but with a true magician of the theatre, with one who possesses that special eloquence, that sacred gift of speech, which differentiates the writer for the theatre and sets him above and apart from the journeyman-dramatist, as elect and predestined.

To all of us who have acted the plays of Giraudoux it has been a revelation to see and feel the audience for the first time in a state of easy, constant, moved attention, and to experience for ourselves the charmed silence of a crowd, transported by the magic of incantation that only a poet can create.

We can conclude that the great writers alone give this dramatic stasis, this profound emotion where the auditorium is all at once willingly charmed and fascinated by a word, where the entire audience is profoundly struck by the lyric familiarity of a passage such as, for instance, the one at the dawn of Amphitryon's battle, which describes the odor of the hare pie cooked in white wine intruding between the weeping wife and the children getting out of bed, while the trumpets of war resound.

I often have people say to me, "Do you think Giraudoux will last?" All I can say is that he is here now, and that is all we need to know today. If you were all suddenly seized with the idea of denying your admiration and declaring that you do not like Giraudoux, I should tell you, from all I know and have proved, that you were wrong; that three hundred audiences have been enchanted by the theme of *Amphitryon,* already produced thirty-seven times, and that its success is proof of Giraudoux's art. I say "his art," for from the living analysis we have made by interpreting him three hundred times, it is impossible to find in the pure metal of his plays any other element of success than the dramatic theme and the dramatic word—*imagination and speech*—the two simple elements of dramatic art. Giraudoux owes his success to the magical incantation of the dramatic word. There is no other reason.

I should be much astonished if I found myself in a new life, perhaps as a stagehand or designer, and did not see his plays familiar and honored on the stage of the future, when nothing was left of other successes but the dusty sets. If the language of Racine is still spoken in France two hundred years from now, the works of Jean Giraudoux will still be performed. It is his success that we must consider in order to understand the definition of dramatic mystery. Aeschylus, Sophocles, Euripides, Shakespeare, Racine, Schiller, Goethe, are all dramatic poets, great and less great; Giraudoux is among them, and I do not think you will be astonished by that opinion—for it is we who have played him.

But let us return to this problem of the theatre, success. I wish I were able to describe success in the theatre; that paroxysm in performance from which the tumult of applause is born, that dramatic moment when one soul suddenly grips and crystallizes the entire house through a magnificent, miraculous contagion—that unanimity which engenders a communion of the most dissimilar minds through a shared idea or a shared feeling, the recognition of which exalts and overwhelms us.

Theatre business, in spite of its utilitarian character, has from the beginning of time been a priesthood, with its source in the noblest and most disinterested motives of the human heart. But every priesthood, no matter how glorious, has in its flank an ugly wound which obliges the priest to live from the altar, the soldier from his sword, the lawyer, as well as the doctor, from his clients. Let us say it, therefore: the theatre is a business from day to day, from week to week. A play that makes no profits cannot remain on the bill. In the theatre genius gets no credit, as in the other arts where the painter, the engraver, the musician, the novelist have the right to accumulate in patience and poverty the fruits of their labors and their talents. Not the playwright nor the actor nor the director can live without success, without material and moral approbation: without gate-receipts and without applause. Moreover, the public seldom gives one without the other.

Here, then, is the problem and the law of the theatre: above all other considerations, *the theatre must be first of all a business, a flourishing commercial enterprise—it is only then that it may obtrude into the domain of art.* There is no dramatic art without success. No dramatic work is valid unless it finds a public to listen to it and make it live. The alternative is shocking and exposes the theatre to all kinds of compromises and special inducements, even to those of *fashion.* In theory or in practice, this law of success clarifies all theatrical activity and justifies all dramatic tendencies and procedures. The necessary yet blind collaboration of an audience, which is, at the same time, the object and the reason for dramatic work, subjects the theatre to the necessity to please.

It is neither greed nor vanity that is responsible for this desire to please. In the playwright, and in the actor, too, it is more like a perpetual hunger of the heart which neither riches nor fame can satisfy. We all have need of faces and hearts turned toward us, you may be sure. The baker who sells his bread, the florist who sells his flowers, do it not so much in order to live as to feel themselves less alone, and I do not mention the deeper and more serious need that makes the poet speak, or the more modest but just as imperious need of the interpreter of a role, who tries to live a fiction. All those whose work is with the drama, either directly or indirectly, are motivated by this necessity to please—guided, sanctioned and rewarded by success alone.

Among the torments invented in his *Inferno,* Dante forgot that of the playwright obliged to be played, or the actor required to play, in an empty auditorium, where voices would be mute and where inferior talents would slowly perish from suffocation. To gain consciousness of himself, to progress, to live by his trade both materially and spiritually, the actor, as well as the author, must have a public to approve him.

Molière, who said *"C'est une étrange entreprise de vouloir faire rire des honnêtes gens,"* was himself constrained by the law of success, and he formulated it undoubtedly with a little melancholy: *Le grand art est de plaire."* And such is the new attitude toward success—to succeed in the art of pleasing.

A dramatic work, an entertainment for an evening, is a conversation between author and audience, offering a sort of spiritual proposition to be accepted or refused. It is of first importance that this acceptance or rejection be understood in the same way by the author who writes the play, the players who act it and the audience who listens to it. The playwright is the point of departure and has the principal responsibility, he is at the apex of the trinity, he is the creator: he alone has the right to this title, for the whole derives from him.

If I ever write a treatise on dramatic art, I will limit myself to quoting all those who cooperate in the pursuit and execution of the pleasures ordained in the theatre. The actor for one example—the author's proxy and living witness who translates the thoughts of the dramatic poet—knows a great deal more about how to live on a stage than do many of those who speculate and talk about the theatre. Take this case. One day I suggested to Pierre Renoir that he read a learned critical study on an important classic role which he was going to interpret. After weighing for a moment the praises I heaped on this study, he answered with old-fashioned simplicity, "No, that doesn't interest me." And when I protested, astonished at his refusal, he was silent for a time, and then said, "No, my friend, I assure you it does not interest me. Those people, you see, are not in at the start. They are only at the finishing-post."

And that, in sum, is the difference in the points of view. You have to start from the beginning, run the race and steer the play, in order to know our craft. The audience, like the critic, are only at the goal.

May 1936

HARLEY GRANVILLE-BARKER

*

A Letter to Jacques Copeau

My dear Jacques Copeau,

You are good enough to ask me whether I think you should accept the directorship of the Comédie-Française if it is offered to you. Yes, I do.

Upon principle, you should. André Maurois, that most apt and valued interpreter between my country and yours, has lately quoted with approval one of the minor watchwords of the British Army: Never ask for a job, never refuse one. You have not asked for this. But if you see any reasonable chance of putting the principles you stand for into practice at the Comédie, it is an opportunity and a duty you cannot refuse. Make what conditions you must, but the fewer the better.

Some people may wonder that you make any question about it. How refuse such a prize? But I know very well why you stand in doubt. You did not first sink your literary career in the quixotic enterprise of the Vieux Colombier, nor leave that rather than surrender it to mere profit-making and go out into the wilderness (even the blossoming wilderness of the Côte d'Or) and begin again from the beginning, to be tempted at this time of day by the externals of success. You are asking yourself whether the straight and logical road you have followed (those who think it other cannot have thought about the matter at all) really leads you to the corner of the rue de Richelieu. As you ask me also, I must tell you why I think it does.

You first came to grips with the theatre as a critic; and, being yourself something of a creative artist, you were hard upon anything that seemed to you dead or dishonest art. Yet (for the same reason) you had little patience with the man who could be content with the easy task of giving good advice. You felt you must prove your contention that for the theatre to regain its touch with life and all that was newly alive in art and literature it must cut free from the hectic Boulevard. Hence the Vieux Colombier.

As to what was newly alive in art, I fancy you were at first a little too intrigued by all those clever devices of staging and decoration that were then in their heyday. This was natural. Some of them were very good and others quite amusing. But the game of dressing up your stage in odd shapes is such an easy one to play, and it contributes just as much to the art of the theatre as the costume of the actor does to the playing of Hamlet or Tartuffe—just as much and no more. The art of the theatre is the art of acting, first, last, and all the time. You very soon found that out. It was interesting to see how quickly you absorbed all that was fruitful in the new staging, and I believe what chiefly attracted you to it was that it is essentially the old staging restored. For you are, like all good Frenchmen, like all good artists possibly, a traditionalist (by which I do not mean a Conservative) at heart.

Had I had any doubts about this they would have been resolved when I saw your performances in London last year. You went to Pernand, did you not, because you felt you were not on firm enough ground at the Vieux Colombier. You wanted to "kiss the soil" and regain strength. Well, you construct and perform, you and your actors, one quite primitive play, very simple, very genuine; that is kissing the soil to some advantage. The next day you gave us Molière. It does not become a mere Englishman to speak on the subject; but if that was not a truly traditional performance, with all the spirit and the strength of Molière conserved, and all the dead redundancies of so-called tradition cut away, then I never saw or imagined such a thing. Do you see now why I think you are heading—and always have been—towards the rue de Richelieu?

I wrote to you afterwards, you may remember, begging you to spend no more time kissing the earth or laying foundations, but to go ahead with your building; that is to say, with the interpreting of one good play after another, letting the art of one beget the better art of the next. For—to keep to the apter metaphor—once the strain is sound, that is how good art does naturally increase, and after painful years of gestation it will suddenly come to amazing fertility and flower in a hundred unexpected ways. Moreover all the virtue goes out of a simplicity that is guarded too carefully and too long, and it becomes an affectation of the barrenest sort. Besides, you yourself it seemed to me had by this completed a remarkable apprenticeship, begun when you bound yourself twenty years ago to the single-minded service of your art. There is now nothing in the theatre that you have left untested; criticism, playwriting, staging, acting—you have turned your hand to them all, and no one can talk nonsense to you about them with impunity. But in most apprenticeships a man is trained in the old ways, and he either remains in them distrusting the new, or turns to the new and comes to condemn the old. You have passed from the new thing which first attracted you back to sympathy with the old. You are still for the new thing, I think, but not merely because it is new. You see it in perspective now, while the old, with its tradition, is a living force to you, not a mechanical creed which you have been forced to take for granted. You are fitted, then, if ever a man was, to make the old thing new again; and from time to time, this must be done.

For, to come to the other side of the question, will not the Comédie, on its part, be wise to welcome you? I speak diffidently here. I have on my shelves a book which tells me how the Comédie Française is organized, and details the Decree of Moscow and the rest. That is very interesting. But what I have always wanted to know is how it is really run. We in England never feel less than great respect for the Comédie, and at its best, it commands our unstinted admiration. But those of us who have studied the administration of theatres wonder sometimes, not that it is not always at its best, but how, with such a constitution, it can in these days function at all. Is it by doing lip service to its rules and regulations and ignoring their plain meaning half the time? We English are thought to be experts at that sort of thing; if we tried to run the British Empire, we are told, according to the letter of its laws, it would stop functioning in a fortnight. That is but half the truth, and not, perhaps, the more important half. Every now and then we give legal sanction to inevitable change. Our belief is that constitutions great and small are kept in health by having scope for change, but also that they are held in public respect by having the letter of their law kept not too remote from the practice of it. And if in some of the fine arts we may be to seek, in the art of government we are not unpracticed.

There is, alas, no such institution in England as the Comédie Française; but when we have one, the less it need live in bonds to rule and regulation, the better it will be. Art of all kinds seems to rebel against organization. Yet the art of the drama must, for obvious reasons, be organized. There is no art that is easier to exploit and degrade. If its credit is to be sustained it must be given the dignified shelter of a public institution. You in France have long realized that. We never have. Therefore the standard of your theatre never falls below a certain worthiness; but ours, in spite of much self-sacrifice and the leading of many forlorn hopes, may collapse in the course of a few years from brilliance to ignominy.

But all systems and institutions have the defects of their qualities; and you hint to me—though, indeed, I know it, for the matter is public property—that the revered Comédie is for the time being in a bad way, and at odds with itself. It would only be impertinent for me to discuss the rights and wrongs of the dispute; but let me suggest this to you as an aid to your own judgment upon it. When the human machinery of an institution will not work there is likely to be something else the matter, and it is usually that the institution itself has temporarily lost purpose and direction. I spoke just now about the new and the old in drama, and you may tell me that there should be no such distinction made. I agree. But for the last forty years or so such a distinction has very visibly existed in the European drama, and it is foolish not to recognize it. The difference does not lie so much, perhaps, in the drama itself, as in the point of view of the actors and producers who interpret it to the public. It is about time that these points of view were, as far as may be, reconciled, so that the theatre as a whole—and the public—may gather in the harvest of the good work that has been done in that time and move forward to the ripening of the next.

Two great changes have taken place in European drama during the last forty or fifty years, both beneficent, each in its way a token of vitality. In the eighteen-eighties came the new realism. Ibsen was its prophet. Brieux and Antoine a little later carried the torch aloft in France, Lugné-Poë still waves it. I detest the term realism, it has been so misused. But it still has a fundamental meaning; and no dramatist, director or actor influenced by the movement but has learnt this from it: that a play's business is to interpret life, not to imitate other plays. Periodically, belief in that simple truth must be revived; from this revival of it a new and worthy drama has sprung. And the one movement gave birth to another, the inevitable sequel, though, as a sequel, it has so far been less remarked. Realism in new drama sets one looking realistically at the old; historically, that is to say. The second movement then (but the change it implies is still incomplete) has been an endeavor to give our classics new life by acting them in the old way—according to the spirit of it, if not the letter.

Institutions are not easily affected by such movements. In this lies their strength, for they may be but passing fashions. It is their business, all the same, to distinguish between the ephemeral and the significant. There is no good reason they should not do it betimes. They cannot shut their doors against all change, and survive. But they are apt—this is their particular weakness—to compromise belatedly between past and present by selecting the second-hand. And for that we damn them as old-fashioned; a deadly damnation.

Once again, I am not criticizing the Comédie. I am not competent to do so. I should praise heaven if we had a theatre in England of half its merit. But when I read that a certain play by Jules Romaine was to be produced there, and it never was, I wondered why. A most admirable play, I thought, when I saw it elsewhere if not a play for the million. Will it find its way into the repertory twenty years hence? It must have been about then that I saw at the Comédie an excellent revival of *Les Corbeaux*. I could but think, of course, how much more Becque and the French drama would have profited by the play's welcome there in his lifetime, before those quaint costumes had come to look quite so quaint, and ask myself were there Henry Becques of today qualifying in semi-barrenness for posthumous fame. (I should sometimes sit asking the same sort of questions, I don't doubt, in an English National Theatre, were we lucky enough to have one.) And a performance of Shakespeare there set me wondering why its sponsors should apparently be so unaware of all that has been done during the last thirty years not only in England, but in France—and not least by you!—to clear away the encrusted rubbish of false tradition from the staging of his plays. (But goodness knows an Englishman need not criticize this; most English productions still show an ignorance as great, and far, far less excusable.)

Are these, or something like them, the questions that are troubling you? Are you doubtful whether, once inside the doors of the Comédie, you would have the power to give them the answers that your whole career has pledged you to give? I guess at the difficulties, but I hope for your sake, and for the Comédie's, that they can be resolved. For it seems to me that the drama is perenially in need of these two things: of the artist who is free to follow his star till his talent has matured, and of the theatre in which good work may be made secure. But if the two are never to come together (the organized theatre seldom gives birth to such an artist, and when it does, it too often loses him) both will suffer and the drama will stay impoverished. For without security the artist is likely to find himself ploughing the sands. He produces his plays if that is his bent; they are done with, the actors disperse, next month's or next year's tide washes everything away, and he must begin again. He begins again, and yet again; but it is not in human nature to go on indefinitely beginning again without loss of faith and of power. While as to the theatre, if lacking its security, the artist ploughs the sands, he may be still more certain that with no fresh and free inspiration to revive it once and again, mere organization will stick in the mud.

If the difficulties are definite, I wish you and the Comédie could discuss them in public. Is that a startling suggestion? It would be enlightening to all of us who have the welfare of the theatre at heart and are conscious of the difficulties of advancing it in these changing times. You would, I know, bring your best brains to bear upon the problem whether you were to share in its solution or not. And one of the fine things about a public institution is that its affairs can be discussed publicly, and people will take an interest in them.

I remember so well being present once at *La Cérémonie*. There was a disturbance, in the gallery, begun by an over-vociferous welcome to some actors, a little booing at others who were held to be guilty of—heaven knows what administrative misdemeanor. (Ah, *one* rule I would make in such a theatre. No actor should be responsible to the audience for anything but his acting; nor, if he were wise, would he wish to be.) But a gentleman rose in his stall and, facing the brawlers, called out, *"Respect pour la Comédie"*; and the noise soon died down. Here, I thought, whatever its passing troubles, is a theatre to be proud of, a theatre that claims, as its due, the *respect* of its public.

My dear Copeau, let nothing that is not of vital import stand in the way of your joining it. You would fulfill your career there; and surely it would gain from you—as from whom else but you—that fresh inspiration with which every such society must be revived from time to time, if it is not to perish.

Very sincerely yours,

H. G.-B.

October 1929

* *

IVOR BROWN

*

Dramatic Criticism—Is It Possible?

DRAMA IS the most cooperative of the arts, but it is habitually practiced by people who are wholly incapable of cooperation. That is why most rehearsals are thunderstorms and the dress-rehearsal is a mixture of hurricane and cataract comparable only to the storm in *King Lear*. Yet out of this tumult something is born; out of these angry, jealous, obstructive personalities even artistic truth and beauty may emerge; out of minds which have no comprehension of the play and could not explain the meaning of the lines which the lips so effectively speak may light and lucidity proceed. Out of darkness, blaze. That is the everlasting miracle of the theatre and the everlasting confusion of the critic.

The critic of books and the critic of painting have an abiding, an acknowledged, an inescapable thing on which to work. The author writes his book and passes his proofs; he may have bad luck in its marketing; it may be published at a moment of public crisis and so be submerged in the general excitement about high, political things. But he cannot have bad luck in the presentation of his book. He has finished and passed it. It is his responsibility and his alone. So with the painter. He too may have bad luck in the marketing. But the completed canvas is his own private affair. If it be good, let him be justly praised; if not good, justly blamed. No interpreter, no executant, can get between the book or painting and the public, as he can get between the public and its plays and music. In the case of a book there are no complications. There is no tangle of supposedly cooperative forces which entirely refuse to cooperate. There is no chance of a text or a canvas being ruined on the day of judgment because the scenery falls down or the leading lady has a fit of temperament or temperature or both, or because the leading man forgets his lines and interpolates dialogue of his own. He who writes a play, far more surely than he who marries and begets, gives hostages to fortune. He who tries to judge it is no more fortunate. He is not assessing something static, something coolly considered and signed, but a brew of chances and changes, accidents and personalities. It may be that everything will come out better than right on the night, but it may be disaster, a disaster for which the author is not responsible at all. And how can the critic know that?

Every play is fairly certain to have had an elaborate and exhausting secret history before ever it comes up for critical judgment. The dramatist, no doubt, had an idea and put it down in dramatic form. He composed a text and, if he were an innocent beginner, he thought that was the end of it. But, when he went to market, he found that A. would only produce it if there were a part for Miss B. and that Miss B. would only play the allotted part if it were entirely altered. A director, Mr. C., is engaged and promptly, and no doubt properly, quarrels with Miss B. Over the text fly recriminations; round it creep intrigues. At last Miss B. gets a Hollywood contract and vanishes. So A. abandons the play.

The author and Mr. C. then look round for a new backer (or "angel") and one is found who thinks it a fine play for Miss F., but only if the end is entirely different. The dramatist is cajoled into radically rewriting his third act, and Miss F. starts rehearsing. After a stormy day she throws up her part but with a nimbleness, most characteristic of leading ladies who throw up parts, she manages to catch it again before anybody else gets hold of it. Then somebody falls ill, somebody drops out, there are wars or rumors of wars, and the backer beats a retreat. So nothing happens for another six months. Then negotiations for a star begin all over again and the machinery of rehearsal is cranked up for renewed action, and breaks down owing to an epidemic of influenza or measles. To cut the story short, the play is finally given a trial performance in a suburban theatre with inadequate preparation and is a complete travesty of what the author had originally intended. His darling idea has vanished altogether and he can scarcely recognize his dialogue.

In any chapter of accidents there may be a happy ending. Perhaps what emerges at last just happens to "let go" on the first night; the piece is purchased and reproduced at a central theatre and once more it "goes." In that case the author, whose original play might never have succeeded at all, is in the best of luck; good direction and good acting have made many a dramatist unjustly celebrated in a night. But, of course, the process may work exactly the other way. The new ending strikes the public and the critics as vapid; the director has been so pleased with his own notions that he has entirely obscured the author's, and that poor wretch is then criticized severely for writing a play without an idea, whereas, in fact, he has been striving all the while to get his idea reinserted. The leading players, who have to play passionate love scenes, have had a violent row and are not on speaking terms the moment they leave the stage, and the stage manager has been reduced to such a state of nervous misery that he rings down the curtain a minute too soon on the first act, thus entirely extinguishing what point that act may have had. After that, the nervous misery of the first night afflicts the whole company and the timing of the dialogue goes wholly astray. Result, calamity.

What has all this, it may be asked, to do with criticism? Everything, if the object of criticism in the theatre be the dispensing of justice and the awarding of credit and blame, where these are due, by a discerning interpretation of the article presented. The critic of a book or picture, as was said, has a static and signed piece of one man's work in front of him. But the critic of a play is dealing with a cooperative venture which has a complicated secret history; he may censure the author for a line which the author never wrote, the actor for a make-up or a series of moves and intonations which were forced upon him, despite his protests, by the director, and the director himself for bad lighting, due to an electrician's negligence, or for clumsy interpretations which he has been striving hard to eliminate.

The number of possible traps for the dramatic critic are consequently immense. He ought to know when an actor is scoring in a very easy, effective, or "fat" part and when he is more meritoriously making something of an unshowy, unattractive role. But the critic cannot possibly tell whether the director has given a poor player his good ideas and has literally imposed a fine performance on him or her by dictating the delivery of every line and the making of every move, as does quite often occur. All the critic can do is to record and to assess as fairly as possible what has been publicly presented. That presentation may be a travesty of what one or all of its agents intended. So a hostile criticism will almost certainly be regarded by the promoters and executants of the play as a sign of malice as well as of stupidity, because these promoters and executants, knowing the secret history of the piece, usually believe that the critic ought somehow to have divined it. By some miracle of comprehension he should have made allowances for the fact that some of the scenery never arrived in its finished form until two hours before the curtain rose, and that the leading lady had just failed to get her divorce.

A further nuisance, from the dramatic critic's point of view, is the inability of the general public to realize that every performance of a play is a new one and possibly a very different one. What seemed to go brilliantly at the dress rehearsal may go sluggishly on the first night, and the player who was in grand form on Monday may be careless or below par on Tuesday. The public who criticize the critic are never, unless they were also first-nighters, seeing the performance which he saw. Moreover, some of the players do actually listen to criticism or are made to do so by the director. Consequently they alter their performances on purpose. Thus a member of the public may say to a critic "How could you blame A. for not being audible? I thought he spoke beautifully." No doubt, he did speak beautifully—later on, after having been justly censured for mumbling.

The up-shot of this is the opinion that the criticism of plays, like the production of them, must be, to some extent, a chancy, hit-or-miss business. If criticism of drama is regarded as an administration of justice, then the people who are to be criticized should be prepared to receive inequity, because justice depends on knowledge of all the facts of the case and these facts the critic, coming fresh to it all at 8 or 8:30 P.M. on a certain evening, cannot even begin to imagine or comprehend. Furthermore, if he is working for a daily paper, he has to dash away and write at top speed. That is not an excuse for ignorant or impudent criticism, but it is mentioned as some excuse for slap-dashness. Sometimes speed helps; but sometimes it causes you to write things which you later repent. The better the play, the more it will need second thoughts. C. E. Montague was profoundly right on this issue when he wrote:

And yet for old theatre notices there may be a kind of excuse. You wrote them in haste, it is true, with few books about you, or moments to look a thing up; hot air and dust of the playhouse were still in your lungs; you were sure to say things that would seem sorry gush or rant if you saw them again in the morning. How bad it all was for measure, containment and balance! But that heat of the playhouse is not wholly harmful. Like sherris-sack in the system of Falstaff, it hath a twofold operation; "it ascends me into the brain . . . makes it apprehensive, quick, forgetive, full of nimble, fiery and delectable shapes." At least it sometimes gives you that illusion; below yourself in certain ways, you hope you are above yourself in others.

It certainly works both ways. The authors and players get it both ways too. They may be praised for what they did unwittingly or at the dictation of another, while they may be given a bad mark for something which was not their fault at all. On the whole, as far as the English theatre is concerned, the actors rather than the authors receive the best of the bargain. Criticism more often exonerates them than it does the dramatist when a bad evening has been endured.

Frequently, when sympathy has been expressed for the players who had to appear in such wretched stuff, the truth is that better direction and performance might have transformed the affair altogether. But critics are usually slow to make that assumption and there is a kind of chivalry in this attitude. The cast, after all, suffer the pains of hell when they are acting a comedy at which nobody is laughing and know half way through the first night that the affair is "a flop" and that their labors will be in vain and unrewarded. So the merciful judges prefer to flay an invisible author instead of the poor wretches who have been undergoing *peine forte et dure* beneath their eyes.

Therefore let those who are intending a stage career, either with pen or person, have no hopes of meeting justice in the public comments, and let the critic who wants to be fair and helpful realize no less that the odds are all against his achieving that high purpose. He may succeed in many other ways. He may be amusing without malice, he may inspire the public to playgoing by the enthusiasm which he brings to his job, he may, by his writing, perpetuate the triumphs of an essentially impermanent art and set down precious records and portraits of the master-players before "into the night go one and all." But these activities, in fact, are not really criticism at all. They are essay-writing in general and not the assessment of technical issues. To be a ready provider of first-rate descriptive reporting may be to render the theatre invaluable service. (A good deal of the classic criticism of the English stage is just that.) But to be accurately magisterial, if that is your notion of the job, is beyond any man's scope. The elements of the drama's cooperation are at once so complex and so clandestine that the looker-on can only fumble to the best of limited ability with the issue relevant to the praise of this factor and the blame of that. What he sees and hears on that first night is half a work of art and half sheer accident. So the dramatic critic who sets up to be a justicer must bear in mind that, strictly speaking, dramatic criticism is impossible.

November 1940

* *

WILLIAM SAROYAN

*

How to See

IT IS AN ILLUSION that people with normal eye-sight are able to see.

The theatre exploits this illusion and either gives vision new depth or a fresh dismissal, while the child, the poet and the scientist (all essentially and deeply related) really go about seeing things. They may exclude a great deal more than they include, but whatever *is* included is seen truthfully.

The depth of vision which the theatre sometimes provides is not organically optical—the vision is not the eye's, it is the spirit's—which is very fine. The theatre's dismissal of vision is also all right, inasmuch as it is patterned after the same process operating in most human beings.

A suggestion of a familiar scene is enough for a stage because there is no importance in the familiarity, and once its existence and reality has been agreed upon, the beholder of a stage-set may forget it and watch the play. Since each beholder of a play is in a different part of the theatre from every other beholder of it, closer or farther away or more to the left or right, it is necessary for theatrical emphasis to be on other things than magnification or isolation of images —the camera is the instrument for that.

What is important, however, is for whatever is intended to be felt sharply to be set in reality sharply—a problem of space, color and light. This is so because all the senses are related, and unless one sees a thing clearly, one very often cannot hear the sound the thing makes (speech if the thing is a human being), and in the theatre if you can neither see nor hear clearly, you cannot understand. Not to understand is not to enjoy. And the theatre must be enjoyed, and I mean by *everybody*. No play can please the orchestra and displease the gallery and be effective. Art must reach everybody, but in the theatre it seldom reaches anybody. Even when it has every right to do so—even when it is certainly art and ready to be received by everybody—the inept bungling with the theatre's limits by artistic people and crackpots keeps the work from reaching anybody.

The very nature of play and theatre asks for intimacy, definite contact between those playing and those being played to. Nothing is more absurd than people with opera glasses in theatres. It is like taking a microscope to a bar with which to study a drop of Scotch while one sips a Scotch and soda. In the first instance you are either there—actually *in* the play—or you're not, and no opera glass is going to get you there. And in the other, it is irrelevant what a drop of Scotch looks like under the microscope if you are fond of Scotch. It is chemistry if you are not—in which case the laboratory and not the bar is the place for the research. Opera and field glasses are for vistas, clouds, and otherwise inaccessible areas.

The source of all reality is vision, and no creation of the universe is more magnificent than the eye, which is found in so many creatures or—for all I know—in *all* creatures of the animal world. I suppose that anything which can move has vision, and anything which moves has something of the divine in it. Spirit, or some of the overflow of universal energy. There is no doubt that the mouse knows terror when it beholds the cat, delight when it sees the piece of cheese. All things separate and isolate in space, excepting perhaps certain migratory sea plants, have vision, and even these very likely have eyes (or vision) evolving in them.

We may assume—in fact we must—that the eye has *made* the world. Consequently, we must also assume that the greater part of the world's shabbiness is the result of careless looking. Heedless vision. Blind acceptance. Taking for granted. Remembrance of the form of a thing before it has been understood in its depth. Everybody eats a peach and forgets to *see* and understand it. No thing can be understood until it has been truly *seen*. No thing can be truly seen unless it is truly looked at, and as the reality of a thing becomes full to one sense, it begins to become full to the other senses, so that finally, beginning with seeing, one knows a thing in all the ways that it is enjoyable to know it—and all experience is fuller, deeper and more enjoyable. The beginning of the full exploitation of the experience of living (of being separate, detached, free, and charged with energy) is through seeing. Perfume, as a coarse example, is absurd (because artificial) apart from a specific living human being, inasmuch as to see perfume at its source is both impossible and undesirable, and inasmuch as it has been evolved solely to form a delightful mist about women—either in order to call the attention of the eye to the form of the woman, or to divert the attention *from* the form to something else.

People seem to *see* only the most grotesque images of life and the world, skipping over the magnificences of the ordinary. Nobody thinks of looking at one leaf of a tree, or at a blade of grass, or at a grain of sand, or at one flower, or at one of anything. People do not even see one another. Nobody is educated to see. Before a child has even begun to know objects as themselves he is taken to school and asked to know the words that stand for the objects. This continues from kindergarten to grade school, and from there through high school and college, so that by the time a child may be said to have gotten himself an education, he is away over to hell and gone in meaninglessness. You would think that the objects of reality deserved only to be known through the images of the various letters of the alphabet joined together in a word to stand for the symbol of the object: its name. Leaf. Cow. Human being. Gorilla. That is why circuses are continuously fascinating to everybody, no matter how old or young, how undeveloped or cultured. Words written or spoken have almost no part in the reality of a circus going on. In fact, whenever words *are* used, they are used only by the ringmaster who deliberately or unconsciously makes fun of them, saying co-los-sal, spec-tac-u-lar, and so on, as if the words could never in a million years mean anything.

Most people don't look at anything. Considering the wasteful speed with which most people move around, this is understandable. The contemporary compulsion of society to save what is known as precious time is responsible in part for nobody having time to see anything. All surfaces of things are known vaguely and more or less by heart, so that contemporary reality is without dimension or truth. People never see the streets over which they move every day. To see a street one must look at it in relation to everything on it, near it, and over it—particularly over it. Not to see what is over things is to go, literally, closer and closer to the grave, which is never more than twelve or thirteen actual feet beneath the eye.

It is not my intention to go into this matter in any detail, but this does not mean that the matter is not of the very greatest importance, and I might say *immediate* importance. The props of one configuration of reality are now swiftly collapsing, and if the next configuration is to be an improvement it is imperative for the living to teach themselves and their children how to see. Because an eye is physically healthy does not mean that no attention needs to be paid to the matter of what it is for, how it is to be used, or what its effective use has to do with all other things. From earliest childhood I have made a study of the relation between vision and all other things, and I believe it should be known that it will be impossible for the living to achieve grace or dignity, adulthood or power, effectuality or understanding until they learn to see. To look sharply means to know what you and things are about, and that is the beginning also of criticism. It means establishing your own personal center in things, and being able to establish for others their centers. Seeing one thing whole is the beginning of seeing all things whole, and when you see all things whole you know where the defects are. Knowing where the defects are indicates what needs to be done, and how it needs to be done. All this is so fundamental that nobody, let alone any of the giant intellects like Marx and the others who wanted or want a better world, has ever bothered to fool with it. The problem of the world is inevitably the problem of each person in it, and the place to start improving is *in* each person. Assuming that all people are hopeless fools is a fundamental error as well as an insult. My theory is that potentially every person in the world is the sum of the best in all things, which is a very great deal. And this sum is not by any means inaccessible. The natural equipment of every person is generally complete. It is simply that this equipment is never exercised, developed and used.

Along about now I believe it is time for everybody to return to the beginning of things and work on out, one thing at a time, toward whatever one's natural limits may be. The world is full of messages on how to do all the irrelevant and premature things, such as how to write, how to make friends, how to be a success in the higher accountancy game, or how to make $500. You really don't need to bother about any of that stuff. All you have to do is learn to see. You've got eyes.

March 1941

* *

ARTHUR HOPKINS

*

New Theatre Freedoms

PLAYS OF THE FUTURE will be more concerned with character than event. This is in line with other art forms as well as with scientific research which is seeking the essence of being rather than dwelling on details of its manifestations.

Look at the disproportionate acceptance of *Life with Father* in this light. Nothing much happens in the play, but there is a superficial revelation of the inner workings of human beings which is not dependent upon crisis or situation, the only problem approaching decision being Father's delayed christening.

Another demonstration of this expanding area of drama is the eager welcome of *I Remember Mama* and *The Late George Apley*. Again little happens in either of these plays. Some critics discover that they are not really plays at all, which only means that they are not plays according to past definitions.

Among the new freedoms that are promised the world this is perhaps a major new freedom of the theatre world.

Certainly there is a greater and richer variety of expression in character revelation than in the altered application of long used situations. Someone once took the trouble to enumerate the basic situations available to the dramatist. I doubt if anyone would attempt to catalogue the number of character facets that are employable. It would be like counting fingerprints.

That the inner man is a richer field than his outer manifestations is evident in much classic literature. One of Hamlet's soliloquies unfolds a more exciting panorama than all of the frantic killings in the last scene. The heart is an inexhaustible source of dramatic riches, yet it is the one source most neglected in the flood of plays stuffing the mails of the past decades.

The fuel of the heart moreover has unexpected by-products. *I Remember Mama* is striking evidence of this. Mama lived in her heart. The daughter, writing of Mama, wrote from the heart. What began as a simple story of a simple woman wanders into profound territory without realizing it. Four major problems of today, without being mentioned, find their complete answer in the play, and in each case the answer is the same. Mama's heart.

Countless plays have been written about woman's place in the world, ignoring the fact that God entrusted to woman the continuity of the race. In Mama's presence we realize that this divine election, when fully accepted, exalts woman above any man-given honor.

Endless plays have been written about the divorce evil, about the problem of children left suspended upon the stricken family tree, and about child delinquency. How could such catastrophes visit Mama's family? Where would any of them turn without her? Where would she be without them? Where would Papa turn?

In the play Mama has lifted marriage above the selfish storms that wreck homes. What husband or child would dream of bringing shame to her who never knew shame?

A tragic price is being paid for the mistakes of "getting" civilization. If there is a better world, it will be a giving world. Up to now, only war has aroused men to ask "What can we give?" "How can we serve?" When these questions become the fixed demands of a peaceful world mankind will have thrown off the last demand of war.

Mama has always known the joy of serving. She has never asked what service would bring her. It carried its own reward. The light of a serving heart shines in many directions. It was not worship but wisdom that called Christ "The Light of the World."

So, you writers, make way for the heart, and you actors, too.

A new mania in the theatre of the past twenty years has driven out much of the magic. It is a selling mania. Actors, instead of concentrating on character creation, are busy trying to peddle their personal wares to the audience, trying to attract attention to themselves instead of to the character they represent. This is particularly true in comedy. In the old days of cheap burlesque, frantic comedians beat each other over the head with bladders. Today three-dollar actors beat the audience over the head with bladders. They want to roll the audience in the aisles. Large sections of discerning audiences have rolled down the aisles to the exit and have not returned, except on the rare occasions when a performance is assured.

The whole desperate flirtation has been shameful and degrading. The actor who tries to serve two masters, the character and the audience, ends by serving neither.

Of course, this false striving is due to the actor's fear that he will not be noticed, not appreciated, not singled out for praise, or for a bigger part, or a Hollywood offer; fear of walking the streets again looking for work. Let an epitaph to all these nightmares be inscribed over every stage entrance, "Abandon all fear ye who enter here."

In every dressing room let there be displayed Hamlet's speech to the players. The actor with normal equipment who follows Shakespeare's advice is on his way to creative realization. Listen to it again; an actor cannot hear it too often:

HAMLET: Speak the speech, I pray you, as I pronounced it to you, trippingly on the tongue; but if you mouth it, as many of your players do, I had as lief the town-crier spoke my lines. Nor do not saw the air too much with your hand, thus; but use all gently: for in the very torrent, tempest, and—as I may say—whirlwind of passion, you must acquire and beget a temperance, that may give it smoothness. O! it offends me to the soul to hear a robustious periwig-pated fellow tear a passion to tatters, to very rags, to split the ears of the groundlings, who for the most part are capable of nothing but inexplicable dumb-shows and noise: I would have such a fellow whipped for o'er-doing Termagant; it out-herods Herod: pray you, avoid it.

FIRST PLAYER: I warrant your honour.

HAMLET: Be not too tame neither, but let your own discretion be your tutor: suit the action to the word, the word to the action; with this special observance, that you o'erstep not the modesty of nature; for anything so overdone is from the purpose of playing, whose end, both at the first and now, was and is, to hold as 'twere, the mirror up to nature; to show virtue her own feature, scorn her own image, and the very age and body of the time his form and pressure . . .

In presenting one-hour versions of standard plays over N.B.C., I have learned two significant facts: first, that because of the prevalent careless and slovenly speech on the stage, plays now are being fully heard for the first time; second, that cut versions of successful plays, presented without intermissions or explanatory interruption, frequently have greater impact than in their original form. In no case has any of the thirty plays already presented suffered in mood or meaning.

The second discovery may have many far-reaching effects, new and progressive business methods; a new and larger audience; new forms of playwriting.

The chief obstacle to a people's community theatre has been the necessarily limited capacity of a satisfactory playhouse. Performances begin to suffer when seating capacity exceeds fifteen hundred. Such restricted capacity obviously works against a low price scale and prevents community professional theatre from becoming self-sustaining.

I am convinced that the one-hour-and-a-half performance, with no intermissions, is coming and can solve this problem. It would make two performances a night feasible, thus immediately doubling the capacity without increasing investment or appreciably adding to operation cost. It would likewise increase the area of potential patronage. Seven o'clock performances would permit early retirers to be home by nine-thirty. Nine o'clock performances would be convenient for others whose schedules run into the evening.

Certain classics which should not be so abridged can be done in two parts, the first part of *Hamlet* this week, the second part next week. Such divisions are familiar in opera and not unknown even in our present theatre (remember *Back to Methuselah* and *Mourning Becomes Electra*).

Furthermore not only are theatre prices too high for many people, but the time consumed is often too great for real enjoyment. When we realize that a considerable part of this time is wasted in dull intermissions, it is obvious that the theatre cannot long ignore the accelerations of our day.

Of course, none of this would be worth while if some essential value of plays or performances were to be lost. But I am convinced that neither is necessary. On the contrary, I believe that text values, accumulated interest and impact can be increased by tightening most plays. There is nothing artistically valuable in the required length of the plays we see today. The time element—two hours and a half—is forced upon playwrights, as is often said, simply to fill the hours between a late dinner and an early supper, regardless of the inherent needs of his drama. One of the commonest causes of failure in the theatre is dragging a story, even a good one, out so thin that it cannot bear its own weight. Boredom is a sin against theatre and padding a play never covers up the evil.

As a parting word to aspiring authors and actors, remember that Solomon did not pray for greater knowledge. He asked the Lord for an understanding heart. This should be the prayer of every author, or every actor—an understanding heart.

February 1945

II · HISTORY

* * *

EDITH HAMILTON

*

Tragedy

WHEN A POET takes tragedy for his subject he enters a field peculiarly his own. Only poets have "trod the sunlit heights and from life's dissonance strike one clear chord." The intuitive insight we recognize as poetical is the endowment without which no tragedy can be written. For tragedy is nothing less than pain transmuted into exaltation by the alchemy of poetry, and if poetry is true knowledge (truer than history, Aristotle said) the transmutation in tragedy has arresting implications.

Pain changed into, or, let us say, charged with, exaltation. It would seem that tragedy was a strange matter. There is indeed none stranger. A tragedy shows us pain and gives us pleasure thereby. The more piteous and terrible the events depicted, the more intense our enjoyment. There is food for wonder here, not to be passed over, as the superficial have done, by pointing out that the Romans made a holiday of a gladiator's slaughter, and that even today fierce instincts, savage survivals, stir in the most civilized. Grant all that, and we are not a step advanced on the way to explaining the mystery of tragic pleasure. It has no kinship with cruelty or the lust for blood.

On this point it is illuminating to consider our everyday use of the words tragedy and tragic. Pain, sorrow, disaster, are always spoken of as depressing, as dragging down—the dark abyss of pain, a crushing sorrow, an overwhelming disaster. But speak of tragedy and the metaphor changes extraordinarily. Lift us to tragic heights, we say, and never anything else. The depths of pathos but never of tragedy. Always the height of tragedy. A word is no light matter. Words have with truth been called fossil poetry, each, that is, a fixed symbol of creative thought. The whole philosophy of human nature is implicit in human speech. It is something to pause over, that the instinct of mankind has perceived a difference not of degree but of kind between tragic pain and all other pain. There is something in tragedy that marks it off from other disaster so sharply that in our common speech we bear witness to the difference.

All those whose attention has been caught by the strange contradiction of pleasure through pain agree with this instinctive witness, and some of the most brilliant minds the world has known have concerned themselves with it. Tragic pleasure, they tell us, is in a class by itself. "Pity and awe," Aristotle called it, "and a sense of emotion purged and purified thereby." "Reconciliation," said Hegel, which we may understand in the sense of life's temporary dissonance resolved into eternal harmony. "Acceptance," said Schopenhauer, the temper of mind that says, "Thy will be done." "The reaffirmation of the will to live in the face of death," said Nietzsche, "and the joy of its inexhaustibility when so reaffirmed."

Pity, awe, reconciliation, exaltation—these are the elements that make up tragic pleasure. No play is a tragedy that does not call them forth. So the philosophers say, all in agreement with the common judgment of mankind that tragedy is something above and beyond the dissonance of pain. But what it is that causes a play to call forth these feelings, what is the essential element in a tragedy, Hegel alone clearly defines. In a notable passage he says that the only tragic subject is a spiritual struggle in which each side has a claim upon our sympathy. But, as his critics have pointed out, even this excludes the tragedy of the suffering of the innocent, and a definition which does not include the death of Cordelia or of Deianira cannot be taken as final. What one definition, indeed, can cover, for instance, Antigone; the high-souled maiden who goes with open eyes to her death rather than leave her brother's body unburied, and Macbeth, the ambition-mad, the murderer of his king and guest? Yet these two plays, seemingly so totally unlike, arouse the same response. They have something in common, but the philosophers do not tell us what it is. Their real concern is with what a tragedy makes us feel, not with what makes a tragedy.

When was tragedy first made? The recent writer of a most distinguished book on the subject,* answers: "The spirit of inquiry

* *Tragedy* by W. Macneile Dixon.

meets with the spirit of poetry and tragedy is born." Make it concrete: early Greece with her god-like heroes and hero gods fighting far on the ringing plains of windy Troy; with her lyric world, where every common thing is touched with beauty, her two-fold world of poetic creation. Then a new age dawns, not satisfied with beauty of song and story, an age that must try to know and to explain. And for the first time tragedy appears. A poet of surpassing magnitude, not content with the old sacred conventions, and of a soul great enough to bear new and intolerable truth—that is Aeschylus, the first writer of tragedy. Other poets may, the tragedian must, seek in the visible world signs of the invisible; seek, that is, for the significance of life.

Only twice in literary history has there been a great period of tragedy, in the Athens of Pericles and in Elizabethan England. What these two periods had in common, two thousand years and more apart in time, that they expressed themselves in the same fashion, may give us some hint of the nature of tragedy for, far from being periods of darkness and defeat, each was a time when life was seen exalted, a time of thrilling and unfathomable possibilities. They held their heads high, those men who conquered at Marathon and Salamis, and those who fought Spain and saw the Great Armada sink. The world was a place of wonder; mankind was beauteous; life was lived on the crest of the wave. More than all, the poignant joy of heroism had stirred men's hearts. Not stuff for tragedy, would you say? But on the crest of the wave one must feel either tragically or joyously; one cannot feel tamely. And the temper of mind that sees tragedy in life has not for its opposite the temper that sees joy. The opposite pole to the tragic view of life is the sordid view. When humanity is seen as devoid of dignity and significance, trivial, mean and sunk in dreary hopelessness, then the spirit of tragedy departs. "Sometimes let gorgeous tragedy in sceptred pall come sweeping by." At the opposite pole stands the *Spoon River Anthology*.

But the outside does not really matter. It may be exactly the same in tragedy as in Spoon River. We do not, to be sure, go to Mr. Sinclair Lewis any more than to Mr. Masters for tragedy, but the reason has nothing to do with the familiar sordidness of either Main Street or Spoon River. There is no inherent reason why Babbitt's house in Zenith should not be the scene of a tragedy quite as well as the Castle of Elsinore. The only reason it is not is Babbitt himself.

When the Moscow Art Players presented the *Brothers Karamazov* there was seen on the stage an absurd little man in dirty clothes who waved his arms about and stamped and sobbed, the farthest removal possible from the traditional figures of tragedy, and yet tragedy was there in his person, stripped of her gorgeous pall, but sceptered truly, speaking the authentic voice of human agony in a struggle past the power of human heart to bear.

The dignity and the significance of human life—of these, and of these alone, tragedy will never let go. Without them there is no tragedy. To answer the question, what makes a tragedy, is to answer the question wherein lies the essential significance of life, what the dignity of humanity depends upon in the last analysis. To answer that question, read the great tragedies. They themselves offer the solution to the problem they propound. It is by our power to suffer, above all, that we are of more value than the sparrows. Endow them with a greater or as great a potentiality of pain and our foremost place in the world would no longer be undisputed. Deep down, when we search out the reason for our conviction of the transcendent worth of each human being we know that it is because of the possibility that each can suffer so terribly. What do outside trappings matter, Zenith or Elsinore? Tragedy's preoccupation is with suffering. But, it is to be well noted, not with all suffering. There are degrees in our high estate of pain. It is not given to all to suffer alike. In nothing do we differ more than in our power to feel. There are souls of little and of great degree, and upon that degree the dignity and significance of each life depends. There is no dignity like the dignity of a soul in agony.

> Here I and sorrow sit,
> This is my throne, bid kings come bow to it.

Tragedy is enthroned, and to her realm those alone are admitted that belong to the only true aristocracy, that of all passionate souls. Tragedy's one essential is a soul that can feel greatly. Given such a one and any catastrophe may be tragic. But the earth may be removed and the mountains be carried into the midst of the sea and if only the small and shallow are confounded, tragedy is absent.

One dark page of Roman history tells of a little seven-year-old girl, daughter of a man judged guilty of death and so herself condemned to die, and how she passed through the staring crowds sobbing and asking, What had she done wrong? If they would tell her, she would never do it again—and so on to the black prison and the executioner. That breaks the heart but it is not tragedy, it is pathos. No heights are there for the soul to mount to, but only the depths where there are tears for things. Undeserved suffering is not in itself tragic. Death is not tragic in itself, not the death of the beautiful and the young, the lovely and beloved. Death felt and suffered as Macbeth feels and suffers is tragic. Death felt as Lear feels Cordelia's death is tragic. Ophelia's death is a tragedy only if Hamlet's and Laertes' grief is tragic grief. It is not the conflicting claims of the law of God and the law of man that is tragic in the *Antigone.* It is Antigone herself, so great, so tortured. It is not Hamlet's hesitation to kill his uncle that is tragic. It is his power to feel. Change all the circumstances of the drama and Hamlet in the grip of any calamity would be tragic, just as Polonius would never be, however awful the catastrophe. The suffering of a soul that can suffer greatly—that and only that is tragedy. What else is the supreme tragedy, the tragedy of the Cross?

It follows then, that tragedy has nothing to do with the distinction between Realism and Romanticism. The contrary has always been maintained. The Greeks went to the myths for their subjects, we are told, to insure remoteness from real life which does not admit of high tragedy. "Realism is the ruin of tragedy," says the latest writer on the subject. It is not true. If indeed Realism were conceived of as dealing only with the usual, tragedy would be ruled out, for the soul capable of a great passion is not usual. But if nothing human is alien to Realism, then tragedy is of her domain, for the unusual is as real as the usual. *Desire under the Elms* is a tragedy. A drearier setting, a more typically realistic setting, it would be hard to find, but to see it is to feel pity and awe before a very ordinary type of man and woman, commonplace in everything else but made great by what they can suffer. Ibsen's plays are not tragedies. Whether Ibsen is a realist or not—the Realism of one generation is apt to be the Romanticism of the next—small souls are his dramatis personae and his plays are dramas with an unhappy ending. The end of *Ghosts* leaves us with a sense of shuddering horror and cold anger against a society where such things can be, and these are not tragic feelings.

The greatest realistic works of fiction have been written by the French and Russians. To read one of the great Frenchmen's books is to feel mingled despair and loathing for mankind, so base, so trivial and so wretched. But to read a great Russian novel is to have an altogether different experience. The baseness, the beast in us, the misery of life, are there as plain to see as in the French book, but what we are left with is not despair and not loathing but a sense of pity and of wonder before mankind that can so suffer. The Russian sees life in that way because the Russian genius is primarily poetical; the French genius is not. *Anna Karenina* is a tragedy; *Madame Bovary* is not. Realism and Romanticism or comparative degrees of Realism have nothing to do with the matter. It is a case of the small soul against the great soul and a writer's power *"voir clair dans ce qui est"* against the intuition of a poet.

Why is the death of the ordinary man a wretched, chilling thing which we turn from, while the death of the hero, always tragic, warms us with a sense of quickened life? Answer these questions and the enigma of tragic pleasure is solved. "Never let me hear that brave blood has been shed in vain," said Sir Walter Scott; "it sends an imperious challenge down through all the generations." So the end of a great tragedy challenges us. The great soul in pain and in death transforms and exalts pain and death. Through it we catch a glimpse of the great Stoic's Dear City of God, and of a deeper and more ultimate reality than that in which our lives are lived.

January 1926

* *

ROSAMOND GILDER

*

Merriment from Megara

FOR A MOMENT the stage is empty, the dancer has just finished her performance; the acrobats and tumblers have had their turn. The musicians are resting on their instruments. Into the silence walks an amiable gentleman with a market basket on his arm—bread, a bottle, sausages, all the paraphernalia of a picnic protrude from it. The man's face is ruddy, a bit pop-eyed, his mouth extraordinarily large, his entire expression mildly inane—benevolently imbecile. Roars of laughter greet his mere appearance. His way of walking, his innocent struggles with his over-laden basket, his candid solemnity put everyone in good humor. He selects a convenient spot in the middle of the floor and spreads a tablecloth on which he proudly sets forth his precious meal. The bottle he deposits carefully on his right hand, the loaf, the fruit, the meat all about him. He is gluttonous and hungry—full of expectations of a noble feast.

As he turns to pick up his bottle for a pre-prandial swig, a bald-headed rascal of a thief slips behind his back unseen and snatches away the loaf of bread, crouching down again behind a convenient rock before the unfortunate picnicker has finished his first drink. Smacking his lips with satisfaction, our hero turns to pick up the bread. The loaf is gone! His expression of astonishment and grief is devastating. The audience howls with joy as the poor man searches in vain on the empty cloth, while the thief, popping up on the other side, makes away with the bottle. Just too late the picnicker bethinks him of that sort of comfort. He turns toward it but, alas, the bottle is gone! Meat? gone! Cheese? gone! Fruit? gone! Every lumbering turn allows the more agile thief to spirit away some delicacy. The unfortunate picnicker is left foodless, drinkless, bewildered, whirling back and forth in desperation, to the delight of the roaring crowd.

Is it Ed Wynn on a New York stage, or Maison the Dorian mime performing in the market place of Megara some five hundred years before Christ? Either—or both—for the motives that prompt such profoundly instinctive miming are the same in every age and country, and the methods astonishingly similar through the whole range of recorded time. We can see Ed Wynn, Joe Cook, the already fabulous Charlot and that most recent and most poignant personification of "he who gets slapped," Public Enemy No. 13, on the stage or screen today. All that is left of Maison, the oldest of comic actors, is a name and a small terra cotta statuette in the Berlin Museum dated by the learned professors somewhere in the fifth century B.C. Yet the statuette represents so familiar, so immortal a being that it might be a caricature of any number of members of the hierarchy of clowns that have delighted countless generations of men from that day to this. Fat, ruddy, bald-pated, pop-eyed and large-mouthed, market basket in hand, a permanently startled and vacuous expression on his face, Maison is the perennial victim, fool and scapegoat whose tribulations have been the cause of raucous delight to the groundlings of every age and country. Whatever may be the fate of high tragedy in such a period as ours, whatever blight of mediocrity may from time to time afflict literary comedy, the sources of mimicry remain unchanged and unchanging and from them bubble forever an inexhaustible fountain of laughter-provoking theatricality and show.

Imitation and mimicry are deeply ingrained in human nature and those individuals in primitive society who are especially gifted in this line will be in constant demand. Wherever two or three are gathered together, there the actor among them will leap to his feet, dance a break-down, sing a song, tell a tale, make fun of the boss or imitate the fine lady who has just stepped proudly by. The shortest distance in the world is that which separates the sublime from the ridiculous, and man has always delighted in watching the great and the self-righteous forced by the mimic to take this embarrassing step. The first professional comedians were those members of the primitive group gifted with the mimetic instinct who found it profitable to devote all their time to entertaining their companions. They were given food and clothing in exchange for their antics and learned in the hard field of experience the difficult and often dangerous task of making men laugh.

Such entertainers existed in Greece in large numbers before the theatre as we know it was born. Before Aeschylus created tragedy, before Aristophanes wrote his imperishable comedies, the mimes of Megara, of Sparta, of Corinth and Athens had developed a robust and characteristic art, which has survived in one form or another through wars, revolutions, the crash of empires and the destruction of civilizations. The type was already old when Aristophanes attacked it in 450 B.C. He boasts that he banished the "wearisome ineptitudes and low buffooneries" of the old mimes from the stage. Yet as he fulminates against the "stale jokes stolen from Megara" (perhaps that very one of the market basket that Ed Wynn performs so devastatingly), against those gluttons "always chewing and ever hungry," those knaves and cowards "who allow themselves to be beaten at will," those slaves "set a-weeping so that their comrades might have a chance of jeering at their stripes"—he seems to be describing not the past which he scorned but all slapstick comedy from his own day to ours. These are the very types of Plautus and Terence, of the *commedia dell' arte,* of Harlequin and the circus clown, of vaudeville and burlesque. The battles, blows and custard pies of the movies are one with the horseplay condemned as old and out-of-date two thousand six hundred years ago. Even Aristophanes could not do away with a type of comic acting as old as time and as new as the latest animated cartoon. Though no texts used by these pre-Aristophanic comedians remain—and it is doubtful whether they indulged in written scripts at all—we can see the actors themselves performing their ribald antics before our very eyes. The great series of Phlyax vases dating from the fourth century B.C. are the first complete record we have of the player's craft in Western Europe. They are a set of "stills" of what must have been a very lively and timely form of knock-about farce. With the help of other surviving relics—statuettes, votive offerings and masks from earlier periods—and enriched by Aristophanes' attacks on the "contemptible buffooneries" of his predecessors, we can catch a glimpse of these earliest comedians and their theatre.

Their stage was a wooden platform set up in the market place or open field as vagabond players have done ever since. Even after the great theatres of Greece were built, the mimes were not permitted within their sacred precincts, but continued to ply their unlicensed trade along the highways and in the villages of Greece and her colonies, quite unperturbed by Aristophanic vituperation and the scorn of the high votaries of their art. The stage as we see it on the vases is well equipped with "practicable" windows and doors, with heavy pieces of scenery such as stairways and partitions and a variety of props—couches, chairs, altars, chests and so forth. The platform seems to have had a curtain hung below the stage level, the space inside serving possibly as a dressing and property room. Ladders led up to the stage level and there are indications that it was provided with a trap-door for sudden appearances. The actors' faces were masked or made up to give an exaggerated appearance of reality, as they are in vaudeville and burlesque; the coarseness is accentuated, the grimace widened. Faces are typical, but not as yet stylized, for these Phlyax actors retain a pungent, earthy reality even while they indulge in the crudest caricature.

For costumes they wore the clothes of the common people, farmers, artisans, slaves, tradesmen and town folk for whom their fun-making was designed. The Dorian mimic actor, reputed the greatest of them all, wore a costume traces of which can be found in his remotest descendants of modern times, the Harlequins of England and the Pierrots of France. Long, tight-fitting trousers, a short vest, padding to distort or accentuate back or belly, stripes and splashes to add color and gaiety, these were his typical insignia. On the principle of exaggerations which dictates the hump of Punchinello, the bald head of the circus clown and the huge feet of Charlie Chaplin, an enormous red leather phallus proclaimed his kinship with the revelers who followed the processions of the wine God and did equal honor to Dionysus and Priapus. He wore neither sock nor cothurnus, ornaments of a more stately stage. His general style, in keeping with his saturnalian humor, was free and easy, his costume permitting him to dance a wild measure, arms and legs, head and heels, all in action, to turn a handspring and play athletic tricks in the manner of all good clowns and harlequins ever since. Women's parts, though secondary in importance, were evidently performed by women. No one had as yet thought of excluding them from an occupation so obviously appropriate, and so closely allied with the oldest profession in the world. Their charms were an added means of drawing the crowd and extracting money, and added to the effectiveness of the show. A realistic theatre demanded realism in casting, and dancing girls, flute players, tumblers and acrobats were at hand to take the parts of the housewives and courtesans, the gossips and goddesses with which the Phlyax scenes abound.

The mimes in which these actors performed—for actor and play were so inseparable that they were generally designated by the same term—are chiefly of two types: mythological burlesque and domestic farce. Nothing is more striking to the modern observer than the cheerful levity with which the Greeks treated their revered deities and heroes. Shaw's *Caesar and Cleopatra* in its unheroic treatment of heroes seemed in its day amusingly iconoclastic, "modern." The Dorian and Phlyax mimes did not hesitate to use the same methods in presenting their own gods and heroes in equally domestic and unheroic guise. Yet the heroes they mocked were the very ones to whom they were building temples and were giving their most precious treasure. No shrine was more sacred than that of the Delphian Apollo, yet the mimes did not hesitate to show the god himself in the guise of an effeminate and very much frightened young man perched in terror on the roof of his own temple, while a smirking Heracles tries to tempt him from his perch with sweetmeats that he may the better wang him with the nasty-looking club he hides behind his back. This merry little skit, so uncomplimentary to its subject, was performed some time in the fourth century B.C., when the authority of the high gods was as yet unquestioned, and when the words spoken from Delphi were still the words of God.

Zeus himself was treated with no more respect by the mimic actors than were the rest of the Olympian hierarchy. In their hands he became the prototype of that immortal subject of jest, the amorous old man ever in pursuit of a pretty petticoat. Zeus climbing a ladder to Alcmene's window while Hermes stands on guard; Zeus with white beard and startled eyes cracking open a huge egg in an animated scene of the birth of Helen, prototype of that famous one in *Back to Methuselah;* these and a hundred other lively and sacrilegious scenes from the Phlyax vases show us a highly developed burlesque farce which would certainly not pass the British censor or escape the criticism of New York's Finest.

In reducing the gods to the level of ordinary mortals, the mime kept to its main characteristic—that of picturing the everyday, the familiar, the known, in terms of caricature. There is something irresistibly comic in the commonplace when it is seen through the eyes of the true comedian. Sitting in the theatre today we are convulsed by the struggles of pater familias to mend an electric iron, by Mr. Average Citizen's efforts to get a certain station on a home-made radio. Exaggeration is unnecessary, repetition need hardly be used; recognition of an ordinary, a shared, a routine experience when seen in imitation, set apart, glorified and intensified by the stage, is in itself sufficient to provoke instant laughter.

The mime of twenty-six hundred years ago used the same method as the actor with the electric iron or as the amateur radio fan. Aristophanes alludes scornfully to this theatre devoted to the affair of "obscure private persons," making use of jokes "common on the street," familiar to the audience before they are even spoken. The everyday little world of Greece and Sicily, of Southern Italy and later of Rome itself walks by us on the wooden platform of the mime—here are old men and their money, young men in their cups, rascally tradesmen, quick-witted thieves. Here also is the grinning simple soul, Maison's contemporary and successor, the greedy, childish creature who has become the symbol of mankind—forever receiving undeserved blows from an incomprehensible fate, eager to enjoy life, responsive to the simplest pleasure, yet inevitably hit on the head, robbed, beaten and defrauded by his predatory companions. Maison, Ed Wynn, Victor Moore—and between them that noble army whose names alone evoke a nostalgic charm, Grimaldi, Grock, Marceline, Charlie Chaplin. Nor should Krazy Kat be forgotten and his triumphant and somewhat brash successor—the cheerful Mickey Mouse.

October 1935

* *

ALVAH BESSIE

*

Gilles de Raiz

EXPONENTS OF THE "new" constructivism which has come out of post-war Europe may be somewhat taken aback by the information that its first practitioner flourished in France at no more recent period than the years 1404 to 1440. It is true that this early *regisseur* did not carry his settings to the fine flower of perfection which Meyerhold has attained, but his interest in the theatre was purely personal, and he cherished no illusions about the theatre's mission or its place in contemporary life. To the noble lord Gilles de Raiz, the stage achieved its purpose when it broadcast his name and his attainments, an attitude not entirely unknown today. But Gilles de Raiz, after all, had a measure of achievement to proclaim.

He sprang of two of the oldest seignorial families—the Lavals and the Craons—among whose living representatives the Montmorency family may be counted. He was the wealthiest noble of his time, and not even the king of France could rival his magnificence. He was capable of raising and supporting entire armies and, during the English campaigns, he was Jeanne d'Arc's right-hand man. At the time of Charles VII's coronation in the cathedral of Rheims, Gilles de Raiz, still well under thirty, was appointed Marshal of France, and as an indication of his gratitude, his king permitted him to bear the fleur-de-lys of France upon his crest.

Bernard Shaw made little enough of the Marshal in his play *Saint Joan*. He was content to display him as an extremely elegant and foppish young man who was not too popular among his companions. As a matter of fact, Gilles was extremely well liked by his contemporaries—he was an excellent soldier and tactician, a well educated gentleman and courtier, and he enjoyed the hearty popularity which is always at the command of any prodigal who is easy-going with his money and lavish in entertainment. The novelist, Huysmans, chose to take another view—and the protagonist of his novel, *Là-Bas,* is writing a life of Gilles—laying particular stress upon the satanic aspects of his character. For it is well known that Gilles de Raiz, impoverished by excesses, sought to recoup his vanished fortunes by means of alchemy and black magic. He succeeded only in having himself sentenced to death and executed in 1440, for "the abominable crime of heretical apostasy," and the fact that he had abandoned himself to the frightful practice of "demonic evocation," not to mention his crimes against nature and the avowed murder of 200 little children, out of blood lust or as part of the ritual of "demonic evocation." This is an aspect of his character which is irrelevant to the present context, though it makes fascinating reading.

The bare details of this worthy's life are incredible, though they all seem to have been confirmed by examination of the archives of Loire-Inférieure at Nantes. The local archivist, M. Emile Gabory, the only man who is actually in possession of the facts of the Gilles de Raiz affair, has written a lively biography of him.* Among other legends which have attached to the young Marshal of France, soldier, diabolist and theatrical producer, is the supposition that he was the original of Perrault's famous Bluebeard. Even Shaw, who was fully familiar with the sources, chose to harness him with that epithet, and his stage directions indicate that the actor is to wear a blue goatee! The mere fact that Gilles de Raiz was married only once, and did not even kill his only wife, should be enough to absolve him of this additional *stigma,* but it has persisted for many years, and you may examine the ingenious hypotheses yourself, if you care to look them up.

* *Alias Bluebeard: The Life and Death of Gilles de Raiz,* by Emile Gabory (Brewer & Warren).

The pretext for this article is found in another department of Gilles' activities. It has been indicated that he was immensely wealthy; just how wealthy would be difficult to say, since there is no way of accurately evaluating the coinage of the period. But when he began to sell his estates in order to procure ready cash, over twenty-five castles and their surrounding woodlands went into their purchasers' pockets for ridiculous sums of money. He never bargained, and when he bought he paid three and four times as much as the actual value of any article. He borrowed at usurious rates of interest, and even his companions plundered him.

Gilles was beset with the idea of commemorating the siege of Orléans, in which he had taken an important part. For years he had traveled about the country, giving performances of farces and *soties,* and his munificence was already legendary. His castles were thronged by the poor seeking alms, despite the fact that wherever he happened to be it was later noticed that children had disappeared. (Of course these accumulated disappearances eventually wrought his downfall, but we are ahead of our story.) This was before the period when Gilles instituted his famous collegiate of hand-picked singers and toured the provinces giving concerts of religious music, but even at this time everything he did was done in the grand manner.

In 1434 he was to give the first performance of his specially written play—*The Mystery of the Siege of Orléans*—and he so arranged matters that the commemorative performances took place in the town itself. Here was the first "long-run" play in history. The Greek trilogies were known to have required an entire day for their performance, but *The Mystery of the Siege of Orléans* not only ran all day long but is said to have been repeated every day for a year and a month! Gilles and his retainers lived in Orléans from August 1434 to September 1435. The theatre was erected in the center of the town and was a miracle of construction and management, consisting of a scaffolding five or six stories high and as broad as the greatest stage now extant. On each floor of this structure a different act took place.

Gilles played himself and seems to have broken the rule that there is no reason why an actor should be able to portray a role, just because he happens to have lived it. Wherever he went he was followed by crowds of satellites who shouted his name and praises. Lucullus could have wished no more. In his play he was pictured as a greater general than he probably was in the field, but that is of little moment. You have read in the history books that at the battle of Tournelles, before Orléans, the Maid was wounded by an arrow and a "valiant captain" stayed at her side, extracted the arrow and carried her to safety. That captain was Gilles de Raiz, who had been appointed to the place of guardian for Jeanne by his powerful cousin and ally, La Trémoille.

But the most incredible part of this particular story remains to be told. Here are a few details: one hundred and forty actors and more than 500 supernumeraries appeared in the *Mystère du Siège d'Orléans.* They engaged in great battles and pompous court scenes, and their costumes, contrary to the usual procedure (Hollywood always excepted), were cut from the most luxurious materials obtainable and imported from distant lands. Cloth-of-gold and silver, silks and resplendent velvets, rioted in a tapestry of color upon this sumptuous scene. That is little enough; consider the fact that Gilles de Raiz (if the record speaks truly) did not permit these costumes to be utilized for more than one performance!

After his death, his heirs drew up a *Mémoire* of his expenditures, in a vain attempt to recover some of the wealth he had so heedlessly squandered in the thirty-six hectic years of his life. They mentioned that in the town of Orléans, at that period, "there was great scarcity of viands." We have said that Gilles and all his friends lived at Orléans for over a year at his expense. They occupied every hotel in the town! They were quartered at The Gold Cross, The Black Head, Saint George's Crown, The Sign of the Sword, The White Horse, The Great Salmon, The Little Salmon, The Wild Man and The God of Love. Their expense account was unlimited; anything they chose to purchase they just put "on the check."

Meanwhile, the performances continued. And here is why there was a scarcity of food. Orléans was after all a little town and could scarcely have furnished enough of an audience to maintain *The Mystery* for a year. So Gilles invited anyone who cared to come—the performances were free. And they came from all over France and foreign countries, and if they could not afford to make the trip, Gilles forwarded them their expenses. When they got to Orléans, they lodged at his expense. So for an entire year the town of Orléans held open house—at Gilles' expense. The streets were lined with tables, at which there was perpetual banquet, quaffing of hydromel and hippocras, and the finest fish and venison furnished out the feast. It was an orgy unparalleled in human history.

New York thought it was seeing an unprecedented spectacle when a certain opulent but misguided gentleman generously offered a bad play free to all comers and by his own efforts kept it running for well over a year! His actors would never have played to empty houses had he taken a line from Gilles de Raiz' prompt-book and offered—not hippocras and hydromel, perhaps, not rare venison or gamey fish, not even lodging and a bed—but merely a free lunch.

August 1930

* *

STARK YOUNG

*

Shakespeare and the Venetians

SINCE EARLY in the nineteenth century two of the chief requirements of poetry have been sincerity and naturalness. Does the poet really feel as he says, and is the poem true to things as they are, is what it says said naturally? This is the attitude that most people bring, as a matter of course, to the poetry they encounter.

It is clear how this attitude tends to stress the personal element in a poem, and how it asks most of all what a poem means and then restates this meaning in what seems a natural, direct statement of it. This implies, of course, that it prevents us from seeing the poem first of all as a work of art, which it is; that it leads us to forget that any genuine work of art has its own sincerity and is true to its own nature, which is the only way anything could ever be natural; and that it prevents us from viewing the work of art in its just perspective. The result of all which is that we get the general idea of the poem but cannot clearly distinguish what its style is, and so miss some of its content and meaning, of which the style is an inseparable part.

There are poems, like some of Burns' lyrics, that are so simple and natural, in the ordinary sense, so close to the poet's private emotion, that this test of sincerity and naturalness, as the average man now takes it, leaves them undisturbed. There are poems like some of

Keats', where the thought, extracted and put into plain terms, would shrink to a mere platitude. And there are poems like Spenser's *Prothalamion,* which is completely distorted and denied unless we see it as a work of art created in honor of an occasion, exactly as a pageant might be, or a painted panel, or court ballet, but using words, images, rhythms, cadences, stanzas, tones, instead of garlands, costumes, gestures, colors, or visual patterns, as the case might require. For an extreme and easy example of all these disasters—as regards perspective, thought, style, and the right content of a poem—there is that place in Shakespeare's sonnets where he says that his verse will live forever and so keep the beloved's name alive:

> So long as men can breathe, or eyes can see,
> So long lives this, and this gives life to thee.

What nonsense has been written about these lines, stressing their personal element and missing elements of artifice and tradition! The great poet, we are told, foresaw his immortality. As a matter of fact he is employing one of the common motives of the Renaissance sonnet, from Petrarch on; they used it to deck out their verses as the painters for Lorenzo's court used in their designs the three rings entwined. This sort of made-up significance, oblivious of perspective and traditional motive, is typical of reams of art criticism.

The fact is, however, that the case with poetry is not so simple as might be. Words, which are the medium of this art, are elusive. They are not things in reality but only symbols of things, and they have diverse meanings and associations for every individual. There is the idea, too, in poetry; it stings us, seems real and close to us, and leads us toward saying it over for ourselves in our own way. In poetry, then, it is not easy to see the idea, the feeling, the style, the complete whole, the work of art. As we read Shakespeare we think we are thinking as this sixteenth-century poet does, but we are really thinking in terms of the thought around us. I am convinced that fifty percent of Shakespeare we miss.

Some of Shakespeare we get directly. Some we get as a kind of blurred, general sum; it stirs our imagination and we feel somehow its persuasion and truth. A great deal of Shakespeare we apprehend because of his force or the universality of his interest. His lyrical power and quick, sharp sensitivity give immediacy very often to the boldest and most fanciful excursions into poetic imagery and complex statement. But the remainder we confront with acquiescence, reverence, dismay, confusion, resentment, or fatigue, according to our case. To take examples. We understand directly the main theme of *King Lear*. We feel the great, general impact upon us of the scene where the old king wanders on the stormy moor. To comprehend the scene as it is written, is another matter. When Shakespeare writes that Lear stands

A poor, infirm, weak and despised old man,

it is the way ourselves might think it. But it is another matter when he makes Lear say to the storm:

You sulphurous and thought-executing fires,
Vaunt-couriers to oak-cleaving thunderbolts,
Singe my white head! And thou, all-shaking thunder,
Smite flat the thick rotundity o' the world!

This is full Shakespeare, writing out his inspiration, but writing also out of his period.

In many of Shakespeare's passages we could profit by viewing his work in the light of some of the painting of the Renaissance. We should see thus not the profound thought, of course, not that so much, but we might see more readily the elements of style, artifice, artistic design, ornament, pure arrangement, for what they are in a work of art. For this practical use a picture has certain advantages. It is seen in a single sweep and seen whole, and it is seen quickly. Its purpose is patently decorative and pleasure giving; and if its beauty is carrying enough, we accept it, and along with it accept its style, and see what this style is. And everything about a painting makes it more easily detached from us than a poem is. It is easier for us to think of a painting as period than to think of a poem so.

We had best begin with Shakespeare as Renaissance art, not earlier, for he is the child of that elaborate and vaulting time, at once so sophisticated and so strangely fresh. We all know the complexity of designing, the copious abundance and the taste for imagery and learned illusion that the Renaissance artists displayed. In Perugino, Raphael, Ghirlandaio, Ghiberti, or a score of other artists of the Renaissance, look at the classical borrowings; the ornate column in the background here; the intricate rhythm of the group of figures there, with their careful feet, their bent and straight knees and eloquent arms, and their studied folds of drapery or erudite properties; the conceits in the phrasing of the design; the grotesque fancy of the monkey or little dog beside those declaiming figures; the anatomical academics; the skillful accessories to the main scene; the counterpoint of tones; the direct arrangement in one part, the elaboration of the rest. Shakespeare belongs to all that. . . .

If we read in Dante the story of an incident—of Ugolino, of Paolo and Francesca, there are many—we find a certain narrative concentration, like that Giotto possessed above all painters. In his beautiful picture of *The Death of St. Francis* there are many figures and diverse rhythms, but one single theme: the entire composition moves toward that dying face on the bed. Shakespeare's narrative is not like that. In *Macbeth* he made use of a story that was more or less ready-made to his hand; and it is often for a moment straitly told. The king is dead, Macbeth says that simply, and states the flaw that remains in his scheme,

Banquo, and his Fleance, lives.

But the strait directness is never long secure or assured. The next moment we forsake that border balladry and naive concentration of the simpler legend, and blossom into the full style of the period.

There's comfort yet; they are assailable;
Then be thou jocund: ere the bat hath flown
His cloister'd flight; ere to black Hecate's summons
The shard-borne beetle with his drowsy hums
Hath rung night's yawning peal, there shall be done
A deed of dreadful note.

For the most part narrative in Shakespeare is in this style. Most of Shakespeare's narrative is like that of elaborate and graceful tapestries, or like the murals of the full-blown Renaissance. He tells an incident in the manner of Raphael, Correggio, Veronese—who came when that chaste, unerring design of Piero della Francesca was no longer the ideal and the ardent simplicity of Fra Angelico or Giotto was no longer the way men felt. In these Renaissance frescoes or tapestries the line is there, the narrative is stated, sometimes more, sometimes less; but they remain as free as they choose from any natural bonds; their waving plumes, their standards and banners, garments and scarves turned into gracious rhythms, as are the postures and studied limbs of their people, whose light feet step on an earth that never was except for princes and dreamers and lovers of beautiful walls; the whole scene is accoutered, arranged, decked out with detail, sometimes only suave, sometimes poignant and profound, but always accoutered thus, arranged and searched out for fair design. It is the same in Shakespeare.

Take one of his young pieces. The death of Lucrece, after all, is hardly a light matter, with the noble wife violated by the tyrant Tarquin and driven through shame and despair to take her own life. We will see then, how it goes. Tarquin has pressed his suit threatening, if she will not yield to his desires, that he will force her to it and then kill her and a vile groom, saying that he found them thus, together, to her eternal shame, her husband's and her children's. . . . The crime is committed. Lust, Chastity, Hecate are brought in, and Philomel apostrophized. Tarquin leaves and Lucrece has some four or five hundred lines about her woeful case; and there are many more lines describing and addressing a tapestry full of figures and incidents of the Fall of Troy, which now becomes a background to the scene. Then there is the scene with the maid, and then the husband and his knights, to whom Lucrece speaks in image after image, classical allusions, allusions to nature, flowers, fire and water, conjuring them to avenge her. . . . Then we have the blood, like the purple fountain that Brutus drew the murderous knife from, and two stanzas of details about the designs in which it flows. At best it is a period death, this of Lucrece, as elaborate and mannered as any tapestry in Florence, despite the fact that the touch in the imagery is fresher and more poetic. And what a rococo treatment of the blood motive!—in the midst of its glamorous senses and gorgeous taste the Renaissance had a strong stomach. This, of course, is earlier and less successful poetry, and for that reason the manner and artifice special to the period are more readily evident.

Or, take that most pitiful of all incidents anywhere in Shakespeare's plays, the death of Ophelia. Ophelia, tragic girl, her mind shattered and her heart broken, has drowned herself; and the Queen, the mother of the lover who caused it all, a woman whom, by a divine insight, the dramatist makes also to love Ophelia, tells the story. . . .

Considering the moment, the passage is as bad, as over-ornate and deviously wrought as anything in Bernini. And to apply to it any strict rule of fact or feeling would make it seem only more strangely false. It has its own pathetic truth, no doubt, but you must swallow it, if you can swallow it, in the light of its period, and even then some of the conceits and fanciful details are excessive and in our way. We cannot rid ourselves of our epoch enough to pass them easily. The virtues inherent in this method, either in painting or poetry, are a certain rich inclusiveness, a dilation in the variety and range of appeal, a gain in texture. The vices of an artifice that grows hollow through lack of imagination and lack of direct emotion are obvious.

And what shall we say of that trial of Shylock in *The Merchant of Venice,* whose crudity, eloquence, luster, barbarism, romance and tragedy make it such a delicate matter to combine with that child's game of the pound of flesh! Taken one way, the Trial Scene is perplexing if not, for adults at least, quite absurd. We can hardly be asked to take it seriously; and it is an unprofitable business to take good art with half condescension, or with an appreciative indulgence, as if we were humoring a child. It will be useful to consider this scene in the light of some Venetian painting in which the older and harsher incident has been softened out from its earlier rigor, the story of it left, but mellowed and embellished with color and decorative detail. Such a process went on for centuries in sacred painting, as you can see by following any saint's martyrdom from Duccio to Titian. Where Duccio may have labored and wept and prayed, the Venetian is easy and at home in the world, gorgeous, fluent, rich-hued, somewhat casual in his conception and design, loose in his invention, abundant in texture and tone. In the light of this Venetian quality we can gauge the Trial Scene, for the unity it may have, the varied ornament, and the degree of its profundity.

And those councils of kings and statesmen in palaces, and of great warriors in tents, that are scattered through Shakespeare's plays, what elegance and facetious invention and tropes, or what inversions of the direct way of stating things, or what intricacy of pattern, they display! Take that conference of Antony and Augustus. The lord of the world, Julius Caesar, has been stabbed in the Capitol, the fortunes of the world are in the scales, the two leaders of war meet to treat with one another, and the picture begins, with its suavities, dialectic manipulations, graces and spoutings, and is forty lines coming to the point, which arrives at last in this intricate flourish:

CAESAR: You praise yourself
By laying defects of judgment to me, but
You patched up your excuses.
ANTONY: Not so, not so;
I know you could not lack, I am certain on't,
Very necessity of this thought, that I,
Your partner in the cause 'gainst which he fought,
Could not with graceful eyes attend those wars
Which fronted mine own peace. As for my wife . . .
So much uncurable her garboils, Caesar,
Made out of her impatience, which not wanted
Shrewdness of policy, too. I grieving grant
Did you too much disquiet.

All the councils and parleys in Shakespeare follow such curves and ornate reality.

Go on in the play to the fourth act and read the battle items, and then, for the pleasing uses of comprehension, look at Veronese's *Apotheosis of the Battle of Lepanto,* with that posing and involved figure of Venice and her crown; the Doge in adoration, his rhythmic, corner-filling page boy beside him; the banners, cherubim, laurels, clouds, marbles, loves—all suave figures in the design, with the graceful Divine Judge in their midst; and far down to the left in the picture, the glint and color of the battle, almost forgotten but not without its ornamental part in the scene. The Roman fighting in Antony's battle drama has about the same relation to the Shakespeare scene as Lepanto has to Veronese's.

The Venetian direction is a good one in which to turn this argument. That side of Shakespeare that is intricate, academic, cerebral, packed with metaphors and puns, subtle, far-fetched, entrancing, or excessive, is easier for us to understand and place than is this other quality of his: I mean his way of relaxing from rigor, and from spiritual grandeur and bursting into a golden stream and flight. This is what the great Venetians did every time they took up their palettes and brushes, and there is more or less of it on almost every page in Shakespeare, whether it be in a word, a phrase, a passage or a scene. It is not always good in either Shakespeare or the Venetians, but it is always characteristic. . . .

An immense power and tragic insight underlies the whole of *Antony and Cleopatra*; the volume of magnificence for that last half of the play, where it deals with the lovers, is overwhelming. It has the violence, the light and the dark, the frenzy and torment and passion, of Tintoretto at his best. But there is a certain blandness of temper not so violent or grand as Tintoretto and more like Veronese. There is all through *Antony and Cleopatra* the complete and easy articulation, the glow, the glaze on glaze of tone, that we find in Veronese.

In Shakespeare this quality of color, richness and ease runs off at times into a sort of barbarism and excess; in the Venetians it can diffuse itself into mere casual lassitude and degeneration.

We must note how Shakespeare when he chooses will put in an entrance, a speech, a piece of inventive metaphor, loosely enough related to the scene. In that too he is like the artists who lived in Venice and who were so much less strict in their design than the Renaissance painters of Tuscany or Umbria. Venetian painters will put half a dog here at the edge of a picture, or turn a head, or throw an arm out there, only to fill some space that cries for less casual composition.

Sometimes Shakespeare's rendering of a moment seems hollow enough, if we think of it on any basis of searching feeling and direct truth, and only moderately profound, even when taken as a baroque rendering of its matter. We must make up our minds to enjoy it as something radiant, decorative, unwounded by the sting of its material, untouched, wholly sophisticated. The most shameless of these scenes is that of Enobarbus' death by his own hand, after deserting his general. We have the moonlit night, the solitary poet, the two figures of the sentinels to fill in the design, and Enobarbus' words, under the moon, as he falls on his sword. Besides the sentinel's short speeches, Enobarbus has only two. . . .

Veronese's *Martyrdom of St. Giustina* is heartbroken, compared to them. And to try to make them wholly natural by laying them to the character's florid and declamatory nature is only to muddle the issue and miss the quality of the scene. . . .

The scene of Cleopatra's death is interwoven here and there with those short, literal speeches that English can bear so well—

> Dost thou not see my baby at my breast,
> That sucks the nurse asleep?

But these only serve to brace and delineate the rich style and to point up the composition.

> CLEOPATRA: Give me my robe, put on my crown; I have
> Immortal longings in me; now no more
> The juice of Egypt's grape shall moist this lip:
> Yare, yare, good Iras; quick. Methinks I hear
> Antony call; I see him rouse himself
> To praise my noble act; I hear him mock
> The luck of Caesar, which the gods give men
> To excuse their after wrath. Husband, I come:
> Now to that name my courage prove my title!
> I am fire and air; my other elements
> I give to baser life. So; have you done?
> Come then and take the last warmth of my lips.
> Farewell, kind Charmian; Iras, long farewell.
> (*Kisses them. Iras falls and dies.*)
> Have I the aspec in my lips? Dost fall?
> If thou and nature can so gently part,
> The stroke of death is as a lover's pinch,
> Which hurts, and is desired. Dost thou lie still?
> If thus thou vanishest, thou tell'st the world
> It is not worth leave-taking.
> CHARMIAN: Dissolve thick cloud, and rain, that I may say
> The gods themselves do weep!
> CLEOPATRA: This proves me base:
> If she first meet the curléd Antony,
> He'll make demand of her, and spend that kiss
> Which is my heaven to have. Come, mortal wretch,
> (*To an asp, which she applies to her breast*)
> With thy sharp teeth this knot intrinsicate
> Of life at once untie: poor venomous fool,
> Be angry, and dispatch. . . .

What glamour and imagination, actuality, prose fact, fire, scope! And all of it immersed in something Aeschylus meant when he said that Prometheus made men cease from contemplating death. We hear the passion and tragedy with awe, watching it move, listening, as if some passage were enacted to the god's music.

January 1930

* *

EDWARD REED

*

Grimaldi

"MICHELANGELO OF BUFFOONERY"

HELLO, here we are again!" The audience, discouragingly apathetic, straightens in its chairs, gathers up its cheer, and beats its palms together. From the stalls to the gods, there is applause and laughter and a response that would be the envy of the most popular player on Broadway. The scene is Covent Garden on any of countless nights during the first quarter of the last century—Covent Garden, a hallowed home of triumphs from its opening bill of *The Way of the World,* but where no man received greater acclaim than Joe Grimaldi, whenever his topknotted head bounced through the curtain with the clown's traditional greeting, "Hello, here we are again!"

He might have been appearing in any one of a dozen pantomimes; from the acclaim you would not know whether it was *Mother Goose, Harlequin and Friar Bacon, Fashion's Fools,* whether Joe was about to indulge in a duet with a mammoth oyster that had been crossed in love, or in hunting the fox on a property horse, or in boxing with a man made of vegetables (a burlesque, this, of Mary Shelley's tale of Frankenstein). All of them received equal welcome from the devotees of pantomime and its leading exponent, that clown in excelsis, the inimitable Joey, who died just one hundred years ago this May 31.

Pantomime—as Grimaldi acted it and as London knows it in a less entertaining if more spectacular form today in perennial Christmastime shows—is a strange hybrid. Literally "imitator of all," the word held to its true meaning as late as the eighteenth century when it came to signify action without words. But speech could not be kept out for long and, although we may still think of pantomime as indicating silent performance (viz., Charlie Chaplin), the English entertainments that went—and go—under the name of pantomimes soon had their dancing and music and scenic effects supplemented by lines. Today, as Willson Disher says, " 'pantomime' is used to imply either a state of affairs far removed from sanity or a representation of life that is far removed from reality."

The biographer of David Garrick gives an account of a typical early pantomime that tells us clearly what form this unique entertainment took:

> It consisted of two parts, one serious, and the other comic. . . . He [the producer] exhibited a story from Ovid's *Metamorphoses,* or some other fabulous writer. Between the pauses or acts of this serious representation he interwove a comic fable, consisting chiefly of the courtship of Harlequin and Columbine, with a variety of surprising adventures . . . such as the sudden transformation of palaces and temples to huts and cabbages; of men and women into wheel-barrows and joint-stools . . . mechanic shops into serpents and ostriches.

The popularity of this form of entertainment grew with amazing rapidity, so that even Garrick, with his audiences for Shakespeare falling away, was compelled to present pantomime; and other producers of serious plays with great actors became accustomed to baiting their bills with pantomimes as after-pieces.

By the time Grimaldi came along, its form was established and its popularity accepted. Clown was the character Grimaldi regularly portrayed; and Clown became the most important figure in the Harlequinade because of Grimaldi, whose genius brought him such various titles as "the Michelangelo of buffoonery," "the Garrick of clowns," "the Jupiter of practical joking."

Grimaldi was the son of an actor-dancer who became famous for his acrobatic dancing at the Haymarket and was engaged for Drury Lane as dancer and as *maître de ballet* not only for that house but for Sadler's Wells and Astley's. He reigned for more than twenty years of pantomime and died in 1788. His son was born December 18, 1778, of an English mother, Mrs. Brooker, and from this English heritage derived the distinctly native appearance which made him beloved in the role of a "hearty English squire" and acclaimed by ultra-patriotic audiences (at the time of the Napoleonic wars) when he represented John Bull and sang of the solid British virtues.

Acting in the serious pieces that preceded the Harlequinade, as well as in the "straight" and "fantastic" divisions of the pantomime, Joe essayed a bewildering variety of parts during his spectacular career—heroes, rogues, ogres, spirits, gluttons, savages, old men, animals. As a tragedian he was likened to Edmund Kean; as a comedian he was held equal to Charles Lamb's favorite, Munden. None knew better than Joe the secret of clownship, the ability to capture and project the droll in the everyday events of humankind. "His exuberance of animal spirits," it was declared, was really miraculous—"what a rich ringing laugh!—the very voice of merriment!" His legs were "eloquent"; his chin "he had a power of lowering, we will not say to what button of his waistcoat, but the drop was an alarming one"; and his smile, fixed on his moon face, began at the corners of his round eyes which were like saucers above his fat cheeks.

Joe Grimaldi made his first public bow when he was less than three, at Sadler's Wells on Easter Monday of 1781. From 1792 on, starting with *The Savage; or, Harlequin Wanderer,* in which he played a dwarf, his name appeared constantly on the playbills. By 1797, although still titled Master Grimaldi, he was listed among the first five members of the Sadler's Wells company, along with King, manager and Harlequin; Dibdin, Pantaloon; Dubois, veteran clown; and Mrs. Wybrow, Columbine. During these apprentice years, trying his hand at every sort of role, he was achieving success in all forms of playing. In the serious piece, *Ko and Zoa; or, The Belle Savage,* he moved one critic to write of his portrayal of the Red Indian, Ravin: "We do not believe the finest tragedian of the day can produce any finer effect or portray a more faithful picture." In projecting songs like "Royal Reasons for Roast Beef" or "Dermot O'Dooley's Description of Egypt," he was achieving renown as a comic singer. And in such a number as his "Comic Dance with Nobody, Somebody and Everybody" he was becoming equally noted as a dancer.

In 1805, after leaving Drury Lane following a dispute over his contract, he joined Covent Garden when Thomas Dibdin induced that theatre to engage the best clown ever seen on the stage and, added Dibdin, "when I say the best, I do not except his father, whose *vis comica* I perfectly well remember." And that Christmas, Clown passed out of his novitiate and took on the sacrosanct robes of his Saturnalian priesthood. It was with a piece lacking the "topographical splendor" of earlier Covent Garden pantomimes: *Harlequin and Mother Goose; or, The Golden Egg,* in which Grimaldi played Squire Bugle, "a rich widower of repulsive manners" who tries to steal the beautiful young Colinette from her lover Colin. *Mother Goose,* with Grimaldi as the keystone, made for its producers a tidy fortune of more than £20,000; and Grimaldi from this time on was the supreme Clown, in whom all mankind saw its image in reverse, and rejoiced.

Off the stage, Grimaldi had simplicity, humility, a homely sincerity that endeared him to all those with whom he came into contact. On the stage he was an unalloyed sinner and villain. He was "a thief, a coward—a most detestable coward, cruel, treacherous, unmanly, ungenerous, greedy, and the truth was not in him." He flattered with appalling guile, he played pranks on his master, he was "the very beau ideal of thieves—robbery became a science in his hands." He was hypocritical in his sympathy for those whom he himself had harmed, derisive behind their backs and, if found out, snivelingly agonized at his just punishment. And at all times he had the backing of his delighted audiences, for standards of morality become arbitrary in judging Clown, who, like the lunatic, is beyond all ordinary laws of morality and justice. Less than human and more than human, real and unreal, fool and knave, butt and bully—all these qualities, and their implicit contradictions, put Clown outside the standards by which we judge everyman. Audiences sitting before Grimaldi agonized over a possible discovery when he was in the middle of some elaborate theft; they cheered when he was safe and away went "the monstrous booty into that leviathan pocket of his, that receptacle of all sorts of edibles, and occasionally of kettles full of boiling water, and even lighted candles" (a quotation that recalls A. Robins, the clown that *Jumbo* revealed to New York a season or two ago, with his capacious pockets disgorging endless bunches of bananas).

Joey's cruelty to the oysters was an especially welcome piece of villainy. The first that he opened made a complaining noise and Grimaldi declared, "Ah, poor thing! I'll put you out of your misery," and swallowed it. When the second made a like piteous appeal, Grimaldi gulped it down, remarking, "Well, I can't make fish of one and flesh of t'other." His gluttony was an outstandingly popular vice. His libelous female impersonations were highly applauded. And his caricatures brought him the appellation of "Hogarth in action."

In most ways the Clown of tradition, if always supreme among them, Grimaldi had the ingenuity to invent a new joke. It has acquired the name of "construction" and attenuated examples of it can be seen today in the "inventions" of Ed Wynn and in the elaborate mechanical devices with which Joe Cook was wont to fill the musical comedy stage. The new joke stemmed from the old pantomime trick of transformation, but reached a more elaborate development in such a Grimaldi characterization as the fierce Hussar, which Joey introduced though a group of genuine Hussars were watching him from a stage box:

> A pair of red pantaloons, which he put on before the audience with the happiest display of blushing modesty, was the only thing which he condescended to borrow of his model: two black varnished coal-scuttles formed his boots, two real horse-shoes shod the heels, and with jack-chains and the help of two large brass dishes or candlesticks for spurs, equipped his legs in a uniform almost as clattering, unwieldly and absurd as the most irresistible of our whiskered propugnatores.

"The strength of Grimaldi, the Garrick of clowns," Theodore Hook wrote, "seems, like that of wine, to increase with age." But even at the age of forty, Grimaldi felt the effects of his strenuous, knockabout stage life. A newspaper that put a qualifying "perhaps" after his name in enumerating the clowns of the day who were true tumblers spoke an unhappy truth, for as he staggered from the stage Joe required assistants to massage his legs: "His sinews were gathered up into huge knots by the cramps that followed his exertions." As early as 1823 he was on the wrong side of the curtain when Covent Garden produced *Harlequin and Poor Robin; or, The House that Jack Built,* with Joe's son, J. S. Grimaldi, as the clown. To this beloved son Grimaldi passed on everything in clownship except a respect for the art. Success came easily to the offspring of a famous father, too easily: J. S. Grimaldi drank himself into lunacy and Clown lost the one exponent, after Joe, who might have kept him in his high station.

There were a few Grimaldi appearances still to come: at his son's benefit in 1826; at a farewell benefit of his own at Sadler's Wells on March 17, 1828, to which he went from a sickbed attended by his doctor; and, finally, at a benefit at Drury Lane where he again sang his eternally popular song, "Hot Codlins," and assumed for a short time the motley which "clung to my skin as I took it off, and the old cap and bells [which] rang mournfully as I quitted them for ever." On May 31, 1837, he died quietly in his sleep.

Fate may not have been unduly kind to the gentle Joe during his lifetime, but it has steadfastly refused to provide a successor worthy of donning the Grimaldi motley. Pantomime after Joe became more and more "tricky," more the spectacle, less the acme of slapstick humor and fanciful merriment. Although it appears yearly on the London boards, it is not the inimitable entertainment of the Grimaldi era. So, in that way at least, by denying a successor, Fate has kept illustrious Joey's name and his fame. A hundred years have not dimmed the magic of this great clown and good man.

June 1937

* *

MARY AUSTIN

*

Primitive Stage Setting

IT IS ONLY by keeping in mind that primitive drama was concerned with getting things done and had nothing to do with story telling that any satisfactory theory of the origin of stage setting can be arrived at. Drama began as magic; as a communal performance for persuading the Universe, under any one of its special aspects, to work together for the advantage of mankind. It was communal in as much as the good of the community as a whole was sought, and both actors and spectators were participants. The performance was rhythmic, since rhythm was an early, empirically discovered method of raising the voltage of group desire. It concerned both gods and men, or if not gods, the invisible Forces which were afterward symbolized as godhead; incalculable, except as they were believed to be alive toward men, and communicable. And this, under whatever shape of the moment, is the function of good drama today; to raise the spiritual voltage of the group, to bring the people into sympathetic communion with the Powers and thus explicate and inform the particular human need that the occasion shows forth. It is in this shape that primitive drama can still be seen going on before the "medicine-lodge," around the kiva, in Amerindian villages of our Southwest.

The act to be dramatically performed is always one of supreme necessity; that the rain may fall, that game may multiply, that the tribe may increase, sickness be taken away and the arrows of the enemy be turned aside. The community is present in whichever of its aspects is most under consideration, as male or female, as hunter, warrior, farmer, housebuilder, giver of bread. The Powers—afterward deified—were thought of as present in spirit, but were brought closer to the actors by being symbolized, in the phallus, the corn-ear, the bow, later by masked impersonators. Man's helpers also appeared as friendly animals or as the spirits of his ancestors. Still later, when the gods themselves had been specialized and named, the community began to appear not as mankind but as particular men, as Oedipus, Hamlet, Oswald, and the aspiration—or the handicap to be removed—signalized as the madness of Orestes, the nose of Cyrano, the beauty of Mélisande.

All of these phases of dramatic presentation had either appeared or been strongly shadowed forth while drama was still primitive; that is to say while movement, color and melody were taking the place that was later occupied by dialogue. This was also before architecture could render any aid, and the play was performed before the huts or tents of the wild tribe. In this period man himself was the only dramatic vehicle. Accordingly he set himself as the stage, the primary object of all stage setting being to isolate the act, to give it cogency and attract the sympathetic attention of the Powers. So man painted himself black to signalize the Earth Power, red and yellow for summer and the sun, turquoise for the sky, or black and white to personate the spirits of the ancestors. Further, he added ornaments and painted or worked designs of appropriate symbol on his skin or his clothing. Very soon he began to isolate the place in which the drama took place; before the tribal altar, on the High-place Shrine, or merely within a sacred precinct variously marked out. Always having it in mind to make an urgent, an unmistakable showing of what he aspired to have or be.

For this is the true use of drama, to make a Showing of Life, that life may be bettered thereby. Thus in the Rain Dance at Sia, men, women and children make a showing of themselves and their desire, "that the corn come up; that the people grow strong; that the people have bread to complete the path of life." In like manner *What Price Glory?* makes a showing of war, that the people may be saved from this madness, *The Silver Cord* makes a showing of obsessive mother-love, and *Abie's Irish Rose* a showing of the folly of race prejudice.

In primitive times man supposed none but the gods able to help life very much. Therefore all drama was what is called religious. It was designed to further the action of men, and so induce the sympathetic activity of the gods. Along this line all stage setting developed. It is not in the earliest stages representative, what is modernly called "realistic," but suggestive. The Papago, before making himself gloriously drunk with sahuaro wine as a way of insuring a wet year, fences in the drinking place with "cloud callers," strings of feathers. The Pueblo dancer will sometimes outline near the dancing place a "god home" in blue cornmeal, or the Navajo erect, for the accommodation of the Yei, a "dark circle of boughs," within which they and the Navajo may meet. But the Navajo did even better. He painted in the floor of the medicine hogan or on the open dancing floor a sand picture of the sacred story which gave rise to his ritual, as bird catchers spread lime on boughs.

When the sand painting is woven into a blanket, as frequently happens, and hung upon the wall of the Medicine hogan, its relation to a stage setting is immediately apparent. It is also from this point that we can definitely begin to spin the threads that connect Amerind drama with what we know of the origins of classic drama in Greece. It has been said that aboriginal drama is not concerned with telling a story. But there is always a story concerned with the play. It is the story of how the ceremonial which is displayed in the dance-drama was originally received by man. Always it is supposed to have been taught to an individual by the Surpassing-Beings, by his totem animal or by one of the animal helpers of primitive man. Sometimes it comes in dreams as the answer to prayer, or in the trance vision of the neophyte, but more often it is given at the end of an adventure with the Surpassing-Ones. It is, in fact, the precious essence of an experience, preserved in song and dance and ritual, remedial for conditions similar to those that called it forth. In the earliest forms, the ritualistic acts and the lyrics or chorals of which the ceremonial is composed are simply shorthand notations of the story, the story itself being utterly unintelligible to the uninstructed onlooker. To the performers, however, the story has been revealed by the priests, or it has formed part of the childhood instruction of every member of the tribe, and serves to explain the ceremonial as the story of the Nativity explains the Christmas tree to the modern child. Ask yourself how much you would guess of the Christ story if, with no other preparation, you suddenly stumbled upon a group of people singing around an evergreen tree hung with gifts and candles, and over it a tinsel representation of a star, and you will realize how little can be guessed of the origin of an aboriginal dance-drama at the first seeing. You might even suppose, in the first case, the chubby masked personage in red, with long white whiskers, found distributing the gifts, to be the deity worshiped in this fashion. So you might suppose an explanation of the Navajo Yabetchi which would be wide of the true story of the young man who was stolen by the Utes and in escaping endured an Odyssey of mythical experiences in the House of the Rock Crystal, or the Rainbow, or behind the Dark Curtain of the Doorway of the Dawn. And having returned home the young man found that his own tribe no longer smelled good to him, whereupon his spiritual guide, Elder Brother, taught him the Yabetchi ritual as a means of restoring him to normal condition. But if you were versed in Navajo symbolism and pictography, you would guess from the accompanying sand painting as much about the play as used to be conveyed by one of George Bernard Shaw's prefaces or, earlier, by such notations as "Towers of Illium in the distance" or "Windsor Castle at the right." It interested me to recall last year, on seeing Robert Edmond Jones' designs for a jazz ballet, that Mr. Jones was directly acquainted with aboriginal art. His method of treating the mechanical background of an amusement park was very much in the Navajo manner, making allowance for the fact that the Navajo is obliged to spread his stage setting flat on the ground, and his medium is colored sands gathered painstakingly from the Painted Desert.

The connection here with Greek Drama is not so instantly perceived. The bulk of Amerind drama is in the condition of Greek drama at about 600 B.C. when historical account of its evolution was first taken. It was composed of ritual acts, dancing and singing, without dialogue; it was confined to one place the locus of which was signalized by the presence of an altar or shrine or other sacred index; it depended wholly on body painting and costume for its explanatory setting. But the most advanced Amerind drama introduces dialogue between the members of the chorus, or between them and a priest or masked personator of the gods. Examples of this can be observed in the dance of The Emergence at San Felipe, The Snake Dance, or Flute Ceremony in the Hopi pueblos, and many of the Zuñi dances. This means that in the most primitive forms of Greek and Amerind drama the story does not appear, but the ritual is addressed to conditions affecting the community, similar to those in which the ritual arose. But little by little the story emerges, until in the best examples of Greek drama it is the story that makes the play. A precisely similar evolution is demonstrable in the case of Mexican aboriginal drama. The identity of the two processes appears beyond question. In classic drama Thespis is credited with having introduced actors into the dance-drama of Athens; but I strongly suspect that Thespis merely improved upon and formalized a tendency which he had discovered developing naturally in Attic drama.

It is necessary to recall so much of the history of classic drama because it has been supposed that the stage, that is a raised platform for the speaker, was introduced by the Greek tragedians merely in order that the speaker might be better heard. I also suspect that this was not so much the case as that the locus of the play had been modified by the temple which had arisen over the shrine or at one side of the sacred precinct. So long as the fetishes and sacred symbols of the tribe were housed in a tent of skins or a hut of boughs there could be no stage other than the ground on which the audience stood and the dancers performed. When there was a temple or kiva within which the more sacred mysteries were performed, its portico or steps would naturally provide a standing ground for actors issuing from its recesses. This can be seen in the Hopi dances as the Snake Priests or the Katchinas come and go from kisi and kiva. It is more than likely that the rigid stone stage of classic drama originated in the equally rigid temple portico, as it can be shown to have originated among Amerinds south of the United States line. Also it is suggested that the Greek habit of having all acts of violence take place behind the stage originated in a previous habit of having sacrifices and other mysteries take place within the cellar or temple proper, out of sight of, or at least somewhat removed from, the crowd.

On this assumption, which in the case of Amerind drama is simple fact, the altar and wall decorations of the temple or kiva become part of the stage setting. As these are dictated by the particular cult being celebrated, details would be tedious. The one thing that can be said of all these settings is that they are invariably *suggestive rather than representative*. They resemble, making allowance for the primitive vocabulary of art, what Robert Edmond Jones tried to do once in an ultra "modern" setting for *Macbeth*; what was done by Covarrubias in *Androcles and the Lion* with a stylized painted curtain for a jungle background.

This was the evolution of stage setting in the drama which remained religious in character and became tragedy in Europe. But stage setting for drama which was modulated into comedy proceeded along realistic lines; its setting was representative or, at the outside, tended toward caricature. From the earliest times comedy seems to have been used as a social corrective, and was in the hands of societies or at least of persons as official and as sacred in character as any other. But the comedy "business," necessarily objective, becomes inevitably realistic. Among Amerinds, however, it was never divorced from that economy of means which distinguishes all their art, the innate capacity for occupying space without filling it. In setting the stage for a Pueblo comedy the absolute article for labeling place or period is invariably selected. Once I saw an impromptu farce involving Apache and Keres tribes, in which the Apache country was indicated by three well placed yuccas, while ten feet away the Keres domain was perfectly characterized by a selection of a single, young pine tree. When it became necessary to indicate the camp of the white man this was done beyond doubt by a scattering of several rusty tin cans. On another occasion a camp of archeologists was successfully located by an old bone and a few potsherds and an imitation phonograph horn. Extremely clever animal representations are managed for comedy, while for the sacred dances only animal masks and symbolic body paintings are used, along with feathers which have always a prayerful significance. In Pueblo drama the complete absence of feathers in costume or setting would positively indicate the comedy character.

One aspect of primitive comedy, if better understood, might throw a helpful light on the vexed problem of the "sex" play. Many primitive plays have to do with fructification of crops, of wild game, of the mothers of the tribe. And to the primitive mind both reverence and laughter are indispensable concomitants of success. A fructification ceremony entered into as a sacrament is not less acceptable to the tribes than a fructification comedy which can be uproariously laughed at. The sort of sex play which can be only sniggered at or suffered in uneasy silence is never seen in Amerindian camps. It is exclusively served to "civilized audiences."

I am sure that the distinction is a sound one, that an attitude toward sex which is of unbroken solemnity is as degenerate as an attitude of uniform salaciousness. The probabilities are that our own difficulties about the whole problem of sex drama arise out of our being so largely bemused by sex obsessions that we do not any more know what aspects of sex ought to be taken seriously and what can be best corrected with whips of laughter. Any sex suggestion or symbol, even the sexual act itself, if done in the presence of the gods, is permissible in aboriginal drama. If done only for or by the people it must be treated humorously.

January 1928

* *

ROLLO PETERS

*

Horse Opera House

THERE IS ONE HOUSE for each of us; a building retained in memory in which is the core of our destiny. Few of us when young are not so affected, consciously or otherwise, by some structure but that we remain always within its influence; snail-like, we carry its four walls upon our back as long as life lasts.

Mine was—and *is*—a wooden Opera House in the old Spanish-Californian town of Monterey where I lived as a boy. Until the other day, when a friend discovered a dusty ledger in a Monterey printing-shop, its magic had faded from my mind. This business record of the Opera House renewed that theatre's past as linked with mine. I saw the place clearly again against the western sky, went into it through the ledger as though it were a door.

On the first page I found this tariff dated 1900, written with faint violet ink in what was then known as "a fine hand":

Regular rental of hall including lights, up to 12.M,	$10.00
Reg. Rental after 12.,	$12.00
Afternoon Rental,	$ 5.00
Show Rental,	$10.00
School Exhibitions,	$ 8.00
Political Meetings,	$ 5.00
Concerts,	$10.00

Here were the harsh economic facts, coupled with a very personal sense of values. Why *not* charge three dollars more for a "School Exhibition" than for a "Political Meeting" where arguments might be washed down with a barrel of Monterey Lager? What, I asked myself, was intended by the contraction, "12.M"? Did it represent noon or darkest midnight? Up to that ambiguous hour the Hall cost only ten dollars, *with* lights. What would be charged if you hired it dark and brought your own lanterns? Turning the pages I saw again, like images in a stereopticon, the house and its owner. After forty years the latter emerged—a ginger-bearded Scotchman wearing golfing breeches, a belted jacket and tweed cap, leaning against an iron hitching-post outside the two-story edifice bearing his sand-dry name—Bagby.

A little taller than neighboring buildings then, Bagby's Opera House was not an unusual structure. In fact its counterpart throughout the United States is affectionately remembered by many of us who were brought up in small towns during the early 1900's. Yet to me it is unique above all other theatres for there, behind the blank white "false front" crowned with a Victorian cornice, I saw my first play and felt those impulses that led me eventually to the stage.

Curving with the bay, Monterey's principal street—named for Governor Alvarado before the Yankees took the town in 1847—follows an ancient cattle path. Fronting on Alvarado Street, with its back so close to the nearby surf that I have known storms to mist its windows with salt spray, stands the Opera House. During the times catalogued in the ledger the building had a double function. On the ground floor, odorous with damp hay, harness and animal sweat, was a livery stable. Above, well fertilized, flowered the Drama in a combination Social Hall and theatre. Nature below; above Art! But Bagby had concealed his exotic blend of manure and culture behind a facade as flatly "U.S.A." as bread pudding upon a majolica platter, a chilly flavorless structure in a setting of cypress, cactus, pepper, banana and palm trees and crumbling, painted adobes.

Today, crowded between newer buildings, almost forgotten as a stable-playhouse, the shell of the Opera House still stands. On the ground floor, replacing stalls and carriage racks, is a neon-lighted Pool Parlor. Above, a Political Club now occupies the dead theatre.

Gone is the bank next door where Mr. Henry cashed my first check. I recall being timid and impressed by the aloof banker who was connected in my mind with far-away, wonderful lands, for at about that time I was told that his daughter, Lou Henry, had gone to China to live with her young engineer husband, Herbert Hoover. Across the street, the Adobe Saloon, rendezvous of my father, Jack London and George Sterling, has been turned to more sober usage —Dry Goods.

It was disappointing to discover that the ledger began with the year 1900. An earlier volume would have disclosed that Bagby built his Opera House about 1875. Reached by a steep enclosed staircase on the left, the hall had a flat floor in order that it might be used for dances and meetings. When actors came to town, a rickety scaffolding with hard, backless seats was erected at the end opposite the stage. Here, in the "cheap seats," I usually sat precariously, drowned in the loves and hatreds of the players—mobile, *round* men and women, not flat figures like those in my cardboard theatre in our house on the hill.

But how *near* I sat to those magical creatures! The Hall, not much more than fifty feet in length, could hold at the utmost three hundred tightly compressed spectators. As there was no loft above the toylike stage, sets of scenery were either rolled up with block and tackle or pushed on from the wings. The front curtain represented a primitive landscape of the Monterey coast, framed in a golden scroll and proudly advertising local merchants.

Kerosene lanterns were replaced in my day by naked electric bulbs.

But this made the place no safer. The Hall, connected with the ground only by a narrow front staircase and a hazardous flight at the back, was a potential furnace.

And worse; the floor, weakly supported by thirty-foot beams set too far apart, sagged like a string hammock. So, in addition to the likelihood of cremation, the spectators were in constant danger of being precipitated through the ceiling onto the backs of horses bedded down below. I would lie at home dreaming of it after a performance, a struggling mass of cattle, soldiers, Mexican ranchers, the town's loose women, actors—and myself!

Remembering that Bagby was prepared against such a cataclysmic chute, I searched his ledger for some note like "10 Pillars, $3.50." There was none. Yet I remember the posts. To offset the strain caused by a large audience Bagby had them set up at intervals between the stalls, thereby assuring himself that the customers remained where they belonged—aloft.

These supports of stout redwood served also as a barometer of his business. A prizefight, calling out the demonstrative sporting crowd, required all of them. When James J. Jeffries came to town in *Davy Crockett,* the stable must have resembled a forest. Less popular troupes of players employed fewer (and probably *walked* to the neighboring town). Pity the company manager, before the curtain was rolled up, passing mournfully between tethered beasts and vehicles, sighing to himself, "God, only *four* posts tonight! Must be the fog. How far *is* Pacific Grove?"

Odors of the stable seeped up between the planks. In those days there were horses the length of Alvarado Street, hitched to posts and verandah rails, as well as below in the stable. Often during a dramatic stillness the well-timed critical whinny of a hack-horse shattered the actors, set the audience shouting with joy so that, to this day, the phrase "horse laugh," has an especial, poignant meaning for me—Horse Opera House . . .

From Bagby's erratic bookkeeping it was difficult to make out what were receipts and what disbursements. For example, towards the front of the ledger I came upon one baffling item, the only reference to his nether business. In the midst of matters pertaining to the theatre, he had set down, "One sack of grain, $1.00." Had a horse wandered upstairs by chance that week? Did the current week's players require a bag of feed every seven days for sustenance? I like to think of the leading man, dark and hungry, shouldering the residue of "One sack of grain, $1.00" as he boarded the train that took him to the next "stand," Salinas.

Perhaps Bagby's vigilance slipped the night he made this entry. In any case, it would not matter, for in those happy days before Trade Unions, Government Control and multitudinous Tax Collectors, such a man as Bagby was "free to run his own business in his own way." Judging by his bookkeeping, he did.

But the ledger is no revealing diary. Bagby emerges only in spite of his bone-dry accounting. He never let himself go, never allowed himself a "jolly good show" or "leading lady shows too much leg in second act." He reveals himself solely as a financier, caring not a Scottish hang for the transient actors in linen dusters, the feminine artists in shabby ruffles and high feathered hats. For instance, with what economy of line Bagby's violet ink etches the opening of our volcanic century:

January	11,	to cash Receipts, Advertising Show, Stereo. Advert. Co.,	$ 5.00
"	13,	Cockatoo,	$ 5.00
"	18,	(No Record)	$ 5.00
"	19,	"	$ 5.00
"	20,	"	$ 5.00
"	27,	Duncan Clarke,	$10.00
"	28,	McMillan, Strong Man,	$ 3.35

Three dollars and thirty-five cents for (or from?) a Strong Man; was that enough? Who was the unidentified artist, Duncan Clarke, that alone among January's stars was able to pay the full tariff, "10.00 up to 12.M"? And the Cockatoo? Had a bird really hired the Hall? We were in New York that winter and so unfortunately I can supply no details of these performers, feathered or fleshed. But on the face of it receipts were slim. Obviously the Theatre was going to the dogs. Or birds. Bryan *should* have been elected. But if January was on the lean side, the succeeding months show little improvement, as witness:

February	8,	Nashville Students.
"	9,	"His Better Half" Co.
"	20,	Foresters Masked Ball.

April	11,	Barlow's Minstrels (Cancelled).	
March	13,	Brehamy Ballard & Opera Co.	
May	1,	Jolly Fellow's Ball,	($12.00).
March	9,	Citizen's Political Meeting,	($ 2.50).
"	17,	Social Dance,	($ 5.00).
"	31,	Social Dance,	($ 5.00).
April	5,	"Iowa" Concert,	($ 7.00).
"	16,	Castell, Hypnotist,	($ 6.50).
"	17,	Social Dance,	($ 5.00).
"	18,	Castell,	($ 6.50).
May	11,	Catholic Entertainment,	($ 6.00).
"	25,	"Young Men's Dance,"	($10.00), (Paid).
June	4,	Public School Exercises.	
"	7,	Fourth of July Entertainment,	($ 5.00), (Paid).
"	10,	Catholic Convent Exercises.	
"	18,	Fire Department Concert.	
July	4,	Fire Department Ball.	
August	23,	Republican Speaking, R. E. Mackinley	($ 5.00).
"	16,	Republican Club, (Rent of Baggage Room, per month, Monday nights,	($ 5.00).

Here, unaltered, is Bagby's jugglery of the calendar during this curious year.

And what were The Nashville Students doing so far from home? Though "His Better Half" Co. is the only play listed, a few others might have slipped in and never been noticed. Up to the "Young Men's Dance" none appears actually to have paid Bagby *anything*.

Next comes an audacious schedule. What metropolitan company today would attempt such a week's repertory as this of the "Incomparable" Erwin Blenkall Company?

Tuesday evening,	Sappho.
Wednesday " ,	Camille.
Thursday " ,	Ten Nights in a Barroom.
Friday " ,	Romeo & Juliet.
Saturday Matinee,	East Lynne.
" Night,	Not Guilty.
Sunday " ,	Shameus O'Brien.

Where did the scenery, costumes and sufficient actors for all these plays come from out of a troupe of ten or a dozen players? Incomparable indeed! But provincial, too. For troupes like the Blenkalls seldom achieved San Francisco, Los Angeles or even Sacramento. This full week's engagement was probably the booking between Salinas and Santa Cruz on the dusty road north from San Luis Obispo.

I remember going on the Friday night. Whether Edna Ellsmere (of the perfect name!) sang between the acts or played Juliet—or did both—I cannot recall, but it was then I saw my first Shakespearean play. Long ago the details have blurred but the essence of that night's excitement returned to me all through the three years I played Romeo.

Much later when our Pacific Coast tour opened in San Francisco, Alexander Woollcott, then drama critic on the *New York Herald,* asked me to write my homecoming impressions. Instead I sent him a memoir of Bagby's Opera House, of that intrepid performance by the Blenkall Company so many years earlier. It was a kind of testimonial to them which Woollcott printed on the front page of his Sunday section. Indirectly but *finally* the Blenkalls achieved New York!

Time, even with Bagby, moved on. Not long after this the ledger dwindles. Lost somewhere in Bagby's haphazard accounts was the Convent play—an odd Catholic idealization of Mary, Queen of Scots—in which I acted my first wordless role.

The ledger ends. The pot of violet ink is dry. It is as though Bagby, fatigued by the gas wagons that outstripped his horses and the flickering screen which shrouds his stage, had laid down his head upon the last page to fall asleep. The husk of his Opera House still stands. All that transpired within it—the player's magic, the dream—survives his casual record. Let him sleep on. Where is the Cockatoo today?

February 1944

WALTER PRICHARD EATON

*

The Theatre Mrs. Fiske Knew

EVERY NOW AND THEN I produce an incredulous stare by stating that I used to see Edwin Booth act. I have seen people positively gape at my mother, when she described Edwin Forrest in *Coriolanus* (my mother is still alive). But the gifted and gallant actress who died this winter, Minnie Maddern Fiske, and who died practically in harness, once acted with Laura Keene, with Junius Brutus Booth, with Barry Sullivan, with Lucille Western. So short, after all, are the links between the old and the new. She who, as a child, learned in the "big bow-wow" school of Barry Sullivan, swept blithely into the twentieth century with the banner of modernism in her hands: this woman whom only a few months ago we were watching on the stage, during her lifetime had been an active—how active!—part of a changing drama, a changing style of acting, a changing theatre organization. She knew the old, the new, the in-between, and one sometimes wonders if she found the differences so great as we, from our all-important isle of the present, suppose. At any rate, she had a pretty shrewd idea of what is enduring through all change.

Mrs. Fiske, who was born, as it were, on the stage, just at the close of the Civil War, began to act at the age of three, and got most of her education in the theatre. Her precocity, of course, explains why she was associated in early years with the old-time theatre. She played, for example, the Widow Melnotte, in *The Lady of Lyons,* at the age of thirteen! She played Dick Deadeye in a juvenile *Pinafore* company, and she acted both in the "classic" repertoire, and in such stuff as *Ten Nights in a Barroom*. There was nothing in this repertoire, and little enough in the acting of it (save when we saw Jefferson as Rip), to train a sensitive child in modernism. Yet when, as a girl still in her teens, Minnie Maddern was made a star, there was something about her playing recognized as different. The late Henry Miller, who was her leading man in *Caprice* just before her retirement in 1890, used to describe the play with ironic amusement, and then discourse with enthusiasm on the wonders of naturalism this wisp of a girl performed in it.

She retired to marry Harrison Grey Fiske in 1890, and it is significant that this was the year Pinero retired to read Ibsen and then to write *The Second Mrs. Tanqueray,* and the year James A. Herne produced *Margaret Flemming.* A change was in the air, of course, and sensitive artists felt it, and felt the need for a new orientation. As Mrs. Fiske, Minnie Maddern presently came back to our stage and for the next decade and a half was in the thick and forefront of two battles, the battle for modernism in dramatic art, and the battle for freedom in theatrical organization. The first battle was won all along the line, and if she had not fought the second she would have become a rich woman. In the world's eyes she lost that second battle, after all her fellow fighters had deserted. But it is being won now, by others, and her instincts are being triumphantly vindicated.

When Mrs. Fiske came back to the stage in the nineties Ibsen was still practically unknown on our boards, William Winter considered the new Pinero a menace to public morals, Ada Rehan was still queening it at Daly's, and the only American playwright with a real understanding of what the new Continental dramatists were trying to do was James A. Herne, and he had to inject a scene of blatant melodrama into *Shore Acres* to make it acceptable. It was only in our rough, popular theatre, in such folk comedies as Hoyt's farces, that the public looked for some reality of method. Further, the bulk of our more serious fare was adapted from foreign sources. Before the century was over Mrs. Fiske had commissioned two Americans to write plays for her (both, to be sure, adapted from English novels), and she had produced them with great success, acting them herself, and causing them to be acted by the rest of the cast, with straightforward sincerity. It happens that I was in college when both those plays, *Tess of the D'Urbervilles* and *Becky Sharp,* were produced. Like all college youths of that period I was a theatre addict. I saw *Tess* eight times in two weeks in Boston. Nor have I forgotten the effect they had upon us all, nor the curiously mixed fare we then enjoyed. The great ones, like Irving and Terry, or Mansfield, in Shakespeare and neo-poetic romances. The Sotherns and Hacketts in *The Prisoner of Zenda* and that sort of romance. Gillette in *Sherlock Holmes.* The Charles Frohman stable of stars in neat little English comedies, or deodorized French ones. *The Christian.* And an occasional glimpse, thrilling, vague, into something new, as *Griffith Davenport* by Herne; *The Wild Duck* acted solemnly by

Ibsen fanatics (at a matinee, of course); Fitch, in *Barbara Frietchie,* feeling for realism of setting and reality of mood; above all Mansfield in *The Devil's Disciple,* by a wild fellow named Shaw; and the acting of Mrs. Fiske. How simple was her Tess, and how heartbreaking! And how magnificent her Becky! Here was high comedy, surely, but not the Ada Rehan version of Restoration artificiality, delightful as that was. It was high comedy because it was a sharp, true character picture of Becky, sparing nothing, painted by two masters of comic irony—Thackeray and Mrs. Fiske.

Well, we youngsters adored to "supe" for Mansfield in *Richard III,* and we adored Ellen Terry, and we adored *The Prisoner of Zenda.* But we sat up till Four A.M. to discuss what "this guy Shaw" was trying to say, and we read Ibsen, and we went eight times in two weeks to watch Mrs. Fiske act. We knew something was aborning.

With the turn of the century, Mrs. Fiske's fight for freedom resulted in her management for several years of the Manhattan Theatre in New York (where Gimbel's store now stands), and there she established the best resident company New York has seen so far in this century, and developed an ensemble not equaled till the Moscow Players appeared here. She set a standard of great value, because it taught us to look for the proper presentation of the play as a play, and not for star performances. Here she produced Ibsen, *Leah Kleschna, Mary of Magdala,* and many other plays of merit, with such actors as George Arliss, John Mason, William B. Mack, Charles Cartwright, in her company. With the passing of that company, it was she who, in 1908, bought and presented the work of Professor Baker's first graduate in playwriting, Edward Sheldon, and helped usher into the theatre the new generation which had grown up in the newer tradition. She acted two of Sheldon's plays, one by Henry James Smith, one by Marion de Forest, and others by young Americans whose work was new. It is an unfortunate fact that none of those who wrote for her could compass anything like her range, either of comedy or drama. It may be that the realistic method can infrequently tap the full resources of a first-rate player. Mrs. Fiske, certainly, needed the heightened style of Thackeray, or Hardy, or Ibsen to tap her full resources. But her method was, to the end, never out of step, and illustrated perfectly what is timeless in the actor's art.

Her last years were sad, because a woman who was still the most skillful player of her country had to troupe about in shabby revivals, when she should have been an honored member of a fine company, playing sometimes, and sometimes giving the benefit of her incomparable direction and training.

And that, of course, is a part of the other half of her story. More even than the style of writing and acting, the organization of the theatre changed in her time, but here was a leader against the change instead of for it. She lost. But her battle isn't over yet.

When she began to act, nearly all large cities had resident stock companies, and nearly all other theatres were locally owned and managed. The manager of such a theatre made trips to New York, saw the current plays, and booked for his house those which he thought his town would like. Many star actors were their own managers, and though the organization of the playhouse may have been somewhat happy-go-lucky, it was free and independent. About 1895 a group of theatre owners, including Charles Frohman who could also class as a real manager, conceived the brilliant idea of getting control of all the best theatres in all the key cities, and then exacting tribute from every company which wanted to make a tour. As all successful plays did then want to make a tour, there being far more profits on the road than in New York, the scheme had merit.

This group was called the Theatrical Syndicate. There was bitter opposition, led at first by Francis Wilson, Richard Mansfield, Nat Goodwin, James A. Herne and Mrs. Fiske, with Belasco and Liebler and Company (George Tyler) joining them. The fight is now ancient history, and we cannot detail it here. Suffice it to say that those who opposed the Syndicate did so on the grounds that the artist's freedom was being curtailed, and that a monopoly control of the American theatre would mean a serious depreciation of standards. One by one the Syndicate tied up the theatres across the land, one by one they bought up the actors who fought them (and truth to tell it came to mean almost financial suicide to oppose), till only Belasco, Tyler and Mrs. Fiske were left.

Belasco had two theatres in New York and one in Washington, which kept him going. Tyler took Bernhardt on a tour and played her sometimes in circus tents. Mrs. Fiske rented the Manhattan Theatre in New York and founded a resident company. Ultimately even these brave people had to give in. But their fight is a noble chapter of theatrical history, and both Belasco and Mrs. Fiske, during it, made their very best productions and demonstrated that the independent artist who is not forced to produce for the greatest common denominator achieves the most admirable results.

The predictions which Wilson, Mansfield and Mrs. Fiske made at the beginning of the fight were, of course, amply borne out. Instead of resulting in better plays for the road, the Syndicate methods resulted in destroying the individuality of local houses and in lowering the standards of plays to the most popular level, except in the cases of a few stars bright enough to insist on personal choice of material. Matters were not in the least helped by the founding, ten years after the Syndicate, of the Shubert rival chain of theatres. Too many theatres, overproduction of poor plays, competitive booking, were some of the evils that followed. The result was, of course, that after the Great War the theatre was ripe for the Theatre Guild, it demanded the stabilization of the Actor's Equity, and it was easy prey for the movies. The theatre in which Mrs. Fiske had grown up, and whose battles she had fought so bravely, had become a football of vulgar and ignorant shopkeepers in New York (or better, perhaps, "realtors").

Well, the members of the Syndicate have passed away, and already their circuit is shrinking to a shadow. The Shuberts are in the hands of a receiver. Mrs. Fiske's last engagement was played in what was once the Syndicate's pet house in Chicago, the Blackstone, and it was independent once more when she played there. The all-powerful Theatre Guild, booking through the Syndicate, calmly insisted on playing in the Blackstone, also, and if the Syndicate didn't like it, they knew what they could do. The days of theatrical monopoly are about over, and one likes to think that Mrs. Fiske realized it during the past year. Now the movie magnates are trying hard to repeat the same disastrous round, and some day the same fate will overtake them. The stars in their courses fight against theatrical, or any other artistic, monopoly. The deeper instincts both of artists and audiences are against it. No one can say what the future will bring forth, but here in the comparatively short lifetime of one actress we see a great swing of the pendulum, and the poise for the return. We see the sincerity of the artist in reflecting life as the element of progress, and the freedom of the artist to invent and create as the enduring necessity. We may assume, I think, that theatres will more and more tend to go back to local control, and that audiences will more and more join with artists to insure freedom. And so much has happened since Mrs. Fiske unfurled her modern banner only forty years ago, we may safely assume as much more of interest and excitement will happen before our children begin to tell theirs, "—but you should have seen Katharine Cornell in *The Barretts of Wimpole Street*!"

May 1932

* *

ALAIN LOCKE

*

The Negro and the American Stage

IN THE APPRAISAL of the possible contribution of the Negro to the American theatre, there are those who find the greatest promise in the rising drama of Negro life. And there are others who see possibilities of a deeper, though subtler, influence upon what is after all more vital, the technical aspects of the arts of the theatre. Certainly to date (1926) the Negro influence upon American drama has been negligible. Whereas even under the handicaps of second-hand exploitation and restriction to the popular amusement stage, the Negro actor has considerably influenced our stage and its arts. One would do well to imagine, therefore, what might happen if the art of the Negro actor should really become artistically lifted and liberated. Transpose the possible resources of Negro song and dance and pantomime to the serious stage, envisage an American drama under the galvanizing stimulus of a rich transfusion of essential folk-arts and you may anticipate what I mean. A race of actors can revolutionize the drama quite as definitely and perhaps more vitally than a coterie of dramatists. The roots of drama are after all action and emotion, and our modern drama, for all its frantic experimentation, is an essentially anaemic drama, a something of gestures and symbols and ideas and not overflowing with the vital stuff of which drama was originally made and to which it must return for its rejuvenation, cycle after cycle.

Primarily the Negro brings to the drama the gift of a temperament, not the gift of a tradition. Time out of mind he has been rated as a "natural-born actor" without any appreciation of what that statement, if true, really means. Often it is intended as a disparaging estimate of the Negro's limitations, a recognition of his restriction to the interpretative as distinguished from the creative aspect of drama, a confinement, in terms of a second order of talent, to the status of the mimic and the clown. But a comprehending mind knows that the very life of drama is in dramatic instinct and emotion, that drama begins and ends in mimicry, and that its creative force is in the last analysis the interpretative passion. Welcome then as is the emergence of the Negro playwright and the drama of Negro life, the promise of the most vital contribution of the Negro to the theatre lies, in my opinion, in the deep and unemancipated resources of the Negro actor, and the folk arts of which he is as yet only a blind and hampered exponent. Dramatic spontaneity, the free use of the body and the voice as direct instruments of feeling, a control of body plastique that opens up the narrow diaphragm of fashionable acting and enlarges the conventional mannerisms of the stage—these are indisputably strong points of Negro acting. Many a Negro vaudevillian has a greater store of them than finished masters of the polite theatre. And especially in the dawn of the "synthetic theatre" with the singing, dancing actor and the plastic stage, the versatile gifts of the Negro actor seem peculiarly promising and significant.

Unfortunately it is the richest vein of Negro dramatic talent which is under the heaviest artistic impediments and pressure. The art of the Negro actor has had to struggle up out of the shambles of minstrelsy and make slow headway against very fixed limitations of popular taste. Farce, buffoonery and pathos have until recently almost completely overlaid the folk comedy and folk tragedy of a dramatically endowed and circumstanced people. These gifts must be liberated. I do not narrowly think of this development merely as the extension of the freedom of the American stage to the Negro actor, although this must naturally come about as a condition of it, but as a contribution to the technical idioms and resources of the entire American theatre.

To see this rising influence one must of course look over the formal horizons. From the vantage of the advanced theatre, there is already a significant arc to be seen. In the sensational successes of *The Emperor Jones* and *All God's Chillun Got Wings* there have been two components, the fine craftsmanship and clairvoyant genius of O'Neill and the unique acting gifts of Charles Gilpin and Paul Robeson. From the earlier revelation of the emotional power of the Negro actor by Opal Cooper and Inez Clough in the Ridgeley Torrence plays in 1916 to the recent half successful experiments of Raymond O'Neill's Ethiopian Art Theatre and the National Ethiopian Art Theatre of New York, with Evelyn Preer, Rose MacClendon, Sidney Kirkpatrick, Charles Olden, Francis Corbie and others, an advanced section of the American public has become acquainted with the possibilities of the Negro in serious dramatic interpretation. But the real mine of Negro dramatic art and talent is still in the sub-soil of the vaudeville stage, gleaming through its slag and dross in the unmistakably great dramatic gifts of a Bert Williams, a Florence Mills or a Bill Robinson. Give Bojangles Robinson or George Stamper, pantomimic dancers of genius, an artistic libretto, score and setting; give Josephine Baker, Eddie Rector, Abbie Mitchell or Ethel Waters a dignified medium, and they would be more than a sensation, they would be artistic revelations. Pantomime, that most essential and elemental of the dramatic arts, is a natural *forte* of the Negro actor, and the use of the body and voice and facile control of posture and rhythm are almost as noteworthy in our average as in our exceptional artists. When it comes to pure registration of the emotions, I question whether any body of actors, unless it be the Russians, can so completely be fear or joy or nonchalance or grief.

With his uncanny instinct for the theatre, Max Reinhardt saw these possibilities instantly under the tawdry trappings of such musical comedies as *Eliza, Shuffle Along* and *Runnin' Wild,* which were in vogue the season of his first visit to New York. "It is intriguing, very intriguing," he told me, "these Negro shows that I have seen. But remember, not as achievements, not as things in themselves artistic, but in their possibilities, their tremendous artistic possibilities. They are most modern, most American, most expressionistic. They are highly original in spite of obvious triteness, and artistic in spite of superficial crudeness. To me they reveal new possibilities of technique in drama, and if I should ever try to do anything American, I would build it on these things."

We didn't enthuse—my friend Charles Johnson of *Opportunity* and myself, who were interviewing Mr. Reinhardt. What Negro who stands for culture with the hectic stress of a social problem weighing on the minds of an over-serious minority could be expected to enthuse. *Eliza, Shuffle Along, Runnin' Wild!* We had come to discuss the possibilities of serious Negro drama, of the art-drama, if you please. Surely Director Reinhardt was a victim of that distortion of perspective to which one is so liable in a foreign land. But then, the stage is not a foreign land to Max Reinhardt; he has the instinct of the theatre, a genius that knows what is vital there. We didn't outwardly protest, but raised a brow already too elevated perhaps and shrugged the shoulder that carries the proverbial racial chip.

Herr Reinhardt read the gestures swiftly. "Ah, yes—I see. You view these plays for what they are, and you are right; I view them for what they will become, and I am more than right. I see their future. Why? Well, the drama must turn at every period of fresh creative development to an aspect which has been previously subordinated or neglected, and in this day of ours, we come back to the most primitive and the most basic aspect of drama for a new starting point, a fresh development and revival of the art—and that aspect is pantomime, the use of the body to portray story and emotion. And your people have that art—almost as a special genius. At present it is prostituted to farce, to trite comedy—but the technique is there, and I have never seen more wonderful possibilities. Yes, I should like to do something with it."

With the New Russian Theatre experimenting with the "dynamic ballet" and Meyerhold's improvising or creative actor, with Max Reinhardt's own recently founded International Pantomime Society inaugurated at the last Salzburg festival, with the entire new theatre agog over "mass drama," there is at least some serious significance to the statement that the Negro theatre has great artistic potentialities. What is of utmost importance to drama now is to control the primitive language of the art, and to retrieve some of the basic control which the sophisticated and conventionalized theatre has lost. It is more important to know how to cry, sob and laugh, stare and startle than to learn how to smile, grimace, arch and wink. And more important to know how to move vigorously and with rhythmic sweep than to pirouette and posture. An actor and a folk art controlling the symbolism of the primary emotions has the modern stage as a province ripe for an early and easy conquest. Commenting on the work of the players of the Ethiopian Art Theatre, discerning critics noticed "the freshness and vigor of their emotional responses, their spontaneity and intensity of mood, their freedom from intellectual and artistic obsessions." And almost every review of Gilpin's or Robeson's acting has spoken of it as beyond the calculated niceties, a force of direct and overwhelming emotional projection. It is this sense of something dramatic to the core that flows movingly in the blood rather than merely along the nerves of conscious effort that we speak of as the racial endowment of the Negro actor. For however few individuals there may be who possess it in high degree, it is racial in the sense of being a characteristic folk capability, a heritage latent at least in a rather unique group experience.

Without invoking the obvious analogies of the contemporary Irish and the Russian drama, we can see in this emotional endowment great resources for the theatre. In terms of the prevalent trend for the development of serious Negro drama, we may expect these resources to be cultivated and claimed as the working capital of the Negro Theatre. They are. But just as definitely, too, are they the general property and assets of the American Theatre at large, once the barriers of discrimination are broken through. These barriers are slowly breaking down both on the legitimate stage and in the popular drama, but the great handicap, as Carl van Vechten so keenly points out in his *Prescription for the Negro Theatre,* is blind imitation with the Negro and with Broadway, stagnant conventionalism. Negro dramatic art must not only be liberated from external handicap and disparagement, but from its internal and often self-imposed limitations. It must more and more have the courage to be original, to break with established dramatic convention of all sorts. It must have the courage to develop its own idiom, to pour itself into new molds; in short, to be creatively experimental. From what quarter this impetus will come we cannot quite predict; it may come from the Negro theatre or from some sudden acceptance of the American stage, from the art-theatre or from the commercial theatre, from an American source, or first, as so many artistic emancipations seem to have come, from the more liberal patronage and recognition of the European stage. But this much is certain—the material awaits a great exploiting genius.

One can scarcely think of a complete development of dramatic art by the Negro without some significant artistic reexpression of African life, and the traditions associated with it. This may seem a far cry from the conditions and moods of modern New York and Chicago and the Negro's rapid and feverish assimilation of all things American. But art establishes its contacts in strange ways. The emotional elements of Negro art are choked by the conventions of the contemporary stage; they call for freer, more plastic material. They have, of course, no mysterious affinity with African themes or scenes, but they do have for any life that is more primitive and poetic in substance. So, if, as seems already apparent, the more sophisticated race consciousness of the Negro should move back over the trail of his group tradition to an interest in things African, the natural affinities of the material and the art will complete the circuit and they will most electrically combine. Especially with its inherent color and emotionalism, its freedom from body-hampering dress, its odd and tragic and mysterious overtones, African life and themes, apart from any sentimental attachment, offer a wonderfully new field and province for dramatic treatment. Here both the Negro actor and dramatist can move freely in a world of elemental beauty, with all the decorative elements that a poetic emotional temperament could wish. No recent playgoer with the spell of Brutus Jones in the forest underbrush still upon his imagination will need much persuasion about this.

More and more the art of the Negro actor will seek its materials in the rich native soil of Negro life, and not in the threadbare tradition of the Caucasian stage. In the discipline of art playing upon his own material, the Negro has much to gain. Art must serve Negro life as well as Negro talent serve art. And no art is more capable of this service than drama. Indeed the surest sign of a folk renascence seems to be a dramatic flowering. Somehow the release of such self-expression always accompanies or heralds cultural and social maturity. I feel that soon this aspect of the race genius may come to its classic age of expression. Obviously, though, it has not yet come. For our dramatic expression is still too restricted, self-conscious and imitative.

When our serious drama shall become as naive and spontaneous as our drama of fun and laughter, and that in turn genuinely representative of the folk spirit which it is now forced to travesty, a point of classic development will have been reached. It is fascinating to speculate upon what riotously new and startling drama may come from this. Dramatic maturings are notably sudden. Usually from the popular sub-soil something shoots up to a rapid artistic flowering. Of course, this does not have to recur with the American Negro. But a peasant folk art pouring out from under a generation-long repression is the likeliest soil known for a dramatic renascence. And the supporters and exponents of Negro drama do not expect their folk temperament to prove the barren exception.

February 1926

* *

MIGUEL COVARRUBIAS

*

The Magic Theatre of Bali

PLAYS AND DANCES AS EXORCISMS

EVERY BALINESE believes that his body, like an electric battery, is only the accumulator of the magic energy called *sakti* that enables him to withstand the attacks of evil powers that seek constantly to undermine his magic health. This *sakti* is not evenly divided; some people are born with a capacity to store a higher charge of magic than others; they become the priests, witch-doctors and so forth, endowed with supernatural powers. The *sakti* can be trained to serve them at will by the systematic study of the arts of magic, but people whose hearts are contaminated by evil use of the magic science to harm their enemies, or simply to satisfy their lowest instincts.

The existence of witches, *leyaks,* is an incontestable fact to the Balinese. The *leyaks* are held responsible for most of the evils that afflict them, including sickness and death. Every Balinese has stories to tell of personal encounters with *leyaks* in various forms. They appear as dancing flames flitting from grave to grave in cemeteries, feeding on newly buried corpses, as balls of fire and shadows of a living white cloth, but most frequently in the shapes of weird animals: pigs, dogs, monkeys or tigers. Witches often assume the form of beautiful mute girls who make obscene advances to young men traveling on lonely roads at night. *Leyaks* are, however, progressive and now they are said to prefer more modern shapes for their transformations: motor cars and bicycles that run in and out of temples without drivers and whose tires pulsate as if breathing. There are even *leyak* airplanes sweeping over the roof tops at night. The most interesting character on the Island is the blood-thirsty, child-eating Rangda, mistress of black magic and queen of the legions of *leyaks*.

A curious ceremony in the temple of a neighboring village introduced Rangda to us. It was well after midnight and although the date for the temple feast was still far off there was a crowd, mostly women, in the courtyard, sitting in a circle around a man who appeared to be in a trance. Next to him sat the old *pemangku,* the temple priest, quiet and concentrating, attending to the incense that burned in a clay brazier before a monstrous mask with enormous fangs. The community, it seemed, was having a wave of bad luck and they were asking Rangda to advise them, through the medium, of what she required to leave them alone. The stillness of the night, the incense and the dim light of the petrol lamp, all aided the feeling that the spirit of the dreaded witch was really there. Soon the oracle began to twitch and foam at the mouth, making painful efforts to talk. The mask was placed on his head and the priest listened with intense interest to the incoherent groans, muffled by the mask, which he translated in a monotonous voice as the words of Rangda, now in the body of the medium. After the offerings that she demanded were enumerated, she reproached the villagers for neglecting to give a performance of *tjalonarang,* the play in which her triumphs are enacted. To end the ceremony the musicians played and Rangda danced; then the man was taken out of the trance and Rangda presumably went back to her abode on the summit of the highest mountain, the Gunung Agung.

Time and again we saw Rangda appear in various magic plays; she was invariably represented as a monstrous old woman, her naked white body striped with black. Rings of black fur circled her long hanging breasts, realistically made of bags of white cloth filled with sawdust. She was entirely covered by white hair that reached to her feet, allowing only the bulging eyes and twisted fangs of her mask to be seen. Her tongue hung out, a strip of leather two feet long painted red ending in flames of gold. A row of flames came from the top of her head. She wore white gloves with immense claws and in her right hand she held the white cloth—a deadly weapon if it struck—with which she hid her horrible face from her unsuspecting victims.

The character of Rangda has its origin in historical facts, now interwoven with fantastic myth. At the beginning of the eleventh century a Balinese prince became the King of Java, the great Erlangga, whose extraordinary mother was a Javanese princess who ruled with her Balinese husband. Erlangga's mother became a widow (a *Rangda*) given to black magic and was exiled to the forest where she collected a band of pupils, *leyaks,* whom she trained in the black arts to destroy Erlangga's kingdom because nobody would marry her beautiful daughter, Ratna Menggali, out of fear of the mother. She hated her son for having failed, in the past, to bring pressure upon his father not to take another wife. She killed nearly half of Erlangga's subjects by plagues brought by her *leyaks,* before she was vanquished by the superior magic of the holy man Mpu Bharada, Erlangga's teacher. It is only in the legend that Rangda could be vanquished; the Balinese perform the story of her struggle with Erlangga in a play, but stop at the point where the tide turns against the witch.

The Tjalonarang. It is in a performance of *tjalonarang,* the legend of Rangda, that the Balinese theatre reaches the height of its magnificence. It combines the fine music and delicate dancing of the *legong* with the elaborate staging, the acting, singing and comedy of the classic plays, besides the element of mystery and suspense. The *tjalonarang* is not an ordinary play, but a powerful exorcism against *leyaks,* because by dramatizing Rangda's triumphs, the Balinese aim to gain her good will. Preparations for staging the great show start days before; it is essential that a "male" papaya tree, which bears no fruit, be first transplanted from the wilds to the middle of the dancing grounds, because such a tree is the favorite haunt of the *leyaks*. A tall house on stilts is built at one end for Rangda, reached by a high runway of bamboo, flanked by spears, pennants and umbrellas, all symbols of state. The entire dancing space is covered by a canopy of streamers made of palm-leaf and tissue-paper flags; as many petrol lamps as are available in the village light the stage.

By midnight, the audience is assembled, waiting patiently, listening to the special *tjalonarang* music, perhaps the finest in Bali, played by a full *legong* orchestra augmented with large bamboo flutes. A full moon is propitious for the performance and the company waits until the moon comes out from behind the black clouds, silhouetting the temple roofs, the palm trees and the long aerial roots of the village banyan tree, a hanging black curtain of long tentacles against the sky, the perfect setting for the magic play. Offerings are made beforehand and consultations are held so as not to offend Rangda and to ascertain whether it is safe to hold the performance.

The show begins after midnight and lasts until dawn, when the witch makes her appearance. The play approaches our dramatic literature more nearly than anything else in Bali. It relates the episodes of the mythical struggle between Rangda and the hero-king Erlangga. Dancing interludes by six little girls, the pupils of the witch, alternate with slapstick, the encounters of the king's subjects with *leyaks,* and with dramatic songs by the prince sent to kill Rangda. She is impersonated by an old actor gifted with such great powers that he is able to withstand, in his own body, the dangerous spirit of the witch herself.

Towards dawn the atmosphere becomes surcharged with mystery as the old actor goes into Rangda's house to enter into the trance. Watchmen are appointed to wake all the children that have fallen asleep, lest their tender souls be harmed; a priest stands ready to conjure the Rangda who will make her triumphal appearance at the end of the play. A flickering lamp can be seen through the curtains of the house and there is an occasional groan from the actor as he undergoes the painful transformation. Meantime below, as the music becomes violent, the prince advances across the dancing space with his kriss drawn. With a yell of defiance he starts up the bridge, just as a blood-curdling howl is heard inside the house, the voice of Rangda. Unexpectedly, fireworks, strung on invisible wires all over the trees, begin to explode over the heads of the crowd. The audience is on edge as the curtains part and the frightful form of

Rangda appears, shrieking curses upon the prince who is put to flight as the old witch descends.

The Barong. The witch has a contender for supremacy in a fantastic animal, a mythical lion called *barong*. Because of an ancient feud with Rangda he sides with human beings to thwart her evil plans and the Balinese say that without his help humanity would be destroyed. While Rangda is female, the magic of the "left," the *barong* is the "right," the male. Rangda is the night, the darkness from which emanate illness and death. The *barong* is the sun, the light, medicine, the antidote for evil.

Every community owns a set of the costumes and masks of both characters. These masks have great power in themselves and are kept out of sight in a special shed in the death-temple of the village. They are put away in a basket, wrapped in a magic cloth that insulates evil vibrations, and are uncovered only when actually in use, when the performer-medium is in a trance and under control of a priest, and not before offerings have been made to prevent harm to the participants. Like the Rangda, the *barong* is treated with great respect and the Balinese address him by titles such as Banaspati Radja, "Lord of the Jungle," or Djero Gede, "The Big One," rather than as *barong,* which is only a generic name for his sort of monster.

Despite his demoniac character, the *barong* materializes in a trance play in which he is made to act foolishly and to dance for the amusement of the crowd. His costume consists of a great frame covered by long hair with a sagging back of golden scales set with little mirrors. A beautifully arched gold tail sticks out of his high rump, and from it hang a square mirror, a bunch of peacock feathers and a cluster of little bells that jingle at every move. Under a high gilt crown is his red mask, too small for his body, with bulging eyes and snapping jaws. The power of the *barong* is concentrated in his beard, a tuft of human hair decorated with flowers. The *barong* is animated by two specially trained men who form the front and hind quarters of the animal, the man in the front operating the mask in his hands.

In Pemetjutan the *barong* play began with a performance of *djauk,* a group of boys wearing grinning white masks, who dance to the delicate tunes of a *legong* orchestra called in this case *bebarongan.* After the dance the two *barong* performers went under the costume that lay inanimate on two poles, the mask covered with a white cloth. Like a circus prop-horse the *barong* danced, wiggling his hind quarters, lying down, contracting and expanding like an accordion, snapping his jaws. After his gay outburst of animal spirits, he began a long dance, staring around as if astounded by magic visions that filled the air. He was constantly on the alert for invisible enemies, growing more and more alarmed, clicking his teeth like castanets as the tempo of the music increased. Firecrackers began to explode at the far end of the arena, startling the *barong,* and when the smoke cleared the figure of Rangda appeared, yelling curses at the *barong* who appeared humiliated by her insults. But eventually he reacted and they rushed at each other, fighting until the *barong* was made to bite the dust.

In the meantime a group of half-naked men sitting on a mat went into a trance. They were the assistants of the *barong* against Rangda. A priest consecrated some water by dipping the *barong's* beard into it, and sprinkled the men, who shook all over as if in an epileptic fit. With their eyes glued on the Rangda they got up, drawing their krisses, advancing like fidgety automatons toward the witch who awaited them with her white cloth, her weapon, ready in her raised hand. Suddenly she ran after them, but just then one of the priests on watch noticed something unusual in her behavior and passed the word that she was out of control; she was caught by a group of strong men and led away, but not before she had put a spell on the entranced men by joining the thumbs of her outstretched hands and yelling a curse.

The Kriss Dance. By the spell, the krisses in the hands of the men turned against them but the magic of the *barong* hardened their flesh so that, although they pushed the sharp points of the daggers with all their might against their naked chests, they were not even hurt. This was the explanation the Balinese gave of the strange exhibition and it seemed inconceivable that they were faking, such was the earnest force with which they seemed to try to stab themselves. Some leaped wildly or rolled in the dust, pressing the krisses against their breasts and crying like children, tears streaming from their eyes. Most showed dark marks where the point of the dagger bruised the skin without cutting it, but blood began to flow from the breast of one, the signal for the watchmen to disarm him by force. It is said that only by a complete trance can the dance be performed with impunity, otherwise a man may wound himself or hurt others. They were closely watched and if one of them gave signs of returning consciousness he was quickly and violently disarmed. Possessed as they are, they have a supernatural strength and it takes many men to hold them down. Even after the kriss has been wrenched away they continue to dance with a blank stare and with the right fist still clenched as if still grasping the kriss handle. To take the men out of the trance they were led, one by one, to where the *barong* stood; someone sucked the bleeding chest of the wounded man and stuck a red flower in the cut. The *pemangku* wiped the face of each man with the beard of the *barong* dipped in holy water, and gradually the hysterical men came out of the trance, dazed, simply walking away is if they did not know what had happened to them.

The Sanghyang. Toward the end of the Balinese year, during the last months of the rainy season, epidemics of malaria and tropical fevers make their appearance because evil spirits and *leyaks* are in the ascendancy; then even the earth is said to be sick. This is a propitious time for the *leyaks* to prey on human beings; because of the predominance of evil forces the village is then magically weakened. The dogs gather at the crossroads and howl all night and the owls hoot, predicting deaths in the village. Quantities of offerings are made to placate the devils, and the benign spirits are implored to come down to earth, through the body of a medium, to advise and protect the community.

A performance of *sanghyang dedari* is one of the most effective exorcisms; two little girls, trained to go into a trance, are chosen by the temple priest, the *pemangku,* from among all the girls of the village for their psychic aptitudes. Choruses of men and women are formed and the training begins. Every night, for weeks, they all go to the temple where the women sing traditional songs while the men (*ketjak*) chant strange rhythms and harmonies made up of meaningless syllables, producing a syncopated accompaniment for the dance that the *sanghyangs* will perform. By degrees the little girls become more and more subject to the ecstasy produced by the intoxicating songs, by the incense and by the hypnotic power of the *pemangku.* The training goes on until the girls are able to fall into a deep trance and a formal performance can be given. It is extraordinary that although the little girls have never received dancing lessons, once in a trance they are able to dance in any style, all of which would require ordinary dancers months and years of training. But the Balinese say it is the goddesses who dance in the bodies of the girls.

When the girls are ready, they are taken to the Death Temple where a high altar has been erected, filled with offerings for the Sun. The *nemangku* sits facing the altar in front of a brazier where incense of three sorts is burned. The little girls wear earplugs of gold, heavy silver anklets, bracelets and rings. Their hair is loose and they are dressed in white skirts. They kneel in front of the altar on each side of the priest. The women singers sit in a circle around them, while the men remain in a group at the back. Their jewelry is removed and is put in a bowl of water; small incense braziers are placed in front of each girl. After a short prayer by the priest, the women sing:

Fragrant is the smoke of the incense, the smoke of the sandalwood, the smoke that coils and coils upward towards the home of the three gods. We are cleansed to call the nymphs to descend from heaven. We ask Supraba and Tundjung Biru to come down to us, beautiful in their bodices of gold. Flying down from heaven, they fly in spirals, fly down from the North-East where they build their home . . . our thoughts shall rise like smoke towards the *dedari* who will descend from heaven . . .

Soon the girls begin to drowse and fall into a sudden faint. The women support their limp bodies in a sitting position and after a while the girls begin to move again, as if suffering intense pain, then trembling all over and swaying faster and faster, their heads rolling until their loose hair describes a wide circle. From this time on the girls remain with closed eyes and do not open them until the end of the ceremony when they are taken out of the trance. With their bare hands they brush off the glowing coals from the braziers, making inarticulate sounds that are taken to be *mantras,* magic formulas, mumbled by the heavenly nymphs that have entered their bodies. From now on they are addressed as goddesses. Women attendants remove the white skirts and replace them with gilt ones; the waists are tightly bound in strips of gold cloth, and each girl is given a jacket, a golden bodice and a silver belt, in all a *legong* costume. The jewelry that lay in the bowl of holy water is put on again. The holy headdresses of gold (*gelunggan*) are brought in on cushions decorated with fresh frangipani flowers and the girls are guided so that they can put them on themselves while the women sing about the beauty of the headdresses and the elegance of their clothes.

The *sanghyangs* begin to dance with closed eyes, accompanied by alternating choruses of the men, who sing in furious syncopation:—kechak-kechak-kechak . . . chakchakchak—chak . . . , and by the women who sing:

The flower *menuk* that makes one happy, the white flower, it is—it is—it is white and in rows, like the stars above, like the constellations, like the constellation Kartika that scintillates, they scintillate, scintillate and fade away, fade away and disappear, disappear, disappear because of the moonlight. Lengkik lengkik lengkik says the plaintive song of the lonely *dasih* bird that was left behind. Oh, how he cries! he cries, cries like the cry of a child who must be amused, amused by the dancing of the *dedari*. Lengkik lengkik, swing and sway . . .

The *sanghyangs* may suddenly decide to go to another temple or tour the village chasing the *leyaks,* followed by the singing men and women. The *sanghyangs* must not touch the impure ground outside the temple and are carried everywhere on the shoulders of men. They stop at a second temple where a pile of cocoanut shells burns in the center of the court. The *sanghyangs* dance unconcerned in and out of the fire, scattering the glowing coals in all directions with their bare feet. They may even decide to take a bath of fire, picking up the coals in both hands and pouring them over themselves.

When the fire is extinguished, the girls climb on to the shoulders of two men who walk around the courtyard, the girls' prehensile feet clutching the men's shoulders, balancing themselves and dancing gracefully from the waist up, bending back at incredible angles. In this manner they give the illusion of gliding through the air. The temperamental girls may suddenly decide that the dance is over. Then they must be taken out of the trance with special songs. As the *sanghyangs* become ordinary girls again, they distribute flowers from their headdresses as amulets and sprinkle the crowd with holy water.

The ceremony lasts for two or three hours, but despite the intensity of the performance the little girls give no evidence of exhaustion and the explanation they give comes back to our minds: the dancers, fascinated by their own rhythm, move in a supernatural world where fatigue is unknown. In ordinary life the little girls are normal children. However, they are forbidden to creep under the bed, to eat the remains of another person's food or the food from offerings, and must be refined in manners and speech. Their parents are exempt from certain village duties and are highly regarded by the rest of the community.

August 1936

* *

HALLIE FLANAGAN

*

Federal Theatre Project

THE FEDERAL THEATRE PROJECT is based on the belief that there is intelligence, skill, experience and enthusiasm in the thousands of theatre people now on relief rolls, and in the hundreds of other theatre people who will cooperate with them. It is based on a belief that this intelligence, experience and enthusiasm will swing in under a nationwide plan in which such elements of strength are needed. It is not a relief project in which artificial jobs are dealt out to people of inferior talent, but rather a plan which begins by saying: in re-thinking theatre activity in terms of the art and economics of 1935, we need theatre enterprises which will supplement our already existing splendid New York stage. We need throughout America a number of theatres, experimental in nature, specializing in new plays of unknown dramatists, with an emphasis on regional and local material. We need Negro theatres in Harlem, St. Louis, Alabama; vaudeville and specialty acts in connection with some of the great recreation centers where dance orchestras, recruited from ranks of unemployed musicians, will play for unemployed youth. We need a theatre adapted to new times and new conditions; a theatre which recognizes the presence of its sister arts, and of the movies and the radio, its neighbors and competitors, a theatre vividly conscious of the rich heritage of its past but which builds towards the future with new faith and imagination.

The Federal Government allocated $4,800,000,000 for relief under the Works Progress Administrator, Harry L. Hopkins. This appropriation included as its first project $27,000,000 for putting musicians, writers, painters, sculptors and theatre people to work in their own vocational fields. A Federal Director has been appointed for each of the arts: Nikolai Sokoloff for music; Holger Cahill for art; Henry Alsberg for writing; myself for the theatre. Each Federal Director plans to work through regional directors who will be at the head of some twelve areas throughout the United States, and because we are eager to work together in close cooperation, we are using, as far as possible, the same regional divisions. Responsible to the regional director, and through him to the project head in Washington, there will be administrative directors of individual theatre projects.

These projects will be as various as the needs of the localities planning them, and the creative imagination of their directors. Plans are under way for an Ibsen repertory theatre in Minneapolis; a traveling Shakespearean company in the Dakotas; a cycle of Restoration drama in a great university in the mid-west; historical and regional projects including a marionette theatre dealing with the local history of New York State; one for remodeling the oldest theatre in the United States to house presentations, in period, of the plays of the first theatrical season in America.

In putting these various units into operation we shall use first of all the theatre people who, due to the economic situation, have been out of jobs for several years. According to the general ruling governing the disbursement of the funds, eighty percent of all money allocated to a project must be spent in wages to theatre people now on relief rolls. Another ten percent will be paid to other theatrical workers who will be used in directorial and administrative capacities in the actual carrying forward of projects. The remaining ten percent will be spent in production costs of theatre enterprises which, it is hoped, will prove so vital to the communities involved that they can continue to function beyond this year.

It may be appropriate to mention exactly what Federal funds can be used for in such a project. In no case may they be used to finance or loan to private theatre enterprise, however excellent; they may be used to pay labor costs at the rate prevailing at the nearest W.P.A.

office; a small number of directorial salaries; and ten percent of the total labor costs of the project, for production costs.

The ten percent allocated to production is, any practical theatre worker will remark, a small amount for production costs for enterprises so vast. Here the professional theatre, the state, the cities, the universities, civic organizations and other public bodies have been asked to come into the picture and, in almost every case, have accepted enthusiastically. Actor's Equity, the American Federation of Actors, the League of New York Theatres, the Stagehands' Union, offer cooperation, advisory committees and office space; the National Theatre Conference places at the disposal of the Federal Theatre Project data on plays and technical matters. Cities, towns and universities are offering leadership, theatres, storage and rehearsal space for companies of players. Everywhere there is willingness to cooperate in a plan so vast that cooperation is imperative.

Practically, the Federal Theatre will operate through the regional plan suggested for years by the National Theatre Conference, THEATRE ARTS MONTHLY, and through the pages of that magazine by George Pierce Baker, Edith J. R. Isaacs, Frederick Koch and E. C. Mabie. Focal centers for theatre activity already exist in such organizations as the Cleveland Play House, the Pasadena Playhouse, the North Carolina Playmakers, the Iowa University Theatre, the Hedgerow Theatre and other university and civic theatres. In other words, while recognizing New York City as the center of American dramatic art, the Federal Theatre Project believes that the theatre horizon is expanding to include the Santa Fé desert, the Rocky Mountains and the valley of the Mississippi; widening to include a consciousness of the social scene as well as the social register; widening, in short, to include the impossible—that same impossible which has led our contemporaries to soar to the stars, whisper through space and fling miles of steel and glass into the air.

Because it deals directly with human beings the theatre, of all the arts, should be the most conscious of economic changes affecting human beings. Painters during the last few years have turned increasingly for subject matter and technique to industry and economics; William Lescaze writes: "The social scene and its implications dictate my architectural renderings"; Martha Graham in her new ballet, *Panorama,* presents "three themes of thought and action which are basically American," that is Puritan religious fanaticism,

Negro exploitation and awakening social consciousness. The theatre, however, aside from the rapidly developing left-wing group, has remained curiously oblivious to the changing social order. It is time that the theatre is brought face to face with the great economic problems of the day, of which unemployment is one.

In a play written by college students and presented recently on a college stage, there is a scene in which an intellectual, strolling alone, meditating on art, is suddenly confronted by a woman who emerges from a motionless, attentive mass of workers. She says, "Is this the appointed hour? Is this the time and place where we should meet?" The intellectual, courteously removing his hat, remarks cautiously, "I do not think that we have met before." To which the woman replies, "I've walked the world for six years, not growing weaker but growing stronger. I've noticed you. I knew that someday you would notice me."

Is it too much to hope that the Federal Theatre Project in America, 1935, may be indeed, for two great forces, in need of each other, the appointed time and place?

November 1935

* *

ROSAMOND GILDER

*

American National Theatre and Academy

IF CONVERSATION LAGS in any theatrical milieu—a rare event, it must be admitted—one need only toss in the question, "What is, what might be, what should be a national theatre for America?" to induce an instant explosion. There are as many theories on the subject as there are pebbles on the beach. Opinions range from a scornful assurance that no such thing is possible or desirable to glowing visions of buildings of baroque splendor or blissful hopes of lifelong employment. Discussion is running particularly high these days, with half a dozen organized theatre plans under way and with that chartered entity—so far not much more than a dream on paper—the American National Theatre and Academy beginning to take up the challenge inherent in its title.

It is eleven years since President Roosevelt signed the Federal document that brought an "American National Theatre and Academy" into theoretic existence. The President himself, the legislators who had voted for the charter in Congress and the group of citizens, art lovers and patrons of the arts who inscribed themselves as its "incorporators" were full of high hopes. The American National Theatre and Academy was, in the words of its preamble:

A people's project, organized and conducted in their interest, free from commercialism, but with the firm intent of being as far as possible self-supporting. A national theatre should bring to the people throughout the country their heritage of the great drama of the past, and the best of the present, which has been too frequently unavailable to them under existing conditions.

The charter was and still is a very precious document. Not more than two or three such Federal charters exist and it is unlikely that more will be granted. The theatre was honored indeed by the governmental accolade—only the theatre did not know it. There was not a single theatrical leader on the list of founders. This was a deliberate omission, intended to prove the entirely disinterested attitude of the group seeking the charter, but it had its serious disadvantages as time was to prove. There was also no money in the bank. The charter carried no Federal grant and the founders, very naturally, waited for a plan of action before supplying the necessary funds.

A great deal has happened during the eleven years that have elapsed since that July day in 1935 when the President affixed his signature to the charter. The Federal Theatre, spending millions for relief between 1935 and 1939, filled the entire theatrical horizon with one of the greatest experiments in organized theatre that this country has ever seen. But, founded on the need of supplying work for the unemployed rather than on any principle of theatre need or development, it could not serve as the base of a national theatre, as Hallie Flanagan and many others who worked for it had at first greatly hoped. After the dissolution of the Federal Theatre by Congress, the Executive Committee of the American National Theatre and Academy, which had in the interim constituted itself a "holding company" for the charter, invited Robert Sherwood to take the presidency and set up a Board of Directors, now largely chosen from the theatre. Mr. Sherwood began at once the difficult task of gathering an effective professional advisory committee, testing plans, exploring possibilities. Then came the war and once more the national theatre idea was laid aside for grimmer issues.

This, briefly, is the story (told more fully in the January 1940 issue of THEATRE ARTS) of the American National Theatre and Academy. Depression and war prevented the maturing of plans to implement an idea in its very nature difficult and complex. There is no single highway to an American national theatre, nor can it be built overnight. But now, surely, is the time to lay the bases of a structure that will be both broad and durable and that, while taking into account the needs of the present, will provide amply for the future.

An American national theatre can never be a single entity, a structure, set down in New York or Washington, housing an expensive repertory company and playing stately classics. It must be a thing of flexibility and range, allowing for individual initiative, yet setting and maintaining standards. It must be both a stabilizing influence and a training ground for talent. Above all it must have a nation-wide as well as an international vision. With these requirements in mind the Board of the American National Theatre—ANTA for short—devoted a succession of meetings to debating a number of plans brought to its attention. It argued, consulted, "havvered" in good democratic style and finally agreed on a series of moves which taken altogether will in time compass the objectives required.

A National Theatre Foundation is the broad base of a far-reaching scheme. This plan evolved by Robert Breen and Robert Porterfield was printed in the October 1945 issue of THEATRE ARTS at about the same time that it was formally presented to the Board of ANTA as a possible method of procedure. The idea is essentially simple, and one which has been applied successfully to other fields of activity in this country. What the great foundations have done for education and medicine can, it is believed, be done for the theatre if a large sum of money is made available for the specific purpose of encouraging sound theatrical enterprises all over the country. A Foundation dedicated exclusively to the theatre would have as its objective the development of the theatre as an art, as an educational medium and as a form of civilized and civilizing recreation for the people. It would have as one of its major objectives the bringing of the best of theatre to the greatest number of people. A similar scheme was successfully tried in England during the war. The Committee for the Encouragement of Music and the Arts, which received, incidentally, its initial gift from an American source, the Pilgrim Trust, came into being to prevent the collapse of art projects, music, theatre, fine arts, which were threatened by the war. CEMA's funds were derived from government sources, as well as from the Pilgrim Trust. With the cessation of hostilities, CEMA was not discontinued; it had proved its value. It was reorganized and re-baptized as the Arts Council of Great Britain—with an important section devoted to theatre. Through its administration, combined with the successful flowering of the Old Vic, which it had to a certain extent underwritten during the war, an English national theatre is coming into being. The methods and functioning of the Arts Council is perhaps the most useful example of a national theatre for Americans to study. England, like America, had talked long and on the whole ineffectively about a national theatre until the stress of war necessity and the idea of giving assistance to existing enterprises rather than starting new enterprises made the whole movement coalesce.

The Foundation plan seemed, therefore, one which might well be attempted here. The Board of ANTA accepted the idea "in principle" and set to work on the long road of working out its details and of organizing the first steps toward a nationwide fund-raising campaign. The scheme would require raising a large sum of money running into the millions, which would constitute a sort of artistic lend-lease for enterprises which came within the scope of a nationwide, non-profit organization such as ANTA. The objectives of the groups which received help would have to be identical with that of ANTA itself—"to bring to the greatest number of people the finest possible theatre at the lowest possible prices." The methods of achieving this end admit of infinite variety, from giving material, moral or advisory assistance to new professional resident stock companies to underwriting the tour of a distinguished professional company in an outstanding play so that it might cover territory not commercially profitable and therefore long denied the spoken drama.

The Foundation scheme is a large project, as indeed any plan for a national theatre in the United States must be. While working at this major objective, which will require at least a year of discussion, exploration, argument and nationwide planning to launch, the Board of ANTA has several specific projects under way. The first and most urgent of these is the establishment within the year—and this again is dependent on raising the necessary funds—of a graduate school or, since the word is already incorporated in the charter, an Academy for aspiring young actors who have already devoted years of school and college work to the theatre. One of the striking weaknesses in our theatre system—or lack of system—is the fact that there is no bridge between training for the theatre and the profession itself. Something in the nature of a post-graduate course or apprentice system is needed to fill the gap.

ANTA has no intention of starting another theatre school; there are many excellent schools and college drama departments all over the country. But what it will offer to the most outstanding of the students thus trained will be an intensive two-year "laboratory" course under professional theatre direction. Fired by the idea of helping young talent to its fullest development and thereby enriching the whole field of the American theatre, Rachel Crothers and Raymond Massey, both members of the Board, worked out the practical details of the plan. The students or apprentices, no more than fifty to begin with, would be directed in a series of plays by three or four resident professional directors, supplemented from time to time by work under directors not on the faculty but able and willing, as several have already stated, to give the time needed for the direction of one or more plays a season. After the first year the best of the young actors would be formed into a National Theatre Company and, again under professional direction, rehearsed in a series of plays which would be toured through nearby communities, playing in schools, community centers, granges or other auditoriums outside the professional theatre limits. All this would provide invaluable training for the young actors, who would have the inestimable advantage of playing under a variety of directors. At the same time they would be under the careful supervision of the staff of the Academy, who would see that they had the extra training in voice, diction, body movement, fencing or dance that they might need.

It is not the intention of ANTA to train more actors and directors for an already overcrowded profession but to give to the young people who have already demonstrated their talent and ability and the seriousness of their interest in the theatre an opportunity to perfect themselves in their chosen profession under the guidance of leading practitioners of the art. The training would, it is believed, result in making available sound and versatile actors for Broadway, for the professional resident companies now developing all over the country, for the much-to-be-desired repertory companies which are beginning to take form and finally for that hoped-for American national theatre of the future which will have its headquarters in New York, its affiliates all over the country and its first-rate companies touring among the smaller towns and cities.

That dream may be very far away—it may be only a mirage—but it is worth working for. And ANTA is taking first steps in that direction. It has rented the little Princess Theatre in New York, an ideal location for the graduate Academy; it is working on the structure of a National Theatre Foundation fund drive; it is serving as a means of contact and a center for the exchange of ideas, and possibly of acting companies, between America and the national theatres of other countries; it is enlarging its board and membership and working on a broader organizational structure which will adequately represent all phases of the American theatre and serve as a broad and democratic base for nationwide action.

September 1946

III · PLAYWRIGHTS AND PLAYWRITING

* * *

PAUL GREEN

*

Drama and the Weather

Chapel Hill, North Carolina
July 6, 1934

Dear Mrs. Isaacs:

If you've ever been down in the country during a severe summer drought, you have noticed how the crops stood lifeless and how the leaves and limbs of the trees sagged under the wilting heat; and how the chickens in the barnyard sat slothfully on the ground, and the cattle in the shadow of the buildings looked out at the world with dull and inert eyes. The farmers themselves seemed testy and irritable about the house, and with reason, for day after day the sun rises like a ball of fire, swims across the brazen empty sky and goes down beyond the rim of brown hills—a burning curse to animal, earth and man. The world itself is perishing for rain, but there is no rain.

Then one morning a different feeling is in the air. After breakfast you walk in the lane, and a change is over everything. The flowers and the trees have perked up their heads, the chickens step about lively and the pigeons no longer quarrel under the eaves. Down in the pasture the cattle move briskly around biting off sweet willow tips, and the farmer and his sons are long ago abroad looking to their dikes and ditches. You go down to the village for the mail. More than once you hear a store loafer say, "The air feels like rain." Being a summer boarder, you read the morning papers, then an article or two in a magazine about trouble in Europe, and after lunch sit on the front porch and take a rest. Looking off across the heat-filled fields about two o'clock, you see low on the horizon edge a faint little wad of cloud, no larger than the cloud Elijah or Polonius saw. And as you sit there watching, another little cloud appears swimming up the sky, to be followed by another and then another. Soon the whole southwestern horizon is marked by these little upboiling racks. And in less time than it takes to tell, a low dark swollen band begins shoving itself up above the line of sycamores along the river. Presently there is a roll of low ominous thunder below the earth, and the windows rattle in their sockets. The moments pass, the dark wide stretching cloud now reaches from north to south and pushes up until it touches the edge of the burning sun. Then it obscures the sun. A flash of lightning marks a sudden fiery crack from sky to earth. The elm trees around the house shiver with a strange delight. The chickens start going into the henhouse and the doves fly into their cote. And then up from the meadow the old bell-cow comes leading the other cattle, her head high, her tail arched merrily. Another roll of thunder sounds, a gust of dust cuts a little jigging whirlwind down the lane, trying to keep up with the swift edge of the cloud which now has raced across the sky and passed over the house. The wind blows more strongly, and somewhere a door slams. You continue to sit there, waiting for the rain to fall. The wind dies out, the thunder is no longer heard, nor is there any lightning. Everything is breathless, expectant, still.

Now with a sudden clatter like stones on the roof the rain begins. A fine mist of dust is beat up in the yard, and in the lane and out across the fields. Like a morning ground-fog it is. And then it too is wetted down to earth as the rain settles into a steady pour. A sheet of wetness begins to blow in on you. You pick up your chair, lean it against the wall and enter the house. There you stand by the window looking out where a world is being refreshed and where a snake of yellow water has started wriggling down the dry road ditch. The drought is over. In a few days everything will be green again.

And as with the rain so with writing a play—so with any work of art. It comes pretty much when it will come, is absent when it will be absent, and no man can provide its presence at his will. So if I may be personal in replying to your question, "Why do you write plays?", I can on first consideration easily say, "I don't know." It's much like the weather to me—the what and why, the wherefore and results. About the only answer I would venture is that I seem to need to. If I were certain that the drama were the one means of gaining honor or wealth or mental stability there would be some obvious common sense in spending one's life trying to set down lines for people to speak on a stage. I believe I should want to write plays though if little or nothing came of them, but naturally I want a lot to come of them.

Of course, your question goes further than any easy answer or any meteorological metaphor. It raises the whole problem of aptitude and calling. I think all people are by nature artists; that is, more or less so. The usual European designation of the American builder and business man as a money hog, for instance—a creature who takes pleasure only in dollar profit and pain only in dollar loss—seems to me obviously false. There is more to it than that—always more. Sinclair Lewis in his latest novel, *Work of Art,* tries his hand at showing that one Myron Weagle with his dream of a perfect hotel might be considered essentially an artist. There is a lot of human truth in his contention and it partly accounts for his book's being a best seller.

Now if all of us have this so-called artistic urge, then why do some of us become hotel-keepers and others banjo-pickers? The answer is perhaps that circumstances always play their part. One child happens to have access, say, to a piano on which he begins to give voice to his yearnings. Another has a piano near at hand but finds his fingers too stiff or too short ever to allow of his becoming a performer. Perhaps he turns to composing, or bricklaying. And so it goes. Each of us could make some sort of statement as to his proper calling. Take your own case—you run a drama magazine. All sorts of odds and ends of circumstances and people went into your choice of that career.

Two incidents happened to me years ago, I remember, which turned me to writing plays. Norman Foerster, who was one of the finest English teachers ever to appear at the University of North Carolina, announced in class one day that the seniors had decided to do a play at commencement and were holding a contest for original scripts. He advised me to try my hand. I took a chance at the thing and happened to win out. The play was produced in the forest theatre and I was thrilled to death. After that, though, I did not set my heart on playwriting, for I had always been more interested in poetry and short stories than anything else. Then in 1919 "Prof" Koch came riding in from the Dakota prairies, his arms full of plays and his head full of dreams. In no time a stage was up, and everybody near and far, little and big, black and white, realized for the first time that he was an artist of some sort—mainly a dramatic artist. Some went in for designing, some for acting, some for writing. I chose the last. And after a few productions I was caught fast in my choice and had struck acquaintance with all the terrors that inhabit the shadow of the stage like bats.

Your next question is easier to answer. "Why do you write the plays you do?" The answer is—that's the only kind I know how to write. Most of the plays I have written can be designated as folk plays, and I know this seems a narrow boundary. Perhaps it is, but since the "folk" are the people who seem to matter most to me, I have little interest in trying to deal with others who are more foreign and therefore less real. Not for a moment do I claim to have done justice to an inspiring subject matter, but the challenge is there, clearer, sharper and more compelling every day. For do these people not live closer to a terrible and all-wise nature than their brethren of the sidewalks and opera houses? I think so. If I were seeking a philosophical statement for the matter it would be somewhat as follows:

The folk are the people whose manners, ethics, religious and philosophical ideals are more nearly derived from and controlled by the ways of the outside physical world (cf. Synge's *Riders to the Sea*) than by the ways and institutions of men in a specialized society (cf. Schnitzler's *Anatol* cycle). And the outside natural world is the fountain of wisdom, the home of the fruitful all-mother, the omnipotent God. (Also it is the dwelling place of those two malignant devils—hazard and chance. Don't you think so?) The line of demarcation between the folk and sophisticated drama is not always easily distinguished. But as extremes they can be definitely contrasted; to instance, once more, Ferenc Molnar's *The Guardsman* and S. Ansky's *The Dybbuk*. And between the last two I'd always choose *The Dybbuk*—even though technique should shift for itself.

I don't claim that sophisticated drama may not be great in its own right, but somehow I never thrill to it as I do to what I like to term the folk-drama—and of course I mean the kind of folk-drama the Greeks wrote; the kind Shakespeare and Tolstoi and Hauptmann wrote; the kind Alexis Granowsky used to produce in Russia with its lovely burden of folk imagery, music and song. In reading *Lear,* for example, I always feel a sudden lift when we come to the heath scene. There is something grand and universal in the naked relationship of the old king to the powers of nature around him. And as characters available to my purposes, to repeat, those who live as it were with their feet in the earth and their heads bare to the storms, the lightning and the gale—those who labor with their hands wresting from cryptic nature her goods and stores of sustenance—these develop a wisdom of living which seems to me more real and beautiful than those who develop their values and ambitions from rubbing shoulders in a crowded city. And that wisdom it is which seems important—a wisdom which is consciousness of the great eternal Presence (good, bad or impersonal) by which men live and move and are allowed their existence. And if the playwrights who tell of captains and lords, kings and queens, dolls or manikins do open up the doors of crowded buildings, cut through the filmy arras that conceals our human instincts and hopes and fears and go to the first principle of human identity—then it's true they raise the hair on our heads with their voice from the sacred grove of Colonnus. And no longer do we think of man as sophisticated or folk but man—man alone with his destiny. And when this happens—and rare is Shakespeare, rarer than heaven—then the matter is all one, and listeners are all one. But the present clang and confusion of wheel on iron, yelling and clamor of tickers and tellers, the secrecy of vaults and locks and braggarty of monoliths of incorruptible concrete and steel—these all make it harder for us to see and hear the God who is the principle of our lives. Maybe I'm crazy on the idea of God, but aren't we all? I refer you to the wild pell-mell rush every evening out of New York when thousands and thousands are fleeing from the city to the country—to the country where the birds are, where the grass is and where there is peace.

Now you catch me almost carrying on into a scheme of social philosophy. And if I wanted to apply this half-surmised aesthetic theory to the control and arrangement of peoples I should say there ought to be plenty of trees and land and outdoors for every man. For only in the outdoors can we associate with power and mystery in their most sublime manifestation. And heaven knows we ought to sense in any way we can whatever touch of sublimity there may be vouchsafed unto us in this darkness.

It seems that after all I'm saying for myself that folk-drama as such is or can be more significant than sophisticated drama. Not at all. I mean to repeat, with a difference, that in the last analysis it is a question of neither folk nor sophisticate—but of man, man in his environment. And I would say that indoors sooner or later man must perish and outdoors there is more of a chance for him. To make another dogmatic statement, I would say that cruelty, scorn and evils of all sorts are more native to the great cities than not, and therefore we should be better off without any great cities—I mean close, skyscraper-bedlam cities. (There's something other than politics behind Russia's efforts to create the ideal commune, don't you think?) And all the little towns that get too large for their britches and so full of metropolitan urges and apings that they cut down all the trees on their main streets and cover the grass and ground with concrete will be better off when they tear up the concrete, reset the trees and grow grass again. And maybe now that we have evolved wheels and telephones and radios and machinery of long-distance cooperation we can all begin to live among trees again and yet keep in touch with each other enough for our sophisticated needs. Then haply now and then we may also have a word with the Great Presence where he walks smoking his cigar by the river bank at evening.

As to the next question of "What happens when you turn your play over to the director, designer, actor and see them add their form to yours?"—it is more than easy to say that sometimes you are pleased with what they do and sometimes disappointed. It is never possible for the image-picture of your characters to be duplicated on the stage. Their habits, their actions and appearance are always different from the production, and necessarily so. But the production as often improves the play over the author's mind as it is likely to hurt it.

Your last question as to what the playwright should be to the theatre and to the world he lives in uncovers a huge wheel-full of spokes of diverging thoughts. Briefly, though, he should be, don't you think, the same to the theatre as the gardener to his garden, or the blacksmith to his smithy or the farmer to his field? And as for the world he lives in—his business is to express in dramatic form the serious struggles, both evil and good, that exist in that world. In other and Aristotelian phrase, he is a maker, and his business is to fashion or make his material fit the imaginative demands of his craft. And in these two words of material and craft all the trouble lies, of course. But the trouble is not final, however mysterious and difficult the matter is—do you think so? For in the great outside universe around us nature is always solving these dualistic antagonisms whether it be raining or whether it be dry, and from her we may no doubt derive both the axiom and the dream.

Now it occurs to me that I make no place for comedy (which includes melodrama and farce). Well, it apparently belongs to another point of view, just as the grotesque requires still a third kind of judgment. Comedy seems to belong entirely to man's world and to have no place in nature's world. In fact one might say that it arises from man's delight in and prankishness with himself and fellowman in so far as he forgets that he is a part of an all-powerful and demanding universe. Its basic pattern is a non-harmful incongruity which man himself provides, and that would seem to justify the definition. For nature is never funny nor playful, not even when she smiles, is she?

As for the grotesque (the hysterical), it disappears before definition and stands representative of nothing more than the frightful effort to combine the comic and the sublime (or the finite funny with the infinite serious) into the body of one piece.

You see your letter has stirred up a whole hornet's nest of trouble for me. And now that I've had to take refuge in the quagmire of metaphysics, I'd better stop. So I'll conclude by—yes, I'll say it—the play's the thing after all, whether it's indoors or outdoors.

Sincerely yours,

PAUL GREEN

August 1934

BARRETT H. CLARK

*

Letters from Sidney Howard

A FEW DAYS after Sidney Howard's death in the summer of 1939, I came home at midnight after taking part in a memorial radio broadcast. I went to my files, got out the Sidney Howard folder, and read over a hundred pages of letters and notes, some of them written in that nervous, strong and often nearly illegible handwriting of his; some on yellow copy paper which he had hurriedly typed himself; several on telegraph blanks, hotel stationery, backs of envelopes; a few that had been dictated, neatly typed and dated. Here in one bundle were nearly all of his communications to me from the day before we first met in 1919 until a few days before his death.

Out of these letters, leaving them just as they are and with as few comments as are necessary to clarify the contents, I have tried to arrange a small fragmentary biography, to be published shortly, that would indicate something of what Sidney Howard was and how he worked. Here are just a few of the letters, those that concern his plays especially, beginning with one about *They Knew What They Wanted,* for which he received the Pulitzer Prize in 1925:

"Thanks for your note and the grand notice you gave the play. As to cutting Joe, there you raise the most interesting point that has been raised yet. I did cut him a good deal because he tended to overbalance the others . . . which was not good because the play is really about Tony and Amy. I daresay you agree to that, and I don't think that I cut anything of value. I am inclined to think that the trouble may be in his being *too* actual. I knew the man and reported him over-faithfully and there were moments when I stuck so close to him that, odd as it may seem, he ceased to be theatric and became improbable. After all, the play is a little (and unimportant) treatise on the obsessions which make the world go round. The woman's obsession for security—the man's for a dynasty, on the one hand (Tony), and for rebellion on the other (Joe's). It is always dangerous to stick too closely to an original and I may have got Joe into the trouble you find by just that process. . . . For myself, I like best in the play my mediaeval morality at the opening of the third act, where capital, rebellion and the facts of the case, pragmatic church, are all worsted by the woman's knowledge of the day of the week. I am boring you with all this because your review is the very best thing the play has had, the most searching and the most understanding. When Bob Benchley covered both *Desire Under the Elms* and *They Knew What They Wanted* as French triangles I was outraged for both O'Neill and myself. I'm delighted, too, at your review of *Desire. There's* a fine play! There's rather a showing, these days, for American plays, isn't there? There may not be any *great* ones—though Stallings and Anderson are pretty near—but there are four of them—doing big business and earning at least serious respect —and that's *not* bad. Isn't Pauline Lord a great actress? *Really* a great actress? She's had an awful effect on me. Every word I write seems absolutely flat. I hear her say 'let go of my skirt,' and I'm gone, absolutely gone for the day. I can't get her out of my mind."

Half Gods, for which Sidney hoped so much, was written after his separation from his first wife Clare Eames. It was produced by Arthur Hopkins in 1929, but did not achieve the success of *They Knew What They Wanted*. The next letter was written from his sister's home in Berkeley, California, and dated June, 1929:

"Two letters of yours sit here unanswered and have been sitting these past I don't know how many days that I have been writing so hard. One of these asks if you can do something about foreign rights on *They Knew What They Wanted*. Of course you can if you care to lose money on the postage. Why don't you buy the amateur rights to the piece? It does very well by amateurs. In Santa Barbara they got the local fish man to play it and he was a triumph. In Dallas the other day it won a prize. The other letter is harder to answer. I shall pause, now, light my pipe and read it again. I have read it again. Since I wrote you I have spent a blissful month on a play called *Half Gods,* in which I am trying to get down some of American womanhood's revolt against marriage, kidded of course, but still pretty much as I see it. I don't know that it is going to be much of a play. I never have had that feeling of writing a masterpiece. The excitement lasts while I am working and wears off into nothing, not even depression. But I do know that I have had a swell time of it and that I am beginning to be able to work again after what seems to me an interminable time. I don't believe that I shall give up writing for the theatre until the theatre gives me up. That is to say: I have got through with melodrama, with reporting and even with the strong story play. I think I am interested, now, in trying to dramatize what these people of ours are thinking about, not in a critical sense, but as it is, heightened by some kind of intensification that comes automatically with dramatic condensing. I am eager to go ahead with four plays and eager to get on to a novel. I dread my impending return to Hollywood. I dread it so that I have a strong feeling that I shall, somehow, try to back out if I possibly can. I see my daughter, though, as a more important job than any number of plays that *I* can write. . . . I have got *Half Gods* a little better than half-done and the worst scenes, except the final one, are licked. About August first I shall ship it off to you to read and stamp upon or like or whatever. I can't get off my track even if I had some exalted vision of my talents and wanted to do so, because I am and shall always be an earthbound pragmatic stoic without any aptitude for the empyrean. I have had a bad time for two years. If I can still write for the theatre without Clare's invaluable . . . guidance, I shall certainly go on. . . ."

In answer to a request of mine for some personal memoranda to use in a little book I was working on, Sidney wrote his own revealing autobiography in "a long wallop of a letter—a fine picture of one who knows not what he wants nor where he is. However, things will come straight, they always do." This letter also dates from spring, 1929:

"Letters like yours are terribly hard to answer. The general dope and facts and dates are all in *Who's Who,* I expect, so we can omit them. I don't know what urged me to write. I grew up in a mess of books. My father was a self-educated man. There is a story, I think true, that he began his education working in a second-hand book shop after the hours he spent working on the wharves of the 'Philadelphia and Reading' in Philadelphia. He was twelve then. He was what is called a 'great reader.' I inherited two of his three enthusiams. I inherited books and gardening. His third and greatest enthusiasm, science, skipped me except that I have a kind of curiosity about people rather than rocks and plants. I began writing poetry pretty early in life. I think that I always fumbled around for some kind of artistic expression. I liked music better than anything and always raged because I wasn't able to get ahead with it. I gave it up, like a fool. I could have great fun now, if I were able to play a piano even badly. I grew up in California. I was next to the youngest of six of which one sister was the oldest. I went to public schools and read books and camped in the high Sierras and rode horses and went to British Columbia and Mexico. I was taken to Italy when I was seventeen. I was sickly a good deal as a kid and never did well at sports. That's always given me a complex.

"My father discouraged my wanting to write. I know that he would have liked having a writer son more than anything, but his standards were high. He would think very little of my talents, I may tell you. And he would be quite right about them. Once he gave me an edition of Ibsen which I very much wanted and added that I was to wash the taste out with a very good draught of Huxley. Young Raimund von Hofmannsthal has just blown in and out to say good-bye, as he starts from here for Vienna via Java and points east and thinks that if he could get a great novel written on the way, his father [the poet-playwright Hugo von Hofmannsthal] might be kinder to him. He is hurrying home to be there for his twenty-third birthday. He takes me back rather. We hadn't much of any money in our family but a sound example of hard work. Oh, and a great deal of music. Both my father and mother were pretty fair musicians. My mother had long earned her living as a professional, an organist and a piano teacher. Quite successfully. My father was a Handel hound. We had to learn Handel choruses as kids and keep time. On both sides we were pioneer stock. My mother's family came across the continent before '49. My father opened the first steamship line to Alaska. My grandfather opened Oregon and Washington by putting the first boats on the Columbia River.

"I can't remember very well how I first got interested in the theatre. I just was, somehow, for no very good reason. Oh, yes, I had a toy theatre, but then I had a toy everything else. I wrote plays in college when I went to California and was rather talked into going to the 47 Workshop course. I didn't like that, in which I was wrong and I have since eaten my words against it. I came very much under the influence of Sam Hume and his first new stagecraft show. But I chucked any idea of the theatre to go over to drive an ambulance in France. Later, much later, when I was working, after the war, for *Life* and *Collier's Weekly* and doing labor investigating in the period when I first knew you well, I translated D'Annunzio's *Fedra* for Nazimova and Hume again. That got me interested again and

*The Rivet** came along. In time Vildrac's [*S.S.*] *Tenacity* started me into an alley where I could function somehow for the theatre, and there I've been since. Always about to tumble out into a world I like better than the theatre and always picked up and put back. Clare held me hard to the theatre, of course.

"I'm in for this, here [in Hollywood], for the present excepting some time this summer when I shall write some plays, but my heart seems to have gone out of that kind of writing and hasn't yet got fixed in any other kind. I am marking time for the moment, not liking it but being well paid and so not complaining. I always need someone with a club, and at the moment there isn't anyone. I never acted and never wanted to. I am torn between the West where I belong biologically if you know what I mean, and the East where I am not bored as I am in the West. I miss orchestras in the West, and people, and being near Europe. I've always been lonely and rather unpopular. *Das, aber, macht nichts aus.* I have the hell of a conscience but don't do well at abstractions. Not at all well. In the philosophic sense, I mean. I have a vague plan, now, which includes saving money here . . . and working for some time on a novel or two. I should think that I might presumably drop out of the theatre altogether, simply because there isn't anything much to hold me to it and there is so much about it that I find intensely uncongenial. That, I guess, comes from shyness. There are so many close personal contacts in the theatre. I don't function well with so many. I've liked one thing out here. I've been so much left alone, which I like awfully. I am going from here to the world's most beautiful garden (my sister's) where my young daughter is waiting now for me. There I shall finish my Yellow Fever play and a comedy about marriage and a tragedy about the conflict between the artist and the amateur. You'll read and see them both in due time. I discussed all that with you a year ago but it's been two years that I haven't been able to write, because I couldn't get adjusted to the break in my life and peace of mind. I'm ok now. Is this hooey of any value at all?"

Alien Corn and *Yellow Jack,* two of the plays mentioned above, were under way, and Hollywood became a disturbing element in a

* A play Sidney and I wrote together in 1919-20, based on Cabell's novel, *The Rivet in Grandfather's Neck*. It was sold but never produced professionally.

creative life, though its rewards were needed. The next letter was from Santa Barbara, February 18, 1931:

"The news of me is brief and to the point; I am hard at work on *Alien Corn* and though it is still in a very crude state, believe hard in it and think that we shall have something to think about very shortly. Though I am not going to send it to the Guild until it seems really in shape. I hope they like it and want to do it. Who gets the Pulitzer Prize, Lynn [Riggs] or Phil [Barry]? . . . I thought of you yesterday in Hollywood when I heard King Vidor say he plans to produce *Street Scene* as a picture. With Rice to cooperate Vidor might even make a good thing of it. I seem to have to do one more picture this spring, but shall not start it until *Alien Corn* is finished, and possibly not until *Yellow Jack* is finished likewise. I have been offered plenty of work but none of it interests me in spite of the dough. I have good plans and really feel that I have never worked better. In fact, life looks awfully well at the moment."

Sidney's account of a play he wanted to write about the Peace Conference at Versailles gives almost as clearly as the play itself could have done his feeling for American life and its problems—its ideals matched against its politics. He had always been a Woodrow Wilson worshipper, and wanted to "pin down" Wilson on paper (Santa Barbara, March, 1931):

"Last fall in Vienna I decided to write a play about the Peace Conference at Versailles. My scheme, which is an ironic tragedy, excites me more deeply than any idea for writing that has ever crossed my mind. . . . I am preparing for it with my head in a shelf of books some hours daily. I have discussed it with no one and I ask you to keep it to yourself. Last December I read in the *Times* about a play on Wilson by Emil Ludwig. It sounded in its résumé like propaganda for the League of Nations. As such it caused me little if any uneasiness and I am so keen on my own scheme that I believe I should go ahead in the teeth of Shakespeare."

(*A few days later.*)

"Thank you for your letter about the Ludwig play. . . . Since I have already said so much, I may as well submit a night letter more about my scheme. I aim at the ironic tragedy of the defeat of the Wilson idea that a great nation in the heyday of its power might dedicate itself to the service rather than to the conquest of humanity. This, I believe, was what caught the world's attention when the war ended and made Wilson the figure he was at the time. This certainly was what Wilson believed the American people to be capable of and this, just as certainly, was what, for various reasons, the American people fell down on. Is such idealism beyond the spiritual strength of any people, one asks, and the answer is probably yes. Not, however, that idealism per se is beyond a people, but that anything abstracted is beyond. The idea that we think with our memories and speak in phrases but act as usual according to the scattered patterns of our individual lives and the example of men with the force to lead us in ways which we can follow without thinking at all. I grow diffuse. Excuse, please. I think I know what I mean.

"I want to tell the story of Wilson's stand for open covenants openly arrived at because that stand seems to contain all the others and to be the most promising of dramatic material. There is, for point to the play and immediacy to the American public, an ironic analogy to be drawn between the secret connivings of the old European diplomacy and the secret connivings of the old American politics. Wilson set out to defeat the one and was destroyed by the other. By his unwillingness to meet the other, his determination, once he had taken his most lofty position, to defy it. I want, for example, to begin with that most moving interview which actually took place between Wilson and Frank Cobb of the *World* on the eve of Wilson's message to Congress in which he asked for the declaration of war as nobly as man ever asked for anything and in what seems the most striking of all the expressions of his ideal for America's service. The European diplomats and the American politicians furnish the body of the play with a gold mine of dramatic obstacles to place in the path of the central figure. I want to end at Boise Penrose's bedside when the telephone brought from Chicago the cheers which greeted Harding's nomination and the restoration of the old order in politics on this side of the Atlantic. Thus, the American aspect of my play is quite as important as the European or international and Ludwig is not likely to tackle that or even to understand or be interested in it. . . . Wilson was not a hero. He was a great idea, an idea worthy of godhead (with which he clearly thought himself endowed) tacked on to the personality of Gregers Werle, and Ibsen ought to be writing about him, not Ludwig or me. If my play *Yellow Jack* turns out to suit me, I shall do Wilson in that same abstracted, pseudo-Chinese technique of acting and production about which I am so excited. . . .

"I ought to be able to get my play done by somebody. . . . I have to take time out this summer to write and shoot two pictures. Thus, the best I can do before I come back in September is *Alien Corn* and *Yellow Jack* both finished and pray God to somebody's satisfaction. *Alien Corn* is drawing nicely to a close and should start on its way East very shortly. After that, I believe that I shall be finished with shooting for realism, at least for some time to come. I am further engaged in knocking out a synopsis for a heroic farce which opens with a young couple who murder their cook because they can get no other satisfaction against her and other members of the servant class and who eventually find themselves made a test case for civilization with the Deity as judge and Lenin as prosecuting attorney, the late Lenin. Only I am tired of saying how full of ideas I am and, as I said above, not delivering. Last week I took four days out to drive to and about Death Valley and found it unimaginably magnificent and remote. There is this point to life in the West; you can take three days off, or four or five, or even one, and use them to go to some part which blows your head off and returns it to you dry-cleaned and improved. You can't do that or get that effect from a week-end of rest in Atlantic City, even with the gin in the suitcase. Life is quite fine. I got back . . . to a party for Jennifer's birthday and survived even that."

One of the most successful of Broadway playwrights and Hollywood script-writers, Sidney Howard was always an enthusiastic supporter of the younger playwrights and of what was going on in the experimental theatres all over the country. There is no space here to print the letters in which he asks detailed questions about the "promising" youngsters of the twenties, nor to tell of his successful efforts to find jobs for many of them. The plan spoken of in the next letter was one of many variations on the theme I had conceived, attempts to persuade the professional managers and playwrights to give serious thought to the important work being done in the best of our little theatres, colleges and universities. It was a rather ingenious plan, I think, involving production of new plays by established writers at various focal points throughout the country, and the statements I brought together and published were by no means perfunctory puffs. O'Neill, Hopkins, Green, Riggs and Howard were my spiritual sponsors. The next letter was sent from New York, March, 1932:

"I read your piece with interest and admiration. Lynn [Riggs] came yesterday to talk at greater length about the plan and about what the Hedgerow people are doing for him. I naturally conclude that your tongue must be hanging out to hear what I think of it all. Need I say more than that I don't see how the younger playwrights are possibly going to get anywhere without it? What you are offering Lynn and company is what the Provincetown outfit offered O'Neill with the addition of the personal note. . . . Your scheme, too, comes most happily in these days of Broadway bankruptcy. The youngsters are clearly going to have a harder and harder time, particularly those, like Lynn, who have a fresh way in dramatic storytelling. I clear my throat and proceed. Everything I see about me now seems passé in the most jaded sense, producers, criticism, audience. Thursday afternoon the Metropolitan gave *Götterdämmerung* the most lofty and thrilling performance I have ever seen of Wagner, and who, but Howard and the standees, gave a damn. Snobbish remark, that. Broadway actors are jaded. Any freshness that appears among them is promptly swallowed by Hollywood. To free the playwright of this atmosphere is certainly to benefit the good health of playwriting. The country needs other lying-in wards than Broadway. The alleged native drama is going to become a great deal more native when it sees the light and takes its first steps in hardier neighborhoods and under a more selfless tradition. Lynn's superb new play perfectly demonstrates the rightness of your scheme. . . . Such men as Jasper Deeter [director of the Hedgerow Theatre] are the white hopes, and I am inclined to think that the best of them will offer the young writers something more than any of us had on either thirty-sixth (or was it thirty-fifth) or MacDougal Street. Let me know if I can write, say or do anything to further matters. I am going West in a few days to make one more picture. *One* more? Well, another. I should be so glad to talk with Gilmor Brown."

The last of the letters I am using here is a characteristic note dating from the early thirties:

"Thank you for the Shakespeare, which we are looking forward to eagerly. The text does not matter so long as it is all uniform, because I am putting the plays to a low use, namely that of dividing up the parts among the kids, who then give daily dramatic readings, an act a day, between their supper and bedtime. Love to the family."

April 1941

* *

HOWARD LINDSAY

*

Notes on Playwriting

THIS IS not going to be a lecture on playwriting. I came into the theatre through the stage door, and all I know about it is what I learned there through thirty years or more. I am just going to talk about that.

The three basic things about playwriting are the organization of the emotions of the audience, story progress, dramatization—and the organization of audience emotions is the most important. Let me illustrate that:

Years ago I used to go to wrestling matches, and here is what happened. A man in green tights and a man in black tights would get into the ring and the match would start. They would make a few tentative passes, try a few holds, each testing the other's strength and skill, and then, fairly early in the match, the fellow in the green tights would suddenly kick the other man with his foot and hit him in the face, and the crowd would yell, "Why, the dirty dog, why, the dirty dog," and would immediately begin to hope that the other fellow would wipe up the floor with him. They had organized the emotions of the audience. They had a hero and a villain immediately. It was tremendously exciting to watch them do that. The fortunes would change through the match, and then toward the end the man in the green tights would have the other at his mercy, the crowd would get angrier and angrier. It would look as though there would be no chance whatever for the fellow in the black tights to survive, but at the last second he would come to life, throw the man in the green tights around, get him down, pin his shoulders to the floor, and the crowd would go mad. The reason was that their emotions had been organized. They were stirred in favor of one of the opponents.

The first job the playwright has in the theatre is to engage the emotions of the audience favorably towards one or more of the characters. The theatre is an emotional institution. You come to hear a story told in terms of acting. An audience wants to be emotionally interested in the characters of your story. *And they want a reward for their emotions.* It is the feeling with which people who have come to spend their time and their money leave the theatre that makes your play a success or a failure. It is their satisfaction, their emotional reward, that is the test.

The reward can come in one of two ways. It can either come through the satisfaction of having the character they are sympathetically interested in win out over circumstances or other people, or be tragically defeated; but if he is tragically defeated, their reward must be a depth of pity and compassion that is satisfying. The play that ends in mere frustration for the people in whom the audience is emotionally interested will not satisfy them, for frustration is one of the most unhappy experiences in our lives.

When you start writing your play you must know how it is going to end. Somebody said to George Kaufman, "I wish you would look at this and see what is wrong with my third act," and George said, "I can tell you now. Your first." What he meant was that the fellow didn't know where he was going when he started. I get pretty impatient at scripts with good first acts and good second acts but in which the author has no third act because he didn't know where he was going.

Bill Maguire started writing a play some years ago which never came to town. It was built around a situation between two women. The husband had given up his career to be with his wife so she could have her career. Then the husband got fed up with it and met another woman. Bill could end the play either way, send him back to his wife or keep him with the other woman. The mistake was in not knowing before he began the play which woman was going to win out. There are two things that lick a play. One is that the audience doesn't believe it, and the other is that they don't care. If the audience does not care about the people or what happens to them, you haven't any play. They must care.

When you have created in the audience an emotional interest for a certain character, you must then excite the audience. You threaten its emotions by threatening your character, pitting him against circumstances or other people, so that it looks as though he is going to be defeated in some way, is going to be hurt. The audience should be very frightened, if the playwright is a good playwright, and when the character overcomes the disturbing circumstances, then comes the warmth of the audience's satisfaction. The amount of that warmth is the product of their affections multiplied by their fears.

The easiest threat against the audience's emotional sympathies is against something they agree is to be held precious. We all know how we fight for life even when we are desperately ill. Everybody does. Life is a very precious thing. So, if you threaten a character with death, you have a pretty good threat. Here's another: We are still a romantic race. We believe that the consummation of love is a very desirable and precious thing. So, if you have threatened your characters with the loss of that consummation, you have a pretty good threat. That still works, thank God. We have a pretty good threat today in the liberty of the individual. That, we have discovered, in the turmoil that the world is going through, is a threat that we can take very seriously.

The speed of the progress of your story must have a direct relationship to the depth of the emotional response. The more shallow the response that you have created, the more swiftly must your story pass given points. Farce must move faster than drama. Think of story points as telegraph poles that you are passing on a train. In farce you have to pass those poles quickly. The story has to keep going forward all the time; your scenes are very much shorter; you are jumping from one situation to another, to another, to another, to another.

Booth Tarkington wrote some very fine plays, especially when he was writing them with Harry Leon Wilson, but not all of his plays were very successful. The critics used to complain they were thin. Finally I staged a couple of his plays. Each was delightful, so charming, so amusing, that you couldn't cut a line. But Tarkington could write so well that he could write ten pages to a scene that should have taken only three. If he had only been able to write three, he would have had a swifter story and more story.

There is a playwright today whose handicap is that he writes too well. When he gets a couple of people together and they begin to play a scene, he can write such amusing talk that they talk a little too much. That slows down a play and thins out the content. Don't write your scene beyond its point. When you are through with it, you are through. Get into your next scene as quickly as you can.

Don't make your scenes too long. When we tried out *Life with Father* out of town a little over three years ago, we thought if we could get through the first act and get into the second, it would be all right. We didn't expect anything of the first act and were very surprised on the opening night because it went like a house afire. We were jubilant. We said, "Now we are all right." When we got to the second act, it didn't go nearly so well; it was way under par. When we began to examine why, the reason was obvious: every scene was a little too long. We had to take two lines out of this scene, four out of that and six out of that. Just a couple of lines can make a scene too long, four lines make it very much too long, and six can make it impossible. Merely by cutting the second act, our play was improved tremendously.

It is a very unwise thing to have your central character an unsympathetic person. Everybody wants to write a play about a bitch, and almost everybody does. Lillian Hellman did, but you had better be sure you can write as well as Lillian Hellman before you do it. Keep in front of an audience the people they like to spend their time with. If you have disagreeable people, people that the audience does not like, and they are in there to help you with your story, get them on, let them help you with your story and get them off.

The greatest reward for audiences watching a play is conviction. When an audience forgets it is seeing a play, when it is just believing what is happening on a stage, that is the greatest pleasure you can give. You can get conviction in two ways, one with sheer veracity where your writing and acting is so true that they believe in it as it goes along, and the other where you create a will to believe by being entertaining. We have found this out in practice.

Brooks Atkinson, writing about *Reap the Harvest* and trying to analyze why he didn't like the play more than he did, said he supposed it was because he didn't believe in it. He spoke about a clock that didn't move, and about an automobile horn that didn't sound anything like an automobile horn, and about a woman in the play calling upon a character to help her move a table which she could have moved herself, only they had to get another character on the scene. I wrote a letter to him, saying, "Tsk,tsk,tsk,t'ain't so. You have got the cart before the horse. You believe in a play because you like it."

It wasn't a very bright thing for me to do, because it was only half the truth, but it is true that if you like the play, you do not quarrel with those things. The minute we bore an audience, they begin to question. Their eyes look around the set and they say, "Good God, that chandelier shouldn't be that high!" Well, we have to hang chandeliers high so that people in the gallery can see the people on the stage. If there is a clock on the stage, they look at it when they are bored and see that its hands haven't moved. They hear an automobile effect and say it doesn't sound like an automobile. If they are interested and entertained, they don't make those observations. This demand for conviction on the part of the audience gets tougher every year. Every time we give them something better than they had before, they will not retreat. So there is this tremendous demand on the part of the audience for conviction, and you have to respect it.

If you are going to write a farce, get as much conviction as you can early. At the start of *She Loves Me Not,* I tried to convince the audience that it was really happening. You can't start on a broad basis and then get narrower. You can't start with a farcical comedy, and then end with light comedy. I am talking about the ordinary rules of playwriting. I am warning you, if you are going to break these principles, write as well as Thornton Wilder does.

The basis of all dramatization, which is probably what I should have started with, is the audience's well-known motto, "Don't tell us; show us." Have it happen on the stage in front of them. Create the incident. Bring that incident on the stage. You can always do it. No reason for it happening down at the corner, or very little reason.

Make your own exposition pay its own way. The first act is the hardest act to write, the hardest to act and the hardest to stage, because we are pushing so many facts across to the audience. They are not yet acquainted with the characters. They are not yet acquainted with their relationships. They are not yet acquainted with the circumstances. The first act must pay its own way either in humor or in excitement. The characters can't sit down and say, "As you know, my dear Gaston, this is the year 1793, and La Belle France is torn with internal dissension." Don't do it through discussion. Do it through incident which will reveal to the audience what you want revealed.

I find it easy to think of a play in terms of story and plot. Your story is the story of the personal relationships among your characters, how they vary, how they change, and the accumulation of it all at the end. Your plot consists of the incidents that affect those personal relationships. Your plot must be in key with your story. You can't suddenly, in the middle of a light story of a boy's and girl's love affair, have somebody come in with a gun and threaten to shoot one of them in order to reveal the fact that the boy loves the girl. That is going too far. Sometimes your plot device is too broad; sometimes too narrow. And *the climactic situation must always break in key with the quality of the story.*

When you are writing—for the benefit of the stage director—see your people in the process of living. Don't just have them come into a room and talk. That gives the poor director the job of having to think of what in the world he can do to make those people seem real and natural and human. Give them some employment yourself.

What to write about? I don't know. It is a very difficult thing to decide. Choice of material can be a happy accident, or an unfortunate selection. Knowledge of the theatre develops an instinctive feeling towards material. Owen Davis has said that a play is a success or failure before the author starts to write it. That is something to give us all pause. Once in a while you hit upon an idea that is fresh, that is novel, that has some unusual quality in it. The freshness of a play can be found in its plot, characters, story, timeliness, threats to the audience's sympathies. Watch for freshness. It is an important thing.

A play doesn't have to point a moral. Human nature is a good enough theme. You don't have to define God or tell what is wrong with the world. It is enough to see human beings acting in the circumstances of life. If you *are* going to write what is called a propaganda play, don't let any character in the play know what the propaganda is. Act it out. Don't talk it out. The minute you let one of your characters know what the propaganda is that you are trying to put across, that character will start talking, you can't stop him, and your play will become self-conscious.

Here is one more important thing. Don't send your play right out on the market as soon as you have finished it. Don't send it right out to the producer or to the agent. I know from experience that when you have finished a scene, and pulled it out of the typewriter, you say to yourself, "This thing is swell!" You think it is about as good as you can possibly write. Let it cool for at least two months, and then go back and read it. Let it cool, and then go back to it. Do your rewriting before the producer gets it. It is much easier all around.

May 1943

* *

ASHLEY DUKES

*

Journey Through Theatre

VII—SUCCESS STORY

YEARS BEFORE 1914 I had made the plan of a comedy whose motive should be the meeting at an inn of four people, master and man, mistress and maid, and their setting to partners for the night. Put like this, it would be hard to find a more ordinary theme, or one more apt to invite every sort of obvious treatment, from the purely cynical to the rosily erotic. My plot allowed for the cross-pairing of lovers in a way that every modern playgoer would expect; but the choice of partners was to arise from character rather than type. The comedy was imagined as a "costume play" from the start, yet it was meant to break away from prevailing theatre fashions. Producers for instance were talking of Shakespeare in modern dress; but this was to be modern thought in period setting. Dramatists were putting contemporary slang into historical drama; but this period play was not to be historical, and its speech, though without any gadzooks, was to fit the dress and the setting. The four personages, destined to play their comedy with a conventional innkeeper and wife for background, were to be four people like ourselves, born of the social and political revolutions made in the uneasy intervals between wars, and well aware of the inheritance.

Granted the setting to partners as an accomplished fact, man to mistress and master to maid, I wanted to leave to these four the answer to the question, what should happen to them in the morning. Their pairing-off could be either brief or lasting; either surrendered at the call of social necessity, or broken by mutual disgust, or maintained in the face of the world; but these were things they would have to decide for themselves as modern people should. I knew the treatment could be neither wholly cynical nor wholly sensual, remembering how the comedy had first come to mind in those far-off years.

The part of the Lady in it was meant to be played by Nora, my friend of the time around 1911, namesake of Ibsen's heroine and daughter of Charles Charrington and Janet Achurch, the pioneers of *A Doll's House*. We had talked of the play from that angle, and I had imagined her stooping beautifully to a manservant whose hard sincerity in love should awaken response in her own sophistication. After Nora's death in 1914 about the time of our joint birthday (she had been five years the younger), the idea of this unwritten comedy lived on sadly, bereft for a while of significance. But as a soldier in France I began sketching out scenes for it in Army notebooks, and by 1919 its outline had acquired almost the pattern of a workable scenario. Now here already was 1924 and the comedy still unwritten, though meanwhile I had been working in the theatre for years, and at thirty-nine had burned the boats of every other sort of profession behind me. It was high time to begin, as I reflected at the outset of a day's walk over the Chiltern Hills, every step of which was to be given to thinking out the composition.

A title for a play, as every dramatist knows, is useful from the start because of its power of suggestion. Climbing over a Chiltern stile with this thought in mind, and perhaps feeling a noonday thirst, I remembered marching in 1915 as a soldier past some roadside alehouse called *The Man with a Load of Mischief*. It may have been either near Cambridge or on the Berkshire downs; the sign was once not uncommon among English inns, and on the site of Selfridge's store in Oxford Street such a house had been embellished by Hogarth with a painting of a man "loaded with mischief." Here, anyway, was a title for a comedy; and it gave me the idea that a manservant (The Man) might be loaded with mischief by his master (The Nobleman) in being bidden to make love to a mistress (The Lady) for her discomfiture, while the master himself should make love to her pert follower (The Maid). In two strides, here was a plot fully elaborated. All that was needful was to link it up with the past of the four chief persons, and leave them to work out their future for themselves. Should the comedy be in verse or prose? Irregular rhyming verse tempted me greatly, but prose is more difficult and for that reason won the day. For period, the Regency would surely be best; and if nobody but myself would see the double irony of the title, the loading of mischief upon a man for his master's ends, no harm would be done. Everyone would see the irony of the man already in love with a woman commanded to make a pretence of wooing her; for that is one of the classic though rare motives of comedy. Everyone would taste the bitterness of the manservant next morning, when his noble master yawns over breakfast and laments the fleeting character of carnal pleasure. Dialogue began to run through my head, something this way:

NOBLEMAN: Sympathy, remember. Speak of me—none too kindly for she hates me.

MAN: I will not speak ill of your lordship.

NOBLEMAN: Have no scruples. Say your worst.

MAN: Servants often speak ill of their masters. I think that is not the way to my lady's confidence.

NOBLEMAN: A nice point. Yes, you have the finer touch.

MAN: I would rather rely on my own merits than your lordship's shortcomings.

And so it is that plays contrive to get themselves written, after maturing sometimes through years of personal experience and emotional impulse, to which a technical understanding of the writer's craft is more or less unconsciously added. Being built of all these things, my comedy sailed perhaps into deeper waters than I had meant to navigate in the beginning. Before half an act was finished, the ending was already determined by the need of making the love of a man and woman the motive of an action where all else was masquerade. The play became liable to be called romantic, although the lovers sought nothing but reality in themselves and one another. It varied from the plane of high comedy to that of the comedy of feeling; which in turn made it none too easy a play for the actor and actress, confronted by one realist obstacle after another to be taken in the stride of their emotional perception.

The Man with a Load of Mischief found a publisher at once, and ran into several impressions as a reading play before it was seriously considered for the stage. During the summer of 1924 the script had been shown to three or four London producing managers, all of whom said there was not a penny in it; an opinion I entirely shared. Nigel Playfair, however, offered to arrange some matinee performances at his theatre in Hammersmith if he could get the right cast, and Norman Macdermott at the Everyman was willing to face ruin by giving the play an evening run. I preferred to hand it to the Stage Society—a step which gave it the final stamp of highbrow non-commercialism, but at the same time offered the hope of first-rate casting if it should ever be produced. The Society announced it as the first production of the season 1924-1925; and when I modestly suggested that Fay Compton and Leon Quartermaine should be asked to play in it, they astonished us all by accepting immediately. Fay Compton was afterwards obliged through other rehearsals to give up her part; but we went forward with a good cast, luckily small enough to enable us to afford the scene and costumes designed by Aubrey Hammond, which gave a distinction hitherto unknown to a Sunday evening play production. Another motive for this little extravagance was an American offer received for the play during its rehearsal weeks; the advance royalties were promptly spent in setting it forth to advantage.

Meantime I had also to rehearse *No Man's Land,* which the St. Martin's management had commissioned me to translate from *La Terre Inhumaine* by François de Curel. This was the work of a notable French dramatist who hitherto had been played only by the Stage Society in England; and the most I hoped for was that his play should have a run, whilst my comedy perhaps might score a success of esteem. Actually *No Man's Land* was a failure, not from its own fault but from casting and other causes. *The Man with a Load of Mischief,* after its two Stage Society performances, was acquired by Frederick Harrison for the Haymarket, where it was presented the following summer, June 1925, and began a first run of eight months. The theatre was more or less sold out for the rest of the London season; and thanks to the contract which had been offered me by the courtly old manager, the last of his line in the West End, I found myself suddenly with an income of close on a thousand pounds a month, more than I would normally require in a year. It was all very surprising, and rather like winning a Derby Sweep by one's own exertions if that were possible.

I tried to live up to the part of successful playwright, visiting the theatre now and then, and giving little supper-parties; but in fact I made few contacts with the new world in which I found myself, even though total strangers wrote and asked me to their homes. On the other hand I fell in the estimation of high-brow friends, who were accustomed to argue that West End success and triviality were one and the same, and felt that I must have been writing down deliberately to the public. I cannot say this troubled me much. Of that summer when the play was running, I seem best to remember a day spent in walking to and from Ascot races through Windsor Great Park, and lunching out among the gipsies and bookies on the far side of the course. I inspected the men in grey top-hats and their ladies in picture-frocks with quite a new interest, knowing that most of them would go to see my comedy because it was the thing to see, and hoping that some of them might even like it. The only visible connection of Ascot with the theatre was the name of Lord Howard de Walden, a patron who had once enabled Herbert Trench to put on plays by Maeterlinck and others at the Haymarket. One of his horses, the race-card told me, was running in the next race; and sure enough there it was, with a jockey in apricot, cantering to the starting-post. The tip was altogether too good to miss, and I enriched myself a little more by the victory of a fantastic outsider. After this, it was sensible to reflect again on luck in the theatre, and the overwhelming part it plays. Where would my comedy have been without Fay Compton and Leon Quartermaine and Frank Cellier, backed by the authority of the Haymarket? A title in the archives of a Sunday evening play society, at the very best.

The problem of continuing to write for such a medium of expression, as an independent author submitting his work for the approval of a producing manager, was sufficiently complicated. As an old dramatic critic I knew how few playwrights register more than one or two hits, even though they give their whole lives to the business. I knew also that what I really needed was to work in the theatre with a group of artists, actors and directors and craftsmen, and to write for them, sometimes at my own suggestion, sometimes at theirs, without surrendering that absolute creative freedom of the study which is the dramatist's right. There was nothing new about this idea; indeed all Elizabethan drama had come into being by such means. Creative directors in our own time had tried, and were still trying, to broaden the basis of theatre so that the stage should not merely translate the realist picture in the playwright's mind into realist fact and furniture. But I questioned very much, and still question, whether it is possible to form such a creative group under satisfactory conditions in the existing proscenium theatre and with existing players whose style is already formed. One would probably need not only dramatic schools and workshops of a new type but also playhouses differently constructed and proportioned, with a new relation between stage and auditorium, to embody the new theatre conception. The more photographic reproduction of a dramatist's or director's picture could be left to the screen. Failing any such movement in our theatre of 1925, which was imagined to be solely the dramatist's mouthpiece and instrument, I could only go on trying to bring it into effective being; but it was an advantage to back my opinion with the freedom of a practising playwright, as well as the experience. As royalties continued to pour in, I began to think of theatre management and direction.

This modest success, which had not otherwise changed my way of life, gave me the chance of a first visit to America. Aubrey Hammond and I sailed on the old Celtic in September 1925, with a vast crowd of returning tourists of those days. Ostensibly we were going to see the New York production of my comedy with Ruth Chatterton and Robert Loraine, but really we meant to learn something more about the world than we knew already. We were innocent enough of the Atlantic to imagine that this aged liner, in which as first-class passengers we slept above each other's heads, represented the normal comfort of ocean travel. As we arrived at the pier, it was cheering to see the yellow covers of THEATRE ARTS waving above the heads of the crowd, and to know that we were among friends, most of whom we met for the first time. We lived at the Algonquin and lunched with the dramatic critics, who welcomed us with the kindness always extended to children escaped from Europe. We visited Niagara, Toronto and Atlantic City during the out-of-town tour of the comedy (I shall always cherish the memory of the Boardwalk and the Heinz pier), and we behaved neither more nor less unwisely than other newcomers to Broadway and its life.

I cannot say that Broadway and Shaftesbury Avenue seemed to

me essentially different; in both of them I met numbers of producers, directors and players whose main interest was the stage, while my own interest was the theatre. Noel Coward was there with *The Vortex,* which I had liked very well a year earlier in London; and among the actors was Herbert Marshall who had played in *The Machine-Wreckers* for the Stage Society. As for my own comedy, I had registered a private vow in mid-Atlantic that any money made by it in America should be devoted to subverting the theatre as we know it in the West End of London and elsewhere. The theatre does not forget such vows, and knows how to defend itself. The comedy failed after a few weeks, though I remained to pay for my seats at other people's plays and to meet writers for the theatre and critics, among whom were Sidney Howard, Stark Young and John Mason Brown. The visit had been a stimulating adventure, and I could have forecast at that time the arrival of the American dramatists in Britain and their conquest of our stage in the years between 1935 and 1940. Just before beginning the homeward journey, I was able to accept a cabled offer of the Home University Library to write their book on Drama, which occupied me on the boat and for three months afterwards.

The ambition of a dramatist is generally to go on writing plays, each as successful as possible, and to draw royalties upon them until eventually the copyrights become extinguished by the passage of time, both on the professional and amateur stage. I share this ambition to the full; and in this year 1941 I am still earning a small income from copyrights created in the early 1920's. But the casualties in such a career are heavy; and when I think of the months spent in writing and rewriting plays never to be performed, or maybe to receive one or two fugitive presentations only, the endurance of perennial hope in the dramatist's mind seems to be the chief marvel of his profession. Among the full-length plays I wrote in the years following 1925 were *The Song of Drums* or *Ulenspiegel,* which managed to get itself performed in the Royal Flemish Theatre at Brussels but not in London; *The Fountain-Head,* which had a short run in a club theatre; and *Matchmaker's Arms;* or *House of Assignation,* played in successive versions by Sybil Thorndike and at the Mercury. The first and third of these were more or less based on picaresque masterpieces in narrative, the *Légende* of Charles de Coster and the *Celestina* of Fernando de Rojas respectively.

There were also the many adaptations commissioned for me by producing managers in England and America, nearly twenty in all. Most of them reached the stage and ran for various periods from a fortnight to a year, whilst others were gradually forgotten by the men who had commissioned them, and still lie somewhere in the dusty files of theatre offices. None of this was hack work in the ordinary sense, for I declined every play or subject that would not give me pleasure in the writing; but much of it was work done in the spirit of the Elizabethan play-craftsman for a kind of theatre almost unknown in our time. The plays that succeeded owed their success to outstanding personalities in the cast; and those that failed were mostly overladen with scenery or costume or some other element inimical to the effect of the spoken word. Had I been given a free choice, I would have had none of this dramatic work performed on a proscenium stage, but on a platform stage resembling that of the Florentine or English Renaissance. And although these notions may seem queer to the reader familiar with one type of theatre architecture only, they are based on the experience of a practical playwright who has always had one foot firmly planted on the commercial stage.

This has been a very personal chapter, for which I make no apologies. Needless to say, many things happened in our London theatre of 1924-25 besides *The Man with a Load*. To this time belong *Saint Joan, Our Betters,* the rise of Noel Coward, the appearance of the *Chauve-Souris,* Stark Young's *The Colonnade* at the Stage Society, *The Emperor Jones, Juno and the Paycock* and many other lively happenings. The General Strike, that strangest of social and economic phenomena, was still before us. The world had not yet embarked upon the orgy of confident speculation that succeeded Locarno, and was so abruptly ended in 1929-30. We had not reached midway in the passage between our wars, and the swell of optimism was still evident, even though it might forecast heavy seas. Most of Europe was quiet too; and to the reflection of this mood in continental drama I shall come very soon. The spring of 1926 found me free to come and go in any country or continent, to write or cease from writing as I pleased. No man of forty-one could have desired a greater liberty than this, or have been more resolved (I hope) to make use of it.

July 1941

JEAN-PAUL SARTRE

*

Forgers of Myths

THE YOUNG PLAYWRIGHTS OF FRANCE

IN READING the newspaper reviews of Katharine Cornell's production of Jean Anouilh's *Antigone,* I had the impression that the play had created a certain amount of discomfort in the minds of the New York drama critics. Many expressed surprise that such an ancient myth should be staged at all. Others reproached Antigone with being neither alive nor credible, with not having what, in theatre jargon, is called "character." The misunderstanding, I believe, was due to the fact that the critics were not informed of what many young authors in France—each along differing lines and without concerted aim—are attempting to do.

There has been a great deal of discussion in France about "a return to tragedy," about the "rebirth of the philosophic play." The two labels are confusing and they should be rejected. Tragedy is, for us, an historic phenomenon which flourished between the sixteenth and eighteenth centuries; we have no desire to begin that over again. Nor are we anxious to produce philosophic plays, if by that is meant works deliberately intended to set forth on the stage the philosophy of Marx, St. Thomas, or existentialism. Nevertheless, there is some truth attached to these two labels: in the first place, it is a fact that we are less concerned with making innovations than with returning to a tradition; it is likewise true that the problems we wish to deal with in the theatre are very different from those we habitually dealt with before 1940.

The theatre, as conceived of in the period between the two world wars, and as it is perhaps still thought of in the United States today, is a theatre of characters. The analysis of characters and their confrontation was the theatre's chief concern. The so-called "situations" existed only for the purpose of throwing the characters into clearer relief. The best plays in this period were psychological studies of a coward, a liar, an ambitious man or a frustrated one. Occasionally a playwright made an effort to outline the workings of a passion—usually love—or to analyze an inferiority complex.

Judged by such principles Anouilh's Antigone is not a character at all. Nor is she simply a peg on which to hang a passion calculated to develop along the approved lines of whatever psychology might be in style. She represents a naked will, a pure, free choice; in her there is no distinguishing between passion and action. The young playwrights of France do not believe that men share a ready-made "human nature" which may alter under the impact of a given situation. They do not think that individuals can be seized with a passion or mania which can be explained purely on the grounds of heredity, environment and situations. What is universal, to their way of thinking, is not nature but the situations in which a man finds himself; that is, not the sum total of his psychological traits but the limits which enclose him on all sides.

For them man is not to be defined as a "reasoning animal," or a "social" one, but as a free being, entirely indeterminate, who must choose his own being when confronted with certain necessities, such as being already committed in a world full of both threatening and favorable factors among other men who have made their choices before him, who have decided in advance the meaning of those factors. He is faced with the necessity of having to work and die, of being hurled into a life already complete which yet is his own enterprise and in which he can never have a second chance; where he must play his cards and take risks no matter what the cost. That is why we feel the urge to put on the stage certain situations which throw light on the main aspects of the condition of man and to have the spectator participate in the free choice which man makes in these situations.

Thus, Anouilh's Antigone may have seemed abstract because she was not portrayed as a young Greek princess, formed by certain influences and some ghastly memories, but rather as a free woman without any features at all until she chooses them for herself in the moment when she asserts her freedom to die despite the triumphant tyrant. Similarly, when the burgomaster of Vauxelles in Simone de Beauvoir's *Les Bouches Inutiles* has to decide whether to save his beleaguered town by cutting off half of its citizens (women, children and old men) or to risk making them all perish in an effort to save them all, we do not care whether he is sensual or cold, whether he has an Oedipus complex or whether he is of an irritable or jolly disposition. No doubt, if he is rash or incautious, vain or pusillanimous he will make the wrong decision. But we are not interested in arranging in advance the motivations or reasons which will inevitably force his choice. Rather, we are concerned in presenting the anguish of a man who is both free and full of good will, who in all sincerity is trying to find out the side he must take, and who knows that when he chooses the lot of others he is at the same time choosing his own pattern of behavior and is deciding once and for all whether he is to be a tyrant or a democrat.

If one of us happens to present a character on the boards it is only for the purpose of getting rid of it at once. For instance, Caligula, at the outset of Albert Camus' play of that name, has a character. One is led to believe that he is gentle and well-behaved, and no doubt he actually is both. But that gentleness and that modesty suddenly melt away in the face of the prince's horrifying discovery of the world's absurdity. From then on he will choose to be the man to persuade other men of that absurdity, and the play becomes only the story of how he carries out his purpose.

A man who is free within the circle of his own situations, who chooses, whether he wishes to or not, for everyone else when he chooses for himself—that is the subject-matter of our plays. As a successor to the theatre of characters we want to have a theatre of situation; our aim is to explore all the situations that are most common to human experience, those which occur at least once in the majority of lives. The people in our plays will be distinct from one another—not as a coward is from a miser, or a miser from a brave man, but rather as actions are divergent or clashing, as right may conflict with right. In this it may well be said that we derive from the Corneillean tradition.

It is easy to understand, therefore, why we are not greatly concerned with psychology. We are not searching for the right "word" which will suddenly reveal the whole unfolding of a passion, nor yet the "act" which will seem most lifelike and inevitable to the audience. For us psychology is the most abstract of the sciences because it studies the workings of our passions without plunging them back into their true human surroundings, without their background of religious and moral values, the taboos and commandments of society, the conflicts of nations and classes, of rights, of wills, of actions. For us a man is a whole enterprise in himself. And passion is a part of that enterprise.

In this we return to the concept of tragedy as the Greeks saw it. For them, as Hegel has shown, passion was never a simple storm of sentiment but fundamentally always the assertion of a right. The fascism of Creon, the stubbornness of Antigone for Sophocles and Anouilh, the madness of Caligula for Camus, are at one and the same time transports of feeling which have their origin deep within us and expressions of impregnable will which are affirmations of systems of values and rights, such as the rights of citizenship, the rights of the family, individual ethics, collective ethics, the right to kill, the right to reveal to human beings their pitiable condition and so forth. We do not reject psychology, that would be absurd; we integrate life.

For fifty years one of the most celebrated subjects for dissertation in France has been formulated as follows: "Comment on La Bruyere's saying: 'Racine draws man as he is; Corneille, as he should be.'" We believe the statement should be revised. Racine paints psychologic man, that is without ever allowing moral considerations or human will to deflect the inevitability of their evolution. His dramatis personae are only creatures of his mind, the end results of an intellectual analysis. Corneille, on the other hand, showing will at the very core of passion, gives us back man in all his complexity, in his complete reality.

The young authors I am discussing take their stand on Corneille's side. For them the theatre will be able to present man in his entirety only in proportion to the theatre's willingness to be moral. By that we do not mean that it should put forward examples illustrating the rules of deportment or the practical ethics taught to children, but rather that the study of the conflict of characters should be replaced by the presentation of the conflict of rights. It was not a question of the opposition of character between a Stalinist and a Trotskyite; it was not in their characters that an anti-Nazi of 1933 clashed with an S.S. guard; the difficulties in international politics do not derive from the characters of the men leading us; the strikes in the United States do not reveal conflicts of character between industrialists and workers. In each case it is, in the final analysis and in spite of divergent interests, the system of values, of ethics and of concepts of man which are lined up against each other.

Therefore, our new theatre definitely has drawn away from the so-called "realistic theatre" because "realism" has always offered plays made up of stories of defeat, laissez-faire and drifting; it has always preferred to show how external forces batter a man to pieces, destroy him bit by bit and ultimately make of him a weathervane turning with every change of wind. But we claim for ourselves the true realism because we know it is impossible, in everyday life, to distinguish between fact and right, the real from the ideal, psychology from ethics.

This theatre does not give its support to any one "thesis" and is not inspired by any preconceived idea. All it seeks to do is to explore the state of man in its entirety, and to present to the modern man a portrait of himself, his problems, his hopes and his struggles. We believe our theatre would betray its mission if it portrayed individual personalities, even if they were types as universal as a miser, a misanthrope, a deceived husband, because, if it is to address the masses, the theatre must speak in terms of their most general preoccupations, dispelling their anxieties in the form of myths which anyone can understand and feel deeply.

My first experience in the theatre was especially fortunate. When I was a prisoner in Germany in 1940, I wrote, staged and acted in a Christmas play which, while pulling the wool over the eyes of the German censor by means of simple symbols, was addressed to my fellow-prisoners. This drama, biblical in appearance only, was written and put on by a prisoner, was acted by prisoners in scenery painted by prisoners; it was aimed exclusively at prisoners (so much so that I have never since then permitted it to be staged or even printed) and it addressed them on the subject of their concerns as prisoners. No doubt it was neither a good play nor well acted: the work of an amateur, the critics would say, a product of special circumstances. Nevertheless, on this occasion, as I addressed my comrades across the footlights, speaking to them of their state as prisoners, when I suddenly saw them so remarkably silent and attentive, I realized what theatre ought to be—a great collective, religious phenomenon.

To be sure, I was, in this case, favored by special circumstances; it does not happen every day that your public is drawn together by one great common interest, a great loss or a great hope. As a rule, an audience is made up of the most diverse elements: a big business man sits beside a traveling salesman or a professor, a man next to a woman, and each is subject to his own particular preoccupations.

Yet this situation is a challenge to the playwright: he must create his public, he must fuse all the disparate elements in the auditorium into a single unity by awakening in the recesses of their spirits the things which all men of a given epoch and community care about.

This does not mean that our authors intend to make use of symbols in the sense that symbols are the expression either indirect or poetic of a reality one either cannot or will not grasp directly. We would feel a profound distaste today for representing happiness as an elusive bluebird, as Maeterlinck did. Our times are too austere for child's play of that sort. Yet if we reject the theatre of symbols we still want ours to be one of myths; we want to attempt to show the public the great myths of death, exile, love. The characters in Albert Camus' *Le Malentendu* are not symbols, they are flesh and blood: *a* mother and *a* daughter, *a* son who comes back from a long journey; their tragic experiences are complete in themselves. And yet they are mythical in the sense that the misunderstanding which separates them can serve as the embodiment of all misunderstandings which separate man from himself, from the world, from other men.

The French public makes no mistake about this, as has been proved by the discussions engendered by certain plays. With *Les Bouches Inutiles,* for instance, criticism was not confined to discussing the story of the play which was based on actual events that took place frequently in the Middle Ages: it recognized in the play a condemnation of fascist procedures. The communists, on the other hand, saw in it a condemnation of their own procedures: "The conclusion," so they said in their newspapers," is couched in terms of petty bourgeois idealism. All useless mouths should have been sacrificed to save the city." Anouilh also stirred up a storm of discussion with *Antigone,* being charged on the one hand with being a Nazi, on the other with being an anarchist. Such violent reactions prove that our plays are reaching the public just where it is important that it should be reached.

Yet these plays are austere. To begin with, since the situation is what we care about above all, our theatre shows it at the very point where it is about to reach its climax. We do not take time out for learned research, we feel no need for registering the imperceptible evolution of a character or a plot: one does not reach death by degrees, one is suddenly confronted with it—and if one approaches politics or love by slow degrees, then acute problems, arising suddenly, call for no progression. By taking our dramatis personae and precipitating them, in the very first scene, into the highest pitch of their conflicts we turn to the well-known pattern of classic tragedy, which always seizes upon the action at the very moment it is headed for catastrophe.

Our plays are violent and brief, centered around one single event; there are few players and the story is compressed within a short space of time, sometimes only a few hours. As a result they obey a kind of "rule of the three unities," which has been only a little rejuvenated and modified. A single set, a few entrances, a few exits, intense arguments among the characters who defend their individual rights with passion—this is what sets our plays at a great distance from the brilliant fantasies of Broadway. Yet some of them find that their austerity and intensity have not lacked appreciation in Paris. Whether New York will like them is a question.

Since it is their aim to forge myths, to project for the audience an enlarged and enhanced image of its own sufferings, our playwrights turn their backs on the constant preoccupation of the realists, which is to reduce as far as possible the distance which separates the spectator from the spectacle. In 1942, in Gaston Baty's production of *The Taming of the Shrew,* there were steps going from the stage to the auditorium so that certain characters could go down among the orchestra seats. We are very far away from such concepts and methods. To us a play should not seem too familiar. Its greatness derives from its social and, in a certain sense, religious functions: it must remain a rite; even as it speaks to the spectators of themselves it must do it in a tone and with a constant reserve of manner which, far from breeding familiarity, will increase the distance between play and audience.

That is why one of our problems has been to search out a style of dialogue which, while utterly simple and made up of words on everyone's lips, will still preserve something of the ancient dignity of our tongue. We have all barred from our plays the digressions, the set speeches and what we in France like to call the *"poésie de réplique"*; all this chit-chat debases a language. It seems to us that we shall recapture a little of the pomp of ancient tragedies if we practice the most rigorous economy of words. As for me, in *Morts Sans Sépulture,* my latest play, I did not deny myself the use of familiar turns of phrase, swear words, even slang, whenever I felt that such speech was germane to the characters. But I did attempt to preserve, through the pace of the dialogue, an extreme conciseness of statement—ellipses, brusque interruptions, a sort of inner tension in the phrases which at once set them apart from the easy-going sound of everyday talk. Camus' style in *Caligula* is different in kind but it is magnificently sober and taut. Simone de Beauvoir's language in *Les Bouches Inutiles* is so stripped that it is sometimes accused of dryness.

Dramas which are short and violent, sometimes reduced to the dimensions of a single long act (*Antigone* lasts an hour and a half; my own play, *Huis-Clos,* an hour and twenty minutes without intermission), dramas entirely centered on one event—usually a conflict of rights, bearing on some very general situation—written in sparse, extremely tense style, with a small cast not presented for their individual characters but thrust into a conjunction where they are forced to make a choice—in brief this is the theatre, austere, moral, mythic and ceremonial in aspect, which has given birth to new plays in Paris during the occupation and especially since the end of the war. They correspond to the needs of a people exhausted but tense, for whom liberation has not meant a return to abundance and who can live only with the utmost economy.

The very severity of these plays is in keeping with the severity of French life; their moral and metaphysical topics reflect the preoccupation of a nation which must at one and the same time reconstruct and recreate and which is searching for new principles. Are they the product of local circumstances or can their very austerity of form enable them to reach a wider public in more fortunate countries? This is a question we must ask ourselves frankly before we try to transplant them.

June 1946

PADRAIC COLUM

*

Poet's Progress

W. B. YEATS IN THE THEATRE

FOR OVER a quarter of a century the greatest poet writing in English has had under his control a theatre which he himself was instrumental in creating, a theatre which is not merely an adjunct to a writer's study, but is popular, and with an audience that has memories, traditions, national consciousness, and that can react strongly to what is presented to it. A poet wishing to express himself in dramatic terms could hardly be more favorably placed. How has this particular poet profited by his enviable position? What progress has he made as a dramatist, and how has his theatrical experience affected his non-dramatic poetry? The question is of the greatest interest, and one turns eagerly to *The Collected Plays of W. B. Yeats* for an answer to it.*

The opening play in the collection was produced before Yeats had a theatre under his control: it was revised afterwards; but fundamentally it is a play written by the poet while still outside the theatre and so it gives us a measure by which to estimate his theatrical progress. *The Countess Cathleen* is a play that with theatrical experience on the part of the poet could have been a classic. The opening scene is perfect: the legendary quality in the theme is rendered completely, hauntingly. Grave and kindly, the proper lady of a legend, Cathleen enters. The lines she speaks and the lines that answer hers must be remembered for their beauty and significance:

CATHLEEN: God save all here. There is a certain house,
An old grey castle with a kitchen garden,
A cider orchard and a plot for flowers,
Somewhere among these woods.

MARY: We know it, lady.
A place that's set among impassable walls
As though world's trouble could not find it out.

* *The Collected Plays of W. B. Yeats:* Macmillan.

These lines "situate" the action—it is in that Ireland where the mediaeval world has lasted until the seventeenth century, a world that is in the poems Yeats wrote before he discovered the world of heroic legend and the world of symbolism. The other scenes are not so telling. There is the love of the Countess Cathleen for Aleel the poet. This might have been used to give rise to a series of developing situations which would reinforce the main situation. It does not come near doing anything of the kind. Aleel is an alien in the theatre, being a lyrical poet's and not a dramatic poet's idea of a character: if Yeats had been accustomed to the theatre he would have known that a dramatist's characters have to be recognizable types; Aleel is not recognizable, being too indeterminate.

A play that impressed this outsetting dramatist, and helped him towards a convention different from the one he had begun with, was the mediaeval morality, *Everyman*. It was a pity that he did not see *Everyman* before he gave *The Countess Cathleen* a form in which there are several changes of scene and a lapse of time: played on a platform with a single scene, as in *Everyman,* and no time-intervals, *The Countess Cathleen* would have been better gathered together.

The King's Threshold was the first poetic play produced after Yeats had actually worked in the theatre (the prose one-act play *Cathleen-ni-Houlihan* was produced when he joined the group that was to establish the theatre for him). *Everyman* had suggested the form—a single processional action played without a break. There is an element in this play which in the original production prevented an audience's complete sympathy going to the central character. The poet Seanchan has resolved to die by hunger. He brings his teaching back to the minds of his pupils who have come to ask him to give up his hunger protest. The poets, he has told them, hang images

> About the child-bed of the world, that it,
> Looking upon those images, might bear
> Triumphant children.

Then, if these images were not shown,

> The world that lacked them would be like a woman
> That, looking on the cloven lips of a hare,
> Brings forth a hare-lipped child.

The poet must not permit these images to be insulted in his person. So far the argument is convincing. But the answer amounts to casuistry. It is a rationalization, and not a very good one, of the action of a man who is going to starve himself and make a disturbance in the state because bishops, soldiers and men of law do not believe that a poet is entitled to a place at the King's council. Nobody really believes that the existence of poetry depends upon its prestige at Court. This is a fantastic element that often comes into Yeats' plays and detracts from the audience's complete sympathy: by fantastic I mean the intrusion of the dramatist's private notions.

Yeats foreshadowed in Seanchan's situation the heroic defiance of Terence MacSwiney. Fourteen years after he had produced this play he witnessed a life flicker to martyrdom through hunger. And witnessing this his vision became uplifted and solemn. He perceived that what Seanchan was striving for was something more than the restoration of an ancient right. It was to make obsolete for ever a whole array of ancient wrongs. As it was first produced the play ended with Seanchan winning over the King and being brought back to the Council Table to a fanfare of trumpets. But a poet in so triumphant a role is not a sympathetic personage; the play that had such an ending was not poignant. And in *The King's Threshold* as given in this collection Seanchan dies, and his death gives rise to solemn poetry:

OLDEST PUPIL: Not what it leaves behind it in the light
But what it carries with it to the dark
Exalts the soul; nor song nor trumpet-blast
Can call up races from the worsening world
To mend the wrong and mar the solitude
Of the great shade we follow to the tomb.

The verse of *The King's Threshold* has strident music—the sound of trumpets as compared with sound of harps which is the music of *The Countess Cathleen*. The poet has now got the rhythm of actual speech into his verse—a speech to be declaimed as the speech of *The Countess Cathleen* is to be chanted.

To read *The Hour Glass* with the first version of it in memory is to realize how essential it is for the dramatic poet to have such a workshop as a theatre under his control. In its original form *The Hour Glass* was an elementary kind of drama; it was in prose, in the convention of a morality, and it lacked conflict and contrast. In the course of several productions this play was developed into something with contrast and character, something belonging to the poet's own world. The play is now mainly in verse, and is more elaborate, on a higher level of creation than the first version. The Wise Man, who before had no particular individuality, is now a Yeatsean Wise Man, one who is startled back into a conviction that must have been in him originally, the conviction that the phenomenal world is no more than a reflection of the real world.

If he has profited by his franchise of the theatre, it has to be said, too, that Yeats has occasionally misused that franchise. There is the case of *The Shadowy Waters*. Originally this was a beautiful and dramatically sustained piece of poetry, capable of being delivered as a dramatic recital. Well, the poet has changed all that. He attempted to make theatrically effective a conception that might have been embodied in a Mallarméan dialogue. The result is that everything becomes muddled. Instead of the lovely dramatic poem, we have in *The Shadowy Waters* of the present volume prose and verse speeches that seem plagiarisms from some Abbey Theatre play:

SECOND SAILOR: . . . It is a hard thing, age to be coming on me, and I not to get the chance of doing a robbery that would enable me to live quiet and honest to the end of my lifetime

FORGAEL: My grief!
DECTORA: Have I not loved you for a thousand years?
FORGAEL: I never have been golden-armed Iollan.
DECTORA: I do not understand. I know your face
Better than my own hands.
FORGAEL: I have deceived you
Out of all reckoning.
DECTORA: Is it not true
That you were born a thousand years ago,
In islands where the children of Aengus wind
In happy dances under a windy moon,
And that you'll bring me there?
FORGAEL: I have deceived you;
I have deceived you utterly.

I can imagine some young writer sending this to the Directors of the Abbey Theatre in the fond belief that he was writing as well as the Synge of *The Playboy of the Western World* in collaboration with the Yeats of *The Wind Amongst the Reeds*.

Nor can I praise the play that follows, *Deirdre*. The verse has high excellence: indeed it is a long way back to the time when verse as fine as this was spoken on the stage:

NAOISE: Such words and fears
Wrong this old man who's pledged his word to us.
We must not speak or think as women do,
That when the house is all a-bed sit up
Marking among the ashes with a stick
Till they are terrified.—Being what we are
We must meet all things with an equal mind.

The lyric that makes a chorus for this play is amongst the greatest of Yeats' lyrical poems. But, to me, *Deirdre* is exasperating. One can do almost anything with an heroic legend that one is treating for a modern audience, except to make the people in it undignified. In *Deirdre* there is not one character that has real dignity: Conchubar is depraved into treachery by senile lust; Fergus is a credulous babbler; the singing-women are out of a green-room; Deirdre has the self-consciousness of a prima-donna; Naoise is a pure fool. These statements call for some backing-up, and unfortunately, it is easy to give them that. Deidre's first words in the play are:

Silence your music, though I thank you for it;
But the wind's blown upon my hair, and I
Must set the jewels on my neck and head
For one that's coming.

When she would get Naoise out of the trap they have been led into she pretends that her object is to captivate Conchubar:

Look at my face where the leaf raddled it
And at these rubies on my hair and breast.
It was for him, to stir him to desire,
I put on beauty; yes, for Conchubar.
NAOISE: What frenzy put these words into your mouth?
DEIRDRE: No frenzy, for what need is there for frenzy
To change what shifts with every shift of the wind,

Or else there is no truth in men's old sayings?
Was I not born a woman?

Naoise has been Deirdre's husband for nine years; he would know, of course, that what she was saying was not true; she would know that he would know it, and so would not say anything of the kind.

There is a good deal of this self-regarding phase in *On Baile's Strand,* but this play about Conchubar and Cuchulain has a vitality that seems over-stimulated in passages but is always to be felt. The weakness of the play comes from that fantasy into which Yeats is so often betrayed. Cuchulain fights a young man who turns out to be his son—fights him and slays him. But he does not want to fight him—he likes him, the boy reminds him of a woman he loved, and he would like to have him for a comrade. And what reverses this feeling? "Some witch is floating in the air above," and then Cuchulain:

Yes, witchcraft! witchcraft! Witches of the air!
Why did you? Who was it set you to this work?
Out, out! I say, for now it's sword on sword!

And on this piece of senselessness Cuchulain and the young man whose appearance has so appealed to him go out to do battle.

Yet the play has the impressiveness of a thing that has inherent character. In Yeats' development as a writer of a high kind of poetic eloquence this play is the peak, above *The King's Threshold.* The exchanges between Cuchulain and Conchubar, between Cuchulain and the Young Man, are magnificent pieces of tirade:

CUCHULAIN: Are you so changed,
Or have I grown more dangerous of late?
But that's not it. I understand it all.
It's you that have changed. You've wives and children now,
And for that reason cannot follow one
That lives like a bird's flight from tree to tree.—
It's time the years put water in my blood
And drowned the wildness of it, for all's changed,
But that unchanged.—I'll take what oath you will:
The moon, the sun, the water, light, or air,
I do not care how binding.
. . .

CUCHULAIN: For he that's in the sun begot this body
Upon a mortal woman, and I have heard tell
It seemed as if he had outrun the moon
That he must follow always through waste heaven,
He loved so happily. He'll be but slow
To break a tree that was so sweetly planted.
Let's see that arm. I'll see it if I choose.
That arm had a good father and a good mother,
But it is not like this.

The characters in *On Baile's Strand* have not heroic stature. Is Yeats, then, not capable of creating in the heroic? The answer to that is in another out of his Cuchulain cycle, *The Green Helmet.*

This play is one of Yeats' complete dramatic successes: it has not any deliberateness, intentionalness, self-consciousness; it has spontaneity that goes well with high and heroic exploit. The heady verse admirably conveys this. It is a real innovation, rhymed verse in ballad-meter through which the characters can be humorous and spirited. Again Cuchulain is the center of the play; with him are his peers, Laegaire and Conall. These heroes have real heroic stature; they have humor, bravery and a fantasy that is proper to them. And unlike the people in *Deirdre,* the people in *On Baile's Strand,* they convince us that they are Irish. Indeed, the spirit of the Irish heroic saga has never been better brought out than in this impetuous and humorous play which at once satirizes Irish tribalism and celebrates the heroism which often transcends that tribalism. The helmet of the title is to be given to the hero who will redeem the honor of the land by laying down his own head for the Red Man to sweep off. Cuchulain of all the heroes is the one who will take the helmet up on the Red Man's terms. But the Red Man does not take his head off; he designates him Champion of the land, and his words ring like an heroic dedication:

I have not come for your hurt, I'm the Rector of this land,
And with my spitting cat-heads, my frenzied moon-bred band,
Age after age I sift it, and choose for its championship
The man who hits my fancy.
And I choose the laughing lip
That shall not turn from laughing, whatever rise or fall,
The heart that grows no bitterer although betrayed by all;

The hand that loves to scatter; the life like a gambler's throw;
And these things I make prosper, till a day come that I know,
When heart and mind shall darken that the weak may end the strong,
And the long-remembering harpers have matter for their song.

With the production of *The Green Helmet* a period in Yeats' career in the theatre came to a close: up to this his technique had envisaged the normal stage with players having normal equipment. Afterwards he brings in lyricism, masks, the dance. But before dealing with this development there are two prose plays to be mentioned.

The Unicorn from the Stars is a reincarnation of an earlier play, *Where There Is Nothing,* and it has no distinctiveness: indeed it might have been written by some of the other Abbey dramatists, by Lady Gregory, for instance. But *The Player Queen* is Yeatsean and it is good theatre; it has flow, high spirits, and with its combination of poetry, intellectual conception and fantasy, it is a new kind of comedy. At the opposite pole from *The Countess Cathleen,* it yet reminds us of that first play: it might take place in a town in Cathleen's territory, and the Queen in it might be some relation of the Countess. *The Player Queen,* in short, is by the author of *The Countess Cathleen* who has made himself into a writer of comedy; the Countess Cathleen's world is here, viewed by a poet older, more gleeful, more worldly.

The plays of the new period, Plays for Dancers, are for some place less formal than the theatre, a drawing-room or a studio. The dramatist no longer aims at creating and developing a dramatic situation: these plays are evocative rather than dramatic, calling up some high, remote mood. An effect of loneliness which could not be obtained on the stage of the regular theatre is in them. They move to the sound of drum, or gong, or zither.

As these plays go on they depart more and more from the formal dramatic pattern, they become ritual rather than drama. More and more they seem to be written for some magnificent lyric that gets uttered by one of the players. Such a lyric is the one that begins "I saw a staring virgin stand" in *The Resurrection,* and "I cannot face that emblem of the moon" which is in a play that is not given in the present collection, *The King of the Great Clock Tower.* And so this poet works back through the drama to the lyric. But now it is a different lyric from the one he was writing when he turned to drama so that he might gain "a more manful energy." Energy is what these lyrics have.

Yeats as a poet has been a leaven in the theatre, putting into it that element that is essential if the theatre is not to be trivially entertaining—exalted speech. And the theatre has transformed the poet. The living speech with a rhythm which has the modulation of the natural voice becomes the vocabulary of the later lyrics, giving them a directness of statement that has not been in poetry in English since the seventeenth century. There is a magnificent succession of such lyrics: the core is meditation, but the form is always dramatic:

> At midnight on the Emperor's pavement flit
> Flames that no faggot feeds, nor steel has lit,
> Nor storm disturbs, flames begotten of flame,
> Where blood-begotten spirits come
> And all complexities of fury leave,
> Dying into a dance,
> An agony of trance,
> An agony of flame that cannot singe a sleeve.

With such magnificent lyrics as a by-product and with such plays as product there is cause for rejoicing that this poet was able to take possession of a theatre. The plays represent the greatest amount of dramatic poetry given the English-speaking world since the close of the Elizabethan age.

December 1935

* *

SEWELL STOKES

*

W. Somerset Maugham

THE APOCRYPHAL STORY most often related about Somerset Maugham finds the distinguished author and dramatist in gentle argument with a friend—the subject of the argument being his own merit as an artist. Evidently the friend believes that Maugham does not do himself justice in this respect, and says so; to which criticism the accused replies as follows: "Would you rather I wrote books like *War and Peace* and lived in modest comfort—or am I to be allowed to write the popular stuff I do, and by it earn the luxury I enjoy?"

The answer to that one, of course, is that Maugham couldn't write books like Tolstoi's masterpiece if he tried; and what is more, nobody is as keenly aware of this fact as Maugham himself. It is doubtful if there ever lived a man with fewer illusions about his own work; and possibly it is just because he never loses an opportunity of indulging in self-criticism—a habit singularly few authors manage to acquire—that a number of professional critics, out of sheer perversity, insist upon elevating him to a position in the literary world that is hardly justified by his achievements, brilliant as these often are. Indeed, there is a school of thought in England that regards Maugham as the Grand Old Man of Letters; but against this are numerous admirers of his, who, with the best will in the world, can describe him as nothing more than a master of magazine fiction. And so it is with Maugham the dramatist. Arguments about his place in the theatre never cease, despite the fact that the subject of the argument has not only given up writing plays, but has firmly stated his reason for doing so.

Unlike those popular dramatists, Henry Arthur Jones and Arthur Wing Pinero—both of whom outlived their popularity and died bitterly reproaching a public that dared to find them hopelessly outmoded and boring—Maugham gracefully retired from the stage in 1933, and since that time has always referred to himself as an ex-dramatist. Would it not be kinder, therefore, to respect his wish that the plays be allowed to die a natural death, instead or reviving their memory by insisting upon their shortcomings? Much kinder; and wiser, too, seeing that none of them—with perhaps two exceptions—is likely even to be noticed by historians of the early twentieth-century theatre in England. And yet, such a provocative figure has Maugham become, largely because of his objective attitude towards his work, that a critical estimate of him ought almost certainly to produce implications whose significance must be of interest, of value even, to students of the theatre in our time. When writers who have failed to master dramatic technique—Henry James and George Moore, for example—declare the stage too crude a medium for the interpretation of their idea, one does not pay them too much attention. But precisely the same declaration, coming from a playwright who has been a favorite with audiences for over forty years, is a very different matter; and what we ask ourselves then is why the author of thirty plays, nearly all of them hits, should turn at last with a sigh of relief from the workshop that has appeared for so long to be his natural home. For it is not even as if Maugham, at the age of sixty, laid aside his pen with a tear of regret for the glorious days that were past. Not at all. Once he had made up his mind to leave for good the theatre that had so richly rewarded him, his feelings were more akin to those of a man suddenly released from a long term of imprisonment. Here, in his own carefully chosen words, is what amounts to nothing less than an expression of gratitude for his deliverance:

"When for days you have been going through a mountain pass, a moment comes when you are sure that after wandering round the great mass of rock in front of you, you will come upon the plain; but instead you are faced with another huge crag and the weary trail continues; surely after this you will see the plain; no; the path winds on and another mountain bars your way. And then suddenly it lies before you. Your heart exults; there it stretches wide and sunny; the oppression of the mountain is lifted from your shoulders and with exhilaration you breathe the more spacious air. So I felt when I had done my last play. I had won great notoriety and perhaps even a passing fame. I might have been satisfied. But there was one thing more I wanted to achieve and this it seemed to me I could not hope to reach in the drama. Perfection."

To judge a man accurately, one needs some knowledge of his antecedents; and whereas we are most often denied this in the case of the average citizen, with a professional man, and particularly with a man whose profession is the theatre, we have the advantage of dealing with someone whose life has been lived more or less in public. This is so in Maugham's case; and we shall not be wasting our time, therefore, if before attempting to discover what lesson is to be learned from his attitude to the drama, we examine in some detail the experiences through which he has passed, and which must in some degree be responsible for the conclusions he has come to at the end of a long career as a playwright.

Born exactly seventy years ago, Maugham had what is considered an excellent education: King's School, Canterbury; Heidelburg University; and St. Thomas' Hospital—where for a time he was a medical student. He was a student at a time when Oscar Wilde's plays were drawing all London, and it is fairly safe to assume that the Irishman's wit, and the brilliant success it was having, had something to do with the young man's decision to give up medicine and become a dramatist himself. What is certain is that once he had chosen to devote a part of his time to the theatre—the rest he gave to his novels and stories—Maugham lost no time in finding out how the trick was done; for a trick, and a little more than a trick, he believed it to be. And here he was again following the Irishman's example, since Wilde himself is alleged to have said that in order to learn the technique of writing for the stage, he shut himself up alone for a week-end with the works of the most popular French dramatists and, on emerging from his seclusion, knew all that they had to teach him. As it happened, the youthful Maugham was even more painstaking than his master, for he not only read other people's plays in an endeavor to discover the secret of their success but even went so far as to copy them out in his own hand. This laborious exercise, he told the present writer long ago, he found extremely useful as a guide on many points relating to dramatic construction. One can believe him. The pity is that more aspiring dramatists do not strive as diligently to master their craft. If they did, fewer manuscripts whose shapelessness makes them useless for stage presentation would litter the offices of the managers. At the same time, admirable though this method of self-instruction is, its adoption by Maugham in his prentice days at once gives us a clue as to what *kind* of dramatist he started out to be. Unlike Chekhov, Shaw, O'Casey and Saroyan—men who preferred to invent their own technique, and by doing so risked failure—he made an obvious bid for success. His ambition was to become a successful playwright; not a playwright who might, if chance favored him, turn out to be a success. And how well he succeeded in this endeavor was proved in 1908, by which time he had four original plays running in London concurrently: *Lady Frederick, Jack Straw, Mrs. Dot* and *The Explorer.*

No doubt remains that Maugham, from the start, set himself up in business as a playwright. Had he inserted in the newspapers an advertisement which read: "You want the best plays—I write them!", he would have spoken no less than the truth. A manufacturer of smart plays for smart audiences is what he quickly became; and his specialty was what is known as High Comedy. Instinctively, he knew the value of an amusing epigram, and if a finished work of his had not a sufficient number of these, he decorated the manuscript with additional ones, as easily as a dressmaker adds sequins to a gown that needs brightening up. One can imagine him smiling—less from satisfaction at his own brilliance than from the knowledge that he had the trick of getting a stage laugh when he needed it—as he set down such a neatly contrived little piece of dialogue as this utterance of Lady Frederick's: "I wish I knew how she manages to dress so beautifully. It's one of the injustices of fate that clothes only hang on a woman really well when she's cast every shred of reputation."

That kind of epigram—Wilde and water at its best—had them rolling in the aisles around 1908, and indeed for some time to come. Lonsdale did very well with it as late as 1925. A laugh for its own sake is always popular in the commercial theatre; the trouble with it is that it is likely sooner or later to go out of fashion, with the result that what once caused merriment comes to cause embarrassment, if not bewilderment. In time it finds its author out, exposing him for what he is, which too often is far from what he appeared once to be. This has been Maugham's experience. He knows it. And the fact leaves him unmoved, since it has always been a conviction of his that in any case the stage play is merely a reflection of the fashion prevailing at the time it is written and therefore of small account once that fashion has changed. Into the validity of this opinion we will look more closely in a moment.

Few managers ever made a mistake in backing Maugham's plays. They dealt with him for years, like customers faithful to the firm whose goods never lose their quality. It was possible even to order a particular brand of play from this most accommodating dramatist, who wasted no time seeking inspiration but executed the commission with promptitude. Charles Frohman once suggested to him a modern version of *The Taming of the Shrew* and, thinking the idea a good one, he wrote it. For this play he embroidered a theme that had come to him when a companion of his aunt decided to give up her post and go to live on her brother's farm in Canada. While on the farm the ex-companion married the hired man, and what the two made of their married life became, by the time Maugham had finished with them, a play called *The Land of Promise*. This play, like so many of his others, was a success. And nobody will blame him for that. No, one's quarrel with Maugham, if one quarrels with him at all, is not on account of the thirty plays he has contributed to the theatre—we can take these or leave them, according to our taste—but on account of his oft-repeated assertion that the theatre is not a medium in which an artist can expect to attain perfection, or anything like perfection. He persists in looking on it, quite objectively, as a box of tricks that nobody who aims at anything higher than the creation of an amusing charade need bother about. Can the theatre as an institution be dismissed as lightly as this? Or must Maugham, for holding such an opinion, be dismissed himself—as a critic of no consequence whatever? The question is not too easily answered; and before investigating it, it will be helpful to look once at the curious career of this theatrical conjuror with whom we have to reckon.

The kind of comedy that Maugham kept alive for so many years, with the dexterity of a juggler keeping a number of balls in the air at once, was finally driven from the stage by the arrival in England of what can be best described as the "domestic drama." Dodie Smith, and her many followers, were largely responsible for this type of harmless entertainment whose characters, unlike Maugham's svelte and witty creatures from Mayfair, resembled in detail the very housewives who themselves made up an audience and who, tired out after a day's shopping, found delight in watching people like themselves wrestling with problems that might easily have been their own. It was only to be expected that when Miss Smith's suburban housewives walked on the stage, Mr. Maugham's elegant ladies would walk off. The fashion had changed so definitely that any return to the old milieu would have spelled financial disaster.

It is true that Maugham had from time to time varied his steady output by attempting to write plays with a more serious theme, such plays as *For Services Rendered* and *Sheppy*; but these were out of his usual genre and added nothing to his reputation. The fashionable comedy was his line of goods; he was quick to note a drastic change in its style and, being by that time weary of it anyway, he shut down that department of his business and continued with the novels and short stories that had all along kept pace with the plays. He had forgotten the theatre almost as soon as the theatre might have forgotten him—had he not written two comedies that somehow managed to get the better of his well-worn tricks and insisted on coming to life in spite of them. *The Circle* was produced in 1921, revived with great success in 1931, and in 1944 found a place in John Gielgud's repertory, beside *Love for Love* and *Hamlet.* The other comedy, *Our Betters,* first presented in New York in 1917, and not in London until 1923, is generally, and rightly, considered his masterpiece; and it is likely to make his name known to theatregoers as yet unborn.

It is the belief of some critics—and perhaps of Maugham himself—that the best work of which he is capable has gone into his novels. If this is so, one cannot avoid the conclusion that their creator is capable of achieving little more in literature than he had done in the theatre. Exceedingly well written as a number of the novels are, not a spark of genius struck on their pages. For the most part, they are *feuilletons* whose polished style is likely to deceive the average reader into praising them beyond their deserts. And why should not the average reader prove untrustworthy in his estimate, when professional critics are not above making the same mistake? Sir Edmund Gosse was human enough to fall into this trap once—when the trap was set by no less a master of romantic hocus-pocus than Sir Hall Caine. Not that Maugham isn't a vastly superior writer to the author of *The Manxman,* whose novels sold by the million; he very decidedly is; what he just fails to do is take his seat with the giants, just as Arnold Bennett failed before him. Even so, Maugham will not escape the notice of posterity. His undeniable genius for the creation of character in short-story form should place him on a pedestal not an inch less in height than one occupied by Maupassant.

What, however, makes Maugham more interesting to students of drama than any of the plays he has published—and the technique of these is not inconsiderable—is his dictum on the theatre: that it is not a medium in which to strive for the attainment of perfection. And, mind you, he adds a rider to this pronouncement of his, which is that he excludes plays written *in verse.* If, he says, a man can express himself in musical prose that lends itself to the actor's powers of declaration, then by all means let him unburden his soul in terms of theatrical art; but lacking that rare gift, he can expect no more than transitory fame. In short, it is Maugham's contention that the fundamental passions of men can only be expressed in words that soar heavenwards; and one takes it that, had this gift of lordly language been his, great tragedy, instead of flippant comedy, might have claimed him. Tragedy, he says, endures; but comedy, being merely a reflection of the manners and customs of a period, becomes meaningless when those manners and customs have changed.

To refute his argument that comedy does not endure, what could be simpler than to confront him with the works of Sheridan, Congreve and Goldsmith? These gay spirits would not, one feels, shake his belief in a theory that it has taken him the experience of a lifetime to develop. Somewhere—it may be in one of the prefaces to the collected editions of his plays or in his autobiography, *The Summing Up*—he has written that most people enjoy revivals of such plays as *The School for Scandal, She Stoops to Conquer* and *Love for Love* only in the sense that they enjoy seeing an object in a museum; and that while to see a popular actor in the revival is entertaining, the play, as a play, is not greatly enjoyed by an audience for its own sake—though an audience, unwilling to admit this stark fact, may unconsciously pretend otherwise.

Remembering the handful of plays that have escaped oblivion, might there be some truth in this credo of Maugham's, shocking though it may at first appear to lovers of the theatre who have never stopped to give it consideration? Each must answer the question for himself. Some will agree with Maugham that the theatre is a box of tricks, and is used as such by most modern playwrights. Others will violently disagree with him. But perhaps, after all, what he means is that our theatre lacks the poets who might make it so much greater than it is, if only they would give their time to it. And none, surely, will contradict him on that point.

February 1945

CARL CARMER

*

George Kaufman

PLAYMAKER TO BROADWAY

PLAYWRIGHTS generally approach their work from one of two angles. Either they have something to say in play form and they hope that audiences will receive it, or they have studied the playgoers' taste and "give the public what it wants." Of the group that would gauge popular desire no American dramatist has been more successful than George Kaufman.

Endow a young man with an observant mind, a sense of the ludicrous, an ambition to become a playwright, and contemporary American life, regardless of his environment, will heap material of the drama upon him. With such an equipment George Kaufman graduated from a Pittsburgh high school, studied law impatiently, held jobs as surveyor, a window clerk in the Allegheny county tax office, a stenographer, a traveling salesman, a newspaper columnist. In that experience lay a wide cross-section of living in the United States, much to be written in the notebook or packed away in the storehouse of the mind.

Journalism led, as it usually does, to New York, and New York led, almost as inevitably, to writing a play. Conscious of his own inexperience Kaufman sought a collaborator, a procedure that has since become something of a habit with him. With Irving Pichel he wrote *The Failure,* which never reached production, and with Larry Evans *Someone in the House,* which was unsuccessful. A play solely of his own making provided him with the initial impetus toward success. Burns Mantle, then reader for a play broker, recommended Kaufman to his firm and persuaded him to submit to them a play entitled *Going Up*. In his compendium, *American Playwrights of Today,* Mr. Mantle summarizes the result:

"It did not sell. But among those who read it with favor was John Peter Toohey, at that time an associate of George C. Tyler, the producer. Mr. Toohey in his enthusiasm called Mr. Tyler's attention to the snappiness of Mr. Kaufman's dialogue and his excellent sense of comedy situations. Mr. Tyler, being convinced, sent for Mr. Kaufman and from that meeting came the writing and production of *Dulcy,* which served as Mr. Kaufman's introduction to fame and a growing fortune."

Dulcy, written by Kaufman and Marc Connelly, seemed to demonstrate the superiority of the two-mind theory. To the long series of collaborations which began with this play Connelly brought human sentiment to complement Kaufman's accuracy of observation, a poetic fancy to balance the sense of the ludicrous. It would be truer to say, however, that three intelligences were responsible for this first success, since the dean of columnists, Franklin P. Adams (F.P.A.), had already made bromidic Dulcinea widely known. Indeed the influence of Adams' wit is not to be underestimated, for through this play the elastic formula was established which Kaufman has been able to use with success again and again, a method based on the humor that is to be found in accurate reporting of the conversation of commonplace characters. The formula involves the selection of a main character, an easily recognizable type, lovable as a rule but utterly lacking in common sense, a protagonist at whom the audience may laugh with the jolly feeling of superiority and tolerance. The unpleasant complications which confront the character as a result of his stupidity are completely overcome at the end of the play with a magnificent stroke of luck, frequently occasioned by this very thick-headedness.

From *Dulcy* onward, no matter who the collaborator, this recipe has served to fill the theatres of Broadway. Sometimes it works more successfully than others. Kaufman and Connelly scored their second hit with it in *Merton of the Movies*; Kaufman did well with it alone in *The Butter and Egg Man*; Kaufman and Ring Lardner were successful with it in *June Moon*; Kaufman and Moss Hart made it tremendously popular with *Once in a Lifetime.* When plays built on it have failed, the formula has not been at fault. As in the case of *The Good Fellow,* which Kaufman wrote in 1926 with Herman Manckiewicz, in which the audience were embarrassed to see the rituals of the national fraternal orders burlesqued; there were too many lodge members in the audience.

It was not merely in its main character that *Dulcy* became a model on which other plays could be patterned. The playwrights realized that if the laughable qualities of their satiric portrait were to be fully appreciated by a Broadway audience, they must be pointed out and accentuated. In the part of William Parker, Dulcy's brother, they made an interpreter who should help the playgoers to an appreciation of the play's humor, one who indicated his complete understanding of the foolishness going on and who, though frequently exasperated by it, found it amusing.

LEACH: Yes, I'd love to see you framed against the glowing splendor of a twilit garden.

BILL: My golly, the man even makes love in sub-titles.

Such characterizations, embodying what the members of the audience would like to think their own attitude, give the playwright plenty of opportunity to exercise his talent for dramatic irony, a device not the most to be admired in a dramatist's repertory, but particularly effective with not-too-intellectual audiences.

DULCY: Oh, that was the most wonderful picture I ever saw! . . . I mean heard! Eight marvelous reels!

BILL: What a picture! My God, what a picture!

In this first product of the extended collaboration, moreover, appeared characters who were to become types in the plays to which Kaufman contributed his talent: the successful business man, the beautiful, brainless girl, the rich and socially prominent young man, the unusual servant, all excellent foils for the laughably silly central figure and the sensible character whose function was not unlike that of the ancient Greek chorus.

Dulcy found so warm a welcome on Broadway that its authors immediately cast about for other subject matter on which to exercise their talents. Kaufman must have supplied a large share of the background and color in the ensuing comedy, *To the Ladies,* out of his experiences as a traveling representative and in a politician's office, for the play lampooned those unimaginative mixers of business and society, the Rotarian business men in their more inspired moments at the banquet table. It contained all the selective truth that sometimes emerges from accurate observation and literal reporting, but American audiences in 1922 were either Rotarians themselves or still looking on Rotarianism as a movement in the advance of civilization, and they considered the play more impudent than funny.

Perhaps realizing then that if they were to make money out of the business of writing an American *comédie humaine* they had better attack native society in smaller segments, the co-workers turned their attention to Hollywood and the motion pictures. In Harry Leon Wilson's story, *Merton of the Movies,* they found a character ready-made to fit into their formula. The pathetic country-boy who had romantic yearnings to be a movie star, who talked the sentimental patter of the movie magazines and who, by acting a part seriously, became famous as a burlesquing genius, was perfectly suited to be the main character in the pattern. The wise, hard-boiled little extra who elects to stand between him and the cruelty of the world is a feminine counterpart of Bill Parker—the interpreter for the audience. The other characters in the cinema world are painted broadly and in much the same caricaturing manner as the minor roles in *Dulcy.* Performances were crowded and the authors realized, from two successful ventures out of three, that they had a reasonably sure method of making a popular play, one to which they could revert at any time (and did once more before they parted company, with a too slight play called *The Deep Tangled Wildwood*). Ambitiously they went on to more experimental and less certain productions.

The Butter and Egg Man, the first play on the formula which Kaufman wrote alone (in 1925), is an excellent index to the qualities that its author supplied in his collaborations. In some ways it was a re-working of *Merton of the Movies,* in others a prototype of *Once in a Lifetime.* Like Merton, an ingenuous young man from the Middle West has ambitions. As Merton went West to Hollywood to become a movie star, Peter Jones comes East to New York to invest in a play. As Merton was championed by an extra girl, Peter finds an ally in a stenographer. As Merton, by a grotesque happenstance, wins fame and fortune, Peter accidentally outwits those who would defraud him and makes a handsome profit as well. About Merton cluster the temperamental leading lady, the arty director, the ignorant producer of the cinema. About Peter are the same group as they exist in the business of the legitimate stage.

The Butter and Egg Man is particularly prolific of that distinctively American stinging kind of exaggerative humor called the "wise-crack." Kaufman is a master at fashioning this type of warmly personal retort. One need only listen to the conversation of the character who fills the interpreter-role in the formula, Fanny-ex-vaudeville juggler and now wife of producer Joe Lehman—to hear Broadway repartee at its low-level best:

FANNY: You got a show there that's going to make history, do you know it? They're going to date things from the time you open this one.

LEHMAN: . . . I ain't asked you what you think about it!

FANNY: . . . I caught that bit where the leading lady was supposed to be sixteen or something, climbing up apple trees. The stuff to make them trees out of is reinforced concrete . . .

LEHMAN: I don't want no advice! Go on home!

FANNY: All right, then—go on and produce it. Produce it with some butter and egg man's coin and that dame of the Colonial Revolution that you got in the leading role.

LEHMAN: Never you mind about Martin! She's going to make the hit of her life!

FANNY: (*entirely too sweetly*) I ain't got nothing against her. I suppose she either had to join up with your troupe or go back to her original role in *The Two Orphans*. Who tipped you off to her, *The Evening Post?*

Fortunately for modern American drama, Kaufman has not always seen fit to rub his Aladdin's Lamp. His magic formula has served him well by filling his coffers but he has been as aware as his critics of its lack of artistic value. His career has been studded with variations from the norm. Each one of these has been important, none more so than his last collaboration (save for the book of a musical comedy) with Connelly, *The Beggar on Horseback*. This combined the best qualities in both dramatists. The pathos and imagination, the poetry and understanding, which Connelly was to show later in *The Wisdom Tooth* and *Green Pastures* were foreshadowed in this fantasy out of the American scene. All the penetrating observation of dialogue, the knowledge of character, the sense of the humorously incongruous, which have made Kaufman an important figure on the stage found expression here as well. Although many of their favorite characters peopled the play, the rich business man, his silly wife, their silly daughter, the nice, sensible, comradely girl, their well-tried method had been discarded for one less artificial and more imaginative and literary. From a suggestion which Winthrop Ames found for them in a German play, Paul Apel's *Hans Sonnenstoesser's Holenfahrt,* they built a play that has become a landmark in the history of modern American Drama. The pitiful barrenness of big business had been attacked before with the weapons of cruel realism, but never had it been dealt such a blow as by this dream-play with its impressionistic sort of fancy. The hideous nightmare of bad taste, conceit and subservience to wealth visited by the god of trade upon his worshippers had been recognized for its true self. Two young commercialists of the theatre had suddenly turned poetic and had found the change profitable.

Kaufman again turned from his usual methods when he joined forces with Edna Ferber. *Minick,* while not a strong play, emphasized the complementary qualities of talents which, united, became a powerful alloy. The play served as an excellent trial flight for the two dramatists who were soon to produce that modern classic, *The Royal Family.* The fable of the latter is significant, the progressive realization by three generations of an actor-family that the stage is the most powerful influence in their lives. While the parallel between the characters and the members of a well-known American family group is obvious, the basis is one of general appeal, and the piece would be quite as effective if it provided no opportunity for identifications. *The Royal Family* contains less of the material that the public has come to recognize as characteristic of Kaufman than any play on which he has worked. His characters in many cases in the past had been so general as to be, in a literary sense, composite photographs made from the lives of typical people. The very subject of this comedy required individualization. Only the speeches of the rich suitors of the mother and daughter are echoings of the talk of their kind. Probably due to Miss Ferber's skill as a narrator, this is the most workmanlike of the dramas to which her collaborator has devoted his abilities. It moves forward briskly and efficiently, never stopping for the effective speech merely because it is effective as a speech—a weakness sometimes noticeable elsewhere in Kaufman's work. The wisecrack is supplanted by shrewdly thought-out dialogue in character, the bludgeonings of satiric burlesque by the keen wit of comedy. The over-sentimental emotionalism into which the story might easily have been led, however, is avoided through a sureness of treatment and a businesslike theatricality which is attributable, with a fair degree of certainty, to the more experienced dramatist. *The Royal Family* remains, a few years after its original production, a thoroughly enjoyable not-dated play, more than can be said of much other work for which Kaufman has been at least partially responsible.

With the production of *The Royal Family* Kaufman first began to be taken seriously as a director. The same straightforward simplicity, swift rhythm and pointed expression which his journalistic experience contributed to his playwriting asserted itself in his directing methods. His is a quick-fire, certain, theatrical manner and whatever drama he is employed upon is assured of his getting out of it all those qualities which have been associated with the expression "good theatre."

Ever since 1923, when, probably due to the influence of Connelly (who had already tried that sort of thing), the two produced the book for a summer musical comedy, *Helen of Troy, N. Y.*, Kaufman had been working at light musical forms. After *Be Yourself,* which he and Connelly wrote in 1924, he had confidence enough to write the entire book of *The Cocoanuts*. The presence of the four Marx brothers was a fair insurance of its success, but its tremendous popularity proved that the writer of the lines was able to produce that combination of satire and mad inconsistency which those gifted clowns find most congenial. It was the beginning of a vein which was to lead to the Pulitzer Prize in 1932.

The last two years have seen two crowning productions, one in each of the fields to which Kaufman has devoted himself, which prove him a hard worker at refining and developing his talents. *Once in a Lifetime* would seem to be the ultimate goal of the old formula begun with *Dulcy*. It is the essence of Broadway theatricality, the wisecracking comedy at the top of its bent. As an exposé of the insanity of Hollywood it had those who have been there explaining that things identical or quite as impossible really happen there constantly. With an almost incredibly stupid young vaudeville actor—a "dead-pan" comedian—as its main character, with a charming and experienced young lady who sees life about her in its true perspective and remarks on it with bitter wisdom, with an unassuming author (first played by Kaufman himself) to help her make clear to the audience what a mad, hopelessly topsy-turvy world the talking cinema has created, with many of the silly beings that America's fourth biggest industry nurtures providing local color, it is a hilarious satire on the grotesquerie that may exist wherever values are ignorantly determined. The play is a complete justification of its author's method—at least as far as entertainment and box-office receipts are concerned. It brings the realization with it that, given equally rich material, Kaufman could fashion a hit out of it as readily as a tailor makes a suit. His imitators have already had a few unsuccessful tries at the most obvious current subject, the world of the radio. He may yet turn to that and show them how to succeed.

The committee on the Pulitzer Prize drama for 1932 defended its choice against those who claimed that a musical comedy was not eligible by declaring that the winning piece was a play. Their argument has strong support, for it is easy to find in *Of Thee I Sing* much of the technique that Kaufman has put into comedies without music. The silly, well-meaning central character is this time Alexander Throttlebottom, candidate for vice-president. Written for a more sophisticated and intelligent audience than his previous formula-comedies, the work contains no interpreter to point the satire with caustic comment. But the act-of-providence climax—the birth of twins which saves the President from impeachment—is reminiscent of all the other unforeseen events which have provided the Kaufman comedies with happy endings. Moreover, much of the matter of the play is reminiscent of his legitimate comedies. Just as in *The Butter and Egg Man* the producers call in Kitty, the hotel telephone operator, to ask her for suggestions on their play, the politicians in *Of Thee I Sing* ask the hotel chambermaid for suggestions on their platform. The group of Supreme Court Judges in the musical comedy are successors to the jury in *The Beggar on Horseback*. And the lunatic inconsistency of Kaufman satire which has been growing steadily funnier throughout his career reaches its climax in the series of inspired non-sequiturs of the election returns:

Waterville, Mass.
First election district gives:

Wintergreen 12
Scattering 1

Atlanta, Ga.
16 election districts, out of 184 give:

Wintergreen 12,736
Jefferson Davis 1,653

New York, N. Y.
126 election districts report:

Wintergreen	72,639
Bryan	128
Absent	4
Late	2

Hollywood, Cal.

Wintergreen	160,000
Mickey Mouse	159,000
Gloria Swanson's First Husband	84,638

All of the play does not keep to the high level of its best passages. Frequently the characters, echoes of American mediocrity, are not as keenly observed as in previous plays; their humor is too obvious, too superficial, too slapstick. Too often the satire is directed at political idiosyncrasies which others have ridiculed for years—mellow oratory, honeyed hypocrisy, trickery, and the insignificance of the vice-president. Indeed, the last joke is hammered home so many times that only a performance of genius saves it from being dulled. Aided, however, by George Gershwin's music and Ira Gershwin's lyrics which give audiences the impression that at last they have something native that is close to Gilbert and Sullivan, *Of Thee I Sing* deserves the encomiums which hail it as America's most sophisticated and intelligent musical comedy, the first of a new genus of satires with music—comedies of manners designed to laugh out of existence the silly practices of modern life.

So long and consistent a record as that of George Kaufman in the modern theatre ought to provide some logical basis on which a prophecy as to his future might rest. If a reckoning may be taken now it would seem to point to a few simple conclusions: that a playwright who has always written with the ticket-buying public in mind and has pleased that public is not likely to change his method; that a playwright who, through over a decade of steady production, has displayed a limited number of talents will, in all probability, not add to them; that a playwright who has been able to develop the powers in his possession through over ten years of hard work to the point where they are largely responsible for two of the most popular successes of recent times will continue to develop those powers; that a playwright with so thorough a knowledge of the theatre, a dramatist who is also a successful director, should be treasured by those who look for a theatre renaissance.

Kaufman has found two forms in which he is skillful. He seems to be satisfied with the number. They have brought him material rewards and literary recognition, though he has never sought the latter. No living American is more adept than he at spanking the silly vagaries of his contemporaries. Scholars may feel that his rod of correction is too much of a slapstick to allow of his endeavors being dignified by the term, comedy of manners, but their purpose is very evidently the same that Congreve claimed. Modern America continues to provide exactly the sort of material that he can use most effectively. The pattern which he first used in *Dulcy* is still in the mode. At the time this is written he is announced as co-author and director of a comedy written with George Oppenheimer and entitled *Here Today,* and as co-author and director of *Dinner at Eight,* written with Edna Ferber. Whether his undertakings this season be type-satires or musical comedies, it is likely that one of our native and popular institutions will suddenly find itself shorn of its assumed dignity and quite involuntarily wearing the motley.

October 1932

* *

EDITH J. R. ISAACS

*

Meet Eugene O'Neill

AS SOON AS I have three dollars of my own," Eugene O'Neill wrote to the editors of THEATRE ARTS, "I am going to subscribe to your magazine. It is good to see *The Emperor Jones* in print." That was in January, 1921, just before *The Emperor Jones* was moved uptown from its first home at the Provincetown Playhouse.

Within a few months O'Neill had not only three dollars but a wide recognition of his talents; he had ceased to be the most spectacular of a group of local celebrities experimenting in theatre-ways, and especially in new forms of playwriting, in a tiny Macdougal Street playhouse, and had become the acknowledged white hope of the American theatre. Within a few years he was more than that; he was a successful playwright with a large following and also with a busy host of audible enemies who objected violently and with regularity to the characters, the themes and the method of treatment of each of the plays which, year by year, O'Neill loosed before astonished audiences. It is hard to say whether his friends or his enemies made the most noise in the press and the public forum, but they helped, about equally, to spread the news of every new play by O'Neill that found its way to the stage. His audiences mounted; his plays were in print almost as soon as they were produced; they went around the world as no other American playwright's ever had—to France, Sweden, Russia, Czechoslovakia, Japan. Wherever they went they enlisted the services of famous actors, of talented directors and skillful designers. And wherever they went they pleased and enraged both the public and the critics. They kept the censors open-eyed and often fired them to action.

O'Neill himself had in the meantime become an almost legendary figure through no effort of his own or of a publicity agent in the manner of the movies. With his close friends and his co-workers he was simple, lovable, open-hearted. Not many successful playwrights have earned and held the deep devotion and admiration which his friends had for "Gene"; not many who have achieved such fame as his so quickly suffered so little from the small pin-pricks of envy or the personal spites that are apt to torment successful theatre folk. But he was shy, high-strung, nervous, thoughtful, eternally perplexed, hard-working and distinctly overproductive, so he had neither the time nor the temperament for crowds. You could not imagine O'Neill sitting, day after day, at the round table at the Algonquin exchanging wisecracks with Alexander Woollcott, George Kaufman and their coterie. A corner in a quiet saloon in Greenwich Village, with a crony or two, was more to his taste.

He was not even a familiar figure in theatre lobbies. It is recorded that he seldom went to the theatre, even to watch the rehearsals of many of his own plays. He had clear and insistent ideas of what plays should look like and should sound like—both his own and those of other dramatists. He read avidly all the classics, the Restoration dramatists and especially the dissident moderns—Shaw, Ibsen, Strindberg, Wedekind. But the commercial theatre's realities disturbed and confused him; they were so seldom what he saw in his mind's eye. And since most of the life around him also disturbed and confused him he kept out of the stream as much as possible. Except for a few interviews, a few letters he wrote for publication about his own plays and the printed comments of his friends one needed to go directly to his plays to know Eugene O'Neill.

There was no lack of plays. Steadily they mounted in number, in scale, in length, power and success. For more than a dozen years the whole American theatre—its playwriting, design, direction, acting and criticism—was stimulated and even a little intoxicated by the work, the personality and the influence of Eugene O'Neill.

The one-act plays of the sea (later united under the title of *S. S. Glencairn*) and certain others of less importance had preceded *The Emperor Jones* at the Provincetown Playhouse. *Beyond the Horizon* came and went almost unnoticed by audiences, although it attracted keen attention from a few men of insight and won the Pulitzer Prize. What might well be classed as "certain other plays," for want of a better title, seemed indeed each year to come and go almost unnoticed without interfering with O'Neill's growing prestige. He is said to have destroyed, moreover, almost as many finished plays as he permitted to be produced. It might have been better if he had taken more pains in the writing of a few, but that was not his way. He was too full of things he wanted to say. So plays that came—and stayed—also followed in regular succession. Arthur Hopkins, then at the top of his flight, produced *Anna Christie* (the second Pulitzer Prizewinner), with Pauline Lord. The Provincetown Players brought on *The Hairy Ape,* with Louis Wolheim; *All God's Chillun Got Wings,* with Paul Robeson; *Desire Under the Elms,* with Walter Huston.

A little later O'Neill formed a producing partnership with two of his friends, Kenneth Macgowan and Robert Edmond Jones, and among their productions was *The Great God Brown.* Then the Theatre Guild found O'Neill and—in 1928—gave him a lustrous production of *Marco Millions* and followed it almost at once with *Strange Interlude,* which consumed five hours of playing time (and for the third time an O'Neill play won the Pulitzer award). The Pasadena Playhouse—braver than its commercial rivals—dared to do *Lazarus Laughed.* Then, again under the banner of the Theatre Guild, *Dynamo, Mourning Becomes Electra*—a trilogy for three successive nights—and *Ah, Wilderness!,* an unexpected and relaxed throwback to youth in Connecticut. In 1934, *Days Without End,* and since then, nothing.

Shortly after this O'Neill left New York to live quietly in the West. There have been two persistent reports about him as the empty years went by. One said that he had not been well; the other that he was working on a series of plays, no one of which would be produced until the cycle was complete. Both were probably true. After he left the scene of his unrivaled triumph, O'Neill's plays continued to be presented abroad and in the summer theatres and the tributary theatres around the country. There were a few, not too successful, revivals. *Anna Christie, The Emperor Jones, The Long Voyage Home, Strange Interlude, The Hairy Ape* have been made into movies of varying value. Dudley Nichols is at work on a film version of *Mourning Becomes Electra.*

Generally speaking, the shift away from O'Neill—in the theatre itself—has been as decisive as his rise to fame, and the O'Neill influence in playwriting and in play criticism seems to have vanished, although the disciples of Chekhov, Ibsen, Shaw continue to thrive. Theatre theorists no longer seem to use O'Neill's experimental methods as their springboard; many reviewers whose columns for years measured other men's plays or characters by O'Neill's seldom mention him today. And yet the question arises: why, if O'Neill has really lost his fascination for us, are we all so eager for his new play, so sure that, whatever it is, *The Iceman Cometh* will have something to offer which we have missed in our theatre since O'Neill left it, something that the theatre had while O'Neill reigned there—had not only from him but from other playwrights, from the actors, directors, designers who worked with him, and from others who watched the results of their work.

In the twelve years since *Days Without End* the whole line-up of our theatre has changed, not only the producers and the actors but the audience. Probably a large part of the audience for *The Iceman Cometh* will be seeing an O'Neill play for the first time. Suppose that, in their desire to know something of what O'Neill meant to his first audiences, they are doing what many of us (who *did* see the plays) are doing now, namely going back to the published plays for understanding. How will they picture Eugene O'Neill himself as he was in his thirties? One may surmise that, after reading all the plays that contributed anything of importance to O'Neill's reputation, and after studying the familiar photographs of his very interesting face, this new audience may think of him as—in appearance—not unlike his own description of Michael Cape, the word-bound husband in *Welded:*

Michael is tall and dark. His unusual face is a harrowed battlefield of super-sensitiveness, the features at war with one another—the forehead of a thinker, the eyes of a dreamer, the nose and mouth of a sensualist. One feels a powerful imagination tinged with somber sadness—a driving force which can be sympathetic and cruel at the same time. There is something tortured about him—a passionate tension, a self-protecting, arrogant defiance of life and his own weakness, a deep need for love as a faith in which to relax.

And they may well supplement this by the belief that O'Neill was revealing much of his own temperament in Dion Anthony's self-analysis in *The Great God Brown:*

DION: (*with a suffering bewilderment*) Why am I afraid to dance, I who love music and rhythm and grace and song and laughter? Why am I afraid to live, I who love life and the beauty of flesh and the living colors of earth and sky and sea? Why am I afraid of love? Why am I afraid, I who am not afraid? Why must I pretend to scorn in order to pity? Why must I hide myself in self-contempt in order to understand? Why must I be ashamed of my strength, so proud of my weakness? Why must I live in a cage like a criminal, defying and hating, I who love peace and friendship? (*clasping his hands above in supplication*) Why was I born without a skin, O God, that I must wear armor in order to touch or to be touched? . . . Or rather, Old Graybeard, why the devil was I born at all?

If a portrait of the young O'Neill, etched of these materials, is to their satisfaction, how will a new public go on to think of his stories, his characters, his style, his essential theatre equipment, his philosophy of life and of art? How closely, after the upheaval of a second World War, will they agree with earlier verdicts upon the worth of the various plays and the importance of the problems that seemed so agitating and disruptive after the first war?

They will be sure—beyond the shadow of a doubt—that in his early impressionable years O'Neill knew poverty, illness and the sea and that all three have left their mark on his mind and heart and have been a guiding force to his pen. They will believe that he has not outgrown the mysticism of an Irish Catholic heritage and training; that he has left the Church but has never for a moment been without the imperative need for some tie with the powers that rule men and nature; that he has not cast off his faith in confession and the forgiveness of sin, though he will allow no man to mark out, for him, the boundaries of good and evil. They will recognize the religious struggle as the strongest element of conflict in his markedly iconoclastic nature. By the time they have read *The Great God Brown* they will know that sooner or later he will either join the Church again or will at least find release, as an artist, in a play like *Days Without End,* in which a man divided within himself at last recognizes that only "In Thy will we find peace."

They will see in O'Neill a man driven by an unnamed force towards an unseen goal, in other words a rebel, not against any special social system or political or ethical theory but against any locked door or barred road because he believes that we cannot know whether they lead to good or evil unless they are wide open. Reckoning with that rebellion, a newer audience will not think, as so many of his earlier critics did, that O'Neill was not a master of theatre techniques simply because of his determined opposition to established forms and traditions. The theatre was obviously an art that he both loved and despised. He would not accept its conventions or obey its laws, but he knew exactly what he was doing, and why, with every experiment he tried, though many of them must seem fruitless today.

They may well believe that there were other things besides the theatre that O'Neill despised and loved—including women, in whom he seems to recognize only one quality, appetite, in many forms, and only one value, sex. Even his lovely and loving Princess Kukachin in *Marco Millions* is fantasy, not reality, a dream of what woman might be, not what she is. His Earth Mothers never have any contact with nature in any form but the human body; it is men, like one of the brothers in *Beyond the Horizon* or the father and son, Ephraim and Eben Cabot, in *Desire Under the Elms* (two of O'Neill's most finely etched characters), who love the soil and nourish it.

Every audience must feel, always and everywhere, O'Neill's deep and broad human sympathies; his sense that—whether in failure or success, or even in mere futility of endeavor—a man's worth is measured by the intensity of his aspirations and his passions. It is so obviously the dream and the search, not the achievement, that interests O'Neill. In consonance with this same spirit they will feel in all O'Neill's writing the poet's hunger but not its satisfaction. There is hardly a sentence in all of O'Neill's plays that an actor cannot speak; he knows well the sound and rhythm of theatre speech. But there are many speeches that must embarrass an actor because they are so purple or so trite, and there are only a few that really touch the height of poetry, as in *Lazarus Laughed* where he writes:

> As Man, Petty Tyrant of Earth, you are a bubble pricked by death into a void and a mocking silence! But as dust you are eternal change, and everlasting growth, and a high note of laughter soaring through chaos from the deep heart of God! Be proud, O Dust! Then you may love the stars as equals.

Or again, in the same play, the single line:

> If you can answer Yes to pain, there is no pain.

No one will need to go far in seeing—or in reading—O'Neill's plays to discover that he was deeply involved with German thought from Nietzsche to Freud—perilously involved, indeed, because he was so much more sensitive and contemplative than profound, more honest and sincere than judicial, more adventurous than affirmative. And they will note with a sigh of regret that he has absolutely no sense of humor.

Among different audiences, as within the same audience, there will always be differences of opinion about the worth of plays. And with a dramatist like O'Neill, who thought of a play in terms of its presentation as well as of its words and its theme, there will be certain plays for which only performance in a theatre can afford a fair test, even for readers with well-developed visual imagination and considerable theatre experience. This is certainly true of his highly mechanized plays like *The Great God Brown,* which depends for effectiveness largely on the use of masks; or *Strange Interlude,* which leans heavily on the "thought-speeches." The stories and the characters in these plays look naked on the printed page. At once you sense the risks involved in trying to make men and women symbols and individuals at one and the same time; they are so apt to appear like clay idols. Reading *The Great God Brown,* instead of seeing it, makes it easier to doubt O'Neill's fundamental thesis—that Dion Anthony was a genius—without which there is no play. It is also easier to deny the validity of the form of *Strange Interlude,* or at least O'Neill's application; to conclude that instead of delving into the unconscious O'Neill was only reporting what good manners or self-protection keeps his characters from saying aloud and what any adequate actor could express without words. The people of *Strange Interlude,* seen against the background of war, must surely seem inexpressibly banal, and surely no mature mind will today accept Nina Leeds as a marvelous woman.

But such criticism does not hold in the plays where O'Neill succeeds in making you believe in his characters as well as in his thesis. There, audiences will no doubt still follow him breathlessly no matter how exotic or romantic, tragic or exalted his way. One can go a long road accompanied by *The Emperor Jones,* by the satiric pageantry of *Marco Millions,* the friendly ease of *Ah, Wilderness!,* by the stark earthly tragedy of *Desire Under the Elms.* And when a new audience knows *Mourning Becomes Electra,* in which O'Neill rises to his full stature, they will understand why we wait again for a new play by O'Neill. When O'Neill stops thinking of himself as Jeremiah he can be a consummate storyteller.

If anyone cares to look outside the plays for further evidence of O'Neill's idea of the modern playwright's material and his responsibility to it, he may find it in these two paragraphs:

> In his infancy of helplessness and terror Man could not face the inexorable; and facts being of all things the most inexorable he masked all the threatening ones as fast as he discovered them; so that now every mask requires a hero to tear it off. The king of terrors, Death, was the Arch-Inexorable. Man could not bear the dread of that. . . . How he fixed the mask of personal immortality on the face of Death . . . we all know. And he did the like with all disagreeables as long as they remained inevitable. Otherwise he must have gone mad with terror at the grim shapes around him. . . . And the greatest terror prevailed whenever some realist, bolder than the rest, laid hands on a mask which they did not yet dare to do without.
>
> An interesting play cannot in the nature of things mean anything but a play in which problems of conduct and character of personal impor-

tance to an audience are raised and discussed. People have a thrifty sense of taking away something from such plays; they not only have had something for their money, but they retain that something as a permanent possession. Consequently none of the commonplaces of the box-office hold good of such plays. In vain does the experienced acting manager declare that people want to be amused at the theatre; that they will not stand long speeches; that a play must not contain more than 18,000 words; that it must not begin before nine nor last beyond eleven; that there must be no politics and no religion in it . . . and so on and so forth.

It is easy to recognize O'Neill in this. But the trouble is that O'Neill did not write it. Shaw did, part of it in the 1891 edition of *The Quintessence of Ibsenism,* part of it in the second edition twenty-two years later. And Shaw was—of course—talking of Ibsen and himself. And yet he was, unwittingly, talking to—and of—O'Neill who was still in his cradle when Shaw first affrighted the conservatives with these revolutionary ideas. (And he was still unborn when Nietzsche wrote that love was folly and marriage only the end of many short follies, being one long stupidity.) And yet Shaw's words do interpret O'Neill. If their date is further proof of what should have been obvious enough without it—that O'Neill as a prophet was already a little old-fashioned before he began his preaching—it is also proof of how slow our American theatre was to accept ideas which, thanks partly to dramatists like Ibsen and Shaw, were already current all over the world. And, moreover, of how badly we stood in need of a fearless, gifted, hard-hitting, passionate iconoclast to break through the conventions of every kind—spiritual, literary, social and technical—that hedged us in. It was the blare of O'Neill's trumpet that cracked the fortress walls.

October 1946

IV · MUSIC AND THE DANCE

* * *

ANDRÉ LEVINSON

*

The Spirit of the Classic Dance

NOTHING IS more difficult than to reduce the essential aesthetic realities of the dance to verbal formulas. Our ordinary methods of analysis are of very little use in dealing with this art, which is primarily a discipline of movement. The dancer in motion is a harmony of living forms, masses and outlines, whose relations to each other are continually varied by that "motion which causes the lines to flow." We are exceedingly ill equipped for the study of things in flux—even for considering motion itself as such. We cling to things at rest as though they were landmarks in a turbulent chaos. A modern engineer, for example, who wishes to study the mechanism of a revolving screw, would doubtless begin his studies by stopping the motor and taking it apart, in order to understand clearly the technical methods employed by the designer.

The dancer has a fairly wide technical vocabulary, but it is one that is useful only to himself. Even the most expert spectator can decipher its hieroglyphics only with great difficulty—not because of ignorance or unintelligence on his part, but because these technical terms invoke no corresponding muscular association in the layman's consciousness. It is because the art of the dance is so peculiarly inarticulate that it has never possessed a proper aesthetic philosophy. Choreographic thought—and here we fall straightway into the use of an improper and misleading term—has always been condemned to expression through paraphrases—high-sounding but inaccurate. It has had to content itself with the shifting, uncertain expedient of the analogy, which is, according to Nietzsche, the surest way of falling into error. We approach the dance by aid of analogous hypotheses and the habits of thought employed in our consideration of other arts with the inevitable result that we substitute the obvious facts of a static art for the elusive dynamics of the dance.

The great Noverre—called the "Shakespeare of the dance" by Garrick and "Prometheus" by Voltaire—who is still the most vital and thorough theoretician who has written on the subject, desired above everything to incorporate the dance into the group of "imitative arts." Carlo Blasis, who established the theory of classic instruction, struggled manfully to evolve some plausible connection between the spectacle of the dance and the poetry of the spoken drama. Others have conceived the dance as strictly limited to the expression of definite ideas, thereby sacrificing it to and confusing it with pantomime. It seems as though everyone has piled upon this art mistaken attributes or supplementary burdens in his efforts to redeem—even if only in a small way—the actual movements of the dance.

I cannot think of anyone who has devoted himself to those characteristics which belong exclusively to dancing, or who has endeavored to formulate specifically the laws of this art on its own ground. Those famous dance historians whose names I have mentioned have listed, described and analyzed a certain number of fundamental dance movements and set down the empirical laws which rule the execution of their elements. The grammar of Zorn is complete in its descriptive matter and the recent treatise of Cecchetti is invaluable as a method of instruction. But no one has ever tried to portray the intrinsic beauty of a dance step, its innate quality, its aesthetic reason for being. This beauty is referred to the smile of the dancer, to the picturesque quality of his costume, to the general atmosphere surrounding him, to the synchronizing of his bodily rhythm with the beat of the music or again to the emotional appeal of the dramatic libretto of the ballet: but never is it shown to lie in the contours of the movement itself, in the constructive values of an attitude or in the thrilling dynamics of a leap in the air. All the other arts are foisted on the dance as instructors. Blasis even insisted that a dancer should, at any given moment, be a suitable model for the sculptor Canova. But a statue is motion captured and congealed, the eternal prison of one specific form. And while it is true that every movement does break up into moments of action and moments of rest, it is only these moments of rest, of stable equilibrium and not the complete movement of the dance that can be said to find an analogy in sculpture.

I am sure that an artilleryman, thoroughly familiar with the motion of projectiles, able to calculate accurately the trajectory of a shell, the force of the explosion that sets it in motion and the range of the missile released, could much more easily discover the principle of a dancer's leap than some loose-thinking poet, however magnificent his style. For the gunner operates with a knowledge of dynamics. Doubtless his aim is wholly material—destruction, pure and simple—while it is the desire of the dancer to create beauty which causes him to make use of his knowledge of mechanics and finally dominates this knowledge. He subjects his muscles to a rigid discipline; through arduous practice he bends and adapts his body to the exigencies of an abstract and perfect form. In the end he brings the physiological factors—muscle contraction and relaxation—completely under the domination of the sovereign rhythm of the dance. This is what makes it so difficult to separate the gymnastic elements of the dance from its essence. The technique of a dancer is not like the mechanical workings of a jointed doll; it is physical effort constantly informed by beauty. This technique is no supplementary reinforcement to his art, nor is it a mere device designed to gain easy applause, like (according to Stendhal) the art of the versifier. It is the very soul of the dance; it *is* the dance itself.

Of all the various techniques it is that of the so-called classic dance—a term designating the style of dancing that is based on the traditional ballet technique—which has prevailed in the Western world. It seems to be in complete accord not only with the anatomical structure of the European but with his intellectual aspirations as well. We find this technique in all those countries where man is fashioned like us and where he thinks in our way. The little definite knowledge we have concerning the system of gymnastics of the ancient Greeks warrants our identifying certain of their "modes" with those of the contemporary dance. Today the universality of the classic style is disputed only by the oriental dance, that finds in the Cambodian ballet its highest and most complete expression. The superb efflorescence of the dance in Spain is in itself a vestige of an oriental civilization repelled but not annihilated.

Opponents of the classic dance technique pretend to consider it an academic code imposed on the dance arbitrarily by pedants and long since obsolete. It is true that it does recapitulate the experience of centuries, for we find that certain of its fundamental ideas were accepted by the dancing masters of the Italian Renaissance. It was they who first broke away from the so-called "horizontal" conception of the dance, based on outlines and figures marked by the feet of the dancer on the floor—what you might call his itinerary. The outlines of the choreographs of the seventeenth century, reproducing on paper the curving path drawn on the ground by the feet of the dancer, are the last vestiges of this "horizontal" idea, which was gradually displaced by the vertical conception of dancing—the configuration of motion in space. This important process, so fruitful in its developments, lasted throughout two centuries and strangely enough has never been even touched upon by any of those many chroniclers of the dance, who, as I have said before, invariably prefer to approach the subject as writers, musicians or historians of folkways and manners. Inasmuch as the verbal formulas that serve to designate dance movements and attitudes have remained practically unchanged all this time, the superficial observer is apt to overlook this development.

As a matter of fact there is no question but that the meaning of these formulas changes with each generation. The five fundamental positions, which are the abc's of the dance, may seem to be the same for Feuillet, the choreographer of the *"grand siècle,"* and for Mademoiselle Zambelli—to mention one of the fairest flowers of contemporary classic dance. But this is not actually so. In the outlines of Feuillet that have come down to us, the feet in the first position make an obtuse angle. In the modern, they are in the same straight line in the first position, and in the other positions in parallel lines. This may seem to be a trifling detail of growth and change, when one thinks of Isadora Duncan dancing a Beethoven symphony. But this almost imperceptible difference, this slight shift of a geometrical line, these feet pivoting at an angle of so many degrees, represents an enormously important advance, capable of infinite combinations and variety. This trifling detail is actually a realization of that essential principle and point of departure of classic choreography which took two centuries to prevail—that of turning the body, and more particularly the legs of the dancer, outward from its center.

I find myself at times looking at the history of the modern dance as though it were some charming but infinitely obscure romance which needed a key to unlock its mysteries. This key is an understanding of what a dancer means when he speaks of turning out the body. The movement of the oriental dance is concentric. The knees almost instinctively come together and bend, the curved arms embrace the body. Everything is pulled together. Everything converges. The movement of the classic dance, on the other hand, is ex-centric—the arms and the legs stretch out, freeing themselves from the torso, expanding the chest. The whole region of the dancer's being, body and soul, is dilated.

The actual manifestation of this can be readily seen or even felt in the trained body of a classical ballet dancer. The dancer spreads the hips and rotates both legs, in their entire length from the waist down, away from each other, outward from the body's center, so that they are both in profile to the audience although turned in opposite directions. The so-called five fundamental positions are merely derivations or variations of this outward turning posture, differentiated by the manner in which the two feet fit in, or cross, or by the distance that separates them. In the fifth position, where the two feet are completely crossed, toes to heels, you have the very incarnation of this principle of turning outward—that is to say, of the spirit of classic dancing. The fifth position is Taglioni; the third was Carmargo. A whole century of experimentation and of slow, arduous assimilation lies between the two. The orthopedic machines, true instruments of torture, that were used to turn pupils out in the days of Noverre would not be tolerated today. But it does take several years of daily exercise, beginning at the age of eight or nine years, to enable a dancer to perform this mechanical feat easily.

At this point, the reader may demand precisely what is gained by this hard-won victory over nature. Just this—the body of the dancer is freed from the usual limitations upon human motion. Instead of being restricted to a simple backward and forward motion—the only directions in which the human body, operating normally, can move with ease and grace, this turning outward of the legs permits free motion in any direction without loss of equilibrium; forward, backwards, sideways, obliquely or rotating. The actual extent of motion possible is considerably augmented, and since the feet are thus made to move on lines parallel to each other there is no interference, and many motions otherwise impossible are thereby facilitated. As a good example of this, I might cite the entrechat—that exhilarating movement where the dancer leaps high in the air and crosses his legs several times while off the ground. This effective "braiding" movement necessitates the turning outward of the body—otherwise the dancer's legs would block each other.

What a tiresome recital, you may be saying, about so elusive and illusive a thing as the dance! But I assure you it is justified, for the very illusion of this enchanting art—which seems to ignore all natural laws—depends on an intelligent ordering of physical effort. The dancer is a body moving in space according to any desired rhythm. We have seen how the turning outward of the body increases this space to an extraordinary degree, pushing back the invisible walls of that cylinder of air in the center of which the dancer moves, giving him that extraordinary extension of body which is totally lacking in oriental dancing, and multiplying to an infinite degree the direction of the movement as well as its various conformations. It surrounds the vertical of the body's equilibrium by a vortex of curves, segments of circles, arcs; it projects the body of the dancer into magnificent parabolas, curves it into a living spiral; it creates a whole world of animated forms that awake in us a throng of active sensations which our usual mode of life has atrophied.

I have not tried to explain clearly more than one of the salient and decisive characteristics of the classic technique. The rich development of the dance that increases its sway from generation to generation corresponds to the gradual elaboration of this principle of turning outward.

If at the beginning of the classic period the dance served merely to give law and style to the carriage and deportment of the perfect courtier, or if at the time of the *fêtes galantes* it was still skipping and mincing, it has gradually become exalted and transfigured until it is now called upon to express the loftiest emotions of the human soul.

When once the enthusiasm of the romantic period had created the idea of the dance of elevation, it was only one step further to make the dancer rise up on his toes. It would be interesting to know at exactly what moment this second decisive factor entered in. The historians of the dance, unfortunately, are not concerned with telling us. It is, however, evident that this reform was at least a half century in preparation. The heel of the shoe was raised up, the instep arched, the toe stretched down—the plant no longer was rooted to the soil. What happened was that the foot simply refused to remain flat any longer. It strove to lengthen the vertical lines of its structure. It gave up its natural method of functioning to further an aesthetic end. And thus it is that when a dancer rises on her points, she breaks away from the exigencies of everyday life and enters into an enchanted country—that she may thereby lose herself in the ideal.

To discipline the body to this ideal function, to make a dancer of a graceful child, it is necessary to begin by dehumanizing him, or rather by overcoming the habits of ordinary life. His muscles learn to bend, his legs are trained to turn outward from the waist, in order to increase the resources of his equilibrium. His torso becomes a completely plastic body. His limbs stir only as a part of an ensemble movement. His entire outline takes on an abstract and symmetrical quality. The accomplished dancer is an artificial being, an instrument of precision, and he is forced to undergo rigorous daily exercise to avoid lapsing into his original purely human state.

His whole being becomes imbued with that same unity, that same conformity with its ultimate aim, that characterizes the arresting beauty of a finished airplane, where every detail, as well as the general effect, expresses one supreme object—that of speed. But where the airplane is conceived in a utilitarian sense—the idea of beauty happening to superimpose itself upon it—the constant transfiguration, as you might call it, of the classic dancer from the ordinary to the ideal is the result of a disinterested will for perfection, an unquenchable thirst to surpass himself. Thus it is that an exalted aim transforms his mechanical efforts into an aesthetic phenomenon. You may ask whether I am suggesting that the dancer is a machine? But most certainly!—a machine for manufacturing beauty—if it is in any way possible to conceive a machine that in itself is a living, breathing thing, susceptible of the most exquisite emotions.

March 1925

ROBERT EDMOND JONES

*

The Gloves of Isadora

"So runs the world, the ardent and the lofty. We are beyond earth's story as it's told, sir."—HENRY BROCKEN

IT IS THE LATE AFTERNOON of a winter day in the White Mountains of New Hampshire. The sky is pale and as cold as marble, and the room in the old farmhouse where I sit is filled with a shadowless light thrown back from fields drifted deep in snow. In this clear icy quiet the seasons that are gone return to mind, colored and glowing. In spring the air is clouded with lilac and in summer the stone walls are tangled in wild roses and in autumn the maples burn red and gold by the river. Now the earth is locked in whiteness and silence. It is like a pause between heartbeats. Everything rests. The great North comes down over the hills.

The sense of the past is strong in the old house. Thoughts of other days close over the present, veiling its sharpness. I sit idly turning over the contents of a battered traveling trunk, with initials picked out on its lid in heavy brass nails. Here are my great-great-grandfather's waistcoats of faded brocade, and here are mitts and lace parasols, and heavy gold bracelets that lock, and fragile Chinese fans. Presently I come upon a long flat box of black-and-gold lacquer. Inside is a package, carefully wrapped in many layers of white tissue-paper. I unfold the wrappings, leaf by leaf. The dreams begin.

Thirty years melt away. It is a warm spring afternoon in 1915 and I am recovering from an operation that has brought me close to the edge of death. I lie in a little clean white bed in a little clean white room, a drowsy convalescent, half way between the other world and this. Somewhere, aeons ago, I have heard a voice that said, There will be no more pain. But I have forgotten. I am very weak. My hands on the coverlet are like transparent wax. Clouds of sleep lift and fall about me as I wander through fields of asphodel, past amaranthine meadows, in a trance-like region just this side of Paradise, all shining in a light like the light in the heart of an opal. Time has no meaning any more. The hours go by. . . .

Presently I am conscious of a new and alien vibration in the atmosphere. I have a vague feeling of disturbance, an unfamiliar sense of stress and urgency. The dream is broken. My visionary world of blurred outlines and shimmering veils is invaded by another and more definite world of clearer forms and harder edges. I look up. Isadora Duncan is standing in the doorway.

I come back from the amaranthine meadows with a rush. I see her with a singular distinctness. The impact of her presence makes me gasp with astonishment. It bites into my mind like acid. She is wrapped from head to foot in a great mantle of violet velvet and her hair—coarsely cropped as if by the shears of some shepherd on the hills of Hymettus—is crudely dyed with pure henna. On her arms she wears long gloves of violet suede reaching to the shoulder, of a style that was once called *mousquetaire*. A figure of mourning and flame.

I know this woman as the world knows her, the divine Isadora, enhaloed in legends of beauty and passion. I know how freely and how completely she has given herself to art and to artists. I have heard that the movements of her dances are the movements of antique statues come to life; that she is the embodiment of Galatea, of the Elgin marbles, of all the enchanting figurines of Tanagra; that she has breathed the rhythms of the classic world until her very life has become a vision. All these impressions have built up in my mind a phantom figure not unlike the figure of Poe's Helen, standing in her perfumed window-niche, statue-like, hyacinthine, dewy-eyed, breathing the Naiad airs that bring the wanderer home. But here is no phantom, no statue, no elusive fey dream born of weakness, no colored image of life to smile at in passing. Here is one of the great figures of the world at the height of her power and her wonder and her terrifying woman's mystery. Here is reality, utter, raw reality. And the touch of it burns and stings.

My first impression is one of violence. There is a suggestion of fierce movement about her, an atmosphere of storm. She is like the corposant on a mast-head. She is like the calm in the heart of a tempest. Then she looks at me and all other images fade away before the sheer intensity of grief that is in her eyes. I am face to face with ruin, with unending bitterness, with woe beyond description. *Against Death shall man call for aid in vain. . . .* This woman has felt the sorrows of Niobe. She has looked upon the last horrors. She has gone beyond despair. Now she no longer cares. I think she hardly even knows where she is.

I begin to tremble with awe and weakness. Then I hear her voice. It is unexpectedly light in quality, allusive, not sharp, and oddly *absent*. It is an American voice, an Irish voice, and in some curious way a humorous voice.

"You have been ill, very ill . . . you are getting better . . . you will soon be well, I know it . . ." Then suddenly, querulously: "Don't you know what's wrong with you? It's those hideous brick buildings across the street! They would make anybody sick! That's what's the matter with you Americans! Why do you live in such ugliness? You are all going to die of it some day. It is going to kill you all, every last one of you. . . . Where have you been all of you, all your lives? Haven't you ever gone anywhere? Haven't you ever seen anything? Haven't you ever loved anybody? Hasn't anybody ever even been kind to you? What *is* it that makes you willing to live with such hideous things around you?

"Just you wait!" she continues. "I'll give you something to take your mind away from those buildings! In a little while you'll forget there *are* any buildings!"

The great mourning figure vanishes.

A Western Union messenger arrives with a long narrow flat box of black-and-gold lacquer. I open it. Inside are the long gloves of violet suede that Isadora was wearing—crumpled, fragrant, just as she pulled them from her arms.

Now it is a summer evening, cool and fresh, with a soft rain falling, and I am alone in the Lewisohn Stadium in New York. I have been designing the costumes for a gigantic pageant-festival which is to be given on the occasion of Shakespeare's Tercentenary—some three-thousand costumes in all—and I have come here to be by myself and to see in my mind's eye how they will look when they are viewed by an audience. (Strange, how much of a stage designer's life is taken up with just such previsionings!) A huge superstructure has been thrown over the stage. Platforms and pinnacles and flights of steps lose themselves in the thin mist. Here and there a point of light picks out some architectural detail. The air is filled with the clean smell of new pine boards. The grass in the great bare oval is green and untrodden. I am standing at one side of the stage, by the base of the great curving staircase, below the high platform of the forestage. Far away rises the murmur of the city, like something half-remembered. Suddenly out of the darkness overhead I hear the strains of an orchestra, loud and sweet and commanding. There on the stage above me, in the soft summer rain, stands Isadora. She is dressed in a plain, white garment that just touches the floor. Over this she is wearing a peasant's cape of a kind that is called *Loden* in Austria, long and full, with bands crossing between the breasts. Her hair—no longer flaming red, but dark—is parted in the center, falling in waves over her shoulders. She is dancing. Tiny raindrops glisten about her in the faint light.

As the cold shadows lengthen in the winter afternoon, the memory of that strange moment comes to me again. I have always thought of dancing in terms of performance—as an amusement, perhaps, or as a branch of athletics, or as a quasi-Grecian ceremony painstakingly enacted by earnest white-robed undergraduates bearing wands and torches and garlands of flowers. But this dancing is different. It is not a performance at all; it is an incantation. These invocations, these gestures of welcoming, these grand simple relatings of the human body to the music and the spaces and the darkness, the atmosphere of gravity and solemnity and triumph they evoke, all seem to belong to a ritual whose patterns were traced in other ages, more innocent than ours. The figure moving there is calling upon unseen, immemorial presences. *Come, O Songs! Come, O dreams! Call to them that sleep!* Their shadows hover over the dark stage. They draw closer in the night.

Then the vision fades. I am in New York again, and this is a rehearsal. The little figure moves to and fro in the soft summer rain.

Now I see her dance at the Metropolitan Opera House. It is many years since she has appeared in America. The auditorium is crowded. The air is charged with an unusual sense of expectancy, an oppression, almost a foreboding, as if we were about to witness a cataclysm of Nature. I hear the plaintive notes of Tristan's sad shepherd. The gold curtains slowly part and lift. The stage is hung with the legendary blue draperies that are called the soul of Isadora, wide and deep, a dreamy blue, filled with illusion, warm and soft, blue like the falling dusk, blue like the sea at evening. The heavy folds rise to a vast height—high, high, as far as the eye can reach—and are lost in cathedral-like distances. A figure in white moves between them. . . .

Again I see that Isadora's dancing has nothing to do with performance. Its ease is so complete that all thought of performance vanishes from our minds and we are given over to wonder and the delight of the moment. This woman is exercising a power over us that is so strong that it is almost a compulsion. It is not physical, it is not mental, it is not even what is commonly called spiritual. And yet it is a thing of the spirit—so much so, in fact, that it is really psychic. Once and for all, the difference between Isadora Duncan and the other dancers of our time—a difference that no effort on their part can ever bridge—is that she dances with her spirit while they dance with their brains. Brilliant, remarkable brains they often are. But the difference is a difference in kind. Brains alone cannot animate the body. They can only galvanize it.

This dancing has, in the strangest way, the quality of a remembering. It seems to remind us of a beauty we have always known. It tells us of a sublime order and harmony of which we are a part, if we can only recall it. When the last movement has sunk into stillness and the last echoes of the music have faded into silence we are left with the memory of something unutterably precious that we once possessed and have thoughtlessly laid aside. She has given back to us something that once was ours. More than this, she has said to us again and again, in the trancelike exaltations of the evening, *You told me this. Do you remember? Do you remember?*

We saw her saying it.

Now the performance is at an end and the great audience streams homeward. I am bidden to a supper-party Isadora is giving at the Plaza Hotel. We are taken to a small salon, beautifully paneled in white. There are candles everywhere and masses of white flowers and champagne in coolers. Isadora is all naïveté and innocence, girlish and gay. She is dressed in white, and her hair is bound close to her head with a wreath of the most beautiful flowers I have ever seen. (I learn afterward that they are white cyclamen, the flowers Duse loved.) We sit down to a supper that is delicate and dreamlike, in the soft candlelight. Flowers, champagne, crystal . . . The world is far away . . . The hours pass . . . A young man is at the piano, playing Chopin . . . Suddenly Isadora says, I will dance for you. She stands in front of a white door. And then—how shall I express it?—creation after creation, incarnation after incarnation, falls from her, one after another, as petals fall from a rose. Our hearts beat faster. We are not lonely any more. Presently it is finished. We go away in silence. Isadora does not notice our going.

High over Central Park, wonderful, troubling, immense in the summer night, shines a strange new word, DIONYSION. Always when I think of Isadora Duncan I see that huge calm steady word burning over the roof of the Century Theatre. Isadora's friend, Lohengrin, in a mood of Renaissance splendor, has presented her with the theatre and an incomparable orchestra, and there she dances, night after night. Sometimes she is alone, sometimes her group of young girls appears with her, the six Isadorables, dreaming children of the woods. The atmosphere of these evenings is strangely disturbing. We come away from the theatre enchanted and shaken. For what we are seeing is not a festival of the dance but the celebration of an unsuspected power in us which can suddenly make the life we know seem petty and mean, a power that can transform us, that can recreate us—proud, urgent, exultant, terrible, breaking down everything we cling to, destroying and reshaping in a breath. No wonder we are afraid of it, this rapacious, remorseless, pitiless energy that would carry us far, far from our familiar surroundings. Come away! her dancing says. Come out into the splendid perilous world! Come up on the mountain-top where the great wind blows! Learn to be young always! Learn to be incessantly renewed! Learn. Learn to live in the intemperate land of song and rhythm and rapture! Say farewell to the world you know and join the great passionate spirits of the world's history! Storm through into your dreams! Give yourself up to the frenzy that is in the heart of life, and never look back and never regret! *You shall become sweet and mad as a lover. . . .*

Thoughts and emotions like these stream from the stage of the Century Theatre, borne on the strains of the world's great music, imparted to us in movements that are like the movements of winds and tides and the stars in their courses, before the blue curtains that are the soul of Isadora. Other forces are summoning us to other destinies. We are being made aware of "earlier and loftier beauties." We too can free ourselves from this crowding pettiness. We too can know the world well lost.

The sky widens in the fading light. The drifts of snow are solid as granite. There is no sound anywhere.

Years have passed. It is the summer of 1924 and I am at the Hotel Adlon in Berlin. As I go into lunch one day I see Isadora in a booth at one side of the corridor that leads to the dining room. Her eyes flash at me from under the brim of her big flat hat. She recognizes a familiar American face. We talk a few moments. She has just arrived by plane from Moscow with her new Russian husband, Essenin. She invites me to a dinner party she is giving that evening at a famous restaurant in Potsdam whose name I have now forgotten. There is a long ride through the gathering dusk, and then a beautiful room banked with flowers. There are many candles, and fruit in high silver epergnes, and food and wine fit for the gods on Olympus. Isadora is at the head of the table, dressed in black. She is incredibly changed. I hardly know her. What has become of the great dancer, the prophetess, the new muse? She is enormous. She is like a tree. For a moment I am lost in melancholy reflections. What stupid tricks time plays on us all! Essenin sits at her side, tall and blond and likable. The party grows larger. Now there are ten people, now there are twenty. Now the room is crowded. The food and wine take us into a region of delight, and there is music and singing and laughter, until the dawn burns blue at the windows. We begin to prepare for the long motor ride back to Berlin. All of a sudden Essenin becomes involved in a ferocious altercation with his Russian acquaintances. They yell at each other, they scream with rage. Finally they come to blows. The quarrel is climaxed by Essenin's clinging fast to the bars of an iron gateway. We tug at him. We beg, we plead, we threaten. We beat his hands until they bleed. Lights flash on in the windows of neighboring houses and oaths are heard. All the while Isadora stands beside her husband, motionless and silent, swathed in heavy veils. She is tragedy incarnate. Images of Antigone and Cassandra rise in the dimness. But somehow I know that this figure of woe she presents to the cold blue German dawn is a piece of acting and that she is secretly rather enjoying herself. There is nothing more to be done. It is simply not possible for us to pry Essenin loose. He has grown fast to the iron bars, a new kind of gargoyle. Blood drips from his hands. Presently I take Isadora back to the Adlon. She is abstracted, far away in some lonely sad region of the heart. Or is she acting again? I am too shy to try to talk to her. I say good night at the door. In the morning she is gone. In the pocket of my coat I find a pair of long gloves of white suede, of a style that was once called *mousquetaire*. Gloves of Isadora.

The years go by and she is in America once more. I see her dance a farewell performance at Carnegie Hall. How different it is from the last time I saw her! The atmospheric blue curtains are gone. Brutally obvious lights glare down on rented draperies of some nondescript color, carelessly hung. A figure with flying hair and the eyes of a Maenad dashes to and fro, pursued and pursuing, whirled about the stage by a furious energy that annihilates walls, background, space itself. Here is something new in the world, new and heart-shaking—an evocation of raw force, a design strong as steel. Here are vast and harsh intimations of worlds in travail. Passions flash out that carry us to the edge of madness. Blood is all around us, and the color of blood. Black clouds are shot through with fierce lightnings. Multitudes are marching, cheering, singing. . . . Then we see the last dance of all. She looks at us from across a great purple veil which she holds in her outstretched arms. She has passed beyond us. It is as if we were her memories.

When the feverish violent performance is over I go back to the stage. It is dimly lighted and it throbs and pulsates with echoes like a great hollow shell. The curtains are closed. In the center of the stage stands Essenin, stiff as a ramrod, motionless, staring straight before him. Isadora, in her scant, filmy scarlet draperies and floating scarfs, clings to him, her arms around his neck, her head on his breast. With a swift sensing of the incongruity of it, I see that she is wearing a wreath of common asparagus, oddly like a halo, somewhat askew, over one eye. All around the rim of the stage in the half-light stand hesitant, silent figures—poets, artists, adorers, waiting to offer her their homage. Some of them carry great bouquets of flowers in their arms. No one moves. No one speaks. The silence continues, becomes embarrassing, becomes unbearable. I go toward Isadora, timidly, the gloves in my hand. I have kept them these many years. Now I will give them back to her. Perhaps the spell will be broken. Perhaps we will be able to tell her what her dancing has meant to us.

She throws me a quick glance, a flash from her painted eyes. Suddenly she sees the gloves. What is this? A packet of money? Another benefactor? (Money . . . greenbacks . . . luxury . . . splendor . . . freedom—!)

I hold the gloves out to her.

No. Not money.

Only some old cast-off gloves.

With a petulant swift gesture she strikes them to the floor.

The sky has receded to an infinite distance. Barely discernible pulsations of light move across it. The silence is like death.

Again the years go by. One afternoon I am walking up Broadway in the rain. As I pass the entrance of the Strand Motion Picture Theatre I become aware of a knot of curious people gathered about the ticket-window. They are staring at an outlandish figure wrapped in a shapeless peasant coat of some thick dark red material and wearing on her head the largest *shako* outside of Russia, rather like a Brobdingnagian tea-caddy, so huge that it seemed to dwarf her. From under the heavy fur brim comes the flash of those unmistakable eyes and I see again that bitter, abandoned, humorous look. It is Isadora. Isadora Duncan, standing in line to buy a ticket for a Broadway movie. She catches sight of me. Again a familiar face. Any face. "I'm stranded in this damned town!" she says. Again and again she repeats the phrase. "I'm stranded in this damned town!" Her voice goes on and on, tonelessly, like an automaton that has been wound up and forgotten. *Stranded in this damned town, stranded in this damned town, stranded in this damned town. . . .* Obscene street-signs wink and leer and jiggle—clitter-clatter, flash, clock-clock—through the hot spring rain. Essenin is behind her, tall and blond and alien. Impatient crowds press toward the pair. I know with an unexplainable intuition that I shall never see her again. All at once the figure of Io stands before me—great Io, in her eternal anguish. Lost—alone—burning. . . . *Why am I stung with frenzy that drives me unresting forever? Let fires consume me; let the deep earth yawning engulf me . . . I have wandered enough, I am weary . . . Shall earth nevermore conceal her buried dead?*

I turn away. Her voice follows me above the rising murmur. *Stranded in this damned town. . . .*

I fold the gloves in their wrappings, the violet and the white, and lay them away in the box. I close the lid of the trunk on this memory of motion and music. *Ruin calls his brother Death. A rare and regal prey he hath prepared. . . .*

Do they increase in stature, do their eyes grow more brilliant?
It is dark now and the room is cold.

October 1947

* *

ARGENTINA

*

My Castanets

FROM MY EARLIEST CHILDHOOD I had a horror of castanets, not of their range and their aesthetic, but of the noise they made. I have spoken of this sound as noise before, and I stick to it. That is what it was to me. My ears suffered from it; it gave me a distinct physical discomfort. When I was about five years old I received a pair of tiny castanets from my father as a toy. "See if you can get anything out of these," he said. I already knew how to use the horrible instruments, and without false modesty I may say that I got the same effect as from regulation castanets—with a smaller volume of sound, of course, since these were hardly bigger than an almond, while the ones in use at that time (a date which I refrain from giving through coquetry) were enormous.

According to the size of the castanets, the concavity which produced the sound was more or less accentuated. I soon discovered, from this plaything of mine, that the usual relation between size and concavity was of no value but was, on the contrary, the cause of the imperfection in tone which I found so distressing. It seemed to me that by lessening this concavity one could proportion the volume of sound to the size of the instrument and at the same time obtain a tone of altogether different quality. I kept the secret of this discovery to myself for a long time for fear that I might be considered simply Mlle. Know-it-all. But about four years later, when I was nine years old, I decided to tell my father my secret and my desire to make some experiments in this direction. He did not take me too seriously but did not oppose my plan. At this point the adventure becomes more picturesque. For if my father simply showed a kindly incredulity, "the master of castanets," as they called the manufacturer, received my idea with mistrust and hostility—a natural reflection of his pride ruffled by the claims of a child to teach him his trade. The master who supplied my father was a small, bitter, dried up old man with the air of a decayed dancer. This appearance was heightened by certain mannerisms which he had copied from the men and women of the choreographic world with whom he came in contact through the sale of his wares. It was funny to hear him talk Dance like an expert in the art. But his trade had not enriched him and he carried his castanets in his handkerchief knotted at the four corners. I can still hear the clatter they made as he came along the street or up the stairs with them. With unbelievable determination I managed to persuade him to what he called my fantastic notion. I made him diminish the castanets' size which, besides being to a large extent the cause of the noise I hated so, also prevented the play of the fingers each time one tried to obtain an unusual effect. Then I begged him to make a pair slightly less concave. This was not enough, and to achieve the perfection of this single detail and get exactly the quality of tone I wanted required the making of at least ten pairs of castanets with gradually lessening concavity.

At this point I began to have a real taste for the instrument and to love it. Yet I was not satisfied. There were still improvements to be made. In the old castanets there was a large surface of contact between the two parts. I made the castanet master lessen this surface a little at a time until it became very small and achieved a much more musical sonority. Then we went on to another detail. The holes through which passed the string that holds the two parts together and goes over the fingers, did not seem right to me. If the holes were big and the cord thin the tone was shrill and one lost control of the instrument. If the holes were small and the cord thick the tone was choked. So we made the holes of medium thickness with a cord in proportion. The tone of the castanet varies with the material of which it is made. Some castanets are made of ebony; once they were made of ivory but their tone was ugly. The best, those with the greatest variety of tone and the finest nuances, are made of the wood of the pomegranate tree.

Castanets are capricious and I do not yet know why, in each pair, there is one which sounds like a violoncello, the other like a violin. This is not an exact comparison but one which will suggest the difference in sound. In theatre parlance we say that one is male and the other female. The latter gives the more delicate sound and is worn on the right hand. The other on the left hand has the deeper tone. Its role is to play the accompaniment.

Gradually, in spite of protestation and ridicule, I have succeeded in making out of the abhorred castanets an instrument that thrills me with its musical possibilities and that seems a perfect collaborator with my choreographic art.

January 1932

* *

AGNES DE MILLE

*

The New Ballerina

THE DAY of the great romantic solo dancer is unquestionably on the wane. Pavlova is dead and before many years are gone the last spangled skirt will have swirled into history to join the tradition of Camargo, Taglioni and Genée, utterly lovely, magical women whose presence epitomized the romance and beauty of their epoch, who were not only expert performers but the distillation, the feminine ideal, of the culture that produced them. The grace and science of their movements were not more wonderful than their clothes, their complexions, their charm, wit, taste, erudition and emotional force. Heroic courtesans! What were they but the spiritual mistresses of the audiences they played for—Barbarini, beloved of Frederick's court, Camargo, who danced so proudly at Versailles, Taglioni and Elssler of the Romantic Salons? Their art was the flowering of whole social systems. Poets learned from their graces; cities courted their smile. Their tambourines have set the tune of music.

When Pavlova took the scene the Russian empire rose behind her. She trod the stage in glamour. Her beauty was the culmination of great traditions. Her toe-shoes, her tarletans, her bow, her smile even, were not her own inventions but a heritage as surely as the five classic positions conceived and developed by women dead two hundred years. Her applause was not her earning alone. Pavlova on her "points"! Bearded nobles who fought Napoleon had clapped to see in the light of candles the same sheen of arched feet, the same winking of diamonds under dark hair. Because of the ghosts which moved behind her, because of this added glory, great theatre existed where Pavlova was, as it had existed always in the presence of the great Imperial dancers irrespective of their own personal transcendent technique.

The solo dancer of today without glamour, without tradition or background, tries to fill a place held for the last three hundred years by one or another sure-footed enchantress. There is little of the charmer about her now. Severe, self-sacrificing, she no longer considers the dance a vehicle for the display of her personal attractions but a cult, a rite, the apotheosis of the forces around her. Two factors have combined to bring about this change: the lack of subsidized organizations to foster and display the art of the old-fashioned ballerina, and a consequent reconception of the function of the dance itself.

Anna Pavlova developed her technique in a school under the supervision of the Czar. Her girlhood was passed in gracious contact with the painters, musicians, writers and rulers of the country. When she was graduated at seventeen she spoke three or four languages, knew a scholarly amount of music, literature, painting and history, and had years of stage experience behind her. On leaving the school room she fell heir, with the other students in her class, to a subsidized theatre devoted entirely to ballet dancing, a working organization of experts, a large repertoire of roles, and an audience trained since birth in the highly technicalized vocabulary of her art. The mechanics of her business adequately cared for by others, she had only to keep her mind on dancing better than any other living persons.

Karsavina in her biography, *Theatre Street,* writes of the ballet theatre and its audience, ". . . The ballet had become fashionable. A competition for seats, for the right to be a subscriber, well proved the interest it aroused. To obtain a seat, a petition to the Chancery of the Imperial Theatres had to be filed; the chance of success was so small that big premiums were constantly offered by advertisement to the original holders of the stalls. . . . No outsider could ever penetrate into the first rows of stalls without a sesame, a favor of a *balletomane* friend. . . . The seats were handed down from father to son, the name of *balletomane* once given in derision, was becoming almost a hereditary dignity. . . . A very knowledgeable, exacting, conservative and somewhat dogmatic public, *balletomanes* were capable of high enthusiasm. . . . One could feel from the stage how the whole audience stiffened in breathless expectation of a favorite passage. The passage well executed, the whole theatre burst out clapping in measure to the music."

In all the forty-eight states of the Union there are only two critics, equipped to write on dancing, who are hired for this purpose by daily newspapers. In all the audiences who witness dancing there are but a handful of students who take the trouble to inform themselves about what dancing is or has been before they attend a concert of dancing. Furthermore, there are no endowed dancing schools in America. The last situation affects the dancer immeasurably more than the other two, important as they are. The concert dancer of New York begins her studies usually in the studio of some transplanted ballet-master, where she learns a bastard version of the classic technique distorted to meet the demands of acrobatic and tap students who wish to get on with all possible haste to the business of making money. Most of her associates are commercially-minded children and their ignorant, commercial mothers, specialty dancers from night-clubs and vaudeville, and fat women who want to reduce.

At about the age of sixteen, if she has talent, she will become dissatisfied with the trade she has been learning and make the heroic decision to abandon all she knows in order to study some new kind of dancing. She will learn, for instance, to stand and walk with relaxed knees instead of the stiffened ballet leg turned outwards forty-five degrees in the hip socket, to lift her foot from the floor without instinctively flexing the toe so that the instep swells into a high arch. She will learn that one hip may rise above the other, that one shoulder may lift out of the parallel composure in which it has functioned for so long. What patience is involved, what heart-breaking patience! The reflexes, the very abc's of bodily movement to be learned over again from the beginning and all this with the pressure of time eating on her mind, the knowledge that she is behind in her schedule, that she will soon be in her twenties and the work of her childhood not yet finished! She flounders from technique to technique in frantic haste while she waits on tables or goes without the proper food and clothing in order to pay for the lessons. She starves herself. She forgoes culture and education. She wastes herself in drudgery that can help her in no way professionally.

Hitherto a dancer trained in one style, the classic ballet, and varied it with folk and character steps that were superimposed on the ballet formula. No matter what the type of dancing she never changed her fundamental method of handling levitation, balance, speed, direction and dynamic impetus. Today there are any number of disciplines with the same problems taught as contradictory systems that destroy one another. The Italian and Russian ballet methods teach that the point of control is low in the back, the arms and legs rotating outwardly from the spine like wheels on a shaft, the spine and horizontal unchanging hips maintained as the constant axis of all movement. The Duncan school contends that the base of all control is the solar plexus, and that the arms and legs must function naturally as in running or walking. The Wigman method trains motion through the body in tensions and relaxations so that dynamism may be said to be gathered up and dispersed in a constant ebb and flow of muscular contraction. The Graham school builds all gesture on a percussive stroke proceeding from the hips that releases movement like an after-beat through the shoulders, arms and legs—very much the way continuous action is sent the length of a whip by a single jerk of the handle—the body maintaining its balance by thrusting the hips, not outward as in ballet dancing, but forward over the bent knees which act like a spring flexing and relaxing as the hip impetus drives motion through them. These systems are opposed in the fundamentals of muscular control and cannot be learned one after the other naturally, but require as complete a reconditioning of unconscious muscular response as would be involved in suddenly learning to write with the left hand if one were born and trained right-handed. A knowledge of various techniques does not always enrich the student. It frequently renders her uncertain, hesitant, without defined style or reliable craftsmanship. And if it does not do this it in any case prolongs the period of apprenticeship far beyond its natural span.

At seventeen, then, the age when Pavlova, as a graduated technician, was placed in stellar roles at the Ballet Theatre of St. Petersburg the concert dancer of today finds herself with an unfinished training, confused notions of form and expression, small chance of contacting the leaders in her own art or any other, no means of studying creative backstage work and faced with the prospect of starving in order to appear three or four times a year on the stage. At last, of necessity, she joins a group of students who, like herself, bewildered and ambitious, have banded together under the leadership of someone who can serve as their teacher. With this experimental direction she rehearses nightly for three or four months in order to make a single concert appearance. She is paid for the four months' work what her teacher can give her, the price, say, of a hat. Personal recognition is neither expected nor received. The likelihood of her ever having enough money to finance a recital of her own is small. The certainty that no commercial theatre in the United States will offer her a chance to display the type of work to which she is devoting her life stands as an almost final barrier to success. If, however, she has talent enough and energy enough, if she possesses personal magnetism and meets no small amount of luck, she will win through. She will take the stage as a great dancer, many years older than the premières of the past, sobered by hardship, driven by ideas more important to her than commercial success or quick fame, conscious always of the group from which she sprang, the group which she in turn must create to perform her works.

And having won the stage what will she do with it? Will she pin roses in her hair and flirt with the audience? Was it for this that she endured a youth of grey tears and hunger, that she might in the full creative power of maturity wear short skirts with more devastating grace than any other lady in town? Long ago in the struggle for bread she forgot to think of herself as set apart from the people by a life dedicated to the soul yearning of the romanticist. She is no longer interested solely in the relation of her spirit to abstract beauty. She is interested in the relation of her spirit to humanity and the social forces that have gripped her life. She dances hunger, agony, the passion and resurrections of civilizations. She dances folk themes, "Steerage," "Strike," "Heretic," "Primitive Mysteries," "Sketches from the People," "Pessimist and Optimist," (Martha Graham); "The Study of Woman," "The Chosen—based on the old Shaker Ritual," "The Life of the Bee," (Doris Humphrey); "The Witch," "Gypsy Songs," "Seraph Song," (Mary Wigman). One has only to compare these titles with those of the old order to recognize the amazing difference—"The Spirit of Champagne," "The Girl with the Enamel Eyes," (Genée); "The Death of the Swan," "The Fairy

Doll," "The Dying Rose," "The Dragonfly," "The Coquetteries of Columbine," (Pavlova); "Carnaval," "Le Spectre de la Rose," (Karsavina).

The first of the great moderns was Isadora Duncan, who brought back religion to the stage, and the second was Ruth St. Denis, who reproduced thereon specific rituals. And now, on the stages of the world, dancers who feel themselves the conscious representatives of their community are bringing into the artistic form folk material significant of the lives of the people for whom it is played.

Every summer in New Mexico the Pueblo Indians dance the corn dance for rain. Every winter around their blazing fires they dance the meeting of heaven and earth and the fecundity of man. On the levees of the south and in Harlem night clubs the Negroes dance a decadent version of their mating dance. And these are the last of our great spontaneous folk actors. Not less than these, not less in any way, Martha Graham, as a conscious artist on the New York stage, dances the problems and hungers and convictions of the people among whom she lives. The German dancers dance folk themes. Has not the dancer, Vera Skoronel, written, "There is no gain—saying that there exists a mysterious cohesiveness between the primitive cult dances and modern choreography"? The Duncan dancers of Moscow create to Soviet Labor Songs and folk music, yes, and sing them as they dance, lustily in unison, in the grand old tradition of the Singing Game. In this country Benjamin Zemach devotes himself to forming a Hebrew ballet which has as its avowed purpose "the interpretation of Jewish life and thought through the forms of the dance, deriving its material from three sources—Jewish Daily Life, Ritual-Legend-Myth, The Bible." In legends, parables and satires which have almost completely replaced the romantic phantasy and picturesque revelry of the old repertories the great aristocratic stars of the Diaghileff ballet seize and develop the experiments of the unsubsidized groups.

There is, of course, a difference between the primitive unconscious folk dancer and the creative artist, but it is one more of purpose than of form and content. The primitive dances to rouse and manipulate the forces of life directly through the dance; the artist manipulates the forces of life through her audience. But the folk dancer creates purely to satisfy himself and his gods, while the artist creates not only to satisfy her gods, that is, her spiritual needs, but to win for herself admiration for the act of creating. Today the artist is closer to the folk dancer than at any time during the last four hundred years because, unlike the old-fashioned ballerina, the modern wishes the emphasis thrown on the created work and on the individual's performance as a projection of that work instead of on the individual's performance as an end in itself. In other words, as in any folk performance, the dance and not the dancer dominates. Individuality, charm and pretty personal mannerisms are lost in action. If the stars of the great ballets consider their virtuosity inadequate to the effects they want, they duplicate their appearance, wear masks, and spell one another in the same roles as in Diaghileff's *Renard*. If the adolescent, vibrant-bodied dancers of New York discover sex and personal appeal to be hackneyed and commercial, they undress alike, cover their hair, cease to be people, and become samples of coordinating anatomy. If the well-muscled heroines of Germany find they can function better in pants and rompers than in female clothing, into pants and rompers they go, or they strip like gymnasts, forgetting everything but the idea they wish to project.

Bereft of femininity and other theatrical standbys the dancers employ now only what they cannot do without. . . . A shift, a crown, a scarlet robe, a mourner's veil, a flag, a workman's cap, these suffice for costume; and for scenery, a ring of light, a wooden platform, a scaffolding of steps, or a plain painted drop of lines and washes. The modern dance setting is as significant and simple as a mediaeval stage with "Heaven," "Hell," "Limbo," marked over the various doorways, as primitive and simple as the markings of corn on the floor of an Indian Kiva. As the dance leaders stalk on to the stage in their one piece dresses and begin mounting or descending their platforms one can almost hear the rumble of the Mystery Wagons coming down gabled streets when whole cities stopped their work to act out for one another the stories of their faith.

The fact that the soloist no longer belongs to a dedicated class but is often self-managed and self-taught lessens the barrier of mystery between the performer and spectator. The fact that the modern technique seems less miraculous than dancing on the points, simply because it is based more closely on natural gesture, gives the audience the interested feeling of watching what they are themselves capable of performing. The dancer has become their proxy and her dance is theirs, potentially. They sit with the jealous, exacting eyes of a lay community watching their official representatives.

The tambourines have ceased to tinkle. The ruffled skirts lie in the wings. The stage is stormed by shafts of light, naked motion, companies and companies of unknown dancers and their leaders working in common spontaneous purpose. Folk dancing has left the public square and is in our theatre. The people are again taken into the dance. It has come back to its ancient traditional place of a communal rite.

May 1931

* *

LINCOLN KIRSTEIN

*

Balanchine Musagète

[*One of two articles by Mr. Kirstein on the work of George Balanchine.* —THE EDITORS.]

THE POSITION of a living choreographer is hard to establish with any independent accuracy. By mid-career, the relative achievement and prestige of painters or musicians become fairly obvious. But choreographers must depend upon conditions of performance unnecessary to painting or music. It is difficult for a choreographer to hold a retrospective one-man show. There is no Museum of Modern Art for the dance; choreographic scores do not exist. Ballet companies are not nearly as widespread as symphony orchestras or even chamber-music groups. Since a choreographer is usually attached to a single company, at least temporarily, his work is largely restricted to the few parts of the world where his company travels. Because of the recent war, with its breakdown of communications in the field of art, only a single repertory is known to each country after almost a decade's interval. Americans, for example, know scarcely anything of the ballets of Frederick Ashton, Robert Helpmann, Serge Lifar, Feodor Lopoukhov or Aurel Milloss. England, conversely, has seen no ballets by George Balanchine later than those composed in 1932, and even these were not presented for nine years until they were given, this past year, in a sad state of disrepair. Balanchine's position as a choreographer, therefore, rests largely on his achievements in the United States.

Balanchine came here in 1933; he left Russia in 1924. Three years earlier he had graduated from the State Academy of the Dance in Petrograd, which he had entered (as the Imperial Ballet School, attached to the Marinsky Theatre) in 1914. Born in 1904, he is barely middle-aged, yet in forty-three years he has experienced what few men in his field can claim. As a student of the ballet school he was attached to the Czar's household; he performed as a child upon the same stage with dancers who established the prestige of Russia as the criterion for ballet in the twentieth century. While still a youth he served as Diaghileff's final ballet-master. Last spring, as an American citizen, he was the first of his country to be called to the Paris Opera as *maître de ballet.*

After Russia (both ballet school and Revolution) Diaghileff was Balanchine's most influential teacher. Imagine what the call to Diaghileff must have meant to a boy who had just emerged from Russia on what was presumably a summer's vacation spent performing around German spas! And then, after brief appearances in Berlin and Paris, what it must have meant to be named ballet-master to the greatest impresario of his epoch! Diaghileff was not a fool. He had long recognized unknown and undeveloped talent, and Balanchine even then was not a nonentity. First of all, he was a fine classic dancer, the head of his class, a type of trained male dancer of which we have few today, one destined from childhood to appear on preeminent stages in responsible roles. He had a splendid physique, a surpassing musical gift and ten years of solid training in theatrical establishments which can only be compared in discipline and subsidy to West Point or Annapolis. Thus Balanchine entered Western Europe fully prepared. His youthful insecurities lay entirely in questions of taste, never in technique. This is important to consider in an age like ours today, when many a student presumes to make choreography, and when virtually every young choreographer has good taste and displays it successively in works which are presented for a single season.

The taste of Balanchine when he settled in France was the taste of a young Soviet Romantic revolutionary of his period—the epoch of Miaskovsky, the Suprematists and Constructivists, the first Cultural Program of Lunacharsky. He adored Rachmaninoff and Scriabin; yet until Diaghileff showed him the Louvre and Italy he had hardly noticed painting. In the realm of architecture the palaces of Great Catherine's town and the façades of Rastrelli and Stassov will always be in his mind, not as stupendous decor but as home. Memories from the world of Pushkin will always haunt him, as they have his exiled colleagues in art and music; theatrical splendor echoes in his imagination in terms of the blue-and-gold interior of the Marinsky Theatre. Compounded in his personal taste are also the nostalgia of Slavic Byronism, the independence of the Caucasus, the ironic elegance of the Statue of Bronze.

Balanchine's taste was developed, and even to a certain degree formed, by Diaghileff—both positively and negatively. To understand the effect of his dominant personality upon Balanchine we must picture Diaghileff, toward the end of his career, chancing across a young talent fresh from Russia, where Diaghileff, once court chamberlain and editor of the Annuals of the Imperial Theatres, had not been for fifteen years. Diaghileff always said that he wished to return to Russia; he had been invited officially but age, uncertainty and insecure health prevented. In his last two seasons he produced two large works commissioned from Prokofieff, then official Soviet composer for export, the Shostakovitch of his day. Massine's *Le Pas d'Acier* (1928) was a danced salute to the USSR's program of electrification and industrialization. Balanchine's *Le Fils Prodigue* (1929), with Rouault's memorable decor, was Diaghileff's last complete synthesis of music, paint and plastic movement, a synthesis which started with *Schéhérazade* nearly twenty years before.

From their first association Diaghileff welcomed Balanchine as his final collaborator, a revivifier for his declining years. To the young choreographer Diaghileff was a revelation. The era of grandeur, of the diplomatic glory of the pre-war Paris and London seasons, of Pavlova, Nijinsky and Karsavina, of Lady Ripon and Deutsch de la Meurthe was long lost. After the first world war Diaghileff had a small troupe, comparatively inferior in quality except for a few soloists. To Balanchine, accustomed to the huge machinery of the state-subsidized Soviet theatre, the apparatus with which he now had to work seemed feeble. But there was compensation in the intense atmosphere surrounding Diaghileff and his general staff—in the vivid interchange of new ideas and influences, in the association with the painters of the School of Paris and with the musical group centering in Les Six.

In Russia art had always been official. For Diaghileff, who had long suffered from the Professional deformations of officialdom, art was merely an extension of private and personal interests. An elegant taste based on discovery, novelty and shock was its only standard. No longer was it desirable—it was even harmful—to employ a gross machine inertly controlled by a Bureau of Culture or a Ministry of Fine Arts. What ballets had the Soviet Union produced comparable to *Parade* (1917: Satie-Massine-Cocteau-Picasso) or *Les Biches* (1923: Poulenc-Nijinska-Marie Laurençin) as expressions of the age in which they were created, even judged in the crassest terms of Marxian dialectic?

Diaghileff's last epoch was the period of *musiquette;* of Cocteau's first rehabilitation of the commonplace (after his early exoticism); of the calculated use of banality, of the *faux pompier,* of shocking bad taste; of the cinema and early jazz; of cyclists with telegrams and aviators in cellophane. The chief artists of the time were attempting to extract a myth from a combination of industrial middle-class urban society and the negligent aristocracy of the Côte d'Azur. All excitement and intensity was in *today,* in the public demonstration of personal and fashionable discoveries. Ballet was no longer either the apotheosis of a national legend or an editorial; there were no Boris, Peter, Catherine and Holy Mother Russia to praise, no patriotic prestige to enhance through the subventioned instrument. Society was international; its capital was Paris, its scale was domestic and diminutive and its cultural effect was enormous. The delicious libertinism of the Riviera beaches, the accidental, the improvised, the unexpected, the anti-heroic; extravagant social sophistication as the loving parody of the vogue: this was Balanchine's second school.

To say that he was happy in it would be an oversimplification. He was confused. At the age of twenty-one he found himself entrusted with great artistic responsibility. The technical competence which has never deserted him was unperturbed even by the united opposition and virtual revolt of Diaghileff's troupe at his unexpected imposition as ballet-master after the prestige of his predecessors, Massine and Nijinska. Yet young Balanchine felt ridiculous. Was this nonsense which Diaghileff proposed—this deliberate identification with the preposterous, this rejection of everything he had been prepared for? It seemed to be; yet Diaghileff, for whom every creative act had immediate historical significance, seemed entirely convinced of the importance of the ephemeral. It was not easy for an inexperienced youth from early Soviet Russia to understand such depths of cynicism, such heights of disinterestedness based on so much human experience and cultivation and breeding.

But Apollo, Lord of the Sun and the Lyre, took pity on one of his struggling votaries and revealed himself in an unmistakable if unfamiliar guise: as Olympic champion. Dignity was restored; nobility was made possible. There reappeared the significance of gesture in itself as a new potential for classic dancing. Balanchine's sense of the creative act as responsible to a continuous tradition, a tradition not abandoned in pique but salvaged for use, became clear. It was clarified through Igor Stravinsky.

Fresh out of school, Balanchine had mounted *Pulcinella* in 1921. (Except for infrequent performances of *Petrouchka* Stravinsky was then and is now almost unknown to the Soviet theatre or symphony audiences.) The first task Diaghileff set for Balanchine was restating Stravinsky's *Le Rossignol* for Alicia Markova, then a "baby ballerina." But *Apollon Musagète* (1928) was a more serious endeavor on a superior level. *Apollon* is a work of capital historical importance in the arts of the first half of the twentieth century. It is also a work of beauty. The combination is rare. (One recalls by contrast Picasso's "Les Demoiselles d'Avignon" or Eric Mendelssohn's Einstein-Turm at Potsdam, in all their hideous historical influence.)

Apollon Musagète introduced to ballet in its time a spirit of traditional classicism absent since Petipa's last compositions almost thirty years before. It demonstrated that tradition is not merely an anchorage to which one returns after eccentric divagations but the very floor which supports the artist, enabling him securely to build upon it elements which may at first seem revolutionary, ugly and new both to him and to his audience. *Apollon* has now lost for us the effects which offended, irritated or merely amused an earlier public. We forget that much of the "modernism" of adagio movement in our classic dance derives directly from *Apollon;* that many ways of lifting women, of turning close to the floor, of subtle syncopation in the use of *pointes,* of a single male dancer supporting three women, were unknown before *Apollon.* These innovations horrified many people at first, but they were so logical an extension of the pure line of Saint-Léon, Petipa and Ivanov that they were almost immediately absorbed into the tradition of their craft.

Glenway Wescott said that instead of *Apollo, Leader of the Muses* the ballet should have been entitled *Apollo's Games with the Muses.* The mimed athletics, the strenuous atmosphere of violent physicality recall the nervousness of runners before a race. Each variation seems a training for the final translation to Olympus. In the chariot-race finale which evokes memories of the profiles on Roman coins and cameos and of the decathlon, visualized in the newly extended idiom of the Russian ballet, a transformation of the Olympic games into contemporary dancing takes place.

Of all Balanchine's works *Apollon* is the most significant historically, the most compact, the most influential, the least appreciated in its full importance. Or perhaps one should say that of all his work it has been the least clearly observed. Although it has been performed with increasing frequency in recent years, chiefly because it provides a generous role for a male classic dancer—perhaps the single one in our repertory which fully exercises capable physical endowment and discipline—its success has always rested not on its virtues as music or as choreography but on the chance it gives its hero to perform. Balanchine has always known so well how to fit a role to a particular performer that his dances are continually identified or confused with his dancers. This has occurred repeatedly throughout his career. The first success of *Le Fils Prodigue* (1929) was Lifar's; of *Mozartiana* (1933), Toumanova's; of *Night Shadow* (1945), Danilova's. As for *Apollon,* Serge Lifar in his various autobiographies, and in the frantic journalism which he still commands, pretends it was he who made the choreography, not alone for his own part but for the others as well. This is not true: the work was composed by Balanchine as a vehicle for Lifar—at that time Diaghileff's newest male dancer, who had as yet received no frame worthy of his powers—and for three ballerinas. It is an indication of the extent to which Diaghileff's troupe had shrunk at this time that this important classic work had to be composed for only three women (Doubrovska, Nemchinova, Tchernicheva) without corps de ballet, since they were almost the only well-trained executants left to him.

No one acquainted only with Lifar's recent shameful political career and present status can have any notion of the impact of his personal quality in 1928. (Mme. Misia Sert, who originally placed Lifar in the Paris Opera, spoke his epitaph: *"Serge, tu es le spectre d'un faune dans l'apres-midi d'une rose."*) With the angular, small violence of a Cossack colt, petulant yet gracious, insolent yet appealing; with a nervous energy which was never completely controlled, but seduced in *Apollon* by Balanchine's masterly study of his personal limitations into an enormous expressiveness, Lifar had an astonishing hard plastic muscular beauty. His performance in *Apollon* was unrivalled since Nijinsky's Faun of sixteen years before. Lifar's individual success, the dreamed-for dazzle that comes once in a career, and hardly more than once in a whole audience's lifetime, obliterated the prime importance of the two factors most responsible for the triumph—Stravinsky's music and Balanchine's movement.

Stravinsky has long been on record concerning his opinion of Balanchine: *un juif connait un autre juif*. But many people thought (and still think) that in *Apollon* Stravinsky went to the market of his memory and came back with nothing but a basket of Délibes, Handel and Tschaikowsky; that Balanchine had sat too long in the perverse courts of Diaghileff watching films of American sporting events. André Levinson, who, despite his persistent nostalgia for the Marinsky Theatre, had a considerable knowledge of tradition and its incessant renovations unlike more recent critics, saw little of interest in the ballet save Lifar's behavior. Those music critics (and one wonders how they manage to go on writing so long after they have become deaf) who consider that Stravinsky lost his "power" after the early Russian nationalist scores never listen to *Apollon* with clean ears. They (and their kin in the dance columns) are impervious to conscious, constructed and deliberate art; improvisation and expressionism is their red meat. Cautious, cerebral, de-energized themselves, they need buckets of blood in the form of big, gutsy symphonic pantomimes to convince themselves the ballet is still alive.

Those dance critics who write as if dance criticism were penal servitude insist that the choreography of *Apollon* is pastiche, a parody of *Lac des Cygnes,* a transient echoing of "Parisian smartness." This last it certainly is, if one translates smartness not as smart-aleckness but as essential human elegance. *Apollon* has its chic; it partakes of the permanent international elegance characteristic of French thought, letters, painting, dress-making and cooking, upon which neither American industrialism nor military defeat has had the slightest effect. The dancers in *Apollon* were dressed by Mme. Chanel, who cinctured them with Charvet's striped cravats. They were Olympians of 1928; they remain Olympians in 1948. In the successive fluent variations of the male dancers and of the three soloists, in the grand duet and in the apotheosis, Balanchine touched those electrical motor impulses which the genius of Stravinsky had imbedded in the music.

November 1947

* *

GEORGE W. BEISWANGER

*

The New Theatre Dance

WITH THE ROUNDING OUT of a five-year cycle of production at the Bennington School of the Dance it becomes plain that the modern dance has succeeded in reaching its most important objective, the creation of an American theatre dance. To those who identify theatre with the existing commercial stage, this statement may seem ill-considered. In order to comprehend what the modern dance is doing by way of genuine theatre art, we need a definition which, while it may slight some of Ibsen and Shaw, will serve to include the essential theatric values of vaudeville, the circus and the minstrel show, of the motion picture, the radio drama and the dance, not to mention that considerable bulk of Maxwell Anderson and O'Neill, of Shakespeare and the Greek dramatists, which breaks through the narrow confines of the stage play.

As a starting-point, let us say that a theatre art, in contrast with a predominantly personal or "recital" art, is distinguished by the fact that its materials are already to a considerable extent embodied aesthetically in forms belonging not so much to the personal artist as to his audience. Theatre material already lies half-formed in the body of general culture. There are story rituals there: pursuit, danger and escape; virtue tried and triumphant or tempted and redeemed; the hero who suffers, dies and rises again. There are heroes, then, and villains as well: the honest son of toil, the rascal, the rebel, the tyrant, the benevolent ruler; the Corn King and the Spring Queen.

The superman and the divinities who walk on the screen or whisper through the microphone or stalk across the footlights already exist in the popular song, the gossip column and the confession magazine, that is to say, in the trade arts which administer first aid to the imaginative needs of the folk. It is the business of true theatre to take these fabulous creatures and give them the chance to "live out" the full significance of the myths whose folk-land of story they inhabit.

In short, theatre art from Punchinello to King Oedipus is an immediate and direct presentation of "life" as a folk sees it when imaginatively stirred by its own legends, divinities and ideals. It is a ritual "imitation" (to use a badly misunderstood word), a passionate display, of the patterns which experience falls into when it is made to issue out of the possibilities imaginatively allowed to it by a group culture. The aesthetic force of that imitation lies in its evocative power: the magical powers and personalities which inhabit the folk imagination are made to walk the boards, and this living illusion of their being in turn calls forth in the spectator a rapt sense of intimate participation in the otherwise secret forces and processes of life.

What I have just said is, of course, not to be interpreted in any esoteric sense. Theatre simply presents with transparent conviction what the imagination is always doing with experience when at its depths the ambiguities of everyday life are cut away and the fundamental forces are allowed to operate according to their own logic. In the theatre, the juggler is made to be inordinately clever; thus we can see how and why juggling can be a meaningful way of life. In theatre, the fool's folly touches the skies; we see why men must slip on banana peels and get tangled up with their golf clubs. In theatre, the vicious impulses are made satanic; we see why the bad man has to be what he is and why we must hate him. In theatre, the defeated man becomes heroic in dimension; we see why he must suffer and how he can triumph in death. So O'Neil in *Mourning Becomes Electra* is true theatre, and Dreiser's *Jennie Gerhardt* and *American Tragedy*. Thomas Benton in the Frankie and Johnny of the Missouri murals is true theatre, and so is Diego Rivera when he paints the class conflict. Many other examples might be given. All point to the fact that the theatre, which is a magical thing, an afflatus that lifts those who participate in it out of the confines of separated personality into a richly communal experience, can be created only in a certain national or folk environment. It is obvious, I think, that a repressed or imaginatively impoverished people are incapable of genuine theatre. Nor is it possible to a people who lack history, who live so close to the edge of the struggle for mere existence that they dare not take time out to contemplate the land in which they walk or to dwell upon the past out of which they have come. Such people in dying do not look with regret upon the "dear land" they are about to leave, nor are they "gathered to their forefathers." And so they lack a theatre art.

If the modern dance, then, has actually achieved a theatre art, this fact in itself is of the utmost significance in interpreting the present state of American culture. It means, when taken in conjunction with our new architecture, our reborn mural art, our Federal Theatre projects, our multiplying orchestras, our vigorous regional schools of painting, our industrial arts, our Thomas Wolfes and even our Hollywood, that, despite all that disappoints and galls one in the present scene, we are actually in the midst of the renascence for the signs of which our prophets still anxiously scan the horizon.

It is therefore significant that the impulse towards theatre has been present in the modern dance from the start. It was implicit in the urge which led to the rebirth of the dance, the desire to find a dance which would communicate American meanings and values to an American audience. With Isadora Duncan the endeavor to make of movement an autonomous art medium had a quite practical and even utilitarian purpose; discovering what it was we had to say to ourselves that could be said in dance. Only by exploring the movements of an emotionally charged American could the meanings and the sources of that emotion be uncovered and expressed.

In order to create a genuine theatre dance, it was therefore necessary to reject the theatre dance as it then existed and to go for a time another way. We are beginning to see, I think, why these revolutionary artists had to dissociate themselves from ballet and declare their independence of the "story dance." As a matter of fact, none of them rejected theatre or story in and of itself, nor irrevocably cut themselves off from the forms and the vocabulary of the ballet. The modern dance sought significant story from its very inception, as the programs of the late twenties abundantly testify; and it never really took its eyes off the stage. What these artists actually turned against was the stage and the story of outworn rituals and faiths; the tales of little loves and impotent passions; the theatre of tinsel and conspicuous display; the hollow traditions that cluttered the nineteenth-century graveyard of the past.

Like all artists of the recent decades, these dancers had to go for a time underground. When Martha Graham and Doris Humphrey and Charles Weidman left the Denishawn company for the garret, the studio and the recital hall, and when Hanya Holm left her native country for a foreign land, they deserted the only audience which dance at that time seemed to have. To all appearances it meant exile, and for generations there had been no "exile's return." What these artists risked, therefore, was another mournful episode in the history of "modern art": the starved artist and the moribund art; the aesthetic manifesto and the little cult; the personal tragedies and the post-mortem exploration; another *ism,* another religion of art, another series of spiritual, and even physical, suicides.

That none of this actually happened is, of course, the miracle of the modern dance. Instead of meeting the fate of the self-isolated artist, these dancers succeeded in reaching their goal, the creation of a new communal art. The factors accounting for this happy culmination are numerous, as one might expect. For one thing, these artists did not actually expatriate themselves, in either a physical or a spiritual sense. The decision, for example, to leave the Denishawns was in effect a decision to return to America. For the company had been essentially a venture in exoticism; the dance had tried to find its salvation in past cultures and foreign lands.

In the second place, Graham, Holm, Humphrey and Weidman had been thoroughly steeped in the sense of the theatre by their years with the Denishawns or the schooling in the tradition of Van Laban; it was in their blood. For all their act of revolt, they still wanted to create a theatre dance; and for all their isolation, they were never entirely cut off from the commercial stage. Although there were few opportunities to carry the new art into the established playhouses, yet as one thinks of the absolute isolation of a Cézanne or a Henry James, one is impressed not so much by the solitariness of these artists as by the luck which from time to time brought them even into Broadway productions. Furthermore, they saw to it from the start that they did not work alone. While for a time only the solo recital was practicable by way of a public performance, yet each artist gathered his or her own group, and thus continuously confronted the problems of the theatre dance.

In the third place, these artists were fortunate enough (again I am thinking of the tragic lives of so many of the nineteenth-century writers and painters) to make almost immediate personal contact with those who were to serve as the evangelists of the new dance and bring it into early contact with its natural audience. They were twentieth-century Americans, of tough fabric and sound stock, to an unusual extent unembarrassed by sensitive skins and the personal vagaries of the romantic artist. For them, to dance meant to dance with a group and for a people. They were thus ready to accept the challenge, for example, of the Bennington project when it came, if in fact they did not actually create the occasion for that challenge by a hearty reception of the teachers of dance in their own studios, and a readiness to take their dance at every opportunity into educational circles. They had the good judgment to see that a community comprising a cross-section of American life and including all kinds of ambitious dancers, from real talent to the "dub," was their métier. And one can in all justice say that Bennington served them well. It not only helped to build them a country-wide audience, but it presented in tangible, concrete form the need for an enlarged theatre dance.

To complete the story, this dance came to fruition in the days of the thirties, in the depression years, these years of taking stock and digging deeper into the American soil. It is a product of a time when the prodigal son came to himself and said, "I will arise and go to my father." So, it not only responded to the pressures of the economic, political and social stirrings under the New Deal, but felt intimately, and in a sense helped to create, its reborn Americanism and its renewed vision of the American dream.

What exactly is this theatre dance like? The answer to this question raises fundamental problems. How can dance have theatre content at all? How is it possible to express through movement alone that which exists originally in the form of the inner dream? How can dance become genuine theatre and still remain dance?

The past five years in dance have largely been spent in working out the solutions to these problems. The shrewd person will naturally suppose that there can be no right way to the exclusion of all others, and this guess is strikingly confirmed by the mature and highly characteristic work which the summer at Bennington brought forth from each of the major artists. *Opus 51, Dance of Work and Play* and *Dance Sonata, American Document,* and in its own vein *Passacaglia,* are all theatre dance, as we have defined it; all evoke feelings and passions, legends and presences which are deeply embedded in the American spirit. But no two approach the problem of the theatre dance in exactly the same way, and no two are alike. They are consequently worth studying as indications of the wide area of experience which the theatre dance is able to invade and occupy.

From the historical standpoint, the immediate import of Charles Weidman's *Opus 51* is its assimilation of the theatrical structure of the ballet. I have in mind not the forms of the court dance out of which the ballet grew, but the kind of spectacle which the ballet became, especially in its later development. *Opus 51* opens with a "Promenade"; it has a short solo recitative; it continues with a "Comedia," a pantomime in the authentic mode; it uses a solo and a duet form without introductory or transitional material; it concludes with a "Spectacle." The women are not afraid to look lovely; the men revel in acrobatics. Pantomime pervades the whole piece, pantomime reflected upon and abstracted until its chief point is dazzle of movement and the effect of irresistible aliveness which it evokes.

All this is in the spirit of the ballet. How then does *Opus 51* differ from the customary work in this form? Obviously, the vocabulary of movement is new, and it is immeasurably more vital and resourceful. From the standpoint of theatre, two other differences are even more significant. For one thing, the dance is surcharged with the spirit of the three-ringed circus (as John Martin in his review acutely observed); that is to say, an indigenous American entertainment-pattern dominates the artificialities of the old form and bends them to significant use. What pulls *Opus 51* together and gives it point is the myth of the ringmaster, embodied in Weidman with extraordinary energy and wit. He makes of himself a theatric presence around whom the life of the dance revolves and at whose beck and call it comes into being. It is a mature example of what his central artistic intent has perhaps always been, for Weidman belongs to the genus of lively spirits who in vaudeville, circus and burlesque have made the stage an excuse for the comic display of the vehemence that characterizes the American man of action, who builds far-flung empires and leads wild animals by the nose.

The material of his dance is thus inescapably American and as contemporary as the comic sheet. Weidman's art is, of course, built on an allusive base. Every movement has some subtle affinity to the gestures, the walk and the patter of the native American. The "dance" of it lies in the fact that the affinity is not labeled as such, so that one's conscious mind recognizes and identifies the gesture offhand. Gesture does become pantomime, but the pantomime in turn is transformed into dance by an identification of the dancer with the movement which he caricatures. Comedy is permeated by dance because the artist has succeeded in penetrating gesture to its core; he has got the essence of the ways in which men move. The result is that in its highest reaches, for instance the solo at the heart of *Opus 51,* the dance becomes an affirmation which another more believing age would have called godlike in quality and power. I trust that this does not sound too labored and esoteric, for that would imply a pretentiousness in Weidman's touch which is never so much as hinted at.

At first glance, the dance which Doris Humphrey has composed to Bach's *Passacaglia in C minor* might seem to signify that the artist has turned away from the interests which created *Theatre Piece, With My Red Fires* and *New Dance*. Actually, this is not the case. As one studies this latest work, it becomes apparent that it really furnishes the vantage point from which to inspect the particular theatrical quality that pervades the trilogy. For the *Passacaglia* is not a homage to Bach, a commentary on the notes of the music or an interpretation of it in terms of movement. What one experiences as the dance unfolds is an evocation springing directly from the rhythmic pattern that pulses measure by measure throughout the whole composition, and so worked out that the spiritual forces operating within the music come alive in the dance and make their presence magically felt.

In essence, music is the drama of passionate inner movement articulated in sound. Isadora Duncan was therefore on the right track when she turned to it in her search for the first movements of the dance. This is not the only road, as we shall see when we come to Martha Graham, and the artist who takes it has to sacrifice that type of the theatre which presents these same inner forces in dramatic conflict with outer circumstance. But there remains the inner drama which results when under favorable circumstances the energies of life flow freely according to their own laws; and Doris Humphrey has amply proved that this drama can be made the substance of theatre art.

Let it be further noted that theatre of this sort speaks with unusual directness to the American of today who is in any sense a cultivated person. Few other contemporary peoples have so wholeheartedly taken possession of the world of music. Its rhythms, its values, its very legendry impregnate and energize our present culture: they transform jazz at its best into the most intricate and elegant of folk music; they build a tonal land through which the motion picture walks; they send the college student out into the night to sing, as I have heard him do, the melodies of the *Ninth Symphony*.

The breath itself, felt as the pulse of time, is the germ of music, and it is out of this that Doris Humphrey builds her dance. I have intimated that the *Passacaglia* furnishes the best clue to the type of theatre which results from a dance so generated. The work is a mirror in which one comes to see how largely her trilogy (of *Theatre Piece, With My Red Fires* and *New Dance*) lies outside the region of drama when it is narrowly and technically defined. If the point of the trilogy actually were the external story—the conflict, for example, of the rebel artist and the maternal woman as they fight it out for supremacy—then I do not think that it would ever really come off. To carry across in that way, costumes, characterization and dialogue would have to be added, at least by the imagination, and the product would no longer be in the realm of the dance.

What the *Passacaglia* helps one to see is that Doris Humphrey's purpose really lies elsewhere. The conflicting forces, which on the stage or in the dance drama would become personages in the round, take form in the trilogy as movement themes whose interplay is as inner and harmonious as the motifs in a musical composition. Her theatre, in short, is not a matter of things, forces and events. It remains essentially personal and inwrought. The inner or symphonic drama constitutes the essence of her dance.

Hanya Holm, in her preoccupation with the delight of movement in space and with her remarkable sensitivity to that which is most vivid among the characteristics of the American people as a folk has, in *Dance of Work and Play* and in *Dance Sonata,* succeeded in bringing into being the substance of a theatre dance which has the vigor and the delicacy of a fairy tale that is not so much told as listened to. Obviously, I am using such terms as fairy tale and folk dance in a definitive rather than an historical sense. Hanya Holm derives none of her matter from the folklore of the past, and she is too intelligent and centrally organized an artist to go borrowing from the Savoy or the country barn.

Because of this she creates in many ways the most immediately exciting theatre of the contemporary dance, as those who witnessed *Trend* will testify. In her work one can always find rhythms that are dramatically conceived and developed, melodies in movement that take the breath away, and a stage which isn't a stage at all but the rallying ground of the openness which surrounds it, a center towards which dancers spring but from which they also continually fly. And never-ending movement; martial movement, waltz movement, rondo movement, grazioso movements. This is the dramatic force out of which her dance is generated. The plots-in-movement which result are as simple in their basic choreography as the folk dance; but their working out is subtle and refined, for this is the most tuneful and decorative of all these highly individualized idioms, and the most congenial to the suite basis on which the sonata is built.

One can say, then, that Hanya Holm has caught the American folk in its moments of pure excitement, exuberance and animal joy. Her dance is master of the mode of the "sheer": sheer pleasure, sheer good spirits, sheer dread, sheer anything you might choose to mention, provided it is all simple and direct and naïve. Whenever she can translate a question, a menace, a catastrophe, into a theme in space, she is ready to dance; and the audience dances with her in spirit. For we like to take our joys and our troubles out into a space which is as order-conscious as that which we have built with our complicated techniques, but which has regained the spontaneity and freedom of the great outdoors; and this is the theatre of Holm's dance.

The kind of theatre which *American Document* creates is, in my judgement, the most difficult challenge which the dance can accept. Dance is conceived as an expression of the power of the human spirit in actual relation with the external forces which aid or hinder man in his effort to live. Martha Graham's goal is thus a stupendous one: dance for her has to become what music was for Richard Wagner, a theatre presentation of the drama of man's experience, not in closed and locked innerness, but on the stage of realized things, forces and events.

Part of the difficulty which was bound to confront anyone who sought a dance of this sort was the universal prevalence in dance of a false method of approach. I refer to the traditional "dance drama," which involved the working out of stage plots through the medium of movement. Obviously this meant an attempt to suggest the actor, and the play as well , by a sort of half-revealed, half-hidden pantomime and a kind of intense emotionalism. Conceived in these terms, the dramatic dance was bound to fail; for when it was dance it was not drama, and when it was drama it was not dance.

The search for a dramatic dance was made more difficult by the fact that nothing else existed by way of a respectable American form which even indicated a solution along more valid lines. American art was singularly lacking in those techniques by which feelings are projected into things, and the very desire to do so was inhibited and repressed so far as conscious art-making was concerned. Even the dramatists who, like Eugene O'Neill, sensed how absolutely necessary it was, for the sake of art, to break down the wall of separation between passion and gesture, between motion and emotion, could manage to do so only by an act of violence. The melodrama of his plays is a measure of the effort required to storm the barrier and hold it against all inner attack.

The first thing Martha Graham had to do, therefore, was to expend her energies, regardless of the cost, on one objective, the forcing out of her deepest feelings into the light of day through the power of expressive movement. It was impossible to use a traditional alphabet of gesture in which movements were arbitrarily assigned meanings, nor was it sufficient simply to manufacture a new set of symbols. It was equally inadequate, as far as her particular quest was concerned, to allow mere movement to generate its own exciting life, as Weidman and Holm have done, or with Doris

Humphrey to create a ritual of the inner drama alone, valid as each of these approaches was for the particular artist who used it. A more radical departure had to be made.

I have said that Martha Graham found no help at this point in the recognized art traditions and values of her own country. This is true so far as her own race was concerned. But she did find a clue in the dance of the American Indian. It lies in even so small a matter as the difference between the American and the Indian way of taking the walk, the jump or the leap. The American habitually rises from the floor in order to fall back into it again; it is a negation of life (Martha Graham would say), a return to the earth unilluminated by the flight which has been made and uninformed by its joy. The Indian on the contrary habitually goes into the floor in order to spring from it into the air; for him, it is an affirmation, a sending forth of emotion into the open world. This difference she discovered in everything that the Indian did. She learned that he felt nothing which did not immediately and naturally spring into movement, which was not already of the nature of movement. It was this which made his dance dramatic.

From these beginnings, a long path had to be trodden before a dance like *American Document* was possible. One had to learn how to use the group and all its possible subdivisions as dramatically as one used oneself. A way had to be found to objectify the rhythm which sustained the life of the dance, so that its beat never died down or leaned solely upon the accompanying instrument. Since words are objectifications of feelings and values, the voice had to be used in a way that laid bare the roots of vocalization in movement and made of the word a *dramatis persona* in its own right. For the eye as well as for the muscles, the dance had to be so ordered that it would reveal, as in modern painting and architecture, the organization which feelings are capable of projecting into things. Finally one had to discover, if one could, a natural American art-form, indigenous but perhaps culturally unrecognized and by that very fact of serving as a vehicle of communication and as a mold into which the dance forms borrowed from western Europe could be poured and thus completely naturalized. All this had to come experimentally, with many uncertain starts and incomplete conclusions, while a partially bewildered public sensed both the power of the effort and the intimation of surer triumphs to come.

It is *American Document* which brings the long and arduous search to its consummation. Within the framework of the minstrel show it creates the most profoundly moving and completely satisfying dramatic dance which the writer has ever witnessed. The use of a despised and neglected folk-form is a touch of sheer genius; for it not only represents a triumph of communication but affords the most elastic structure conceivable for a documentary dance. The "Walk Around," in which the minstrel strut is transformed into a thing of transparent pride, introduces and concludes the dance and binds together its several segments. The end-men have become a diminutive pair whose unbounded energy and impudent thrust raise the traditional roles into a realm of delight. The interlocutor furnished the necessary excuse for the introduction of the voice; and what happens after it is there makes one realize that only an excuse was needed, for its presence is amply vindicated by the integral role which it plays in the dance.

Within this framework, then, the dance unfolds. The introductory theme of the "Walk Around" is immediately taken up by the two principals (*American Document* is Martha Graham's first use of a man dancer—Eric Hawkins of the American Ballet Caravan—in recent years) who transform it into an affirmation of the energy and faith out of which an independent republic was forged. Then, to words from the Declaration of Independence, comes a statement of the revolutionary spirit which, dispensing with the melodrama of battles and debates, asserts the passion for freedom and the determination to defend one's rights.

In the same directness and simplicity of manner, the Indian figure of the next dance evokes the love of the dispossessed for the country which was taken from them; the statement is deepened and enlarged by the interlocutor and group in *Lament for the Land*. As the occasion for the Puritan Episode which follows, the voice of the interlocutor brings the words of Jonathan Edwards and the "Song of Songs" into ironic opposition. The "Walk Around," always taking up the transition, opens the way for the next episode, a dance of emancipation.

A quick transition, and the interlocutor calls to mind "things we are ashamed of . . . Sacco-Vanzetti, share-croppers, the Scottsboro boys . . ." to the eloquent accompaniment of the group dance; and enumerates the grounds for our pride: "Our land, our rights, the word, Democracy." The new age finds expression in a haughty variation on the cake-walk, punctuated by the end-men with cart-wheels. Then we face today with its challenge of injustice, want and war. "We are three women; we are three million women; we are the mothers of the hungry dead; we are the mothers of the hungry living"—done with voice and movement in antiphonal response. We are confronted with ourselves. "I am a man; I am a million men. I have a fear; it is you. I have a faith; it is myself. I have a hope; it is you"—again with voice and dancer in dramatic duet. The dance of Declaration returns and, for the last time, the "Walk Around," amplified and heightened for a quick climax and "Good-night."

I have gone into some detail because only by outlining the content of the work can one gain some conception of the magnitude of the conquest here achieved in the dramatic dance. It is the old dance drama in essential aim, but completely transformed by the integrity of an art which has swept away all excrescences and subterfuges and relied solely on the resources that dance is able to summon and order. With *American Document* the most difficult problem of the theatre dance is solved. What we do with that solution remains to be seen.

January 1939

* *

CECIL SMITH

*

The Maze of the Heart

IN HER FORTNIGHT'S SEASON at the Ziegfeld Theatre, Martha Graham spread out a panorama of her dances, ranging chronologically from *Primitive Mysteries* (1931) to her newest works, *Errand into the Maze* and *Cave of the Heart.* It was revealing to discover that in so generous a survey of her repertory she chose to include only *Primitive Mysteries* as a representative example of the long list of abstract, non-theatrical compositions to which she de-voted herself in her earlier years. Not a single dance composed between 1931 and 1939, the date of *Every Soul Is a Circus,* was given a place in her schedule. Clearly she now regards herself as a theatre artist, and does not feel that the early pieces—many of which were magnificent examples of "pure dance"—are suited to her present following.

Many admirers of more familiar kinds of dancing find it hard to discover and become reconciled to the clouded subliminal world of experience into which Miss Graham's artistic instinct impels her. An initial obstacle to many, no doubt, is the fact that her movement and choreography are seldom superficially decorative, and certainly decorativeness is never their main quality. Unlike ballet, Miss Graham's choreography does not consist of variants upon authorized steps and positions and leaps and lifts, nor does it concern itself with the surface details of simple narratives. It displays the body as a dynamic and often tortured organism, not as a lovely and graceful spectacle. It is less intent upon inducing pleasure than sympathy, compassion and an aesthetic satisfaction bordering on tragic catharsis. For these reasons extensive acquaintance with ballet is frequently more of a hindrance to the appreciation of Martha Graham than a preparation for it. Those who approach her art without a predilection for the utterly different gratifications of ballet are likely to meet her half way more readily than those who expect to find qualities in her dancing which are not there nor meant to be.

Each of Martha Graham's more recent compositions—to employ an Aristotelian description—is an imitation of the movement or progress of certain passions in the human soul. For instance, when she derives the theme of *Deaths and Entrances* from the cramped life history of the Brontë sisters, she does not fabricate a choreographic biography. No outward happenings in the lives of the sisters are specifically portrayed as they would be in a story ballet; nor do the various dancers in the cast represent actual people the sisters knew. Underneath the frustration, the lonely bitterness, of the three sisters there are unuttered hopes and half articulate dreams which come to life in memories of the past. Through pure dance movement, aided by evocative costumes and a goblet and some chess men to which the sisters attach memories, we understand or at least sense the repressed gaiety, the love implicitly proffered but never asked for or accepted, the festering ingrown hate, the ultimate madness when womanly feelings are irrevocably thwarted from fruition, all of which constitute the sum total of these three tightly circumscribed lives. Yet to grasp the meaning of *Deaths and Entrances* one need never have heard of the Brontës; other human souls have known the same "restless pacings of the heart," the same "deaths and entrances" of hopes and loves.

All of Martha Graham's dances—even the comic ones, *Every Soul Is a Circus* and *Punch and the Judy*—take place in this veiled and perplexed world of the inner consciousness. Though she is essentially a dramatist, she is not concerned with the development of a plot. Her dances are dramas of character, and the figures in them are like Hamlet or Hedda Gabler, in that we are asked to be more interested in the state of their souls than in their practical actions. We encounter the converse of *Deaths and Entrances* in *Letter to the World,* in which the addition of Emily Dickinson's verse to the dancing results in a poetic sublimation of frustration. We see the nameless fear of the unknown in *Herodiade;* the triumph over fear in *Errand into the Maze;* the love which destroys its object in *Cave of the Heart;* the frankness of sexuality in *Dark Meadow;* the optimism and exaltation of new hope in *Appalachian Spring.*

The whole rich complexity of Miss Graham's scrutiny of the secret heart does not always make itself completely clear, even to the initiated, on first seeing. Through years of painful and self-abnegating creative exploration she has gradually found the only way in which she can say exactly what she means to. She has a right to expect us not to be trivial or impatient in our effort to discern and experience the nature of her discoveries. And the effort is deeply rewarding, for her compositions vivify and transfigure the turmoil of personal emotion, in isolation from the distracting attributes of particular people, events, times and places.

The Graham idiom permits the body to move without using a predetermined vocabulary of steps, leaps, attitudes and sequences of all these devices. A constantly variable and plastic movement is based upon such principles as the acceptance or rejection of the pull of gravity, tension and relaxation of the muscles and extension or contraction of the arms and legs. The particular movement employed at any moment has a double reason for its choice: it must be the physical corollary of the facet of the emotions that is to be revealed; and it must be related as visual thematic material to other movements employed in the formal construction of the piece.

No movement or succession of movements is ever selected because it is dictated in advance by the external requirements of a style. It would be misleading, nevertheless, to imply that no such thing as an identifiable Graham style exists. If it did not, Iva Kitchell's hilarious parody, *Soul in Search,* would have no point, nor would Miss Graham's frolicsome spoofing of her own mannerisms in *Every Soul Is a Circus.* Obviously, the kind of subject-matter which preoccupies her causes certain genres of movement and gesture to appear frequently enough to be characteristic and recognizable. On the other hand, ballet devices seldom appear at all, for their presence might arouse associations which would deflect the spectator's attention from Miss Graham's quite different goal. In theory, the idiom of ballet is part of the total range of movement upon which she is entitled to draw, but in practice its stylizations are never safe around for her unless she wishes deliberately to invoke its light and frivolous implications.

As I have already suggested, Miss Graham's way of evolving a consecutive, organized form involves a double reference. In each work, appropriate solo or group movements follow one another as reflections of the succession of passions which makes the work a psychological continuity; and the same movements relate to one another as purely constructional elements, much as the themes in a symphony are structural materials at the same time that they are emotionally expressive.

Because her processes of composition closely parallel those of the musical composer, Miss Graham has been able to achieve a remarkable integration of her dances with the musical scores. (In ballet an equally incontrovertible unity of music and dance is found today only in the choreography of George Balanchine.) There is no rule of thumb about her adaptation of the dance to the music. Each score presents a new challenge to find the treatment which will bring choreography and music most intimately together without inhibiting the full realization of either.

Her musicianship has developed slowly. In *Letter to the World* and *Deaths and Entrances* the Hunter Johnson scores may best be described as utility music. They enable the dancers to function successfully, and they evoke some appropriate mood and theatrical tension, but the composer propounds no particularly arresting musical ideas, nor does he grant his themes much more than a rather primitive and repetitive sort of development. In Louis Horst's scores for *El Penitente* and *Primitive Mysteries* the musical values are much more delectable, but this music can scarcely have presented much of a problem to Miss Graham, since years of association with her as musical director of the company have given Mr. Horst, as both composer and conductor, a phenomenal intuition of her needs.

The more recent scores by Aaron Copland (*Appalachian Spring*), Samuel Barber (*Cave of the Heart*), Gian-Carlo Menotti (*Errand into the Maze*) and Paul Hindemith (*Herodiade*) are quite another matter. Composers of this stature are not willing to obscure their individuality, water down their ideas or stunt the normal development of their materials. Yet in every one of these works Miss Graham has been able to preserve the phrasing, structure and eloquent design of the music without either merely borrowing its patterns or allowing it to diminish choreographic spontaneity. The score of *Herodiade* was the hardest to cope with. Mr. Hindemith, who always likes to invent obstacles to be overcome in his own compositions, required himself to write music which rigorously follows the rhythm of the Mallarmé poem which furnished the original suggestion for the dance. The trouble with this tour de force is that the finished dance has little to do with the poem and nothing whatever to do with its word rhythms.

Only once has Miss Graham been forced to ignore a score. The Carlos Chavez music for *Dark Meadow* is largely an old string quartet taken from the shelf to fulfil a commission from the Library of Congress. Since the music has little or no choreographic implication, she met the difficulty—rather than affront Mexico's leading musician by rejecting his contribution—by devising one of her most faultlessly organized dances, letting the music play along harmlessly while the dance carries the whole burden.

The enigmatic title of *Errand into the Maze,* the only totally new work of the New York season, comes from a poem by Ben Belitt, describing the "errand-journey into the maze of the heart in order to face and do battle with the creature of fear." The scenario, deriving from the myth of Theseus and the Minotaur, requires only two dancers, Miss Graham and Mark Ryder. Mr. Menotti has written his best score, demonstrating a far more resourceful command of theatrical expression than he showed in *The Medium*. But *Errand into the Maze* is still imperfect and unfinished, for there is no real choreographic tension between the Creature of Fear and the protagonist.

For herself Miss Graham has created a crescendo of terrified movements, twisting distractedly about the stage at first, and finally developing the power and thrust which enable her to overcome the Creature. It is essentially a solo dance, and before it can assume final shape Miss Graham will have to decide either to dispense with the puppet Minotaur altogether or to give him something more meaningful to do.

It will be a more commanding achievement the next time we see it, if it follows the example of *Cave of the Heart.* When this latter work was first given at Columbia University, under the title *Serpent Heart,* it was a daring but wayward and uncoordinated experiment in high-voltage theatricality. Now, a year later, its ambiguities and obscurities have been eliminated, it has been improved in taste and its action moves in a straight line to a truly awesome denouement, in which Miss Graham's Medea-like figure reveals the horrid blood-lust of a soul which must destroy the one it loves. Although it awakens memories of *Salome, Cave of the Heart* is not a fabrication of sensationalism, for it now possesses a sufficient idealization and aesthetic detachment, and even a certain moral force.

The revival of *Primitive Mysteries* indicated that we have lost as much as we have gained by Miss Graham's abandonment of abstract and universalized materials. A series of three profound religious celebrations danced by Miss Graham and sixteen girls, its simple but wonderfully varied and fluid geometric configurations realize an undisturbed beauty of group movement which she has never again attained so completely. I should select *Primitive Mysteries* as her supreme masterpiece, and certainly it is one of the great dance compositions of our time.

May 1947

WILL MARION COOK

*

Clorindy, the Origin of the Cakewalk

[*When Will Marion Cook, composer of many favorite songs, died, he left an unfinished autobiographical manuscript. This excerpt tells how the first all-Negro show came to Broadway in 1898.*—THE EDITORS.]

WHEN BERT WILLIAMS and George Walker met in California, the Negro god of comedy and drama must have opened his thick lips and wide mouth and laughed loud, long, raucously! After failures around the country in medicine shows and cheap vaudeville houses, the team found themselves at French Lick Springs where Canary, George W. Lederer's partner, happened to catch their act. Immediately he put them on a train for New York and Lederer's Casino Theatre, where the famous producer introduced them between the acts of *The Gold Bug*. They swamped New York and then went on to one of the longest runs that had ever been made at Koster and Bial's. That was where I came into the picture.

Since I had come to New York to learn to write good music, I met Williams and Walker and gave them my ideas on creating a story of how the cakewalk came about in Louisiana in the early Eighteen Eighties. *Clorindy, the Origin of the Cakewalk* was the result and though, when the time came, Williams and Walker were unable to play in it, it was for them that I wrote the show.

But all that came later. At our first meeting Williams and Walker made a few suggestions to me and then introduced me to their manager, Will McConnell, who lent me ten dollars to go back home to Washington. I was barred anyhow from the classes at the National Conservatory of Music because I wouldn't play my fiddle in the orchestra under Dvorak. I couldn't play; my fingers had grown too stiff. Dvorak didn't like me anyway; Harry T. Burleigh was his pet. Only John White, the harmony and counterpoint teacher, thought I had talent, and insisted that I attend his classes.

With McConnell's ten dollars I returned home with my tremendous idea. After a long siege of persuasion, I finally got Paul Laurence Dunbar to consent to write the *Clorindy* libretto (which was never used) and a few of the lyrics. We got together in the basement of my brother John's rented house on Sixth Street, just below Howard University, one night about eight o'clock. We had two dozen bottles of beer, a quart of whiskey, and we took my brother's porterhouse steak, cut it up with onions and red peppers and ate it raw. Without a piano or anything but the kitchen table, we finished all the songs, all the libretto and all but a few bars of the ensembles by four o'clock the next morning. By that time Paul and I were happy, so happy that we were ready to cry "Eureka!" only we couldn't make any noise at that hour so both of us sneaked off to bed, Paul to his house three blocks away and I to my room.

The following morning, or rather later that morning, I was at John's piano trying to learn to play my most Negroid song, "Who Dat Say Chicken in Dis Crowd?" My mother, who was cooking my breakfast, came into the parlor, tears streaming from her eyes, and said:

"Oh, Will! Will! I've sent you all over the world to study and become a great musician, and you return such a nigger!" My mother was a graduate of Oberlin in the class of 1865 and thought that a Negro composer should write just like a white man. They all loved the Dunbar lyrics but weren't ready for Negro songs.

After the writing of *Clorindy,* many days are to elapse before I get any kind of action. Williams and Walker come through Washington with the Hyde and Behman show, on their way to the coast. They listen to my music and, after praising it highly, again get McConnell to lend me ten dollars, so that I may go to New York and play it for Isidore Witmark, the head of Witmark and Sons, then located in Thirty-seventh Street just beyond Broadway.

That weekend I go to New York. McConnell makes an appointment by telephone for me for Saturday afternoon at one o'clock which was the Saturday closing hour. After keeping me waiting for two hours, the cooling-off process, Isidore Witmark comes into the large front professional office and curtly says, "Go ahead! What's you got?" I am not now and never have been a great pianist, and I could sing only a little bit, but for forty minutes I struggled to give this man some idea of the songs and ensembles. At last, starting for the door of his private office, he interrupted me long enough to say that he thought I must be crazy to believe that any Broadway audience would listen to Negroes singing Negro opera.

There I was, on a Saturday afternoon in New York, with only a few pennies in my pocket, and no place to eat or sleep. I started to walk to the Twenty-third Street ferry, hoping for some good luck and found it. An old pal of mine, Sol Johnson, was on the same boat, on his way to the Penn Depot in Jersey City, where he was a porter on the Washington train. As his train did not leave until night, I loafed about for a while. Later he locked me in a closed dining car, telling me to be quiet until we reached Washington.

And so I got back, hungry, mad with the world and heart-broken at such a failure. It took me some months to recover my spirit, and by this time my brother John, who worked at the pension office and was always good for a touch, became disgusted with the whole idea and wanted me to go to work at something that would at least take care of me. What was more tragic, he even refused to lend me any more money! Bill Higgins, secretary to Congressman White, one of the last colored congressmen from North Carolina, lent me ten dollars. Higgins had been a classmate of my brother at Howard University.

This time it's do or die. So I hunt up Sol Johnson again, and again he hides me on his train, but he charges me two dollars for the favor, since I seem to have become a regular passenger. A long, long struggle and much suffering is to ensue until George Archer, head usher at the Casino Roof Garden, says, "Why don't you go to see Ed Rice? His office is in the Standard Theatre Building at Sixth Avenue and Thirty-second Street. He runs the show up on George Lederer's Roof and needs an outstanding attraction."

For weeks, whenever I could get three or four of my prospective cast together or find a place to rehearse, I had been teaching them the *Clorindy* music. I taught them with or without a piano; sometimes just singing or trying to sing the different parts. But this was a genius aggregation, Negro talent that had made much of little. And besides, they believed in me.

As directed by George Archer, I went to see Ed Rice, and I saw him every day for a month. Regularly, after interviewing a room full of people, he would say to me (I was always the last): "Who are you, and what do you want?" On the thirty-first day—and by now I am so discouraged that this is my last try—I heard him tell a knockabout act: "Come up next Monday to rehearsal, do a show and, if you make good, I'll keep you on all the week."

I was desperate. My feet, with soles worn through, were burnt black by walking on the hot cobblestones of New York streets. I was hungry almost all the time, except when I could meet Harry Burleigh, who had recently become soloist in St. George's Church. He only made a small salary but always had enough to treat me to coffee and crullers at a little dairy called Cushman's, on the corner of Fifteenth Street and Third Avenue, or to a twenty-five-cent dinner at a German restaurant near Union Square.

On leaving Rice's office, I went at once to the Greasy Front, a Negro club run by Charlie Moore, with a restaurant in the basement managed by Mrs. Moore. There I was sure to find a few members of my ensemble. I told them a most wonderful and welcome story; we were booked at the Casino Roof! And I sent them to contact all the others. Everybody was notified to be at the Casino Roof Garden on Monday at eleven a.m. Only Ernest Hogan, my comedian, could not be reached because, unless he was working (and sometimes even then), he stayed up all night carousing. Consequently he slept all day. Just to play safe, I sent him a note in care of his landlady. "We were booked!" I exclaimed. That was probably the most beautiful lie I ever told.

Hogan, whose real name was Rube Crowders, had become my comedian because Williams and Walker, for whom *Clorindy* had been written, had been delayed on the Coast by the terrific success of the Hyde and Behman show. I had come in contact with Hogan one day in the back room of the Greasy Front where I was playing "Who Dat Say Chicken?" for a couple of unimpressed comedians. Suddenly I heard a full-bellied laugh and a loud but musical voice: "That's great, son! Who are you? Come on and have a glass of beer."

As I went into the front room to join the man who had called me, Charlie Moore whispered: "That's Ernest Hogan, leading comic with Black Patti's Troubadours, and the man who wrote 'All Coons Look Alike to Me.' He's a great comedian and can do lots for you." That same night Hogan learned "Who Dat Say Chicken?" and my "Hottes' Coon in Dixie."

Back to *Clorindy*. On Monday morning, in answer to my call, every man and woman, boy and girl that I had taught to sing my music was at the Casino Roof. Strange to say, Hogan was the first one to show up.

Luckily for us, John Braham, the English conductor of the Casino orchestra, was a brick. And, still more luckily for us, Ed Rice did not appear at rehearsal that morning until very late. When Braham had finished with the smaller acts, he turned to me questioningly. There I sat, orchestra books in hand. In two minutes I told him how I had studied violin under Joachim, a bit of composition under Dvorak, harmony and mighty little counterpoint under John White. I explained that I had some new music, a Negro operetta. Right then he stopped me, turned to his orchestra men and said: "Gentlemen, a new composer!" He held out his hand for my orchestra parts. Again I got his ear and told him that my singers understood my direction, they understood my gestures and that I was afraid . . . He again turned and announced: "Gentlemen, a new composer and a new conductor."

By this time my singers were grouped on the stage and I started the opening chorus, an orchestral and choral development of "Darktown Is Out Tonight." Remember, reader, I had twenty-six of the finest Negro voices in America, twenty-six happy, gifted Negroes, who saw maybe weeks of work and money before them. Remember, too, that they were singing a new style of music. Like a mighty anthem in rhythm, these voices rang out.

Rice must have heard the voices and the pulsing Darktown rhythm as he came up Broadway, but his only comment when he came was shouted to Braham: "No nigger can conduct my orchestra on Broadway!" And Braham—God bless him! and He must still be blessing him if there be a place for the great-hearted—simply said: "Ed, go back to your little cubby-hole"—Rice had a little pagoda at one end of the roof, where he "entertained" some of his pretty girls after the show at night—"Go back to your little cubby-hole and keep quiet! That boy's a genius and has something great!"

Well, we didn't get on that Monday night after all. It rained pitchforks until about nine o'clock and the Roof, which was uncovered, was in no condition to receive the high-class habitués. We were sent home about nine-thirty. A more disappointed bunch of people you've never seen. I was heartbroken. Another failure! Was I never to get going? Only Hogan was in good spirits. He had taken charge of things by now, and had spent the day staging the different numbers. Naturally, he had eliminated Dunbar's dialogue, for a lot of dialogue on an uncovered roof garden after eleven p.m. would have been impossible. Hogan also hurriedly gathered three or four sensational dancers. He seemed to know everybody. In short, it was just as well that we didn't go on that night, for Hogan really needed the extra time to whip the dancers into shape, especially the cakewalk. After all, our subtitle was "The Origin of the Cakewalk" and we mustn't fall down on that part of the performance.

Our opening for Rice was postponed until the following Monday and by then all was ready. About 11:45 Mr. Price, Rice's manager, made the simple announcement that the Negro operetta, *Clorindy, The Origin of the Cakewalk,* would now be produced for the first time on any stage. Immediately I struck up the introduction and opening chorus. When I entered the orchestra pit, there were only about fifty people on the Roof. When we finished the opening chorus, the house was packed to suffocation. What had happened was that the show downstairs in the Casino Theatre was just letting out. The big audience heard those heavenly Negro voices and took to the elevators. At the finish of the opening chorus, the applause and cheering were so tumultuous that I simply stood there transfixed, my hand in the air, unable to move until Hogan rushed down to the footlights and shouted: "What's the matter, son? Let's go!"

So I started his strut song, which began and ended with an ensemble, "Hottes' Coon." This was hardly Dunbar's finest lyric, but the chorus, the dancers and the inimitable Ernest Hogan made that Broadway audience think it was. The rest of the performance kept them at the same pitch, especially "Who Dat Say Chicken in Dis Crowd?" This number (which Rice had thought too slow) had to be repeated ten times before Hogan could leave the stage, and there were encores galore when Belle Davis sang "Jump Back, Honey, Jump Back!"

The Darktown finale was of complicated rhythm and bold harmonies, and very taxing on the voice. My chorus sang like Russians, dancing meanwhile like Negroes, and cakewalking like angels, black angels! When the last note was sounded, the audience stood and cheered for at least ten minutes. This was the finale which Witmark had said no one would listen to. It was pandemonium, but never was pandemonium dearer to my heart as I stood there sweating in Charles W. Anderson's old full dress coat (Charlie weighed 200 pounds; I, 126), Harry T. Burleigh's vest (Harry was very short; I, quite tall) and my own out-at-the-seat and frayed-at-the-cuffs light street pants, and the same feet-mostly-on-the-ground shoes. These, with a clean shirt and tie (thank heaven), completed my evening clothes.

But did that audience take offense at my rags and lack of conducting polish? Not so you could notice it! We went on at 11:45 and finished at 12:45. Boy, oh boy! Maybe, when the pearly gates open wide and a multitude of hosts march in, shouting, laughing, singing, emoting, there will be a happiness which slightly resembles that of *Clorindy's* twenty-six participants. I was so delirious that I drank a glass of water, thought it wine and got gloriously drunk. Negroes were at last on Broadway, and there to stay. Gone was the uff-dah of the minstrel! Gone the Massa Linkum stuff! We were artists and we were going a long, long way. We had the world on a string tied to a runnin' red-geared wagon on a down-hill pull. Nothing could stop us, and nothing did for a decade.

September 1947

* *

RICHARD RODGERS

*

How to Write Music in No Easy Lessons—A Self Interview

AS AN ALLEGED COMPOSER I am asked certain questions with regularity. It appears that the average person considers musical composition either one of the darkest of the black arts or the result of heaven-sent compulsion. There is never any between ground. Resorting to analogy for answers doesn't help much, but I try it. I say: "Look, you have to write a letter to your Aunt Tessie, a rich old gal who will eventually die. You'd like the letter to be a good one. You have certain equipment at your disposal, such as pen, ink, paper and, most important of all, your knowledge of the language. You're on your own, and the quality of your letter will depend largely on how well you are able to use your equipment. My problem is the same, only translated into terms of music. Aunt Tessie is the public or, frequently, my own satisfaction. My equipment consists of paper, pencil, piano, the ability to hum, whistle or sing (horribly) and a knowledge of musical language acquired in the theatres, on the streets and in serious study." I lean back with a glow of self-admiration, having drawn what I consider a pretty clear analogy. Then the next question comes: "But, Mr. Rodgers, where do you get your inspiration?" So I take a drink.

Another time-consumer is, "Which comes first—the words or the music?" The worst part about this query is that it makes sense. It is logical and it demands a logical answer. Actually, there is no set procedure whatsoever. My favorite blight and partner, Mr. Lorenz Hart, often hands me a completed lyric to be set to music. More often I have a tune ready for him to work on, the tune being what it is because it seems to fit a given situation in a musical play and not because the composer was the victim of a rush of hot inspiration, brought on by a beautiful girl or a breath-taking sunset. (I guess you can see I'm pretty sensitive about inspiration.) Sometimes we sit in a room and hate each other until we get a title; then I throw Larry out of the house and fool around until I get a satisfactory melody, inspired entirely by the title and not by nostalgia for Venice in the spring.

"Don't you and Hart ever fight?" And how! Though I must explain that the fighting is all on a theoretical basis. It is difficult to prove this, but in over twenty years of coping with each other we have never had a disagreement over policy or credit or money or, for that matter, any of the things that cause partners to part.

"How did you happen to meet?" That is a bad question because the answer is just what it ought to be. When I was sixteen and still in high school a friend of mine, Phil Leavitt, told me he would like to introduce me to a fellow called Hart. It appeared that this Hart knew something about lyric writing but had no composer. I knew something about composing (Leavitt speaking) but had no lyricist. We ought to get together. On a Sunday afternoon I was taken to Larry's house. Larry came to the door himself, dressed in his Tuxedo trousers, an undershirt and house slippers. He was shy, as he still is, and I don't believe the ice was broken until a disreputable cat ambled into the room. "That's Bridget," said Mr. Hart. "She's an old fence-walker!" He chortled with glee at the joke and rubbed his hands furiously together, a nervous habit of his. There was a sudden crashing "BONG" that lifted me out of my chair. Hart told me not to be frightened. It was his mother's clock and it just did that. Bridget has long since gone to her cat-heaven where fences are brought to her, but that clock still bongs and I still jump.

Well, we sat around and talked theatre and song-writing. I played some tunes for him, about which he was highly agreeable, and he told me his ideas about lyric writing. He was violent on the subject of rhyming in songs, feeling that the public was capable of understanding better things than the current monosyllabic juxtaposition of "slush" and "mush." It made great good sense and I was enchanted by this little man and his ideas. Neither of us mentioned it, but we evidently knew we'd work together, and I left Hart's house having acquired in one afternoon a career, a partner, a best friend and a source of permanent irritation.

"What do you feel like on opening nights?" That's a cinch. Like death! Larry is more fortunate than I am on these occasions since he is able to work off the nervous tension by walking up and down in back of the audience, cursing softly if a joke fails to get a laugh and rubbing his hands vehemently if a song goes over well. I seem compelled to take it sitting down. I cringe in the last row where I can run to the nearest exit in case of mis-fire. The awful thing about an opening night is that you can't trust anyone or anything to supply you with an accurate indication as to the success or failure of the show. It is madness to listen to people since they are invariably the victims of wish-fulfillment, wanting the piece to be good or bad, depending entirely on their personal attitude toward you. After hearing ultimate failures cheered passionately on an opening night and seeing great successes received with complete coldness you can't even trust the evidence of your own ears. I was badly confused the night *I Married an Angel* opened. I was sure the audience didn't like it and I said so. It took great reviews in the papers and weeks of capacity business to convince me.

"Do tunes come to you in the middle of the night?" NO! No tunes have ever come to me anywhere. I've had to go to them. I've heard about the boys who get swell ideas in taxis, bathtubs and my-baby's-arms, but not me. I have to beat myself into submission by picturing the boy and girl on the stage and imagining what they are singing to the accompaniment of a full orchestra in the pit and a full audience in the house. Then I am ready to start searching for a melody that will conform to a number of arbitrary conditions. To begin with, I write scores and not isolated song numbers; therefore the particular song in question must bear a family resemblance to the other musical material in the piece. However, since change of pace is almost the first rule of showmanship, I must see to it that this number is in sharp contrast with the one preceding it and the one to follow. These conditioning elements have obviously narrowed the scope of choice, but that is not the end. Who is to sing the song? If our soprano has sound vocal ability she may be given something with range, otherwise it is best to confine the melody to the conventional octave. The size and instrumentation of the orchestra have their bearing, since this is to be a composition for voice and orchestra.

There was a time, in Victor Herbert's day, when scores were orchestrated by their composers. A successful operetta would run for a year or two or three. Thus the composer had time for the laborious business of orchestration. All that has changed. Shows do not run as long, and sheet music stops selling after a few months at best. That means more shows, if a living is to be made, and no time for orchestration. Fortunately there are fine musicians available whose work is to orchestrate for the theatre, and it is this process which I must bear in mind as I write. With the aid of the piano I can readily hear the orchestra. I make a rather complicated manuscript of the song, indicating orchestral figures, and I confer at length with the orchestrator. All that insures the absence of nasty surprises at the first orchestra rehearsal.

If all these problems appear to be obstacles, let me assure you that that is not the case. They are a definite aid in the sense that they provide sign-posts, speed-indicators, warnings and helpful hints along the otherwise nebulous road of composition. They also must make it obvious why "tunes do not come to you in the middle of the night." As for my sparkling collaborator, not once in all these years has he called me on the phone to say, "Hey, I got a great idea for a song!" so I guess it goes for him too.

"Do you think the critics are fair?" Eminently so. I do think, however, that many of them approach a new musical comedy with certain handicaps. Most of them fall into the "I don't know anything about music but I know what I like" category. It's true that the majority of the audience also belongs in that class but, considering the fact that music is less capable than words of appreciation on first hearing, it would be helpful if the boys had a somewhat sharper musical perception which would enable them to tell the public what to expect from a score. On the other hand the critics are enormously appreciative of novelty, whether in a scenic device or a little twist in a lyric. The obvious value of this attitude is that by encouraging the writer to experiment it prevents the theatre becoming a static and inevitably moribund medium.

"Do you get a kick out of hearing your songs played?" Only a liar would say he didn't. There are few experiences so soothing to the ego as that of turning on a radio and hearing something you've written come jumping out at you. This pleasure is sometimes sharply balanced by pain when some maniacal "arranger" goes to town and orchestrates your work out of existence. There has in the past few years been a curious development in the dance-orchestra business which has apparently made it imperative for each band to have its particular personality. Because one saxophone player sounds relatively like another on the radio, the only way in which this personality stamp can be acquired is through orchestration. Turn your dial and get "Gus Gump and His Gurgling Goofs." Gus has decided that he wants his band to be recognized by the fact that his music gurgles, therefore both "Jeepers-Creepers" and "Smoke Gets in Your Eyes," though dissimilar in intent, sound like soup being drawn through Jo Davidson's beard. One bright lad has found it useful to make his saxophones play flat as a means of identification! I cannot believe that this is not deliberate as nobody could play as flat as that by accident. This sourness combined with an over-warm vibrato produces the same effect as herring with chocolate sauce, but the man is famous. Consider, also, the exhibitionist who is convinced that his harmony is better than yours. Over your signature he endows your melody with harmonization that is generally in bad taste if not downright unsound. It is as though the editors of this periodical took this article and invested it with incorrect spelling, bad grammar and more vulgarisms than it already possesses. (*Note to Ed.*: Please check grammar and spelling.) To offset the damaging influence of such relations, there are many times when a mediocre composition is lifted into importance by a brilliant orchestration and a loving performance.

All in all, writing musical shows is a fine way to earn a living. There are many complaints about union unfairness but nobody mentions the fact that the quality of theatre musicians is extraordinarily high, and that stage-hands are invariably capable. There are letters to the *Times* mentioning only the lack of politeness in box-office treasurers but nobody realizes that they are patient, good-natured people for the most part, who go to work behind the grille of a hit show at eight-thirty in the morning and leave for home after midnight. With the lurid tales about chorus girls' activities nobody seems willing to believe that they are the kindest, most loyal group of people in the world. Out of something like thirty shows only once has a producer tried to cheat me. You would be amazed if I told you his name.

Yes, it's a fine way to earn a living, even if you do have to answer a lot of questions.

October 1939

* *

IRVING KOLODIN

*

Folk Songs

VARIATIONS ON A THEME

IT IS A CURIOUS THING, considering the exhaustive literature of folk-song, that so much attention has been devoted to assembling the contribution of a single locality or country, and so little to the comparative study of these creations or to the basic phenomena of the folk-song itself. More than anything else, it is engrossing to consider the eventual destination of the folk-song—whether it is ever absorbed in sophisticated art-literature or whether, once a thought attains its ultimate folk-form, it remains a thing apart.

It is well known that much of the early liturgical music (as recently as the middle of the sixteenth century) was based on folk-tunes, street songs and worse, whose occurrence during a service often recalled distinctly uncanonical texts to the devotees. In fact, the Council of Trent, sitting in 1555, was called upon to aid in stamping out this rowdy practice from the organized Church, and it was one of Palestrina's supreme achievements to establish the model of what a mass should be. In the Protestant Church, the custom persisted as late as the time of Bach, nearly two hundred years afterward. His "In dir ist Freude" was originally a *Balletto* from a collection of Giovanni Gastoldi, as was also his "Jesu, wollst uns weisen." Another of his eloquent chorales, "Was mein Gott will, das g'scheh allzeit," was in its first form a French love song, and the equally devout "Durch Adams Fall ist ganz verderbt" came into being as a soldier's chant at the battle of Pavia.

Such resurgences are comparatively infrequent in the music of our day, save they be introduced frankly as extraneous material for the precise purpose of lending a national character to a formalized work, as in the "Rasoumovsky" quartets of Beethoven, the misnamed "New World" Symphony of Dvorak, certain of the Tschaikowsky symphonies; and the reason for this is not remote. The apparent exhaustion of the secular influence (in its unconscious aspects) is coincident with the rise of secular music from the seventeenth century onward. Previously there had been only formal church music and undisciplined folk-expression. The *same* folk-impulse manifested itself in the works of Bach, Handel, Mozart, and so forth; but it expressed itself through an individual with a specialized training and a definite identity, rather than through an anonymous spirit of great eloquence but limited means of expression. The blending of the contrapuntal technique of the church-musician—which had been developing for eight centuries—with the rich vitality of the folk-spirit gave to the world a kind of music it had never possessed before—the literature we know, in all its permutations, as Western music, from Bach to Sibelius. Yet the number of potentially valuable spirits who were exposed to a formalized training was necessarily limited; and so there has remained an accumulating folk-literature, just as there has remained an accumulating literature of church music.

That any infusion of culture is fatal to the retention of the pure folk-song quality is excellently illustrated in our own country, with its great variety of races and influences. While it is true that folk-songs exist, in a sense, in the midst of our most highly mechanized society (in the play-games of children at school, for example) yet as a fact of life, an experience and expression of the people themselves, they still thrive only in the rural communities. And the more remote the settlement from the centers of civilization, the closer the perpetuation is to the form in which it was first given to the world.

This is aptly shown in the folk-song known in English as the "Briery Bush" (and as a variety of other things in Finnish, Russian, Sicilian and Esthonian) of which the first verse is:

O hangman stay thy hand
And stay it for a while
For I fancy I see my father
A-coming across the yonder stile.

In Virginia, where the song is preserved at second-hand by the Negroes (since they took it from the white settlers) it is now sung:

O hangman hold your holts I pray,
O hold your holts awhile
I think I see my grandmother
A-coming down the road.

In North Carolina the variant is:

Hangman, hangman howd yo' hand
O howd it wide and far
For there I see my mother cooming
Riding through the air.

However, in the less accessible Kentucky Mountains, the father is again the chief protagonist, and the original rhyme scheme is more nearly preserved:

Ropesman, ropesman slack up your rope,
Slack it up for a while
I looked over yonder and seen paw' comin'
He's walked for many a mile.

In these mountains, too, the Elizabethan ballad still flourishes, not only as a heritage from the distant forefathers of the present inhabitants, but as an enduring, active form of expression. When, during the life of the present generation, a particularly vicious feud engrossed the attentions of the mountaineers, it was immortalized in a ballad (or Ballet, as it is locally termed) titled the "Rowan Country Trouble," which is wholly Elizabethan in design. It has since been accepted into the standard repertory of ballads in that region.

Despite the wide range in types and origins of the folk-songs familiar to our continent (a recent volume* offers examples from the Southern Appalachians—Virginia, the Carolinas, Kentucky, Tennessee—specimens of the pioneer songs of the west and southwest, cowboy songs, songs from the Great Lakes region, vaquero songs, sea-chanteys from down east, and so forth) it is instructive to notice how frequently the evidence of a common folk-consciousness is encountered through the recurrence of an especially meaningful thought or image. There is, for example, a stanza in the literature of the American folk that is phrased thus:

Jack o' Diamonds, jack o' diamonds,
I know you of old,
You've robbed my poor pockets
Of silver and gold.

Except for the lack of the dialectic indications, this is obviously a quotation from the Negro work-song "Water Boy," which Hall Johnson declares he heard daily from the chain-gangs as they worked along the road in front of his boyhood home in Georgia. Yet, equally, it might be presented as folk-material from North Carolina or the southwest. For it is quoted, in a collection of Carolina mountain songs (edited by Marshall Bartholomew), to a tune entirely different from the Negro; as the first stanza of a song with several succeeding verses that have no relation to it. Also, it is included by the Messrs. Lomax as an incidental part of a cowboy song called "Rye Whiskey," which is wholly dissimilar in tune and context from both examples previously instanced. In fact, the cowboy's chant is a reworking of an English folk-tune titled "The Waggoner Lad."

Apparently the "Jack o' Diamonds" motif had a particular significance, a curious aptness for each of these folk, some meaning which it has, certainly, no longer for us. A similar persistence of an image is to be discerned in a pair of songs from the Lomax collection, the first of which, a mountain song entitled "Every Night When the Sun Goes Down," offers this outcry of a deserted woman:

It's once my apron hung down low
He'd follow me through sleet and snow

* *American Ballads and Folk Songs,* by J. A. and A. Lomax. Macmillan.

It's now my apron's to my chin
He'll face the door and won't come in.

Fifty pages further on in the volume is a Negro blues from a widely-separated region ("Dink's Song") which contains this passage:—

When I wo' my ap'ons low
Couldn't keep you from my do'

Now I wears my ap'ons high
Sc'acely ever sees you passin' by

Now my ap'ons up to my chin
You pass my do' and you won' come in.

The tune in each instance is quite individual; and there is no further resemblance between the texts, save for the general character of lamentation. Here again is an image which has passed from the urban mind and speech; but its expressiveness for the singers of these songs is obvious.

The strongest feeling one has after a continuous absorption in folk-material of many origins is that the orbit of influence such material possesses today is sharply limited. Folk-songs can be, and still are, transmitted from one group to another, but each of these groups is certain to be found within definite social strata, generally the agrarian or the peasant class. The time seems to be past for folk-songs to be adopted by the more cultured populace as a part of their emotional resources; their place in the need for aesthetic expression has been usurped by art-products (regardless of quality) which are more consistent in form and philosophy with contemporary urban existence.

Within that orbit, the transfusion is often effected with results that are curiously revealing. Almost without exception it demonstrates that the folk are more sensitive to the large, generalized aspects of an emotion than to a particular nicety of speech, an especial aptness of phrasing, a colorful choice of words. Thus, there is the familiar "Shoot the Buffalo" whose refrain, in the lowlands, is sung "We'll rally round the canebrake and shoot the buffalo"; and in the mountains, as gaily, "We'll rally round the *cambric* and shoot the buffalo." There is always this tendency for the singers to supply, in a song imported from another region, a local reality for a more esoteric original reference; or, if nothing plausible suggests itself, to slight or abuse the alien words. Of the first tendency, this Virginia variant of the ancient English "Robin Hood Rescuing Will Stutley" is a first-rate example:

> Will Stutley he surprised was,
> In Aiken prison lay,
> Three varlets whom the king had hired,
> Did basely him betray.

This was the first form:

> That Will Stutley surprised was
> And *eke in* prison lay,
> Three varlets whom the sheriff had hired
> Did likely him betray.

The change demonstrates the process by which the archaic English speech has almost disappeared in American folk-songs, even in the less accessible regions. Moreover, the substitution of a "king" for the "sheriff" of the English version shows plainly whom the Virginians thought it safer to malign. And the choice of a word which preserves the long *a* sound for "eke" (Aiken, that is) demonstrates that the tradition for this version dates to the time of Chaucer, when that pronunciation was in vogue. In a sea song which became popular inland, a ship which "sprung a leak" was regularly described as having "sprung a *leap*." A "pen-knife" became a "penny-knife"; but the lengths to which such mistreatment may go can be best summed up in this comparison between an old English folk-song and its contemporary Tennessee version. The English of the sixteenth century knew it as:

> A Nobleman near Exeter,
> He had a comely daughter fair:
> And at the age of sixteen years
> She courted was by Lords and Peers.
>
> But none of them her heart could move
> Till a young sea captain he did prove
> To be the master of her heart
> And caused it both to bleed and smart.

In the south this has been altered, adapted and reduced to:

A rich man exter tire
Had a beautiful daughter fair
Courted was she by lords and spears
None her favor could remove
Till a young sea captain did approve.

In this latter, there is a remarkable resemblance, both in rhythm and meter, to the "hill-billy" ballads that have recently risen to fame on the radio, and the mutilation lends credence to the theory enunciated by Ernest Newman (among others) that, rather than growing by a process of accretion, folk-songs degenerate through the years from an originally fine individual expression to a commoner mass version. Since there is a smaller number of superior minds in any heterogeneous group, this is reasonable; but I would add to this that occasionally one of these can operate on a previous creation, and give to it a new vitality. Something of that sort would seem to have occurred to a seventeenth century song by Martin Parker (dated 1635) titled "The Old Maid's Song" which is preserved in Pulaski County, Kentucky, in this form:

Let none be offended, nor say I'm uncivil,
For I needs must have one,* be he good or evill;
Nay, rather than faile, I'le have a tinker or broomman,
A pedlar, an inkman, a matman or someman
Come gentle, come simple, come foolish, come witty,
O let me not die a maid, take me for pity.

How many hands must it have passed through before emerging in this form, to a different tune, in but an adjacent county (Letcher) of Kentucky? Here it is the wail of a maiden whose ugly sister has long been married, a grandmother before sixty. Yet, of herself, she mournfully concludes:

No tinker and no tailor
No fiddler with his bow,
No plowman and no sailor-man
Has bid me yes or no.

* Man.

Come gentle ones, come foolish
Come lame ones and come halt,
If ere I die a withered maid,
It sure will be your fault.*

And finally (to complete the cycle) it is possible for these simple mountaineers to appropriate a folk-tune and verse whose origin is completely obscure to them, to sing it wholly unchanged, and yet find in it a new emphasis, a different meaning. As the Revolutionary soldiers picked up a "Yankee Doodle" which was flung at them in derision and, to its insolent lilt, marched a new nation into being, so in Kentucky a favorite song of the play-party is an old Jacobean tune to which some unruly subject of Charles II set these mocking words:

Charley's neat and Charley's sweet,
Charley he's a dandy,
Every time he goes to town,
He gets his girl some candy.

Over the hills to feed my sheep,
Over the hills to Charley,
Over the hills to feed my sheep,
On buckwheat cakes and barley.

But in Kentucky, the song is one of sentiment, and even affection; to the same tune, and with not a word changed.

As this powerful folk-force travels in its orbit, it is only natural to speculate whether it ever casts its shadow on our everyday world of calculated expressions; and it is gratifying to find that the evidences of such an influence do exist, in the field where they logically should—in jazz and our popular songs. In the Negro spiritual "Lay Dis Body Down" there is a verse which sighs,

I know moonlight,
I know starlight
I'm walking t'rough de starlight,
Lay dis body down.

* *American Folk-Song Series; Set No. 14,* by J. J. Niles. Schirmer's.

There is an echo here, and more than a remote one, of Gershwin's "I Got Rhythm":

> I got starlight
> I got sweet dreams.

Whether the lyricist was familiar with this spiritual is difficult to say; it appears to me rather improbable. I certainly should prefer it that way, with the added privilege of believing that something inherent in the Negro psyche, obsessing him as this lyric was being fashioned, dictated the words and image to his groping fancy. Also, among the "Songs of Childhood" in the Lomax collection is one entitled "Hardly Think I Will," detailing the cogitations of a miss about a young man of her acquaintance. One passage states:

> His name is not so scrumptious
> In fact it's common Bill.

Again, it seems, the folk have been plagiarizing from a somewhat later Broadway; specifically from the Wodehouse-Kern "Bill," out of *Show Boat*. And even a wholly new school of thought in popular exaltations may be traced to the humble precincts of Texas, from whence springs "Rattlesnake" and these lines:

> A nice young ma-wa-wan,
> Lived on a hi-wi-will,
> A nice young ma-wa-wan,
> For I knew him we-we-well.

The idea is developed through the dozen stanzas of the song. Generally the eminent Eddie Leonard (minstrel and vaudevillian) has been awarded the honor of inventing the wah-wah technique in singing, but this evidence would seem to bestow the wreath on some less celebrated bard. In his wake (and the "he" might be either Leonard or the anonymous singer) have come the Calloways, the Ellingtons, the Crosbys, the hi-de-hos, the boop-a-doops and their ponderable influence on the national life and thought. Certainly if the arty American composers still consider our folk-expressions unworthy of cultivation, those of our musicians who *have* won a wide audience sink their roots in a rich soil.

February 1935

* *

LEHMAN ENGEL

*

The Musician in the Theatre

WRITING MUSIC to order for the theatre in our time poses a problem that is much like a first-class mystery. Usually the conditioning factors lie far away from music itself and in some respects away from the theatre proper. Rather they belong in the sphere of economics or human relations. The composer must look and listen carefully to find out the style of play he is writing for and what opportunities and responsibilities it entails. He will probably not be told, for example, whether the play is period or modern; whether it is stylized or realistic; whether the music is to be incidental or thematic; whether there are to be songs and, if so, whether the cast can sing; or even approximately how many or what kind of instruments he will have to work with and how many rehearsals he can count on. Often even the clues he seeks are matters of taste and point of view which will be picked up first in conversation with the director and spring into clearer focus with one peep at the scenic designer's sketches. For directors generally know better how to order the stage designs than the musical score.

In fact, scene designers often influence composers to a considerable degree through the period of preparation and even rehearsal. The style of their scenery is sometimes more clearly expressive of the mood and period of a play than the director's instructions. In a multi-scene show such details as the rapidity of change condition all the transition music. Here is an absolute. The curtain is never held for completion of a musical piece. If fifteen seconds are allowed for a change of scene, the music that covers it must be no more and no less, and in that time the musical idea must be clearly stated, developed and concluded.

Actors, too, have an effect on the music for a play though usually a limited one. Some actors—big enough stars to command attention—do not know how to speak to music, and when this difficulty arises the axe is taken to the score. In Shakespeare, many older players decry new songs because they are convinced that the old songs are the authentic ones. In all but two or three cases this is erroneous and most of the familiar songs were written for famous revivals in the nineteenth century.

The director exerts the most powerful single influence on the theatre composer. A few personal experiences will serve to illustrate this. Halsted Welles (*Murder in the Cathedral*) and Melvyn Douglas (*Within the Gates*) both allowed me to create what I thought best suited to the plays, and nothing was actually changed in rehearsal. Such a procedure was easier in these two plays than in many others because nearly all of the numbers were "set" pieces—that is, they had definite beginnings and endings dependent on "set" lyrics.

Orson Welles, on the other hand, virtually dictated the twiddles I composed for *Shoemaker's Holiday*. Often he tapped out rhythms for a particular spot and no less often described the quality of the melody and the number of measures. The production that resulted from his method was always one definite idea made up of the scenery he designed, the play he revised, the acting he postulated in detail, and the accompanying twiddles he indicated. This was a very stimulating kind of theatre and it achieved exactly what its founder intended.

Margaret Webster, with whom I have worked again and again, is critical of music in great detail. She discusses the play in advance, describes her point of view, mentions special places where she wants music and listens to suggestions from the composer. In rehearsal she frequently stages scenes so as to accommodate a musical passage she likes, and thereby prevents unnecessary cutting. When she (or Maurice Evans who is also astute about music) dislikes something, she is usually articulate and replacement is facilitated.

Of the thirty-three shows I have done in New York in the past six years, twenty-four had scores of my own composition, the others were conducting chores. Of the twenty-four, two alone had orchestras of more than seven players, and they were both productions of the Federal Theatre. Two others had no orchestra—only voices—and nineteen used four or five musicians. The Musicians' Union requires a minimum of four men if any are to be used and some "contract houses" agree under union contract to employ four players for every show whether or not music is specified or required by the script. The fact, then, that a composer has at least four musicians to work with is not a matter of choice but rather a kind of dialectical Olympian award—a gift of the Union gods.

The kind of instruments is conditioned by a dozen influences—often unsuspected—so that not only size but quality are the composer's inheritance. When Maurice Evans engaged me to do a score for *Hamlet,* he had been performing *Richard II.* His composer for that play employed a flute, two trumpets, drums and a Hammond organ. Four of these five players were considered a permanent part of his theatre's contract so that I was free to exchange only one. The result was that *Hamlet* used the *Richard II* instrumentation, substituting an oboe for a flute.

When Orson Welles opened the Mercury Theatre, his first bill was *Julius Caesar* with score by Marc Blitzstein who used horn, trumpet, drums and Hammond organ. Since the Mercury was a repertory theatre, I had exactly that same combination to write for in *Shoemakers' Holiday,* the second bill. There is no need to dwell on the differences between the two plays. One was tragedy, the other comedy; one Elizabethan produced in a modern setting, the other made to suggest its own period. I solved the problem by writing an entire score of duets for trumpet and horn with occasional percussive folderol.

Certain playwrights "orchestrate" their own music. In *Macbeth* Shakespeare indicates in the cauldron scene "noise of hautboys" (oboes); in the second scene of the witches:

> A drum, a drum
> Macbeth doth come,

and there are fanfares and alarums which demand some brass instrument of the trumpet family. With only two vacancies to fill, I chose a second trumpet, and for fullness of effect and general musical texture I had the inevitable Hammond organ.

I do not complain of these limitations, though any composer will tell you that it is easier to write for a full orchestra, where any desired effect is obtainable in thousands of tried-and-tested recipes.

In a curious way the limited and imposed conditions may even be healthier. But it was a wonderful experience each time the bans were lifted. When Halsted Welles and the Federal Theatre produced *Murder in the Cathedral,* the government played Lady Bountiful. There was an orchestra of nearly thirty, a backstage chorus of singers and unneeded actors numbering close to fifty, and an on-stage speaking chorus of a dozen or more women. No substitutes here: brass was brass, a woodwind choir not an organ, a string choir not a quartet. Having the resources at our command, we underlined the excitement of the spoken choruses with an orchestral accompaniment, punctuated them dramatically, and provided interludes which helped to sustain the action. The Federal Theatre no longer exists and nothing else has arisen to take its place. For the theatre musician it is a great loss because through it alone, in the theatre of our time, have musicians been able to draw upon any quantity of resources. . . .

A play like *Johnny Johnson,* in which the playwright and the composer, Paul Green and Kurt Weill, pooled their problems and collaborated in their solutions so that play script and music script were integral parts of the same work, is a bridge between the play for which incidental music is composed to order and the musical comedy. For *Johnny Johnson* Kurt Weill did his own orchestration and I conducted from his complete score. For American musical comedy, on the other hand, the composer seldom does his own orchestration and the problem of musical presentation is approached from a different angle. Composer, author and lyric writer usually make a draft of an entire show before production begins, but the composer often writes only the melodies or also indicates certain trends in the harmonization. Then, as the producer, director and actors get to work, a new figure steps in: the "arranger," whose business it is not only to give the music the texture, color and speed the show requires at each particular point but to give variety enough to the verses of a lyric to make it hold and grow or carry a dance along with it, to build a bridge between lyrics, to reorganize a song to fit a special actor's voice and to attend to a hundred other difficult technical details. . . . The importance of this new figure in modern musical comedy is indicated by the reputations both in and out of the theatre that have been achieved by such gifted men as Russell Bennett, Ferde Grofé, Hans Spialek.

Many if not most of the musician's problems in the theatre are really inherent not in the work itself but in the system under which theatre music of all kinds is presented on Broadway. One of the greatest difficulties, of course, from which many others arise is the conflict between the unions and the producers. But, in spite of much talk to the contrary, it is by no means only the unions that have created the difficulties. (It took only two of my earliest jobs to send me scurrying to Local 802 for protection. My first show, and one of my most successful, paid me $175.00 for the composition of an entire score and rehearsal, and then gave me billing second to someone else who had contributed a single melody. My second producer simply did not pay his bills.) Yet it is undoubtedly out of the question, with present union requirements, to undertake the production of a show requiring a sizeable orchestra (twenty to thirty players), an adequate singing ensemble (sixteen to twenty-four) and a crew of stagehands sufficient to negotiate several important scene changes, except when a show has considerable box-office appeal. This condition is badly limiting, since it restricts production to money-makers addressed to the relatively small public which can afford to pay high entertainment prices.

No one would suggest that union restrictions should be eliminated, but with so much theatrical unemployment the various unions could well do one or all of three things: 1. allow cooperative production where it can be definitely established that a real cooperative is intended; 2. establish a producing unit within the union as an aid to employment, limiting its efforts to the best of those works found impossible for regular commercial trial; 3. establish a joint board made up of representatives of all theatrical unions where plans for shows in the non-profit category may be submitted and, if found suitable, be allowed production at appreciable scale reductions.

Such treatment would stimulate new forms of musical enterprise. Composers and playwrights would conceive works along less stereotyped lines. Employment in general would be stimulated and a new public, hitherto excluded from the theatre by prohibitive prices, would find itself for the first time enjoying a long dreamed-of pleasure.

June 1942

V · ACTORS AND ACTING

* * *

ROSAMOND GILDER

*

La Nostalgilder

SOME LETTERS OF ELEONORA DUSE

ELEONORA DUSE has already taken her place among the figures of dramatic legend. We think of her as Duse of the Beautiful Hands, Duse whose voice was tuned to the sorrows and sufferings of mankind, whose gestures spoke of a knowledge beyond pain, of a wisdom beyond experience; the great artist, the subtle and powerful actress, remote, glamorous, passionate, the almost mythic figure of tragedy and pain. To my mother, Duse was all these things, but she was her friend as well. Between these two women there was a bond stronger than that created by the exchange of courtesies. Undefined by either, but recognized by those near to them both, it was as though twin souls had met and spoken. It was a likeness that escapes definition, that crumbles under the hard touch of words; yet when I saw Duse walk on the stage, I thought it was my mother's shadow, and when I talked of my mother to one who had not known her, my friend exclaimed, "But it is Duse whom you describe!"

This kernel of strange kinship served only to accentuate the differences of temperament and training—the unlikeness of their uses and their destinies. Yet in my mother's presence Duse found relief from the pressure of an existence which always seemed too heavy to be borne. Secure in that unspoken understanding, she came and went at will in my mother's house, a lovely, graceful figure of trailing lines and bubbling laughter. She appeared at odd hours and in every possible mood, strolling in for a cup of tea at two o'clock in the morning, spending an afternoon curled up in the corner of the library sofa, or a morning playing with the children in the nursery. Unexpected but never unwelcome, changeable but never changing in her warm friendship, she showed her friends a side of her nature which is sometimes forgotten in the sombre outlines of a stormy and sorrowful life.

It is to recapture something of the gay and humorous qualities of the great tragedienne that I have preserved these letters written to my mother during Duse's first visit to America. They are fragments, exclamations, bits of phrases tossed to a friend with whom the important things would be discussed at the next meeting—yet they are as vivid today as when the postman brought those long blue envelopes mightily scrawled upon by an impatient hand to the door of our house on Clinton Place. They are all written in fluent and idiomatic French, the language that my mother and Duse used with equal ease, and they are indited with a cheerful disregard of time and space that makes each letter a picture of the writer's mood. The printed page may diminish their ardor, for no type could cope with the extravagance of capitals and underlinings, the furious architecture of words and phrases with which the emotions of the moment are recorded, but the living word is there, and with it a glimpse of that *"sauvage apprivoisée"* who was the delight of all who knew her—and the wonder of a generation.

Duse came to New York in 1893. She opened at the Fifth Avenue Theatre (on the corner of Twenty-eighth Street and Broadway) in *Camille* on the evening of January 23, before a large and critically minded audience, ready to deny her the laurels which had been conferred on such favorites as Sarah Bernhardt, Modjeska, Ellen Terry or Clara Morris. Salvini had already accustomed New York theatregoers to listening to Italian, but Duse had been wiser than Salvini and had brought an excellent and well-directed native company to support her. She had not been on the stage five minutes before the discerning realized that here, in the familiar situations of this well-worn play, a new genius was made manifest. "Long before the end of the evening," wrote the dramatic critic of the *Evening Post,* "(Duse) had demonstrated her right to be reckoned among the few living actresses of the first rank. . . . In her farewell to Armand, she exceeded all actresses seen here. . . . The curtain fell on a success as brilliant as it was in many cases, at least unexpected." She played during this first engagement (it was before the advent of D'Annunzio) an assortment of French tragi-commedies the moral tone of which was exceedingly painful to those critics who were not carried away by her genius. The neurasthenic heroines of Sardou's *Fedora* and his *Divorçons,* of Dumas' *Fernande* and *Françillon* were relieved only by the tragic Santuzza of Verga's *Cavalleria Rusticana* and the irrepressible Mirandolina of *La Locandiera* by Goldoni, in which Duse demonstrated her exceptional gifts as a comedian. . . .

So determined was Duse to avoid the usual spectacular entry that she succeeded in outwitting her managers, Carl and Theodore Rosenfeld, by slipping into New York alone a few days before her company arrived and hiding herself in the Murray Hill Hotel. Here some days later my mother called on her at the instance of Mrs. Arthur Bronson, my mother's older sister, who lived in Venice and had known Duse for years. Duse was out, but the following message was dispatched by hand immediately upon her return:

Thursday [*January, 1893*]

MADAME:

I deeply regret having missed your visit. I thank you—and I am most grateful to Mrs. Bronson and dear Mademoiselle Edith [Mrs. Bronson's daughter].

But, greatly as I appreciate your kind invitation I am not able to take advantage of it, as I *never* go out "dans le monde." It would give me the greatest pleasure, however, to see and know you, and if you wish to come to see me, please write me a line telling me at what hour and on what day I may expect you. I will remain at the hotel to receive you at any time you name.

With warm appreciation for your kindness and

sincere greetings

E. DUSE

As the letters are all undated, it is impossible to tell exactly what disagreeable incident prompted the following note. It may have been some expression of disapproval for one of the French farces which so disgusted the worthy critic of the *Tribune* that he felt the judicious use of eggs, in the same condition as the play, would be a healthy antidote.

[*January, 1893*]

DEAR MRS. GILDER:
I thank you from the bottom of my heart for your note—but I am too sick with disgust for so coarse—so vulgar an audience as that of tonight.

If I go to you I would like to be able to give you in return a little of the kindness that you give me—but—there's a bitter taste in my mouth—I can no more. . . .

This does not prevent my understanding your goodness of heart—your delicacy— Thank you!

Until tomorrow Eleonora

It is delicacy and goodness itself that speak through you.

Thank you—

Deprived of the usual interviews, photographic séances and spectacular sallies of the well-trained star, the reporters were called upon to use their own invention in the matter of material about "La Duse," who had sprung into such sudden and dazzling prominence. Her hermit-like disposition was, therefore, featured as much as possible and a legend grew up that she never saw even her managers, but insisted on conversing with them through the keyhole. Perhaps the legend originated up from the occasion, referred to in the following letter, when she kept them waiting while she sent in all haste for my mother:

In bed—the 26th—Morning
[*February, 1893*]

MADAME:
I need you. I cannot move from my bed today—and I *must* talk to you. Will you be so good—will you answer my prayer—will you come to me today at any hour you wish?
I have something I want to ask of you, and also I want your advice. Perhaps you will consent. Please answer—and what is more, please answer *quickly* for the Impresarios are waiting my answer, which depends on yours—and they will not let me alone.

You can come up at whatever hour is most convenient for you, because I will not go out at all—as I am ill and in bed.

Yours always, Madame,
E. DUSE

As Madame Duse's popularity increased, it did not seem wise to her friends, who knew the ways of the press, simply to refuse to see the reporters without some sort of explanation of her attitude. On one of her now frequent visits to the house, my mother suggested that she write a short letter to a particular woman reporter who had begged an interview, a letter which would make her attitude clear to the public. The following memorandum is in my mother's handwriting, but written at Duse's dictation:

[*1893*]

I love freedom as though I were myself an American—but I am a slave—the slave of the public which pays to see me act—the slave of my professional engagements—the slave of the author whose play I am interpreting—above all I am the slave of my temperament which, alas does not permit me simply to "play" my parts, but, much against my will, forces me to suffer with the beings I represent.

For this reason, dear Madame, when I return to my house I have but one desire—to forget everything even remotely connected with my work. You can understand that interviews with journalists will not contribute toward such forgetting. And so, with all respect for the rights and privileges of the press, I beg the reporters not to insist upon interviews.

Que voulez vous, Madame, I have never taken any interest in practical affairs—I have a pronounced antipathy for everything that resembles advertising. I leave it to you to judge whether I am right or wrong.

Her interest in practical affairs would revive, however, when it came to helping a friend or fellow-worker in need. A hastily written note was brought to my mother one day:

[*February, 1893*]

Dear woman—dear Madame—dear friend—
Dear Mrs. Gilder:
Do you know a gentleman by the name of X—?????
If "yes"—
Well, I wish to see him and talk to him.
What shall I do??? R.S.V.P.
Une sauvage apprivoisée

My mother did know all about the gentleman in question, and blue-coated messenger boys flew between the Murray Hill Hotel and 55 Clinton Place (now so tamely labeled 13 East 8th Street) with my mother's answer and with Duse's reply which follows:

[*February, 1893*]

Thank you dear friend for your answer—
It is said
And it is understood—about that Individual.
Now I will explain to you that the name was given to me by an ex-actor of my troupe, a poor devil who is in New York without any means of earning his living—ill—almost in the street.

Someone told me that the individual in question could give him a place in the museum, and the ex-actor asked my help to get an interview with the Individual. My heart told me that there was little good in it—but—well, that's the reason I asked your advice. We'll talk of this, for I would like to be kind to my poor ex-comrade who is trying to earn his living—

I will go to see you tomorrow—now I must run—to earn *my Liberty too!*

ELEONORA

—and your baby—Francesca, how is she??

Duse was very fond of this small black-eyed infant and would often drop in to play with her, even when my mother was not at home. During an absence of my mother from New York, Duse came every day to see that all went well with the children. Little notes of reassurance were dispatched to the absent parent, interspersed with affectionate hopes for a swift return. The following memorandum which she left one day on the library table has that delightful touch of wit and unexpectedness that every word she wrote is able to convey. It is written on my mother's own notepaper and is therefore headed:

55 CLINTON PLACE

I owe you:
(for I don't know what) 1. dollar
Expenses for the entrails of my watch 20. "
To buy pieces of happiness—
Let's say 5. "
Blue or green cretonne for 2 windows and a table 3. "
(bankruptcy!)

Having thus regulated her affairs, and incidentally closed her New York engagement, Duse went to Chicago about the middle of March, 1893. The World's Fair was then in progress, and both my father and mother were wildly enthusiastic over its beauties. They were anxious that Duse should see the Exposition buildings and reverse her judgement on the general ugliness of American architecture. Her expressions of exaggerated horror of all things Chicagoan in the bombardment of letters from that city (of which the first and last follow) were largely playful. They were her teasing response to my mother's desire that she should find something beautiful in the American scene.

[*Chicago, March, 1893*]

You write to me—you say: "Well—how goes it?"
Well?
Well!—*I die*
and that's all.
"Eh"—"what?"—"How?"—"why?"—Say no more!
I DIE
Two words—two syllables—and all is said. Let's talk no more about it. If you knew what it is like to suffer from Nostalgilder—that most exasperating of diseases—worse than influenza—you wouldn't dare ask me how I am.
DO YOU WANT ME TO PERISH? Well, then—no—no—NO.
Not here—I beg of you
I DIE

Voilà!

[*Chicago, April 2, 1893*]
Sunday

Dear—We are bankrupting ourselves in letters and telegrams! I hope to get yet another letter from you tomorrow with my European mail.

And you. What is this "plan of campaign" that you haven't the courage to talk about. Why?

Bankrupt yourself and come to Boston! Remember that life is short. When will you find another Duse? Well, then? Ruin yourself—come to Boston!

Your Chicago is awful—with or without the Exposition buildings—with the buildings it is even more horrible! I obeyed you and I asked Mr. H—— to go with me. Coming back from the Exposition, having seen so many *horrors,* I said as much to him. He thought I was lacking in amiability—yes—that's true—but . . .

"What a beautiful sunset we saw, the Gilders and I, in New York!" That was my answer. As for the Exposition buildings—they *are horrible*. So much for that.

Now, today, I've made peace with Chicago—a bit—I've seen one beautiful house. The owner is called James M. Ellsworth. He seems to be a fine man—and his house contains some beautiful things. I was sorry I could not talk very much with Mr. Ellsworth, but he doesn't speak French—and I can't speak English, so Mr. H—— had to carry the whole burden of interpreting for us. Now I have obeyed you, I have seen everything, I've swallowed everything—and now—enough of your Chicago!

Come to Boston. We'll talk about your Chicago Exposition! If you come to Boston I'll become gay—like Francesca, good, like you—and amiable, like Mr. Gilder.

I'm not even making money here—but it doesn't matter.

And as for the sun—I don't know where it has hidden itself, nevertheless, the fact is that today is Easter.

PEACE

Sweet festival—sweet word. Peace to hearts and souls,
Peace, too, to my pen—and to you who read! Amen.

Music!
Trumpets!
Fanfare!
Hallelujah!

If you come to Boston. And if you don't come? May the Lord forgive you—Don't speak of it. Don't do mediocre things. Come to Boston—Bankrupt yourself. Life is short!

[*Chicago, April, 1893*]

I DIE

Au revoir.

P.S. In another letter I will give you the address of the hotel in Boston.

Rejecting the mediocre, my mother went to Boston and stayed with Duse during her short engagement there. My mother's birthday was on the fourteenth of April and on that day Duse sent the following characteristic note to my father, who was alone in New York:

[*Boston, April 14, 1893*]

Today I think of you—and I feel that it is indeed "your life" that I have in my hands.

Here, too, she is beloved and for my part I often ask myself, with all the sincerity of my heart—if ever I will be able to do something good—something serviceable for her.

ELEONORA

Shortly after this they both returned to New York. Duse's first American tour was drawing to an end. The last messages flew between hotel and house:

[*April, 1893*]

Come! I cannot go out. I have Nostalgilder!

[*April, 1893*]

Dear

It is evening.

The hour of departure—the hour of memories, of prayers. One must hide everything and go to work. May God keep my daughter and every woman from such an existence!

Au revoir—until this evening.

It is good to be able to say "this evening."

E.

Finally the parting came, Duse sailed on the 22nd of April. From the boat, by hand, came this hasty scrawl:

April 22, 1893
Compagnie Generale Transatlantique

Faith,
Friendship,
Courage,
Affection!

Au revoir—

Tender greetings to you! and kisses to Francesca.
Thanks for everything—With all my heart—

ELEONORA

And then, by cable from the other side:

LONDON, MAY 10, 1893

AGAIN THANKS FOR EVERYTHING. GOODBYE. WRITE. ELEONORA.

LONDON, MAY 20, 1893

I BANKRUPT MYSELF TO TELL YOU THAT I LOVE YOU. ELEONORA.

June 1926

VELONA PILCHER

*

Dame Ellen Terry

EARLY ONE MARCH MORNING Spring stepped into the garden of a cottage in Kent and performed a wonder for a guest who stood upon the threshold looking along a lane of six little cherry trees standing barely root deep in shallow snow. Behind one's back shouted and spluttered a fresh fire noisily greeting its daily ration of young tree's trunk, censering the air as though it were a fire of flowers, and sending a shadowy stream of gold out onto the lawn whose snowy shift lay frailly where it had fallen secretly and surprisingly during the dark. And then suddenly—as one gazed, ravished, at the tapering cherry branches spreading lace-like this lovely silver raiment that dawn had discovered upon them; and as one looked through this lacy handiwork into a field beyond where many sheep lay waiting for their lambing hour—suddenly, at that miraculous moment, there shot across this scene a naked sword of sun. A shaft of strong sun came down from heaven like an annunciation and touched with its tip the tips of all the cherry tree boughs and lo! living pearls poured upon the ground; slowly and deliberately, delicately and softly, all the fingers of the trees dropped jewels into earth's lap—great golden drops melting, petals of water wilting, blossoms of blown snow—all dropped deliberately one at a time along the path between the trees with a stately stepping motion, like the walk along the path of a very aged and lovely lady.

And nearly every evening when warm weather has come to this countryside to stay, Dame Ellen Terry—just such a lovely lady—does walk along this path.

It is pleasant to be meekened, and made a worshiper, before some exquisite accident in the life of the earth; to be so grateful for a wonder performed that we want to say grace. And I think that is how we playgoers of today feel in the presence of this high and gracious player of the past; before Her Highness we are all grateful guests. We adore. She is a glorious force of nature, a mysterious conjunction of the gentlest elements, an exquisite accident in the life of mankind. That Dame Ellen Terry still walks above the earth with us, enters our playhouses, bows to our salutations, is part of us the public, sits with us as audience, sees what we see upon the stage, shares our aspirations for the life of the theatre, and is, along with us, a living London playgoer . . . this is our proud inheritance, a splendid privilege that is ours by right of birth.

Nor do we ever forget to say our grace. When she comes into a public place we do with one common impulse what we do also only for Bernard Shaw—we rise to our feet and applaud in a sort of frenzy of thanksgiving. (How one's heart thumps against the ribs even in the solitude of the study, remembering such entrances!) These two we know we love, and to these two at least we are agreed to give old Job's great phrase—*the honorable of the earth.* And once, what is more, we saw them together. Yes. We saw them both, Terry and Shaw, sitting chair to chair on a platform and whispering and giggling, and nodding their heads with mirth, like two ancient jesters shaking clown-sticks at each other . . . until Mr. Gordon Craig, whom they had come to hear open the International Theatre Exhibition, began to speak and then his two elders were quiet. Another time, when Messrs. Ervine and Cochran had a public debate and made rude remarks to each other for an hour or so, she also sat on the platform; and half the fun was watching how bravely she sat behind their blows, listening with infinite amusement, turning swiftly to her neighbor for news of any word missed, and looking up wickedly at the bristling backs now and then, peering up askew from behind her big glasses like a whimsical fairy godmother watching the youngsters have it out at last. But these two appearances were some years ago.

One of the more recent times when we stood to her—rising to our queen-mother of the theatre as she entered the box her presence made royal—was when Miss Edith Craig produced *The Verge;* and that evening she accepted our long tribute ("Thank Heaven!"—a man growled aloud next to me—"Thank Heaven she is still with us, that priceless spirit!") with a shake of the head; we had misunderstood and were applauding the wrong thing, and she begged us with wide gestures please to watch what the others were going to do, and attend only to the play. Sometimes, too, for charity's sake she will herself still play us a scene from Shakespeare . . . but these words are only about her as a playgoer among playgoers.

And most rememberable of all, in this matter of acting as audience, is how she was to be seen among us on those few unforgotten afternoons when the Duse came for the last time. (Good Lord, yes! There *have* been glorious souls among us on the earth in our day. And shall Theatre, whom these two heroines have served, ever be offered less than others' best?) Then for the last time we saw the Duse's hands, palms turned away from the world and us, only the backs of the straight long fingers—like bare boughs—vouchsafed us, and the fingers always falling toward the earth in a sign of renunciation; and there was the Terry leaning far forward in her seat, head flung back as though drinking at a fountain, hands held out as always in a gesture both begging and bequeathing, the palms open upward, and the fingers curled a little as though feeling forever for something there.

"Yes, but, my dears, don't be *too* solemn!"—Dame Ellen would say if she should overhear us, and she'd prick the black bubble of our melancholy with some sunny thrust of wit, and laugh merrily to see it melt. For if the shadow of age comes fearfully into the vision of the young who watch, freezing the heart, freezing young blood, making the heart heavy as if hung with icicles . . . it comes to her majesty with the sweet naturalness of all things in nature, and is only a change into another sort of lovely life. She seems unconscious of it, unafraid of it. Trees hold up their heads to the sun and snow and then bend obediently under both inexorable blessings when the time comes. It was Matthew Arnold who, writing of her long ago, coined the golden phrase for her genius, I think—*spiritual vivacity*. Today, too, this is her crowning quality; a shining something that ravishes those whose privilege it is sometimes to meet her. Others writing of her acting used to say (and graciously she has acknowledged the criticism) that it lacked repose—but never response. A radiant response to all that touch her is the miracle of her personality today. Is there, on the earth now, another human being with such a quenchless thirst for the waters of life?

Hers is a heavenly gaiety, a holy joy. Her love of fun is, as Arnold implied, of the spirit. If, seeing her absorbed, you should for a moment forget her presence of mind and say something too solemn or stupid or ungenerous—thinking, perhaps, she does not hear, and is using for a little while that most blessed power of age that can send the senses to sleep against the insignificant—pat! into the empty place you opened she will drop a word of wit that will light like lightning on your wooden head, and set the room ringing with wise laughter. Or if by chance you should happen to be amusing and retell a good story well, how hungrily she will press forward to hear it, hugging the comedy of it to her heart, and at the same time almost unable to wait till you have finished and she may unfold her arms and release her laugh, and then top your tale with another and a better. And she has plenty of her own, because all the best jokes of theatreland are saved up, like precious things, for her pleasure; you will hear the latest being passed about back stage, tried on one tongue and then another and then another until—pronounced perfect and especially appointed to royalty—some present-day player will approach Miss Craig and, with the air of a courtier who knows his gift is good, announce—"Here's a funny story for your mother." Or if now and then by chance you should happen to say something sensible, and say it simply, she will open her eyes wide to look at you, as a child looks at something for the first time, and you will receive an understanding that passes understanding. As for the art of the theatre, that she honors as all who practice that art honor her; it is the theatre that absorbs her; concerning the theatre nothing is insignificant; and intimates who often see her say that since last Christmas, when one of her gifts was Stanislavski's *My Life in Art,* she is seldom to be seen alone or abroad without that big book under her arm.

It was last Christmas, too, that a few guests whose happiness it was to wish her a happy New Year saw a scene that may well be shared, I think, with all who desire news of the present of this player of the past. Her health drunk, the jokes failing, the last Christmas crackers popped, and the hours of the old year lessening, she at last said good night and went to bed. A little later, the guests began a gramophone dance around and around the deserted dinner table to the tune of Paul Whiteman's Band, and around and around they went absurdly, not very gracefully, the paper caps wilting foolishly on their heads . . . when suddenly in the doorway swayed a silver figure wrapped in a long loose cloak of snow-white fur. The head was high, flung back defiantly from the bent body; the white hair haloed it and moved as it moved to the rhythm of the record; one poised hand beat the beat, poised like an Angel Gabriel making the sign annunciate . . . and as the little group of earthly dancers fell back in a sort of fear from this dream whose sleep had been disturbed and stood struck still before this pre-Raphaelite figure drawn back into life by music and mirth, Dame Ellen Terry began to dance; silently once around the table she danced—slowly, stately, delicately, pouring beauty from her bones, bearing her years like a burden of long-stemmed lilies, moving like a blossom of snow blown down to its rest on the ground—and then silently passed again out of the door.

October 1926

* *

ASHLEY DUKES

*

A Doll's House and the Open Door

WITH TWO LETTERS FROM GEORGE BERNARD SHAW

[*This article has been kindly and extensively revised, as every reader between the lines will see, by the hand of G.B.S. It would have been better if he had written it all himself; my part of it exists, where it exists at all, only by way of introduction to the two letters, dating from his liveliest period, which he now permits to be published for the first time.—A.D.*]

TO OUR GENERATION Janet Achurch and her husband Charles Charrington are dimly remembered names, shadows flitting across the luminous page of a Shavian preface. The dramatic and social history of the eighteen-nineties has been thoroughly expounded by Bernard Shaw himself; but the purely theatrical history of the Ibsenite movement remains unwritten. It was natural enough that the battle of controversy should have centered in the visible emblem of the play. The strangely moving success of *A Doll's House* in London in 1889 did not save *Ghosts* from being received with execration, *Widowers' Houses* with a queer mixture of hoots and cheers that continued in the press, especially the hoots, for a fortnight, and *Mrs. Warren's Profession* with prohibition by the censorship; but what biographer has recounted the lives of the stage pioneers who helped to create the new drama? They braved even greater odds than their authors; for they were dependent for their livelihood on the old commercial theatre whose conventions they flouted. The playwrights, living in a world of their own deliberate choice, were well able to take care of themselves; but the actors and producers, who were in the everyday theatre but not of it, were the true vanguard of the advancing movement.

Let us take up the tale where Bernard Shaw drops it in his preface to the *Plays Unpleasant.* "It was in 1889," he writes, "that the first really effective blow was struck by the production of *A Doll's House* by Mr. Charles Charrington and Miss Janet Achurch. Whilst they were taking that epoch-making play round the world, Mr. Grein followed up the campaign in London with his Independent Theatre." This was the theatre which produced *Widowers' Houses* and so gave birth to the contemporary English drama; but the original pair of players were flown. They were touring the cities and provinces of Australia with one-night-stands of Ibsen. When the famous door of *A Doll's House* was banged at curtain-fall and Helmer (by way of explanation) exclaimed "She's gone!" the fervent voice of some backwoodsman might be heard to declare "So's my blasted money!" Such are the trials of theatrical pioneering.

Janet Achurch (born in 1864) was the grand-daughter of Mr. and Mrs. Achurch Ward, who in their time were managers of the Manchester Theatre Royal. There was perhaps an echo of Lancashire in her speech, which did no harm, since Nature had never cast her for a heroine of the Mayfair drawing-room; but she was in no sense a woman of the people. She toured the provinces for a year or two before joining F. R. Benson's company, in which she played Lady Macbeth and Desdemona before she was much past twenty-one. Next she appeared in Adelphi melodrama and in several of Beerbohm Tree's productions at the Haymarket. She was once married, not unhappily, before her meeting with Charles Charrington, who produced *A Doll's House* at the old Novelty, now the Kingsway, in 1889. Ibsen, writing to him from Munich in May of that year, gave his authority to the enterprise. Janet Achurch here created the part of Nora on the English stage; and she and Charrington became for the moment the leaders of the new movement among the theatrical profession. They were soon challenged by Miss Horniman, Florence Farr, and Elizabeth Robins; but Miss Robins was soon snatched from the stage by her sudden success in literature, leaving Janet

Achurch, whose vocation was unequivocal, supreme as an actress of genius, while Charles Charrington was something of a scholar and thinker, an early Fabian, a competent if too thoughtful actor, and one of the founders of the Stage Society, whose first production was to be *You Never Can Tell.*

At this time Bernard Shaw, red-bearded and nearly forty, was dramatic critic of the *Saturday Review.* Some of his appreciations of Janet Achurch's acting may be found in *Dramatic Opinions and Essays,* others are still buried in the files of that lively periodical. After the Ibsen success she and her husband and Shaw became intimate friends in spite of his merciless candor and Charrington's Irish pride. Janet's daughter, inevitably named Nora, was a secular godchild of the critic-dramatist. He made the mistake of keeping *Candida* unacted for Janet for several years, withholding it even from Elizabeth Robins, Mrs. Patrick Campbell and the girl Sybil Thorndike because of a rash promise made to Janet on her saying "I could be that woman—for two hours." When she at last created the part, he said, on being asked how she played it, "She did not play it: she kicked it round the stage. But she was wonderful in the second act." When she created Nora Helmer she was a beautiful woman of nearly thirty, approaching her maturity as an actress. If she failed to take the foremost position in the English theatre to which her gifts entitled her, that was not only because she was consciously a rebel artist on a reactionary stage. Her husband had a good deal to do with it.

Charles Charrington (his real name was Martin) had a most disastrously and incongruously compound character. He was a stage-struck Irish Puritan, who ought to have either shunned the theatre as the gate of hell or been inoculated with the tolerance and morals of Charles II. Janet chose him and clung to him not merely because he was stagestruck and utterly devoted to her, but because she hoped that his Calvinist conscience would fill the void left by the absence of that steadying organ from her own moral anatomy; for there is no denying that Janet, though her pride and the dignity of her talent and brains made her contemptuously refuse all her opportunities of obtaining money and patronage in the most obvious way, was to all ordinary business intents and purposes gloriously unscrupulous.

Unfortunately Charrington failed her as a moral anchor. He was a courageous and clear-headed thinker; and he saw that as there was little money in the new drama he had no chance of bringing it and Janet to the front by fair commercial means. Quite deliberately, knowing well what he was doing, he not only begged and borrowed what he could from credulous enthusiasts, and gambled desperately in pioneer play production with it, but, what was less pardonable in the profession, he gambled with the livelihood of his fellow actors by engaging and rehearsing them without having a farthing to pay their salaries in the event of the pay-boxes not proving fruitful, which they seldom did. Finding that as a barrister he could get the credit which would have been denied him as an actor, he went into debt head over heels for properties, scenery, costumes and the rest of the stage necessaries. At his last attempt as a London manager he bought his first meal that day with the first few shillings that went into the gallery pay-box. He was a familiar figure in the county court, where he generally obtained sympathy as an unlucky gentleman-idealist, and avoided an order by convincing the judge of his destitution. Only once did his forgetfulness of a judgment summons force his friends to save him from prison by paying the debt. He was regarded as an old friend by his pawnbroker. When little Nora's grandfather tried to amuse her by springing open his gold watch under her nose, he elicited, not the expected laugh of ecstasy, but the very serious assurance that "Mr. X would give you thirty shillings on that, grandpa." When one of Janet's prosperous sisters sent her a roll of splendid material for a dress, it went to Mr. X unopened. Charrington's chief contribution to the propagandist literature of the Fabian Society was a tract proposing municipal pawnshops.

In such ways, and on principle, Charrington ended by making himself and Janet professionally impossible. Let those who blame him remember that as the time was unripe for his work, he could in no other way have hacked out the little breach in the theatre dykes that subsequently let in the flood. The hardest part of it for the two pioneers was that when the flood at last did come it was fifteen years too late. Their youth and novelty had passed: they were associated in the public mind with forlorn hopes and perpetual Ibsen, and in the professional mind with unforgiven financial betrayals. Janet's powers had reached a pitch at which she played everyone else off the stage, whilst her reckless recourse to morphia whenever she did not feel up to the mark made her more and more dependent upon it, though she was curiously proof against its worst effects and finally

ived on it with oriental complacency. She was not jealous of other
ctresses; but Charrington was: he was always writing under a sense
f the world's injustice to her great talent, and was beyond reason
nd self-control when her position was in question. When the new
novement at last took hold under the management of Vedrenne and
Barker at the Court Theatre in 1904, the most devoted friends of the
Charringtons were forced to recognize that they must be ruled out
s unemployable until the venture was sufficiently established. Both
Charrington and Janet did actually appear at the Court Theatre
nder the Vedrenne-Barker management, he as the Jaggers-like
arrister in the last act of *You Never Can Tell,* and she as the old
voman in *The Witch,* in which she achieved at least one demonstra-
ion of her extraordinary powers; but both appearances were entirely
ncidental and did not replace them in the center of the pioneer
tage.

Charrington presently inherited a modest competence and had to
dmit that he was too battered by Fate, and Janet too old, to throw
t away on pioneer management. Janet, who had produced a wonder-
ul effect as Cleopatra by dying seated, one day, whilst chatting with
er husband, sat down quietly and did actually put off her mortal
oil as she might have taken up a newspaper. Charrington survived
er long enough to marry again and see his modest competence re-
luced to the old incompetence by war deflation before he too died,
orgotten at last even by his ancient creditors.

Among his papers was found a letter from Shaw to Janet, a relic
f the odd friendship between the industrious, fact-facing, financially
crupulous, vegetarian author and the woman whom he has de-
cribed as the most thriftless genius he ever met or heard of. The
ircumstances under which it was written must be explained. Shaw
ad his first great success in America with the production of *The
Devil's Disciple* there by Richard Mansfield. Mansfield, whose posi-
ion as the leading serious actor-manager in New York had been
laced beyond all question by this success, asked for further parts.
Shaw wrote *The Man of Destiny* for him; but he refused it as too
hort, and perhaps too like himself in his tantrums. Shaw then pro-
osed that he should, by a tour de force, play the boy poet in *Candida,* with Janet in the title part. Mansfield went so far with this
ather dangerous suggestion as to engage Janet for the season at the
hen very handsome salary of £80 a week. When she arrived he at

once saw that it would be impossible for him, in such a part, to maintain his artistic supremacy in the cast against so formidable a competitor playing a much more suitable part. He gave up all intention of producing the play, but continued the rehearsals with the object of provoking Janet to throw up her part and thus release him from his engagement to her and Shaw. But Janet clung to her £80 a week with a tenacity that baffled him, and drew it regularly to the end of the season, when she returned to England without having had to earn a farthing of it. Shaw proposed then that Mansfield should produce *Caesar and Cleopatra* instead; but Mansfield did not dare assume the mantle of Julius; and a cablegram from Shaw, "Farewell, Pompey," ended the correspondence, though not, as might have been feared, the amicable relations between the author and the actor.

Meanwhile, however, Janet was for a time in New York, casting about her for some means to make herself known there. One of her plans was to lecture on Ibsen; and Shaw, then at the height of his practice as a platform speaker, proceeded to coach her as follows, frankly giving her a scenario without assuming any scruples of any kind on her part.

G.B.S. ON HOW TO LECTURE ON IBSEN

29, Fitzroy Square, W.
23rd April 1895

Charrington has just been here, with the dire news that you want to lecture on Ibsen. Now if you get a chance of making a speech under auspicious circumstances in New York, by all means do so. If there is any artistic club that you can address, get them to ask you to address them. Don't let it be a dinner, because after-dinner speaking is difficult and inconvenient; and the audience is always half drunk. But don't get a lecture agent to announce you as a lecture with a charge for admission; and don't let yourself be put into the position of a professional lecturer for a moment. There must be no money in the transaction.

Suppose, then, that you are in for a speech, what had you better do? To begin with, don't write your speech. If you attempt to read a lecture on Ibsen, you will embarrass yourself and bore your audience to distraction. If you haven't sufficient courage and simplicity of character to chatter away pleasantly to an audience from a few notes and your own experience, then let the platform alone. You can, without much preparations, get a very entertaining turn on some such lines as the following.

First, you hope nobody expects that you are going to deliver a lecture. For that, it is necessary to be a critic, an essayist, a student of literature, like the clever gentlemen who write about the drama for the New York papers. Besides, you are not conscious of your art as these gentlemen are. You took to the stage as a duck takes to water. When people want a lecture on swimming they don't go to a duck for it, but to a professor who probably doesn't know how to swim at all. In the same way, if people want a lecture on the drama or the stage, they must not come to you for it, but to one of the dramatic critics. Not that you mean to suggest that they cannot act; on the contrary, it is clear from the way they write that they are all accomplished actors; and you would go a long way to see a performance of a classical play with all the parts filled by critics. The subject that you are really going to talk about is yourself—a favourite subject of yours. Perhaps they (the audience) think that an impertinence—oh, it is very kind of them to disclaim that feeling; but you are sure some of them think so; and if they don't they ought to. But you have a justification ready.

The justification is that the actress really does take a very important part in the history and development of the drama. The drama progresses by a series of experiments made on the public by actors and actresses with new plays. The public may determine the result of the experiment; but the public never makes the experiment. It does not come to you and say, "Produce a play of Ibsen's, and see how we will like it." The initiative comes always from the actor or actress, who says, "I do so long to play Nora, or Hedda Gabler; and I must try whether the public will support me in it." If Ibsen had not interested *us,* the actors, his plays would still be on the book shelf; and I should have been celebrated for my impersonations of Pauline Deschapelles, and Adrienne Lecouvreur, and all sorts of nonsensical heroines instead of for my Nora in *A Doll's House*. So you see it really does matter what *we* like and what *we* think; and that is my excuse for getting up here today to give you a piece of my mind. If any lady or gentleman present will write a play with a part in it which I feel I *must* play, that play will be performed some day, even if every one else in Europe or America said worse things of it than Herr Max Nordau says of Ibsen (Here endeth the exordium).

Now you (the audience) perhaps want to know why I am bent in thrusting plays like Ibsen's on the public when there are so many excellent plays, by Shakespeare and other clever people, which were good enough for Mrs. Siddons and ought to be good enough for me. Well, I can't tell you why any more than I can tell you why I have different ideas from my grandmother. Perhaps the change may be for the worse; but that doesn't alter the fact that there is a change, and that the change is taking place in you as well as in me. If I were to revive some of Mrs. Siddon's popular parts for you, you would be the most astonished audience in America before it was half over. You would find the sentiment of the play as much out of date as its rhetoric, so much so that you would think me mad in producing such a work at the present day. Now what all the world feels about the plays of a hundred years ago, a few people feel about the plays of twenty-five years ago. I need not tell you that an actress has to play parts in many plays of which she has no very high opinion. Sometimes the author has not written one single line right: the actress has to invent the part for herself and play it *between* the lines, or else speak her words with a pathetic intensity that makes you forget that the actual words do not mean anything pathetic at all, affecting the public as Sarah Bernhardt affects people who do not know a word of French or Duse people who do not know a word of Italian. Sometimes the author has only succeeded in a single scene, though that scene may be worth producing the play for. Then some bits of a play wear out faster than others. In Shakespeare there are parts—like that of Helena in *All's Well* for instance—which are still too genuine and beautiful and modern for the public; but there are also many passages which are tedious and impossible, though we all pretend to like them. These are terrible bits to get over on the stage when they cannot be cut out; when I come to them I am only *pretending to act,* which is the most horribly dishonorable feeling you can have on the stage, though perhaps that will not be easily understood by people who think that acting is all pretense. But I assure you that is how I feel; and the result is that a part that I can play from beginning to end with conviction attracts me more than the most popular play in which my faith is imperfect. Consequently I get strong preferences for one play over another; and I will try to make the nature of my preferences clearer to you by comparing certain passages in those modern plays which show the influence of the great movement of the past half century for the better education and freedom of women, with passages from other plays which date in feeling from before that movement.

Now here I (G.B.S.) must leave you (Janet) to make up the real stuff of your speech for yourself. The idea is to quote the sham womanly stuff from *The Lady of Lyons, Adrienne,* and so on, and contrast it with passages from Ibsen's plays. A comic performance of the death scene from *Adrienne* would be good. Do it exactly as you do it on the stage, telling them previously that they must not laugh, and assuring them that what you are going to do is to the eighth of an inch what you have so often set the house weeping with. They will probably laugh like anything. Then give them the sharp, businesslike death scene at the end of *Hedda Gabler*. Allude to Dickens's Esther Summerson and Agnes Wickfield as the sort of thing that women dislike, and show how the women on the stage are making constantly for the sort of work which, even when it makes them unamiable, at least makes them unamiable human beings, which is better than making them amiable impostors.

You might then, very carefully and slyly, point out, on the lines of my preface to Archer's book (proof of preface enclosed in lecture of C.C.'s which goes to you by book post this mail) how the men on the stage dislike the plays in which the women's parts are real parts, and how women are being driven into management by this, with the likelihood that we shall presently have half the theatres managed by actor-managers, with no chance of a good woman's play being produced, and the other half managed by actress manageresses, with the men at the same disadvantage, and the drama thus worse off than ever. The moral ought to be desirability of management with artistic aims, the object being the production of the best plays and not the exhibition of this or that performer. And be sure to disclaim, in as amusing a way as possible, any pretense on your part to be fit to be trusted with management on those lines. Say that wherever you are in charge, they may depend on having actress-management at its worst.

If you can get an invitation to address a society of women, speak on acting as a profession for women, and show them as many stage tricks as possible. Remember, you cannot give yourself away too completely to please an audience; nor is there any method by which you can convey so strong an impression of modest amiability, of unconscious strength. You must honestly not try to make a success in the stage sense on the platform.

The post hour is come; and—thanks to this confounded project of yours, which you will have abandoned before this reaches you, probably, I have not had time to say a word to please myself. You are a hard taskmistress for an unfortunate literary man.

I went to Battersea Park yesterday to bicycle; and Nora came to see me fall. Florence Farr was there, caracoling on her machine with surpassing elegance, to the admiration of all the park. The Webbs also struggled with their new machines. But I must stop.

G.B.S.

After returning to England, Janet Achurch played in *Little Eyolf* at the Avenue in 1896, and later appeared as Cleopatra in Louis Calvert's Shakespearean production in Manchester. By this time Bernard Shaw was in the midst of the *Plays Pleasant*. The part of Lady Cicely in *Captain Brassbound's Conversion* was not originally intended for Janet, but she played it at the Stage Society's original performance; and here is the author's criticism of her work:

G.B.S. ON BEING A LADY IN HIGH COMEDY

Piccard's Cottage, St. Catherine's
Guildford. Xmas Day 1900.

My dear Janet,

I saw the performance at the greatest possible disadvantage from the back of the worst box in the house. However, perhaps I am none the worse able to tell you about it for having seen the thing too close.

There is no doubt that you did, in a sort, begin to act high comedy for the first time in your life in the sense of carefully composing a picture instead of merely looking into a mirror in a volcanic manner, and saying: There! there's your Nora, Candida, etc. And you were so excited at finding the thing coming off, that each laugh produced the effect of a tablespoonful of brandy and soda; so that, if the graver touches had not brought you back to your seriousness, dignity, and power, you would finally have made Lady Cicely an exceptionally obstreperous maenad. You made points, rammed them home, and rollicked and clowned in a way that would have scandalized John Nash. Of course the audience liked it; but they knew no better: their delight was the measure of your condescension. A well trained French audience—say an aristocratic Gluck and Molière XVIII-century audience—would have been shocked. There were moments which you enjoyed amazingly, at which Sir Howard and Lady Cicely quite vanished, and what remained was "a Christian dorg and his woman."

The fact is, you tumbled to the trick of comedy acting suddenly and luckily; but the mere trick of it will carry you no further than—. You can save the situation by falling back, in *my* plays where the opportunities are mixed and the comedy tissue is shot with reality and tragedy, on the great Janet; but in a St. James's fashionable comedy you wouldn't get the chance. And that is why you would not suit the St. James's, because your comedy is not delicate enough, your parts are not studied enough, and your heavy qualities not wanted.

Before you can play Lady Cicely perfectly, you will have to do what the author did, and do it much more minutely and personally than he; that is, make a careful study of the English lady. Mind: I don't mean the English bourgeoise, nor the English artist-Bohemian; I mean the great lady. It is very difficult to say a thing like this to a charwoman, because she immediately flushes indignantly and says, "I ham a lidy." And as every human being has something of the charwoman's vanity and folly left, especially in their haughty youth, it is probable that the real reason that you have never dispassionately studied the great lady as an Icelander might study an elephant is that you have concluded that one lady is like another, and that since your father kept a gig (so to speak) you have nothing to learn. As a matter of fact there are no two animals in the whole human fauna more completely different in every trick and touch than a great lady and Janet Achurch.

I am like Molière in point of always consulting my cook about my plays. She is an excellent critic; goes to my lectures and plays; and esteems actors and actresses as filthy rags in comparison to the great author they interpret. Consulted as to Lady Cicely, she at once said: "No: she wasn't right: when she sat down she got her dress tucked in between her knees: no high lady would do that." Now that is an excellent criticism. You played the whole part, as far as the comedy went, with your dress tucked between your knees. Of the dress itself I say nothing; for we must do what we can afford in that way, not what we like; but although you solved the difficulty of looking well on artistic lines—on *Liberty lines*—on simple, sensible lines, such lines are quite wrong lines for Lady Cicely, who would associate that sort of dressing with Fitzjohn's Avenue and professional people who don't go to church. The directions in the play, to the effect that Lady C. does not wear a tailor made tourist's suit, and that she dresses as she would in summer in Surrey, mean that she is too conventional to regard dress as a wholly adaptable-to-circumstances matter. She would wear petticoats and drawers, just as she would say her prayers, for half a century after all the working women in the country would have taken to knickerbockers and agnosticism.

She would hardly ever show real excitement, or lose her distinction and immense self-complacency and habit of patronage. She wouldn't, for instance, if a fly bit her, go for it with a cat-o'-nine tails as an Australian drover goes for a fly on the flank of the furthest off bullock with his stockwhip. She might have plenty of tricks, and silly tricks too; she might be childish, and make little jokes and puns that only courtiers laugh at; she might even go on with men in a way which in a shop-girl would lead to overtures and be understood to have that intention; she might do forty thousand things that no woman who was not either above or below suspicion would do (the coincidences between the tramp and the aristocrat are very interesting); but in everything external she would be distinguished from the middle-class woman, who lives her whole life under suspicion and shortness of cash. Until you have mastered all these marks of caste, and can imitate them as easily as you can change a number five stick of grease paint for a number ten, you will not be able to do Lady Cicely as finely as a very obvious housemaid at the Théâtre Français can do the Queen in *Ruy Blas*. It is not that court ladylikeness is difficult; but it is antipathetic to the free Bohemian middle-class *revoltée:* the essence of it is flunkeyism, upper-servantism; and you will have to become as heartless as I am before you can study it quite dispassionately and put it on quite mechanically. But it is worth doing, as it involves a good deal of technical refinement along with its moral slavery.

Meanwhile, to be able to do Eyolf's mother and not a commonplace comedy is to have something of Laurence Irving's fault of never being able to strike less than twelve, which means being out of an engagement for 22 hours out of 24. Lady Cicely is the first sign you have given of reaching the wise age of comedy and being able to play the fiddle as well as the trombones and drums.

I went out of town dead beat, immediately after the Sunday performance, and did not see the Thursday one, nor get your letter in time to act on it. Was the Thursday performance worse than the Sunday one? I expected it would be. You may have observed that the critics have shaken down at last into something like a firm opinion about me, the favourable ones playing up strongly and the unfavourable ones saying boldly out that the thing is a failure. That's a great advance on the help-a-lame-dog-over-a-stile business.

Barker was *very* good. We must stick to Barker.

Yrs, dear Janet

G.B.S.

Janet Achurch died in September 1916, and Charles Charrington in the same month ten years later. Nora, their only child married an actor and went on the stage, but died in 1914, at the age of twenty-four. The race of these theatrical pioneers of Ibsenism is thus tragically extinct. Only a few elderly authors and producers know what they contributed to the drama of our day.

January 1928

* *

OTIS SKINNER

*

Kindling the Divine Spark

IT IS A MATTER of gratification that our theatre has no specific rule for comedy acting. Could we turn out our comedians like Packards they would all be paragons. I can imagine nothing more ghastly. It is an art that cannot be taught; it is as variable as the wind, more unpredictable than the gambols of a kitten. It knows no law.

And yet for several hundred years on the French and Italian stages comedy action was only to be found in definitely prescribed types. Spectators of the *commedia dell' arte* demanded certain stage tricks from its Scapino, Dottore, Pantalone and Capitano which were familiar not only to themselves but to their grandsires, clichés handed down from generation to generation, indelibly labeling each character.

Moreover, if you would see tradition in its stereotyped perfection today, go to the Théâtre Français for a revival of any Molière comedy. It is as rigid as a religious ritual—the removal of the plumed hat, the snuff box, handkerchief, walking stick, the position of the hands, arms and feet follow the directions established by Jean-Baptiste Poquelin himself.

The formal street salutation by a pair of greeting gallants, for instance, never varies. The long walking stick is planted at arm's length to the left, held by the two middle fingers and thumb with the forefinger resting on the top; the right hand is swung over the head to the left, grasping the hat's broad brim on that side; the hat is then lifted as one raises the lid to a basket (so that its removal may not disarrange the carefully curled peruke) and with a full-armed swing brought around to the saluter's heart. It is then extended to the salutee and returned to the heart, whereupon, as each bends his torso in greeting, that hat once more circles the air and is restored to its original resting place with mathematical precision.

And against this background, hung upon this traditional framework, the figures of Tartuffe, *Les Précieuses Ridicules, Le Bourgeois Gentilhomme* come to life not alone in their own colors but as each performer paints them. Constant Coquelin's Mascarille was as different from other and lesser Mascarilles as day from night.

Even the horse-play that Hamlet deplored in the clowns who "made the judicious grieve" must conform to prescribed standards. But does not all this apply to the tragic muse as well? Assuredly. Nevertheless, in spite of established modes in acting, the Macbeths, the Hamlets, the Juliets and the Lady Macbeths have been as varied and multicolored as seashore pebbles.

However, it is the intellectual rather than the sentient appeal that Comedy makes to an audience who, when spectators of rapturous, thrilling or tragic scenes, may be stirred mainly by their sensuous fire. Before you take your seat at the performance of an emotional drama you may, if you will, check your critical faculties in the cloak room but beware of doing that at a comedy. It won't be necessary to carry your hammer, your axe or your scalpel, but the more alert your mind the greater the sum of your enjoyment in the lines and the acted scenes.

Swept along in an emotional or tragic part an actor may be effective through a nervous intensity alone; a species of hysteria that acts as a smoke screen to his limitations becomes contagious with his audience. Many indifferent players have had wonderful first nights, but the day arrives when hysteria will come at their beckoning.

I remember with infinite amusement my early invocations to the bogey man of inspiration. There was one hurdle that grew higher and higher the farther it receded from my first performance—Laertes in *Hamlet.* Laertes has a terrific handicap to overcome: shortly after the opening of the play he disappears and for an hour and a half must sit in his dressing room drenched with inertia. At the end of Act IV, he comes tearing on the scene like a runaway horse, shrieking for vengeance for his father's death. This is a pretty large order for anybody—it was especially so for me. For a while, after my first acquaintance with this fiery young man, I was all excitement about him. My reception in the part was gracious and my press notices were fine. Then something happened. I had lost something. Where was the fire that had nearly consumed me a month ago? Only its embers were faintly visible.

Dismayed, I resorted to every expedient to revive the dying flame. I went through violent calisthenics in my dressing room, put on boxing gloves for a bout with my fellow players, tried deep breathing exercises until I was weak. Once I donned my street clothes, ran a mile out of a western town and, returning, scrambled precipitantly into my stage costume. I bolted onto the scene breathless, with my heart pounding like a trip hammer. I was certainly a very excitable Laertes that night, but I never tried it again. It was all very childish.

I was discovering that passionate impulse in the actor is dynamite, excellent when properly handled but liable to blow him to pieces unless skillfully controlled. A fine, sensitive reaction to the emotions of a character is a priceless possession for the player, but if he drowns himself in grief and gives all to Hecuba, he is far from the purpose of playing. He is the driver of a spirited team of feeling but he must keep a cool head and hold a tight rein. Tears and thrills are for his audience, his the business of administering them. Too copious a shower back stage will produce a drought in front of the curtain.

Sarah Siddons, Melpomene's majestic daughter, once said to a talented associate, "Kelly, you feel too much; if you feel so strongly you'll never make an actor." This august lady, who at the domestic dinner table stabbed her boiled potato as if she were murdering King Duncan and who once, while pricing calico, terrified the mercer's clerk by demanding in Lady Macbeth's sepulchral tones, "In God's name, sirrah, will it wash?" wore her crown "with a difference," but she was never so torn by her tragic woes as to upset her mental balance. To quote William Winter, "When playing Constance she wept over Prince Arthur so copiously that his collar was wet with her tears; yet when she rushed from the stage in the full tide of overwhelming anguish she would walk placidly to the green room taking snuff with the utmost composure."

Even our high priests and priestesses of ecstasy, the elder Booth, Matilda Heron, Fanny Janauschek and Clara Morris, never lost themselves in the flood. Morris could turn on the taps at will but her clutch on the gauge was always sure and steady. It is singular that so eminent a practitioner as Henry Irving should have held to the theory of free abandonment to deep feeling in acting.

The gifted Garrick, who held the supremacy of Old Drury for over three decades, would sometimes, after he had lifted the audience from their chairs with an outburst as King Lear, turn up stage waiting for applause to subside and say to the actor playing the Fool, "This is stage feeling. It got them, Joe."

I have never known a great actor to "lose himself in his part" (as the phrase goes); he may be in a state of great exaltation but unless he has completely lost his self-control he can never forget that he is on a stage, before an audience, and has a part to play. This notwithstanding the legends concerning those intrepid explorers into Alcoholia, George Frederick Cooke and Junius Brutus Booth, whose adventures in that misty land were wild and hilarious.

However, we are talking about Comedy. What have tears and strides, elocution, woes and passions, ambition and grandeur to do with the comic mask? Everything. Thalia and Melpomene are coupled and inseparable, but the little hussy, Thalia, is the fairer sister; she can say with Beatrice, "There was a star danced and under that I was born." They must both present themselves for favor before an audience. Comedy, however, demands more of both audience and player than her somber mate; she's a fickle jade and you must be mentally alert if you would catch her moods, quick to detect her surprises, the subtle wit of her sayings and the quiet but eloquent suggestions in her pantomime, tolerant even when she beats you with a bladder.

Tragedy may take you into a bleak barn and move your heart to pity, sympathy or terror, but Comedy must furnish her house with meticulous care and be mighty busy about it. She has the more difficult job to do.

When the curtain goes up on a comedy of wit, of manners, of amusing character or situation for the first time, the chances are that it is only partly prepared. It hasn't met its associate director—an audience; that audience will be the final arbiter to tell author, actor and producer what is right and what is wrong. The higher its intelligence the more vital, of course, becomes its assistance. But it must be remembered that acting is not a one-sided affair. It is a collaboration between actor and audience that makes for cohesion and unity, and it is the business of the actor's art to keep this partnership a secret to himself. Too open an avowal of it defeats his aims and breaks the connection.

A comedy may be rehearsed fifty times and its every nuance and detail worked out with microscopic direction but behind the first night's curtain there is always a huge interrogation mark. I do not refer to the open verdict whether or no such and such a performance is a failure or a success. The audience is the *unconscious* barometer by which the actor judges the even running of his machine. He must time his pace to its mood. He has learned by experience in other plays what is effective and what is not, but every new part is an experiment. There is no such thing as an abiding rule, and he is never quite sure.

Before the premiere of *Kismet* my wife, who had watched the rehearsals, felt sanguine about the outcome. She had no fears for me and said as much to manager Charles Frohman. "Mrs. Skinner," he replied, "you never know. Otis may sneeze at the wrong moment."

The performance of any new comedy is filled with surprises on its opening night, even to its author; things showing positive brilliance will ebb into ditch water. Disaster may overtake a humorously risqué phrase by undue emphasis rendering it offensive. On the other hand, lines completely ignored at rehearsal become highlights in the performance. The player, perhaps, will be stopped by a burst of delight midway in a speech that has seemed utterly trivial.

There may also be occasions when he finds by that sixth sense which defies analysis—merely something vaguely felt—that he is playing a character at a non-adjustable angle to his audience and must alter his entire conception of the part's possibilities. It was once my fortune to have this untoward upset happen to me as Colonel Phillipe Bridau in *The Honor of the Family*. In studying the part I found him, as I thought, the typical swashbuckler; he was a familiar character to me. I had played many such. He smashes through the play, relentlessly hewing away all obstacles.

We opened for a tryout at New Rochelle on a terribly stormy night, almost unannounced, to a sparse audience. The first act dawdled along until my appearance—a melodramatic burst upon the scene one minute before the curtain. I know I couldn't fail, it was one of those flawlessly written, actor-proof situations. I was prepared for the applause that followed. It was a small riot drowning the racket of the rain on the theatre's roof. There were a half a dozen recalls for the company and when I took my own I was greeted with a howl of glee. The play continued; the moment I reappeared in the second act the howl broke into a general hearty laugh. That laugh revealed my real identity; I was no romantic hero. "Good Lord," I said to myself, "this Colonel Bridau is funny!" From that moment my part was easy. Through the weeks that followed, *The Honor of the Family* developed into an unusual success and more and more on the comedy side which I elaborated bit by bit. It took many weeks to reconstruct the play. Thanks to the wise stage direction of my audience I played the Colonel for four seasons.

To a comedy long runs are always detrimental, sometimes fatal. The players grow careless, allowing their minds to stray away from their work. The original spirit and freshness drift into inertia or else into exaggeration and over-stressing of points.

While playing Mrs. Malaprop to Joseph Jefferson's Bob Acres, Mrs. Drew, to her distress, found her comic speeches going very flat. She consulted Mr. Jefferson. "I'm not getting the laughs I used to get," she said, "what's the matter?"

"Mrs. Drew," he answered, "it's because you read the lines as though *you* thought them funny. Try reading them seriously."

I asked Jefferson how he managed to keep himself alert and spontaneous as Rip van Winkle and Bob after thousands of performances.

"I have a very simple method," he said. "I force myself into the belief that I am playing them for the first time. I say, 'This is an interesting fellow. I'm glad I met him.' You set the tone and tempo of your acting from your various audiences, and you must not be caught napping. Work like the dickens when you're studying your effects, but don't carry your tools into the theatre. Leave them in the workshop. Most anybody can be funny but real comedy is the most serious and difficult business in the whole world. It's a shy thing—comedy—chase it too hard and it runs away from you.

"I found that out when Billy Florence and I were a two-star team in *The Rivals.* I had been used to work all the tricks of terror in the duel scene, shaking knees, ghastly face, and so forth, as Acres sneaks off with his courage oozing from his fingertips. They used to laugh tremendously at it and, of course, I liked the laughter—but I must be fair to Florence. I must give him a show as Sir Lucius O'Trigger. So I didn't work at all. I gave Sir Lucius a look and turned and walked quietly into the wings and, by George! they shouted louder than ever."

"Never rush your comedy points," he once told me. "The more quiet and deliberate you are the better your effect."

There was an occasion when I pursued a laugh for two weeks before I captured it. As the beggar, Hajj, in *Kismet* I was thrown into a stygian dungeon. After bemoaning my fate for a few moments and calling on Allah to avenge my wrongs, from out the darkness came the jeering voice of my dearest foe. With a yell of triumph I responded with, "Allah is good! We shall end side by side. I die content." Sheer melodrama—nothing particularly comic in that. One night a slight titter from out front caught my ear. Sensing a humorous slant in the line, I began experimenting. Night after night I tried every inflection, pace and vocal pitch to call it back. It still eluded me. At times the laugh was more pronounced but never spontaneous, until I struck the exact technique—a high-pitched initial note descending, like a skier shooting down a slide, to the finish. It was pure vocal trickery. Comedy imposes many tricks.

The notable controversy between Irving and Coquelin regarding the expenditure of deep personal feeling in acting is still remembered—Irving on the emotional side, Coquelin the advocate of carefully planned and delivered effect. There should really have been no dispute at all. Both were right. It was the tragedian arguing against the comedian.

There is no such thing as "natural acting," if by that you mean the photographic and cinematic reproduction of the individual in everyday life. It is entirely an artificial process, however colloquially presented. To a young eighteenth-century farceur who claimed that his success lay in acting as nature dictated, the old comic, Munden, retorted, "Nature? Nature be damned! You make them laugh." To my mind a performance is perfect only when the player is keyed to great and resilient elation, when his heart is beating a little faster, when the emotions of his character expose themselves clearly to his eye and color his movement. In that clarity new things born of the moment's impulse suggest themselves and become incorporated in succeeding performances.

But—and here is the paradox—possessing all these he must still be the cool-minded and alert technician whose efficiency is brought about by long study and experiment.

Those who had the good fortune to witness Gertrude Lawrence's brilliant performance in *Susan and God* saw technical invention at its best. Its variety was infinite, its timing perfect and its spirit irresistible.

I recall the late Mrs. Fiske's strikingly individual methods in many plays. Learning her vocation from childhood she became mistress of comedy expression that never failed her. She saw life through the lens of the acted scene. Although her nature was "subdued to what it worked in like the dyer's hand" her instinct for truth was unerring. When all is said, acting, tragic or comic, knows no definite rule. Genius submits to no restraint. In its last analysis it is a case of Personality.

September 1938

CEDRIC HARDWICKE

*

The Moribund Craft of Acting

IN A SEASON so distinguished as the present, with performances like Robert Morley's Wilde, Maurice Evans' Hamlet, Raymond Massey's Lincoln and Walter Huston's Stuyvesant, it is perhaps a little far-fetched to suggest that acting as an art seems to be dying. But I think of the younger actors when I say this.

Nor is it more than passing strange that in the midst of all this superb performing one should complain of slow strangulation: great art, great acting, always come at the end of an epoch, not at its beginning.

It may be possible that the younger actor will be able to meet the many new obstacles in his way and emerge as equal to the artists of any generation. But the way is difficult, more difficult perhaps than he realizes. Fashions have changed; points of view have shifted. It would not be amiss at this time to set forth what is in the way of good acting and what seems to be strangling it.

Today the mode is to say that the actor is merely one cog in the machine, like the designer, the director, the author and the ticket-taker. Recently when the Moscow Art Theatre celebrated an anniversary the hat-check girls applauded equally with the directors and the actors. No one denies the cooperative nature of any theatrical enterprise; still less does he wish to make the function of the actor more important than it need be. But we seem to forget that it is the actor and only the actor that can make the play breathe. Until he speaks and moves, the play is a closet-drama, interesting, perhaps, but utterly lifeless.

It is therefore with some slight amusement that I have heard playwrights say that a good play should be actor-proof. I have never heard a composer declare his concerto pianist-proof, but it has always made me think that, if our playwrights feel that the actor is an unfortunate handicap in the creation of a work of art, a kind of necessary evil, they would be better off writing novels. The novel *is* actor-proof.

The novel, too, has many advantages which the theatre cannot offer. It is more free; it gives the writer greater scope. The novel is a better form in which to handle ideas or propaganda. The theatre, being the most explicit of the arts, demands ideas and truths in their most abstract form: poetic truths.

Since Ibsen, however, playwrights have been more pleased to enlighten us than to stir us. We have received sermons on divorce, youthful sinning, getting married and a variety of topics. The theatre for its own sake seems just a little shameful and not quite worth the attention of an intelligent individual. Of course, a propaganda play can be great theatre; Ibsen and Shaw are master dramatists. But the same cannot always be said of those who have been influenced by them.

In its search for realism the modern theatre has discarded many old techniques. The term *theatric,* for example, has come to be one of derision. Today all motivations tend to be clear, and all characterizations sharply etched. Shakespeare knew better. Lear is one of my favorite parts, but I cannot for the life of me understand why the old man should be so foolish as to ask his daughters which of them loves him most. It is the actor's task, however, to make this preposterous situation credible: nor is it surprising that a good actor does just that which we, in the quiet of our study, cannot do. And as for *theatric,* what could be more unrestrained, more turbulent, than the picture of Lear at the end of the play? What contemporary modes of underwriting and underplaying could convey the old man broken by tragedy, wild with grief?

Shakespeare always allowed scope to the actor's art, always left hidden, secret meanings for the actor to bring to light. Hamlet, of course, is the classic example; the pundits are still learnedly mulling over his motivations and his character.

I have been playing Canon Skerritt in *Shadow and Substance* for more than a year now and I confess that outside the theatre there are many things the Canon does and says that I cannot fathom the meaning of. Brigid will have left him one moment quite charmed by her and the next the Canon sees of her he will be sharp and cross to her. That is, however, as it should be. Before the footlights there exists another world, not the "real" world, and it has its own laws and meanings, its own spatial and temporal limitations. Mr. Paul Vincent Carroll has been willing to trust his effects to the actors; many of his contemporaries, I daresay, would not be so eager.

Nor are the playwrights alone in their distrust of the actor. In England I have directed plays, and when I chide the director I can take part of the blame. To the man who stages a play the actor is a kind of mimic who parrots back his every inflection and gesture. There was a time, I suppose, when actors champed under this kind of treatment but it is not evident today. I once directed a play in which the actors were given their sides some days before the first rehearsal. They came to that first reading, each one knowing every word of his part perfectly but without one bit of sense to it. They studied words mechanically; the rest they left to the director.

Can I hear the voice of the playwright say, "That is just the reason why a part must be actor-proof. That is why we cannot trust our effects to the actor, why we must be sharp and precise. Leave it to the actor and you will have nothing more than a senseless repetition of words."

But, I contend, the reason one encounters actors like these is that one has playwrights and directors like those who flourish today. The actor must bring to his part no intelligence, no understanding and a minimum of sympathy. He must look right, speak right and be able to follow directions. From long, sad experience the fledgling star knows it is wiser to study nothing more than words.

In our day we have witnessed a hundred theories about training actors, most of which have been advanced by directors, *régisseurs*. There is much in these theories that is valuable. What is true in them is not particularly novel nor does it often consist of more than a technical restatement of verities our common sense tells us are true. One or two of them, like that of Stanislavski, have added to the body of knowledge about the craft of acting. But what I distrust in all of them is their tendency toward cultism, toward forming special little groups which, though they give lip-service to "studying life," do nothing more than function as circles where one may talk shop interminably. For after an actor has mastered the few principles of his trade, the place for him to study is in the world, people, if you please. A portraitist, after he has learned to put brush to canvas, is better off studying people than other portraitists. You would never have had Goya's mordant studies of Spanish royalty, Greco's pictures of the aristocrats, had they done all their studying inside their studios. How can a man whose every friend is an actor, who lives in an hotel or apartment with other actors, eats where they eat, wears what they wear, reads only the theatrical pages, play anything but an actor?

The modern theatre puts yet another obstacle in the way of the young actor. That is the stage designer. Now there are stage designers and there are men to whom a play is an excuse to erect some kind of circus, preferably on a revolving stage, which they must necessarily suffer actors to punctuate with speeches before the scene can change to permit another round of applause. What is wrong with some of these magnificent designs we have all admired? They are impressive, they are expensive, they are ingenious. Their only flaw is that they so reduce the actor in stature as to change the focus of the whole play. Impressed by the technical dexterity of the designer we do not hear the actor or the author. That is why, incidentally, a mediocre play must have the best and most impressive settings money can buy.

The very nature of the modern stage, even when the case is not so extreme as I have made it, relieves the actor of his old function of scenewright. When we can build a magnificent castle for our audience to see, why should our playwrights trouble to describe it as beautifully as Shakespeare does in *Macbeth?* Shakespeare had no modern lighting board, nor could he call upon the genius of the scene-builder; so to create a magic island he had to create magic poetry for the actor who played Prospero. In a sense, therefore, the technical progress the modern theatre has made is the actor's irreparable loss. Necessarily, he is called upon to do less and less.

Though I am not an antiquarian and though I do not suggest to modern playwrights that they employ old devices when they have newer techniques at hand, it is interesting to point out that one of the most beautiful plays of our day, Thornton Wilder's *Our Town,* used a stage much like the Elizabethan and achieved much of its eloquence because the author asked of the theatre that it give him nothing more than four walls and a few lights; for the rest he depended on his own genius.

As well as being sinned against the modern actor sins against himself. Since the theatre began striving for realism, the actor, always an humble fellow, began striving for lifelike effects, too. His voice fell from the declamatory to the sweet, sugary tones of a crooner. Instead of gesturing and posturing, he now limits himself elegantly to flicking the ash from a cigarette or adjusting his shirt-cuffs under his jacket. It is, of course, perfectly true that there is no longer any necessity for the excessive gesturing of yesterday when stages were poorly lit and acoustics bad. But here is another instance where progress has hurt the craft. The result is that today an audience must comprehend a play entirely with its ear and, since it has given up adequate gesture as being too theatric, acting has tended to become more and more inarticulate. The cult of the inarticulate reaches its height in Chekhov and it is not surprising that the modern actor is always little less than perfect in the Russian's plays.

Behind all this lies the contemporary trend toward realism in the theatre. No one wants to go back to the days when every room was the size of a room in Buckingham Palace. And it is quite natural that in a democratic era our theatre should concern itself with life as everybody knows it and lives it. But we have gone further. We have *excluded* the colorful, the dramatic, the excessive, because it is too theatric. The fallacy behind the realistic theatre, I think, is that there is no reason to go to the theatre if it must consist only of the drab and commonplace, of events that could occur to any individual in multitude. The world outside is too exciting, too full of conflict, of drama, of struggle, for us to care very much about the prosy problems of some petit-bourgeois merely because they transpire on the stage.

Today the world is a theatre: we see men in politics as personalities engaging in a great drama in which we are at once spectators and participants. Politicians rant, they cry, they storm the very Heavens, they threaten, they perform before vast multitudes. Only the realistic theatre is still anxious about the problems of the little man.

This is not to say that our theatre is all realism. Everywhere one sees evidence of growing poetic awareness on the part of dramatists, a growth of vision, a working with newer, more heroic materials. Maxwell Anderson comes to mind for his historical plays and Robert E. Sherwood for his beautiful evocation of Lincoln, the hero.

But these hopeful signs are not the rule. Otherwise, the realistic theatre is another evidence of the moribund craft of acting. In this country these problems take on a very special significance. I have outlined all the new problems the younger actors must face today; in America they are especially acute. You have so much here that is matchless, such an audience, such technical perfection, such a body of vastly talented young people, that you will forgive an Englishman for inquiring where—with some very honorable exceptions—are the American actors? Your actresses are the best in the world. But what of the men?

Alfred Lunt is a joy to watch; Walter Huston is a grand actor and there are many others that one could list easily and confidently. But one October day I glance at the theatrical page and I see that Messrs. Massey, Evans, King, Lawson, Keith, Brice, Digges, Morley and Bateman are engaged in leading roles. We await Messrs. Merivale, Kortner, Sokoloff, Homolka, Lukas, Waram, Oscar and Daniell. There is not an American actor in the list. What is it that makes the New York managers seek outlanders?

I think Americans must soon ask themselves whether the very structure of their theatre is not unnecessarily adding to the burdens under which acting is laboring. Does the American theatre hinder the development of the craft in so far as it offers no training for the very young actor?

In England we have touring companies. It is possible for a young actor to master his craft in many years of touring and playing a multiplicity of roles. We have repertory theatres all over the country. An actor can gain poise, technical assurance and authority by actually working before audiences. The young American actor Orson Welles began his career by taking advantage of the opportunities our theatre offers younger actors. An actor will never gain the experience he needs by interviewing managers, playing before cameras or lunching in the right restaurants.

What, then, do you offer the younger actor here? Your tributary theatres, as you call them, can offer him some employment; but it is exceptional, not usual. Unselfish, theatre-wise people like Katharine Cornell and the Lunts are developing what amount to repertory companies and offer untold opportunities for the younger actors in their companies. The Mercury Theatre offers similar opportunities; the Group Theatre has developed a number of actors. There are in the hinterland, I am told, a few stock companies which employ professionals.

But all this is not nearly enough. You have to develop hundreds and hundreds to get one great artist. The system must by its very nature be superabundantly generous. It requires more than individual effort. Today the only way a young American actor gains experience is to be the perfect "type" for a play and, luckily, find the play a hit.

In a country where the psychology of the frontier still exists, most people, I daresay, expect success early and lavishly dread the day-to-day work it demands. Thus I have often heard young American actors tell me that they have turned down jobs with stock companies in, say, Louisville or New Orleans because they "would just be wasting a year." It makes me wonder if I wasted a year playing in churches, hotel dining rooms and lecture halls in South Africa in 1913?

Now you can say that all these things I have been pointing out are true enough but that it has been ever thus with supreme genius —yet somehow it will emerge, whatever the conditions. I will not deny it. There is something mystic, unknowable about genius: the spark is there and it fires us. An inexperienced child can make technically competent people seem cold and lifeless. But in truth I have not presumed to speak of supreme genius: that does not bear speaking about except perhaps by geniuses, of which I know I am not one. I have really been speaking of competent, fine craftsmen. *They* must be developed. And we can tell how well the system functions by examining the performances in the lesser parts.

Our theatre can learn much from yours, but in almost every English play you will find the small parts played to perfection. The dramatist Somerset Maugham, when he came to writing his artistic testament, *The Summing Up,* singled out only one actor for special mention, not a star, sometimes not even featured, an actor who has played small roles in Mr. Maugham's plays and played them perfectly: Mr. C. V. France. When a dramatist does that, he does more than pay polite respects to a few stars: he pays tribute to an institution. And the reason you will find these small parts played so beautifully is that the English theatre, for all its faults, gave the actor just the training and experience he needed to do his job well.

Where—lacking a system of touring companies, stock companies, repertory theatres—is America to recruit its leading actors ten or fifteen years from today?

People are afraid of a "shortage" of good playwrights. It is a justifiable concern. But how much more acute not to have actors—trained, capable actors! Mr. John Golden and the Dramatists Guild are giving some thirty fellowships to young playwrights. Americans must now ask themselves if they are doing enough for their younger actors. Are they being given every opportunity to master the tools of their craft? The very nature of the modern theatre, as I have shown, militates against the growth of the art of acting: it now stands still and indeed loses much of its old function. But the structure of the theatre, which is man-made, should not as well be permitted to hamper the development of a body of fine actors.

February 1939

* *

SERGEI EISENSTEIN

*

The Enchanter from the Pear Garden

MEI LAN FANG'S POPULARITY extends far beyond the boundaries of China: his portrait or silhouette you can find in the house of every intellectual Chinese family in San Francisco, in the little stores of Chinatown in New York, in the fashionable Chinese restaurants in Berlin, in the taverns of Yucatan—everywhere where there beats a Chinese heart that remembers its country. Everywhere Mei Lan Fang is known. Everywhere you can find copies of the statue-poses in which, following the Chinese theatrical tradition, he performs episodes from his remarkable dance-dramas. But it is not only among his countrymen that Mei Lan Fang is popular. The greatness of his art captivates people of other countries and of different cultural traditions. Charlie Chaplin was the first to tell me about the remarkable work of this great Chinese artist. . . .

Articles and stories about the Chinese theatre usually stress those "peculiarities" which strike the superficial and unprepared tourist accustomed to the routine of the European stage. These "peculiarities" are never considered to have any connection with Western-European theatre and its art, and yet the influence of the Chinese theatre upon Western theatrical art, particularly upon the Soviet theatre, is well known. But that is not what I want to speak about here. Nor do I want to describe those marvelous and unexpected things that the Chinese theatre holds in store for the uninitiated spectator. The technique and system of the Chinese theatre deserves more than a catalogue of its peculiarities. It deserves a deeper look into that philosophy which is expressed in art forms apparently so removed and yet so near to us which, although not always understood, are always profoundly experienced. Otherwise, how can one explain the magnetic creative force which has made this art overlap national boundaries. Should we enter deeper into its meaning, these peculiarities would indeed soon lose their strangeness. How many tourists, for instance, have been amazed by the fact that the audience in the theatre was seated in profile, facing a long table that extended perpendicularly from the stage. Yet there is nothing strange in that. According to the ancient tradition the ear and not the eye should be turned toward the stage; one went to the ancient Chinese theatre not to see a drama but to hear one. A somewhat similar theatrical tradition we have in our own Moscow Maly Theatre. The older generation still remembers Ostrovsky, who never looked upon his plays from the auditorium but listened to them from back stage.

The ancient Chinese theatre was always synthetic: the dance was organically related to the song. Then a separation was effected. The vocal aspect of the theatre began, at the expense of the plastic, to root itself in the north of China. The visual aspect flourished in the south. Thus, even today, a northern Chinese speaks of going to "hear" a drama while a southern Chinese goes to "see" a drama.

Mei Lan Fang was confronted with the problem of creating a synthesis of these two tendencies. A profound student of Chinese culture, he revived the ancient Chinese theatrical tradition. He resurrected the visual aspect of the theatre, adding to it a complex blending of dance and music and thus restoring the ancient Chinese synthetic theatre. But Mei Lan Fang is not merely a restorer. He knows how, in restoring the perfect forms of the old traditions, to endow them with a new content. He tries always to broaden the thematic content of his plays and he tends to emphasize social problems. Several of the hundreds of plays in which Mei Lan Fang performs speak of the difficult social status of the woman, the exploitation of the poor, and so forth. Some of them deal with the struggle against backwardness and religious superstition. These dramas, although played in the old conventionalized style, because of the temporary themes and problems they present, are of a poignant sharpness and splendor. The theme of the woman is presented in his plays from many angles. His ability to depict a variety of female types is a great achievement of Mei Lan Fang's art. Usually there is a specialization and a limitation in the actor's field, but Mei Lan Fang is a master over a wide range, and while adhering strictly to the traditional style in depicting his female characters, he has added a number of details.

Chinese theatrical tradition knows six basic female characters:

1. *Ching-Tan*—a kind matron, a faithful wife and devoted daughter.

2. *Hua-Tan*—a younger woman, usually a servant. Whereas *Ching-Tan* represents a positive type, lyrical and melancholy, depicted usually through songs, *Hua-Tan* represents a frivolous type. She is usually depicted through fast and lively movement.

3. *Kuei-Men-Tan*—a girl, graceful, elegant and kind.

4. *Wu-Tan*—a heroic girl; a female soldier and military commander.

5. *Tsai-Tan*—a cruel and intriguing woman, a servant always ready to betray her masters. Although she is endowed with great beauty, she is nevertheless extremely base.

6. *Lao-Tan*—a very old woman, usually a mother. This is the most realistically presented woman on the Chinese stage. The part is played with great tenderness.

All of the names of these female characters end with the symbol *Tan*. In ordinary translation this symbol designates one who performs a female role. This, however, does not explain the complete meaning of the word. The symbol *Tan,* as Mei Lan Fang emphasizes, while it describes the concept of woman on the Chinese stage, stands primarily for a stylized, aesthetically abstract image of woman, altogether unrealistic.

The realistic depiction of woman is not part of the Chinese actor's art. Instead, the audience is treated to an idealized, generalized female image. Realistic in its own specific sense, capable of touching upon familiar episodes of history and legend, as well as upon social and everyday problems of life, the Chinese theatre, nevertheless, is conventionalized in its form, from its treatment of character to the minutest detail of stage effect. Indeed, no matter with what aspect of the Chinese theatre you deal, "each situation, each object is presented abstractly and often symbolically." Pure realism has been banished from the Chinese stage.

Let me cite a few examples from the ancient theatre.

Ma-Pien is a riding whip. When an actor holds a whip in his hand he is supposed to be riding horseback. The mounting and dismounting is depicted through established conventions of movement.

Che-Chi is a cart. It is depicted by two flags upon which there are painted wheels. Two servants hold the flags on each side of the rider who may either stand quietly or move about.

Ling-Chien is the messenger's arrow. When in ancient times a military commander would dispatch a messenger, he would entrust him with an arrow to indicate the authenticity of his news and also to convey the command that the message should be delivered with the speed of an arrow.

Similar symbols are used in the stage directions. For instance, if a Chinese actor is to show that he is passing through a door, he limits himself to raising one leg as though he were crossing a threshold. If, at the same time, he is supposed to be opening the door, he spreads his hands towards a non-existent door. When he is closing the door, he brings his hands together. These conventional stage directions are identical whenever a door is part of the business—for entrance or exit, for inside and outside, and so forth.

A realistic depiction of a dream is considered unaesthetic. If an actor is required to show that he is dreaming, he does so by leaning his head on a table. The act of battle is characterized by the following basic traits: "The art of the duel on the stage consists first of all in the fact that the enemies never touch each other." The duel consists of swiftly changing, synchronized rhythmical movements which give a conventionalized concept of the duel. Finally, in the old drama the taking of food was never presented realistically. Eating was usually depicted through a song or through several tunes on a flute. Such examples as these will show how certain objects have acquired definite symbolic meaning.

More interesting are the cases where the meanings are multifarious, where one and the same object, depending upon its use, may have more than one meaning. Such, for instance, are a table, a chair and a broom made of horsehair. "A table or *Cho-Tzu,* more than any other object, can depict all sorts of things: sometimes it is an inn, sometimes it is a dining table, a courtroom or an altar." A table is used when it is necessary to show that a man is climbing a mountain or jumping over a fence. When it is turned sideways (*Tao-I*) it symbolizes a man sitting either on a cliff or on the ground in an uncomfortable position. When a woman is climbing a mountain, she gets up on a table. Similarly several chairs put together represent a bed.

Even more varied are the functions of *Yingch'en*—a broom made of horsehair. On the one hand *Yingch'en* represents the attribute of a demigod. Only gods, demigods, Buddhist priests and spirits of various sorts are entitled to possess it. In the hands of a servant, on the other hand, it becomes merely a household object. . . .

This aspect of multifariousness and elasticity is even more striking than the conventional method of acting. What is still more significant is the fact that this multifariousness is not a trait of the theatre alone. Its meaning is rooted much deeper. It is part of the Chinese "thought process" and its influence upon the theatre is merely incidental.

By "thought process" I do not mean the prevalent ideas which are conditioned by the national and racial interests of the Chinese. What I refer to is that aggregate of concepts with which the Chinese operate in the cultural and ultra-rational sphere. Its nature is deeply rooted in the social history of China and in that original social phenomenon according to which forms reflected in consciousness from earlier stages of social development are not discarded by later forms but are canonized by tradition. This, I repeat, is true primarily of the cultural field which is, however, broad enough to include problems of speech, morals, and so on. In this original aggregate of concepts, the structure of the pre-feudal system was preserved. It was shaped into a hierarchical system of thought in the post-feudal periods and finally in the eleventh century into a finished system of philosophy—a justification and legalization of the reign of the rising Han dynasty.

Such order of succession is to a certain degree typical of any system of thought. Particularly is it true of art. The question is, however, one of degree: in Chinese culture these traits are so strongly emphasized that they are strikingly impressive, even outside the boundaries imposed by specific fields of culture. They are essential to an understanding of the complex and exquisite hieroglyphs and emblems of China. Moreover, the multifariousness of meaning that astounds us when we examine the Chinese theatre forms the basis of any Chinese method of expression. In these traits, as well as in a number of other characteristics, the pre-feudal traditions and concepts are strikingly imprinted; you will find traces of them no matter what branch of Chinese culture you examine.

Let us begin with the first means of cultural communication—speech. Here this trait is to be found in practically every word. The Chinese language belongs to the so-called monosyllabic languages. It has 460 monosyllabic words which do not change in speech. They convey definite meaning only when they are pronounced with a certain intonation, with a certain accent. A Chinese expresses each monosyllable in five different intonations. As a result, out of 460 indefinite sounds he acquires 2000 so-called root words, each of which conveys a definite meaning. Since, however, these root words are not sufficient for purposes of speech, there also appear in the Chinese language a number of synonyms, each conveying from four to twelve different meanings. For instance, the designation of a chatterer, a fire, a ship, and feathers are expressed by the word *chou.* The word *hao,* depending upon the intonation with which it is pronounced, may mean "to love," "good," "charity," "friendship," "very." . . . One has to guide oneself by the general context or by the arrangement of the words. Similar phenomena, incidentally, are found in the cultural traditions of other countries, as, for instance, in the English language, the language of a country that is also steeped in traditionalism.

In this connection I remember a humorous poem about a Frenchman who tried hard to learn to pronounce properly the "ough" with which so many words in English end:

> I'm taught p-l-o-u-g-h
> Shall be pronounced "plow."
>
> Zat's easy when you know, I say,
> Mon Anglais I'll get through.
>
> My teacher say zat in zat case
> O-u-g-h is "oo."
>
> And zan I laugh and say to him,
> Zees Anglais makes me cough.

He say: Not coo, but in zat word
O-u-g-h is "off"!

Oh, sacré bleu! Such varied sounds
of words makes me hiccough!

He say: Again mon friend ees wrong!
O-u-g-h is "up."

In hiccough. Zen I cry: No more,
You make my throat feel rough!

Non! Non! he cry, you are not right,
O-u-g-h is "uff."

I say: I try to speak your words
I can't pronounce them though.

In time you'll learn but now you're wrong,
O-u-g-h is "owe."

I'll try no more! I shall go mad,
I'll drown me in the lough!

But ere you drown yourself, said he,
O-u-g-h is "ock."

He taught me more! I held him fast
And killed him with a rough!

In the Chinese language the syntax, unlike that of Western Europe, is still in a rhythmical stage. The rhythmical pronunciation of a whole phrase decides its grammatical meaning—the phrases themselves mean anything you please, like the broom made of horsehair.

A word, a sign, an object and a phrase are not used to convey a definite meaning. While European logic attempts to establish the exact meaning of a given sign, the Chinese sign pursues a different goal. The Chinese hieroglyph serves first of all to convey an emotional impression perceived through a whole aggregate of accompanying impressions. The purpose of the hieroglyph or the symbol is not to give a rigidly defined idea. On the contrary, its purpose is to give a diffused image which is perceived indirectly. The role of the multifarious image is to allow each concept to inject its emotional experience, communicating with its neighbors in the most general terms. It is interesting to note that this method which is based, first of all, upon emotional communication and presented by a symbol which lacks intellectual rigidity could become a method of communication only among the numerous peoples of the orient. The languages of north and south China or of China and Japan are so different that they find it hard to understand each other. The general symbolisms of these languages, however, are similar over the whole great territory. Similar concepts exist in Chinese art and in the theatre. In the light of these traits all the "peculiar" aspects of Chinese theatrical technique become quite explicable.

What then is the practical lesson that we can derive from studying this theatre? For us it is not enough to admire its perfection. We seek in it a means to enrich our own experience. At the same time, we are in entirely different positions. We, in our creative practice, believe in realism and, what is more, in a realism of a higher form of development—socialist realism. The question then arises: Can we derive anything from an art that is altogether steeped in convention and is seemingly incompatible with our system of thought? And if we can derive something from it—what is it?

Whenever we deal with the problem of enriching our experience through other highly developed cultures from which we cannot borrow directly, we must first of all find out where there is a common language and in what specific field of our art we are nearest to this culture. Such a problem, for instance, arose in our relation to the technique of the Japanese Kabuki theatre. In an altogether original way, the Japanese theatre has influenced the aesthetics of our sound cinema.

The experience to be derived from the Chinese theatre is even wider and deeper. In its own sphere it is the acme of perfection, the sum total of those elements which form the kernel of any art work—its imagery. The problem of imagery is one of the main problems of our new aesthetics. While we are fast learning to develop our characters psychologically, we still lack a great deal when it comes to imagery. And here we come upon the most interesting aspect of

Chinese culture—the theatre. Imagery in Chinese art is emphasized at the expense of the concrete and the thematic. This emphasis is the antithesis of the hypertrophy of imagery upon which our art is still based.

Is the polarity of these two approaches incompatible? Not at all. They are just two extremes in the development of those traits which, when they will blend into one harmonious whole, will give the highest phase of realism. And this extreme which is imprinted upon the past cultural traditions of China is highly instructive in its examples of pure imagery, its multifarious and conventionalized symbols. The system of imagery in the Chinese traditional culture is inseparable from us historically. In her great tradition there is imprinted a stage of complex conceptions through which sensibility always operates. The traditional Chinese culture has brought us vestiges of a system of thinking through which every culture must pass at a certain stage.

October 1935

* *

SYBIL THORNDIKE

*

I Look at the Audience

I SUPPOSE the art of the theatre is the only form of art of which the public is an integral part, the only form that is not complete without the spectator. In the fine arts of painting, sculpture or letters, the work is complete without any effort of the outside world. It is very helpful to the artist, no doubt, when good hard cash is paid down and the work is sold; but nothing that the purchaser does or feels or thinks about the particular work can alter it. It is a complete and perfect thing, materialized from the artist's imagination and soul. In music the composition is a complete thing in itself—even a performance of a work can be finished without the public participating, though here again appreciation is extremely pleasant, and helpful, both to pocket and self-esteem.

All forms of art seem to exist completely and separately. They may be understood or not, they may rouse sympathy or not, but the created thing is there. I believe this is why they are called the Fine Arts.

The popular art of the theatre, however, stands on quite another footing. (I do not include the Cinema, because that is also a finished product before it reaches the public, and the performance can never be altered however differently the audiences are feeling about it. In fact, I don't know how to place the Cinema and its canons. I do certainly feel it cannot be judged as the art of the theatre, which depends on interplay between actors and audience. Neither is it a Fine Art. It is, I suppose, a growth from the theatre, but it must be judged separately.)

A play is not for all time, it is for the actual moment. (Reading plays to one's self, by one's own study fire is a pastime of the intellectual which, with a great many people, has taken the place of visiting the theatre and joining in performance—what a great pity this is!)

It may be that a particular play is chosen to be played again and again through the ages, but the rite of performance is the important thing, and it is newly created with each performance. It may be, and most frequently is, that the actors choose the same outward signs and movements—vocal or otherwise—at each performance, but these must be freshly selected and born at the moment, and not just copies of those of previous performances.

Many actors will tell you of that curious sensation we have when entering the stage, as of one's other half-being waiting to be transformed. An expectant force is there, not just separate men and women but an entity, a personality made up of all those men and women who have sunk their separate individualities in the larger common soul of the mob, and this thing has to be shaped and used and made to move by the mind directing. Don't think this absurdly fantastic. I know many widely differing types of actor who feel this in common with me. This mob-soul is a force that is continually baffling us, it is always an unknown quantity. On our first entrance, before a word has left our mouths, we are conscious of this large thing confronting us. Sometimes one knows it is a thing to be fought and struggled with in order to move it and use it, and on these occasions the performance is a big effort, as every sensitive actor will tell you. At other times one is conscious of a something that is feeding one with life, and if the actor is well equipped technically and sensitively, and has something to express, it is on these occasions he can rise to heights greater than he thought possible. He is being given greater life, and the audience get what is often called "a great performance."

I think audiences realize extraordinarily little how much they make or spoil performance in the theatre, and sometimes I wish—and especially do I wish this when the play is of large vision—that (as in Church one has, or is given, a little manual to show what one's attitude of mind should be, and hints how to behave, that the service may not be unfruitful) members of an audience should be handed a few choice words, setting down that too much eating of chocolate, too much blowing of nose and clearing of throat, too much fidgeting of any sort, will prevent the full enjoyment of the play. And let it also be pointed out that these things and their like are a constant source of irritation to fellow members of the audience and induce in the unfortunate actor a feeling closely akin to murder. A quiet body, with few beads and chains to jangle (the dreadful days of the bangle are over, we hope), a quiet, untrammeled mind and a quiet tongue—these three good things will give an atmosphere in which imagination can work. Shakespeare in his Prologues tells the hearers how to receive the play and conduct themselves.

"Don't forget we've come out for an evening's entertainment, will you?" my friends in the audience will say. No, I don't forget that, and I realize there are differences of approach to various entertainments. I am told that a good dinner, with good wine, is the best way to prepare for the enjoyment of a good play. A good dinner—a choice, spare dinner—maybe, but a large dinner and a full content makes the feeder a hard thing to move, and only the most obvious cast-iron humor will reach him, and only the most obvious sentiment will cause the tears to flow down his cheeks.

For the enjoyment of sensitive, subtle humor or sentiment—in order to appreciate the full flavor of Gracie Fields or Edith Evans—I suggest spare feeding, because through these artists, and their like, you will be filled to overflowing with a food of life which will the better spread to all parts of your body if it is not clogged with meat, poultry, suet and ice-cream. For the healthy and normal-stomached, a not-too-vigorous fasting is an excellent preparation for enjoyment. It whets the appetite for exercise, and the mind and body prepared for exercise are the sort of mind and body the actor hopes to encounter as he leaps or crawls or saunters on the stage, ready to give forth the superabundant creative energy that he can scarcely restrain.

Who was it that said of actors "Poor pale ghosts—shadows of Life?" I think that is what our rather hectic, over-busied, over-catered-for life asks of the theatre. "Be ascetic in your life, that in your art you may be violent," said a great French writer. That's better! Give us not pale ghosts or shadows, give us creatures with greater life than we know. Give us a larger-sized life than we actually experience, give us violences, shocks; beings that surge with vigor and electricity, that touching them in spirit we may be charged with that same energy and our grasp and scope be larger.

How wonderful if an audience asks this of its actors. "Give us more," is a cry we seldom hear, but the opposite we hear always and then we wonder why the actors of great energy are all swallowed by revue and music-hall—part of the theatre certainly, the only part that does demand abundant vitality and strength, but, don't let us make any mistake, only a part.

In the Tragic Theatre of England we have nothing which compares with the energy and life of the Comic Theatre in our midst. Comedy and Tragedy (the words Tragic and Comic include all forms of drama) are the whole, and until we embrace both we are one-sided cripples—one part dead—disused; delicate and ailing.

Whose fault is this? The actor knows it is the audience; the audience knows it is the actor, it is probably a bit of both. But how often do we hear that stupid refrain, "But we have tragedy in real life. Why should we have it in the theatre?" Every time this is said to me, with sickening, irritating regularity, it is only by the grace of God and amazing self-control that I am prevented from hurling myself on the speaker.

"You are the servants of the public, you actors. Give the public what it wants." We answer "We are not servants of anyone who does not demand the fullest life. We are the servants of the theatre, of which the public is only a part, and the public doesn't know what it wants till it sees it. Our business is to discover its needs—a very entertaining, intriguing and heartbreaking business. Servant of the public by all means, if by that is meant one who seeks to serve those who do not know what to ask for. The theatre serves those who say 'Show us life and that will suffice us.'"

January 1932

MORTON EUSTIS

*

On the Road with the Lunts

IT WAS A TUESDAY AFTERNOON in the Ellis Auditorium, Memphis, Tennessee. The large arena, which had housed 7,000 people for a boxing match the night before, was shut off from the stage by a steel curtain. An audience of about 2,000 people filled most of the orchestra and balconies of the smaller, but still vast auditorium, except for some blocks of vacant seats in the side sections where the sight lines were such that it was impossible to see more than half of the stage.

There was a burst of applause as the curtain fell on the "original New York cast and production" of *Amphitryon 38,* a comedy from the French, in which Alfred Lunt and Lynn Fontanne were making their first appearance in the southern metropolis. There were ten curtain calls, well earned by a superlatively good performance—the best I have ever seen the Lunts and their company give. Backstage there was gratitude and more than a little astonishment, too. The company was exhausted. After a sixteen-hour train journey from San Antonio, Texas, they had played the night before in Little Rock, Arkansas, in a school auditorium in which the acoustics were so bad that they had, almost literally, to "scream at the top of our voices," as Lunt put it. The night journey to Memphis had brought little sleep; the loading of the scenery was a long and noisy procedure and the road was bumpy after the train started. Disheartening news had greeted them in the dressing rooms—the box-office was "light" and the house enormous. But their fears had not been realized.

"Wasn't the audience *wonderful?*" said Lunt, as he peeled off Jupiter's beard. "And *what* happened to us? I wish you'd tell me. I've never given a performance that satisfied me as much. I've never seen Lynnie better, but *never!* And Dicky and Sydney, the whole company—and we were all so tired we could hardly stagger out of our dressing rooms. Oh well, it will probably be awful tonight." . . . "We've never," said Miss Fontanne, "given a better performance, any one of us, that I can remember. I suppose we were *so* tired that we just—you know, it's this kind of thing that makes trouping worth while."

"A superlative treat," wrote the critic of the Memphis *Commercial Appeal*. "The receipts stood at $5,200, every penny of which was well spent." . . . "A Jovian revel, as brash and gay as anything ever unmasked before a Memphis audience," declared another Memphis paper, and, in conclusion: "Memphis has never seen a production more aptly and unstintingly staged."

If proof were needed that road audiences recognize the finer and more subtle points of plays and performances—that the road cannot any longer be fooled by third-rate productions and bad supporting casts—the press and the public, in the one-night stands of the so-called "sticks" in the South and Southwest which the Lunts visited this year, gave it over and over again. The audiences in almost every town were intelligent and understanding, and their appreciation was based on a sound theatre knowledge and sense, on a culture and sophistication which was just as keen as, and often less jaded than, Broadway's. Anyone who has trouped through the hills and prairies of the theatre's "open spaces" knows that this is true. It is likewise a fact, whatever you may hear to the contrary in Broadway's saloons, that the road public is willing, able and eager to pay the theatre's prices if the "big names" of Broadway will go trouping with good plays and sound productions. Grosses of $30,000 to $35,000 a week can result from one-night stands in the Cotton or Bible belts. But taking all this for granted—as, indeed, it should be—the press and public on the road take more for granted, including much that they have no right to treat so casually. They seem to believe that the best Broadway has to offer should be theirs by right, as well as Broadway's, with none of Broadway's responsibility for the second best (quite different from the second-rate), the growing, the experimental.

"It's simple"—this question of "the survival of the Fabulous Invalid as it gasps and pants for breath below the Mason-Dixon Line"—according to the critic of the *Austin* (Texas) *American*. "A solid company, not one hastily assembled for the provinces, a production intact" and people like the Lunts who have the quality "that revitalizes the road, that makes all speculation about its preservation just so much chatter." . . . "We love the Fontannes, the Lunts, the Cornells, the Hayeses and the Hustons," the critic goes on to say, appraising the company the Lunts have surrounded themselves with, "but how much better and more satisfying an evening in the theatre it is when they bring along, also, the Sydney Greenstreets, Richard Whorfs, George Meaders and Barry Thomsons." True enough. But you need to be out of New York—trouping with such first-rate troupers, through towns that often can't even offer them a real theatre to play in before they go on to the next one-night stand—to know that the answer is less "simple" than the *Austin American* claims.

"A solid company" and "a production intact" are, in themselves, difficult attainments, as the annual 75 percent of failures on Broadway attests. A production, too, to a seasoned player, is never quite "intact." Always it is undergoing change, being tightened, expanded, refined and enriched. The Lunts, last autumn, reworked their whole production of *The Sea Gull,* even though it was a success, and added new business or subtracted old bits all during the tour. In Atlanta, in February, they sat up half one night, working over a scene from *Idiot's Delight* that had never jelled since the opening four years earlier. And still they were not satisfied. As to "a solid company," it took the Lunts over five years to integrate the group of actors playing with them this spring, and good as the cast is—and it has a fluency attained only by companies which have played together for years—it still can be, and will be, improved. Add to these fundamentals the complexities which touring involves, and the reason so few plays venture far from New York becomes increasingly clear.

There are distinctly two sides to the question: one of them, constantly under discussion, is what New York owes to the road; the other, less frequently mentioned, is what the road owes to Broadway, especially to its actors and its technicians. There is no question that actors like the Lunts, Miss Cornell and Miss Hayes have the artistic standards, technical experience, glamour and integrity that "revitalize" the road, or Broadway. But with conditions in the provinces as they are today, *only successful actors* can afford to go trouping at all *and only the very best,* who have enormous technical ability and reserve resources, can hope either to make enough money to pay the heavy overhead of trouping or, more important, to play well enough so that they can project their parts in huge, impractical, badly equipped auditoriums, with wretched sight lines and worse acoustics.

In a week of trouping, accompanying the Lunts from Little Rock to Montgomery, Alabama (during which the company grossed almost $30,000), here were a few of the "conditions"—fairly typical, according to reports, of conditions in the South and Southwest generally. Some of them are trivial. Others merely amusing. All of them, coupled with the Lunts' vitality, enthusiasm and sense of humor, were fun to cope with. But they are indicative of serious aspects of the situation which must be changed and soon, if the theatre is to flourish in one-night-stand land.

The only "theatre" in Little Rock is the auditorium of the high school, about two miles away from the business section of town. Tickets for *Idiot's Delight,* accordingly, are on sale in the lobby of the American Exchange Bank on Main Street, where Mrs. Frank Vaughan, booking agent for the town, cajoles everyone who enters the doors. At least a third of the prospective audience of 2,200 are out-of-towners who have ordered tickets by mail—many of them living as far as 100 to 150 miles away, six coming a distance of 1,000 miles. If there is a sell-out, which Mrs. Vaughan confidently expects—"if it doesn't rain"—the house will gross about $3,600 at $2.75 top. She gets 25 percent of this sum out of which she pays her expenses and furnishes twenty-six stagehands. This does not, she says, leave much margin for profit—not enough, even, to pay the $100 necessary to bring the auditorium the additional current which the lighting for *Idiot's Delight* requires. So the lighting has to be cut down.

When the weary stage crew, traveling with the show, arrives at the auditorium for a 10 A.M. "call," they find that all the scenery, props and costume trunks have to be carried up three flights of stairs. They discover, also, that the stage is a gymnasium, with three basketball courts alive with players, and that Broadway must wait until the 11 o'clock school recess. The "grid" is just high enough to squeeze the set beneath; there is no space to "fly" any scenery. "That doesn't matter for this show," the company manager says, "as we have only one set. But three weeks from now, when we come back with *Amphitryon,* I don't know what we'll do."

The proscenium is about ninety feet wide, the auditorium even wider, so that the set, which was large and massive in the Shubert Theatre in New York, has the appearance of a cameo when it is masked by some thirty feet of black velvet on each side. From the side-seats down front, one can hardly see the set at all; further back, not more than half of it is visible. In front of the playing line a fourteen-foot apron extends into the auditorium, which makes the actors feel they are playing to a not-too-inanimate sounding board instead of to an audience. The setting up of the show, difficult enough as it is, is further complicated by the fact that the stage and auditorium are filled, off and on all day, with excited students, peering and poking at everything—asking questions and practically mobbing the Lunts when they come out in the afternoon to inspect proceedings. It does not help matters much to be told at the last moment that the house is full of "dead spots," and that it is difficult to project the voice across the apron without getting a reverberation from the back wall. But the Lunts laugh that off. Bad acoustics are a familiar hazard.

The only dressing rooms are the gymnasium locker rooms down a cold and draughty flight of stairs, so two canvas ones are installed under the basketball nets for Miss Fontanne and Edith King. Lunt, Whorf and Thomson are assigned to the "Visiting Team's" quarters.

Despite Lunt's dire predictions that there will be "nobody out front," the house is sold out at curtain time, even the bad seats, and there is a solid line of standees. In the first act, while the company is struggling to find the "pitch" of the house, it is difficult in certain sections to hear the actors, particularly in one block of seats where all conversation from left-stage seems to emanate from the rear of the auditorium. But it gets better as the actors warm up.

In the second act the fuses blow, unable to stand even the reduced load, and the balcony lights go off, leaving Lunt and Miss Fontanne to play their big-scene in semi-darkness until the lights come on again, twice as strong as before. Nobody seems to mind, however. The show goes over with a bang, to $3,600 in receipts. The stagehands, exhausted by now, carry the sets down to the waiting trucks and the whole party is off in the early hours for the matinee and evening performances at Memphis, the next day, and then on to Chattanooga.

Watching the train load or unload is a lesson in theatre economics. The accessories alone which accompany a troupe are no small item in the transportation bill—which, this week, will amount to about

$2,700. In addition to costumes, props and scenery the Lunts took with them such items as: six dozen straw hats (one is smashed every night), several rounds of ammunition, six cases of sheets of glass, a sewing machine, ironing boards, a flock of extra casters (costing $3.50 each), drum trunks, a harp case, a piano (which has to be tuned at every stop) and a cooking box. These details, of course, are mere "chicken feed" compared to the expenses for trucking and transfer of the scenery, railroading, musicians, stagehands and advertising (the last named averages from $200 to $300 in each town), but when the gross is not of smash proportions, they are big enough to cause worry.

The only "worry" in Chattanooga, fortunately, seems to be a state or local tax, which cuts down the overhead by a few hundred dollars. The 1,850-seat movie house—the best theatre of the week, so far—has been sold out solidly for over a week and *Idiot's Delight* goes over with the usual "bang," even though the bombardment is less effective tonally than usual, owing to lack of space backstage to shoot off the ammunition and break the glass. The manager of the theatre here reports that he will not book legitimate shows unless there are "big names" in the cast, or unless the plays themselves have received national publicity of the type accorded to *Green Pastures* and *Tobacco Road*. "There just isn't an audience here for any other kind of play," he asserts, "I don't care how good it is." But the perceptive attentiveness of the audience at *Idiot's Delight* makes you wonder if he is right.

The Erlanger Theatre in Atlanta, the next day, is the first "legitimate" house that the company has played in for some time. It is large and well-equipped, has a nice theatre smell when it is empty and an even nicer one when it is full, as it is for the night's performance of *Idiot's Delight* and the matinee and evening of the next day for *Amphitryon*. The local musicians, hired to augment the four men traveling with the company for *Amphitryon,* do not seem to be able to read Sam Barlow's score—judging, at least, from the awful sounds that emanate from the orchestra pit. But since the music is only "incidental" this is not the major catastrophe that it would have been for a musical show, though it does bring one unexpected, and unwanted, laugh when Lunt has a line: "What was that?" spoken with agonized expression, which happens to follow a peculiarly strident blast from the trumpet.

The company entrains next morning early for Montgomery to an assured sell-out, according to advance reports, and they go on to another sell-out for *Idiot's Delight* in Jackson, Mississippi, in a high school in which the stage is so small that it is impossible to use any scenery except drapes. And so it goes, for ten more weeks.

After covering much the same territory with his touring company of *Kiss the Boys Goodbye,* Brock Pemberton, quoted by Lucius Beebe in the *Herald Tribune,* had this to report: "If we live long enough and we have the brains—and by 'we' I mean the responsible New York producers—to organize the road the way it should be organized and give it authentic shows, the road one of these days is going to be more important to the legitimate theatre than New York ever was. It is potentially a greater consumer of stage goods than Broadway and all it requires to exploit this market and demand is some little sense on the part of New York producers and, above everything else, some plays worth sending on the road."

What Pemberton says about Broadway's responsibility and its potential market is obviously true. He should be the first to admit, however, that the road must do its own share of organization or, better still, reorganization. Authentic shows are one essential. Authentic, well-equipped theatres, with decent accommodations for the actors and technicians, are another. The road has a deeper responsibility, too. If it expects, and believes it has the right to expect, the great people of the theatre to travel on these inconvenient and physically fatiguing circuits, it must be willing to welcome the near-great as well. Because it *is* the road, it will never have to attend the exasperating ineptitudes that Broadway—the theatre's testing ground—sees night after night, for no producer in his right mind would attempt to tour one of these Broadway fizzles. But, assuming that New York producers do not cheat the road (and the indications are that they have learned their lesson on this score), the road audiences, in their turn, must respond by supporting all the good plays and productions that are sent out, regardless of whether their favorite "stars" are billed or not. The watchword cannot be: "The best and nothing but the best!"—for no art or business could long be sustained on that basis.

As for the actors, they will always turn to the road. For every actor who is not lazy—and no good actor *is* lazy—loves trouping. He is willing to leave friends and family, to live on trains and in hotels, because of the stimulation he gets, the experience and training he gains in playing to a public that, almost every night, is a "first-night audience" and yet completely individual. It is on the road, also, that he gains the national reputation so essential to lasting Broadway success. And, finally, there is the excitement and good fun the road provides, and the lure of cold cash.

Players like the Lunts, who would rather troupe than eat, would be the last to stress—as this article has done—the difficulties rather than the delights of trouping. For the difficulties to them are part of the delight. They like nothing better than to meet and surmount them. Each one is a challenge. Each one teaches them something new. Playing in a vast hall, like that at Wichita, Kansas—"which looked like Madison Square Garden"—they can learn how to project an intimate comedy scene into a huge space without losing the intimacy, or seeming to shout. Forced to play without scenery, they can discover how it is possible for the actor to supply the scenery. Acting every night in a different-sized theatre, without rehearsal, they can learn how to judge the "pitch" of a house so that they know instantly, by second sight or sound, when to raise or lower the volume of their speech. There are, however, only two Lunts, and only a handful of other players with their skill. And road audiences must learn to recognize the fact that actors less expert *but still extremely competent*—able to give more than satisfactory performances under normal conditions—have not got, and should not be expected to have, the technical facility or ingenuity to overcome the road's handicaps.

Broadway, as Mr. Pemberton says, "must sell a straight bill of goods." It must also—as the American Theatre Council realizes—have enough goods on hand each season to meet the present demand and to create a new and even greater demand. But while the Council is attempting to make this possible, while it is trying to iron out Broadway's own complex relationship with the road, to reduce transportation and other excessive overhead costs, the road might take time out to think about its share of these problems. For unless they are solved somehow, the Fabulous Invalid will continue to "gasp and pant for breath," no matter what Broadway does.

June 1939

RAY BOLGER

*

Strictly for "Round" Actors

IN THE VERY GOOD COMPANY of Little Jack Little, famous pianist-composer-orchestra-leader, I have just finished the most thrilling and satisfying engagement of my career. For five months we have flown, jeeped and sometimes mushed through ankle-deep mud to entertain, under USO-Camp Show auspices, the men in our armed forces stationed in the far reaches of the Pacific.

We managed, by cajolery, sob stories and fast talking, to get ourselves transported to most of the isolated posts that comprise the South, Southwest and Central Pacific War Areas. It isn't easy to "hook a ride" down there, because of the millions of pounds of material that have priority on the planes. But "sweating out transportation" is another story. Suffice it to say, we went a lot of places, saw a lot of guys and had a wonderful time. It was fast. It was exciting. And those kids, babies most of them, were such wonderful audiences that it was hard to tell whether they warmed our hearts or broke them.

But don't get the idea that there is anything soft about anything or anybody on those hell-spewed hunks of coral. "Rugged" is the word they use and, after the war, Roget's *Thesaurus* will have to add about ninety synonyms to cover all that it means. "Terrible, terrifying, miserable, mosquito-ridden, poisonous, Jap-infested, sweat-making, lousy, lonely" are just a few mild ones that are printable. Rugged it certainly is, and will continue to be. That is where we come in.

Never before in its history has the theatre had such an opportunity to serve itself by being of great service. No other branch of the entertainment world is so well equipped. Its people are ready, willing and able. And the need for their warm, human, personal talent for entertaining, under any and all circumstances, is terrific!

The wonderful part is that they can serve their country *and* their art at the same time. To illustrate, I would like to point out that Jack Little and I have not only appeared in places where no "flesh," or live entertainment, had ever been before, but we have played to boys who had never seen live entertainment before they joined up. Many had never heard of a Broadway show nor of any of us ingredients for same. It's kinda hard to take but this bit of dialogue tells all:

"Colonel, Sir?" said Private Hoskins to the Special Service officer.

"What is it, Hoskins?"

"Colonel, Sir, what do we have tonight, flat actors or round actors?"

"Round," was the Colonel's laconic reply. Then, gravely and solemnly, he explained to me that flat actors were those on the screen, round actors—us!!

Before we took off on the first leg of our journey, Little Jack Little and I had never met. Facing each other across a packing box aboard a bomber, we studied the situation and each other. We decided to postpone mapping out our show until we reached Australia, where we hoped to find proper facilities for rehearsal. I got into a gin-rummy game and Jack proceeded to go to sleep. This continued, with small variation, for twenty-two hours, until the Captain handed me a radio from our next stop, where we were due in about an hour.

"Would Bolger-Little do show for us while plane is serviced?", it read. "Oh, noooooo," we groaned, in perfect concert. But we made the mistake of looking at each other. Jack grinned. There was a challenge in his bloodshot eyes. Well, I've been challenged by experts, so I turned to the Captain and said, "Okay. But tell 'em it's strictly a break-in date."

From then on it was a frenzy of trying to put something together that resembled a show. But the more we struggled for a routine that we could do together, the more it sounded as though we ought to sell medicine and rattle a tambourine. Finally, I quit digging.

"Listen, Jackson," I said. "You can play 'Swanee River,' 'Sweet Sue' and 'Melody in F,' can't you?"

"Sure, Ray," replied Jack, "in any key."

"Okay. That's all I need for twenty dances. You have a flock of songs you can play and sing. Between us we know a lot of funny stories. Let's go down and see what those fellows want."

"Roger," snapped Little the lingoist, and we both turned our attention to the business of landing on the fly-speck far below.

It was dark when we rolled onto the tiny landing field of the island, a ten-mile strip of coral, decorated by a single, dwarfed and desolate tree. Stiff and tired, but filled with the same anticipatory excitement that precedes an opening-night performance, we climbed out of the plane. A group of officers, clad in tropical shorts, greeted us enthusiastically and rushed us to their mess hall for some food. Then they escorted us to the "theatre."

A picture was just unwinding its final reel from the makeshift projection booth. It was a war picture. An airplane was doing some impossible maneuvers to the accompaniment of scathing and vitriolic comments by the GI's watching the screen. The handsome, intrepid hero of the movie was obviously winning the war single-handed, unmindful of the invectives hurled at him by the jeering throng. This was to be our audience. Would we be received in the same manner?

"Scared?" said Little Jack Little.

"I would be if I hadn't played the Windsor Theatre in the Bronx. If you can handle those kids, you can handle anybody!" I whispered.

"Yeah. I feel the same way about the early show at the Earle Theatre in Philly."

The picture was over. A light came on, spraying the screen with an eerie glow. We saw the stage for the first time. I heard a sigh of relief at my side. There was a small piano—Jack had not quite mastered the accordion he carried. But the stage! It was a small platform about three feet above ground, not quite eighteen feet wide and eight feet deep. Slightly smaller than my long legs were accustomed to galloping around on. I started to hum, "Don't Get Around Much Anymore." This was going to be an experience.

It was more than an experience. It was an education. What we learned gave us the clue to all our future shows. I climbed onto the stage, greeted the boys, introduced Jack, and two hours later we were still answering requests for more. Don't ask me what went into that first performance. Neither of us knows. We do know, however, that we came away with an infallible recipe for the boys' entertainment.

First, take several good, fresh jokes. Add a large measure of real entertainment, mix well with a pinch of salt, a dash of vinegar, a bit of spice. Keep stirring the risibilities, toss in a little sugar but go easy on it and never, never use syrup. Then, turn on the heat and for a finish you will have a dish every gang of servicemen will go for.

We found the best source of humor to be the boys themselves

Their living conditions, gripes, pet hates, and so forth, furnish wonderful material and at the same time serve as a bridge between you and your audience. For instance, as you know, there are no South Sea Island Paradises. So, one of my opening lines was, "I am delighted to be with you in your South Sea Island Paradise." A storm of groans, good-natured boos and wise-cracks always followed and from then on the boys were a part of the show. Sometimes the cross-fire was pretty fast and I had to be on my toes to think up the answers. Occasionally, I would be "topped," much to the delight of all concerned, whereupon I would insist that the victor come up on the stage and take a bow. This invariably evoked much applause and heightened the spirit of camaraderie.

We also found that mentioning towns was a sure way to get the boys with us. I used such a device in introducing Jack, to wit:

"You have all heard Little Jack Little on the radio in your hometowns. Station WLW, Cincinnati—" An enthusiastic yell from the Ohio boys. "Station WGN, Chicago—" Another yell. "Station KDKA, Pittsburgh, h'ya, Smokey?" The Pennsylvanians roared. "Station WJZ, New York and Brooklyn" always brought a terrific "Yay" (which leads me to believe that Brooklyn is really winning this war). I would answer in my best Brooklynese, "H'ya Brooklyn, whatya doing gout here, anyways. Cheest, it's good to hear ya verce!"

With their minds turned toward home, the boys were in a mellow mood for Jack's soft inimitable style of singing and playing any and every song they asked for. But we didn't let nostalgia reign very long. Jack told stories in between songs, then I did request dances and told more stories—until finally the right moment arrived to make the boys in the audience sing. It isn't easy to get them started, but once you do, they never want to stop. And the release that comes to a bunch of guys singing is really something. It's the greatest morale builder of all, I think. Laughter is fine, yelling is swell, but nothing breaks up that hard little kernel of nerves that grows in a lonely, home-hungry, battle-scarred fighting man like raising his voice with his buddies in a good old song.

It occurs to me that all this talk of songs, dances and funny sayings may be discouraging to you of the legitimate theatre. Even now, you are saying to yourselves, "I should love to go overseas to entertain the armed forces. But what can I do? I don't sing. I don't dance." Ah, but can you do a card trick, can you do a monologue, can you play a sketch using soldiers in the supporting parts? Can you do imitations, can you turn a hand-spring (Tallulah can!), can you talk a song (Bette Davis can and does), can you tell a funny story?

In your theatrical background there must be a hundred tricks that you have had to master before you became the artist that you are. Drag 'em out! Parlor tricks. That comedy monologue you delivered at dramatic school. The bigger you are, the more the boys will love anything unusual, away from your regular acting, that you do. And, of course, there is nothing they appreciate more than fine acting. (Captain Maurice Evans and Miss Judith Anderson have proved that with their highly successful presentation of *Macbeth* to soldier-audiences in Hawaii.) A good dramatic sketch will find a warm and hearty reception, I assure you.

In sum, our servicemen are starved for real, first-rate entertainment of all kinds. They have enormous respect for real talent. But they despise the phonies who glibly mouth, "I'm sooo glad to be here with you sooo wonderful boys who are doing such a magnificent job for the folks at home. I'm soooo sorry I cawn't sing or dance. But I can say Hello—and keep up the good work!"

Go out there, good people of the theatre. Go out with an honest, sincere approach and a spirit of informal good fellowship, and do the finest job you have ever done. You will be rendering desperately-needed aid and comfort to the finest of American manhood. You will be winning new respect and interest for the Thespic Arts. And you will have the tremendous satisfaction of looking at yourself in the mirror and saying, "Nice work, you old 'round' actor!"

April 1944

ATHENE SEYLER

*

Fans, Trains and Stays

A SERIES OF LETTERS ON THE ART OF 'PERIOD ACTING'

[*Impressed with the superiority of English to American actors in the technique of so-called "period acting," the editors of* THEATRE ARTS *asked Athene Seyler, co-author with the late Stephen Haggard of* The Craft of Comedy, *for her theories on the actor's interpretation of plays of other times, and on the adaption of a particular period. She responded in the following series of letters written during her tour of England in* Lady Windermere's Fan—THE EDITORS.]

MANCHESTER

I SHOULD LIKE to oblige, but oh! my first reaction is that so much too much is written and said that is only chatter in print and not of any value. I've really no idea why British actors play period pieces better than Americans—if indeed it is true! What can one say? That the continuity of tradition in this country tends increasingly to influence us? (I don't believe it!) That we have an innate conservatism in this island that preserves a cultural line of thought? (What a phrase!)

I suppose in America you have so many originally alien influences at work, so many different backgrounds, that the particularly English idiom expressed in our seventeenth- and eighteenth-century plays, and nineteenth-century too, is lost in its purity. I suppose it is true that a certain crispness of speech and a precision of movement—an elegance of gesture and an assumption of artificiality—come more easily to an English-bred actor than to one who is used to more loose slang, to easy drawl in speech and more freedom of manners. We have kept a clipped reserved tradition of speech and manners through our aristocracy and public-school system, which has to be sacrificed in a land of more progressive democratic ideas. And without saying that one is better than the other it may help us over the smaller issues of period acting.

I've been coaching our new Lady Windermere in how to use a

fan in the nineteenth-century way, and someone (for John Gielgud's New York production of *Love for Love*) in how to use one in the seventeenth-century manner! . . .

ADELPHI HOTEL, LIVERPOOL

Why should one set up to know anything about the use of the fan in any historical period? I very certainly have never read any descriptions, nor do contemporary pictures give more than an indication here and there. I suppose one bases any guesses one may make about these periods on what one knows of their customs and background and of the spirit of their times.

In England we are never far from history. All day long we are in touch with historic customs, with buildings and traditions still surviving from bygone centuries. Think of the civic functions, of the openings of Parliament, of our coronations and royal occasions which must foster in us almost unconsciously a sense of continuity in formal manners. One cannot enter any art gallery or any of the great houses open to the public without constant reminders of the fashions and particular attributes of different centuries, shown in contemporary portraits and period furniture.

For instance, the use of a fan must have indicated and reflected the same attitude towards life as shows in the style of the hairdressing, of the clothes and of the dances of any given age. The late seventeenth-century women wore a mass of shaking curls, bared their bosoms and evidently had flung themselves out of Puritanism with a gay vengeance. So what more reasonable than to suggest in a Restoration play that one should flirt one's fan and flutter it gaily around one's curls, or gaze archly over it?

In the next century one would gather from its more formal and exaggerated character, from the grace and dignity of the minuet and the pomp of the hair styles, together with the idiosyncrasies of the huge hats, that fans were also larger in proportions and, as we know, exquisitely painted. So perhaps a more measured movement in their use—and a pose held with them at arm's length, to display them to the fullest advantage—would be correct.

Victorian influences substituted demure bonnets for Gainsborough hats, and dresses which emphasized delicacy and weakness in women's behavior. What more suitable than to use a fan to ward off difficulties (or over-heat), with a modest stirring of the air around one's temples and a discreet shadowing of one's face from the bold gaze of one's partner?

At least so I see it! And if this is not strictly what the real ladies of those days did with a fan, at least it will give an audience the spirit of the times and will be in keeping with the manner of the plays of these periods—which is what an actress sets out to do.

LEEDS

You ask about the "period acting" of the French in comedy and whether they are similar to us or different in their "period" traditions, and I have to confess that I have never seen a Molière comedy done by the Comédie Française, and in fact have actually seen only two productions from that theatre: once in 1914, I think—Hernani—and once last time they were over here—*Ruy Blas.*

Each time I regret to say it seemed to me that tradition weighed so heavily on the shoulders of the actors that behind I could see a long line of identical arms making the same gestures on the same cues, with the same inflections and pauses, as one sees oneself repeated unendingly in mirrors that face each other. The repetition was, I am sure, of some originally fine inspiration, but to me only the mechanics were left. I had the impression that the technique of tragic acting (and perhaps I should have felt the same about comedy) was far more detailed, cut and dried, and inexorable than our own. Perhaps this comes from their having had for so long a static academy of acting where technique was perfected and then—I was going to say pickled—at least preserved intact from a former age.

In England we have no such museum of acting—alas! I think much of value has been lost for this reason, but it has left us a little more elastic and varied in our attack—witness Mr. Gielgud's season of repertory in 1945, when his Hamlet had quite a new angle, from which we could see what was intrinsic in his performance ever since he first played it many years ago, but now newly informed and considered.

When one compares Sir Laurence Olivier's performance of the same part one sees at once that there is no common tradition of tragic acting such as I felt I recognized at the Comédie Française, and in a lesser degree I expect this to be true of classic comedy. The precision and intellectual tidiness of the French mind is so unlike our own that their comedy acting may well be much more formalized and clearly defined than ours, for national characteristics I believe are clearly shown in the art of different countries.

The wealth of natural gesture that the French use in acting (as in their normal life) and the greater mobility of their facial expression must give more force to their comedic expression. Our tradition is much more in understatement and oblique methods, and in comedy may seem to have less emphasis. But surely in pantomime and expressive by-play the French must be as superb in classic comedy as they certainly are in modern plays. . . .

THE QUEEN AND CASTLE, KENILWORTH

About wearing period costume: The most important thing is not the dress one wears but what one wears underneath it, and in one's mind. That is to say, the best Edwardian creation put over a modern elastic belt, and worn by someone who crosses her legs and throws her chest in or stands with her weight on one hip, will never look in the least right. On the other hand, give me a pair of boned corsets high under the bust and to a point in front and laced tightly to the waist, and at least three full stiff petticoats, and I shall be able to wear a tablecloth and a lace antimacassar with a good suggestion of 1870.

But of course I must have the line of the train on the floor and remember to kick my skirt neatly ahead of me with my feet as I walk so as not to tread into it. I must hold my head erect and my back very straight, sit with one foot a trifle in front of the other on the floor, never lounge (even if one could in corsets), never put my hands on my hips but keep them neatly folded on my lap.

I am wearing a train at the moment of writing which is quite a yard long on the floor and incredibly heavy. How the modern young actress gets scared of this and says she can't move this way, or get round that chair, because her train is in her way! One must, however, never be train-bound. The normal and correct thing to do is to pick up one's train and throw it around one out of the way or, if it is a shorter day-gown of light material, to catch it at arm's length behind and quietly lift it as one walks. It needs quite a deal of practice to get a train properly to heel, if I may put it that way, with elegance and neatness.

Do you realize how different a shape one's corset makes one? The modern "girdle" gives a pear-shaped line behind, increases one's waist measurement and leaves one's bust to uplift or to constraint. When one puts on stays of the Victorian and Edwardian period, one's waist is two inches smaller, one's hips correspondingly bigger, and the line of the bosom is raised quite two inches again and neatly thrown into a shelf under one's chin when one sits down! So you can see how important it is to have one's shape the correct foundation for a dress to hang on.

I believe that in the sixteenth century, stays were not made of whalebones but wood, and that long stiff line in front on which the slender Elizabethan torso was molded gave women quite a different line again. I've never worn wooden corsets with an Elizabethan costume, but probably we would all look less like fancy dress and more like the originals if we did.

Shoes, of course, are of great importance in giving one the correct poise for a dress. Impossible to swim with tiny steps under a crinoline in modern high-heeled court shoes or wedge heels. One must have either flat sandals with ribbons crossed up the ankles or such low heels as to be nearly flat. The seventeenth century had square toes and perhaps one-and-a-half-inch heels, and not till the eighteenth century did one have higher ones, and even so these were "Louis-shaped" and did not tilt one forward as the modern shoe does. One's walk and stance are quite determined by one's shoes, as one can see when one changes from brogues to evening slippers nowadays. So how important they must be to an actress in assuming period dress!

I've rather left men out of this discussion, but I am not altogether popular with younger actors when directing them in an 1890 play and forbidding them to put their hands in their pockets! But perhaps I had better leave them to one of their own sex for instruction as to how to negotiate a top hat, a cane and a four-inch collar!

All we want in Kenilworth at the moment is a mackintosh and snow boots—how simple to wear! . . .

THE GRAND HOTEL, PLYMOUTH

You asked me about producers and production, or as you say directors and directing? I've never worked with John Gielgud, but having come into one of his nineteenth-century productions (*Lady Windermere's Fan*) and seen his other Wilde plays I guess that he stresses mainly style in directing any period play. Now, I find that the question of keeping the balance between the artificiality of the period and the true characterization and humanity beneath the surface wit is as debatable a subject as the age-long discussion of "sound versus sense" in speaking Shakespeare! There must be a happy means whereby one can joy in the form and fantastication of the dialogue and yet bring out all the meaning of the lines. I am sure myself that the modern throw-away method is no use to dramatists such as Wycherley or Congreve and that the fullest value must be given to every single word. But in doing this one is apt to use forced inflections and unreal tones—it is just the trick of accomplishing the one and avoiding the other extreme that constitutes the charm and difficulty of speaking period plays. A fastidious ear and a simple heart should be the successful combination.

What about setting? Stylized or naturalistic? I believe I can play Restoration drama in either, happily, and have indeed done so. Nigel Playfair favored the first kind of approach, and I remember a delightful set in which we did *Marriage à la Mode* where he had a permanent Renaissance bridge across the back of the stage with two flights of steps leading up to it each side. This enabled him to invent my entrances and exits as Melantha, the ridiculous Frenchified lady—up one flight, across the bridge and down the other side each time—and as I had bunches of curls hanging each side of a huge hair arrangement, they bobbed and flew about with each step up and down and made a perfect visual gay joke of one's appearance. That I consider true and imaginative production, for it used legitimately a device to emphasize the peculiarities and modes of the time.

A great deal of space and room to move in is a boon to an actress in a seventeenth-century play, for breadth of gesture is essential. A stage cluttered up with furniture is probably quite wrong in that century. The scenes are obviously intended to be played very often with sweeping movements and on the feet more than in the modern "sits settee left" type of acting.

I like a lot of light for artificial comedy—and footlights—and every gay help of music and color to add to the theatricality of these old plays. No subtle shadows or half-lights, no modernistic crudities; preferably, for me, should a setting be "pretty," with any coarseness in the text softened by a charming background.

I do not believe that the old plays—essentially forthright and straightforward in essence as they are—need or, indeed, allow of fantastication or of distortion in their setting. Everything about the production should be as sparkling and lucid as possible. With which few notes I leave the field clear to any of our more adventurous producers who care to challenge my theories in practice.

November 1947

* *

MARIAN RICH

*

Natural Speech

NOT LONG AGO, a group of professional actors and a speaker presented a sketch and a speech to an assemblage of social workers. After the performance, one of the social workers approached the group with a problem. She wanted to teach social work by recording interviews between case-workers and their clients. But when the actual recordings were made, the case-workers and clients, instead of sounding like real people doing a real job—as they were—sounded artificial, stilted, "unnatural."

"I noticed," said the social worker, "that all of you, actors and speakers, although you were talking to a large group and acting in a large room, just seemed to be conversing in an everyday tone. You were natural. That's what we tried to do, but somehow it didn't come off."

Most professionals recognize that speech is an art. And as in other arts, the test of success is to seem simple, spontaneous, direct, at ease. To seem natural under unnatural circumstances involves a training and a technique as clean cut and arduous as the techniques for dancing, music interpretation, painting.

The art of speech, like the art of music interpretation, must communicate something to someone. This something communicated in acting and speaking is a combination of feeling and concrete idea. As Stark Young says of the actor, "the word he speaks gives the concept; the gesture he makes exhibits a single phenomenon; but the voice may be anger itself or longing, and may go straight, as music does, to the same emotion in us."

It might seem, at first, that to achieve natural speech under unnatural circumstances was a purely physical problem—one of talking over greater distances, to more people. This is a misapprehension which deludes all too many speakers and actors. The physical problem is only a small part of the whole. In its technical aspects, communication in speech does, indeed, imply a vocal instrument of varying range, volume, rhythm and timbre. It implies a technique of producing tones that is physiologically correct. Incidentally, the voice in song or speech differs in this respect from other musical instruments, in that technique and instrument building are one and the same. Bad vocal technique ruins the instrument. Every sound and series of sounds contributes to the quality of future sounds, for good or ill.

But not only are there techniques of sound production but of word production also, involving correct pronunciation and clear articulation. This is the technique of speech. Yet while speech and voice training can help to mitigate the physical problems of distance and numbers, they are still only part of the answer to the problem of effective and natural communication.

Most people speak badly. They get by at home, at the grocer's or their club, in the course of everyday business, because they are part of a group. Put them in the spotlight, alone, and their troubles begin —also those of their audience. Their voices are strained—tight, high —their articulation impure, undisciplined. Their pronunciation is faulty, local, and the melody of their voice, for any length of time, monotonous. But, strangest of all, there is no "expression"—or what there is sounds false.

A too loud voice in a small room, a too soft voice in a large room, a too charming voice dealing with objective material, a too cold voice on a personal subject, all are disturbing. The overdramatic announcer may pass muster when telling of the horrors of war, but he strains his audience's credulity when applying the same tones to the virtues of a shaving cream. The "I love me" voice may coo its praise of a perfume, but it offends when its honeyed tones surround the latest reports from the Pacific. True communication implies a balanced relationship between the speaker, his material and his audience. This balance is easily achieved in ordinary conversation, because there is an immediate contact between the speaker and his audience and an inherent relationship between what he feels, the sounds he makes to express it, and the words he chooses.

Among the most modern teachers of acting, there is a phrase often repeated to the effect that "if the emotion is felt and correct, the external expression will be." The fact that this is what happens in ordinary life is the basis for the assertion. And if a theatre were a drawing-room, or the audience a few feet away from the speaker's platform, the maxim might hold. But such is not the case, any more than the voice recording into a microphone is the voice of a face-to-face interview. Feeling must be amplified to fit the enlarged sound. But feeling is not enough to enlarge sound, any more than louder tones in and of themselves can convey feeling to an audience.

Any instrumentalist knows only too well that expression and feeling can exist only when there is complete physical freedom and technical expertness. I remember a few years ago being in the Green Room after a Koussevitsky concert. The great conductor was receiving the usual enthusiastic acclaim for the evening's performance. But he was not satisfied.

"No," he said. "Tonight it wasn't good. There was a long rehearsal this afternoon and the men were tired and tense. There must never be tension here," he said, pointing to the arms and shoulders. "It must be here"—pointing to the heart.

Too often physical tension is mistaken for feeling and emotion. But the performer's emotional charge is no promise of his artistic achievement. It may as easily blow a fuse, or never come to light. Neither the nervousness of stage fright, nor the personal, individual emotions of the actor himself, are the real emotions of the artist. They only tie up his throat and interfere with his freedom of expression, as the over-anxiousness of a tennis player or a golfer or a violinist tends to tie up his arms. To the Greek poets and philosophers, pity was connected with the abdomen, courage with the beating heart, and intense thought with the diaphragm. The recreation of these emotions by an actor or speaker is the subconscious result of physical freedom and inner awareness—not of effort.

Only when the voice and articulative mechanism are well trained, when the senses are sharpened and the mind alive, only then can the speaker aspire to the art of sounding natural.

July 1945

CORNELIA OTIS SKINNER

*

"I Saw Your Father in Kismet"

ACTORS, on being met by the public for the first time, are quite frequently accused of being distrait and even (a far worse term of opprobrium) "high-hat." This lamentable fallacy—and I'm a loyal enough lodge member to maintain that it *is* a fallacy—is due largely to the fact that actors are simple souls who don't know any better than to get themselves involved in those gruesome gatherings, sometimes social, sometimes for charity, usually crowded and always terrible, when they are "being met." Nobody, not even a candidate running for public office, is much good on such occasions and actors, who often as not are retiring by nature and desperately ill at ease in any milieu other than the theatre, show up worse than most celebrities because they're expected to be so much better. They are bored and unhappy, and their attempt to hide this ennui results in that "high-hat" expression. They shake hands with swarms of people they say they're glad to meet when they aren't; then if by good fortune they manage to hook up with some kindred spirit and are about to start enjoying themselves, someone comes up with another someone "they just *have* to meet" and, what makes it all hopeless, they do just have to. One should abide by the Charles Frohman principle that "actors should be heard and seen but never met."

Things get off to a bad start and never advance beyond it. I daresay authors, musicians and anyone in what is termed the public eye find themselves in the same sort of jam. The root of all the trouble lies in the fact that one is constantly being overwhelmed with remarks to which there is absolutely no reply. When average individual meets average individual he, or she, generally tries to start the conversational ball rolling, shoving it along with certain polite, if trite, utterances that will enable the other person to respond with further shoves. When these same individuals, however, meet players, they seem to labor under the illusion that they must greet them with something special and the greeting turns out to be so exceptionally special that it leaves the actor high and dry. This is too bad because certain starry-eyed devotees of the theatre still believe all thespians are brilliant creatures of wit and repartee. Well, even if they were, nobody meeting them gives them half a chance. It's like expecting one to exchange sparkling badinage with a sand bunker. For instance, some bustling member of the sandwich committee will lead a beaming fellow member up to the captive lion saying, "Miss Jones, do you know Miss Barrymore?" Whereat Miss Jones, her beams by how becoming pure infra-red, gurgles, "I know Miss Barrymore, of course, but Miss Barrymore doesn't know me." And what in the name of dear kind Emily Post is Miss Barrymore to reply? "So what" is obviously the answer but one can't jeopardize the box-office.

Actors live and blossom on praise and any who tell you it means nothing to them should be suspended from Equity. "I had a superb time at your show" or "I loved your performance"—such phrases, heaven knows, are blessedly welcome and an easy pleasure to reply to. Without them we wither and pine away into character bits in the Federal Theatre. Occasionally, however (and maybe it's with an idea that we ought not to be pampered), someone will stand before us and in the tone of a prosecuting attorney—all but pointing an accusing finger—will say, "I saw you last year in Pittsburgh." And nothing further. They don't follow the announcement with a reassuring "You were swell." They don't even say, "You were terrible." They say just that and then stand waiting for a rapid come-back. I have yet to find one. One can't say "Thank you," and "How nice" doesn't sound right somehow. "Oh" goes by unnoticed and "Did you?" merely brings forth a "Yes," after which they're still waiting for you to utter a gem. It's an awkward moment for everybody. "I saw you once before" or "I'm coming to the matinee tomorrow" falls into this same category of stalemates. Then there are those discouraging comments to the effect that "I saw you years ago when I was just a tiny child," to which one could rally with "Well, you don't look so darned young either" but one doesn't. Sometimes the people who meet you launch forth into a little excursion in autobiography. . . . "I remember seeing you because it was the first year I was married and my husband bought tickets to celebrate my having made my first cake." . . . All of which is very pretty indeed but there's still no answer to it.

Then there are the exclaimers to reckon with. These are the little women full of enthusiasm and good intentions who rush up, seize one's hand, forget to let it go and, after gazing at one for what seems minutes with speechless rapture, exclaim "Well, Well" or "Oh my dear, my dear!" or even just repeat one's name as if it were a priceless discovery, like radium. And that's very bad indeed.

One non-replyable remark is constantly being made to me in particular. People tell me they've seen my father in *Kismet*. This is very nice and I for one am always glad to hear it, but as my father played that play for three years to packed houses the length and breadth of the continent, the statement is not particularly staggering. "You'll be interested in meeting Miss Brown," a hostess will exclaim, her eyes dancing with suppressed excitement, "she has a special message for you" . . . as if it were a T.L. And Miss Brown's special message will turn out to be that she too saw Father in *Kismet*. This announcement is always made with such flourish, such an air of bringing glad tidings, it would be boorish indeed not to appear overwhelmed with happy surprise . . . to refrain from exclaiming "Not Really" in tones that imply "Great God, No!" Sometimes (and to be sure, it adds variety), they tell me they've seen my sire in plays he never even saw himself and nothing will persuade them that he never appeared in *The Garden of Allah* nor in *Omar the Tent Maker*. One lady told me she laughed herself sick over Father's rendition of *Casey at the Bat* and when I timidly suggested that she must be thinking of DeWolf Hopper she grew indignant and practically told me I didn't know my own father. The best policy, I find, is never to doubt their word, especially as they disbelieve not only me, they sometimes won't even believe my father. To his politely firm "No, dear lady, I did not play in *The Man from Home,*" they've been known to protest, "But you must have forgotten, because I saw you in it." So why spoil their fun?

Musicians and lecturers I daresay come in for these opening remarks that are about as open as the Mormon Temple. An author I know who lectures tells me he finds himself pretty baffled when people say to him, "I've got your book but I haven't read it yet." Fond mothers are always bringing their children around to meet great musicians because they're "starting piano"; and there's the story of the Philadelphia debutante who, on being presented to Stefánsson, the explorer, gasped "Oh, I'm so glad to meet you, Mr. Stefánsson, because we keep a Swedish cook." Perhaps it's a sort of panic or that curious state of awe that for some reason overwhelms some people when they find themselves in the presence of anyone whose name appears in print. It's flattering if you like, but at the same time a little trying to those same persons who, in spite of the frequent publication of their names, are of perfectly standard clay and who, if given a chance, will react like any other human beings. The trouble is, no one will give them even half a chance.

October 1941

VI · THE FILM

* * *

DUDLEY NICHOLS

*

Death of a Critic

THE REPORT of his death the other day, confined in a lonely paragraph and buried humbly in the depths of pages of advertising, brought to my mind the memory of my first meeting with Henley James. I recall that at first I did not wish to see him. Contrary to the general impression, when one is engaged in film production and faced with its multitude of harassing decisions there is no time to talk to anyone who is not directly concerned with the job at hand. Fortunately Henley James bore a letter from Hermine Rich Isaacs of THEATRE ARTS and that was the open sesame. Had I been a little less preoccupied I should have remembered his name in connection with several brilliant pieces of film criticism which I had read in obscure journals.

He entered, an ordinary enough man until his eyes caught your own. Then you realized you were looking into knowledge and imagination, into a source of light that tolerantly evaluated you and everything it glanced upon.

As I came to know him I marveled at his visual power. He derived more joy from his eyesight than any man I have ever known. Perhaps painters and astronomers—and great film-makers—share that faculty. He had a fresh and unprejudiced way of seeing things. I felt embarrassed when he would casually point out something that had been under my very eyes—the meaning and implications of the human scene.

Everything is before us, he would say—the universe and all its secrets, man and all his mystery, his tears and laughter—and yet we neglect to see them. Don't make a dead-set at seeing, he would say. Don't use will-power. The will is destructive in the realm of feeling and imagination. Only desire can open the doors of the heart and mind. Love seeing and you will gradually begin to see. But be careful how you point your visions out to others, they won't thank you for it. Men, he said, really don't want to see anything new, just as they loathe experiencing anything new. You will really be disliked, said James, if you offer men a new experience. That is why the way is always hard for pioneers and innovators in the arts, for art of course offers us new emotional experiences.

Yes, he was intensely eye-minded. He cared little for the sound of words, only for their color and images, and he confessed this was a shortcoming. For one thing it had made the study of music difficult for him. He finally knew a great deal about music, learned it doggedly for he felt it was essential to the knowledge of film—that great film was in itself a sort of visual music. It was this principal defect, he held, that had kept him from becoming a film-maker himself. But I believe the real reason was that he was a born critic, a discerner of values, loving the whole of architecture too much to play with blocks. Perhaps a perception of values can be more important than creation.

His whole life had become a search for values and he concentrated this search in the field of cinema. He called himself a moralist and said it was absurd for anyone not a moralist to be interested in the theatre, for the eternal subject-matter of the drama is the conflict of good and evil. Of course, he would add, there are large moralists and small moralists. The small moralist is insufferable because he believes man is born good and that evil is something baleful outside him, from which he must be protected as a child learning to walk must be protected from bumping into chairs or tripping over rugs. He trusts neither himself nor humanity and so in mortal fear goes through life disclaiming the evil that is in himself by accusing it in others. The large moralist faces his own guilt without fear and thus armors his own portion of goodness and strengthens it in others.

But though a moralist for man and his works, James held no ethical view of the universe. He liked to quote Conrad's paragraph on the aim of Creation being, perhaps, purely spectacular . . . "In this view there is room for every religion except for the inverted creed of impiety, the mask and cloak of arid despair; for every joy and every sorrow, for every fair dream, for every charitable hope. The great aim is to remain true to the emotions called out of the deep encircled by the firmament of stars, whose infinite numbers and awful distances may move us to laughter or tears . . . or again, to a properly steeled heart, may matter nothing at all."

"Man," said Henley James, "is God's creation. Art is Man's. A knowledge of the first is essential to the second creation—but let no artist or critic confuse the two. Nature is the miraculous tree and art—man's work—is the flowering that makes the mystery and wonder of the tree manifest. Art—or, to make myself clearer, that poetic faculty which is the animating spirit of all the arts—is always that which renders the invisible visible and intangible tangible. Music, for example, is that which makes Time audible. Sculpture makes Space visible. Literature strives to make life intelligible.

"An artist," he said once, "is a born liar who uses his lies to tell the truth of his time. A critic has the harder task of telling the truth without the liar's gift."

Clearly Henley James was born to be a critic, but why not a critic of the drama, or of literature, or of music or painting? He was gifted to go in any direction. The answer is that he loved the cinema. Love is a mystery. A man loves a woman and forever after her face is stamped on every dream. A man falls in love with archaeology, say, and spends the rest of his days digging in desolate places for the remains of ancient man until perhaps he himself is caught in some cave-in and sealed away until another lover of his mistress—some future archaeologist thousands of years hence—shall dig up his bones and rejoice over the remains of another ancient man. James made no attempt to explain his passion for film. He scorned any critic who did not love his chosen medium. It is hard to believe that a man will practice film criticism if he does not love the cinema or book reviewing if he does not love books, yet there are some. Only more insufferable to him than the film critic who secretly dislikes all films was the critic who secretly likes any film. Discrimination and the perception of values were his religion. He quoted G. B. Shaw, in his memorial essay on William Archer, defining the essence of genius as the "perception of values."

James, who could have been a fine literary critic, was derided by some of his bookish friends for devoting his talents to the cinema. He retorted that in his opinion the cinema was the most important art form of the twentieth century and that it could and should integrate all the arts. He also said that film criticism was the most difficult career a man could choose, not only because it demanded a knowledge of all the arts but for the reason that there were so few films worth criticizing. Besides, the film-makers feared true criticism. Every film is launched like a squid in an obscuring cloud of spectacular publicity. No critical appraisal is wanted. No sound evaluation is possible.

I frequently heard James despair of finding intelligent editors with any respect for the cinema. Reviews and magazines of standing have their heads in the cultural clouds, forgetting that every culture is rooted in the people whose dreams are shaped in no small degree by the glut of movies they get, overlooking the plain fact that what happens on the land masses below ultimately affects even the highest-sailing clouds. Such publications either hold snobbishly aloof from so mundane a thing as the movies or they assign a staff member who writes intelligently, literately and entertainingly—but is, alas, in no way equipped to practice film criticism.

James would not review films as they came along in their endless bulk because he practiced discrimination in his subject-matter. He pointed out that the literary critic, as distinguished from the book reviewer, did just this. The presses of publishers whir at an appalling rate, just as do the cameras of film-makers around the world. Does the literary critic report on every issue of *Red Book* or *The Saturday Evening Post,* on mystery novels and detective fiction and confession pulps? He respects these phenomena for what they are and, keeping one eye on the great literature of the past, directs his attention on what is important in new production.

Yet James had no exclusive or snobbish attitude towards the cinema. He said that the medium by its very nature was not for the few but for the many. He wanted films to be better so that the many could have greater enjoyment. Most Hollywood films were bad, he held, not because Hollywood wished to make poor films but because it did not know how to make them better. Hollywood workers did not understand their own medium and its unimaginable possibilities. They were not entirely to blame. They lacked penetrating criticism which would aid them to understand what they had done. And how can we have penetrating and informed criticism when there is no one to encourage or publish or support the critic?

First-rate criticism has always been a thankless task in any department of the arts. Those who for the sake of entertainment and success exploit their wit and personalities until their own gifts are exalted above their subject-matter stultify their profession. The true critic, who must combine the heart of a poet with the intellect of a scholar, must find his reward in his work, in his sense of growth and discovery, in winning the respect of a few people whom he respects. It is strange that gifted people should ever choose the career of criticism. Perhaps it chooses them and they have no escape save in the suicide of going against their bent, as is the case with every true artist. Yet the artist has it easier. His are the rainbows, however wretched his life may appear to himself.

The compulsive artist, who pours his dreams and passions into various forms which reflect the realities hidden behind the appearances of things, thus releasing us from the blindness and chaos in which we eternally walk, such a man may make not only his fortune but his name a household word; though often his fortune is only for his heirs and his fame for the obituary columns. But the equally compelled critic, a man no less devoted to high and passionate aims, who spends his mature life in service to the great realities of art, sorting out and examining the abundance of man's and not God's creations, evaluating and integrating achievements so that a culture may keep on growing and continue on its path and climb mountains, such a man may live and die and yet be known with honor to very few.

Yet these few have shaped and will continue to shape everything that makes life worthwhile. Nothing is completed, no caught dream can be secure, no work of art or letters be certain of itself, until these few in every generation have stamped its value and arranged its place, have traced its pedigree and clarified its features, have rendered clear its meaning and related it to life as well as to art. And the process is continuous in the sum of the generations as long as culture is developing. When it fails or falters you may be sure the culture is dying.

"There is nothing peculiar," said James, "in the fact that the artist is not always sure of where he is going or why. If he stopped to ask he might never do it—so dangerous is the critical faculty, which must always keep one eye open, so to speak, to the creative faculty which sees best when both eyes are closed—for only then are imagination and intuition fully awake. Naturally artists at times work blindly and compulsively. The poet tracing the hidden truth of some experience or following the footprints of some savage dream is Kit Carson in the wilderness of his own heart.

"The artist desperately needs the critic because he cannot contain him. And the people need him just as urgently because neither can they contain him. They are blind to values without him. They can in fact more easily contain the artist because the poetic faculty is instinctual in mankind whereas the critical mind is based on knowledge and must be consciously trained and developed.

"My function?" he said one day when I had asked him. "I'm a middleman. A window-cleaner for the mass, a mirror-polisher for the film-makers. It's all the same glass, but there are two ways of looking at it, depending on where you stand. For the public I scrub and squeegee with all my wits and say, 'Look, a new constellation is in the sky. Look, that dim little star you thought was a speck of dust on the windowpane is going to grow brighter than Aldebaran and will change the horoscope of our time. Look, those bright lights you see are not the sun, moon and stars but a neon sign down on the corner advertising another gaudy lie.'

"For the artist I give the glass an extra rub and he either breaks the mirror in a rage or lifts up his heart and turns encouraged to another piece of work; for the mirror reflects not only what the artist has done but what he really is, and once he has looked he cannot stand upon a pile of dollars or a heap of dung—or even on a mountain of publicity—and pretend he is strutting on Olympus."

James had great enthusiasm for the film library of the Museum of Modern Art and for the critical writings of Iris Barry about that growing collection of films. "In the early days," he said, "film criticism was possible because the critic had direct knowledge of all that had been accomplished in the medium. Today the young critic would be ignorant of the past, he could gain no historical perspective, if he had no access to this library of world films."

The last time I saw James he admitted the cinema had got itself into a blind alley but he had no doubt of its eventual emergence.

"The medium is more powerful," he said, "than those who work in it. It will always force its way ahead. From the beginning people have confused it with the stage but in the early days there was less confusion because film did not talk. It was pure dream and the dream compelled the invention of its technical devices—the dissolve, the fading out and in, cutting to successive images, camera movement, the long shot and the close-up. This silent film attained a higher artistic development than sound film has approached because it was not confused with the stage, and because the mechanism of its creation was simpler. The less machinery the artist has to deal with, the purer will be his art. Sound film complicated and multiplied the mechanism. The present-day film-maker is still too aware of his machinery. He must learn all there is to know about it and then forget it. This will come in time. Today it accounts for the slick professional products that pass for film.

"And the confusion with stage continues. At first the cinema began to dominate the theatre—though those who are wedded to the stage will hardly admit it. But the loosening-up of stage techniques, revolving or sliding stages, cutting to quick successive scenes by means of lighting effects, expressionism itself was a result of the influence of cinema. Now the influence is the other way and the stage begins to dominate the cinema. I suspect you will find the stage in the next decade returning to its classic form and the cinema regressing from its own classic form until it suddenly realizes its mistake and discovers again its pure direction. I have no objection to the photographed play, when it is done with cinematic skill, but it is not true cinema."

After that visit ended, I never saw Henley James again . . . yes, he is dead. He is dead of course because he never lived. I wish he had. . . . And if you are annoyed by this deception let me plead that I knew of no other way to describe the kind of film critics we need—and he would have starved to death before this time anyway!

April 1947

* *

CHRISTOPHER LA FARGE

*

Walt Disney and the Art-Form

WALT DISNEY'S animated cartoons and graphic movies have come so close, so often, to an absolute artistic excellence that it seems a hard judgment to say that they have fallen short of the mark. Actully, however, it is a high compliment to say so, for it supposes that he attainment to such excellence is within his capabilities—and this after much evidence publicly presented) is not true of any competiors now in his field.

When he first began to show his cartoons, there was apparent at nce a remarkable quality both of imagination and draftsmanship, nd this was soon followed by evidence of a color-sense above the verage. Compared with the work of his competitors and imitators, e also displayed a further requisite for the creation of an art-form: aste, that almost indefinable quality that lifts a conception above the evel of merely common appeal and gives it the greater (and incluive) universal touch. Nevertheless, although he has grown in all hese manifestations of his talent—imagination, draftsmanship, colorense and taste—he has not grown enough to have passed the diffiult line that always lies between the popular success and the work f art. The fault, or weakness if you choose, can be traced largely to aste, which controls both conception and execution; and to an as yet ncomplete analysis of what he wants to do and why he wants to lo it.

The phrases, "what he wants to do and why he wants to do it," re descriptive of the unavoidable process of mind through which ll artists must go before they can intelligently practice their art in ny medium. Looking back now on the lengthening history of the notion picture, it seems apparent that when, at any stage, the industry has been able to answer those two questions of *what* and *why,* hey have refused to apply their answers to the production of their ilms except momentarily. The result has been obvious to most obervers: in spite of gigantic and steadily enlarging advances in the echniques of production, they have as yet failed, as Disney has failed vith them, to produce an art-form in the true sense of the word. That is to say, they have not yet consciously produced the film which s inevitably the product of the motion-picture technique, could not onceivably be produced in any other medium as successfully, and s married to its medium as finally as mosaic to a Byzantine chapel, tained glass to a twelfth-century French Gothic church. I mention hese two examples of media because they were both the products of a technique that required many craftsmen to execute, as is true of the motion picture. An example analogous to the failure of the notion picture to achieve this end is that phase of tapestry weaving, begun in the late fifteenth century, where by the perfection of tec nique it was felt possible and admirable to reproduce paintings i woven form. The painting suffered distortion in color and in draw ing; the tapestry suffered by being essentially untrue to its prop function and limitations.

This is not to say that the movies have never produced an "artisti film. They have; but such films have been rare and have appeare more or less as happy accidents and not in any continuous and i creasing flow—a flow that would indicate a consciousness on the pa of the producers that there were certain definable limitations to the art and that they had recognized these limitations. Actually it h been the unexplored terrain of the movies that has made their jo the hardest: so far, the limitations of the medium have been s rapidly overcome as they appeared that it has led the producers int the natural error of believing that there were virtually no limits t what could be done. It is a truism, however, that the limitations c a medium of art form its artistic quality and inform its excellenc

Curiously enough, one can find examples of the successful use c the moving picture almost as far back as one can go in its histor These examples take most often the form of humor or of fantas or both. It was discovered almost at once that the motion pictur was the answer to the magician's dream. Form and matter could b changed, dissolved or made to vanish; motion could be controlle or reversed beyond human possibilities; the law of gravity could b overcome; the monstrous and the fabulous could be given reality. I the field of low comedy, the rare skill of a Fratellini, who could los his trousers in a somersault on the stage, was no longer necessary the trick could be done by the unskillful with the aid of the photc graph. The complex timing of humorous coincidence could be con trolled to a split second—and would remain fixed at its apogee fo each performance. The perfecting of all these tricks of humor an magic produced, immediately before the advent of the sound-track a use for pure pantomime that was incredibly fine and culminate more or less, in the work of Chaplin, some of whose best silent film are "works of art," having a timeless quality of perfection and, mor important, being of a sort impossible to conceive of in any othe medium.

I do not want to go too far into study of the history of successe and failures in the motion-picture industry. Mostly we all recogniz that a poor play, or a poor book, is sometimes bettered by the movie version, and that that version is yet far short of excellence. Mostly too we know that a fine book or a play is rarely as fine, as moving, in the picture version. The point to see is that the movie from a book or a play approaches artistry, at no sacrifice in intensity, almost always when it had better have been a movie first and a book or play afterwards. *Becky Sharp* from *Vanity Fair* via Mitchell's play, *Abe Lincoln in Illinois* from Sherwood's play, *Cavalcade* from Coward's play were all less intense, less moving, less excellent than their prototypes. I will risk the criticisms I shall provoke by saying that *The Grapes of Wrath* was better as a movie than as a book because the theme and its treatment were originally better suited to the moving-picture medium. On a lower scale entirely, *Gone with the Wind* was almost level with its book and would have been level except that the book permitted the reader to create for himself the images of its otherwise unbelievable characters and the movie inevitably made those characters too real.

All this, then, is another way of saying that Disney's work began as a branch from the parent stalk of the movies, following consciously or unconsciously that line of peculiar success made visible in the fantastic movies that punctuated the history of the films. But it is not going to remain as a branch: it has almost become (and can become) a separate entity, in no way competitive with its parent. It can become, perhaps before the movies proper achieve to that distinction, an art-form in its own right. This is the possibility I wish to examine.

If Walt Disney, when he first began to be able to control this new technique of the animated cartoon, had been content to limit his productions to the fantastic and the magical, he would still be but a branch of the motion pictures, dependent for his popular support merely on the difference between a drawn and an acted character. That difference would consist in two parts: the first, the actual difference between a drawn or painted image and the photograph of a human being; the second, a difference in the degree of impossibility he could achieve. The first of these, then, would have provided merely a change from real actors photographed in color or not—a pleasant and at moments undoubtedly a refreshing change, but no more. The second, the degree of impossibility or absurdity, could at almost any moment have been lessened if not altogether abridged by the astonishing technical advances of photography. And even if Disney could always have kept a little ahead of the movies proper, the difference would largely have been confined to the field of slapstick humor and would have been unimportant in the field of fantasy. The technical virtuosity of that otherwise poor movie, *The Vanishing Man Returns,* is a case in point.

What quality, then, most distinguishes the animated cartoon from the fantastic movie? It is the quality of abstraction, which I shall define as the stripping of action and mood to its essential characteristics until the point is reached where all that remains is the concentrated essence. This is what all the great artists have succeeded in doing. It was carried to a logical extremity in the greatest days of Chinese painting, when men and animals, their moods and motions, even scenery and climate were reduced to the essential abstractions so successfully that the artist was free to fit them into patterns of beauty that never sacrificed the intensity of motion or of emotion. I believe it to be incontrovertible that until the day of the slow-motion camera no reproduction of the action of a horse has even approximated the accuracy of the abstracted Chinese drawings.

I remember seeing, some years ago now, a Disney Silly Symphony which was called (I believe) *The China Shop.* In it there occurred, at the magic midnight hour, a ballet-pantomime by the china and crockery figurines stored on the shelves of the shop. The hero and heroine were a Dresden china shepherd and shepherdess. The villain was a green china Devil. In color it was the best I had yet seen, in drawing and in smoothness of animation far superior to any Disney had then achieved. Its particular excellence, however, lay in the fact that for once he animated some of the magically moved china characters in a fashion dictated not by ordinary human motion but by the sort of motion one could imagine for a china figure. *The Wizard of Oz,* acted by human beings, attempted also to portray china figurines in action; in that case the illusion was poor and the effect nothing but banal. But Disney, with his drawn characters, *abstracted* the motion and thus gave it a quality utterly its own, as original as it was pleasing, and a quality quite beyond the reach of any possible human-acted motion picture. Suddenly, before our eyes, we saw something altogether new, altogether of its own kind. Yet—only in part. The abstraction was not maintained. The Shepherdess grew more and more to resemble an ordinary pretty chorus girl. The

Shepherd became more and more human and like a chorus man or a matinee idol perhaps—the animals that came to life alone maintained their abstracted quality. Only in its finale, when—after a fierce battle—all the figures were chipped and broken, did the film return to its first beauty, and then the shepherd and his love, battered and broken, took on again the characteristics of china and abandoned the commoner aspects of a rather ordinary humanity.

Since that day I have waited for a Disney movie which would follow the best of that one and follow it throughout. I have not yet seen it—flashes of it, yes, but never the whole maintained. Donald Duck comes close to it, often, but Donald Duck and his peers are and must remain a lesser branch of Disney's main work. In *Snow White,* the Princess was distressingly human and so was the Prince. The Seven Dwarfs were sometimes wonderful, but sometimes they degenerated into rather cheap vaudeville clowns, not alone in what they said or sang but in the way they were drawn to move as human beings. Pinocchio himself was never, after his original animation, the wooden doll in magic motion but a small boy—with an odd nose, to be sure—yet a small boy just the same. Compare Pinocchio with Jiminy Cricket and you will see what I mean. I think back now with real distaste to the Good Fairy, who was merely like a dull, middle-aged actress in an English Christmas pantomime. And yet in *Snow White* and *Pinocchio* there were passages where the motion was magnificently abstracted into a convincing, fairy-story unreality, and for those passages the audience was suddenly transported into a world unique in kind. For the most part, these passages in both films concerned animals and vegetables; commonly, with the advent of people, even though they were magical ones, the story dropped into the banal and tasteless and, far worse, came suddenly into the field of comparison with human-acted movies.

Fantasia, while it raises other questions, is another example of the failure of taste and of analyzed conception. I am of those who believe it succeeded in proving beyond further necessity of proof that to illustrate music with drawing is impossible and useless but that music can be used magnificently as an adjunct to drawing. Anyone who has studied his program notes and interpretations at a concert will know what I mean: such notes can be almost unbearably irritating and misleading. I choose to create my own magic world as I listen to music.

But leaving that aside, together with the tiresome repetition of Stokowski's silhouette, it is interesting to note the great heights to which Disney rose in *Fantasia* and the great depths to which he fell—always because he either followed his best instincts of abstracting his art or abandoned them to compete with the movies. The abstractions of motion shown in the Frost Fairies, the Dancing Leaves, the Sorcerer's Apprentice are almost beyond cavil; the Creation of the World was so remarkable, except for its color, that I dare say that never before has a scientific speculation been better or more clearly given in graphic form. But what shall we say of the boneless Centaurettes who batted their eyes? The Beethoven section was cheap, ordinary, commonplace. It was a travesty on classical myth, but an unsuccessful travesty. It is true that it would be difficult if not impossible to make centaurs gallop even in the movies, but these figures were made as nearly human as their shape allowed and throughout that section of film all the characters were of the same tasteless stamp.

One must add a comment on Disney's color. It is so far superior to that of his competitors that one is tempted to say it is good. But it is not good in the absolute sense. It is not bad but it is safe—almost always safe. It is pretty color—harmonious, charming, amusing. It lacks the vitality of his drawing and it falls short of the demands of art. Perhaps he is not a colorist: I don't know. I suspect that he has been feeling his way and that his color expresses, so far, the same indecision that has marked all his productions. Until he decides what he wants to do and why he wants to do it, it will be impossible for him to bring his color up to the pitch of his draftsmanship—and until he decides to use his draftsmanship to create stories only in a manner that is impossible in any other medium, he will not achieve that artistic excellence at which I am sure he aims and which he has so often approximated. When that day comes, he will have created almost single-handed a new art-form.

September 1941

PAUL ROTHA

*

Films of Fact and Fiction

IT TOOK a world depression to shake our belief that public affairs jog along smoothly enough without much worry by the ordinary citizen. It was the depression, with its personal as well as national tragedies, that brought a ripening of social responsibility in country and city. From that memorable year of 1929 there has been a growing public thirst for information about current affairs. The constant repetition of labor wars, of political scandals, of exposés of brigandage by industrialists, of undeclared but bloody wars all over the outside world, of the darkening menace of the dictator states—all these things have urged the citizen to ask what's happening beneath the surface, and why. Public issues have at last become of public interest.

To meet this demand, new techniques have been developed in all modern mediums for communication of fact. From the straightforward presentation of news to the dramatized expression of an editorial opinion, there have been experiments which might not have been made if aesthetic purpose had been the sole urge. The success of pictorial journalism in such papers as *Life* and *Photo-History,* of dramatic rendition of current events over the air by "The March of Time" and of such sociologically important occasions in the theatre as "The Living Newspaper," *Pins and Needles* and *The Cradle Will Rock* is proof of the existence of an alert public interest in public affairs. The film industry, usually slow to catch on to new movements, has played a leading and influential part in this dramatization of fact. The camera-work of newsreel and documentary films has been mainly responsible for the great strides made in photo-journalism. Today, the movie as a medium for presenting fact, as a reflection of reality, offers more stimulating chances for creative experiment than the socially constipated fiction film.

Regular moviegoers know what is being done to bring reality to the screen. "The March of Time" swings along with its pendulum beat. The newsreel, still shy of public reaction to screen controversy, scores an occasional success by a cameraman who has the luck and toughness to be on the spot, like the Chicago steel riots and the "Hindenburg" disaster. The documentary film grows out of its infant stage of romantic impressionism and gets down to using human beings instead of machines. But at each step forward the makers of factual films are met by the same problem—the representation of the individual and the relating of that individual to his social and economic background.

The closer the movie gets to a dramatized expression of reality, and I mean current reality, the more acute becomes this problem of the portrayal of the individual. In the newsreel, facts are represented simply in terms of their physical appearance in time. While current they are news, but they soon become history. The drama lies in the vitality of the material and not in the method of presentation. "The March of Time" monthly film issue made its appearance in America in 1935. The reel adapts from the newspaper a reporting purpose which claims to give the inside story behind current events and borrows from the fiction film a dramatic method of presentation. Using partly the same naturally shot material which is the stuff of newsreel and partly staged dramatic scenes with both real people and actors, it tries to present a selective picture of an event which implies a comment, often ironic, upon the event itself. Like the newsreel, it uses also the method of the personal interview but bends the individual to fit its editorial purpose, as with the junk merchant in the Scrap Iron item recently issued. Its narration is written in a highly descriptive, provocative style and delivered with a breathless emotion which does not always coincide with the subject of its visuals. But its journalistic insistence on speed leaves little time for treating individuals; the reel lacks human quality almost as much as the newsreel from which it springs.

In Russia the dramatization of fact has been a first aim since the industry was nationalized in 1919. Many of the earlier Soviet films dealt with what was to their sponsors and creators the greatest event of modern history—the Workers' Revolution of 1917 and the historic events that led up to its success. Pudovkin's *Mother* was based on Gorki's novel of the 1905 revolution; Eisenstein's *Potemkin,* on the Black Sea mutiny of the same year. It was worth noting that both films, along with others, departed freely from actual fact.

The physical effects made possible by rhythmic arrangements of shots, as had been first used by D. W. Griffith in his film *Intolerance* in 1916, were exploited to put across in a semi-sensational, semi-hysterical manner this blood-and-fire material. Analysis of their editing methods showed Eisenstein and Pudovkin a way in which the film medium could conform to the fundamental principles of Marxist dialectic reasoning. Their films of mutiny and uprising were largely based on the clash of class against class, the mob versus the military. Their drama was conflict. And so long as their subject material was the stuff of revolution, their methods were successful.

In many of the early films natural actors were used. While they were running around in the mass, they ran as well as any trained actors could have run. But when individual characterization was required, new and serious problems arose. People as individuals in relation to their social and economic background demand psychological understanding and screen direction which cannot always be achieved by tricks of editing. Thus the Russians found themselves up against both a technical problem in film direction and a philosophical problem of the place of the human being in society. In interpreting human beings in films the Russians had also to interpret the individual's attitude towards the State and his economic and social relationships, a problem that had not before been met in movies. In most American and European fiction films the subjects did not reflect the social conditions of the period, except in such rare cases as the modern story in Griffith's *Intolerance* and in Von Stroheim's *Greed*. But once the Soviet directors, like the British documentary film-makers later, decided that their films should deal with real life, they were inevitably involved in the bigger philosophic issue.

Recent events have shown that the solution to this problem depends largely upon the development of social and economic problems in the Soviet State itself. The enthusiastic self-criticism so popular in the Russian arts has continually expressed dissatisfaction with these efforts, and at the Moscow Film Festival in 1935 it was stated that the films of Pudovkin and Eisenstein were undramatic and coldly intellectual. The crowd must no longer be the hero; it must be represented through the character development of its leader. The theory and practice of montage which had worked so well with non-actors and mass movement must be reconsidered in the light of the emotional powers of the professional actor. "We need actors with great passions," proclaimed Dinamov; and *Chapayev,* with its actor-hero Boris Babotchkin, was the film of the year, although technically it was inferior to the work of the better-known directors. The subsequent development of this trend produced films like *The Youth of Maxim* in which story and acting illustrated the developing intellectual and emotional experiences of the chief protagonists as they reacted to changing social occurrences.

Pudovkin attempted to meet the difficulty by going straight to the individual himself, studying his behavior, trying to understand his reactions and then to build the character filmically by editing methods. He got his actors to externalize their feelings before the camera by using various trick stimuli. Eisenstein, on his return from America, did not resume production but assumed the role of professor and developed a series of methods (the "internal monologue," the creation of a class character who will act as *pars pro toto* for the mass) by which he hoped to emotionalize and humanize the ideological film. Thus actors and acting returned in full force to the film studio. Stories and plots were invented. With this sudden swing from one use of the medium to another there has inevitably resulted a technical and aesthetic setback. The recent Russian films have had more human qualities than those of ten years ago but they have not equaled the technical brilliance that made *Potemkin* and *Storm over Asia* world-famous.

In England, the documentary film-makers are at present faced with this same problem of the individual. Technically and aesthetically, the documentary film includes most of the innovations of the past ten years but it is important to remember that, like the Russian cinema, aesthetic purpose has come second to sociological aim. Through historical research, social reference and economic understanding, they try to bring the ordinary citizen closer to the world which is intimately his own. Like the Russians, they aim to interpret the modern scene but their basis of production is different.

Although subsidized, these documentary films should not be confused with commercial advertising pictures such as are produced in England and America. The documentary film is an outcome of a public-relations movement and results from a conscious desire on the part of government departments, industrial firms and various public bodies to create a deeper sympathy between their activities and public understanding. Their makers take only subjects which are of acknowledged national interest and pursue the line that their films provide a basis for discussion on some of the more vital social issues of current living. By creating on the screen a dramatic picture of how people live and how public services work and what part the ordinary citizen can play in everyday life, these films have achieved a certain civic value. During the last six years films have been made on such divergent subjects as airways, shipping, unemployment, slum clearance, radio, postal communications, electricity, gas, education, book publishing, railroads, nutrition and city administration. Thus while such social problems as unemployment and slum clearance have been discussed in Parliament and press, the living fact of each as it affects the people has been brought to the screen, making audiences conscious of their vital concern in current public affairs.

Most of the early documentary films, like *Industrial Britain* and *Contact,* used the individual simply as an uncharacterized type. He may have been given a name and a place by the commentator but he was invested with no human feeling and related to no background beyond his immediate job. In many cases, the interest of the film director lay in the job and not in the man who was doing it, unless it was to make him the romantic figure of a craftsman as did Flaherty with his glass-blowers and pottery-makers in the Black Country. Most often the documentary film-makers were embarrassed at the thought of handling their people as people and took the easiest way out by treating them as symbols ("the man behind the machine").

In addition, most of the directors were young and lacked familiarity with the materials of the movie. When Grierson made *Drifters* in 1928, he confesses that he did it "without knowing one lens from another." Again, the romantic style most nearly approached the "interest" pictures and travelogues to which audiences were accustomed and thus the films made in this style, like *Contact* and *O'er Hill and Dale,* were at first the most popular. It was not long, however, before simple lyric films like *The Country Comes to Town* were developed into such an aesthetically satisfying film as Basil Wright's *The Song of Ceylon,* and the striving after social analysis made something more of *Shipyard* than just a descriptive film of shipbuilding. This trend continues to be developed, using new techniques of sound and speech, and has resulted in such emotionally exciting and sometimes sentimental films as *Nightmail* and *The Future's in the Air,* although the place of the individual is still largely ignored.

The personal interview with camera and microphone, first used in Elton and Anstey's *Housing Problems* in 1935, cut right across this impressionist style. Here were human beings spontaneously speaking and gesturing right into the lens and microphone. This was not acting but normal behavior as far as a consciousness of the camera would permit. Sociologically, this was important; but the method deprived the documentary film of much of its cinematic quality. It became an illustrated lecture studded with personal interviews which provided "documentary" evidence that the commentator was speaking the truth. To set up camera and microphone and to record what is placed before them, occasionally cutting away from the portrait of the speaker to visuals of what he is talking about, is nobody's creative fun except that of the newsreel cameraman. *The Nutrition Film (Enough to Eat?), Smoke Menace* and *Children at School* followed the same method although the last staged small scenes in which professional actors were used. Valuable as sociological documents—and it is important that they are being made—these films contribute little to the fundamental problem of the dramatic presentation of human beings. Aesthetically, they mark a conscious effort to break with the sentimental approach of *Coal Face* and *Nightmail.*

This danger of journalistic reporting and the snapshot influence of "The March of Time" were recognized by Cavalcanti. In *We Live in Two Worlds* he tried to combine both the interview and the impressionistic style in an intimate globeside chat with Mr. J. B. Priestly. But even this was not using the individual as actor. The Swiss peasants were as uncharacterized as the glass-blowers in *Industrial Britain.* The attempt to humanize the postal workers, especially the nervous trainee in *Nightmail,* was more successful but so far only two of these English documentaries have got down to the problem.

The Saving of Bill Blewett, a story of fisher people in a small Cornish village, is perhaps the best example of the handling of natural actors in documentary. But the plugged publicity angle of the Savings Bank was so incongruous beside the honesty of the people themselves that, despite its subtle introduction, the audience was resentful at being fooled. For all the genuine quality of the acting and the technical skill of Cavalcanti and Harry Watt's production, the film never got beyond being a publicity film as did *Nightmail* and *The Song of Ceylon*. *Today We Live,* a film of social-service activities, carried a slight story based on fact and alternated between two locations—a town in a depressed mining area in South Wales and a country village in the Cotswolds. The characters were played by unemployed miners and country villagers. None of them was required to do anything which he or she did not do in ordinary life, with the result that, although sincere, their "acting" was without emotional appeal. By nature of its dual location, moreover, the film lacked the time to develop human characterization in each sequence and would have succeeded better, I believe, had its sponsors agreed to tell one story instead of two. Despite this, *Today We Live* gave a true picture of life as it is lived in two widely differing parts of England and, for almost the first time in documentary, had intentional humor. The characters grew out of their surroundings and their economic circumstances determined their actions. It is doubtful if professional actors would have done the job better.

The few available American documentary films do not contribute much to the discussion. The Mexican-made *The Wave* used nonprofessional actors but either lack of direction or the superimposition of a philosophical argument on persons who did not fully understand its implications resulted in a picture of embarrassing awkwardness. Neither of Pare Lorentz's well-known films, *The Plow That Broke the Plains* or *The River,* had any attempt at characterization. Despite its difficult production circumstances, Joris Ivens' *The Spanish Earth* had considerable human feeling which arose, I suspect, from the very nature of the material.

In retrospect, we must not overlook the films of Robert Flaherty. It is true that he is mainly interested in the reenactment of dying customs and crafts by semi-primitive peoples, but Flaherty, more than any other documentary film-maker, has known how to handle his people in front of the camera. He is helped, of course, by the fact that most of us are unfamiliar with his people and it is only when he treads on the home front, as in *Industrial Britain* and *Man of Aran,* that we realize his shortcomings. But his habit of digging himself in, absorbing the background and letting the theme emerge gradually is, without doubt, a sensible method if the production budget permits.

As far as the individual in the studio-made fiction film is concerned, we shall find that few fiction films deal with subjects which have their roots in reality. While subjects have little in common with real life, this discrepancy does not matter. But when the movie touches social reality in the gangster film, Cagney cannot be just Cagney. No more can Muni be just Muni when the social background becomes real (or pretends to be real) in *Zola*. Here was a character who must needs be deep-rooted in his background. Relation of character to background is a familiar matter to the stage actor but it is more difficult on the screen. More difficult because the illusion of background on the stage is known and accepted as an illusion, whereas the screen can present a background that, for all its studio artifice and back-projection, is very close to the real thing, in fact, often is. A wide difference exists between Muni playing Zola with the aid of an elaborate make-up and weeks of historical research, and Cagney playing Tom Powers in *The Public Enemy*. The first was a deliberate fake; the second was real. I am not suggesting that Mr. Cagney is, or was, a gangster but I am saying that he, like so many other born New Yorkers, knew what he was acting about. He knew the smell of the thing because it was contemporary and real. As a result, he was able to create a closer relationship between character and background than did Mr. Muni, whose performance was nearer to that of a filmed photoplay than a film. I doubt if it is the screen's function to show dressed-up history. The medium is perhaps too real.

I have raised, I hope, a whole series of questions that go right to the heart of the movie. Can the studio-made fiction film with actors and sets come as close to presenting reality as the factual film? No matter how faithful the sets, how convincing the acting and how accurate the research, can a studio reconstruction achieve the dramatic intensity which is inherent in the real thing? Could the trick department restage the burning of the "Hindenburg" so as to give us that same sense of horror which we got from the newsreel? Should we not always be aware of the fake? Then is it possible to bring about a blending of the two methods; or should the fact film and the fiction film pursue their divergent courses? Only on such rare occasions as Pabst's *Kameradschaft* have the two approaches been married with success. Pabst's mixing of actors with real people, or real exterior backgrounds with faked studio interiors, was so perfectly done that the audience was not aware that it was not seeing reality. It is surprising that so little has been done to develop Pabst's theories, theories which he himself has been unable to develop owing to the unsuitable subjects of his later films. But *Kameradschaft* does suggest a logical development of the realist film which takes the best from both the fiction and the fact film to meet the present demand for public discussion of public affairs.

March 1938

* *

ARTHUR L. MAYER

*

People to People

AS IN THE PAST, the great stories of World War II will be told long after the war is over. They will be told by its participants, for in the ranks of the armed forces served the Hemingways, Dreisers, Scott Fitzgeralds of the future. They will use any mediums, but those who wish to speak to the millions will use the medium with the widest circulation ever known to man—the motion picture.

They will take advantage of the magic mobility of the camera to overcome the limits of time and space, of its technical proficiency to portray the movements of fleets and armies the like of which have never been seen before on land or sea, as well as the agony or redemption of a single soul. They will use its coordination of sight and sound to speak in a language which all people can understand and to which all people respond.

And what stories of heartaches and heroism, loneliness and love, confusion and consecration they will have to tell. A generation of young Americans, long misunderstood and underestimated, will be perpetuated for the tears and laughter of posterity. Not that they considered themselves at all heroic—they were foul-mouthed, unruly, ill-informed and boastful. They were also gay, gallant, generous, resourceful and unselfish.

For a man to sacrifice his life in battle to capture a murderous machine gun or to cover a retirement is nothing rare in American annals; but the devotion that leads a sailor to risk a week in the brig to get his buddy back on ship before liberty expires, though less sensational, is equally characteristic. The humor of the barracks would not meet with the approval of the Legion of Decency, but I strongly disagree with those who think that war brutalized the sailor and soldier, that it transformed him into a machine with only one purpose—the destruction of his enemies.

The contrary is far nearer the truth. A deep instinct of preservation made the erstwhile civilian seek constantly to forget his new vocation and his dedication to death. He sought beauty and understanding and tenderness in all about him. By nature of his occupation he became intensely aware of the transient nature of life. Its daily uncertainties magnified his sensitivities to where, believe it or not, he flocked to Shakespearean performances, loved classical music, picked flowers by the wayside, cuddled every vagrant cur and made a fuss over children regardless of whether they were dark because of natural color or unnatural dirt.

Dreaming so avidly of the past, fearing so gravely for the future, he sought to extract the utmost joy from the passing moment. In the midst of thousands of his comrades he was lonely, and yet he sensed that he had become a member of a vast fellowship, a brotherhood that had given much and justly asks today for a little in return—homes, food, clothing, at reasonable prices in reasonable abundance. He built himself a nostalgic faith in a Mom overflowing with love, hot water, clean linen and apple pie; a sweetheart, the acme of lacy femininity, always understanding, incredibly beautiful and equally virtuous; an old home town, replete with friendliness and good will; and an economic system where all who wanted to marry and rear children could do so, where all who were frugal could seek and achieve security.

This was more to him than a dream of a never-never land. It was his vision of the future. To its fulfillment, if we hope to live harmoniously with our ex-warriors, we must all dedicate ourselves. Mothers and sweethearts who find their sons and lovers strangely changed will have to acquire the wisdom and patience to rebuild and enrich the old intimacies. Educators, priests, statesmen and publicists must remodel our schools, churches and social institutions to bring them closer to the veterans' yearning for peace abroad and fair play at home for men of every race and creed and color.

And the movies will have to do their share in forging this fine new world. Of course, they must continue to tell stories of romance in the moonlight, but the lovers need not be cardboard figures endowed inexplicably with 1948 model cars and thousand-dollar gowns. They can be young people leading, or planning to lead, significant and interesting lives. Of course there must be belly laughs, but they can be at the expense of the stuffed shirts and the blue noses and the would-be fuehrers among us. God forgive us, there can even be horror pictures, but they can deal with the real horror of poverty and misery in the mill towns, or the tortured struggle in a man's psyche between his aspiration and his limitations, far more harrowing than the synthetic horror of crazed scientists and clutching green hands emerging from a hidden panel.

Our pictures must be propaganda in the best sense of that misused word! subtle propaganda for democracy and for freedom of speech, press, religion and assembly. While they entertain, they can also serve to make our people fierce in their love of liberty, tolerant of all except those who preach intolerance; lovers of beauty as well as of mechanical progress; aware of the fateful participation of every one of us in world affairs; as ready in the future to live for our country as only yesterday we were prepared to die for it.

I cannot magnify the dangers, the responsibilities that confront us. I cannot magnify what we—the little people—must do. For the responsibility for making the motion picture a mighty instrument of mankind's hopes and salvation lies today where it has always lain—not with producers, distributors or exhibitors, not with authors, directors or critics, but with an audience. It is the audience that will determine whether the progress that the movies made in war both as entertainment and as information shall blossom forth into leaves of olive and laurel. It is the audience that will decide whether the motion picture can be as potent as atomic energy—as potent for human destruction, as potent for human salvation.

I have said that the Hemingways and Fitzgeralds of tomorrow, as well as the Capras and the Fords, are now coming out of the ranks of the armed forces. They will want to use the picture medium to record their experiences and recreate for the entire world all that they and their comrades performed and suffered—all that they hoped would be achieved by those performances and those sufferings.

But what if old man box-office tells another story? What if he whispers or even shouts that the people are tired of war and democratic dogma on the screen? That they want to forget about it all? What if the theatre receipts begin to say that there is no market for films of the public and private virtues that made our country great; that there is no demand for the celebration of free institutions as the Nazis and totalitarians celebrate their regimentation; no sale for films which hymn the beauties of nature and of art or those which dare to pioneer in new techniques and new forms of expression? Suppose, when Hollywood studies its grosses, they indicate that people are not interested in such things? That all they want are false glamour and superficial gaiety, fairy tales empty of content and sentimental symbols of self-indulgence?

That is what the box-office said in that terrible let-down into lethargy and self-complacency that followed the first war. It might do so again.

But the box-office is us. It is you and me and our relatives and our friends.

You may despise it and disparage it, but it is an unfailing barometer of what we want in our heart of hearts—frippery or meaning, shadow or substance. In spite of certain inequities in picture distribution, pictures are as good as the picturegoing public. A trivial people will have trivial pictures. A great people will demand and will get great pictures.

To get good pictures on the screen is like getting good government. It is not a mysterious feat or legerdemain but the simple, arduous, uninspiring task of getting out the vote. To get out that vote, to get out those potential patrons, what we must do today is to clarify our thinking, intensify our efforts and, above all, acquire a sense of timing and strategy. For time is running out and strategy alone can get things done fast enough to save us.

Responsible members of the motion-picture industry are making a greater effort than ever before to import into the United States films made in the other countries of the United Nations—films like the Swiss *Last Chance,* the Mexican *Portrait of Maria,* the Italian *Open City.*

The American public has never cared greatly for foreign films and those of us who are importing these films are taking a chance—a last chance, you might say—for an open market in ideas. Perhaps the public still won't like pictures from other countries, but if it rejects them it will be doing more than just registering that it does not care to be entertained by foreign films. It will be signaling the people of all these countries that Americans are indifferent to what is happening in the rest of the world; that we don't care to know our neighbors or understand their problems and their aims. We will be saying that we do not seek to evaluate any way of life save our own, or any viewpoint save our own. In this shrinking world we will be trying to shrink ourselves down to a pinpoint of isolation so that we will not have to share anything with our neighbors—not wheat or bomb formulas or even ideals.

Remember, too, that those of our own American films which we make successful by our attendance are the films which will tell the rest of the world what makes America tick. If we support only films glorifying materialism and moral indifference, those will be the films which will disclose us in all our nakedness to our former allies and enemies, to Germans and Frenchmen and Russians, to the teeming millions of Asia and our neighbors in South America.

Our responsibility is much more than a mere matter of taste in entertainment. The movies, like everything else, are tangled up in the mighty cords which are binding the people of the earth together, whether they like it or not. If we welcome—not in words but in attendance figures—films which other countries send us to tell us what they are like; if here at home we support—not in the drawing-room but at the box-office—American films which give a true account of our honest problems and highest aspirations, then we will help to educate the men and women of every nation to be citizens of the world. We will make our motion picture a symbol and token of all striving humanity—a living voice speaking among the people.

June 1946

JOSEPH FREEMAN

*

Biographical Films

IN THE PAST SEVEN YEARS Hollywood has produced more than forty films which are biographical in the strict sense of the word. The story deals not with imaginary figures in imaginary situations but with historic personages in historic situations; and the conflicts of private life are replaced in part by those of the body politic. Some of these films have been unusually successful; it was probably the triumph of *The Life of Emile Zola* and *The Story of Louis Pasteur,* pioneers in the field, which launched the biographical avalanche.

Biography, always an important branch of literature, bids fair to become a permanent branch of the film. It is bound to be especially important today. Everyone is thinking and talking about "history in the making," and people are ready to follow the stories of historical figures on the same screen which shows them the adventures of the Hardys, the Aldriches and young Dr. Kildare.

The basic elements of film are those of drama. Theatre and screen follow essentially similar laws in developing the moral problem, the conflict, suspense and resolution. On one score, however, the screen has transcended the theatre infinitely; for the film presents action as it moves not only in space but in time.

In the biographic film the element of time is particularly crucial and the moral problem takes on a special character. In contrast to the drama of private life, the biographic film develops the action of public figures. That, as Hollywood well knows, makes all the difference in the world. In *Northwest Passage* Spencer Tracy as head of Rogers' Rangers says: "I am not a man now. I am a soldier commanding troops. Some day, when you will meet me as a man, I'll need a great deal of your charity." Clearing the wilderness for the American people gives social value to actions which in private life might be considered crimes.

The Greek dramas about the House of Atreus raised precisely such moral problems. Orestes, Oedipus, Electra, Medea—all these are biographies of public figures. They are also social dramas by any definition of the term we care to make. They deal, among other essentials, with the great political struggle in which patriarchal replaced matriarchal society. Here the process was vivid enough and the Greeks made no bones about it. They knew that to touch biography is to touch history, and to touch history is to touch society at its roots.

Shakespeare's historical plays are in the same tradition. His chronicles about the House of Plantagenet give us—over and above the great poetry, drama and character—insight into a country and an age. So far the development is direct. The biographical drama deals with members of dominant social groups and governing houses. You cannot dramatize the story of a prince without involving in the most fundamental way the politics on which his very existence depends.

The real change in the biographical drama was made by the Renaissance. As the merchant enters the social arena, his son, the artist, takes the stage. In *Hamlet* and *Richard II* we get for the first time (though still in princely dress and still directly in the main stream of politics) a biographical drama whose hero is the artist. But the hero still carries his own historic name, and the fable of the play is still taken from official chronicles. To be sure, the poet transcends and transforms his raw material; that is his genius. Nevertheless, the material is taken from history, not from private life.

The nineteenth century brought, along with modern industry and its specific democratic forms, what Diderot called "the bourgeois drama." The hero is no longer the ruler but the private citizen. He bears no historic name; he is anonymous. He appears on the stage as a type whom the author invents and names Dr. Stockman, Uncle Vanya or John Tanner. The profound revolution which ushered in the century separated the individual from history in literature as well as in society. The actions of rulers now belonged to formal history and biography; the novel and the drama concerned themselves with the private affairs of the anonymous citizen—his successes and failures in the struggle for love, money or social standing. Very likely, as you go through the plays and novels of the century which ended with 1914, you will find that the hero becomes progressively unheroic and progressively divorced from the major social conflicts of his time.

This was the tradition which Hollywood, in the nature of things, was compelled to pick up for the content of its films. Whatever technical innovations the American film has made, its basic ideas are those of the novel, the magazine story and the theatre. Most movies, from the story of John Bunyan to the chronicle of Andy Hardy, have dealt, humorously or seriously, with the actions of the anonymous citizen confined to the world of his private concerns.

The first important break in this pattern came when the world war of 1914 made men conscious once more of the history they were making. *The Birth of a Nation* and *Intolerance* were great efforts to film history imaginatively. The second of these films even attempted something vastly more important from a technical standpoint, something which only the movies can do and which for some reason they have since neglected: it cut across time and illuminated history by counterpointing four different epochs.

Biographical films which came later treated the historic figure as if he were simply an anonymous citizen, as if the most important thing about Napoleon-Boyer was his affair with Walewska-Garbo. Or, as Sergei Eisenstein, a truly great director, once said: "The lady and gentleman are put in the foreground and the historic event in the background."

It took the turbulent Thirties to alter attitudes toward history and, consequently, toward the historic film. Revolution and counter-revolution, invasion and civil war, the collapse of an economic system and the dissolution of an entire culture centered men's thoughts on the historic process and the historic hero. It was under these circumstances that the serious biographical film was born. *Zola, Juarez* and *Abe Lincoln in Illinois* reverted to the drama which shows not only the wholly private concerns of the anonymous citizen but, in part at least, the public actions of the social hero who appears under his own name and in his actual historic setting.

Significantly, all three films came during the great popular movement for the preservation of nineteenth-century democratic ideals against the onslaught of fascism; all three centered around great nineteenth-century figures; and all three took as their central theme not so much the life of the hero as his embodiment of the nineteenth-century ideal of liberty. Given such a theme and such heroes at a moment when millions were preoccupied with the democratic dream, and there was every prospect for successful biographic films.

What gave *Zola* its motive power was a theme in which past and present fused at white heat; a central idea which the makers of the film and its audience could understand, feel and believe with all their being. They thought Zola wanted exactly what they wanted. They were mistaken; but that could not diminish the effect of the film. Art needs a commonly accepted *mythos* to be effective. The sanctity of the man-of-letters uttering truth was still valid, and they shared Zola's sentiments about justice for the innocent, his hatred of intolerance, his abhorrence of war.

But time cannot be ignored, especially in the film which more and more tends to acquire the time-qualities of daily journalism. Take, for example, this speech by Zola in the movie:

> The world is about to hurl itself to destruction, the will of the nations for peace, a powerful brake, stopping it on the brink! You don't believe it? Wait! To save Dreyfus, we had to challenge the might of those who dominate the world. It is not the swaggering militarists! They're but the puppets that dance as the strings are pulled! It is those others who would ruthlessly plunge us into the bloody abyss of war to protect their power. Think of it, Alexandrine, thousands of children sleeping peacefully tonight under the roofs of Paris, Berlin, London, all the world! Doomed to die horribly on some titanic battlefield unless it can be prevented! And it can be prevented! The world must be conquered, but not by the force of arms, but by the ideas that liberate. Then we can build it anew, build for the humble and the wretched!

Obviously the spectator could not be so deeply moved if he thought only of the historic Zola saying this in Zola's time. In that case we should get only irony. All the liberating ideas of the nineteenth century could not prevent the first world war. What the audience really heard at this point was not the voice of the historic Zola speaking for his generation but the voice of Paul Muni speaking for ours.

In *Abe Lincoln in Illinois* author and director managed to convey the image of Lincoln as the democratic man of destiny, each of whose experiences and choices contributes to the final goal; but in *Juarez* the problem was more complicated. To some extent, this film betrayed its nominal hero. Juarez was placed in the background and the "lady and gentleman" in the foreground. The Mexican spokesman for liberty was only a kind of Greek chorus to Maximilian and Carlotta, two charming aristocrats whose private lives obscured the historic drama in which they were engaged. The real hero wore the uniform of an Austrian prince, but he was the anonymous citizen after all, just like the Austrian hero of *Mayerling*. The biographical form was here too lightly imposed on love's old sweet song, and we did not see enough of the real Juarez, or the real Mexico he represented, or the real struggle which centered around him. This film was nearer to *The Private Lives of Elizabeth and Essex* than to *Zola,* yet the moment was so astir with talk about democracy that Juarez' lines on that theme held audiences spellbound and the net effect was that of an unusual film.

Perhaps it was awareness of the difficulties inherent in political biography which led Hollywood to fall back on another great protagonist of modern culture. This time it was the scientist, the success story of the truth-seeker who triumphs over both the mysteries of nature and the prejudices of man. And again, Pasteur, Ehrlich and Edison are all taken from the nineteenth century.

Films about scientists have not been as successful as those about liberators. The conflict in which the latter is protagonist generates its own emotions. The scientist, on the other hand, deals with the conceptual, even when he invents a phonograph or cures syphilis. It is difficult to present the real drama on the screen because it is primarily a drama of ideals which goes on in the hero's mind. The screen can only show us the by-products, not the real conquest. The conflict with nature and with outworn scientific notions is overshadowed by the conflict with men over the acceptance of the new idea.

So far the biographic film is not really biography, the way *Goodbye, Mr. Chips* is biography. It is not a chronicle spanning a lifetime but a drama in which the liberator or the scientist is shown at the highest point of his career, at the moment when his work meets the world in conflict and the past meets the present in sympathy. If the Ehrlich film was not a great box-office success, it was probably because the hero was important in the history of medicine without being significant as a popular symbol of the march of civilization. Various factors also contributed to the lukewarm reception given *A Dispatch from Reuter's.* Yet this picture, for all its shortcomings, opened new horizons for the biographic film. William Dieterle, its gifted director, managed to span four decades without losing dramatic interest, and he moved the story from city to city, from land to land, without breaking the sense of unity.

Among recent films, *Sergeant York,* a big box-office hit, was unique in several respects. It selected its theme from America instead of Europe, from the twentieth century instead of the nineteenth. Its hero was an actual historic figure in the sense that his living prototype had distinguished himself in an historic action. But he is not a major historic figure, like Lincoln or Zola; his significance, both in life and on the screen, is that of the common man rising to heroism when the future of the world is being decided by force of arms. The film is thus a tribute to the anonymous citizen and an appeal to his deep-seated capacity for heroism which needs to be activized at this moment. But since, in our civilization, the heroism of the anonymous citizen is recognized only at such crucial moments, *Sergeant York* takes only one episode from the actual life of its nominal hero. Around this it creates fiction which may be essentially true of this kind of life but is not true to the biography of the hero. In this sense, *Sergeant York* is not strictly speaking a biographic film. It is an epic about the anonymous citizen who loses his anonymity by assuming the name and the heroic act of Sergeant York. Name and act become links between fiction and reality; what we get is an effective, deliberately created myth.

Citizen Kane does the precise opposite. Here the alleged life-story of a living man, who for some reason hastened to identify himself with the hero of the film publicly, is recreated into fiction. Some of the events are actual, others are imagined; but the use of a fictitious name and the extensive liberties taken with the material remove the film from the realm of genuine biography and place it in another class altogether. It is a movie version of the novel cast in biographic form which the western world has known for several centuries. Strict biography sets limits to the imagination, but it has the advantage of giving us historic fact. Fictionized biography sets the imagination free, but we no longer get the values of historic fact. *Citizen Kane* was not a clear choice. To the extent that it is bound to the realm of fact, it could not soar freely in the realm of truth.

What gives this film its unique power is not the biography as such but the film as such: a camera which reveals the visual world after Cézanne; the influence of the newspaper, which begins a story with a lead and moves from high point to high point regardless of sequence in time; psychoanalytic techniques in the treatment of Kane's love-life, the use of symbols, the sharp alternation between past and present; and finally a suave treatment of the social theme. Each of these factors has been developed in previous films, here and abroad. But their combination is new, and their use by a dramatic talent of the first order gave us a first-rate film.

Where *Citizen Kane* falls down is precisely in its biographic aspects. Many of its failures on this score arise from the fact that the alleged prototype is alive; under the best of circumstances, this is bound to cramp one's style. But the problem is further complicated by the fact that the hero is not—like Zola, Lincoln and Juarez—an undisputed symbol of the good life. Is Kane a hero in that sense at all? Welles apparently never made up his mind about him. Where the film is technically original, strong and clear, the character drawing of the central figure is vague, confusing and contradictory. We are asked to remember that there is a good side to the worst of men; if Kane's victims are sorry for him, why shouldn't we be? This is true about men, and it is one of the functions of drama to show us this truth. It is true also about historic figures, and it is one of the functions of biography to show us this truth. But we can do so only in fiction or in biography at a distance. When the subject is as close as Kane, the evil of his public career is too close for us to shed tears over his private life. It is difficult for us to identify ourselves with the man who says, "You provide the pictures, I'll provide the war," no matter how unhappy he may be with his wives. And somehow one feels that the author himself has an ambivalent attitude toward his hero; we are never quite sure what the hero really wants or the author really thinks.

Despite these shortcomings, *Citizen Kane* opens the way for a new type of biographic film which deals with what is perhaps the major theme of our times: the problem of power. Obviously, it is not necessary to confine the biographic film to the nineteenth century or to cramp the story in Ibsen's form. It is not hard to think of several great Americans whose biographies, following the time-scheme of *A Dispatch from Reuter's,* could take us across Europe and the United States, and across a good part of the nineteenth century into our own. This would illuminate the present and its moral problems with the utmost dramatic intensity. It would even be possible to deal with some great figure of the past who envisioned not only our present but also our future.

The biographical film has only begun. It has unusual possibilities ahead of it, provided vital personalities, moments and problems are chosen. Provided, too, that the hero is not crucified on a formula but comes to us moving through genuine, basic experience, truthfully seen and truthfully presented. The technical equipment is there in abundance, and the box-office has shown that public enthusiasm is also there. What is now needed is a deeper realization that if the biographical film is essentially an attempt to dramatize history imaginatively, we must understand history more imaginatively.

December 1941

* *

THORNTON WILDER AND SOL LESSER

*

Our Town—From Stage to Screen

(A CORRESPONDENCE)

[*This lively and friendly correspondence between Thornton Wilder, author of* Our Town, *and Sol Lesser, who made the screen version of the play, provides an illuminating insight both personal and technical into the translation of an excellent play into an excellent motion picture. . . . It is obviously only a part of the exchange . . .*—THE EDITORS.]

NEW YORK, Oct. 7, 1939

DEAR MR. LESSER:

Forgive my delay in answering these letters and reporting on this material. . . . Considering the screenplay pp. 1-79 (the second installment is waiting for me in New Haven, and I shall find it there this afternoon):—

I feel that now the point has come in the work, as I foresaw, when my feelings must often give way before those of people who understand motion picture narrative better than I do. It's not a matter of fidelity to my text—since I doubt whether there has ever been a movie as faithful to its original text as this seems to be—it's just a matter of opinion, and my opinion should often give way before that of those who know moving pictures thoroughly.

I. For instance, in the opening. Mr. Morgan appearing at the door of his drugstore, and saying: "Well, folks, we're in Grover's Corners, New Hampshire . . ." seems to me far less persuasive and useful than the opening over the jig-saw puzzle. The puzzle opening has the advantages:

(1) Of setting the background against the whole United States, that constant allusion to larger dimensions of time and space which is one of the principal elements of the play; and

(2) Of giving the actor and audience that transitional moment between talking-one's-thoughts and addressing-a-theatre-audience from the screen, that Sacha Guitry found necessary, too. It would seem to me that each occasion that Mr. Morgan addresses the audience directly should have some such preparation: from monologue to address.

II. In the episodes during the evening it would seem to me that (pp. 38ff) there should be constantly maintained by the camera the view of the whole town—our feeling that *there* is choir rehearsal; *there* are the children at work; *there* is Dr. Gibbs reading. These episodes are very slight to be received in succession; but all gain when they are given with an air of being simultaneous. At present the camera directions don't pick up the whole town until page 49. . . .

III. As to the date.

1919-1923 would be all right with me. It closes out those horse-and-buggy pre-automobile days which may have been a part of the much-discussed "nostalgia" which people found in the play. I can't for the life of me think of any events that could substitute for the Treaty of Versailles and the Lindbergh Flight. Death of Grover Cleveland? . . .

In the meantime, all my cordial regards to you and your family and to Frank.

Sincerely ever,
THORNTON

CULVER CITY, October 11, 1939

Telegram to Thornton Wilder

YOU PERSUADE ME TO RESTORE JIGSAW PUZZLE OPENING. AM TRYING TO FIND DEVICE TO MAINTAIN FEELING OF WHOLE TOWN AT NIGHT. . . .

SOL LESSER

NEW HAVEN, CONN.
Oct. 9, 1939

DEAR SOL:

Returning to New Haven I found the yellow pages of corrections and now have everything before me.

The cuts in Mrs. Gibbs-Mrs. Webb shelling beans are all right with me; also the transferred speeches from the Stage Manager to Mrs. Gibbs in the last act. Also the omission of the Birthday Scene from the opening sequence.

My only worry is that—realistically done—your wedding scene won't be interesting enough, and that it will reduce many of the surrounding scenes to ordinary-ness.

Did you ever see a wedding scene on stage or screen that followed through normally?

Either it was interrupted (*Smiling Through* and *Jane Eyre* and *It Happened One Night*), or it showed the bride hating the groom (*The Bride the Sun Shines On*), or some other irregularity.

On the stage with *Our Town* the novelty was supplied by:

(1) economy of effect in scenery.

(2) the minister was played by the Stage Manager.

(3) the thinking-aloud passages.

(4) the oddity of hearing Mrs. Soames' gabble during the ceremony.

(5) the young people's moments of alarm.

You have none of these things—by a close-up of Mrs. Soames even her gabble will lose its oddity and shock. Here is a village wedding and the inevitable let-down when it all runs though *as expected.*

Now, Sol, it's just you I'm thinking about; will you have as *interesting* a picture as you hoped?

This treatment seems to me to be in danger of dwindling to the conventional. And for a story that is so generalized that's a great danger.

The play interested because every few minutes there was a new bold effect in presentation-methods.

For the movie it may be an audience-risk to be bold (thinking of the forty millions) but I think with this story it's a still greater risk to be conventional. This movie is bold enough in the last sequence, but apart from the three characters who talk straight into the audience's face, there's less and less of that novelty and freedom and diversion during the first forty minutes. I know you'll realize that I don't mean boldness or oddity for their own sakes, but merely as the almost indispensable reinforcement and refreshment of a play that was never intended to be interesting for its story alone, or even for its background. . . .

All my best to all, as ever,

THORNTON

October 19, 1939

DEAR THORNTON:

Tomorrow I am sending you a revised first draft script, in which you will note that we have re-captured those elements omitted from the first rough draft, and in which we have incorporated the further suggestions made in your letters to me. You will also find several new ideas which I hope will please you. . . .

It was a great satisfaction to me today when we rewrote the wedding scene and used the technique of exposing the characters' thoughts. I see now, more clearly, the purpose of the wedding as you originally intended. I ask you also to edit these lines with the fullest sense of their import. The more I consider this scene, the more value I see in its original form.

I urge you to point out to me wherein you think the picture lapses into conventionality. While this is only our Revised First Draft, I feel we can, without danger, add boldness and novelty, even though our thoughts up to date have not produced anything further than the script shows. . . .

Frank Craven has just done a picture for Paramount in which he played the part of a druggist. Whether this would identify him as the same druggist in our picture I can't say, but I've decided to play safe; so instead of establishing Mr. Morgan as a druggist we have played him as the proprietor of the general merchandise store. I give you this explanation now so you do not fall over backwards when you read the establishing scene of Mr. Morgan in the script.

I know you will not hesitate to speak your mind freely, and I await your further comments, criticisms and suggestions with eagerness.

Gratefully,

SOL LESSER

NEW HAVEN, CONNECTICUT
October 29, 1939

DEAR SOL:

The "Revised First Draft" is before me. Before I speak of it in general I shall take up the few notes I have made. . . .

Page 106. I hate to seem like "Vain Author thinks every Word Sacred," but it does seem to me that the cuts in the Death-and-Immortality speech do something to it—in its present shape it reads like a sweetness-and-light Aimee MacPherson spiel. I don't feel violently about this, but suggest omitting "lot of thoughts . . . but there's no post office," and restoring after: ". . . There's something way down deep that's eternal about every human being." Some of the original lines there, and placing "Yes, all these important things . . . grow kinda pale around here" to its position after the "Something eternal" paragraph—and then omitting the "And what's left? What's left when memory's gone . . . and your identity, Mrs. Smith?" In other words: The idea of the Relinquishing Earth-Associations follows the Something Eternal-Passage.

However, as I say, I don't feel very strongly about this, and I leave it to your judgment. . . .

The Wedding Scene is better. I still think it's not fresh enough. I don't think that realistic boys in a realistic village would hoot and guy a friend on his way to his wedding. That's Dead-End-Kids city life. And its pretty sententious of Mr. Morgan to say out loud to a friend. "There are a lot of things to be said about a wedding. And there are a lot of thoughts that go on during a wedding." . . .

The papers say that this script has been sent me for my approval. My approval it certainly has. My demurring is just between you and me, Sol, not as to whether it's good treatment and a faithful transcription—that it already is—but whether for your joy as well as mine, it is a movie that beats other movies—and which the public and the critics will receive as a deep movie experience. For that I feel that there is still some more work to be done.

All my best to you all, as ever, THORNTON

NOVEMBER 2, 1939

DEAR THORNTON:

. . . I do hope you will not permit yourself to feel, to use your own words, "any inexperience in movie values." While agreeing that the medium of the screen is entirely different from the stage, still I hold that if we properly translate the situations from stage to screen, audience emotions will be the same looking at the picture as looking at the stage play. I might use this as an example of a difference: A person might attend a Hollywood Bowl Concert and hear *Aïda* played for fifteen minutes by a full symphony orchestra, and thoroughly enjoy it. That same person attending a motion picture theatre and hearing *Aïda* played by the identical orchestra in identical fashion might be thoroughly bored before it is half finished. There is an important difference. One will grow tired of looking at the orchestra on the screen. Something must accompany it which would entertain through the eye as well as the ear. . . .

I now come to a question which needs your guiding answer. It has been suggested that for movie purposes a means be found to attach the third act to circumstances already within the play. I suppose by this it is meant that perhaps there should be a problem affecting the married life of Emily and George growing out of the differences in their mentalities. I cite the following only as an example:—

Emily is brighter than George; in her youth she has the best memory in her class—she recites like "silk off a spool"—she helps George in his mathematics—she is articulate—George is not—she is "going to make speeches all the rest of her life." . . .

Query: Could it be Emily's subtlety in the soda-fountain scene that causes George to make the decision not to go to Agricultural School? The audience gets this, but George feels it is his own voluntary thought. He makes the decision not to go.

Could Emily, after death, re-visit her fifth wedding anniversary . . . and now see her mistake?

Emily in life is likely to have been over-ambitious for George, wanting him to accomplish all of the things he would have known had he gone to Agricultural School, but which he has had to learn mainly by experience. In a single scene we could establish that George did not develop the farm as efficiently and as rapidly as Emily thought he should have. She continued to get ideas out of newspapers and books as she did out of her school books, and had tried to explain them to George, but he was slow in grasping them. She had been impatient very often. Someone else's farm may have been progressing faster than George's and she may not have liked that. . . .

Now she sees this. She remembers she was responsible for his not going to Agricultural School. She has overlooked many of George's virtues—she took them all for granted. All this was her mistake. . . .

Could there be a great desire to live, to profit by what she has just seen, rather than go back to the grave—should she long to live—would the audience, witnessing this picture, pull for her to live—and she does?

Others tell me that this, or something like it, would give the picture more appeal for the forty millions, and that it would only change the expression of your philosophy, not the philosophy itself, which would be retained.

Now tell me frankly, Thornton, what do you think. Would it help or hurt the structure? Does it give rise to something that you think might be done within the scope of your original purpose? . . .

Sincerely,
SOL LESSER

NEW YORK
Sunday, Nov. 12, 1939

DEAR SOL:

My letters seem only to make you unhappy about the work and God knows I don't mean that.

The important thing is that I do think it's a very good script as it is now, and when I do express some reservation about some portion or aspect of it, I don't seem to be able to offer anything concrete to propose in its stead.

However, I feel pretty concrete about trying to dissuade you against showing Emily returning to her fifth wedding anniversary and regretting that she had been an unwise wife.

(1) It throws out of the window the return to the twelfth birthday which you feel is sufficiently tied up with the earlier part of the picture, but which is certain of its effect.

(2) It introduces a lot of plot preparation in the earlier part of the picture that would certainly be worse than what's there now. Scene of George running the farm incompetently. Scene of Emily upbraiding him.

(3) It makes Emily into a school-marm "improving" superior person. The traits that you point out are in her character, her "good

in classes," her desire "to make speeches all her life"—but I put them in there to prevent her being pure-village-girl-sweet-ingenue. But push them a few inches further and she becomes priggish.

(4) The balance of the play reposing between vast stretches of time and suggestions of generalized multitudes of people requires that the fathers and mothers, and especially the hero and the heroine, be pretty near the norm of everybody, every boy and every girl.

If this is made into ineffectual-but-good-hearted-husband and superior-interfering-wife, the balance is broken.

It's not so much new "plotting" that is needed, as it is refreshing detail-play over the simple but sufficient plot that's there. . . .

Cordially ever,
THORNTON

HOLLYWOOD, DEC. 4, 1939

Telegram to Isabel Wilder

WHAT MAKE OF CAR WOULD THORNTON LIKE FOR CHRISTMAS?

SOL LESSER

NEW YORK, N. Y., DEC. 5, 1939

Telegram to Sol Lesser

THORNTON DOESN'T DRIVE ANY MORE BUT HAS ALWAYS SAID IF HE HAD CAR WANTED A CHRYSLER CONVERTIBLE WITH RUMBLE SEAT

ISABEL WILDER

December 26, 1939—10:34 P.M. E.S.T.

DEAR SOL:

Just to show you that I'm not stuck up because I own the most beautiful car in town (even the Cartwrights turn their heads when I go by now) I'm writing on my old paper. All my sisters were back for Christmas and you never heard such squeals. Everybody had to be taught all the gadgets. When they found there were little red lights that went on when your oil and gas were low—that slew 'em; and the two speeds on the windshield—oh, and the defroster; and a top that goes up and down without anybody losing their temper. Well, well—first I was so astonished I didn't know what to do, but ever since I've been getting more proud and pleased every hour. A thousand thanks, Sol! I wish you were here to see what a big success it is. . . .

THORNTON

January 5, 1940

DEAR THORNTON:

Your two letters, December 26 and New Year's Eve, arrived at the same time, and I feel confident that from them we have achieved the desired result; so the changes have been incorporated into our script, which now takes the form of a Final Screenplay. A copy of this will go forward to you within the next two or three days.

We decided to change the opening of the picture in order to eliminate all mechanical feeling. Our minds out here have all agreed that this final choice is smoother and better. I fought right along to retain the jig-saw puzzle opening to get the illusion of the many small towns that make up the United States, but unquestionably this will assert itself in the picture proper. Our conclusion was that this sort of thing has been done too many times to make it worth while, even though it would serve a purpose.

The picture itself will be treated in an unconventional manner with regard to camera set-ups, following our original idea of introducing properties intended to accentuate the moods and to visualize something deeper than just the mere dialogue. . . .

SOL LESSER

January 9, 1940

DEAR THORNTON:

Under separate cover I am sending you a final shooting script of *Our Town*. Even though it says "final" we are still working, not only for new bold effects but also for simplification, and I will appreciate very much any further word from you in criticism or suggestion.

I have a feeling that it might be helpful to you in visualizing this script to meet Harry Horner who could show you a number of the sketches that he has prepared and which in a great many cases have acted as a stimulant to our art designer here. I can't commence to tell you my enthusiasm for the sketches that have so far been prepared. They are indeed artistic, and I think we will get a very unusual result.

Most of the conversational scenes will be played in very close shots, eliminating scenic proportions, in order to capture the original purpose of the play—the non-use of scenery—but at the same time we will have a beautifully scenic production in the places where scenery will serve its purpose. . . .

With all good wishes, I am,

Cordially,

SOL LESSER

January 9, 1940

DEAR THORNTON:

Does it occur to you that we should expose as a premise early in the picture "that human beings do fairly move about in self-preoccupied matter-of-factness—admitting that human beings are inadequate to experience"—all as demonstrated in the last act? If this could be accomplished subtly, yet thoroughly understandably to the forty million, perhaps the third act will take on a still added value.

As an example, Craven says: "And there comes Howie Newsome and Bessie delivering the milk"—adding—"Howie, you know, does one of those services that we just naturally take for granted."

While I realize that this premise "cannot be taken as a motto for this picture," do you feel, as I do, that it is an important collateral—which when exposed should have everyone in the audience right where we want him?

Think this through for me, and let me hear.

Cordially,

SOL LESSER

Jan. 13, 1940

DEAR SOL:

. . . Re planting unobtrusively the notion of everybody's inevitable self-preoccupation.

I should suggest that the idea is not so much suggested by the service a Milkman renders—the American Mind assumes that what you get money for cannot be classed as benevolence—but by some picture of a person's not noticing another's need or claim or call, (Chekhov's plays are always exhibiting this: Nobody hears what anybody else says. Everybody walks in a self-centered dream.) Children perpetually feel it as a rebuff:

"Mama, mama, look what I found—isn't it *wonderful?*"

"Yes, dear, now go and wash your hands."

It is certainly one of the principal points that the Return to the Birthday makes; when I read the script today I'll be thinking over a way to incorporate some advance indications of it in the earlier part of the picture.

All my best,

THORNTON

Monday Morning
Jan. 15, 9:45 A.M.

DEAR SOL:

I hope you're as completely pleased and reconciled as I am to the simplifications in the last act—I append a few notes, but they're not important and not meant to wrinkle your brow now when you have so many other things to think about. . . .

Re the Opening. You have thought it over a thousand times and I defer to your judgement, but this opening lacks the largeness that might be there. On the stage, though the whole U.S.A. was not mentioned, the largeness of design was conveyed by the bareness of the stage and the surprise of the direct address to the audience. It may be that during the work of production you will feel the other opening recurring to you. . . .

So shooting will begin any day now. All my best to all the forces. How splendid Fay Bainter and Beulah Bondi will be; and Tommy Mitchell. . . .

All regards,

Ever,

THORNTON

January 17, 1940

DEAR THORNTON:

I have your letter of January 15th, which arrived in the midst of our happy excitement incidental to the starting of the picture.

The cast is now practically complete:

DR. GIBBS	Thomas Mitchell
MRS. GIBBS	Fay Bainter
MR. WEBB	Guy Kibbee
MRS. WEBB	Beulah Bondi

NARRATOR	Frank Craven
EMILY WEBB	Martha Scott
GEORGE GIBBS	William Holden
HOWIE NEWSOME	Stuart Erwin
MRS. SOAMES	Dere Merande
REBECCA GIBBS	Ruth Toby

. . . We are now energetically employing what remains of our faculties to devise a new opening. We are all of one opinion here now—that the Narrator should not be too much attached to the story as the druggist. He doesn't have the freedom of the original manager, and I am certain we will come up with what will be the right idea before many nights have passed.

We have been searching but haven't found the emotional reason for Craven starting the story back in 1901, nor have we exactly identified the location where we pick him up. Everyone seems to feel that the opening should have a feeling of air, broadness and scope, rather than being confined in a set or in front of a store, but we can't put our finger on it.

And so the remaining major problems are: the opening, and the situation about which I still expect to hear from you, which will lay down early in the picture some advance indication of the premise exposed by Emily's summing up in the last act.

It is difficult for me to convey to you the extent of my obligation to you for the support that you have given me and the value of your corrections. . . .

We should not consider the script settled until the picture is finished shooting, and there is no difficulty at all about changing any scenes. There will be a practiced orderliness, even while the picture is being photographed, which will permit us to improve where the opportunity affords. . . .

Sincerely,

SOL LESSER

January 17, 1940

DEAR THORNTON:

. . . You are going to get a real thrill, Thornton, when you see on the screen the production of the graveyard sequence as designed by Mr. Menzies. There is great inspiration from the time the mourners under their umbrellas come into the graveyard. We never show the ground—every shot is just above the ground—never a coffin or an open grave—it is all done by attitudes, poses and movements—and in long shots. The utter dejection of Dr. Gibbs—we have his clothes weighted down with lead weights so they sag—the composition of Dr. Gibbs at the tombstone is most artistic—and as Dr. Gibbs leaves the cemetery the cloud in the sky gradually lifts, revealing stars against the horizon—and as the cemetery itself darkens a reflection from the stars strikes a corner of the tombstone which is still wet from the recent rain, and the reflection (hilation) seems to give a star-like quality—and the scene gradually goes to complete darkness. We get a vast expanse of what seems to be sky and stars. When this dissolves to the dead people this same reflection of hilation appears to touch the brows of the dead. It is lovely—something quite bold! Well, if it comes out on the screen as we hope, we will get that feeling of joy.

Cordially,

SOL LESSER

Monday, Jan. 22, 1940, 4:10 P.M.

DEAR SOL:

First: Re suggestions for Additional Business. You notice I've noted 14 O.K.'s; 3 O.K., but finicky; and 6 reservations.

"O.K., but finicky" means the kind of detail-business which might get a laugh, or a moment's pleasant "recognition" chuckle, but which might break the curve of a scene or (still more serious) establish the wrong tone for the picture. A few more stealing-doughnuts; dish towel-errors; four-spoonfuls-of-sugar, drinking-coffee-out-of-saucers; mothers-looking-behind-sons'-ears—and the audience would be justified in believing they're in one of those pictures Quaint Hayseed Family Life. (I saw a striking example of this establishing the wrong tone last week on the New York stage. Barry Fitzgerald and Sarah Allgood played the first act of *Juno and the Paycock* in the tone Drunken Irishmen and Tyrannical Wives are very very funny. But Sean O'Casey meant that drinking and shiftlessness are the ruin of Ireland—so when Sean O'Casey got around to showing the ruin in the rest of the play, the audience felt that he'd switched his message, and resented it.) . . .

THORNTON

Wed. afternoon

DEAR SOL:

The new opening's fine.

I shudder at the way you spare no expense. Fences, bridges, nut-trees, distant villages, scarecrows—!

It's fine.

I'm sorry I came home too late yesterday to get my answer off to your telegram about the beginning of work. I wish I could see all those fine actors and fine people gathered together.

And a look at you up in your office when every minute you want to be down in the middle of it.

Sol, I thought I'd found a place to insert that nobody-pays-any-attention-to-anybody motif.

EMILY: Mama, I made a speech in class today and I was very good.
MRS. WEBB: (*Abstractedly*). Hm. I musn't forget that bread in the oven. . . . What, dear?
EMILY: Oh, Mama! You never listen to what we're telling you. I said I made a very fine speech in class today.
MRS. WEBB: What was it about? *Etc. Etc.*

But now I'm afraid of it. Because it puts the burden of self-centeredness on Mrs. Webb again, who bears the burden in the last act. (A woman from California!! wrote me, asking me whether the meaning of the play was that New England mothers were so severe that they had no responsive love for their children!!)

I wish I could attach some such brief hitch in the dialogue to somebody else than Mrs. Webb. Mrs. Gibbs could "take it" but I can't find the place (George's spending-money—Rebecca's "Mama do you know what I love most in the world, do you?") without its unnecessarily blocking the forward movement.

Well, I carry the problem around with me wherever I go and will report to you if I see something.

All my best to 1041 and allied departments.

THORNTON

February 21, 1940

DEAR THORNTON:

. . . We are finishing up this week with those of the cast who did not finish last week. They are dropping off like flies. Another twelve days should see the picture completed.

Everyone—not only the "Yes Men"—yes, everyone is most enthusiastic, and I think we have something quite different in novelty, both from the photographic and story-telling standpoint. Now if the motion picture public wants this kind of a story—all is well.

Cordially,

SOL LESSER

March 21, 1940

DEAR THORNTON:

Well, Thornton, I've managed to work myself into a jam. Or at least I think it's a jam, which is just about as bad, I suppose. Maybe you can help to extricate me. It's a sort of puzzle, and it all comes about with respect to the ending of the story.

The first serious thing to decide is whether we should let Emily live or die. There are two schools of thought here, as naturally there would be. But I find myself bouncing from one side to the other, and I just hate myself because I can't make up my own mind. It is true that we can rely upon a preview, showing both endings alternately, but it is in the event that we choose the happy ending where the problem really lies.

Doug Churchill, who wrote the review for *Red Book,* has counseled me to use the happy ending. He has given us a very flattering review, which he concludes by saying (as nearly as I can remember his words):

"The picture differs from the original play in only one respect: the ending—Emily lives. Those who are purists and who loved the play will be outraged, but to those countless others, like myself, who have during the running of the picture come to love Emily as well as the other characters, it is a most satisfactory and logical conclusion. And since, indeed, this ending has been arranged with the permission of the author, who is there amongst us to criticise? It is a beautiful, inspiring picture." . . .

Cordially,

SOL LESSER

New Haven, Conn.
Easter Night

DEAR SOL:

Sure, I see what you mean.

In the first place, I think Emily should live. I've always thought so. In a movie you see the people so *close to* that a different relation is established. In the theatre they are halfway abstractions in an allegory; in the movie they are very concrete. So insofar as the play is a generalized allegory, she dies—we die—they die; insofar as it's a concrete happening it's not important that she die; it's even disproportionately cruel that she die.

Let her live—the idea will have been imparted anyway.

Cordially ever,

THORNTON WILDER

MAY 9, 1940

Telegram to Thornton Wilder

I AM SENDING THIS WIRE TO YOU AFTER WHAT I CONSIDER A MOST UNUSUAL AND SUCCESSFUL PRESS PREVIEW. THE VERDICT WAS ONE HUNDRED PERCENT UNANIMOUS VERY FAVORABLE FROM BOTH PRESS AND LAY AUDIENCE. . . . DID YOU EVER SEE A DREAM WALKING? THAT'S ME AS I DICTATE THIS WIRE. . . . I FEEL IT IS SAFE TO SAY THAT PICTURE WILL NOT DISAPPOINT ANYONE. AFFECTIONATE REGARDS.

SOL LESSER

November 1940

VII · SCENE AND COSTUME DESIGN

* * *

SHELDON CHENEY

*

Gordon Craig

THE THEATRE'S CHIEF REVOLUTIONARY

THE REBEL of one generation is often the solid citizen of the next, granted that he has had the true vision, a bit of the universal prophet about him; and one might now expect Gordon Craig, whose ideas afforded the battle-cries of all the insurgents in the theatres of the Western world a full twenty years ago, to have slipped into his appointed place in things-as-they-are. Sometimes the prophet slips into place because the world, against its will, has been convinced, has caught up with him, and other times because he himself has softened, has compromised, has seen the worldly wisdom of "fitting in." In the very difficult, grinding life of the theatre, minor revolutionaries enough have stepped over into security in this latter way—one remembers Jacques Rouché directing the Paris Opéra, and Gemier directing the Odéon. But the quality of Gordon Craig's insurgency, the mettle of his vision, clearly is such that compromise has been impossible.

His ideas, to be sure, although called "crazy" twenty years ago by those who presumably knew and loved the theatre best, are espoused in some measure today by almost every theatre architect, stage designer, director or playwright who calls himself in any way progressive. And yet these very men who are practicing in the Craig-influenced theatre may tell you that Craig is not "practical." They more and more, as they test their advance by his writings and his designs of ten and twenty years ago, acknowledge that it was his vision and his urging that made their work the reasonably advanced and acceptable thing it is; but, they say, he wanted a new theatre all at once, instead of gaining it by an evolutionary process: he would not trim to meet conditions existing at the time.

The great figure that does not fit in, that refuses to compromise, may achieve a sort of solid-citizenry in another way. He may become the director from a distance, the "great outsider," recognized as shaping world ideas by sheer force of vision and prophecy, but carefully excluded from participation.

A sort of myth has grown up that Craig was thus becoming the great outsider of the modern theatre, that being too uncompromising to fit in, too clear-sighted and perhaps too proud as an artist to exhibit before the public with an imperfect machine, he had accepted exile from his mother-theatre, had lapsed into the role of outside critic. Even more, that he was becoming truly a hermit, with the hermit's distaste for life and art as lived and practiced, not untinged with bitterness. The English, be it said, keep forward the self-exile thought, for there is something uncreditable to a country in the exiling, by lack of sympathy and cooperation, of its greatest stage-artist. At any rate, the outsider myth has grown and grown; and not quite willing to accept it, I went to see for myself, hot from that Broadway that knows the name of Gordon Craig only nebulously, while acclaiming, quite properly, the achievements of visiting directors like Max Reinhardt who have "made practical" the more showy of Craig's ideas, and of local *metteurs en scène* like Robert Edmond Jones and Norman Bel Geddes, and designers of settings like Lee Simonson and Woodman Thompson, all of whom derive directly from one phase of Craig's inspiration.

I was not thinking of these things as I climbed the picturesque stairs in the Via della Costa di Serretto, between high walls that formed a veritable sun trap, on a hot Italian late-Spring day—for this Englishman, son of Ellen Terry, lives not in London but in Genoa. I was reflecting rather on the spick-and-span trolley car in which I had ridden from the Piazza de Ferrari, and on the clean Italian streets, so unlike those of other days, wondering if these innovations had resulted from some word of the iron Duce to his extraordinarily obedient people. Up a very maze of alley and stairways; and then suddenly a cheery voice from a landing above: "Here you are!" And Gordon Craig, half-way down from his villa to the streets-possible-for-trams, had found his guest before the guest had found his host. His hair had further whitened since our last meeting, at the Amsterdam Exhibition five years ago; but here was the same tall erect figure, picturesquely clean-cut, with his wide-brimmed black hat not wholly concealing the long white hair—a finely set-up and spirited man who would stand out with a natural distinction in any group.

Craig had written me to come, but that it might be just as well if we didn't talk about the theatre—an injunction violated in a running start before we got our hats off, and for five hours thereafter. What had I been doing in the Broadway theatres, had I seen George Jean Nathan lately, what's new in California, what sort of fellow is Stark Young, had I been in Hollywood? But I did my questioning too, about Craig and his relation to the world.

There is more than a shade of truth in the "outsider" conception, the status of one removed from the marketplace playhouse; but there is less than a grain of truth in the hermit and bitter-feeling myth. There never was another so in touch with the world, knowing the immediate latest moves in the theatres from Moscow to San Francisco, never another so equipped and prepared to take his place as leader in a practical theatre. In his home there is such a theatre library, cross-indexed and extra-illustrated, as any director or designer would find a perfect instrument; and in his son, "Teddy," Craig has an assistant and follower of unusual talent, who is already a help in business and technical matters.

I had found Craig indeed in what we of New York, London, Berlin or Moscow designate a "retreat." But the man himself is as alive, as clear-purposed, as eager to be at work in his own theatre, as he has been any time these twenty years. I found him pleased to have been visiting artist recently (modestly he terms his part "Assistant") at the Royal Theatre in Copenhagen, where Ibsen's *The Pretenders* was produced in his settings and after his suggestions; pleased that he found a genuine spirit of collaboration, absolute and sincere courtesy, and particularly a ready response and affectionate regard from the actors, with even an embarrassing willingness to put into his hands every responsibility.

He talks no less certainly of his own theatre and his workshop-school, that he will have when some patron of the arts gives financial support without insisting upon the supposed "right of interference," although he dodges successfully any exact explanation of what his theatre will produce, or how, for he has seen not only his ideas appropriated but his actual designs pirated year after year. He is no whit less scornful of those who clearly followed the surface method and the naked principle set forth in his early books and exhibitions, only to twist them into commercially saleable caricatures, or to dress prettily the old realistic play that will have no place in his new un-realistic theatre. But men like Robert Edmond Jones, who have gone on from "decoration" to the more difficult tasks of stage direction in the larger commercial theatre, find him neither scornful nor critical. In fact, if there is any change in this master-artist's attitude toward the world of his art, any sign of a less radical insurgency, it is only in longer consideration, greater precision of statement and surer basis in authority. He is no less forceful, no less enthusiastic over a discovered old theatre from which the moderns can learn, or over the *commedia dell' arte,* and no less impatient of the charlatans and the born compromisers. But, in general, one recognizes an increased tolerance, a greater value put upon courtesy and reasonableness.

It was as far back as 1905 that the first of Craig's books about the theatre appeared, a slender brochure entitled *The Art of the Theatre* (later included in the larger volume of essays *On the Art of the Theatre* which is still Craig's best known and consulted work). This first volume was not, as so often represented, a theoretical work, but was written after ten years of hard work as an actor, and half a dozen years of producing and designing. About the same time Craig's designs began to be known internationally through exhibitions. To a few it became apparent that here was a fresh light shining in the rather tired world of the stage. The designs were so entirely unlike anything known in the theatres of the day that ninety-nine out of a hundred spectators affected to see in them interesting, sensitive and perhaps beautiful drawings, but things wholly fanciful, impractical for realization upon the stage. His writings, often cryptic, not seldom marked by overstatement, irritatingly frank, had something of the same sweep, the same vast difference from what was known and accepted. While the drawings were serene, quiet, delicate, and later led to endless imitation by their elusive charm, the essays were stimulating, barbed, strangely provocative. Indeed, in the entire twenty years since, Craig's several books and his personal magazine, *The Mask,* have been characterized by a peculiar dynamic power. Every reader feels the urge to be up and doing, to condemn compromise and hypocrisy, and to enlist in constructive theatre work. Only, Craig has always insisted that enlistment must mean service behind the master, obedient and patient help in shaping a new theatre, and not merely jumping into the old to alter the backdrop or stage a play stylistically.

Talking to the intensely alive and provocative Craig of today, one realizes why it was that the fire of the new idea ran so swiftly through the channels that lead to experiment and production. In those early days Craig himself staged a dozen plays—seldom with adequate means for ideal preparation or complete statement. For others the easiest thing to see about his vision was that it embraced a stage cleared of the painted picture setting and cleared of the clutter of real-life detail that Naturalism was just then bringing into the theatre. Stage decoration must be radically simplified and stylized. Immediately the world of critics ran away with the catch-idea that if Craig had any importance it was as a new sort of "decorator." What Germany gained from him by way of improved staging is incalculable. Here in America, those of us who as writers, designers and directors from about 1912 to 1915 felt the direct urge of Craig's spirit and vision, likewise concentrated chiefly on reform of setting. But we know pretty well today that we only half-read his message, applied one part of his idea to a sort of drama that never will belong to his theatre. That is why you will find the artist in our theatre laying down his tools for a year at a time, going back for a new start. Craig believes that one cycle of the new movement, a minor one, is closing. He is ready for a new one, where a vision *beyond* "decoration" is emphasized.

He is quick to talk about those who have brought gifts to the new theatre, and to appraise their contributions: the artists (in the wider sense) including the Duncans, Yvette Guilbert, Adolphe Appia, and designers such as Bakst and Roller; the directors, including Stanislavski, who "best found a form of organization, a core, for his theatre," and Reinhardt, who is more admired for his "professional" qualities—with little said about his productions—and Jessner, Antoine, Dantchenko, and the makers of the Russian Ballet; and so down to the "followers" like Copeau, Pitoëff and Gemier. In any alignment Craig himself prefers to be grouped unmistakably with the *professionals*. It is the traditional theatre that is his home, his training ground, the place for which he has made his sketches and plans. We ran over a group of his designs with this point in mind. "Sound *stage* design," he would say, or "That's nothing—but it does give the actor his chance," or "The actor on the stage—that is what we must play up to—and that is the key to this design." This importance of the dominance of the actor, of an understanding professionalism, of the old-time actors' theatre as a starting point Craig pounds in continually, in his talking and in his articles in *The Mask,* which he maintains as a messenger to the forgetful and the laggard everywhere. These points and one other, concerning the conditions of group work:

"What I ask first now, when people talk of collaboration, is just *courtesy*. That we try to consider one another, not with artificial forms but with genuine, excited and vivid consideration—that seems to me essential in any life as difficult and complicated as that of the theatre. I have just found such courtesy, a grace of manner, and immense activity, in my work on *The Pretenders* with the Royal Theatre troupe at Copenhagen. Moreover, I found there a true authority. . . ."

In answer to questions about the relation of such a production to his own planned theatre, Craig made it clear that this was more in the vein of his earlier work. "Related to my first expressions, and to the production of *Hamlet* with screens in Moscow in 1911, perhaps in a direct line of progression from that. But it is too soon to show what I have recently been planning. A greater freedom, more patient preparation, are necessary."

Talking of this matter led to my comprehension of what is probably the chief shift in Craig's attitude toward the contemporary stage. It is that he no longer attacks the problem primarily as one entailing the bringing of a new art into the theatre, but rather as a question of curing unhealthy conditions in the organization of the playhouse. In a recent issue of *The Mask* he is quoted as saying, "We of the New Movement have still to change the very life of the Theatre. We have changed the art a good deal—we will now change the life. The world of the Theatre is sick; and so only that—the changing of the life—can brace it up."

Craig talks as he has always written, with swift flashes of thought, seldom outlining completely a plan, seldom giving the whole picture, challenging his interlocutor constantly to fill out the sketch from his own understanding. I can imagine the utter confusion of an interviewer seeking afterward to reconstruct the actual sentences and thoughts into a sequence of quotations. It is only with perspective, later, that one begins to piece together an impression of what the man is really after. But I find that I have jotted down these points, as things hot on his mind.

He approves unhesitatingly of Fascism. He stands for absolute respect for authority, whether in the theatre or in a country's organization. A leader proves himself the strongest and the most visionary man in a group; the others obey—that is enough. (One gathers that Craig feels that the delay in establishing his own producing theatre has been caused by the lack of *faithful* followers, ready to abide by authority—they all, when they see the idea, want to elbow forward and be masters of minor houses.)

Natural creation, improvisation, are urgent needs. There is too much heavy thinking going on, particularly to the Northward.

The moving pictures—what couldn't Craig and Chaplin accomplish together?—intrigue him even while irritating him. But they will never dim the glory of the real theatre. Still, Chaplin is the modern inheritor from the glorious *commedia dell' arte*.

The only safe starting point for insurgency is a complete understanding and knowledge of the laws and traditions of the institution revolted against. There has been perhaps too much revolt without either background or vision.

Whether Craig will emerge again from his quiet life of writing, designing, reading—of garden, family and library—into the practical work of stage producing, whether he will again be content to "assist" in a production, as recently he did so happily at Copenhagen, whether he will have this year or next the opportunity to form his group for study and production, and present plays completely, whether he will ever have the means to build a stage after his own vision, without handicap or concession: these are questions unanswerable at the moment.

Though Craig himself talks more of a group of faithful followers than of a concrete theatre, the final consummation, the two together, cannot be far from his mind. He even vaguely hints that it is coming—with the workshop always stressed in his mention of the matter—and one hears rumors from the corners of the world: last year it was the Carolinas, this year Italy, and next it may be London or California. If he came to America, certainly, his stay necessarily would be a matter of years, for not in less time could he train for us a company and with its aid launch a series of productions. At present we have no theatres with permanent seasoned companies, mellowed in years of playing together, with the grace and the authority and the spirit that he noted at Copenhagen. But whether he ever works in our theatre or not, he remains incomparably the greatest single influence up to this time in our progress toward a theatre essentially of today. A visit to him personally, in exile if you choose to call it that, only emphasizes the living quality of his insurgency, the mettle of his theatrical character, the soundness of his theatrical prophecies and vision.

December 1927

* *

The Exhibition of American Stage Designs at the Bourgeois Galleries

[*Following are excerpts from an article and group of statements written for an exhibit of American stage design at the Bourgeois Galleries in April 1919—perhaps the first full-fledged recognition of the importance of the artist in the new American theatre, and "the progress of modern stagecraft in this country." To quote again from the prefatory note signed by Sheldon Cheney, it was "probably as representative and as complete as is possible when an art is young."*—THE EDITORS.]

KENNETH MACGOWAN

*

The New Path of the Theatre

ARE WE to emerge from the war into a new theatre? Are we to harvest in the playhouse, as we are harvesting in other fields of art, the rich seedings of Europe many years neglected? Will we find ourselves in that theatre of beauty and expressiveness toward which Russia and Germany and in less degree France and England were moving in 1914? . . .

Behind the modern art of stage production loom two immense

figures of theory—Gordon Craig and Adolphe Appia. Craig, an Englishman writing in English, gave us the great outlines of inspiration, filled in with the brilliant and provocative art of his pencil. Appia, an Italian-Swiss writing in French, supplied an abstract philosophy and a concrete method. Two nations—Germany and Russia—took up the task of realizing these ideas and prescriptions. Through state and city theatres, through group playhouses, where study, experiment and thoughtful accomplishment were not impossible, modern theatrical art rounded from theories into—productions. From Germany rose the fame of Max Reinhardt, obscuring for us the splendid work of a dozen other producers like Schlenter, Linnebach, Hagemann. From Russia came the ballet of Bakst obscuring only less completely the theatre of Stanislavski. In Ireland, the Abbey theatre opened its eyes to the vision. Barker saw in London, and minor men and playhouses in the English provinces. Rouché, of the Théâtre des Arts, showed Paris that which made him director of the Opéra for the fated fall of 1914. And in France occurred that most remarkable birth of a literally new theatre, the Vieux Colombier of the critic-player Jacques Copeau. At this point, the Great War wrote "finis." Russia under the Soviets has reopened the scroll. America under the Shuberts may yet write upon it. . . .

Indeed, America is at the point where criticism should begin to take the place of indiscriminate enthusiasm. The exhibition of sketches and models at the Bourgeois Galleries in New York and the essays by native stage artists to which this is, in a certain sense, an introduction, demonstrate how far things have already moved. . . .

We must appreciate the potentialities of the stage. That was what the old school didn't do. And that is what some of the new schools also are failing to do when they cling to the old theatricalism, to the old arbitrary four walls of canvas, the forced marriage of pretence and extravagance. We have fought realism. We have berated Belasco. But our fight should go further back—and further forward. Realism can emerge into the expressiveness of the new art. Behind realism lies the greater enemy, the enemy that realism and its Forty-fourth Street high priest fought with us—yes, before us. That enemy is theatricalism. It is the dead-alive theatre of the last century, where the meager materials of side walls, wings and backdrop, were accepted as canvases for the smearing of bad color and worse perspective into a "play-actory" pretence at a marvelous reality. The thing was never life. It was never poetry. It was never emotion. It was a routine rule-of-thumb fake. And in America it still lives.

Two men set themselves to demolish this thing. They were Otto Brahm and David Belasco. They produced actuality. Admirers of the Berlin producer called it naturalism. And it was this light that Reinhardt and Stanislavski first followed. These men made actual rooms and plausible exteriors. A great mass of enginering mechanism, new lights, new stages, new skies, were invented in the process of getting rid of the old fake and putting realism in its place. The two-dimensional perspective of the easel painter was banished from the three-dimensional theatre. The footlights and the borderlights of the picture-frame stage were left to the picture gallery in all their blank staring glare.

Aesthetics, like life, do not come in water-tight compartments. There is evolution. Now it is quite possible to argue that the old theatricalism was always striving to be real, and that hard, intelligent work pushed it over into naturalism. Certainly naturalism, as Reinhardt and Stanislavski practiced it, drifted over into the high expressiveness of the new art. There was a time when Reinhardt produced *A Midsummer Night's Dream* in a forest of real papier-mâché trees. Stanislavski made a Gorki of utter and gutter reality. But they had only to try to add beauty and meaning to their productions in order to be forced, like all the great artists of the world, into a refinement, a selection and an interpretation which is best expressed through the rather awkward term abstraction. The old theatre of theatricalism had tried to reach a vivid and picturesque reality through certain rule-of-thumb abstractions which cribbed, cabined, confined and defeated the purpose. The newer theatre tries to reach beauty and meaning, to win to a vivid expressiveness of the play, through spiritual abstractions. In the old days stretched canvas, painted with pictures of leaves and branches, tried to look like a forest. In the days of realism, actual, modeled, three-dimensional forms of trees did indeed look not unlike an inferior sort of forest. In the third period, however, that same canvas of the old days, treated frankly as cloth, and either hung in loose tree-like shapes or painted with symbols of nature and draped like the curtain it actually is, becomes an abstraction of a forest, full of all the suggestive beauty of which the artist in colors, shapes and lights is capable. . . .

Besides falsities that should be banned and compromises that may be accepted, there are many varieties of style and method possible in the new art. . . . But behind all such conflicts and compromises and differences of method, there remain a few basic ideas and basic methods, without which we cannot have the beauty and the expressiveness of the modern stage art. They are simplification, suggestion and synthesis.

Simplification is the test in almost all great art. Simplification of effect always; simplification of means generally. On the stage, simplification of both effect and means are essential, because the scenery is not the only thing to be seen. Stage architecture is not architecture alone, or stage picture merely stage picture. The setting is the medium for the actor. And it is essential that he shall be properly seen. It is essential that he shall be properly set off by his background and properly fused in it. He must mean more because of the setting, not less. . . .

The complement to simplification is suggestion. Simplify as much as you please; you only make it the more possible to suggest a wealth of spiritual and aesthetic qualities. A single Saracenic arch can do more than a half dozen to summon the passionate background of the Spanish *Don Juan*. One candlestick can carry the whole spirit of the baroque *La Tosca*. On the basis of simplification, the artist can build up by suggestion a host of effects that crude and elaborate reproduction would only thrust between the audience and the actor and the play. The artist can suggest either the naturalistic or the abstract, either reality or an idea and an emotion.

Finally, the quality above all in modern stage production is synthesis. For modern stage art, in spite of all the easel artists who may care to practice the painting of scenery, is a complex and rhythmic fusion of setting, lights, actors and play. There must be consistency that has the quality of progression in it. And there must be such consistency among them all. Half the portrait, half the landscape, cannot be in Whistler's style and the other half in Zuloaga's. The creation of a mood expressive of the play is, after all, the final purpose in production. It can no more be a jumble of odds and ends than can the play itself.

The achievement of this synthesized suggestion of a play's simple, essential qualities has been sought by the great theorists in very different ways. Gordon Craig would get it mainly by design, backed by color. Adolphe Appia fuses his drama in light. Jacques Copeau, whose beliefs and whose work must take a high place in the record of theatrical progress, achieves the play through restriction of means and the re-creation of every element from the theatre building to the actor at each production. . . .

America has its artists, it even has a producer or two, that see this exacting yet catholic new art aright. It is beginning to have an audience, and it must cultivate critics. We are through with imitation. Europe has taught us; we must now practice and create. We are past the Craig period when theories and rather extravagant sketches had their justification in the inspiration they gave. Now is the time for practicality, revolutionary practicality, and for accomplishment and triumph.

* *

LEE SIMONSON

*

The Necessary Illusion

THE ILLUSION of being not at the play but in the domain of the play itself is the essential illusion which the theatre must give. Without it no vicarious experience is possible, that purgation of our emotions, more often romantic than tragic, which is the ultimate and permanent satisfaction that any dramatic spectacle bestows. I find myself a designer of scenery because, even as a spectator, I find the forms in which the players move, and the very light they move through, as essential in maintaining this fundamental illusion of the theatre as their impersonations or the words of the play itself. . . .

Stating it as a doctrine, one might say that quality of a background determines one's emotional reaction to anything that happens in front of it. As such it may seem hyper-aesthetic; yet it is a doctrine we acknowledge daily by the importance we attach to creating appropriate backgrounds everywhere—parks and gardens to idle in, houses to live in, churches to worship in, tombs to lie in. And we try, however fitfully or unsuccessfully, to give them some design or some beauty relevant to the experience they are supposed to shelter. And yet this same public that will save their lovemaking for the prettiest lane, or forget guide books, rapt, in the nave of an alien cathedral, will, once within the theatre, accept the most cherished love scenes and romantic deaths, amid surroundings they would not consider worth printing on a picture postcard, or which would outrage them at the funeral of a friend.

To destroy this strange dualism, this indifference to visual beauty that the theatre seems to breed in most actors and producers, as well as in their spectators, is, I think, the fundamental problem of the scene designer. For the present danger is that the so-called "modern scenery" will be accepted, but never craved—that it will remain a luxurious extra, a dressing-up of the play, and applauded as another tradition of the theatre, and in the end matter no more than whether the costumes of the chorus of *Listen Lucy* are green with black spangles or pink with yellow plumes.

* *

JOHN WENGER

*

The Mission of the Stage Setting

. . . SO TO HARMONIZE with the play, so to correspond with, and intensify, if possible, the underlying motif expressed by it, so to merge itself with the spirit and purpose of the play that it calls forth of itself no recognition beyond the subconscious appreciation of its absorption into the play itself—that is the purpose of the stage setting. . . .

Nature is gorgeous in color, and color on the stage is one of the three essentials which the mind demands. The other two are action and sound. Give the setting all the brilliance that the motif of the play, or opera, demands. No fear that the players won't be seen. They move. The moving object is always more conspicuous than the background, no matter how skilfully the colors blend. Then there is contrasting color. Harmonious contrasts add vigor and beauty to the stage picture.

The background should contain movement. Life is not static.

It is fluid. The stage setting should tend towards that elusiveness in life found in the rainbow, in the play of shifting lights and shadows.

Inbue the stage setting with poetry. Give it an imaginative quality. Let it absorb within it a fluidity, an elusiveness that stimulates the mind. . . .

* *

HERMANN ROSSE

*

Artificiality and Reality in the Future Theatre

. . . PART OF THE APPEAL of the theatre is structional reality, and part is art-for-art's-sake illusion. Where we find the modern theatre lacking is in the poverty of structional beauty in auditorium and stage, and in the overemphasizing of the technical side of the purely artistic beauty of the scene. There are plays now—and it is safe to predict that there will be more soon—for which the pure structional beauty of unadorned building will be very sufficient, will in fact be the only entirely right method of mounting. Nearly all plays of a meditative, analytical nature, all plays of words, could thus be acted on a beautifully finished platform.

The dynamic play, as the dionysian ballet, no doubt will gain in power through being assisted by sympathetic scenery and costuming emphasizing its mood. Making its appeal through motion, through rhythm, anything which will emphasize our illusion of motion in the right tempo will be beneficial to the total impression on the spectator. . . .

The next move in the development of this type of play is the abandoning of the static parts of the stage-picture, and the development of moving scenery. That the abandoning of these static elements means ultimately the elimination of the stage floor, and the consequent disappearance of the actor, does not greatly worry us. This will simply eliminate one factor of expression, which is too likely to be influenced by chance emotions. Our present knowledge of technique seems to lead us to suppose that the purely dynamic play will bring us back again to the picture-frame proscenium. In fact, a crude prototype of it may be seen in the animated cartoons in the moving-picture theatres.

From a purely aesthetic viewpoint the effect of this developing of the background at the expense of the actor will remake the dynamic play. Imagine beyond the proscenium a void in which planes and bodies will develop themselves in limitless graduation of color and shape in one great rhythm with the coordinating music —two dimensional patterns in kaleidoscopic succession, and these fascinating patterns formed by the intersection of solids, darts of color across a somber background, lines, planes or solids, and symbols of man and surrounding nature, all emphasizing the mood of the music! The wholly actorless theatre with its tendency toward the two-dimensional visible art and the abstract in music will be the triumph of the artificial, the decorative, the stylistic. . . .

The deadline of the stylistic stage will be coincident with its canonization. That which will always conquer art is reality, life itself. In the theatre of today two tendencies are very evident— one toward a rare and precious artificiality, and one toward a new and vital realism. The first tendency will probably work itself out in the actorless theatre. The second tendency will probably lead by way of a slow development of the purely constructive stage and the oratory platform to a new type of churchlike theatre, with reflective domes, beautiful materials, beautiful people—to a revitalizing of art by a complete reversal from the artificial to the living real. If we are going to stay true to the spirit of the time, both of these tendencies will develop side by side until reality carries the day— or will time assert itself still further and will the result be a compromise?

* *

ROLLO PETERS

*

If I Must

HOW UN-SIMPLE we have become, we of the "commercial" and "art" theatres, with our exquisite differences and separations. And how many treatises, attacks and counter-attacks are hurled by the one party against the other. The division is futile, and worse than futile.

For there is no "old theatre," nor is there a "modern stage"—there is simply the Theatre, for you, for me, for the other fellow. . . .

In order that they may come to know the Theatre, I advise all actors to turn painters, and all painters to turn actors—(only the playwrights must keep to their cells)—for no matter how bad an actor he may make, the painter will come back to his drawings with renewed life, with a sense of the relation that the actor bears to the scene. The actor will weave into his words the color of the scene and of the light; there will be a mysterious and penetrating relation between his movements and the flowing melody of structural line.

Let us forget our differences, we of the Theatre. Let us enjoy them.

* *

ROBERT EDMOND JONES

*

Fashions in the Theatre

WORKERS IN THE THEATRE have always faced and will always face the same problem: the problem of making a drama live before an audience.

To create an impression of livingness in the presence of spectators, to recall life to them—that is the necessary thing. There are numberless manners of working and there is no real quarrel with any of them. Realism, simplification, stylization, are fashions in the theatre all of which can carry energy in the hands of artists.

The new director will adopt any fashion, any convention, so long as it is a living one. He may come to use masks on his stage, for example, having observed that his actors project essential motion by their movements and attitudes much more freshly and significantly than by the changes in the expression of their faces. He may apply the bird's-eye view of life, made familiar by the motion picture and the airplane, to new visualizations of the mass-soul in mass grouping and movement. He may discover through the study of crystallography unsuspected relations between spacing in the theatre and present-day processes of thought. He may find a new dramatic form springing out of community drama expressed through the rhythms of polyphonic prose. He may see the classic unities of space and time across the modern conceptions of curved space and curved time. No method of working will be too daring or too direct for him to adopt—always with the supreme desire to make a thing on the stage which will live and will draw the life of the audience promptly into its own larger life.

* *

IRVING PICHEL

*

Scene and Action

I REGARD A PLAY as an action taking place primarily in the minds and hearts and souls of a group of characters. In so far as it is a great play, it has action of this type more abundantly than outward physical action. In the same degree, it depends upon or is independent of outward forms, connotative of a specific time and place. A true digest of human emotion and experience is not confined within scenic walls or canvas vistas.

As long as we have our present stage, we must, I suppose, clothe every play in forms of a sort. But, in the case of the play the action of which we do not see with our eyes, I seek, in the setting, forms which connote as little as possible, because I want to be free to see the humanity of the characters, stripped of Romanesque or Gothic or Renaissance or sky-scraper implications.

Very few plays, however, are so written. The great classics of Greece, of Elizabethan England, of Japan—of any great literature, for that matter—might best be viewed from the side of a prize-fighting ring, from all sides and at every moment visible. I am not sure. But that they should be given what they do not absolutely need of scenery or decoration is to place an obscuring screen before them, even in the case of scenery that claims to be "an unobtrusive background." The man must stand up clear against sky only, or perhaps multiplied by mirrors, or backed by more human beings—the audience on the other side of the ring. The only implications must be human. . . .

As a producer, I look upon a play as having begun in the turbulence of a writer's mind. By means of pen, ink and paper, and later, through actors, scenery, lights, sound-waves, this creation of imagination must be drawn through a material welter to issue again—a turbulence of the spectator's mind. If I could bridge across this material pit, and translate from the mind of poet to spectator his fable of poem or dream—an unimaginable osmotic theatre—I should be happy. Scenery stands by way of a footpath we must walk upon when we wish to fly. But we are learning to fly. Soon we may be able to in the theatre. . . .

. . . I cannot conceive of having a style of scenery all my own—it belongs to the play, comes out of the demands of the play, grows as the play grows in rehearsal. Finally, after some two weeks of rehearsal, I am able to give the stage carpenter certain measurements. The scene is set and painted standing. Afterwards, very often, I ask somebody to make a sketch of the scene in colors, or I content myself with an unsatisfactory photograph. And I find that it looks nothing like my stage setting, which vibrated with light and color and the humanity of the characters in the play.

* *

C. RAYMOND JOHNSON

*

The New Stage Designing

THE SUCCESS of the new stage designing is to a certain extent dependent upon the play. The modern successful play is usually trash, as far as true art is concerned, so of what profit is a new motive in the background? Well, it serves as an example of something better. It helps the play along, and is more bearable to look at. Above all, it is more in relation to the action, and comes nearer to reality, being farther from realism.

For me the new movement means a striving for complete unity in the theatre: a new form of expression. We are trying to make the theatre an art, with a form that is of the theatre and not pieces of something else. I feel that we are at the beginning of that art. . . .

I consider the entire theatre, including the building, of great importance. Our usual theatre is far from a thing by itself. For instance, imagine how wonderful and beautiful an auditorium and proscenium could be in relation to the stage. In regard to stage decoration, my feeling is that the things we call "old stuff" are mere representation of detail and a sort of illustration to the play—any old thing to cover up the back wall of the stage, which is oftentimes better than the drop. The significance of dramatic qualities is lost, so far as background is concerned. I feel that the real art of stage decoration is an expression full of mystery and joyousness, and aims at setting the point of entrance into the new world where for an interval there is an illusion, and unconsciously we are lifted to that higher plane where we are moved by that which moves. . . .

I think of progress on the stage, and I see the scene a simple, orderly massing, principally projected by light. Light to me offers the greatest possibilities of all the means on the stage. . . . I seriously believe we are only at the beginning of a great new day in the use of light; and, when the dawn of that day appears, it will seem to be the glorious sun rising to light us on our path of pure joy in work, in creation, and in contemplation.

* *

NORMAN BEL GEDDES

*

The Theatre of the Future

IN THE MIDDLE of the fourth century the theatre went to sleep simultaneously with the downfall of the Greek social system and the idealism of the Greeks. Ten years ago it rubbed its eyes. Since that time there have been indications that its slumber is not peaceful. Ten years hence it will be fully awake.

The theatre, more than any other form of art, belongs to the majority of the people. A painter, sculptor, or poet can produce his gem isolated from humanity. The architect and the dramatic director require company. Because of this necessity their two forms of art are destined to a more general appreciation. At present we are under the misapprehension that great art is an enjoyment exclusively for the minority. Naturally those who most thoroughly understand anything are in the minority, but that is no reason why the entire world cannot learn to enjoy and appreciate. Even a tiny candle held by one person will illuminate a crowd. So evolution constantly develops the unexpected possibilities of art as an integral part of the life of the people.

More than through any other channel the artist in the theatre has direct intercourse with his audience. The extent of his power is beyond present-day comprehension. We have less conception of the possibilities in drama than geographers had of the world in the fourteenth century. There is no form of creative expression which cannot be used to advantage in the theatre. Since it is an aggregate medium, it is destined to hold the predominating position among the arts. Architecture is the most enduring; dramatic production the most delicate, depending almost entirely upon the sensitiveness of human fragility. Up to this time no effort has been made to develop a technique that builds permanently. We can record definitely the spirit of authors, composers and designers, but not of the actor; though cinema and phonograph are elemental, uncoordinated developments toward such recordization.

There is nothing odd in the fact that almost simultaneously artists in all parts of the world have turned their thoughts towards the theatre. There is nothing "new" in what they are giving to it. Art has always had its own little continent in the world of the theatre, though to popular opinion we are just discovering it with the same éclat that the Europeans "discovered" an America already inhabited. Discovery is only the awakening of human consciousness to a reality that always exists. . . .

I am looking to America for the greatest increase in artistic interest. Here the old and the new are balanced relatively. No centuries of tradition bind free meditation. Appreciation has lain dormant under drowsy ignorance, but an unprejudiced freshness predominates. Drama will become more indigenous and intimate with the hearts of the people. We have made the eternal mistake of going somewhere else for our material instead of searching it out here. Theatrical managers have a lower opinion of American intelligence than is justifiable, though there have been plenty of reasons for their attitude.

Just a word as to my own interest in the theatre. It was not a special attraction toward scenery that drew me into it. Under a sudden impetus I wrote a four-act play, first in pantomime and then in dialogue. With the consuming desire to visualize the written conception, I concocted a crude little stage on which I slowly worked out variations of lighting, principal figure compositions, costumes and detailed properties. The effect showed me so many obstacles in adapting my own ideas to the mechanics of the present type of stage that my second effort went into the discovery of a new form of theatre structure, which I developed until I was ready to send the main ideas through the Patent Office. It was that architectural endeavor which induced me to experiment with the lovely realities that such a stage could actually accommodate, and it was the building of a second, elaborate model stage that swung me with emphasis toward the creating of the setting of plays as a more immediate opportunity.

There are plenty of reasons for discouragement in the present standard of theatrical productions. Every form of expression periodically passes through a degenerate period, but the harder the pendulum swings one way, the more vigorous will be its push in the other direction. At present there are many little theatres in the country working away at the difficult task of reaching the public in small, scattered groups until larger organizations are ready to use their more adequate machinery. I predict without a doubt an entire cutting away of the clumsy, tough weeds of the present theatrical system. It is the little green shoots almost hidden underneath and sometimes almost stifled that will become the beautiful, fresh growth of the future theatre. I feel positively that an altogether new form of production, writing and acting will replace what we have.

* *

JOSEPH URBAN

*

The Stage

. . . THE THEATRE of the future must become:
The carrier of the culture of its nation.

The altar to which the best and greatest of a nation offer their energy and beauty, strength and knowledge.

The institution which receives equally the gift of genius and the force of the workman.

The shrine of beauty so democratic that every new cultural element coming, finds there cooperation.

The future stage must be so big and general in its influence that the strength of its conviction goes out to the very frontier and knocks on the door of its neighbor. Who refuses this gift hurts himself and impoverishes his life.

In our future life the stage must have the same influence that the Christian church has had in the past.

April 1919

* *

FRANCIS BRUGUIÈRE

*

The Camera and the Scene

THE VALUE of a properly taken photograph of a stage setting is that it is a closer approximation of what the designer actually creates than even his drawing can ever be. Most drawings by scene designers only approximate their intentions. The lighting of a scene, for example, is generally worked out at the final rehearsals. Moreover, a photograph may be made to present the conception of the designer even when that conception has been distorted by the producer or chief player, as is not infrequently the case.

Many of the photographs that I have made in New York Theatres were made under the direction of designers, and generally the light on the stage was readjusted by them to what had been their original intention. I, in turn, readjusted this lighting to make it possible to record it photographically. Thus the photographs that have been made of these productions show more of the intention of the designers than is seen by the public who go to the theatres.

The readjustments that I make in the stage lighting when I photograph a set are to compensate for the differences between the vision of the human eye and the vision of lens, plate and paper. The new lighting systems which have been installed in most important theatres make it possible to adjust stage light to the requirements of photography. The adjustment is made by taking into consideration the speed at which the different colors travel photographically. Blue, green, yellow and red are the principal colors that have to be considered. These colors as a rule are controlled independently on the switchboard of the modern theatre. To obtain results it is necessary to allow the blue to be exposed for a shorter time than the green, the yellow or the red. Before taking a photograph I study the set to see the color relations. With the electrician I then work out a scheme for cutting out certain lights from the switchboard at certain specified points—the camera remaining open all the while. For instance, I might tell him (depending on the intensity of the colors) to shut off the blue light at the count of five, the green at ten, the yellow at twenty and the red at thirty. In this way the camera will achieve a relation of tone approximating the relation of color in the set.

The time of exposure—say, of blue on the cyclorama—depends on the amount of light that falls upon it. As nearly all cycloramas are lighted in a different way, it is difficult to tell, except by experience, the exact time to give them. But when this time is determined you can have the lights that are on the cyclorama put out, and continue to expose the picture for the other colors that are on different parts of the stage.

In the present system of lighting, with the exception of light on the cyclorama, the main light is directed on those places of the stage where the principal action of the scene takes place. Owing to this, in order to bring out the figures of the actors in relation to the scene, it is necessary to control these lights in the same way in which the cyclorama is controlled. As a rule the light falls from "spots" on the right and left of the stage and from the first border. These spots, by falling on the figures of the actors and on the floor cloth, light the set by reflected light. Unless there are lamps in the balcony or the motion-picture box, it is difficult to get sufficient illumination on the scene by reflected light. Most of the theatres, however, have thousand-watt lamps that can be brought into the auditorium and so placed that the set can be illuminated without materially affecting the quality that the scene designer desires. To the layman's eye the whole scene loses the original look that the designer has worked for, but the camera registers it relatively.

At best, the present position of photography in relation to the theatre is one of compromise. There is no way of taking the scene as it actually looks, for color is a very important factor in all modern productions, and photography has to translate this into light and shade. In the production of *Hamlet* there were continually shifting moods of color through the different scenes. It would be impossible to record these nuances by means of photography. To get even the general effect of, say, the opening scene would require the bringing of special lighting apparatus into the theatre. Most of the lighting apparatus is hired and installed at the time the production is made, and of course photography is in no way considered when this is done.

The Theatre Guild at the present time has the best and the most mobile lighting equipment of any of the New York theatres. In this organization neither time nor expense has been spared to record what Lee Simonson has done, and perhaps the Guild comes closer to approximating the ideas of the scene designer in lighting than any other theatre. It may be for this reason that the photographs I have made there are nearer to a record of what is actually seen than in any of the other productions I have taken.

What might be done with ideal lighting systems, such as are said to exist in some of the German theatres, is an interesting question. Let us hope that as the theatre progresses there will be permanent systems installed that are absolutely controllable. Then it will be possible to get accurate results quickly that will be more in keeping with the ideals of both the scene designer and the photographer.

March 1924

* *

NORRIS HOUGHTON

*

The Designer Sets the Stage

[*Two of a series of eight articles on the working methods of prominent stage designers*—THE EDITORS.]

Robert Edmond Jones

IT IS DIFFICULT to write an account of an interview with Robert Edmond Jones; it is difficult in the first place to conduct the interiew at all. For Jones is an artist, a poet, a visionary, and, as you sit vatching him pace the room as he conjures forth visions, you are nagnetized by a kind of electrical discharge which he emanates; yet vhen you attempt in later tranquillity to put those ideas into com-non prose, to set down the glowing image that he has somehow eemed to snatch from the air about him, the result is stale, flat and nprofitable. And when you try to discover, through conning your otes, what were his answers to specific questions, you find he has nade no answers.

It is quite understandable that the interview should have turned ut as it did. Mr. Jones was in little sympathy with my purpose of he moment. "All of us designers work the same way," he said, when explained what I wished him to tell me. "Nobody is interested in hese processes; the important things are the deeper ones, things that ave to do with our ideas about the theatre, the ideas and the dreams hat motivate our work. It is in them that we differ. You must try to xtract the essence of each of us. That sort of thing is significant, but t has little to do with methods." In that argument itself there is al-eady revealed some of the essence of Robert Edmond Jones.

It would perhaps be most faithful and most serviceable both to im and to the purpose of this sketch if the notes taken during con-ersations with Jones about his methods of work could be presented nore or less as they were recorded. It would be a miscarriage of neaning and intention if the technical processes described were to e magnified beyond the importance they had in Jones' thought.

Designers have been more loath than other artists of the New York heatre—actors, playwrights, directors—to make the sacred pilgrim-ge to Hollywood. The only designer of first magnitude who has pent any considerable time there (Aline Bernstein has made short xcursions) has been Robert Edmond Jones. He had just returned rom there, and it was in the hope that I might uncover some of the lifferences in the technical problems of the cinema art director, as pposed to those of the designer for the stage, that I mentioned Hollywood. Although he could not be lured into a description of novie scenic practices, he was full of impressions.

"Hollywood seems to pulse with eagerness and youth," he said. 'There is all the excitement of college dramatics out there. Everyone is working at top speed and as hard as he can. Even the stage hands seem to like to work! New York by contrast seems strangely old and lacking in vitality." Furthermore, the aggregation of talent packe into the moving-picture studios is tremendous, he points out. Why with the combination of talent, youth and energy which is Holly wood's, is the product not better? Jones believes that "the talent be comes dissipated simply because so many minds are involved. Holly wood is a superb example of the adage, 'Too many cooks spoil th broth.'" But such a situation is inevitable, he contends, because th machine is so vast.

Although he agrees with Hugh Walpole that "there is much tech nically that the movies can teach the stage," Jones contends that, ir the final analysis, "movies and the theatre have almost no connection Certainly at least the theatre cannot become cinematic." With thi thought, he turns back to an explanation of his work in the theatre

Jones' first, his constant, desire as he designs is "to carry the audi ence into that other region where the ideal play takes place." Hence to "find the simplest, broadest, boldest, grandest way to take th audience there and to keep them there" is at the same time his princi pal preoccupation and his point of departure. Jones, never satisfie however, and always seeking and questioning, asks at once, "Is thi simplest, broadest, boldest, grandest way to carry the audience out o reality always and necessarily to be found in the scenic decorations Need it, indeed, ever be the designer's way? May it not quite a probably be acting, even in an empty space, which uplifts the specta tors?"

In Elizabethan times words had the power to transport audiences Jones points out. "The spoken words of literary description coul evoke in the imagination of the Elizabethans scenery far more satis fying than any created with paint and cloth. So settings were *in dicated,* but not *represented* or even *suggested*. Yet the theatre wa very broad, bold and grand. Words have in some measure lost thei meanings for us in these days." Jones wonders, however, whethe the radio may not revive in our time the value of words spoken an thus do the theatre great service. Indeed, he envisions one kind o theatre in which the loudspeaker of radio could be used to replac scenery: "There might be only an empty dome, beautifully lighted and the amplifier of music and other sounds and words might pro vide the rest of the atmosphere. So once again the background fo drama might become evocative and indicative instead of suggestive

"One must continue to bear in mind, however, that we are nowa days particularly eye-conscious," Jones went on. "People's visual responses are much more acutely sensitized than their aural responses; so a theatre in which words and sounds might replace scenery as we know it is perhaps only a dream. If realized in our day, one would want, I suppose, to combine with it color in light and costumes." (One is reminded of Norman Bel Geddes' comment that scenery for him consisted of "three-dimensional plastic space, lighting and clothes.")

Color is important to Jones and when he says that "color is emotion" one concludes that its usefulness to him is far greater than in its realistic application—blue for sky, green for grass, red for bricks. He remarks that he has long wished to design a production for a play of Bernard Shaw entirely in black and white—"Color, being emotional, has no place in the Shavian theatre of the intellect." At last Jones reveals where he actually begins his designing. His conception comes from the feeling, the quality, the mood and intention of the play and the playwright. The ground plan, the director, the technical problems involved are all of little importance compared to the establishment of a kind of rapport between Robert Edmond Jones and the play. Several years ago he prepared a production of *Much Ado About Nothing* which, although carried out even to a dress rehearsal, was never presented. In it he dressed the actors in a kind of actors' uniform—all the men alike and all the women alike—and the entire company appeared before the play *as actors*. They put on hats, cloaks, swords, and so forth, in full view of the audience and at the end laid their trappings aside and appeared again as actors. As Jones read Shakespeare's text, it seemed to him that "such a scheme came closer than any other to carrying out the intention of the poet in this play."

This relationship of Jones to the play is so close that Jones admits to doing bad settings for a play he does not like—not intentionally of course; he simply cannot help but express his reaction in that way. Therefore in past years he has tried, whenever possible, to design only for plays with which he was in love. When this has been the case, then his setting has occurred to him suddenly as he sat reading the script. "All at once the people, their groupings, their clothes, the light, the background, appear to me complete in detail." Thus reading, he envisions the play as though it were being acted out before him. It then but remains to make drawings of these picturings of his imagination which he will take to the producer.

How different is Robert Edmond Jones' process of creation from those of the designers who have preceded him in this series. While the men who work up from ground plans or with architectural or plastic units in space may rearrange their designs a dozen times until they find the most satisfying position for a door or a window, a platform or an action area, Jones has before his mind's eye a complete picture which requires but slight adjustment to be executed and allows little rearrangement. The accuracy of his imagination may be judged by a comparison of his finished product with his sketches. The latter in their proportions, perspective and atmosphere almost perfectly presage their realization on the stage, and this seems possible only because he conceives them pictorially rather than structurally or architecturally. Thus he reverses the procedure of those designers who raise their settings from the ground into the air, by creating his scenery in the air and then mooring it to the floor. Jones moves from picture to plan instead of from plan to picture.

As he develops his settings, Jones seeks to "avoid in scenery the idea behind type casting"—that is, representation (in acting, an old man cast as an old man) as opposed to presentation (which is the essence of real acting, Jones claims). So he contrives decors which may be presentations rather than representations—suggestive rather than literal. "A setting should say nothing but give everything. Scenery as a rule seems to me to be too definite. It should possess powerful atmosphere but with little detail. It must be important but unobtrusive." Such dictums may help to explain his palette and his use of light—much black and gray and chiaroscuro which seem to sink his backgrounds into remote detachment from the world of his scarlet- or golden-clad actors. "Above all else," says Jones, "I seek to avoid doing a 'Jones setting'!"

If certain of these remarks lead one to imagine Robert Edmond Jones as an abstract visionary conceiving in some cloudland of art, that thought should be immediately dispelled. Although perhaps he may dream more dreams than some of our designers, he is adept in the craft as well as in the art of stage decoration. His costume sketch is usually complete only when there are pinned to it samples, chosen by Jones himself, of all the fabrics that compose it; his ground plans and his painter's sketches are prepared with the greatest care and display an accurate knowledge of stagecraft and construction. His fingers have fashioned headdresses and fitted sandals for as many years as his "mind's eye" has been busy seeing visions of the stage.

Jo Mielziner

"Every new play I do requires a new attack, different methods, another point of departure. I can tell you of no set rules that govern the way I begin work on a show," says Jo Mielziner, known as one of the most versatile scene designers on Broadway. The secret of this versatility, which makes him defy pigeonholes—realist, stylist, impressionist—which enables him to satisfy the demands of *On Your Toes* or *Ethan Frome, Jubilee* or *Winterset, Pride and Prejudice* or *Romeo and Juliet,* lies perhaps in this first remark. Mielziner does not announce continual flexibility as necessarily his aim, he merely states it as a fact of his past theatrical experience. By constantly changing his point of departure he has found that he achieves his best results.

"The ideal way to begin, I suppose, would be to forget all about both the back wall and the backer and do a Gordon Craig—allow one's artistic imagination to dictate entirely. But practically it is only very rarely that this is possible. Back wall and backer do exist and must be considered. Sometimes one may govern the designer's solution, sometimes the other; at other times again, it is the play, or the director, or time, or a special scheme of stylization. Time and the back wall need not necessarily be considered as limitations, however," continues Mr. Mielziner. "I think of them rather as the rules of the game; you have to play according to them and the only way anyone can have fun is to keep within them. The only thing I demand is that these rules be specifically stated. When a Broadway producer declares, 'I want the show to be able to go into a small theatre'—how small, I want to know; it's for the good of the design that I should know."

When he reads a play, Jo Mielziner, like Norman Bel Geddes, prefers to skip the stage directions. The ideas for the settings come from other sources than the playwright's instructions. "Often the designer knows better than the writer what the scene should look like when translated onto the stage." As the production proceeds, however, he is glad to place himself under the director, for he believes strongly in the autocratic theatre of the director.

"I used to begin working on a play by creating a visual picture of the *mise-en-scène,*" says Mr. Mielziner. "I have since given that up, and nowadays, after reading the play through once, I go over it again, seeking this time to visualize in my own mind the actors in the important situations of the drama. I hunt out the most telling line that conveys the atmosphere and background. This may give me an idea for a significant piece of furniture, a quality of light or shadow, a color combination; it may not be an entire setting at all—just something that is associated with the dramatic significance of the moment, but which may become the clue to, or indeed the cornerstone of, the whole setting."

Mr. Mielziner contends that scenery really exists for an audience only for about thirty seconds after the curtain rises or during times when the play becomes boring and their attention wanders to it. "I consider vicious the kind of designing which is based on this solo performance of the designer during the first half minute of the scene. I wish to design a setting for the key scenes, the critical moments of the play, for the moments when the audience has forgotten that there is any scenery on the stage at all—a setting, in other words, that becomes part of the highest life of the play." Such an attack, Mielziner feels, prevents him from ever building his setting purely to catch or mask light (the function, as he sees it, of the sculptural setting), or to be either entirely pictorial or entirely utilitarian. The setting designed for the instant when the curtain rises to reveal it may be entirely unsuitable as a background for the high moment of the dramatic action an hour and a half later, whereas the setting originating out of the key scenes will probably stand the first minute's inspection; if it does not, better to sacrifice that thirty seconds of "solo performance" than to harm the great moment later.

Having found the key to his setting in some important situation of the play, Mielziner is now ready to develop his plans. He starts by drawing various groups of figures—"I never cease to thank my father who trained me to be a figure painter"—because "the relation of the human form to the setting and to the furniture, the relation of a person to a doorway, to an opening, to light, is more important than any amount of architectural detail." This, Mr. Mielziner points out, is something that the decorator does not, in the nature of his task, have to consider in a drawingroom. But in the theatre where a thousand eyes are fixed upon a woman as she sinks into her chair upon the stage, the line of that chair, its color, its mass, must be carefully calculated with relation to her figure.

"At about this point I begin to get panicky," continues Mielziner. "I realize that the sets have to be changed in forty seconds, or that there is only another ten feet to the back wall. Then I must turn practical." He emphasizes repeatedly the necessity for practicability. "That it is important for the stage designer to be a craftsman as well as an artist is pretty generally admitted in this country now. But in the English theatre it is quite a different story. The London manager who wants a really swank production will engage the services of some eminent painter outside the theatre—a man like Augustus John, for instance—to do his settings. I have observed, however, that although the painter may conceive a sumptuous decor, more often than not he will be helpless to explain to technicians how it is to be executed. Broadway managers expect designers to be practical craftsmen as well as superior artists, and that is only right."

A further training which Mielziner believes ought to be required for designers is an apprenticeship as an actor and a stage manager. He himself devoted a year to this after he had decided that designing was to be his metier, and he claims that it has been of tremendous value to him.

After he has drawn groups of figures on the stage and made a rough ground plan or two, Mielziner sets to work on "a complete color sketch, with actors portrayed in the setting, with the lighting effects indicated and with twenty-eight feet of theatre dust and everything that contributes to the final illusion." Always, as he draws, it is with a feeling for three dimensions: "I mean I keep in mind, as I draw, that something will be, say, twelve feet from the footlights." This obviously gives added solidity and depth to an otherwise pictorial rendering.

After the complete color sketch is finished, Mielziner draws up his final ground and working plans himself. He says that he is envious of "those among my colleagues who are able to delegate the execution of details to assistants; if I could, I would be able to turn out much more work more easily, but I can't." It is in this way that we come upon what Mielziner considers the greatest working limitation of the theatre. Without a moment's hesitation he says, "Lack of sufficient nervous energy to keep going at maximum efficiency for nine or ten hours without a lag seems to be the thing that stands most frequently in my way." He spoke feelingly, for at the time he had just had two elaborate productions opening simultaneously in Washington and in Toronto and a third on the brink of dress rehearsals in New York; three times in that week he had flown back and forth from one place to the other!

About his studio practices Mr. Mielziner has a few other comments. When a production involves many platforms or contains a tricky problem in the relationship of a figure to mass in side elevation, he uses a scaled model. This model is never completed, rarely even painted, and therefore is never exhibited outside the drafting-room. He makes constant use of a dark room into which he takes materials and sketches for the painters, in order to test their reactions to various colored lights. He considers this a vital part of the preparation of his scenery. As for the lighting itself, he considers it important that he himself should light productions in which he is involved. The short-lived *Daughters of Atreus* earlier this season presented ample proof to those who saw it that Mielziner is a master-artist in the field of lighting the theatre.

When he has time, Mielziner likes to do the costuming of a play as well as the settings. When he does, he tries, if possible, to decide the color scheme of the clothes before he determines the colors of the scenery, preferring to let the former set the note and the latter serve as the accompaniment. This seems to him fairer to the actor and hence fairer to the play.

Mielziner is one of the few artists who design both for drama and for musicals and he sees no reason why more designers should not be able to work in both fields. He finds the technique very much the same. "One uses a different palette, perhaps, sharper, bolder colors for the musical show, but that's about all." But then Jo Mielziner is a particularly versatile person: he can laugh and weep, wax poetic and turn sternly realistic, as the theatre calls to him in different tones. So there is no reason to be surprised that it is equally easy for him to lift up his voice in song!

December 1936

ALINE BERNSTEIN

*

The Craftsmen

A FEW MONTHS AGO we lost one of our great men of the theatre; he was a carpenter, and had his own shop where he built scenery. His name was Bill Kellam. I know of no one, working in the crafts of the theatre, who was held in greater respect and affection. You trusted him and his work completely. Shortly before his death, I traveled back on the train with him after an opening night in Wilmington. He had built the scenery for a play that had many tricky and fast changes, and he had come down to set up the show and make it work. The train left Wilmington station at midnight, arriving late in New York after waits, stoppages and delays, at almost four in the morning. Bill Kellam had done that for three nights, putting in a day's work at his shop on another show that had to be out at the end of the week. He would take an afternoon train to Wilmington, arriving to supervise the evening dress rehearsal of the scenes. One night he collapsed and had to rest on an improvised couch in one of the boxes. He would not rest for long; there was too much to do; and soon he was up and around again.

This is not an extraordinary way to work in the theatre. It is in the nature of the business. I do not mean to say that all of us work ourselves to death; but such devotion to work is typical of people who work in the theatre. In another business, another man who felt as sick as this man did might go home and take care of himself. This man, in this business, did not. I like to think of it as a form of professional will.

I speak as one who loves the business of designing for the theatre. I believe that all designers do. There is no limit to what we can create on the stage. But we could not do what we do were it not for the excellence of the craftsmen who carry out our work. Our ideas are interpreted by them, are translated into the theatrical terms of wood, canvas and paint, and the loveliest costume drawings in the world would amount to nothing as costumes were they carelessly made.

The relation between the designer and the craftsmen is close, and it must be a good one. For it is in the workshops that our dreams come true. I take my T-Square and triangle and I draw a line on the clean paper pinned to my drafting table; and I know that line will soon be a wall, and all the other lines I put to it will be the doors and windows, the fireplaces and the cornices, and the great sky itself. What I have put down on that oblong sheet of paper will, by a miracle of building and painting, become a drawingroom or a kitchen or the palace of a king; or a garden or "another part of the forest."

There are a hundred ways of interpreting a drawing. Drawings for scenery are more exact than drawings of costumes, they have to have their mechanical statements, in feet and inches. Still there is always room to go wrong. Things have a peculiar variation from the ideal. It is difficult, for instance, to imagine space, no matter how precisely it is enclosed, so the set often looks either larger or smaller to the physical eye. Considering the fallibility of human nature it is a wonder that things go wrong so seldom. Of course, it means that there must be close understanding between the designer and the builders and painters, and we have to be on the job from morning to night.

You step from the busy street into the sceneshop, and the noises make the streets seem comparatively quiet. There is the whir of the band-saw and the hammering, the clatter of lumber being handled, the scraping and moving of heavy pieces. There is the indefinable smell of scenery being built; the smell of fresh glue, of lumber, of canvas that has been fireproofed (it has a distinct smell of its own), and the sweet-sour smell of sawdust. It all mingles into the single smell of scenery being built. Everything is clean, there is something almost wholesome about the uncut lumber and the clean new yards of canvas, and the fine sawdust on the floors.

The first visit, we see the flats and some of the set-pieces, the fireplace, the doors and windows. Then the time comes when the entire scene is set up, before it goes to the painter, and both the carpenter and the designer (myself) go over it carefully to see that everything fits and is in good shape. One evening last year I had dinner with a producer-director, and he said to me, "Yesterday I saw the best performance of this play I will ever see, surely the most interesting." I had something to say to that, but I didn't say it for I saw an amused expression on his face. "No scenery, no props, no costumes," he added. I know just what he meant. To me, an empty stage is one of the most wonderful things in the world; but next to it is a set of scenery before it is painted, the beautiful bare white canvas walls, the honey-colored gleam in the raw wood, and the first sight of the proportion and spacing of one's design. He had nothing on me, for I had seen my scene that morning, with no paint, no lights, no actors and no props. It was something of my own, except for the carpenter. "Looks good," he said. "Yes, looks good," I said.

When I say I like raw scenery, it is much the same as a cook feels about the assembled ingredients of her dishes, a bowl of eggs, a quart of cream, the beauty of an uncooked cabbage or a basket of tomatoes. Or a leg of lamb the way Chardin saw it. It doesn't mean that the finished product isn't good. And no public would take the beauty I see in my unpainted scene.

The painter has a more difficult job than any of the other craftsmen. His work is governed not by line and rule but by artistry, combined with the closer supervision of the designer and the designer's taste. The color of the set when you see it on the stage is modified by various conditions: the lighting, the colors of the props—that is, hangings, furniture, wall decorations—and the color of the actors' costumes as they move in and out of the spheres of light and play against each other and the props. A set is never painted a flat tone, as a wall in your room is painted, but the color is broken into varied tones and values of itself, ranging from cold to warm, and light to dark. Yet it must be so harmonized that it does not look as though it had been varied at all; it must only give the effect of atmosphere and of life as the play itself must do. Even an intricately patterned wallpaper design is painted in this manner. Actual wallpaper is never used on a set—it would look all wrong, small in scale and flat; and besides it is not fireproof. It takes a painter years of experience to reach this skill, and it takes something more, a right feeling for the theatre and the rare quality of being able to interpret the designer's ideas.

The smell of a scene painter's shop is nothing like as entrancing as the builder's. When you say the smell of paint, your mind's nose is tickled with something clean and fresh, with turpentine prevailing. But our work is done with watercolor paint: that is, powdered pigment mixed with glue-size; and nothing in the world smells worse than glue-size after it is a day old. It doesn't even smell good when it's new. But fortunately the odor is confined to certain portions of the studio.

It is a shock to come into the studio and see the white canvas splashed with color. The first painting, the underpainting, always looks far from the way it should look finished. Years of experience have not taught me that it will be all right in the end. There is still that first sinking of the heart. The painters begin with their fine work, overpainting with the various methods they use—the rag roll, the spatter, and plain dragging paint on with the brush—darkening the scene toward the top, lightening it at the bottom and center, helping the corners to keep in shadow and pulling it all together. It is all done with a knowledge of what the lights will do to the color and texture, and how it will look across and behind the magic curtain of the footlights. One of the best things the painters can do is the imitation of wood. There are men who are specialists in graining; they'll give you pine, mahogany and walnut so that you are completely fooled, even at close range, still keeping the liveliness and gradations that are necessary to stage illusion.

The term theatrical property, or props, means anything you see on the stage that is not scenery or an actor; in other words, it means the furniture, the draperies, the carpet, the rugs, the lamps and lighting fixtures, the dishes and napery, pictures on the wall, fifty million ashtrays, trunks, pipes, tobacco jars, flowers with vases and bowls to hold them, trays and wastepaper baskets, stoves, grates and fire-irons, strange statues and paintings thought up by the playwright, knick-knacks and gewgaws and all sorts of bric-a-brac; that extra little bit of furniture to fill the foot-and-a-half space that is empty (for a director, like nature, abhors a vacuum, even though the eye occasionally needs a rest). Most of this dread list can be bought or rented from the concerns who deal in such things, but some cannot; so we go to the propmakers.

Wizards. They make everything in the world out of wood and papier-mâché—kitchen stoves, thrones, those odd statues, great silver tankards, busts of great men and ancient musical instruments. That paper stove has to be so good that it looks real beside the real kitchen chairs and table. Sometimes it looks even more real, for they can give it the tone of time. They're expensive, but they're good; and the sky is the limit to what they can do. All props, though, are painted by our scenic artists of local 829. I've seen one of our men add, in ten minutes, ten years to the look of that stove.

A whole chapter can be written about our costumers. At their best, they are great; at their worst, they are frightful. Some people make a costume forgetting that there will be an actor inside of it who must act, walk about, and use his arms, legs, torso, even his neck. That is not funny. It is an element that needs skillful handling. A costume moves, it must look as well from the back and the sides as it looks from the front; and never, under any circumstances, must it hamper an action or a gesture.

The selection of fabric, its truth to your choice of color, the cut, fit, hang and drape of the costume, although closely supervised, are really in the hands of the costumer. Again the intangibles do a large part of the work. It isn't just dressmaking, even the finest dressmaking, that does the trick. It is the skill, the costumer's interest and feeling for the job, and endless patience for dealing with the actor's temperament and idiosyncrasies. Of course, the most important part of a costume is the acting that goes on inside of it, but we must give the actor a break, and ninety-nine times out of a hundred we do.

A living can be made in all of these theatrical crafts; but except in boom times it is not a fat living. No business is more variable. A few of the craftsmen have done very well, many of them just get by, and in bad times a great many can barely keep body and soul together. Just now, the theatre is in the money, and there are barely enough men and women to do the work. The great question now is how these crafts can be learned by the young ones. For years I have raised my voice in favor of establishing the apprenticeship system, even among the actors. It is such a good idea. Some of us old ones would have to do a lot of the training; it would not be easy. But nothing worth doing is easy. We should at least have craft schools run by the unions or in cooperation with them. Maybe it's a dream, but dreams in America have a way of coming true.

Out in the other world, away from the theatre, I meet many people who envy me, knowing nothing of how we work, or what it means to get a show on the stage for them to see. It's that threadbare word "glamour" that they are thinking about. They say to me, clasping their hands, "You must meet so many interesting people, Mrs. Bernstein." And I say, "Yes, I do!" But they think only of The

Lunts and Miss Hayes, and so forth. They know nothing of these friends of mine, these craftsmen, who have helped to make my life in work the great experience that it is.

April 1945

* *

DONALD OENSLAGER

*

Let There Be Light

IT IS DARK. Jake is balanced precariously twenty feet in the air atop a teetering extension ladder. The ladder is anchored none too safely to the stage floor by all of four disinterested fraternal operators. Only Jake's legs are visible. The rest of him, like some disembodied spirit, is lost in the flies. You must be wondering where you are. No, you are not witnessing a circus act, you are in the auditorium of a theatre and we are lighting a scene for a play. Jake is the electrician. He is up on the ladder focusing spotlights and our conversation runs along something like this:

"All right, Jake, give me No. 19 spot on the end pipe. Hit the steps. Now tip it down—further still. Pull your focus back. Sharpen it up more—way back. Watch your spill on that wall. A high hat will help? Pass a high hat up to Jake. Now you've lost your position. Hit the steps again—OK. Give it a combination 53 and 3. Now Joe, are you on the board? Take No. 19 down easy—to 3 points—up a hair. Now gang No. 19 up with No. 15 and No. 11. Jack [he is the stage manager], take this reading: During Act II on cue 6, Miss Bankhead's exit, this hook-up will dim out on the count of 8 along with the circuit of left blue booms. Check? OK, now let's try it!"

That is the staccato dot-dash lingo that travels over the sound waves from the auditorium to the stage to the switchboard and back again. Interminable hours have been spent uncrating and hanging electrical equipment and connecting cables with the switchboard according to blueprinted specifications for the lighting layout. Now finally we are beginning to light the scene.

With the best of planning, lighting remains one of the most

clumsy, time-consuming and primitive phases of theatre production. In only an hour and twenty minutes it will be midnight and the stage crew will go off. The scene is dressed and set. The first run-through with the cast will be in the morning. As usual, little time remains now for actually lighting the scene. Yet proper lighting is one of the most exacting and sensitive of operations. To the uninitiated, lighting a scene seems the most casual and haphazard of operations, requiring nothing but patience and the capacity to "dim up" the pink or "dim down" the amber. Sometimes, in some hands, it is almost as elementary as that. Light control as it is handled on the stage today is inadequate and remarkably crude in comparison to the subtlety of the action of the play which it must accompany, and to the emotional development of which it must be an integral part.

When I say "lighting the scene," I do not mean we are lighting the actual scenery. We are lighting those acting areas on the stage where the actors are to play. The acting areas are always lighted first. This is the most logical procedure, but in practice is frequently forgotten. Scenery should not be featured by light. Light the actors and the scene will take care of itself. I find that the average stage setting plays its role best in the reflection of the acting-area lights. The setting thus maintains its proper relationship both to the actor and to the action of the play, and, incidentally, also appears most effective. Naturally, this principle does not apply to those lighting units which specifically provide background light for scenery, because this pictorial handling of light actually represents scenery.

Just what is the aesthetic or spiritual relationship of light to a scene? Light, we know, moves in wave motion. So does a play on the stage. Also, like a play, light is never static. It changes in intensity, direction and color. The light released on the stage must be of such a fluid and volatile nature that throughout a performance, if carefully controlled and directed, it will both reveal every significant movement of the actor's body and also in some mysterious way fan those emotional sparks that glow within the actor. Whether the performance is a comedy, tragedy or musical, we are aware of a kind of contagious current of response or friction surging between performer and spectator. By consciously synchronizing this response with subtly changing light, there will occur a more explosive experience caused by the actor's heightened emotional fervor playing on the receptive mood of the audience. The influence of light on this state of theatrical combustion between actor and audience bears a parallel relation to the power which sunlight exerts on our manifold activities in the world of today.

Before investigating the nature of light and its dramatic expression, let us first retreat to that neutral, pre-Cambrian era of global gloom when there were no recognizable elements of our world today—and of course no theatre, although the events about to take place were the very essence of drama. It began in darkness. God simply said, "Let there be light; and there was light, and God saw the light that *it* was good; and God divided the light from the darkness and God called the light Day and the darkness He called Night. And the evening and the morning were the first day." It was apparently as simple as that.

On that first "opening night" of creation occurred the first conscious control of light in this world. Was it summoned out of a whirlwind with the same dot-dash of numbers and staccato phrases with which we light our scene? Perhaps that first strange dawn rose slowly on a count of eight beats to scatter the forces of night, although we know today that light comes to us from the sun as wave motion traveling something like one hundred and eighty-six thousand miles a second. Or did that first light issue forth with such a blinding flash that one could not see the miracle for the paradisiacal radiance on every side? One can only conjecture. It must have been infinitely more exciting than witnessing the control and release of atomic power. Certainly dark glasses were not passed around, and Jake was not balanced on the ladder, and there were no light switches to pull.

Today the clockwise miracle of alternating lightness and darkness is accepted ipso facto every twenty-four hours. Like the stop-and-go sign, light dominates our lives. Occasionally, on our own authority, we have ventured to devise for ourselves the corollary which provides light by night and darkness by day. But in spite of our efforts nature has always been far ahead of us. Those creatures that inhabit the dark valleys of the deep seas have, since time immemorial, carried their own headlights. Glow-worms suspended from the vaults of certain caverns in New Zealand summon the distraction of their starry light to protect their safety in darkness. The fireflies' cool incandescence is not wired for sunlight. The world had indeed been slow in discovering for itself the fabulous energy to be drawn from the sun. Not until the seventeenth century did Isaac Newton admit a beam of light through his curtained window onto a prism and produce the ordered colors of the rainbow.

Almost yesterday scientists discovered that our eyes do not detect eighty percent of the recorded wave lengths of light. The infra-red, ultra-violet and x-rays are invisible vibrations and occur beyond the red and violet band of the visible spectrum. We feel the infra-red rays as heat and the ultra-violet rays as cold and call them black light. In many ways these invisible rays of light are put to positive beneficial use. Their ultimate capabilities have not yet been nearly explored. Their use envisions undreamed vistas.

Even today we seem to live far beyond the periphery of the accepted realm of sunlight. But in spite of our blackboard theories of time and of space the frosty corona of the sun's eclipse remains a wonder to us. We are frightened before the uncontrolled bolt of lightning flashing earthward, and the majestic procession of lights on a summer evening parading across dark northern skies is still awesome. Though we can forecast the eclipse, reproduce a destructive bolt of laboratory lightning and explain the cause of the Aurora Borealis, our common submission to the sovereign activity of light in the heavens remains complete. And with all our scientific knowledge of the properties of hot light, cold light and black light we are lost in the dark, timeless universe that bounds us only a few miles distant from the earth's surface. Indeed, we blow a simple house fuse and our darkened confusion before Edison's ghost is immense.

We cannot deny that we live by the sun. Since that first morning of creation we have been sun-kissed. Sunlight is the one element that still remains universally tax free. It is the fifth freedom—shared by all, for we are sun worshippers at heart, hitch-hikers in Aurora's chariot. The whole earth absorbs and reflects the solar energy in a myriad of ways. Are not our bodies, like trees and flowers or wheat, partly composed of light? Our animating spirit feeds on this radiant energy. Every part of us, every gesture, is an active revelation of light—the flashing eyes, the shining face, the burning lips, the radiant smile, the fiery temper, the glowing body, the spark of conscience. The agency of light is a lucid means of communication. It illuminates and reveals those inaccessible reaches of our minds. Artists fire their imagination with this natural energy which is synonymous with creative instinct. Incandescent inner light is the hallmark of fine acting. An actress, we say, illumines a role with her power and the stage with her presence. To enhance her presence on the stage, to spotlight her intuitions with a quickening light, is a most serious responsibility in the theatre. How can it be achieved with more effective results?

It might be appropriate to depart for the moment from those accepted limitations which the theatre imposes on our use of light and turn to the painters, sculptors and architects. Theirs is an unfettered appreciation of light's artistic potentialities. What clear understanding of the manipulation and purpose of light successive generations of distinguished artists have unfailingly displayed in their work! We are magnetized by the perennial attraction of their creative use of light, and even more by the degree of their preoccupation with the character and depth of their particular subject's inner light. They translate this inner light for us through their own dictionary of expression and interpret anew for our eyes the animated material world of color and form.

Rembrandt fully understood the revelatory value of light. In designing a scene, he ennobled with his own humility the most sacred and profane episodes. His etching for "The Crucifixion" remains a revolutionary and profound interpretation of one of the world's most tragic dramas. With an utterly arbitrary use of light, he triumphed over academic traditions of representation. His scene comprises three crosses surrounded by a host of figures. There is neither earth nor sky. The wonder of "The Crucifixion" is that it is fabricated from pure light. Airy space becomes locked in three-dimensional form. It is a monumental abstract expression of overwhelming emotion. The copper plate is etched and cross-hatched with magic splinters of black light, imparting a spiritual radiance to the action of the scene which transcends the limitations of our accustomed way of utilizing light and space.

Van Gogh thought of painting as consisting of all light, prismatic light passing through space. A portrait head of a good friend—an artist of imagination—Van Gogh painted against a sparkling blue sky. Above the head he set a single star swimming in the intensity of a luminous void as a symbol of the artist's unfettered imagination. Here is a pictorial statement of character in light.

Nameless sculptors set friezes of Apsaras dancing along the temple walls of Angkor Wat. Photograph these dancing maidens and they seem frozen in their storied blocks of stone. Reproduce them in plaster and they seem arrested in a trance. But see these sculptured creatures moving in and out of vibrant shafts of shifting tropical sunlight and alternating purple cloud-shadows, and they seem never to have ceased their tireless pursuit of animated grace and beauty. In the same way the Elgin marbles transplanted to a northern climate from Greece seem chill and austere. In British captivity, beneath artificial light, they appear to languish in cold, classic repose. Unable to thaw, they do not impart the contagious warmth of those companion pieces left basking in Greek sunlight, marble fragments still glowing with the original fire of Phidias' genius because they remain on the rocky pedestal of the Acropolis under the original clear light of a cerulean sky.

Architecture too breathes most freely beneath the animating rays of shifting light. In Peiping, the Temple of Heaven is raised dramatically on a formal tier of concentric marble terraces. The circular concave roof of blue tile sweeps upward to veritably fill the azure dome of heaven. The ancient monument stands like a sundial in studied proportion recording the hours of the day and the seasons of the years. To the Chinese this is a beautiful living symbol. The timeless perfection of form matches the accuracy of passing seconds. So under the same sun, but in different climes, the pyramids in Egypt, the Borabodur in Java, Santa Maria della Salute in Venice and the Lincoln Memorial in Washington each in its way derives its animation and peculiar charm from those variable quantities of light which ordained their appropriate form and determined their unique design.

Painters, sculptors and architects intuitively respond to every mood of light and instinctively seize full advantage of its special characteristics. In their hands light reveals character, defines scale, measures time and gives substance to shadow. Light they convert into motion and rhythm. With light they touch off the inner spark of marble, bronze, wood or pigment. They assort the splendors of the spectrum and from a single hue create a tempest or a rainbow. Sometimes, like William Blake, they are endowed with a visionary prescience of the mysterious power latent in the atoms and molecules and ions which the scientists understand but which we only sense but cannot see, feel but cannot touch.

Keeping in mind the constancy of light inherent in architecture, painting and sculpture, come back now to the stage of the theatre. Bring back the interpretative power and the abstract beauty of light with you. Summon it forth onto the scene with the artist's sensitivity. Adopt the bold, visionary approach of the painter, the sculptor and the architect. Handle light with the brush or the chisel or the rule. Conspire with the lighting engineer. Release and set light in motion. Draw light patterns from the empty air like cloud forms. Allow light to clothe the bare stage with visible light, black light, cold light, warm light. Never forget that magic is legitimate in the theatre and that the theatre is a laboratory for the imagination. Reveal to the playwright new forces, new concepts, new directions. On your stage defy space and time. Fire the beacon in the actor's eye. Sensitize the scene.

But how can we achieve this "change of scene" today with our old-fashioned, upright piano-box type of switchboard? We must have far greater light control than present switchboards afford. To my knowledge but one distinguished contribution to light control has been realized for the legitimate theatre in recent years. This is George Izenour's preset remote control board which he has developed and installed in the Department of Drama at Yale University. Mr. Izenour applies entirely electronic intensity control to light. His control is accurate and infallible. What heretofore in the theatre has seemed impossible to accomplish with light because of time limitations and inadequate control is now possible. This compact, simple method of control opens up possibilities in the use of light which the designer, director and playwright have heretofore only dreamed might be accomplished.

But now, given the control board, what of the antiquated equipment which it must control? We are asked to accomplish miracles of light in the theatre with Olivettes, X-rays, Projectors, Fresnels and Wizards. In illustrated catalogues of stage lighting this equipment looks efficient and streamlined. While those instruments may be the best equipment at our disposal, in efficiency they are only a few steps beyond the junior high-school tin-can spotlight. They were designed, for the most part, to reproduce lighting on the stage. With all our aggressive laboratory experimentation and research in illuminating engineering, lighting equipment for the stage remains sadly out of date. Most manufacturers of lighting equipment are unmaginative. They believe that if they invest in the improvement of ld or the invention of new equipment the consumer or producer will not pay the increased cost though it will achieve both more fficient operation and more effective results. Everyone today knows hat this is an economic fallacy. The American consumer demands nd obtains the best in vacuum cleaners and plumbing. The best heatre requires and deserves the best equipment.

The following list of equipment is merely an indication of the ind of improved lighting equipment desirable in the theatre. Some nay now be in the drafting stage; others will not be possible for ome years to come.

1. A simple switchboard with preset control to obtain mobility.
2. A simple multi-capacity electronic dimmer.
3. Suitable mechanical dimmers for fluorescent tubes.
4. Radar control of electrical equipment.
5. A high-wattage lamp that will remain cool.
6. A lamp capable of such control that any desired color can be produced.
7. A lamp that will dim without growing warm in tone.
8. A spotlight with accurate, simple control and focusing apparatus.
9. A spotlight capable of throwing diffused light without spill.
10. Shadowless illumination.
11. Greater variety of heat-resisting glass color filters.
12. Stereoscopic projected scenery to be obtained by better colors and with more compact and more intense light sources.

Light has been flowing through fuse boxes onto the stage of our heatres for many years now. We accept its presence as we accept cenery. We could not manage without it. The conception of light s a medium limited merely to achieving visibility is behind us. On very city block and every farm throughout the nation we are aware of new forces sweeping us into ever larger spheres of perception. The new eye on Mt. Wilson, radar for the blind and deaf, television, tomic power and electronics are only a few of the new forces that control and dominate our contemporary world. Illumination is but one facet of electronics. Electronics becomes a new and revelatory nedium at the theatre's disposal. It is an integral part of the common impulse of scientific progress.

The role we assign to light in the theatre today may be curtailed by technical deficiencies but in the theatre of tomorrow it will shine as a new force as surely as did that first dawn. It will come sweeping in on our own winged trial-and-error insistence on new forms of expression. In the meantime Jake is still up there on the ladder and Joe is on the dimmers. Give them a hand. Let there be light—not tomorrow but today.

September 1947

VIII · ARCHITECTURE

* * *

To Architects: Stop! Look! Listen!

*

[*Concerning Any Project for Building a Modern Theatre, and Concerning Especially the Architectural Competition of the American National Theatre and Academy for a Festival at Williamsburg, Virginia* —THE EDITORS.]

EXPERIENCED ARCHITECTS are accustomed to seek the service of experts to solve their technical problems—such as heating, lighting, plumbing, steel, ventilation or acoustics. But there have been few opportunities offered to American architects to build theatres, and most of them know very little about the highly complex functional problems involved. Today with the recent flexible Building Code of the City of New York and new demands for housing community activities in the arts in an effective and economical building, a new set of problems is added to the old. As Lee Simonson, whose *Basic Theatre Planning* was one of the first attempts to clarify essentials, expresses it: "The theatres that are being built are not just theatres; they are a part of a larger building complex in a building that has to serve a great many other purposes; and the problem is one of general planning in which the technical requirements of theatres have to be incorporated. Every one of these buildings has a different program, and will have a different kind of life in it when it gets built." The real answer, as Mr. Simonson goes on to say, "is that what the architect needs is a theatre consultant who has a feeling for architectural planning, as well as technical experience in theatrical requirements, both maximums and minimums; and that such a theatrical consultant is essential from the development of the original *parti* through to its final form and through the actual installation of the building."

A few "do's" and "don't's" will not answer the problem but they will help to focus attention on some outstanding difficulties. No one knows these problems better than the men and women actually at work in the theatre today. Caught in the wings and in the middle of a rehearsal or at work in shop or studio, these artists and technicians have taken time out to jot down notes on the most crying needs in theatre planning. Their "do's" and "don't's"—the result of years of experience and experiment—will be of great value in charting the architect's course.

ROBERT EDMOND JONES, *designer and director.* Every theatre should have plenty of stage space—depth, width, height; adequate storage space for scenery, costumes and properties; the latest and best lighting equipment; sound-proof, well-ventilated rehearsal rooms; adequate, easily accessible, well-ventilated dressing rooms; traps in the stage floor; a removable apron stage extending over the orchestra pit. *The atmosphere of a theatre, not that of a lecture hall or laboratory.*

LEE SIMONSON, *designer, author of* The Stage Is Set. Don't make the gridiron too low. 60′ is a minimum. Don't fail to leave offstage room on each side equal to at least half the width of the proscenium.

Don't make the proscenium too wide. 32′ to 34′ is ample for most professional productions, and certainly for most amateur ones.

Be sure to plan the placing of the switchboard on the original *parti,* as the wiring conduits have to be laid when the foundations are put in and the walls go up.

Reserve ample funds for an adequate switchboard and lighting control system, for that is the nerve center of the modern stage.

(Mr. Simonson adds, and we agree, that these are only a few of the most elementary precautions and that they are typical of technical problems that can be discussed intelligently only in conjunction with the total design and all the details of the building.)

ORSON WELLES, *actor and director of the Mercury Theatre.* If a permanent houseboard is to be installed, be sure to leave space and adequate wiring outlets for the temporary boards which accompany almost every traveling company. . . . Don't build a permanent cyclorama which makes it impossible to fly a show. A permanent "cyc" is very expensive to keep up and not half as useful as one which can be flown. . . . By all means have a complete counterweight system. . . . A built-in revolving stage is bad, as it breaks up the trap area; it is much more important to have the entire stage trapped, and to use temporary revolving stages which are very cheap to install. A temporary revolving stage can be stored when it is not being used.

The scene dock should be as large as the stage proper, with ample room for storage and painting. Even better to have the dock big enough so that a platform stage can also be accommodated. This would make it possible to set up a scene in the dock and push it directly onto the stage—a great economy of both time and space. . . . Very important to have a flexible orchestra pit, which can be covered and used as an apron stage when so desired. . . . An architectural proscenium which was both permanent and flexible would be of enormous value. If you could change the size of the proscenium, both at the sides and the top, as easily, say, as you can raise the curtain, it would do away with the expensive false proscenium "tabs" made of extravagant, light-absorbent material.

While there should, obviously, be ample leg room between rows, the seats should not be too far apart or too comfortable, as the audience must be made to sit up. If you make a theatre like a cocktail lounge, the play loses a third of its effect. . . . Most house lights are grossly inadequate. The house should be gay and brilliant when the curtain is down, frankly theatrical and gala, and not simply hygienic as is the modern tendency.

SAMUEL SELDEN, *associate director of The Carolina Playmakers, co-author of* Modern Theatre Practice. The new forms in the theatre will probably include a greater use of dancing, music and massed groups in different planes and on different levels. To provide free working opportunities for these new elements, the theatre architect should give special consideration to two points: (a) plenty of simple, flexible space on, and in front of, the stage, (b) good sight-lines from every part of the auditorium to all parts of every possible acting area. Specifically, in regard to the stage, the theatre architect should consider:

1. An ample proscenium opening. The frame should be neutral, free from any kind of ornamentation which might fail to harmonize with scenery and costumes in scenes played on a forestage.

2. Facilities for setting-up of a forestage—when needed.

3. An adequate orchestra pit.

4. Plenty of height on the stage, and plenty of wing and front-to-rear space. All unnecessary projections from the stage walls should be removed.

Such mechanical devices as revolving, sinking, rising and sliding stages are luxuries, to be included only if the budget has a margin. The primary requisite is always flexible space.

HAROLD BURRIS-MEYER *and* EDWARD C. COLE, *authors of* Scenery for the Theatre. It is cheaper to build a good theatre than to build it wrong and then correct it. The following check-list contains a few of the more important considerations necessary to good acoustic design for legitimate theatres:

1. Keep the noise level below 30 db.

2. Beware parallel walls, they encourage standing waves.

3. Beware rear walls which follow the curve of the seats, they often cause focal points.

4. Beware ceilings under balconies, parallel to the orchestra floor, they may cause pockets.

5. Slope the ceiling for purposes of sound distribution rather than any other consideration, and provide even distribution throughout the house.

6. Items 2 to 5 are qualitative considerations. Designs can be checked with respect to them by ripple tank and spark tests on models. The wave patterns must be satisfactory with the sound source anywhere on the stage, in the orchestra pit or at any speaker-mounting position.

7. Choose as your reverberation time that which falls halfway between the optima for speech and music for the cubage in question unless provision has been made for controlling reverberation time.

8. Keep the reverberation times of all frequencies approximately equal throughout the audible range.

9. Keep the reverberation time the same no matter to what extent the house is filled.

10. Keep the house live. It is easy to tone down too live a house. Not even the best PA system can completely cure all the faults of a dead house.

Items 7 to 9 limit the choice of surface materials for walls, ceiling, floor, seats and articles of a decorative nature. It has been found satisfactory to make calculations on the basis of a theatre in which the curtain is up and the set on the stage is an interior, with ceiling and velour side masking.

DONALD OENSLAGER, *designer, technician*. Everyone sitting in the orchestra pays the same price for tickets and is entitled to an equally good view of the stage. Be sure to plan the side walls of the auditorium so that every seat has an equally free sightline of the whole stage scene. Designers, actors and directors should not be forced to work 8′ from right and left of the proscenium to reach sightlines of bad seats.

Be sure to provide more height backstage from the stage floor to the grid than may seem necessary to a non-theatre person. This space, of which the audience is unaware, is utilized by the designer, technician and electrician for storage, to facilitate increased speed in scene changes and for economy in running expenses. The practicality of a production is limited by this area. Just adequate height backstage is never enough.

WARREN MUNSELL, *business manager of the Theatre Guild*. Box-office accommodations in most theatres are completely inadequate, tucked away under the stairs or in some two-by-four cubbyhole. The ideal box-office should be at least 8′ by 12′, with outside ventilation. It should have two ticket windows—one for reservations, one for current sales—close enough to have access to each other, yet far enough apart so that two lines can form in front of them. It should be placed so that ticket buyers will be protected from the weather and will not get in the way of people coming into the theatre. Nearby, if possible connecting the box-office, there should be a room the same size for the company manager and the advance press agent (independent of the house manager's office). A washroom should be within easy access of these rooms.

In the theatre proper, there should be two sets of lounge and rest rooms, one for the audience downstairs, one in the underpass of the balcony. Most theatres provide inadequate toilet facilities, especially for women; there should be ten toilets in each ladies' washroom. . . . The coatroom should be located on the orchestra level.

At least 3″ should be added to the standard space of 32″ required by law between the back to back of seats.

Backstage, *a vital thing* is to have adequate loading and unloading accommodations—a large enough driveway for two trucks, doors at least 12′ high and 8′ wide, with the stage floor at truck level, so that scenery can be pushed directly from the truck into the stage house without being carried.

ALFRED LUNT, *actor.* I'd like to see an architect plan his stage *first,* and plan it very carefully; then design the auditorium after he is sure the stage is right.

There should be at least four dressing rooms on the stage floor, each of them 8′ by 12′ or the equivalent, with running water and a connecting toilet. Actors have not got time to use hall washrooms.

There should be ample space to hang clothes, *not* in closets. *And there must be outside ventilation.*

I would suggest that they light the house so that people can read their programs and so that the women show off to advantage. Top lighting is unbecoming to everyone except the Venus de Milo.

There should be an ample orchestra pit (big enough to hold at least 25 musicians) which can be covered and used as an apron stage.

The whole front of the balcony, and gallery, should be wired for lights (for the stage). The lower these lights are the better. When you are very young, you are apt to think that spot-lighting from the top is beautifully dramatic. By the time you are over forty, you won't light from the top at all if you are interested in the women in the cast. Footlights, by all means—the kind that you can put in or take out.

A flexible proscenium which would form a part of the architecture of the front of the house would be marvelous. You wouldn't have to use those loathsome black tabs on every set then.

For heaven's sake, have a soundproof, fireproof room off-stage for stagehands to sit in and smoke *and cough* during the show. Many performances have been practically killed by asthmatic stagehands.

STANLEY MC CANDLESS, *Yale University Theatre, author of* A Method of Lighting the Stage.

1. Modern production methods demand a good cyclorama. A good cyclorama is one which presents primarily a smooth, unwrinkled

surface through the entire expanse of the proscenium opening, thus serving to mask the sides and back walls of the stage from sight. It should be large enough to mask without using borders or wings because they tend to destroy the illusion of limitless depth when the cyclorama represents the sky. At other times it can serve as a suitable screen for the projection of patterns of light.

2. Valuable as a full masking cyclorama is, it presents a definite problem of building design. When a scene is to be changed quickly the cyclorama must be "cleared" instantly for removing the present scene and bringing on the new one. This can best be accomplished by "flying" it, so the grid must be high enough to permit sufficient clearance under the cyclorama when it is raised. The grid should be 20′ to 30′ higher than the height of the cyclorama itself. This is a *must* where no compromise is effective.

3. Limited offstage space and limited height to the grid limit the variety of productions and plays that can be staged effectively. Most plays are written today for interior scenes because playwrights are justifiably dubious of the satisfactory staging of exterior scenes. Amateurs should not be expected to show greater ingenuity than the best professionals, yet the stages that most of the former are expected to use are more limited in space than the latter would even consider.

4. Architects should throw away most of their reference material. A most vicious circle has developed where one architect copies the mistakes of another, where equipment companies are forced to list outmoded equipment to supply the "sticks" because architects continue to specify it, and where the youthful glamour of another day secretly leads a middle-aged building committee to remember the day when footlights and borderlights, a few cutout wings and a backdrop were enough. Nor are most professional theatres, where the greatest number of seats on the smallest taxable area is of primary consideration, worth copying. European theatres with their large stages are questionable examples to follow because our production methods differ so completely. The outstanding community and college theatres come closest to providing good examples for plans and equipment.

5. Don't forget to include an adequate amount for lighting equipment in the budget. In addition to seats, carpets, curtains and furniture the stage is of no use unless it has lighting equipment and a flexible switchboard. Footlights and borderlights (generally just

two: one at the teaser and one to light the cyclorama) are essential but they comprise only a small part of a modern layout. Furthermore they should be made in short, easily portable sections so that they can be moved about. At least twelve spotlights of the proper wattage and type, five or six floods and projectors and cable, color mediums and lamps are more essential in modern practice than any footlights and borderlights.

6. A switchboard should have at least twenty-four dimmer control circuits, preferably more, up to forty-eight. Each control unit should have a variable capacity with certain limits, and aside from the house-light control there should be a free interconnection between the load circuits and the control circuits. The board should be mounted where the operator can see the stage easily.

7. Remember to provide plenty of positions where instruments can be mounted. Spotlights should generally be directed diagonally to the acting areas, forty-five degrees in plan and section. The front areas are best lighted from ceiling ports, not from the balcony front.

8. Provide shop space near to, and level with, the stage. Have an assembly room near the stage manager where the actors can be checked in. Allow plenty of wing space, areas at each side of the setting. Provide a signal system centering at the stage manager's desk where he can communicate with all parts of the stage. At this same desk put the control of the worklights and rehearsal lights.

9. Don't expect a stage 4′ above the auditorium level to justify a flat seating area. The stage should never be higher than 3′ above the auditorium floor, better 2½′. The auditorium should always have a sloping floor. Don't specify useless lighting equipment. Long border strips are necessary only where wing-and-border scenery (horse and buggy era) is still in use. Don't provide hardwood stage floors. Every architect should be made to try to work a stage screw into them, just once.

MARGARET WEBSTER, *director, actress.* Don't forget to include dressing rooms in your plans—in some theatres they have been omitted altogether, in many they are too far from the stage for quick changes. Put as many good dressing rooms with proper toilet and washing facilities as near the stage as possible (the toilets not too near!). And remember that even actors need air.

Obviously plenty of room to fly scenery, an adequate counterweight system and good storage space will be needed if repertory is contemplated, as well as rehearsal space in the building. If it is practicable, consider very seriously the enormous advantages of a revolving stage. Permanent switchboards and generous provision for front-of-the-house lighting are requisites. The orchestra pit should be so arranged that an apron stage, with steps leading up to it, can be used when needed. The door into the pit from below the stage should be big enough for actors in costume to walk in and out—not merely a hole to crawl through.

Lines of sight in the house should be carefully worked out so that every theatregoer can see as well as hear. Beware of dead spots in the orchestra. Seats should be silent, if possible, as should the heating equipment. It is hard for the actor to create illusion when accompanied by an obbligato of banging seats and exploding steam pipes—but this is not the architect's problem. One important item is the proscenium arch. Please do not make an elaborate, overwhelming proscenium that catches all the light and throws the whole show out of scale. A flexible proscenium would be splendid.

H. D. SELLMAN, *technical director, University of Iowa, co-author of* Stage Scenery and Lighting. In making new specifications don't follow old ones that are twenty years out of date. Much of the equipment going into theatres is old when installed. Be sure you are specifying well-designed, efficient, flexible equipment that meets the need of modern theatre practice.

The seating capacity, especially in school and college theatres, is more often too large than too small. Be sure to consult acoustical experts. Provide lighting instrument ports or false beams in auditorium ceilings to light the down-stage areas. Provide sufficient slope in the auditorium floor and good horizontal sightlines.

It is almost impossible to have too much offstage space. Enough space on both sides, so that a complete set of scenery mounted on a large wagon can be stored and rolled into place before the proscenium opening from either side, provides opportunity for an excellent scene-shifting device. Be sure to provide a well-equipped shop for scenic construction and plenty of storage space for scenery, properties and lighting equipment.

RICHARD WHORF, *actor*. Almost all shows use electrical off-stage noises today; often the recording is ruined because the audience hears the sound of the needle scratching. I would suggest having a small soundproof room off-stage where the disc recording machine can be placed, with a glass wall looking onto the stage. There should be permanent outlets, like plugs, for loudspeakers on the stage level at both sides and back of the stage wall, also high up in the flies and in the orchestra pit.

Upstairs there should be at least twelve dressing rooms, six on the first floor and six on the next, with one large room, which could be partitioned by sliding doors, for choruses, with washrooms and toilets at each end of the room.

The front of the balcony line should be constructed so that there would be a cut-back (about the width of two seats) where a man could sit and regulate the balcony lights, change them during intermission, etc., either that, or install a system of remote control, so that the gelatins can be changed and the lights focused without getting on a stepladder.

There should be entrances from the stage to the front of the house on both sides of the stage. This is a great convenience while lighting and rehearsing a show; the director and technicians have to go back and forth constantly.

THEODORE FUCHS, *Northwestern University, author of* Stage Lighting. Don't forget to make provision for a director's rehearsal control station at a convenient central point on the main floor of the auditorium, say a center-aisle seat in the twelfth row. This should consist of a box located near the floor beneath the seat in front of that selected as the station. This box should have (1) a duplex receptacle, wired to 115-volt current, into which a light can be plugged; (2) a standard telephone jack connected to similar jacks at the stage switchboard, the stage manager's station on the stage, each of the lighting ports in the auditorium ceiling, and the projection booth; and (3) a standard microphone jack connected to amplifier and loudspeaker facilities on the stage. The telephone circuit should be entirely apart from the regular inter-communicating phone system of the building. Such facilities will permit the director and his assistants to check their various plots and plans in the otherwise darkened auditorium, to keep in touch with the backstage workers and make adjustments without interrupting the rehearsals, and to issue directions to the actors on the stage without the usual shouting. In addition, it will permit contact during actual performances between the vantage point of the projection booth (or lighting ports) and important backstage positions.

LYNN FONTANNE, *actress.* The dressing room for the star should be at least 8′ by 12′ (wash basin and toilet adjoining). It should have a full-length mirror, also a large glass, about 3½′ square, over the dressing shelf, surrounded with 6 bulbs, 2 on top, 2 on each side; directly over the actor's head there should be a drop light with a powerful bulb. (This is important in adjusting the wig.) Wall space for two wardrobe trunks is necessary; also for a sofa for the actor to rest on between the matinee and evening performances. There should be wall plugs and shelf for electric water-heater; no closets but plenty of hanging space (you may have as many as ten changes of costume). Comfort or beauty is unessential; only concession to comfort is to have a rug which can be washed, actors are in their bare feet so much. Ventilation is vitally important; if theatre is air-cooled (and every theatre should be air-cooled today) dressing rooms also should be air-cooled; windows must be curtained and yet easy to open and close.

JAMES W. GRIEG, *stage carpenter for the Lunts.* Most stages are badly equipped for loading and unloading. There should be at least two doors, not smaller than 8′ by 12′, so that props can go in one door and scenery another. This is especially important when you are making quick jumps and have to catch a night train. Alleys ought to be big enough so that two trucks can be backed up at each door.

The counterweight system, alone, is not adequate for many legitimate shows. The best idea is to use a combination of counterweights and hemp lines, every other one a pipe line.

The whole stage area should be trapped *in small sections* so that a trap can be placed at any part of the stage without ripping up the rest, or so that a series of sections can be taken up to form a large trap. Beams and supporting girders should also be in sections so that they may be disconnected and a wide trap put in.

It is very important not to break up the stage with too many doors or obstructions, so that there is no place to stack scenery.

If possibe, there should be a corridor back of the stage, so that actors and technicians can get from side to side without crossing the stage.

A stage should be built under the sanitary conditions of a factory. A great many stages are so badly ventilated that factory workers would refuse to work in them, and entrances are in rat-ridden alleys.

LEE MITCHELL, *director, technician, Northwestern University.* In any theatre where more than one production is in preparation at a time, particularly in a festival or repertory theatre, the provisions for rehearsal space must be adequate. Not only does the company rehearsing need some other space to work in while the technical elements of the production are being assembled on the stage, but the companies for the following productions have the same need.

Rehearsal rooms should approximate the spatial conditions of performance, providing level floor space equal to that of the stage acting area, plus a 10′ margin all around, making a room altogether not less than 45′ by 35′. In order to avoid distortion of inflection in the actor's reading of lines, the acoustical properties of the room should resemble those of the auditorium as closely as possible. In addition, all the rehearsal rooms should be grouped about a common foyer in which the bulletin board is posted.

A large stock of scenic equipment is a desirable thing in any repertory theatre. Many well-equipped theatres today have shops capable of fabricating almost anything needed in the way of scenery or props. But few of these theatres provide anything like the amount of space necessary for storage, with the result that most of the settings must be destroyed when a show closes. Careful consideration should be given to storage in the planning of the theatre. Here are some of the requisites:

Size: the storage space must contain settings for a number of shows while the stage need hold but one. The area should be at least as great as that of the stage and as high as the highest flats—about 24′.

Location: as close as possible to the stage, preferably adjoining it.

Plan: longitudinal aisles at least 6′ clear running towards the stage. Between the aisles, the scene docks, shelves and cupboards.

Entrance: only one door is essential, on the stage side, but if two are possible, the second should open onto an outdoor covered loading platform in the alley. Doors should be at least 6′ wide and as high as possible.

Equipment: docks of 1¼″ pipe, 6′ deep, 2′ wide and 24′ high, for flats; racks of similar construction, 6′ deep, 2′ wide but not necessarily over 16′ high, for parallels and wagons up-ended; shelves, near the floor, 6′ deep and 7′ high, for the steps and practical pieces, with tackle for raising and shifting these heavy pieces; light sufficient to illuminate each shelf, rack and dock, bright enough to read newsprint easily.

MORTON EUSTIS, *author of* B'way, Inc., *etc.* The theatre section of the Building Code of the City of New York, drafted by a committee of prominent architects, engineers and stage technicians, contains the most modern requirements for safe and progressive theatre construction. Many of its clauses relate strictly to building in crowded city blocks, but all architects will find its provisions instructive and illuminating. There is no reason why architects designing a festival theatre should not consider the possibility of adapting the plans so that a similar theatre could be erected in a large city. The Building Code for the first time makes it possible for a theatre to become an economic unit of city life, supporting itself for 24 hours of the day and for 12 months of the year by rentals from shops, offices and apartments built around and over the theatre proper. Copies of the Code may be obtained from the office of the City Record, Room 2213, Municipal Building, New York City, for $3.50 plus postage. If writing, send cash or a certified check.

January 1939

* *

EDITH J. R. ISAACS

*

The New Plant

THE BUZZING, like the sound of many voices, that you hear behind almost every closed door you pass, is probably a meeting of some committee on post-war planning. They are everywhere, these committees, and hard at it. Many of them have their programs already far advanced. There are wonderful plans for post-war transportation, by road, by rail, by air; for new communities, happy little villages with trees and parks, good schools and no skyscrapers, built along roads that go not too far nor too fast but lead everywhere that you might want to go. There are committees on health and preventive medicine, on education in all its branches, on progressive museums and the development of the industrial arts, on music and printing. Many of these plans have already reached the brochure stage, some even the stage of experiment. Only the theatre, as usual, lags behind, with nothing done and little under way. This, then, is the time to begin.

What and where and for whom is the theatre to be after the war? Obviously that is a question that cannot be answered by a single scheme, for the theatre, as has been said a thousand times, is both a means and an end in education, an important form of recreation and a social force to be reckoned with. On each plane it must make its own plans and meet its own handicaps.

The way to begin, then, would seem to be to take stock; of what we have and what we want that we do not have, then of our practical opportunities, and finally of the difficulties that stand in the way of realizing them. But if this stock-taking is to be effective, the theatre must first be divided into the three forms whose purposes, techniques and material equipment are most divergent and each of which requires a separate and divergent approach: the professional theatre, the community theatre, the educational theatre. We should be wise at once to accept the fact that this is the order of artistic and social importance in which—in a perfected scheme—the various theatres must stand. We must never allow ourselves to doubt that the finest plays in the world's dramatic literature, performed by the most excellent artists, under the best possible professional conditions, before the most sympathetic (and therefore the most understanding) audiences would be the apex of all theatre, what the technicians have lately called the "end-product" of all theatre labors. Our professional theatre, however, has strayed so far from these ideal conditions, has become so tangled in the web of commercialism, that we are apt to forget that it is only because the theatre, at its best, is in many ways the most evocative of the arts that it is worth all our social and educational endeavor. Yet it is this *best* theatre that is our final aim—as artists, as citizens, as educators—to create, to value, to encourage and to use for our delight, our instruction, and to give wings to our imagination.

We hear a great deal of noble talk about a people's theatre as an end in itself, about houses big enough to seat "the masses," and performances by "the common man" for "the common man"; but it is not the number of people that see a play at one time nor the number of worthy citizens employed on the stage that give a performance its social and artistic value. And you cannot build a theatre or develop actors or playwrights or audiences by means of the multiplication table. Nor would it be an art theatre or an educational theatre worth its cost if you could. So let us admit at once that the finest professional theatre is our top artistic goal.

Experience should have taught us, however, that you cannot build either a skyscraper or an art from the top down. And our social and economic structure has changed so much in its relation to the theatre, since the days when the professional theatre could lay its own safe and sound foundations, that we must look for more modern ways, ways to build from the bottom up. The educational theatre and the community theatre, used to their best advantage, seem to be the soundest modern basis for fine theatre of every kind. They represent the best medium for the creation and organization of a large, sympathetic, knowing audience for the drama not only as literature but as played on a stage before an audience. They afford the means of training craftsmen in many theatre fields. They stimulate the imagination and the dexterity of the young artist and turn them toward the theatre before the mind and hand settle into other grooves. And all of this is apart from the already well-established value of the dramatic impulse in educational method and of theatre participation as a unifying agent in community life.

When you accept the fact that these three major forms of theatre require different foundations, you see almost at once that a major divergence is in the actual structure, the building that in each case is best adapted to the work in hand. There is no use in pushing aside this material basis as unimportant. It is a first consideration. Even the most cursory study of the subject indicates how haphazard has been our approach heretofore, and how much we might gain now by looking well before we leap, by thinking well about what we want before we build any kind of theatre whatever.

It should be obvious that, apart from monetary considerations, an educational theatre might be hampered or might hamper the full use of an educational structure of which it is a part, if it were as complicated as a building adequate for full professional production. But there are certain elements that must be right: sightlines, acoustics, proportions. Student players can suffer more from poor acoustics, wrong stage proportions (either too large or too small) than professional players who have been equipped to master such defects. And many school audiences have been disrupted or permanently discouraged from theatre attendance by bad sightlines. If the educational theatres are worth the effort and all the money that has been spent on buildings for them during the last twenty years, they are surely worth solid planning and intelligent construction. It is distinctly discouraging to see how many schools and colleges have been willing to budget enormous sums for their theatres and have wasted so much money on poor or outmoded or inadequate buildings and equipment, or on forms not suited to their educational needs. It must be said that the conventional school architect and hidebound trustees are the deadliest enemy in this field. Even today, with so many excellent examples of ways in which the school theatre problem has been solved, reports are still coming in of entirely inadequate plans for post-war theatres.

You cannot plan a high-school or college building along conventional lines and then—after all the offices and classrooms and laboratories and washrooms are provided for—tuck in a stage and audience chamber in some leftover space. A school theatre, to be worth any space at all, must be a workshop, both the stage and the auditorium; the active working spaces, stage house, dressing rooms, scene loft, and so forth, are a part of its integrity. There are only two ways to begin planning for it, depending on whether the building is to be a part of a single educational structure, like a high school, or a separate building closely associated with another educational structure—like the Shorewood auditorium, for example, in relation to the Shorewood high school. If it is to be a part of the high-school building, the architect should know two things before he begins his drawings: first, what are the absolute essentials required for the work of the department; second, (since the stage and its accessories may not be in use during all of every day) to what other purposes in the regular school planning it can advantageously be put: lectures, for example, programs of visual education, student and faculty meetings, and many musical uses. Beginning at this end, you increase to its fullest extent the usefulness of the drama department's space allotment, instead of judging the department's needs by the opportunities left over after everything else is taken care of. And your result will cost you no more.

If the educational theatre is to be a separate building, its problem is both broadened and simplified. In many ways, it approaches the functioning of the community theatre. It is, in fact, in most towns and small cities and in the suburbs of larger cities, the only form of community theatre, and one that has been increasingly successful in its operation as the years go by. The building's uses will, of course, still be based on the educational need that it must serve, but this will be not only the need of the student body but of adult education and often of community recreation and information. There is usually in such a theatre, when it is well planned, equipment for motion pictures, for radio (and soon no doubt for television), for concerts and dance recitals, for lectures and forums and town meetings. In fact, the chief difference between planning structurally for a separate school theatre and for a community theatre is that the school theatre, since it is financed on an educational budget, must "pay out" primarily in educational benefits, while the community theatre is faced, to some extent at least, with something of the same problem that faces the professional theatre, namely that it must "pay out" not only in cultural but in economic value received.

There is another difference between the educational and community theatre which is not exactly structural and yet should influence both the site and the structure. An educational theatre is by its nature a part of the educational unit in any community, even where it serves the community for more general purposes. As a matter of fact, where it does so serve, it is usually a part of a neighborhood in whose life education is apt to be the focal point. A community theatre as a separate entity should by preference be close to the homes of one or more of the other arts, the concert hall, the library, the art gallery. It should be near a secondary rather than a main shopping center, have good transportation and parking facilities. The reasons for most of this is clear. Proximity to other art interests is highly recommended as a way to break down the separation between art audiences so prevalent today. A special interest in art or in music should not preclude an active interest in the theatre, and if the *places* are within easy reach of one another (especially if there are good restaurants and some shopping possibilities nearby), the *people* will more easily find common ground. This matter of site also touches the matter of financing. It should be obvious that there is nothing in the nature of theatre that makes it any less noble if it is associated with industries that help to make it a self-supporting venture. Every community theatre should, to its great advantage, house rehearsal and dance studios, a bookshop, an art shop, a first-class restaurant and a half-a-dozen other related businesses that come easily to mind. These would help to pay for the maintenance of the building, its insurance and taxes and all the other overhead charges that so often make the difference between success and failure in a community group. For no matter how high-minded the producer and players and board of directors may be, the artistic elements will reflect the effect of the box-office and of the theatre's real-estate balance sheet.

When it comes to the professional theatre, this matter of making the theatre pay as a business takes first place in our cities, and there is no use any longer pretending that it does not. It is today an accepted fact that if anything but hit plays are to live in New York, for example, either they must be endowed by some outside interest like the movies, or the buildings that house the theatres must be productively employed for more than a few hours a day, a few days a week, a few months a year. The older building codes made it almost impossible to build a theatre in a way to finance itself wholly or in large part as a building enterprise; they were mindful of the danger to public life and health and security involved in crowded auditoriums, miles of lighting cables and many pieces of equipment, materials not too securely fireproofed, and the gusts that can sweep up through a high stage-house. But all of these matters were brought under control before the motion-picture theatres crowded out the legitimates as centers of public interest, with the result that motion-picture theatres do not suffer from the limitations formerly placed on playhouses. Just before the depression, however, a new building code was passed in New York which makes it quite possible today to erect business buildings of which safe, modern theatres are a component part. Every city that is big enough to make a professional commercial theatre pay should study the New York Building Code and see that its own code has come up to date on all these matters. This is of first importance. A second practical device is a standard stage and standard lighting equipment to cut down the tremendous expense now involved in hauling scenery and equipment around the country.

More important than either of these is the reestablishment of the idea of a theatre unit as a permanent, year-round business, with a permanent home and a permanent staff that is on a year-round and not a weekly basis of pay. This last is a far mightier bunker than appears on the surface, for it means upsetting the present conventions of the theatre unions although the results are all to their advantage. It will take brave work and belongs only to men and women so firmly established as labor's friends that they can face the present corruption and tyranny without fear of revolt. The cause of the evils in the present theatre set-up lies definitely in theatre leadership of past generations. Yet the present turmoil among labor groups, themselves acknowledging no common leadership, is of all things the most damaging to the art and to the industry today. A few smash hits a year can survive on the present basis but they will not make a living for many men at any wage. Nor do feather-bedding and stand-ins add to final security.

It is humbling to admit that we can no longer say that four boards and a passion will make a theatre, or look to Epidaurus or the theatre of Dionysus or to the Shakespeare's Globe Theatre and say that this is all we need. Today's theatre is a part of our complex social and economic life. The more we allow its exteriors to follow the conventions of the time, the freer we shall leave our stages. But the material conventions we follow must not be those that were good enough for our fathers and our grandfathers but only those which we have agreed—in modern architecture, in electricity, in acoustics, in heating and cooling—are good enough for us in our homes and in our public buildings.

July 1944

* *

JO MIELZINER

*

Make the Theatre Building Pay

DURING THE PAST TWENTY-FIVE YEARS a limited few intelligently designed theatre buildings have been erected. Without exception, these new structures have housed every type of production, with the startling exception of the professional metropolitan theatre. So-called "Broadway" has been the most neglected of all.

Although no immediate legitimate theatre buildings are in the process of construction, plans are already on drawing boards. There is no more fitting place than the pages of THEATRE ARTS to cry out a warning to the master minds who will mold the legitimate theatres of tomorrow. Be they architects, realty speculators or just sound businessmen, my plea is: Don't let another wave of inadequate and unglamorous theatres spring up as they did in the 1920's.

This appeal is not to the patron of the arts who might encourage a subsidized project but to the businessmen who, without proper guidance, can so easily cripple and stifle our professional theatre by erroneously assuming that a well-designed house for the drama must necessarily be a losing venture.

I propose to deal only in generalities, not in a specific plan. My plea is for a different attitude toward the problem during the pre-blueprint stage of discussion between the investor versus the inventor —the backer versus the architect.

Our first consideration is the fresh approach to the function of the building which houses the drama. Theatre exists only when a real audience is present. Time and again I have witnessed a technically perfect performance during a rehearsal which seemed completely different the following evening in the presence of an audience. The difference was not necessarily on the stage side of the footlights—in fact, I am inclined to think the change was a psychological one that happened the moment I became a member of the body of the audience. Theatre is a communal experience. The understanding of this is essential to understanding the theatre. The most uninhibited person enjoys a fuller, richer laugh in the presence of 700 equally amused spectators than he did the preceding night, sitting alone at a dress rehearsal. Therefore the half of the theatre that houses the audience is supremely important.

Functionally, this half is merely a place where the audience can be sheltered from the weather, where lighting may be controlled, and with seats on which the audience may sit. But this functional definition is not enough. Being an emotional experience, theatregoing is, in a sense, a ceremony. The excitement of the theatre should begin the moment the audience approaches the entrance to the building which houses the drama. Everything to make the evening an occasion is as important to the fulfillment of the experience as giving the actor a glamorous setting.

The truth is, the performance is really on both sides of the footlights. The ticket window, the hat-check concession and the lobby are as important as the seats and the auditorium itself. Whether the performance is comedy or drama, the essential appeal is one of release from the actualities of daily life. Very few people go for purely intellectual or academic enjoyment. The sooner you take the audience out of the humdrum world, the more complete the enjoyment of the evening, and the less tedious and more exciting the delay awaiting the raising of the curtain or the necessary intermission time.

As for the other half of the playhouse—the stage—it is, functionally, simply the place where the performers are so placed that the audience may see and hear them. But to heighten the art of the theatre we add the visual and aural arts, costumes, properties, scenery, lights, music, plus all the technical equipment to facilitate the handling of these compliments to the drama and all the mechanical equipment of dressing rooms, rehearsal space and the like to aid the performers. Adequate storing and handling facilities for productions other than the one currently playing are additional imperatives. If you gave the theatre all these elements without restrictions, you would have an ideal theatre, on the performer's side of the footlights.

What do we have today in these two halves to house our legitimate theatre? A little over twenty years ago in New York something happened that illustrates better than pages of description the state of the legitimate theatre house as Broadway knows it today. A man interested in so-called theatre development secured a plot of land on 4X Street. Business was booming. It was an ideal time to build a theatre. He had an architect and a contractor and a business manager. The theatre was put up in no time flat. The plan, if there was one, was apparently based on the belief that if you could squeeze in a few more seats the theatre would be that much more successful.

On the day the building was completed, the owner called in a friend who had some professional knowledge of the theatre. He was a producer, and he was the first person with professional knowledge to be consulted. Compliments were passed on the magnificence of the exterior, on the lobby, where thirty or forty people would be as crowded as if on a subway train. The inspection proceeded. The first rude shock came when the visiting party went backstage. The innocent question was asked, "Where are the dressing rooms?" The contractor looked at the architect, the architect looked at the client, and the client said, "You boys better get busy. We've got to have dressing rooms by Wednesday."

This is not a fable—it actually happened in the city of New York. During the same visit an inspection was made of the cellar under the stage, a place usually reserved for the storage of technical properties. The professional friend, being a little embarrassed at having pointed out the total absence of dressing rooms was delighted to find something to praise. There, under the stage, standing almost eight feet high and some twenty feet long, was a magnificent prop rock. It was so realistic and beautiful in detail that he walked over and gave it a slight kick. The contact was an unpleasant one for he was kicking a piece of good old Manhattan Island granite. The contractors responsible for excavations had been a little too hasty in their investigation of the terrain, and although the building proper had been dug out without blasting, this bit of granite, to their relief, was found to be in a position which "didn't matter anyway" as it was under the stage!

I tell this true story not because it was unusual in the twenties but because it reflects the regrettably small amount of thought and planning that went into our legitimate theatres. The basic plan was a rat race between theatre-seat salesmen enthusiastically backed up by business managers, as opposed to the architect and what few professional advisors were ever called in. Not only were auditoriums crowded, with not the slightest understanding of the relation between the audience and the stage, but the stage itself became smaller, narrower in width and shallower in depth. For a nation with our proud record of architectural and engineering achievements, we have the worst theatres of any country in the world.

Like many other fellow designers, my heart sinks when I turn the first page of a new manuscript and read the author's description of the setting—"As far as the eye can reach, the sunlit haze of the Arizona desert stretches in all directions"—and all I can see is a brick wall with a radiator pipe twenty-five feet and six inches away from the curtain.

Our theatre buildings are, to a great extent, owned and managed by people whose interests and training are essentially in real estate and commercial investments, with very little technical and professional knowledge of the problems of theatre-producing.

The approaches to our theatres are appallingly bad in their psychological effect. There is hardly a single theatre with a lobby large enough to hold thirty percent of its audience. Crowded and inadequate box-office facilities tend to shorten the tempers of box-office treasurers and make all the more unpleasant the already difficult problem of getting tickets at the window. Checkrooms are not large enough to hold ten percent of the hats and coats, even if the audience wants to check them knowing that space does not permit a decent handling of the problem at the end of a performance. The average space between the rows of seats is so narrow that it discourages patrons from going out in the intermission if they have to climb over neighbors who are seated. All these things are physical and psychological deterrents from the full enjoyment of the evening.

How much wiser and more progressive are the planners and designers of most of our moving-picture theatres. They discovered years ago that the audience thrives on a presentation and revels in the luxuries of comfort. Did you ever hear anyone say, "Let's go to the X legitimate theatre and see the play there" as they say, "Let's go to the Music Hall (or the Roxy or the Paramount)"? Many movie patrons get attached to a certain theatre, even down in the Roaring Forties. They will fight the traffic problem because they know they will have comfort and luxury once they get there.

Now the solution. I will forego details of technical or mechanical improvements backstage as well as many obvious improvements to the front of the theatre. But to the pessimist who says that if legitimate theatres hardly pay now, with conditions as they are, there is no hope of making money on an ideal theatre, I reply: I believe that not only can the ideal theatre be built to give every sense of luxury and comfort that the legitimate theatre deserves, but this theatre can be incorporated in an architectural unit capable of earning a healthy return on the investment.

We must have a completely new point of view toward theatre building of tomorrow. The first thing to point out is the limited potential earning power of our average theatre buildings today because they are available to the public only *about twenty-four hours each week!* In the same neighborhood a moving-picture theatre is averaging over four times that number of potential income-earning hours. In other words, the theatre is only working three hours per day, six days a week, and even now, in this boom period, only averaging thirty-five weeks per year. In the same location a movie house is using a fourteen-hour day, seven-day week, fifty-two-week year. With the same approximate investment in the building a moving-picture theatre has six times the number of money-earning hours as its legitimate neighbor.

We must find a new concept for the theatre building which will make it available to the public fifty-two weeks a year and at least twelve hours a day, or more. We know that the theatre is a lure; we know that when people buy a ticket to the theatre it creates a mood of both excitement and relaxation. Therefore, why not make of the theatre a focal point for other outlets associated with an evening of relaxation?

I can envision a couple from Scarsdale driving into town for dinner and the theatre. Mr. Smith has bought a pair of tickets for this Theatre of Tomorrow. These tickets are not only theatre tickets. As he steps out of his car, a uniformed attendant takes a section of his ticket, which becomes his check for the parking of his car for the evening. They enter an enormous lobby, which has already earned its keep as a display showcase of luxury goods during the eight preceding daylight hours. From the lobby they enter an attractive restaurant and bar. Part of Mr. Smith's ticket stub is surrendered to the headwaiter, where a table has been reserved in the name of Mr. and Mrs. Smith. Their wraps have been checked on another section of the ticket.

The intermission lobby is large enough to hold the entire audience, not packed in like sardines but free to move about, enjoying concessions of food and drinks. The displays in the lobby can reflect many of the qualities which people admire in a walk down Fifty-seventh Street or Madison Avenue. In what better place, and to what more receptive spectators, could you show luxurious wearing apparel or jewelry or exhibitions of fine arts? Again the space in this super-lobby is not going to depend on two ten-minute intermissions to earn its upkeep. It is large enough for dancing and for parties, being also adjacent to catering service and bars. After midnight it might be turned into an ideal night club. At the end of an evening's performance, if Mr. Smith and his wife so desire, their stub might also entitle them to this supper and night club.

Examine the ground plan of a currently licensed theatre and notice the enormous unused but necessary area given over to fire alleys. There is nothing in the Safety Code that prevents an imaginative designer from turning that area into an additional attraction to the audience and revenue to the owner. Both the stage proper and the auditorium itself need not remain idle during all the twenty-one hours a day when not used as a legitimate theatre. If the stage is sufficiently large to handle and store both current and repertory productions, the same theatre could be used for concerts and meetings on non-matinee days, for fashion shows, trade shows, conventions.

During the hours between midnight and four in the morning, hundreds of thousands of dollars are spent in a city like New York in converted rat holes called night clubs. True, they are a hangover of the Prohibition era, but you cannot tell me that if you had a choice between an over-crowded, badly aired so-called "hot spot," as it exists today, and a magnificent theatre-into-night-club (a conversion which could be made in a half-hour) there would be any question as to which you would choose and which investment paid off best.

This theatre building naturally would take a much larger plot of ground than the average metropolitan theatre now occupies. However, its function as a focal point of attention would make the building a natural location for a hotel or a business building, combined with retail stores. Luxury trades would gain enormously with contact of this sort in very much the same way (and to a larger degree) as the arcades in Rockefeller Center gain prominence from their location in that focal center. There was a time when business buildings were named after towers that attracted attention by their extreme height. Why not attract that attention—and therefore business—by the glamour, the beauty and the popularity associated with a fine theatre center?

Having designed scenery for actors for the past twenty-two years in New York, I have begun to realize that the audience has been a bit neglected. They, too, need a setting in glowing lights and glamorous costumes. The theatre is a brilliant jewel, whose setting today is a little smeared and faded. But the jewel itself is sound and bright, and a new setting would immeasurably increase both its brilliance and its worth.

June 1946

IX · RADIO AND TELEVISION

* * *

NORMAN CORWIN

*

The Sovereign Word

SOME NOTES ON RADIO DRAMA

RADIO IS such a young medium, in every respect save its jokes, that nobody has a right to sound like the Voice of God on any phase of the subject, especially the dramatic. Its techniques are still developing, its forms slowly jelling, its literature is only lately hatched. Most of its tenets, principles and claims are tentative, but the few which look as though they might hang on for a while are sufficiently interesting to bear scrutiny.

First, there is no audience in the world which attaches more value to the spoken word than an audience of the blind—and a radio audience is just that. If a listener at home is moved to laugh or cry, to experience interest or suspense, the effect has been wrought by words alone. There may have been a little help from sound or music, but that support is incidental and supplementary. There is no help at all from sets, lighting, composition, gesticulation, costume, make-up or sex appeal. There are no camera angles, dissolves, multiple exposures or rear projections. The fluttering hands of a Zasu Pitts are frozen; the rolling eyes of a Groucho Marx roll no farther than the microphone; the profile of a Barrymore is wasted on the engineers. You can't make a smash ending to a radio drama by showing a picture of a hand reaching for a butterfly.

Since in radio drama the word has no visual collaboration, it bears the entire burden of communication and therefore assumes far more responsibility and authority than it does in any other dramatic medium. It is story-teller, image-maker, character-delineator, set-builder. If the word fails, the play fails.

In Archibald MacLeish's *The Fall of the City,* the ANNOUNCER, describing the expectancy of the people of the city, says:

> They are milling around us like cattle that smell death.
> The whole square is whirling and turning and shouting.
> One of the ministers raises his arms on the platform.
> No one is listening: now they are sounding drums:
> Trying to quiet them likely: No! No!
> Something is happening: there in the far corner:
> A runner: a messenger: staggering: people are helping him:
> People are calling: he comes through the crowd; they are quieter.
> Only those on the far edge are still shouting:
> Listen! He's here by the ministers now! He is speaking. . . .

These exciting lines, spoken against the movement and noise of a crowd, created a powerful feeling of realism. Had the lines been weak, the whole effect of mass action would have been ruined and the scene made ridiculous. The entire play was a striking demonstration of plasticity in the use of a crowd—something that, up to then, the cinema alone, and then only at its best moments, had been able to achieve.

This dependence of drama upon the word is not especially notable in the theatre, and not all true of the cinema. The morning ablutions of Jeeter Lester are entirely wordless, yet there is no better characterization in the play. The "Now might I do it pat" soliloquy in *Hamlet* is unnecessary. Everything that goes through Hamlet's mind while the King prays could be indicated by face and body and by the handling of sword and scabbard. There are examples aplenty in the theatre. As for the movies, it's almost too obvious to point out that pictures can totally ignore language (as they did for years) and still be effective.

Not unrelated to the stress on word-value is the fact that radio is the greatest disciplining force in modern playwriting. It is a good thing for a man to write simply and clearly, and to write for radio one must do both. The medium requires simplicity, and this has nothing whatever to do with the intellectual level of its audience. It has to do with the normal physical limitations of the ear—the inability of the ear to regress, as the eye does on the printed page.

There is no retina of the ear to carry over syllables as the eye does images; hence the radio writer's imagery must never be too intense, or shot at the listener too fast. It must be directly communicable and easily assimilated, or it has no right to be on the air. The tightly packed imagery of a poem like Mallarmé's *L'Après-Midi d'un Faune* wouldn't have a ghost of a chance.

Writers for other dramatic media can be far more expansive, can take more time, can diffuse more than the radio writer because they know that eventually, when their work is produced, an audience will come for the sole purpose of seeing it. The good people will sit quietly in their seats to the end, unless the performance is too terrible to endure. But the radio writer knows that he must contest with a million attention-wreckers in a million homes. He knows that his audience, to the last man, is subject to the distractions of the home. Phones ring, doors slam, babies cry, there are papers to pick up, windows to look out of, chores to do.

Nor do the dramatists of stage and screen have to hurry out of the way of the next program, as the radiowright does. The strictness of radio's time system imposes a very special kind of discipline on the writer, and this is not because of the exigencies of network operation, either. It just happens that an hour is time enough for any radio drama; indeed, too long for most. The reason is that radio's pacing is naturally shorter; its time compressed; its action foreshortened.

Once, in a documentary script about railroads, I had the problem of dramatizing the setting of the world's speed record for a steam locomotive. The sequence began with the engine idling in the terminal, ready for its run. After getting under way, the speed was supposed to accelerate to 120 miles per hour. The actual time required for an acceleration from 0 to 120 m.p.h. would be many minutes, but 40 seconds of airtime was more than enough. It was not a matter of exercising dramatic license; it was simply recognition of the fact that the ear accepted 40 seconds without any question. Another 10 seconds and the scene would have collapsed into dullness. I mention this because, by the same mechanics, a script longer than an hour would wear out its welcome. Any scene *within* a script cannot run very long without becoming static. The attention must be trapped at the beginning and held constantly, for with radio it's a continual scramble to have and hold listeners, to win them away from opposition stations, and to keep them won.

It is good discipline for a playwright to make his transitions so clear, to keep his characters so distinct and his action so lucid that they can be seen by blind men—and that is what the radio writer must do. Unlike the stage play, which so often begins vaguely and gets going only toward the end of the first act, the radio play starts socko. The more arresting, the better. *The Fall of the City* begins that way:

> Ladies and gentlemen:
> This broadcast comes to you from the city.

and MacLeish's *Air Raid:*

> When you hear the gong sound
> The time will be
> Ten seconds past 2 A.M. precisely.

My own *They Fly Through the Air* puts it right up to the listener with the opening lines:

> Assume it is morning.
> You know what mornings are.

In *Seems Radio Is Here to Stay,* the same thing happens:

> Do we come on you unaware,
> Your set untended?
> Do you put down your paper to lift an ear,
> Suspend what you were just about to say,
> Or stay the fingertip that could snap shut
> The traps of night between us?

In *The Plot to Overthrow Christmas,* there is no time wasted:

> Did you hear about the plot to overthrow Christmas?
> Well, gather ye now, from Maine to the Isthmus
> Of Panama . . . .

Gibson-Gilsdorff's *The Ghost of Benjamin Sweet:*

Bolt the doors. Fasten the windows.
Cut out the lights. Sit down quietly
in the dark. (*Long Pause*) And meet
the ghost of Benjamin Sweet.

Max Wylie's adaptation of Wilbur Daniel Steele's *A Drink of Water:*

It is about Clare Mayo that we are concerned now.

I do not say that all radio plays must begin like a bat out of hell, but it helps. The running start is much to be preferred over such a coldly visual opening as:

It was cold, the sea was gray, and there were fresh northwesterly winds roiling the surface. Mr. Holmes could not look back, not even for an instant because the long swirls, unbroken as yet but running fast and high, with glassy bubbles breaking at the peaks now and then, held his frightened eyes. He became aware of the cook, close to him, as the lifeboat wallowed, panicked by the heavy seas. With all his strength Mr. Holmes held to the tiller, which might at any second be wrenched from his grasp by the pressure of the rushing water against its rudder blade.

This is how short stories begin, not radio plays. The script from which this is quoted turned out to be fine entertainment from that point on, but it ran the risk of losing listeners who don't like to hear a long description before action gets under way at the outset of a play.

It is a fact seldom considered that radio has contributed the greatest stimulation to dramatic techniques since the invention of the movies. It has taken the ancient device of the narrator and developed it to points never reached before, such as in *The Fall of the City, Air Raid, They Fly Through the Air, The Plot to Overthrow Christmas, John Brown's Body* and *So This Is Radio.* In the first two of these MacLeish cast the narrator as a spot announcer and gave him a realism against which the symbolism of the action stood in relief. In *They Fly Through the Air* the procedure was quite the reverse. The realism of the action was superimposed by the omniscient narrator, who enjoyed not only a power of commentary but a mobility whereby he could quit one scene of action for another, or for none at all, without affecting time values in any way. By this I mean that the narrator could say to the unhearing crew of a bombing plane:

> Excuse us; we'll go on ahead to see.
> Allow us to precede you.
> We flash ahead
> As fast as thought anticipates a deed
> And here we are: the city:—

The narrator later finds that while he has been inspecting life in an apartment building in the city the plane has caught up with him and so he says:

> We are caught-up with; the plane is fast.

In *The Plot to Overthrow Christmas* a "sotto voce" character appears throughout to kid the principals, a few radio clichés and himself. In one scene, when the great villains of history are drawing lots at a meeting in Hell to decide who is going to be sent to earth to assassinate Santa Claus, SOTTO VOCE comes in over the background noise and says:

> This is your old friend Sotto Voce
> Visiting down where it's eternal noce.
> (Noce is Spanish for night, you know—
> Merely a reference just to show
> That English isn't all I have to go
> By.)
> Oh, well, I guess I've missed my calling.
> I should have been a lobbyist. You see, I'm stalling
> To give them time to finish the voting.
> —Let's see—the weather—Now I'm quoting
> The Daily Hellion: "Continued heat
> Both overhead and under feet—
> Fresh and moderate gasses blowing
> Up to gale force, and then going
> North by westerly—Light showers
> Of brimstone toward the evening hours."

That's what it says here—I'm not fibbing.
How'm I doing with my ad-libbing?
This is a thing Bob Trout would have fun with.
Say—the drawing should soon be *done* with.
We expect the results at any moment now—
As soon as—

and then he is interrupted by a great uproar announcing the decision.

In the adaptation of *John Brown's Body* multiple narrators were used; one representing Jack Ellyat of the North, another representing Clay Wingate of the South, a third representing Melora Vilas, a fourth speaking directly for the poet, Benét, himself.

In *So This Is Radio* the narrator was assisted by a "running footnote-maker" who helped clear up difficult technical points in an involved exposition of Special Events techniques in radio. Every time the principal narrator said something which was not quite clear, the footnote-maker would sound a buzzer and call the narrator on the carpet for an oversight.

Whether the theatre and motion picture are indebted to radio for new techniques of sound and writing is a matter that may well be debated, but I doubt very much whether a picture like Sacha Guitry's *The Story of a Cheat* could have come about without the inspiration of radio narration. One might say the same thing about Pare Lorentz's *The River* and *The Plow That Broke the Plains;* and it is interesting to note that the deliberately radiogenic form of *They Fly Through the Air* was considered sufficiently adaptable to the movies to be bought by Hollywood. Also bought by Hollywood were the services of radio's pioneering technician, Irving Reis, on the basis of the general originality of his sound and dramatic work in radio.

The stage is indebted to radio for microphone techniques, both in the use of sound and voice, although in both departments its operation is usually ineffectual. This is largely because stagehands or electricians are running the control boards instead of trained sound men.

As for stimulation in the department of writing, the drama now finds itself with new forms: the fifteen-, thirty-, forty-five- and 60-minute compressed play; the radio "strip" serial, with its most distinct structure; the "experimental" piece, such as the play based on sound alone; the play in which not a single sound effect was used; the surrealist show *Surrealism: from Ooh to Aah* produced by William N. Robson; the "augmentation and orchestration" of poetry as in last year's *Words without Music* series, and so forth.

Lately, writers have been perked up to the point where they are trying their hand at new radio ideas. Maxwell Anderson and Kurt Weill are, at this writing, working on a trilogy of "Radioratorios," a new form of music-drama for the *Pursuit of Happiness* program; William Saroyan, Alfred Kreymborg, Stephen Vincent Benét, Lord Dunsany, Dorothy Parker, Arthur Kober and Eric Knight are a few others who have already tried their hands—with varying success. But I believe it unlikely that radio can look to many of the established writers of this generation for topnotch work, since most of them know little of the medium's special requirements and are unaware of its literary possibilities.

I have no doubt that once radio gets around to paying the right kind of money for the right kind of scripts, it will begin to develop a literature as great as that of the theatre, but this cannot happen before adequate facilities are placed in the hands of writers sincerely interested in the medium. In the long run, the great things will come from men who will undertake to study and develop the relatively primitive craft of microphone-drama and who will approach their work wholly without condescension.

February 1940

* *

VAL GIELGUD

*

The Actor and the Broadcast Play

NO PLAY whether broadcast or not exists by writing or production alone. People claim that there are certain plays which should only be read, and a few daring spirits have essayed the theory that the actor should be no more than a robot in the hands of the producer and the author. But whatever may be the case when dealing with ordinary plays, the broadcast play is not and should not be written in order to be read. It must be heard and therefore it must be acted. It seems therefore worth while considering the conditions under which the actor in a broadcast play must work and the methods he must use. As a corollary some form of answer should be found to the question whether the normal actor in stage plays makes the best actor in broadcast plays.

Many factors reconcile the stage actor to the trials and difficulties of his calling. What of his colleague in the broadcasting studio? Here we have no footlights, no limelights, no costumes and no scenery; merely a rather large, rather bare room with one or several microphones in it, and with an audience invisible and intangible—in the circumstances almost unimaginable; an audience which cannot cheer, or laugh, or thrill the player by that astonishing silence which sometimes grips a great theatre in the face of a magnificent performance. Romanticism here has no trappings on which to feed; make-believe is rendered ten thousand times more difficult. The applause has vanished and the actor may never know whether he has thrilled even a single member of his audience. That audience may have numbered millions; it may have numbered dozens. He does not know, and however much he cares it must not affect his work. He does not even have to learn his words. He reads from a script. He is produced, after the first one or two original readings, by a voice issuing from a loudspeaker belonging to his director in a room in a different part of the building. In scenes with the several members of the cast, he must address not them but the microphone. He must move to and fro not as emotion guided by a producer bids him, but as the unsympathetic tones of a balancing engineer direct. Much of the play—I speak now of British broadcasting—not only may be but usually is performed in a studio different from that in which the actor is. He cannot hear those other segments. The various pieces are drawn together by the producer at his dramatic control panel, and there mixed and sent out for transmission; but during the intervals the actor cannot hear the play go on. He must wait in dreary silence for a green light to flash in the studio to give him the cue and then he must take up his part as firmly as if he were entirely conversant with the running of the complete play.

In short, he is part of a machine; and though it should be the job of every broadcasting producer to do everything he can to get the personalities of his actors across the microphone to his audience and to exploit those personalities to the utmost of their ability and his, yet the actor still remains part of the machine. There are, of course, exceptions, as in the case of Herman Kesser's radio monologue *Nurse Henrietta* when Miss Lilian Harrison entirely swamped a play little more than mediocre by the force of her personality and of her superb microphone performance. Only recently Mr. Leon Lion has broken through all the disabilities of broadcast acting by his interpretation of the roles of Jekyll and Hyde in a specially adapted version of Stevenson's novel. And in one of the best microphone plays, Johannsen's *Brigade Exchange,* Mr. Ralph Richardson achieved a personal success as memorable as that of the play itself. There will often be outstanding individual performances, but it is not on these primarily that the significance of the ordinary broadcast play depends. It is on an almost machine-like keenness of uptake and precision in attack; unflagging attention and loyal teamwork. Where the exploitation of personality can be achieved it is of course of the greatest value. But to achieve this with the voice alone is a task formidable in itself; to find plays in which such exploitation can be legitimately and profitably used is a matter of extreme difficulty.

It is evident, then, that the professional actor who works in a broadcasting studio is sacrificing much for the sake of experiencing a new thing. He is of course the first person to whom the broadcast producer turns, because all acting—whether it is broadcast or not—is based on the same principles, and the experienced actor has a practical knowledge of these principles and their application which no amateur, however startling his voice quality or vivid his natural intelligence, can hope to achieve. Most actors in broadcast plays, in Great Britain at any rate, are also professional actors; though it is fair to add that as a rule the broadcast actor who is not a stage actor, when he *is* successful, is the most successful of all. But the backbone of our casts remains and in my opinion is likely to remain the professional actor.

It is astonishing how quickly the professional actor adapts himself to the difficulties of the microphone and to the lack of personal contact with his audience. It must be remembered that, whereas on the stage the actor must get his effects in such a way that they shall be obvious all over the theatre and his words audible in the back row of the gallery, when he comes to the microphone he is dealing with an instrument which exaggerates every inflection enormously and reveals insincerity or histrionicism mercilessly. An actor who may have been trained in the tradition of thinking in terms of the back of the gallery must suddenly think of himself as acting to an audience of millions, each of whom is at his very elbow. And not only is the microphone, in itself as it were, all the members of his invisible audience, but it is also the other members of his cast. This difficulty of lack of mutual support owing to the inability of two actors to play "against" each other, has been obviated to some extent in England by the provision of double or triple branched microphones, by the use of which the actors can at any rate be placed vis à vis during certain scenes.

Apart from anything else the physical exertion of acting in broadcast plays is very considerable; far more so in the event of a big part than in the ordinary theatre. The preservation of absolute silence, the acute concentration, the lack of intervals (for most broadcast plays are played straight through, or the audience is liable to get restless and switch off), induce a feeling of stress and fatigue even in studios ventilated on the most modern principles. In the more old-fashioned studios it was by no means unusual to see a cast working in shirt sleeves, and leaving the studio at the end of the performance with a look on their faces familiar to all of us who have seen people landing after a rough crossing of the English Channel.

But I do not wish to paint too gloomy a picture. In spite of the machine-like qualities inseparable from the environment, in spite of the lack of color and applause, the work has a fascination of its own. No actor with a real love of his work can resist the tremendous challenge to justify his art by means of his voice alone. This greatest difficulty that might well appal usually stimulates. And as more and more actors gain experience of the microphone so the standard of broadcast acting continually improves. Again, though the actor may be deprived of the applause of a thousand or so, he is usually an optimist and finds it difficult to withstand the temptation of thinking that the audience which he cannot hear or see, split up into its units by their several firesides, must be millions at the least. That surely is a harmless gratification of normal human vanity.

February 1931

DAVIDSON TAYLOR

*

Good Radio

THERE HAS BEEN a good deal of discussion as to whether radio is a medium for artistic endeavor. Whether it is or not, it is certain that good radio, like good music, may exist at many levels, and is distinguishable from bad by its harmony with the essential traits of the medium.

Only a fraction of the people employed by radio are concerned with producing programs; yet the lifeblood of radio is the broadcast, and radio is known to the public overwhelmingly by what goes on the air. The nature of these radio programs differs in several ways from products of other means of communication and media of expression. Perhaps an analysis of these essential differences may form a basis for critical evaluation of radio.

Network broadcasting in this country is only about fifteen years old. Before they could become articulate about it, it was necessary for those employed in the industry to realize that they were dealing with a medium which had peculiar capacities and limitations.

Radio did not know how to profit immediately from its handicaps, yet from the start it gave rise to certain products which were unique. One of these products was the ad-lib news broadcast. Oral reporting of events while they were occurring was something new. Even before men were trained for this work, an occasional gifted announcer was able to deal plastically with the processes of time before his eyes. It soon became obvious, however, that only the feature story adapted itself to this kind of handling; large events must be reported with preparation. It is exceptional for a William L. Shirer to be on the scene with a live microphone as Hitler walks into the railway car at Compiègne where the armistice is signed. Generally speaking, the panorama of decisive human activity is too great for a microphone, with telephone line attached, to roam over the whole field and to cover it along with the armies. In consequence, men have been trained for vivid follow-up radio reporting or comment after the event.

It is difficult for these men to produce anything approximating art, for there is nothing judicious in the nature of art. There is nothing calculating or timorous. The artist may decide to be as cautious as he likes; but the decision must be up to him, and not be imposed by the nature of the medium in which he works. Nonetheless, the radio reporters who write out their material and weigh every word often produce telling pieces of spoken literature, which leave a curious and valuable emotional residue. Edward R. Murrow is excellent at this sort of thing.

How, then, is radio reporting different from other kinds of reporting? Wherein do radio drama, comedy, music, education, political speeches, poetry, variety and games differ from the counterparts elsewhere? The answer seems to lie in at least seven main characteristics of the medium which determine its nature.

1. Radio Addresses an Isolated Listener.

Unlike theatre, which is projected with an assemblage in mind, radio is an oddly private thing. In general, it has to do with a personal message delivered to a person, or to a few persons gathered congenially in comparative solitude. It is exceptional for radio to address assembled multitudes; a radio speech heard on a public address system when the speaker is invisible is strangely unsatisfying to the mob. The listeners may cry "Seig heil" at the right moments, but the actual living presences around them impart to the disembodied voice addressing them an air of unreality which they do not seem to feel when they are alone—or with only a few companions.

2. Radio Is a Blind Medium.

Radio is almost unique in that it deals solely with sound. It shares this peculiarity with phonograph recordings, but phonograph records are selected by the hearer, whereas the sender selects the materials of radio. The sender tries desperately to arrest and retain the attention of the listener, but he does so with materials of his own choosing and from four fields only: words, music, recognizable sounds and noise.

3. Radio Operates in Fixed Time Units.

The fact that periods of time are sold as commodities compels broadcasters to operate in definite segments of the hour. The usual units are ninety minutes, sixty minutes, forty-five minutes, thirty minutes, fifteen minutes, ten minutes and five minutes. Obviously the habit of thinking in time units tends to impose form on certain types of broadcasts.

4. Radio Is Continuous.

There are no real intermissions in network broadcasting. The competitive structure of the industry makes it essential to give the listener something every minute, from the time the stations take the air until the time they sign off. Silence has value on the air only in the most minute quantities.

5. Radio Cannot Be Recalled, Recaptured or Reviewed.

The listener must get it right the first time, or he misses what is said. Even when a news analysis follows a straight news program, the same words cannot be received twice. Radio constantly demands some new thing. It is very unusual to repeat even an extremely fine dramatic program, such as Archibald MacLeish's *The Fall of the City,* and the quality of the repetition almost never duplicates the impact of the original broadcast. The reasons for this are clear. Rehearsals are keyed toward a single performance, done at high tension. The lapse of time which occurs between the first broadcast and a requested repetition forbids the achievement of automatic performance by any actor. There is no opportunity for him to choose what reading, in view of all other readings by the cast, is his best. This evanescence of the medium tends not only to compel concentration on the part of the listener, but also to simplify expression on the part of the writer.

6. Radio Addresses Millions Simultaneously.

The enormous audience which radio commands leads the broadcaster to believe that he always addresses millions. This often appals him; much oftener, it excites him; occasionally it inhibits him. He wants to please the many, and indeed in some ways is obliged to do so. He fears, conversely, to displease the many; sometimes he fears too much to displease the few. But he knows that this great democratic audience is impatient. It has a nervous wrist, which spins dials and twists switches. It inclines to be escapist.

Actually, no one knows the total implications of addressing ten million, twenty million or forty million people simultaneously. Of course it means money; of course it means power. But it means something else, something quite mystifying and even frightening.

The maker of art is a solitary man. He puts his work together on his own. The receiver of art is also solitary. Radio men have felt acutely the urge to communicate with the lone listener. Fan mail has helped them. At first they tried merely to adapt the materials of other media to their purpose. This usually consisted of a process of elimination. Those sights which could not be made aural were disregarded.

Some beautiful things happened when radio tried to duplicate the theatre by sound alone. But it was not satisfactory, and it is unsatisfactory still. Radio has always been compelled to create scenes behind the eyes. It is significant that the first successful original play for radio (written by Rupert Hughes for the BBC) dealt with a mine disaster, and the entire action took place in total darkness.

Radio is at a loss to evoke the specific image and the precise gesture; it can, however, infinitely suggest. It has been highly successful with the evocative arts of music and poetry. Although the fidelity of musical transmissions is still not unimpeachable, frequency modulation will practically eliminate any aural sense of mechanical interposition between performer and auditor. And radio has already done better at transmitting in music the import of an art created outside its boundaries than it has with any other art, making it debatable whether music is better when the musician is visible. Much music has been written for radio, but thus far radio has made no great qualitative contribution to music.

There has always been poetry on the air, the worst sort as well as the best. Shakespeare is a radio success. Archibald MacLeish and Norman Corwin have sensed the potentialities of the medium, and have produced for radio works of permanent, not transient, merit. But poets in America have, on the whole, been very remiss in failing to realize that radio reestablishes with their public the contact which made the troubadours and their humbler colleagues socially significant. The wide social function of poetry could be restored through radio, if poets would only prepare themselves to use it.

The rigidity of radio time units, the prevalence of fifteen-, thirty- and sixty-minute dramas, is more than offset by the fact that radio permits the dramatist to dispense with the unities of time and place. The compressions of temporal and spatial impressions which are possible on the air have never been fully exploited, although the listener is ready to accept such condensations whenever they are adroitly proposed.

Radio can give the sense of dream. A great many successful plays for the air have been horror stories, fantasies and stories of the supernatural. The power of the voice from the void, speaking in the solitary room, stirs the night-mind of man.

But it should not be supposed that radio can people the retina of the blind with images of terror only. Because of the intimacy with which it speaks, radio has considerable power to console. The most successful original dramas on the air at the moment are the strip shows—serials which occupy the same fifteen-minute period five days a week. Most of these supply the pleasures of pulp without the pain of reading, but their purpose is to reassure the woman listener as to her own importance and rectitude. In the process of this reassurance, practically all the fundamental situations arise, and it is only a question of time until these issues will be dealt with regularly on the air by artists, and by better craftsmen.

Radio comedy has been enormously successful. Incongruity, one of the keystones of American humor, has free rein on the air. It is possible for Bob Hope to order a driver to stop in mid-air, and for the driver, the great Jerry Colonna, to stop. This surrealist twist to wit is only one aspect of this nation's huge ability to laugh, but it is peculiarly useful in radio. Slapstick, the pratfall, the pie in the face, are not specifically radio comedy formulae.

Radio's greatest educational asset is its ability to stimulate curiosity. Instead of confirming hearers in the opinion that they are receiving a patent pellet of knowledge which is their learning for the day, educational broadcasts can—and should—dissatisfy the listener with what he knows, should lead him to believe that some of the gaps in his equipment are remediable.

The most puzzling characteristic of radio is the fact that it reaches such an enormous number of people simultaneously. What does it mean for all these people to hear the same thing at once? Does it tend to standardize them? Of course they discuss yesterday's broadcasts with each other today. But does some force arise from their mass response? I do not know the precise answer. But it does seem that when a broadcast is good radio, something returns to the performer. Repeatedly I have seen the members of a cast turn to one another after they were off the air, and say, "That was a wonderful program." They feel proud and humble. They are not so much elated as awed. They do not have to wait for confirmation from the listener. They are already in communication with him in some way which is mysterious. There seems to have been a sort of retransmission from the people back to the performer. I am not able to demonstrate this logically, but I suspect that the performer in such cases is sharing the mass reaction, and actually experiencing what he has helped to generate.

There is one further characteristic of good radio which remains to be mentioned. Before listing it, I should like to enumerate a few broadcasts which have seemed to me great, because of the suitability to the medium of their materials, structures and performers. Perhaps from this enumeration the seventh quality of radio will emerge more convincingly than if it were stated baldly. This is—at best—an incomplete and random list.

Some years ago, the BBC installed a microphone by the nest of a nightingale in Pangbourne Wood. From time to time, they would interrupt the regular schedule and turn on the microphone. No engineer was there; the bird was alone. Several times, he did not sing. At last, he sang.

During Toscanini's Brahms cycle with the Philharmonic in his final season there, there was an incandescent performance of the Violin Concerto by Heifetz, in which conductor and soloist did not glance at each other from beginning to end of the extended work. There was a perfect understanding between the three of them—Toscanini, Heifetz and Brahms. The listener did not need to be in the hall to know that he was in the presence of something tremendous and not duplicable.

One night this winter in London, Edward R. Murrow brought to the microphone a young R.A.F. pilot who had bombed Berlin several times, but who had only that afternoon seen bombs fall on his own soil. The cool young British voice recounted his most recent flight over the German capital in simple terms. One knew exactly how it was.

The first performance of *The Fall of the City,* by Archibald MacLeish, directed by Irving Reis, music by Bernard Herrmann, with Orson Welles as THE ANNOUNCER and Burgess Meredith as the FIRST MESSENGER, was unforgettable radio drama.

In 1939, Paul Robeson sang the first broadcast of *Ballad for Americans* on The Pursuit of Happiness, directed by Norman Corwin, and the ovation lasted long after the program was off the air. The writers, Earl Robinson and John Latouche, had articulated something the whole country wanted to have said, and the number, which had been unnoticed in a short-lived WPA revue, became overnight the musical sensation of the season.

There was one Charlie McCarthy broadcast in which W. C. Fields was at the height of his bafflement. I cannot remember when it happened, but it was magnificent, the comic triumph of the inanimate.

The abdication speech of Edward VIII was gripping, but the first address of George VI, although he groped for utterance, surpassed it.

On the night Pope Pius XII was crowned, there was broadcast from St. Meinrad's Abbey in Indiana a Mass for the Coronation of the Pope which stirs me every time I think of it. It was Gregorian, and the sound of the human voices echoing against stone is imperishable.

All these programs share this quality peculiar to the air.

7. Radio Is Always Capable of the Unexpected.

There is a quality of improvisation about even the most finished broadcast. As John Houseman puts it, "At any moment, the Holy Ghost may descend upon the actor, or he may say something unprintable." One never knows, in listening to radio or in making programs, when a great light may flare up, or a great darkness descend. The expression, "the miracle of radio," is no idle cliché. People who have worked in radio for years still cannot understand how certain juxtapositions of talent and history make some broadcasts fabulous, while others are routine.

Good radio visualizes the isolated recipient, it utilizes sound adroitly, the broadcast starts and stops on schedule, it never flags, it is present for a moment and then is gone forever, and it reaches huge and democratic audiences. But beyond one's power to plan, radio may momentarily become the receptacle of inspiration, and in essence it remains mysterious.

Good radio is an art.

March 1941

* *

ROBERT J. WADE

*

Television Backgrounds

WITH DUE ALLOWANCE for the myopia of propinquity, a man involved in designing television settings may not be too preoccupied with work-a-day details to issue prophecies concerning the aesthetic future of scenic backgrounds for this new and synthetic medium. For a synthesis it is: radio with a sight, movies with the zest of immediacy, theatre (intimate or spectacular) with all seats about six rows back in the center, tabloid opera and circus without peanut vendors.

Once it is conceded that these multifarious art or entertainment activities require a background other than the obscure neutrality of draperies or flat studio wall, the question arises as to what kind of setting various television programs need to be artistically effective. We are, for the moment, not considering, and yet not forgetting, the purely decorative or commercial backgrounds employed in the inevitable fashion show, utilities demonstration and video vaudeville. Classroom television programs (already being planned here and in England) and news "Dailies" also require special and ingenious physical settings, animations, maps and *impedimenta* in no way related to an adapted literary, dramatic or operatic televised show that will present "an imitation of nature" in fictional form.

A television setting, unlike the stage set, is rarely seen in its entirety except during an occasional shot to establish locale, period or atmosphere; views of the setting are generally like those of the films, and the photographic techniques are similar. Thus, in cinematic sequence during a musical prelude, Dr. Herbert Graf, at NBC, introduced a scene from *La Bohème* by titles, lettered in nineteenth-century type, to indicate period; turned pages of an enlarged volume of Mürger's *La Vie de Bohème,* for expository description; used a tri-dimensional model of snowy Paris rooftops, to establish locale. A camera shot through high windows caught a full-scale detail of gables, and made the transition into Rodolfo's attic in a matter of seconds; the camera dollied away to include first the poet at his desk, then the fireless, cracked-plaster atelier.

In strictly dramatic scenes the producer may utilize partial settings, definitive props, logically placed posters or similar "dated" material to take the place of much spoken exposition. But, of course, television settings must establish more than mere period or time-of-day: they must be atmospheric and expressive of the dramatic action, and in this respect the scenic conception does not differ appreciably from the basic design-idea or motion picture. Time and experience may create mutations in technique which will be indigenous to this new medium. The "pan" and "track" shots, borrowed from the movies, require a continuous background, a wide-angled interior, street or corridor. When studios are especially designed for television, such borrowed techniques will be adapted or extended to become as much a part of television as the flashback, fadeout or angle shot are of the films.

It is obvious that the roving eye of the iconoscope requires careful set dressing. Three or more cameras, situated at separate station points, may be directed on a single small acting area, and the designer must rely on suggested props to set the scene rather than architectural units: the quill pen supplants the Tudor arch; the table set for dinner, rather than the complete room, reveals the economic status of a family group.

Whether television sets will follow the naturalistic school of the movies or the realistic, suggestive or stylized designs for the theatre depends not so much upon the producer and art director as it does on the scripts that television develops. To date, few original television scripts exist. It was hardly to be expected that the early works for this new medium would be highly imaginative. For a time at least, and under present studio conditions, television plays, operettas and vaudeville are likely to be set against as realistic a production as possible. And it is safe to say that during the period of development, conventional methods will apply to design and execution.

But even now there is no lack of experiment in styles and methods.

Charles McGarrahan, artist at WRGB, has effectively translated Elemer Nagy's gay stage designs for the Offenbach operetta into stylized, black and white (grey) television scenery, and in *Hansel und Gretel* he actually used built-in perspective to achieve depth and related scale in a delightful peasant kitchen scene. At NBC, baritone Hugh Thompson rollicked as Figaro against two settings of cartoon-like overstatement, with frankly painted-on props.

NBC used stage vignettes for *Die Fledermaus,* bits of realism for Ernest Colling's *Mississip'* and *This Singing War,* and a solidly constructed, yet suggestive, simultaneous setting for Dr. Graf's *Carmen.* Mood lighting has been found possible under certain conditions, but must await development of special lighting instruments. For the present, television inscenation is eclectic in style and catholic in scope. It may well be the task of the Hoopers, *et al.,* to discover how much stylization the ordinary television-viewer can stand; obviously the "average family group," which is the statistician's delight, may twist the dials when obscurations appear on the living-room kinescope.

A critical discussion of any phase of television programming must take into consideration present studio limitations in space and in military development in electronics. Materials for the physical setting are scarce, and probably no active studio can be said to be producing under conditions approaching an ideal. It is, therefore, largely due to the ingenuity of engineers and artists that acceptable scenic results are achieved. A brief description of one approach may suffice to indicate a point of departure. N. Ray Kelly, in charge of television facilities at NBC, has developed a series of interlocking architectural units, similar to "stock scenery," but possessing greater adaptability. These elements, constructed somewhat like picture sets, may be wall-papered, marbleized or treated in plastic paints; they are heavier than stage scenery, but still may be painted in conventional distemper. The units and regular scenic "flats," together with special, built-to-order pieces, constitute background material which the designer redesigns for interiors, ancient, and modern, and architectural exteriors. Exterior backings of photographic verisimilitude have been projected successfully in the manner of cinema process shots. Stylized settings may be, as in the theatre, executed on canvas drops with an airbrush.

If again we may judge from current programs, television costumes need not differ from those of the stage or movies, except in certain characteristics. Fabrics that drape naturally, and that have satinlike highlights and deep shadows in folds, are especially effective. Colors are lost, of course, but experimentation has revealed a color palette that yields pleasing grey tones within the present range of the iconoscope. But while the use of colors in setting and costume may widen slightly the scope of the resultant greys, because of physical differences in various studios no experimenter can yet establish a universally applicable rule as to color results. One is alarmed to see blue photograph as an off-white in one studio and as a low dark in another, or to discover that a red with blue in it may go very dark when the exact opposite was expected. The main reason for this color change is that varied types of lighting are used in different studios, some predominantly warm, others cool and bluish in tone. Some standardization will probably be effected as soon as the best type of lighting unit is established. Until then red roses will have to be touched up with black (or blue) to register as "red"; and lipsticks (at least in one studio) will glamorize with touches of deep magenta and raspberry.

The *effect* of pictures in greys cannot alarm a television public. We have long accepted black-and-white halftone engravings and we do not object to non-color films, even after thirty years; it is a sort of unhappy but necessary convention to assume that nature exists in white and dark, that the green of foliage is a medium grey, that the distant violet foothills are light neutral mist. Fortunately, we are used to this arbitrary substitute, and one is even inclined to believe that the less sensitive see a great deal of the world as a study in monochrome. When color television comes (and it is promised) it may well correct and re-educate; it may have a wider color influence than the color film or the four-color magazine page.

To sum up: it seems, superficially, that television producers, commercial or experimental, are attempting to imitate the films by providing realistic backgrounds for all types of programs. Perhaps, with modifications, this will be the final answer; but we must give this new synthesis of the arts a few years' grace in order that its practitioners may create a backlog of their own based on actual programming over a long period. To continue discussion now beyond the realm of immediate experience would be only to speculate, but those who remember the early talkies—nay, the early radio and the early movies—should, by extension, take heart.

December 1944

X · TRIBUTARY THEATRE

*   *   *

KENNETH MACGOWAN

*

Little Theatre Backgrounds

ABOUT the little theatre movement of America there is the atmosphere of the unique. Across a country four thousand miles wide somewhere in the neighborhood of 15,000 amateur actors provide amusement for an audience whose size can only be estimated by multiplying five hundred producing organizations by whatever figure you may care to set as their average clientele. If you guess their patronage at five hundred per bill, your estimate will be 250,000; with only a very little recklessness, you can push the little theatre audience of the United States up to a half a million. All the professional producers of Broadway and the Road do not mount so many plays in any season as these five hundred little theatres with their two to ten bills a year.

If you put the American mania for statistical extravagance firmly in its place, you still find certain things that seem to cut off our little theatre movement from any theatrical phenomenon of the past. It is ninety-nine percent amateur, and it dedicates itself above all things to the newer arts of scenic design and atmospheric lighting.

And yet these symptoms of American geography, American megalomania and American enthusiasm for the newest in current fashions should blind no one to the fact that our little theatre has an ancestry of almost forty years on the continent of Europe, and is only a part—a current phase—of a long story of theatrical rebellion. It is a story in which the amateur actor, the subscription audience and the small auditorium have always played a part.

Free Theatre, Independent Theatre, . . . Literary Theatre, Art Theatre, . . . National Theatre, Stage Society, Repertory Theatre, . . . Little Theatre, Chamber Theatre, Intimate Theatre—behind all the twists of phrase which set them off into families is a common note of rebellion. Strindberg set it down on paper in the eighties. With these words he called into being those rebel playhouses which almost invariably included among the plays of their first seasons the *Ghosts* of the other great Scandinavian playwright: "Let us have a free theatre where there is room for everything but incompetence, hypocrisy and stupidity! . . . where we can be shocked by what is horrible, where we can laugh at what is grotesque, where we can see life without shrinking back in terror if what has hitherto lain veiled behind theological or aesthetic conceptions is revealed to us."

It was against the conventional drama and the conventional acting of the Parisian boulevards that André Antoine—clerk in the gas company and amateur actor—launched the Théâtre-Libre, ancestor of all the little theatres of the world. On March 30, 1887, in a small hall above a café on Montmartre, Antoine and his friends put on their first bill of modern one-act plays. The actor who spoke the prologue forgot his lines, and there were many hitches about the scenery; everything was quite in the soon-to-be-established tradition of the little theatre. But actors appeared as human beings in plays of recognizable milieu, they smoked cigarettes, they even turned their backs on the audience, and through their agency the way was opened for distinguished realistic playwrights like Brieux, De Curel, Porto-Riche and Lavedan.

Brother to the Théâtre-Libre and great-uncle to the American little theatre, the Freie Bühne appeared in Berlin in 1889. Amateurs and critics—Maximilian Harden and Otto Brahm, for example—mingled with professionals in its leadership, and Ibsen, Hauptmann and Tolstoi were given to an audience of subscribers only.

In England George Moore, arch-realist, began to talk of a free theatre in 1891, and before spring had come John T. Grein, the critic, launched the Independent theatre with that performance of *Ghosts* which permitted the reviewers of the London stage to make consummate asses of themselves. The membership in Grein's society included George Meredith, Thomas Hardy, Arthur Wing Pinero and Henry Arthur Jones; the next year Grein produced Shaw's first play—written for this theatre—*Widower's Houses,* and not so many years after its founding in 1900 the London Stage Society, which replaced the Independent Theatre, was putting forth Granville-Barker, Somerset Maugham, Arnold Bennett and St. John Hankin, as well as Shaw, Maeterlinck, Hauptmann, Ibsen, and the rest. Other acting societies followed—the Play Actors, the Oncomers, the Drama Society, the Pioneer Players, etc.—and soon Barker was worming his way into the commercial and professional theatre to give London Galsworthy and Masefield.

In 1897 Russia created the greatest of modern acting companies out of a dramatic school maintained by Nemirovitch-Dantchenko, and a little theatre headed by an amateur actor called Stanislavski. It took about a dozen years for the amateur reformers of the London stage to break into the professional theatre. I cannot say how long the Moscow Art Theatre was a-borning in Russian little theatres, but the strength of that special and finely amateur impulse was evident when, at the height of its success and in the midst of a world war, the Stanislavski company began the organization of its four Studio Theatres where new talent meets special audiences.

In all these efforts the same spirit of amateurism, the same system of subscription, the same parallels with our own little theatre movement are clear enough. The cause is rebellion against the commercial stage. The guiding spirit is amateur. The economic system is based on the subscription audience. And the playhouse is usually a small and cheap one, or an ordinary theatre rented economically for occasional performances. The differences between these European theatres of reform and our own are two: The policies of the European theatres succeeded in breaching the walls of the professional houses and establishing their leaders—Antoine, Brahm, Barker—as directors of commercial playhouses, just as their amateur ventures died; and the chief aim and artistic outcome of these efforts was the development in each country of new playwrights with a distinctly native quality. Our little theatres have their effect upon Broadway, but the necessities of the smaller cities, deserted by good road companies, keep them alive even when their actors or directors move on into new work. As for their product, it is not as yet—worse luck!—a brilliant group of such playwrights as the free theatres of Europe produced; but the rebellion of today is against the realism that the free theatres fostered, and imagination in production, settings and lights opens the way for imagination in playwriting.

Later European efforts than those I have chronicled also link up with our little theatre movement. Within half a dozen years of the founding of the Théâtre-Libre, Paul Fort in the Théâtre d'Art and Alexandre Lugné-Poë in the Théâtre de L'Œuvre were cultivating Shelley, Maeterlinck and Verlaine, and setting their faces against realism. When, fourteen years later, Jacques Rouché founded in 1907 the Théâtre des Arts, and began the exploitation of French stage designers, and when in 1913 Jacques Copeau made a group of amateurs into a fine company on the naked stage of the Vieux Colombier there had already developed in Germany a unique figure —Max Reinhardt—out of a unique aspect of the rebellious and amateur little theatre movement.

However professional Reinhardt may appear as actor and director, it is highly significant that the first theatre over which he exercised complete control was called the Kleines Theater, that he worked in Freie Bühne, and that he bridged the gap between volunteer work with the Freie Bühne and the management of the Kleines Theater by an adventure in the kind of cabaret management of which we have caught a glimpse in Balieff's Chauve-Souris. From 1900 to 1902, while Reinhardt was still a member of Brahm's company at the Deutsches Theater, he was creating in Die Brille and Schall und Rauch two cabarets amateur in spirit and emolument, and exclusive in their special audience. From these efforts, which were vivid and imaginative in quality, it was natural that Reinhardt should venture into the production of short, picturesque plays, and finally into the management of a theatre where vivid realism and imaginative drama utilized the services of the new stagecraft and took advantage of the intimacy of a small auditorium. Oddly enough, the first plays that Reinhardt attempted in Schall und Rauch were by the same Strindberg who sounded the trumpet call of the free theatre and who founded in Stockholm in 1907 a tiny Chamber Theatre in partnership with August Falk.

Of the European backgrounds of our little theatres there remain only the English and Irish ventures which have brought forward the phrase "repertory theatre" as a misnomer for a resident stock company. However professional some of these companies became, the people who served the oldest of them all and the woman who gave them all their financial impulse were amateurs. In 1894 a certain Miss A. E. F. Horniman, who bore significantly the name of a popular brand of tea, put up the money for Florence Farr to produce *Arms and the Man in London*. In 1904 this same woman bought the Mechanics Institute Hall in Dublin, turned it into the Abbey Theatre, and presented it rent free for six years to the Irish National Dramatic Society. This organization, which had come to life through the energies of two amateur actors, W. C. and Frank Fay, which had enlisted W. B. Yeats from the moribund Irish Literary Theatre of 1899, and which had brought to itself John Millington Synge and Lady Gregory, developed in half a dozen years into a professional theatre that sent us the Irish Players, created a dramatic literature of real distinction and, inspired by Gordon Craig, embarked on significant experiments in the new stagecraft.

Turning to England again, Miss Horniman began in Manchester a dramatic movement which even the war has been unable completely to destroy. In 1907 she set up in the Midland capital the Manchester Repertory Company, at the beginning under the direction of B. Iden Payne, later of Lewis Casson. In 1909 Glasgow created the Scottish Repertory Theatre; in 1911 the Liverpool Repertory Theatre came into being under the direction of Basil Dean. The Birmingham Repertory Theatre followed in 1913 under the leadership of John Drinkwater and Barry Jackson. The theatres and certain others that imitated them employed many professional players and turned their first energies to the calling forth of new playwrights; yet their relationship is closer, perhaps, to our little theatres than to any other of the rebellious experiments of Europe.

Though the "provinces" of England could be pocketed in Texas, they correspond fairly closely in their theatrical life to the present state of the far-flung touring system of the United States. London is an exaggerated Broadway. In 1907, when the successes and the stars of a New York season were certain to spend a year at least visiting Boston, Baltimore, St. Louis, Des Moines, Denver and stands between, it was a rare play that came to Manchester or Birmingham with any members of the original London cast, and it was only the most obviously popular pieces which went on tour. In the repertory theatres of the provinces a considerable impulse came originally from playwrights or the hope of playwrights, but the necessities of play-starved audiences had as important a part in calling forth new theatres as they had in our American provinces.

And today, when most of the pioneers are gone, the provincial repertory theatres that remain do so largely in response to a need for dramatic entertainment and not because of a creative impulse among the artists. Play producing societies like the Stage Society still continue to render their special service and a certain few theatres like the Maddermarket at Norwich, the Everyman at Hempstead, the Leeds Art Theatre and the Birmingham Repertory form a link between the older and the newer experimental theatres.

By a terrific effort the history of the rebel theatre in the United States can be forced back to 1892 and the abortive Theatre of Arts and Letters. A little less energy discovers it at work in 1906 and 1907 with the founding in Chicago of three institutions of which two quickly passed away—the New Theatre under the direction of Victor Mapes, the Robertson Players under the direction of Donald Robertson, and the Hull House Theatre under the direction of Laura Dainty Pelham. The years 1909 to 1911 marked the rise and fall of the New Theatre in New York under the direction of Winthrop Ames, and 1911-12 the brief resurgence of Donald Robertson in the Drama Players. But for practical purposes the true start of dramatic reform in the United States must be reckoned 1911, when Thomas H. Dickenson founded the Wisconsin Dramatic Society, and 1912 when Mrs. Lyman Galès Toy Theatre of Boston and Maurice Browne's Little Theatre of Chicago came into existence. After these beginnings, of which only the Wisconsin group still exists, came the Arts and Crafts Theatre of Detroit, and the Little Theatre of Philadelphia (both now passed away), the 47 Workshop of Harvard, the Little Country Theatre of North Dakota, the Dramatic Workshop of Carnegie Institute of Pittsburgh and a long line of experiments that had at their forefront the Washington Square Players, the Neighborhood Playhouse, the Provincetown Players, the Portmanteau Theatre, the Vagabond Players of Baltimore, the Carolina Playmakers, the Pasadena Community Theatre, the Ram's Head Players, the Cleveland Play House, the Dallas Little Theatre, Le Petit Théâtre du Vieux Carré of New Orleans, the enterprises of Sam Hume, Irving Pichel and Maurice Browne on the Pacific Coast, not to mention the Canadian ventures, the Vancouver Little Theatre, the Hart House Theatre of Toronto and the Home Theatre of the Canadian Players.

It seems to me that the impulses and results of the American little theatres are clear enough. Except for a small group of educational enterprises they have come into existence for one of two reasons, and they have continued successfully when both these motives were present. Europe knows these motives. In varying degree they were behind the rebel theatres that began with Antoine.

One motive is an audience that needs and to some extent demands more or better entertainment than its professional theatres provide. In Europe in the nineties it was the degrading "Sardoodledum" of the commercial playhouses that left audiences unsatisfied; in England in the first decade of the twentieth century and in America in the second decade it was the decay of the touring system outside of the theatre capitals.

The other motive behind the American little theatre as well as its Continental forerunners is the creator who cannot find an opening in the professional theatre. Everywhere the amateur actor has always insisted on exhibiting his charms, but in the serious theatre of which I am writing a new type of truly creative amateur appeared. In Europe he was the director or the playwright, and the outcome of his efforts was new drama. In America he has been the director or the scenic designer, and the results have been new and imaginative beauty in production. The difference is only a difference of the times. The rebellion of the eighties and the nineties looked toward the intellectual, the literary and the realistic. The rebellion of today is looking towards the imaginative, the picturesque, the expressionistic, and it takes the visual path first, the written path later.

One type of little theatre distinguishes our movement from the movement of Europe. This is the scholastic. The vigor of the dramatic interest of America finds its sharpest index in the hundreds of courses in playwriting, play producing, acting and design given at our leading universities. These courses have a practical outlet in the producing theatres of men like Baker, Arvold, Koch, Stevens and others whose number and activity increase each year. Even the acting schools begin to see the light and give their pupils the practical experience of appearing frequently in first-rate plays under the general conditions of little theatre performances.

Within the last year or two an entirely new phase of development has opened up for the little theatres which, like Pasadena and Carmel, have grown large enough and sure-footed enough to venture upon new theatre buildings, with complete and modern professional equipment offering great opportunity not only to little theatre directors of professional quality but to progressive professional actors and to playwrights who prefer to have their own roads.

A fine amateurism is at the heart of all this effort, both here and abroad, but in this amateurism certain curious distinctions between the movement in Europe and in America appear. In the European ventures, particularly in the English Repertory theatres, the actors were sometimes professionals, though the directors were invariably amateurs. The American movement began on a wholly amateur basis, and almost (though of course not quite) all of its actors remain amateurs. The directors on the other hand have frequently developed into professionals, like Browne, Hume, Pichel, Hinsdell, Dean, McConnell and others, who shift from little theatre to little theatre.

In Europe the directors passed from their amateur first ventures into important posts in the professional theatre. Antoine became head of the State-subventioned Odéon. Rouché is now the director of the Paris Opéra. Reinhardt conquered the whole German theatre. Dean and Drinkwater found openings in London, and Payne in America. Stanislavski and Copeau quickly solidified their beginnings into the finest professional theatres of their two nations. Perhaps the fact that most of these men worked in the capitals of States was at the bottom of this swift development; certainly it is this fact which accounts for the rapid and solid growth of three New York ventures, the Washington Square Players-Theatre Guild, the Neighborhood Playhouse and the Provincetown Players. In the bulk of the little theatres of the United States it is not the directors but the actors, designers and occasional playwrights who pass on from the amateur to the professional playhouse. It is to these graduates—to men and women like Helen Gahagan, Rollo Peters and Katharine Cornell, Norman Bel Geddes, Woodman Thompson and Lee Simonson, Martin Flavin, Zoë Akins and Eugene O'Neill—that we look for the justification of the ideals and the practice of the rebellious little theatres in the professional playhouse which is slowly but surely being conquered for art.

September 1924

JOHN MASON BROWN

*

The Four Georges

G. P. BAKER AT WORK

IF THERE WERE only one George Pierce Baker, and if he had been the arbitrary teacher of playwriting that some of his critics have imagined he must be because he dared to give courses in the writing of plays, his influence would not have extended beyond his classrooms, if indeed it would have stretched that far. But there have been at least four Bakers functioning simultaneously in the two great universities which have claimed him; and at Yale, as at Harvard, all four of them have been significant.

First there is the Baker most widely known to undergraduates at Harvard, at Radcliffe and at Yale: the formal classroom Baker whose business it was to teach the history of the drama to anyone who might care to learn it. He chose his materials so wisely (they were new when he first presented them) and showed such a happy instinct for limiting his attention only to what was theatrically most significant in each man or period he dealt with, that hundreds of those who have sat under him, and then turned teacher, have been compelled to follow in his footsteps down the straight trail he blazed through history. This classroom Baker seated behind a broad desk, with a sheaf of faded notes before him, and a black brief-case stuffed with dusty books beside him, has been the most professorial of the four Bakers and, for that very reason of later years, the least important of the lot.

For some time now he has been a slightly bored and tired man. Even in his last years at Harvard, his lectures on the essentials of a play, the four tellings of the Electra story (this was before O'Neill had raised the number to five), Aristophanes, *The Cid,* Victor Hugo, or what have you, showed the long-run system can be as dangerous for teachers as it is for actors. When he spoke of Lope de Vega or Tom Robertson he did so in tones that were as mechanical as Joseph Jefferson's must have been when, after countless seasons of playing Rip, he called for his dog, Schneider.

There was much good stuff in these outline courses. Whether the subject was the English drama from its beginnings to the closing of the playhouses in 1642, or from the Restoration to modern times, or a general survey of the world's drama, the facts were all there, earnestly investigated, and set forth with the precision of the man who had edited the Belles Lettres series, who had published an interesting batch of Garrick letters, performed the same service for the Charles Dickens-Maria Beadnell correspondence, written in *The Development of Shakespeare as Dramatist* the most penetrating study of Shakespeare's technique that has yet been written, and helpfully set forth the commonsense essentials of playwriting in his *Dramatic Technique*.

Yellow as his notes may have been, and slightly bored as he may himself have seemed in the classroom, these lectures of Mr. Baker's had the decided advantage of being delivered by a man whose primary interest was the theatre. He never abused dramatic literature by treating it as if it had no connection with the stage. He kept it smudged with grease-paint and, even in his weariness, managed to give the impression that the desk behind which he was lecturing was surrounded by footlights.

Witty as many of his comments were, clarifying as his perceptions proved, and amusing as he used to be when he would roll out long sentences and make a classroom roar at their intentional involutions, the moments one remembers best were those in which he forgot all about facts and tendencies and, abandoning his professorial calm, began to make his points as an actor. He had his favorite characters by means of which he would expose the virtues or the follies of a type of playwriting.

Sir Fopling Flutter in *The Man of Mode* was one of these. When he came to him, Professor Baker's blue-gray eyes would deepen behind his pince-nez, his face would beam with pleasure and his portly body rock with mirth. Still seated behind his desk, with his coat, usually dark gray, tightly buttoned, he would begin to assume the airs and graces of a Restoration fop. His voice would change and take on the mincing tones of Etherege's hero. His hands, which he always uses swiftly, would begin to race in elaborate circles. Artificial gallantries would be slightly indicated in a way that seemed so courtly and was so deliciously right that one could have sworn his sleeves were fringed with lace.

Professor Baker was no less happy when, during his talks on Henry Arthur Jones and Arthur Wing Pinero, those transitional dramatists who were his friends, he could show the strides that they had made as playwrights by quoting from their earlier works. In Mr. Jones's *Saints and Sinners* he used to give as admirable a performance as he did in *The Man of Mode,* and by doing so he pointed out all that was absurd in the older melodramas. Standing up, with his left hand pushed far into the pocket of his coat and still holding a copy of the play in his right, he would act the scene in which Fanshawe, the extremely wicked villain of the piece, confesses in a soliloquy that his intentions toward the parson's daughter are not honorable. A terrific scowl would spread across Mr. Baker's face and seem to take possession of his vocal cords. As he leaned against the blackboard, imitating Fanshawe who was supposed to be resting against a tree, flicked ashes off of an imaginary cigarette and indulged in chuckles that were far more diabolical than any Jones had dreamed of, the classroom turned into a theatre. And on that academic stage, a melodrama of not-so-long ago was spoofed far more entertainingly than have been many of the older melodramas which have recently been revived.

To those who took his historical courses at the same time that they were working with him in other capacities, the reason for his coldness in the lecture hall was clear enough. He was a teacher who had tired of teaching in the ordinary way. His notes were left yellow and unadded to because his heart was no longer in them. They held as little interest for him as a train does for the person who has left it after it has carried him safely to his destination. From the fall of 1903, when he was first allowed to experiment at Radcliffe with a course in playwriting, he must have realized with an ever-increasing clarity that the drama's present, and not its past, was his goal. Undoubtedly he felt indebted to these historical courses he continued to give, because it was by means of them he had been directed to his new field of interest. Perhaps he also hoped they would perform the same service for those who took them that they had performed for him. From an intimate knowledge of the theatre's past might come a desire to contribute to its present-day practice. Be that as it may, the Baker who "walked through" these courses, year after year, was much too much of a New Englander and far too well trained as a professor to succeed in faking what he did not feel. In this respect his acting talents, even his theatrical instinct, failed him.

The man who met his incipient playwrights in an upper room in Harvard's Widener Library did not have to act. He was doing what he liked, and his liking of what he had to do was plain from the moment he hurried in, deposited his black, actor-y hat on a nearby bookcase, took off his dark coat, pulled some blue-covered manuscripts out of his bulging brief-case, and seated himself at the circular oak table around which the students were grouped informally. This second of the four Bakers was beholden to no notes. The job ahead of him required patience, but for some miraculous reason he did not look upon it as a chore. The forbidding, un-get-at-able Puritan who put the underclassmen off was beginning to thaw. The chalky mask of professordom was being laid aside. A new man was emerging.

This Professor Baker who dared to teach such an unteachable subject as playwriting was the least dogmatic of men. He had no Golden Rules of Dramaturgy. He did not pretend to be able to turn out playwrights in ten easy lessons. Indeed he did not claim to be able to turn them out at all. He was among the first to admit that dramatists are born not made. But he did hope to be able to shorten the playwright's period of apprenticeship by granting him the same instruction in the essentials of his craft that the architect, the painter, the sculptor and the musician enjoyed in theirs.

There was nothing oracular about his methods in these seminars. He did not lecture. He dodged the absolute. He issued no proclamations and passed no laws as to what dialogue, or plotting, or characterization, should be. His distinctions between the materials available to the novelist and the dramatist were given in his book. So, too, were his common-sense pleas for clarity, for the scenarios he felt it advisable for playwrights to draft before beginning their actual scripts, and his endless illustrations of what was good and bad in dramatic practice and why.

But what was inelastically stated in *Dramatic Technique,* with that finality which can attach itself to words set down in black and white, was flexible and free when spoken by Mr. Baker and applied to a case in point. His verbal comments had another advantage over his written ones, inasmuch as they could keep pace with the tastes of changing years. Where the date 1919 on the title page of his book was bound eventually to seem printed on many of the pages that followed it, Mr. Baker's point of view remained undated. Born a contemporary of Jones and Pinero, he managed to continue as the contemporary of each class that came to him.

When he had hurried into that upper room at Widener and seated himself at the table, with the window behind him and the light pouring down on the manuscript he held in his hands, it was obvious that his belief in "The play's the thing" was stronger than any Hamlet's has ever been. He spoke briefly, except at the early meetings of the class when he was making his initial assignments and waiting for his playwrights to turn in their first scripts, because his custom was to let the plays speak for themselves.

His program for his beginners was as similar each year as the results were different. Invariably the course would start off with a one-act dramatization of a short story. Three short stories, culled from anywhere, could be selected by each of the tyros for Professor Baker's approval (or his demon assistant's), and always the one presenting the most insurmountable technical problems was the one chosen. Next came an original one-act play and, finally, by spring, a long play. As many others as the students happened to write and wanted comment upon were gladly received.

A sure test of the merits of a play was Mr. Baker's reading of it. He was an exceptional reader, and he made a point, wherever possible, of reading a manuscript at sight, without revealing the author's name. Naturally enough, he got scripts of all sorts and kinds and was forced to be as ready as an old-fashioned stock actor with quick study characterizations and every conceivable dialect. He was compelled to vary French with Irish, Irish with Italian, Scotch with English, English with American, and as an American he was called upon to suggest tough guys of the toughest sort that undergraduates could imagine, prostitutes who made Mae West seem virginal, Indians who grunted about Manitou on the mesa, Negroes who put Mrs. Stowe to shame, and southern colonels who were more southern than the Confederacy. He had to rip out oaths that only occasionally pinkened his cheeks or caused him to hasten madly through a speech, which was his other way of blushing. He had to read love scenes that must have disturbed everything New England in him. And the number of pleas he was forced to make to imaginary juries would undoubtedly have won the envy of Max Steuer.

The wonder was that he never succumbed to the temptation of

making fun of the stuff he was reading. He could spoof the classics, real and pseudo, in his history courses, but he never made sport of his young playwrights' work. He was on their side, was fully aware that their fellow students would tear them limb from limb when the time for comment came, and, accordingly, acted as their defender. He would plunge into the first manuscript on the pile before him (neatly typed in black and red, of course, in order to distinguish the dialogue from the stage directions) and read it through in the dialects required. Or, if none were needed, he would give it the benefit of that deep Boston voice of his which has a surprising way of going Brooklyn in its pronunciations every now and then. Perhaps it should be added that everyone thought Professor Baker was a good reader except the person whose play he happened to be reading. It was not hard to tell who the dramatist in question was. Author's vanity and a poker face are not compatible.

When the last page was finished and the final curtain read, the class had its merciless but helpful say. Mr. Baker merely presided over these discussions, throwing a word in here and there and waiting for his private conference with the playwright to give his own opinion or to make suggestions. Come to think of it, there was not any teaching, as teaching is ordinarily understood, in English 47. The course was as free from pedagogy as the MacDowell Colony. There were only twelve or fifteen people who shared a common interest, who knew as they sat informally around that table that they were aiming at the same goal, and who were aided in their writing (first of all, by the simple knowledge that they had to get their stuff in on a certain date and, secondly, by the reassuring thought that Mr. Baker somehow believed in them, for reasons which were not always clear. There was, of course, more to it than that. All-important was that indefinable evocative gift of Professor Baker's which made him a great teacher even when he did not seem to be teaching at all.

The third of the four Bakers known to his Cambridge students was the tireless Baker who, when he had lectured to his history courses at nine in the morning, spent several hours dictating letters in his small cubbyhole of an office, met with two of his four playwriting courses (he gave an elementary and an advanced course both at Harvard and Radcliffe), conferred with his dramatists, worked in the garden of his Brattle Street home and eaten a huried dinner, used to come rattling up to Massachusetts Hall in the dusty Dodge his energy and his driving had aged so prematurely that it had begun to resemble his wrinkled black brief-case. Once arrived at the Johnson gate, and looking slightly surprised and pleased at having made a safe landing, he would wriggle out from behind the steering wheel, jump to the street, bang the door behind him, rush into the yard as if a host of demons were pursuing him, give a presidential salute to the men and women who were inhaling their last cigarettes and going over their lines beside the unperturbed bust of James Russell Lowell, and scurry through the two-story room that was the Cain's Warehouse of his past productions, prepared to spend the evening rehearsing the better plays his courses had yielded.

Outside, Massachusetts Hall was (and still is) one of the few architectural joys of the Harvard landscape. One of the oldest structures in the Yard, it had the trim grace early New Englanders could give to their buildings. Inside it was, at least in the days when Mr. Baker and his designers worked in it, a fascinating nightmare. Its hollow shell, cluttered with flats and drops which stretched to the ceiling, and smelling strongly of paint and glue, was a defiant contradiction of its chaste exterior. If Bernhardt's heart had beaten in Priscilla's body the effect could not have been more startling than it was to find this topsy-turvy greasepaint kingdom enclosed by brick walls which had housed troops during the Revolution.

In the center of this confusion was a space cleared for a rehearsal stage, and facing it, with innumerable little paint-specked chairs flanking it on either side, was an equally spattered black table behind which Mr. Baker sat with the author. As he took up his position there night after night, half in the shadows and half blinded by the light that beat down from above on the script he held in his hands, the Baker who in his youth was supposed to have resembled Edwin Booth came to life once more. His scraggly gray hair was darkened by the shadows, his long, sensitive face had a rapt intentness about it, and there was something about his straight, tight lips which gave him an expression startlingly similar to the one that forever repeats itself in Booth's photographs.

At rehearsal, as in his sessions in Widener, Mr. Baker was the most stalwart defender his playwrights could find. His job was a far harder one than anyone realized, even as his work as a director was far more skillful than many people gave him credit for. Not only was he working for the most part with scripts that had the right to be bad and took advantage of their right, inasmuch as they were the classroom exercises of dramatists who were still learning the fundamentals of their craft, but he made it his duty to protect these scripts from actors who generally were inexperienced amateurs.

His faith in his dramatists was endless. He never forced them to rewrite, even when it was as obvious to him as it was to everyone else (except the playwrights in question) that drastic rewriting was necessary. His hope was that his playwrights would learn by having had a real production in front of a selected audience, every member of which was supposed to turn in a criticism. Those productions of his were, he knew, his surest means of instruction. They could teach more to dramatists possessed of any instinct for the theatre than hours of idle theorizing.

With his actors, as with his playwrights, Mr. Baker's patience knew no bounds. With them too, though officially it was not supposed to be among his duties, he functioned as a teacher. He was an excellent judge of acting. He was blessed with that alert inner ear all good directors must have. It allowed him to hear a line as it was being read at the same time that it enabled him to hear it as it should be read. He had a sure sense of timing, a shrewd eye for character, and the all important ability to get results from beginners.

When things got too bad, when his actors failed completely to give him what he wanted, he would push his chair back, dig his hands deep into the pockets of his coat and rush onto the scene, with short mincing steps and with one foot put before the other as if he were walking the tight-rope, to illustrate how this or that part should be played.

He did not scold. In fact he hardly ever lost his temper, but when he did it was an impressive display: horribly dignified, chilly as the banks off Newfoundland; devastating as Cotton Mather's threats of brimstone. Almost always he was equability itself. This man who could straight-arm strangers so effectually could be warmly intimate with the few to whom he gave his friendship each year. There was nothing of the palaverer in him. He kept his friendships, like his work, on the gold standard. As a scholar he valued the real meaning of words, and as a dyed-in-the-wool New Englander he had an honest detestation of those amiable phrases which most people render meaningless by squandering lightly.

He was sparing, almost stingy, with praise. His thanks for something he liked or appreciated was a slight pat on the back, a hastily muttered "That's fine." That was all. But it was by means of these few words, which were as treasured by those who earned them as if they were public testimonials, that he reared the astonishing organization which flourished at Harvard; that he persuaded men and women, who received no pay and little credit for it, to sit up night after night to slave on his stage crews; that he got his actors, in spite of the courses they might be taking and the fact that the 47 Workshop counted for nothing as an undergraduate activity, to feel duty-bound to come promptly to all rehearsals; that he mesmerized designers into competing for the privilege of setting one of his productions; and that he built up and held together that loyal Cambridge audience (he has done the same thing in New Haven) which felt itself honored to be allowed to sit in at the performances of what were usually very bad plays.

It was this Baker who inspired more active loyalty than any other teacher at Harvard (not excepting the great "Copey" himself) who was, and still is, the fourth of the four Bakers. This man Baker, with his extraordinary personality, was the keystone upon which everything else rested. He may have put people off. His seeming coldness may have terrified some and antagonized others. But everyone who actually worked for him, and hence knew him—because he was the kind of man who revealed himself only in his work—felt affectionately toward him. He was not Professor Baker to them. He was "G.P.," but always, significantly enough, he was "G.P." only when he was safely out of earshot.

It is because these four Bakers have existed side by side, that there has been—and is—only one George Pierce Baker, as Yale has doubtless learned to its sorrow now that he is retiring, and as official Harvard discovered some years ago when he put the Cambridge elms behind him, and left for New Haven or what Harvard was foolish enough to think for a time was "blue obscur-i-tee."

July 1933

EDITH J. R. ISAACS

*

Paul Green

A CASE IN POINT

IT IS SOMETHING over sixteen years since THEATRE ARTS published Paul Green's delightful play, *The No 'Count Boy* which, later in the same season, won the major prize in the Little Theatre Tournament. This was an annual contest much in favor at that time, that brought representative theatres from various parts of the country to show their best work in competition in New York. Before this victory, Paul Green's name belonged chiefly, if not altogether, to the Carolina Playmakers of Chapel Hill with whom he had received his dramatic training and his first opportunity of watching his plays take shape in production on an actual stage. But prizes are always news in American journalism and productive little theatres were news fifteen years ago. Paul Green's name was carried swiftly across country and he was featured, immediately, as the type of playwright through whom the tributary theatre would soon revitalize the main stream. It was a fortunate beginning, for the fantasy was distinctly "regional" in material and personal in style. It owed nothing to Broadway. If it owed any debt it was to Ireland but only for the impulse to write simply and freely out of the life around you. When *In Abraham's Bosom,* Paul Green's first full-length play presented in New York, won the Pulitzer Prize two years later, the Tributary triumph seemed complete. Again a regional play, this time a drama of Negro struggle suggesting some of O'Neill's in material, power and human sympathy, without some of O'Neill's fine theatrical drive and technical assurance, but with a poetry that O'Neill lacked. It was not only the Carolina Playmakers that showed a pride in Paul Green's work; something of credit for his success was felt to belong to the tributary theatre at large. It was assumed to be only a matter of time before every regional theatre would be running out playwrights just as good.

But that was thirteen years ago and today it seems that we have sung that chorus too long and too loud. Paul Green has grown steadily through the years from *The House of Connelly* to *Johnny Johnson* but there is still no playwright out of all the tributary theatres in all these years who can stand beside him. There are a few talented, earnest men like Lynn Riggs who have contributed some good plays and some less good, and there are many men with smaller gifts struggling honestly to make the professional grade and not quite succeeding, but there is no "regional" playwright except Paul Green who has had the slightest influence on American playwriting and production either in his own community theatre or in New York. It is about time that we begin to ask why this should be so.

It is true that artists are not made in droves. The Provincetown Playhouse begat Eugene O'Neill and a number of smaller men; the tributary theatre has given us Paul Green and a host of smaller men. Perhaps that is enough. Or perhaps playwrights are the fruit and not the flower of the tributary theatre, which has already given so many actors, technicians, designers and other artists and craftsmen to the profession. And perhaps we shall look back another fifteen years and be glad that so many of the hopeful young playwriting talents—fed to the world by college and community theatres—were neglected and had to go into other fields of work, to live deeper into life and into themselves before their real playwriting careers began. It is all quite possible. Yet, even so, it is still time to take stock of fifteen years' experience and to see what contribution to American playwriting we may fairly expect from the tributary theatre during the next fifteen years. It may surprise a good many people to see how much of the answer to this question is indicated in the life, training and ideals of Paul Green, as well as in the special opportunities and the inherent limitations of the tributary theatre.

Paul Green was born and brought up on a farm in North Carolina. His family owned the land, but they worked hard winter and summer to protect it and Paul Green had only a few months a year for school. A short period of teaching; active service in the war between the first and last halves of a course at the University of North Carolina; graduate work at Cornell and back to Chapel Hill again as an Associate Professor of Philosophy. During most of this time, Frederick Koch was in North Carolina and Paul Green was an active member of the Playmakers as he has been ever since, joining philosophy to playwriting, with New York and Hollywood as interludes. Many years ago a letter from Paul Green said: "Eighteen years of ploughing and digging the sandy fields of Harnett County, of pulling fodder and sweating day after day with the Negroes, of watching the sun pass from East to West, sobered me to the bottom. I'll never be up for running off to New York to roost in Greenwich Village. My inspiration and stimulation are here in North Carolina, along Cape Fear River, down in the bottom lands, up in the wide level lands. Everywhere there's something deep here, something of humanity that lasts like the dirt itself, down and right on down." Perhaps the most important things to remember in considering Paul Green's career as a measuring-rod are already clear from the brief biography: he had struck deep roots into his own home soil and he had been close to life's major struggles—of man with nature, of man against man—before he wrote his first worthwhile plays. For it seems increasingly evident that great plays are not written out of cheerful inexperience.

It is important, too, to note how early in his playwriting career Paul Green had a stage to work on, for playwriting is not only a literary technique but a technique of handling men, women and properties in action on a stage. That this factor influenced his career as a playwright THEATRE ARTS has ample evidence. His one-act scripts, almost all about some phase of Negro life, were among the first that came to THEATRE ARTS' desk. There were several plays in the years before *The No 'Count Boy* which showed enough quality to make the editors read them with interest and write encouragingly to the unknown author although the work seemed not quite good enough for print. By coincidence, another unknown playwright, also from the south, was sending in manuscripts on the same Negro themes, at the same time. The scripts were about on a level; both men knew a dramatic situation, both had a keen sense of dialogue; they knew their Negroes, they had the gift of speech. But Paul Green's plays grew broader, better, more mature, technically more secure, one by one; the other man's remained static. We soon learned one reason why. It was after Paul Green came into THEATRE ARTS' office on the way back to North Carolina from Cornell and we saw he was a white man that we discovered that the other playwright was a young Negro. Paul Green was welcome in any theatre where he could pay his way; and he had the stage of the Carolina Playmakers as his Workshop. The young Negro was not welcome in a white man's theatre and he had no theatre of his own; nor did he have a collaborator such as Richard Wright found, years later, when Paul Green helped him in the dramatization of his novel, *Native Son.*

We cannot credit the tributary theatre with Paul Green's need to strike roots where he lived and worked nor with his capacity for hard work nor with his personal power to remake life into plays. But we can fairly say that to the tributary theatre he owed the workshop which made it possible for him to try out his playwriting skills "on his home roots," so to speak, to have the criticism of a teacher, co-workers and an audience, and to be free of the deadening pressure of fashion and convention which are apt to stultify young talent in the market-place. And to the freer air of the tributary theatre must be credited the opportunity to experiment in unfamiliar theatre forms such as lie at the base of plays like *Johnny Johnson* and *Roll, Sweet Chariot.* There are ideas in some of Paul Green's short plays, there are pages in their writing that have never been excelled in American playwriting—for example in *The No 'Count Boy,* the fantastic tale of the youngster in whom the love of freedom and the possession of an imagination that had never known a bridle were made to substitute for honesty and common sense; in *Man on the House,* a mystic and pathetic story of a family on the way to spiritual ruin (much more integrated and effective in this early form than in the elaborated version called *Shroud My Body Down*); and in *Hymn to the Rising Sun,* the bitter picture of death and human waste in a chain gang on Independence Day. Such plays could, it seems, develop only in a theatre where a playwright could take his own time and chart his own course. They are easy plays to produce and rewarding; yet they are distinctly professional plays, and only the most professional and poetic actors could do their variety and their subtle simplicity full justice.

Working on a poorly equipped stage with amateur actors and directors creates its own difficulties for a playwright. There are many possibilities for characterization and for action that amateurs cannot discover in manuscripts and have not the technique to present, even if they do discover them. Moreover, projection across footlights is so apt to be lacking in their performance that a playwright cannot always tell whether he has made a point or not. Above all, there are few amateur directors who understand how to create a pattern of characters in contrast, of time, action, rhythm for an untried play, and few amateur ensembles who can hold such patterns.

Many of these difficulties show clearly as flaws in Paul Green's work. If you read his plays, especially the short ones, you will see how many of the characters are slightly oversharp, as if he had unconsciously given them an edge he could not count on from his players. His stage directions are often so detailed that they interfere with the reader who is trying to visualize the action of the play himself. They create an emotional as well as a mental let-down. This is particularly true with the printed version of that triumphant failure, *Roll, Sweet Chariot*, published under its older title, *Potter's Field*. If you can eliminate from the printed page the major part of the stage directions and let the characters and the action and the music of the speech swing you along with their own momentum, you will find it difficult to believe that an audience and a group of sensitive critics could sit through an extraordinarily fine performance of this play and not see how important it was. The music (by Dolphe Martin) and the words that went from speech to chant and into song were so unified and on so high a plane that it hardly seems possible that only a few years later the same audience and the same critics could listen to so obvious and blatant a work as Marc Blitzstein's *The Cradle Will Rock* and call it original and epoch-making. But if you do not find it possible to skip Paul Green's interfering stage directions, you will probably not be able to act the play for yourself and will find it muddy reading. You must charge that to a habit, too often acquired in tributary theatres and in second-rate professional companies, of forgetting that actors are creative artists and not depending on them to create the characters and the action the words need to complete their meaning.

Tributary handicaps are, however, very small ones to the sensitive playwright who is trying to find the way to his own form, compared to the handicaps he encounters if he goes *too soon* to a professional theatre where everything must move at top speed, where mistakes are so expensive that a few slips may wreck a play, and where a new playwright is not apt to be favored with the expert directors and players who will take pains to help him along the way. The man who comes to Broadway equipped to meet it on its own terms will find the best skills in the world at his command. But the record of failure in professionally produced plays is an evidence of the amount of playwriting talent that is shattered there.

It is all very well to say that genius can work within limits. But genius is not required to accept the conventions of a given time, or of a certain place, as the limits by which his art should be bound. It is interesting in this connection to compare Paul Green and Eugene O'Neill. It bothered O'Neill to be forced to plot a play in a definite number of acts; it bothered him to have a play's length determined by the length of an ordinary theatre evening; it bothered him to have an actor's own face between the actor and the character in a play. Being a powerful playwright and by nature an iconoclast, O'Neill wrote plays to break through each of these mechanical restrictions and release our theatre from the fetters of their conventions. Paul Green is not troubled to destroy such annoyances. What bothers him is the shrinkage which has taken place in the theatre itself. His aim is to dilate the range of our modern theatre until it can do again all of the things the theatre has done. He does not accept the fact that actors cannot dance or sing, that simple words cannot, by adding to their color and their phrasing, be made to do more than they have lately done, that gesture cannot be made free and group movement more meaningful. All of these broader ranges are inherent in his plays' action. He is never afraid to grapple with common prejudices and to make poetry out of the struggle, as witness *Hymn to the Rising Sun*. He is not afraid to write a little play or abashed by a big one. He is more theatrical than most writers of our day, and it is safe to say that of all the American playwrights now writing for the theatre there is none who stands a better chance than Paul Green of writing a play which will be acclaimed as a great work by his contemporaries and be so considered by their descendants as well. He writes out of the life of his day and is concerned with the people about him—all the people—with the lives they live and the deaths they die. His canvas is usually local, "out of the south," but his themes are universal and not tied to time and place, except for such "occasional" plays as *The Lost Colony*, written in celebration of the first English settlement in America on Roanoke Island, and *Highland Call* written in memory of Flora MacDonald and intended to be played at Fayetteville where she lived.

Shroud My Body Down was published in Iowa and E. C. Mabie, whose faith centered in Iowa, writes the prefatory note: "Such plays," he says, "are plays for a truly experimental theatre . . . with a staff sincere in efforts to make honest and significant interpretations in dramatic form." So far so good. But Mr. Mabie goes on to say "Furthermore, these are plays *for* a regional theatre. . . . They challenge the best of imaginations, those which envision a regional theatre as artistically independent of metropolitan centers." Paul Green could never have written that sentence. He would conceive of plays as *out of* a regional theatre but not *for* a regional theatre. A regional theatre can recreate its own characters, problems and ways of life more freely and fully than a metropolitan theatre, with its many converging and conflicting influences, can do the same job. And that regional theatres should do this is of great and essential importance to the whole of the theatre if it is to maintain its power as a social and artistic force in the life of the nation. But plays written *for* a regional theatre, or on the assumption that regional artists or a regional audience are superior to any other, are stultifying both to the artists who create them and to the audience that watches them. Their material is belittled, before they are written, by the playwright's attitude toward his audience. This is true whether the region is North Carolina or Iowa or the province of New York. Paul Green knows this. Some years ago, after a particularly disconcerting experience in New York he left rather hurriedly for Chapel Hill and I must have written to him saying that I hoped the experience would not make him desert New York, for we also needed him here. His answer was characteristic: "No, it is not my intention to desert New York any more than to desert North Carolina. In fact, I am working every day *to bring the two closer together in myself*." The italics, of course, are not his. What that sentence means is simply that the secret of Paul Green's power lies within him. He is distinctly a social being. He believes in the theatre as a good means to interpret men to one another. He is willing to plough and to sow wherever his work is needed; he does not care who reaps the harvest.

At the moment this is where he stands: He is represented on Broadway as collaborator with Richard Wright in the dramatization of that author's *Native Son*. He is finishing a volume of *Life Stories of the Cape Fear Valley*. The state of North Carolina has just, by act of legislature, underwritten to the extent of $10,000 a year the production of his symphonic drama *The Lost Colony,* which opens its fifth season in Roanoke Island on July 3. The Federal government has offered the cooperation of the National Park Service to "make it possible for *The Lost Colony* to reach an ever increasing number of American people." Paul Green has just been elected President of the National Theatre Conference. He has promised this large group of tributary theatres a new play for the autumn which twenty of them have agreed to produce during the season as a first experiment in making various cross-country productions even including New York. He is working actively with a group that is providing directors and building up recreation programs for the soldier camps, because he knows better than most men that we are still physical beings who—probably for many more generations—must "lag behind the dream." All of this shows how Paul Green is working—at half a dozen points—to bring the various parts of the country "closer together in myself."

July 1941

* *

EDWIN DUERR

*

Teaching Theatre

TEACHERS WHO WORK in the American theatre ought to think more about their relation to the potentialities of the American theatre. We ought to re-discover more or less exactly what it is we are trying to accomplish—or we can have no progress, nor expect any which is not accidental. We ought to know what our efforts are adding up to, or what we hope they are adding up to, in sum total.

Sometimes, in thinking about such matters, I find it challenging to begin with the point that many of us—teachers of theatre—do not know what we are doing. And many of us do not know we do not know what we are doing. I say this warily, and very humbly, but also most emphatically because I am reasonably sure that the American theatre of recent times has failed to become the kind of theatre which, with enthusiasm and great vision, we promised ourselves some years back it could and would become through our efforts—mind you, through *our* efforts.

In the 1920's, on top of the high wave of Eugene O'Neill and Gordon Craig, and the new designers, and the Neighborhood Playhouse, and the young Theatre Guild, we took the theatre into the school curriculum. We said the theatre is an important manifestation of man, of his time, of his place in the scheme of things. We said apprentices in culture ought to be instructed in the art of the theatre, and taught to appreciate and to demand genuine theatre. We wanted to flood into American life people who knew and understood the art—people who could enrich it either as artist or audience. We were on the verge of creating, in various guises, what Edith J. R. Isaacs so aptly termed a tributary theatre; a small stream, a source stream, flowing into the main stream.

But today, some twenty years later, looking back on the creative talents and the critical faculties we have developed and set in motion, and measuring their total effect as well as their potency by the theatre we now have, some of us might be compelled to admit that we have done little or nothing to improve our country's theatre, except perhaps accidentally. We might agree that we have failed to augment the theatre with that sense of meaning and beauty which our university thought and discipline should have engendered.

That is why, and not merely to be contentious, I so frequently hazard the supposition that many of us do not yet know what to do with theatre instruction in a university or college. Too many of us do not know what the art of the theatre is in first principles.

Is it not essential to believe with the poet MacLeish that "Art is a method of dealing with our experience of the world. It makes that experience, as experience, recognizable to the spirit. There are other methods of dealing with our experience of this earth which translate it into intellectual terms or extract from it moral meanings. Art is not such a method." Can we not come to some sort of agreement with Robert Edmond Jones, that "this theatre we are working in is a very strange place. It deals, not with logic, but with magic . . . with forebodings and ecstasies and mystical splendors . . . and mysteries . . . and unleashed passions and thrilling intimations . . . and elevation . . . and exaltation and secrets 'too divinely precious not to be forbidden.' "

If there is more than a bit of truth in Madariaga's saying that "humanity can be divided into types, according to the dominance in them of memory, intelligence or creative intuition," may not our job as teachers of theatre be to discover in and for others this creative intuition, this magic, this wonder. . . . May it not be for us to reveal, and to bring others to reveal, "the inscapes of things" in this precinct of art which we work in and call theatre? Perhaps too many of us are trying to understand and to nurture both the art and the artist solely by the scientific method.

In the theatre, and therefore in our teaching of theatre, more of us must be dealers in the imagination as it takes form in sound and sense, in words and pictures and color and movement, as well as in time, on such-and-such a platform before an audience come to hear and to watch and to be moved "at the likeness of things that be absent."

I do not often enough see the beginning promise of such a theatre in the high schools of the country where the teachers we have taught are now teaching. At least I do not see in it the multitudinous high schools where the drama instructors drill their students to be proficient at and to appreciate only the pulp drama, the ten dollar "story" plays written by hack writers as insensitive to revealing experience or theatric form as rocks are. Such instructors are daily exposing our own shortcomings as teachers, because a quality theatre can come into existence only with difficulty so long as that kind of glib and vacuous play is consumed so regularly and with such gusto, consumed in such quantity that the play-brokers to the amateur market, in response to the demand, depend almost for their existence on the abundant royalties garnered from them.

I do not see the bright promise of a better theatre in the common attitude to the stage wares of Broadway. Many of us commit two contradictory wrongs at one end and the same time: (1) we decry Broadway and its professional productions for inept reasons; (2) we ape in almost every way we can the practice and policies of Broadway. Too many theatre teachers coddle themselves by saying to colleagues and students: "We could do such-and-such a play much better here on our own campus," condemning Broadway in terms of mere efficiency. There ought to be a better way of evaluating the professional stage. We ought to have the critical good sense to say, perhaps, not that what Broadway does is often inefficient, but that what it offers is not true theatre.

In order to do that, we must first be able to criticize playwriting, acting, directing and decor, not solely in terms of technical proficiency, but in terms of audience aesthetics: the idea finding its body, the form inherent in the expression, life abstracted and extended into intuitive truth, the emotion pleasurably communicated. . . .

Too many theatre teachers turn everything topsy-turvy—the main stream into the tributary—when they continue to ape Broadway while they criticize it. As often as we produce a New York play, largely because it was successful "on the main stem"—as often as we stage *Margin for Error, Family Portrait, What a Life* and *Charley's Aunt* (after Broadway revives it!)—we too rarely add our own creative contribution; too many of us follow in almost every detail the actual promptbook and the glossy photographs of the New York production. In too many cases for comfort the theatre teacher's aim is Broadway's aim: to get the play competently on the boards, to draw large audiences. Only a few teachers here and there refuse to be rushed into the routine practice of "putting on plays" at specific intervals. These few teacher-directors demand time to create, and to perfect what they create, as well as the most important time of all, time to think about the fundamental nature and the magic-like appeal of theatre.

If more of us do not work that way our students will some day soon say to us: "Don't teach us how to get this play on effectively, how to be practical, how to get by! At a university, studying theatre, we want to learn the right way, the creative way, of bringing its life to this script. The world outside will quickly enough teach us to get by."

Until we can create and judge our work in terms theatrical, our university productions, in too many instances, from San Francisco to New York, our *Holidays* and *Wintersets* from Minneapolis to Memphis, will continue to be more or less identical. Until more of us concern ourselves with a few first principles, we shall go on being artist directors without a sense of form, without style, without independent individualities. We shall all be cut from the same grey average cloth.

How is it that in the field of the modern dance three schools—Hanya Holm's, Charles Weidman and Doris Humphrey's, and Martha Graham's—can come together and teach students three different theories of what the dance might be? Why can that sort of conjunction not happen in the teaching of theatre? Have we no differing theories, or only one theory, or none? Yet, if we have no theories of theatre, no first principles, to teach and practice—what have we?

How else in our practical and technical work can we justify the teaching we do at a university unless such methods are the only or best methods by which certain *theories,* certain *principles,* can be examined and communicated?

If you reply that there were no theories about theatre, and no thinking about its magical nature, in the times of Sophocles and Molière—that their creativeness sprang into being without it—then why do we teach theatre at a university at all?

I am reasonably sure that there is not enough deep concern about the nature of theatre when I read many of the book products—the visible thinking—of my colleagues. During the last twenty years a considerable portion of the books published have been of two non-thought-provoking kinds: the practical manual on how to act, direct, set up lights, design scenery, make-up, and so forth, and the research opus, the footnoted historical study, in which the determination of a play's antecedents or an actor's interpolations is as important as the play's artistic merits. Such studies are supposed to constitute "scientific research." Would it not be wiser and in the long run more profitable for theatre teachers to hold with Robert Maynard Hutchins that "Research in the sense of gathering data for the sake of gathering them has . . . no place in a university. Research in the sense of the development, elaboration and refinement of *principles* together with the collection and use of empirical materials to aid in these processes is one of the highest activities of a university and one in which all its professors should be engaged." We need more books on the method and manner of Stark Young's *Theatre,* Alexander Bakshy's *The Theatre Unbound* and Harley Granville-Barker's *On Dramatic Method.*

What I mean to say, in sum, and with considered emphasis, is that the potentialities of the American theatre can be greatly realized by us only when more of us will do more thinking about theatre. In well-thought-out aims, and not merely in our practice, we can know those potentialities. They are more concerned with first principles than with professionalism. They have more affinity with aesthetics than with efficiency.

July 1941

* *

LYNN RIGGS

*

A Credo for the Tributary Theatre

[*This statement of faith was delivered by Lynn Riggs in an address to the San Diego Community Theatre at the Globe Theatre early in 1940*—THE EDITORS.]

CASUAL as the personal reasons may be which bring the workers in a little theatre together, one dare not be casual about theatre itself. No one should touch any aspect of the theatre without joy, honest-to-God delight. For joy is the very stuff of the creative impulse, and this impulse must be given a chance if the worker and the audience which comes to see his work are to be rewarded.

Certainly no drama group has the right to ask anyone to sit through a production without being in some way changed; not necessarily made over, converted in a moment to something new and strange and unrecognizable, but somehow, somewhere, in at least one cell, different because for a moment something in experience has been made to stand out arrested, fixed in time, made immortal. Theatre people should make these moments happen, or consider themselves failing in their craft.

The stage is a platform for eloquence, on which life is compressed and heightened, made larger and more significant. It is a rocket that flares and sparkles and bursts, its tentacles streaming against darkness. Such revealing, thrilling moments happen in life, but they must be made to happen more often and more grandly in the theatre. The theatre is the place in which to enlarge and illumine life.

But in order that this may be done, life must be looked at: the world crowding around, of sections, of city, of state, of farm and crossroads, of our own country, of the entire globe. One must constantly seek to comprehend the flow of the tides of man in the aggregate, his needs, his impulses and his right to dignity. It's a large order to be alive in the world today. It's strenuous and often demoralizing. But the more we seek to know and to comprehend, and to add what we can to make it bearable for ourselves and others to live, the more revelation we stumble on, and the more we possess the power to change that world.

As revelation comes, we find that we have something to say. As individuals we begin to have a special and unique wisdom. If we are to draw on this, it's time to ask ourselves: what do we know? what have we got to say? how are we going to say it in the theatre? This means a very clear program, not merely of schedule and plays but of policy, of aims and goal. Nothing on this green earth survives without an idea behind it, a burning abstract compulsion, a pure concept, a central motion and aim. This country would be completely disorganized and probably in ruins—certainly at war—we would be many bickering states and tongues—if it had not been for some common ideas and ideals. We now largely believe that every man has a right to live and a right to work; true, we have staggered forward, and back a little, then forward again a little farther, trying to achieve a government truly of the people, by the people and for the people. But the point is that we would not be going anywhere —even staggering—unless we had that imposing ideal. One can't handle it; it can't be seen, and yet it is stronger than flesh and blood, and it outlasts them both.

An ideal, a goal, an intention, an aim—without it, there is no core to an undertaking. It is like a body without a heart to pump food to the farthermost cell. A theatre can stand for a time without any hard and fast intentions, but in the long run, if it is to live, it must have visionary as well as practical goals. Actually, these visionary ideals exist in every theatre group, often formless and chaotic but nonetheless real. The composite need that has brought the group together is a driving force; however inexact and unclear it may be, it directs the whole enterprise. There is no accident about it. Every time we cut a piece of goods to make costumes, or dab paint on a flat, or walk across the stage, or pull a curtain, or put a word on paper, we reveal ourselves, what our nature is, who we are, what we think, what we intend to do.

What a betrayal that can be. I should think that, if nothing else would, vanity at least might make us stop to consider what trivialities of soul we are revealing. I should think we would try to find out what we are doing, that we would wait to use our talents truly and deeply, in order to reveal the exact and the timeless, the important, the life-giving truth. I should think we would take the theatre seriously. I should think we would take life seriously.

February 1941

XI · DIRECTING AND PRODUCING

* * *

MARGARET WEBSTER

*

Producing Mr. Shakespeare

"THE ONELY grace and setting of a tragedy," wrote one of Shakespeare's contemporary playwrights, "is a full and understanding auditory." It is as true today as it was three hundred years ago. His plays, the greatest in the English language, can only be kept alive, in the fullest and most vivid sense, through the living theatre.

With the direction of *Richard III* for Maurice Evans in New York in February 1937, I began to glimpse the enormous opportunities which lie before the producer of Shakespeare in the United States. This play was virtually unknown to American audiences; the most that was hoped of it was an "artistic" success; yet it enjoyed a recordbreaking run in New York as well as two extensive road tours. The uncut *Hamlet* which followed was also produced for the first time in the American commercial theatre, and *Henry IV,* Part I, though it had been done by the Players' Club in 1926, had never been considered as having potential value for the theatrical manager with a living to earn. Yet both of them, as well as the better-known *Twelfth Night,* which was produced by the Theatre Guild with Mr. Evans and Miss Helen Hayes, found eager audiences all over the country. The reputation and personal quality of the stars was undoubtedly a great factor in this result; but it seemed that Mr. Shakespeare was still one of America's most popular dramatists.

The aim of Mr. Evans' productions has been a collaboration with both author and audience. We have tried honestly to interpret the author's intention, as nearly as we could divine it, to the audiences for whom the productions were intended. We have never supposed that we were providing any definitive answer to the problems of the plays, especially those of the inexhaustible *Hamlet.*

We have had to face a number of difficulties of which we only gradually became aware. There was, for instance, the minor one of accent. Several actors went so far as to refuse parts in the production on the grounds that they either could not "speak English," or were afraid that by so doing they would endanger their chances of future employment as gangsters. We tried to obtain some homogeneity of speech that was neither dude English nor localized American, pertaining neither to Oxford University nor Akron, Ohio. We found that actors were plainly frightened of Shakespeare, particularly of the verse, and were initially disinclined to regard his characters as real people. Audiences were frightened, too; but they also proved, I found, eager and swift, very ready to respond, the kind of audience that Shakespeare himself might have wished for.

From both actors and audience we were confronted with the inhibitions which result from regarding Shakespeare as high-brow stuff. At a performance of *Hamlet* in a Middle Western city, the balconies were crowded with school children, noisy, skeptical, restless. Owing to a shortage of ushers, a couple of cops were called to keep a watchful eye on them; the cops were very conscious of their responsibilities, and when the children, as quick as they were critical, began to laugh at Polonius, they were cowed by a fiercely resentful "Shush" from the police force; poor Polonius played frantically to solemn faces throughout the afternoon.

One of the most vital tasks which confront the Shakespearean producer in America is the breaking-down of this unwholesome reverence for the Bard. There is at present no tradition as to the production or playing of Shakespeare, and this freedom is, in itself, an opportunity. The repertory companies which used to tour the country have been forced out of business by economic conditions and the competition of new forms of entertainment. There have been individual, and blazing, performances by stars who have had the vision and the ability to avail themselves of Shakespeare—John Barrymore, Jane Cowl, Katharine Cornell, and others. But there has been no standard against which succeeding actors and directors could measure the truth of interpretation newly divined, little informed knowledge of the plays and of their author. Tradition is sometimes a yardstick. It need not be merely a collection of fusty and outworn shreds from the theatrical wardrobe of an earlier time. The modern theatre, confused and uncertain upon this as almost every other topic, vacillates between excessive respectfulness and a determination to be novel at any cost. Considering its more recent ancestry, this is not altogether surprising.

In America and England the nineteenth century wore itself out in a blaze of star actors, playing Shakespeare very much as he had been played by the preceding hundred and fifty years, using the plays as vehicles for the principal players, blissfully unaware of the power of their craftsmanship as the uncut texts have since revealed it. Edwin Booth in America was the last of the giants, the latest glory of a long period which had been distinguished by superlative actors and ridiculous plays. In England the succession developed upon Sir Henry Irving, whose particular twist of genius was complemented and graced by the radiant humanity of his leading lady, Ellen Terry. Like Booth, he was a single-minded man of the theatre. His productions at the Lyceum Theatre, which he also played extensively in America, followed the long-established precedent. They interpreted Irving rather than Shakespeare.

But even in the eighteen-nineties the voice of rebellion was beginning to be heard, and it was no uncertain one. "In a true republic of art," wrote the critic of the *Saturday Review,* "Sir Henry Irving would ere this have expiated his acting versions of Shakespeare on the scaffold. He does not merely cut the plays, he disembowels them." The prophet of the new scholarship and the new criticism was Mr. George Bernard Shaw.

Mr. Shaw was no Bardolator. "Oh, what a DAMNED fool Shakespeare was!" he wrote, in a moment of exasperation. And repeatedly he inveighs against Shakespeare's "monstrous rhetorical fustian, his unbearable platitudes, his sententious combination of ready reflections with complete intellectual sterility." But he never ceased trying to goad producers, Irving, Tree, Augustin Daly and the rest, into doing the plays as "the wily William planned them." The interchange of letters between Shaw and Ellen Terry prior to her first appearance as Imogen with Irving in 1896 provides an invaluable object lesson in lucid critical thinking, supplemented and humanized by the truth and simplicity of an actress' feeling. The apostle of the new Shakespeare did not have long to wait for the results of his campaign. In October 1897, Forbes Robertson produced *Hamlet,* also at the Lyceum, and the *Saturday Review* greeted him thus: "The Forbes Robertson *Hamlet* at the Lyceum is, very unexpectedly at that address, really not at all unlike Shakespeare's play of the same name. I am quite certain I saw Reynaldo in it for a moment; and possibly I may have seen Voltimand and Cornelius; but just as the time for their scene arrived, my eye fell on the word 'Fortinbras' in the programme, which so amazed me that I hardly know what I saw for the next ten minutes."

Since that time Shakespeare in the theatre has had to undergo a period of heavy upholstery and mountainous realism before the theatre really stripped itself for action, under the influence of the "expressionist" twenties, and the vigorous but erratic impulses of that rebellious period. Scenic design has gained enormously in freedom and flexibility, growing steadily nearer to the Elizabethan spirit as it grew less representational. The theatre has cast a wide net, from constructivism to modern dress, in its efforts to revitalize plays which, in point of fact, have never lost their vitality.

The whole convention of our theatre has changed since Shakespeare's day. The tacit covenant between actor, author and audience is on a wholly different basis. How can we preserve Shakespeare's intention in our modern terms? We may, we must, try honestly and devotedly to divine his meaning. We must know, for that purpose, the instruments of staging that he used, for they shaped his craftsmanship and without a knowledge of them we shall often divine his intention wrongly. But it is not, I think, enough to study the exact way in which he swung his action from inner stage to outer stage, to upper stage and back again; to assess the extent to which the use of the boy players influenced his characterization of women's parts; to scan the Quarto texts for signs of his theatre thinking expressed in cuts, additions to and revisions of his script; least of all to follow the scholars in their passionate disintegration of the texts into "early Shakespeare," "another hand," "a late addition," "a playhouse omission," and so on. Our business is not disintegration, but integrity. For the scholars' "true texts" we are grateful indeed; but it is still our business to transmute them into terms of the living theatre today.

If, however, we were to consider only "audience effect" in its most superficial sense, we should be liable to go as far astray as the great actors of the eighteenth and nineteenth centuries did, and to lose as much of the essential Shakespeare. We have yet to produce a dramatist who is more skilled in audience psychology than "the wily William." We shall be foolish to underrate his methods or to disregard his conclusions.

If a modern producer were dealing with an author with thirty-seven plays to his credit, most of them successes and a dozen or so smash hits, he would at least listen with respect to what that author had to say, and take some trouble to appreciate the workings of his mind. Shakespeare is still one of Broadway's most successful playwrights. His pay-checks, if he still received them, would top the lists of Dramatists' Guild members; although the Hollywood market offers him little, the amateur rights are worth a fortune. He is worth consulting, worth understanding, as a man, as a man of the theatre, and this will take something a little wider in scope than a cursory perusal of the text, even of the New Cambridge edition.

There is a German play in which Goethe, reincarnating himself as a college student about to take an examination on Goethe, fails hopelessly to answer the questions put to him. He either does not remember at all incidents which the examiners seem to consider of supreme importance, or his replies run directly counter to the textbooks of accepted criticism. It is probable that we should be appalled by Shakespeare's inability to satisfy some of our burning inquiries, and that he would be at a loss to understand why we should get so exercised over seeming trifles. But it is unlikely that we should ever find him without an explanation of the purpose of his stagecraft, or a reason for his dramatic intention. I think we are justified in assuming that he would readily suggest modifications to suit our revivals; he would probably understand our audiences as well as or better than we do. We are perhaps too ready to accept current shibboleths as to what an audience will or will not like, what it will pay to see, and what it will stay away from in overwhelming numbers. He probably would find no difficulty in adapting the practice of his theatre to the usage of ours, and if he found it unnecessary to make all the changes we at first demanded, we might well discover in the end that he was right. Since, however, we cannot claim his aid, we must do our best to think with his mind, and bring his standards into harmony with our own.

The principles on which a director must base his approach to a

Shakespearean play are, after all, no different from those which govern his approach to any other play; his method will vary, since the technique of directing is itself subject to every degree of personal idiosyncrasy. I believe that he should determine first the mood of the play, its material and spiritual atmosphere, its structural pattern, the wholeness of its effect. What kind of a world is this of Arden or Elsinore, Illyria or Verona? what forces are at work in it? what values or what standards hold good within its confines? Shakespeare will have employed certain dramatic devices whose origin and purpose we must learn to recognize through a knowledge of the material, human or inanimate, which he employed. But what was the intention behind these theatre devices? Knowing his method, we may guess at his mind; perceiving the familiar, we may divine the transcendental. With the former, we must sometimes take liberties of adaptation; the latter we may not violate, except at our own peril.

The bridge over which we shall travel to Shakespeare's country, like the bridge we ourselves shall build from stage to auditorium is built of human beings. Who are these people? From King Lear to the Third Citizen, we must know them. It is always a sense of closeness at which we should aim, rather than an emphasis of separation.

We shall not have to dress Hotspur in the uniform of the R.A.F. in order to invest him with life; we underrate both our author and our audience in supposing that they can only be dragged into accord by distorting Coriolanus to the image of General Franco; slyly insinuating that there have been abdications of the English throne more recent than that of Richard II; on claiming with gleeful shouts that Enobarbus is an anticipatory Rudolf Hess. The truth of the plays is a timeless truth, and similarity of external circumstances no more than a fortuitous, though sometimes poignant, reminder that the returning paths of history have been trodden by many feet. In these days those who love the theatre and are jealous for its power and prerogative are rightly eager that it should prove itself as a contemporary force. But Shakespeare is not an escapist; he aims straight for the heart. There is singularly little hatred in the plays, and infinite understanding. It would be a barren world which ever felt it had gone beyond his wisdom and compassion.

January 1942

MORTON EUSTIS

*

High Jinks at the Music Box

NOEL COWARD REHEARSES BEATRICE LILLIE IN SET TO MUSIC

"WOA-P!"—Noel Coward claps his hands, runs up the rough ramp connecting the orchestra with the stage, throws up one hand to shade his eyes from the light which floods the stage and stands motionless facing the empty house. The pianist, seated at the left, stops playing in the middle of a beat. Four couples in day clothes, who have been fox-trotting on the stage, which is bare except for a few wooden chairs and some scenery stacked against the walls, stop dancing and look at Coward. The actor-playwright-director holds his brooding pose for a moment of complete silence, then whirls around to the pianist and snaps his finger: "I've got it. Right! Ready to start. Now watch, everybody." The piano player breaks into the opening bars of "The Party's Over Now," a gaily plaintive melody, and Coward, every inch the dancer, paces out steps for the chorus. Once, twice, three times, he goes through the routine, a sweep of his arm indicating to each couple when he is playing their bit. Then—"We'll try it all together now."

He starts the chorus on the dance—it is really more of a walk—and executes it with them, setting the tempo and beat with vibrant, expressive gestures and movements of his feet and body. He does a step in front of one couple, then waves them off the scene to skip across the full length of the stage—without missing a beat—and does the same thing, with variations, with another couple. By the time that he has guided each pair into the wings, and given a one-man show of extraordinary virtuosity in doing so, he claps his hands together; the music stops; the boys and girls stroll on; Coward motions the whole group back to their point of entrance as he chats with the stage manager.

"Do it again, please."—He stands at the left, his arms poised like a band leader. The pianist bangs out the chords; the first couple stroll on. "No, wrong beat!"—Coward hums the opening bars;

his arms drop to his side and he takes two buoyant steps forward. "Get it?" He raises his arms: "Right!" The music starts again. The chorus goes through the number—uninterrupted this time—while Coward taps out the beat with his feet, sways his body and his arms slowly in time to the music and appears to be in another world. The moment the last couple have gone off, he walks brusquely center-stage—all his movements while rehearsing are agile, staccato—"All right, it's coming. Start from the beginning again, please." He comes down the ramp into the orchestra whistling the air, leans over to exchange a joke with Beatrice Lillie, who is sitting in the darkness of the auditorium. He is silhouetted in the aisle against the bright lights on the stage, a lithe and agile combination of Stokowski and Benny Goodman, as he "conducts" the boys and girls—over and over again—in a simple routine that won't play for more than a minute or so when "the show is on."

Rehearsals for *Set to Music* have been in progress for almost a week at the Music Box Theatre; the cast know their lines fairly well by now though some of them still carry their "sides." Coward apparently believes in having the whole company on hand, chorus, principals and all, at every rehearsal, not in the American method of rehearsing a musical comedy all over the town and then assembling the bits in the last frenzied moments before the try-out. He also believes, after the first week or so, in doing the skits as nearly as possible in the sequence in which they are to be unrolled. "It helps to give you a feel of the whole show," he says. Of course, *Set to Music* is not a mammoth spectacle; there are only eighteen show girls, eight or ten chorus men, six or eight principals, and one star, Beatrice Lillie by name. But from the intense and painstaking supervision Coward devotes to each scene—every gesture, even—it seems unlikely that he would ever resort to the method of preparation so common in our song-and-dance theatre.

You have only to watch Coward once rehearsing to realize that, for better or worse, the show that bears his name will be a hundred percent Noel Coward show when it is introduced to the public—even though, as in this instance, he is not appearing in it. His versatility, his theatre sense, is nowhere seen to better advantage than in the grind of day and night rehearsals. He is everywhere; he does everything; he knows exactly what he wants. Singing, dancing—every variety from tap to ballet—playing every part except that of Miss Lillie (and who but Bea Lillie could play that role?), he infuses the whole cast with a sense of his enthusiasm and craftsmanship as he drills them mercilessly, but with patience and good humor. And yet, when the actor has something to offer on his own, he is wise enough to let well enough alone.

"Night is over. Dawn is breaking"—Penelope Dudley-Ward and Hugh French, the juvenile leads, go into the verse of "The Party's Over Now," while Coward, on stage again, paces around them, giving them the beat of the song with a soft tap dance. "Wait a minute," he breaks the number and turns to the pianist. "I don't want it to drag. If it drags it's spoiled. Now try it again and let them hear the melody." They sing it again, and again Coward interrupts. "It's not 'the *mu*-sic of-an-hour-ago,' Hugh. That's Bing Crosby. It's," he sings, exaggerating the emphasis this time, "the *mu-sic of an hour ago.'* Do you see what I mean? You've got to *sing* each word."

French tries it. "That's better. Now start from the beginning and —wait a minute, everybody. When you're singing, remember in your mind all the beginnings of the words. If you jump onto them from the top, get above them, instead of leading up to them, they'll sound like something and, what's more, they'll be heard. Never run a whole phrase into one line. Your line, Pempy, for instance, in 'Mad About the Boy,' you sing it: 'If-he-was-real-enough-I-couldn't-tell.' It ought to go," he sings, "'If he was *real* enough I *couldn't'* —pause—'tell,' then, with emphasis, *'but, like a silly fool* I—*fell.'* And let me hear each word. I know this is hypercritical. But it's important. All right. We'll do it again."

He sings the number with them this time, taking French's part first and then Miss Ward's; then they go into the brief dance routine —all three of them, Coward in front, exaggerating each move and gesture, over-emphasizing every beat a little to point up the effect. Then, watching them: "Would you like to move a little on that beat, Pempy? You don't have to if you don't want to, but I think it might give just a little more zip to the scene."

Miss Lillie, in a red blouse, a black skirt, a green hat with a little veil trailing behind it, saunters on stage for her cue. "All right. Come on, Dicky"—Coward waves French and Miss Ward off, on their cue, and Richard Haydn and a girl come on and sing a new reprise of the song. "That's very nice," Coward clicks his fingers. "All right, Bea-dle-dy."

Miss Lillie appears in the doorway, indicated by two chairs. It's been a *marvelous* party, she tells her hostess effusively. She was the "first to arrive and the last to leave." "Hurry, Bea," Coward whispers, "You won't have enough time before the song cue." She sweeps forward, looks from side to side, throws her arm in the air yells "Taxi," and bursts into laughter. A bored and sleepy taxi-driver saunters on, scolds Miss Lillie for making so much noise. She nestles her head on his obliging bosom, at a peculiar angle, and begins a patter song describing the party she has just attended. Bibulous guests were raffling off various nations, it seems, and "Grace got the giggles"—pause, a heightening of the shoulders, a stiffening of the muscles, a wild gleam in the eyes, a ridiculous gesture—"And gave me . . . JaPAN!" "Japan" comes out in a shriek of astonishment, followed, as her body relaxes, by a gust of inane laughter. "I *could*-n't have liked it more." She puts her arm through the taxi driver's and pulls him off stage, laughing and talking. You can't hear a word she says until, as she nears the wings, one hand shoots up, her shoulders pull back, "I've been to a—" A side glance, almost a wink at the audience; her hand starts a downward sweep—"MAR-velous!" —The swing of her arm rockets her towards the wings, and "party" is pronounced sotto voce as she exits.

"That's good, Bea. . . . Now the whole scene from the beginning —to see how little everyone can remember." Coward's clipped accents interrupt the laughter.

He smiles and hurries down into the house. "And remember, keep the weight on the front of your feet; otherwise you all seem to be pulling back and there's no lift to the scene. *Right!"* He picks up the orchestra leader's baton and literally drives the scene forward; it comes to life; it has swing and precision; the sentimental banality of the song seems charming for the first time. "Don't let it down. Don't let it down," Coward calls as he swings the baton over his head. "That's *much* better. . . . But I tell you what, Dicky," he runs on stage, "We might just as well face it. It's a tragic moment. I think we'll drop your refrain. It's good but it doesn't add anything to the number." Haydn takes the blow good-naturedly;

he had expected the demise earlier. "Don't bother about your entrance, Bea. We'll do 'Opening Night.' "

Now Coward is supervising the placing of the props. "The dressing table's got to be further upstage, Tony, and cheat a little with the angle so that everyone can see Bea when she's sitting there. . . . All right. Start!" He watches intently as three of an actress' suitors, waiting in her dressing room, show her maid the jewels they have bought her. "No. No. No!" he claps his hands and steps forward. "I want you to take your voices *above* what you're saying. I want a sharp sound. Remember you've got to be heard way up there"—he points to the balcony—"and we're going to be in a much bigger theatre in Boston. Now try it again, with a high tone, with sharpness. Get it right up. If you get it too high, I'll tell you." This time they almost shout. "Listen," Coward stops them, "it's a question of *pitch,* not of noise. When you're on the stage you've got to get a little higher edge to your voice than you do in real life, but you don't have to shout. Listen to me now." He speaks the lines, hardly seeming to raise his voice, but each word can be heard clearly all over the house. "See what I mean. *Right!"* He clicks his fingers, strolls to the side. The scene proceeds; it has more edge. "Don't let the tempo drop," Coward calls out; he beats the time.

Applause is heard off stage and Miss Lillie comes on with the line; "Shut it out, Daisy. *Shut—it—out!* I can't *bear* it!" She puts both hands to her head to drown out the sound. "What's the matter, darling?" one of her admirers asks. "Nothing," she responds, with tragic mien, and sits down wearily. "Everything." She turns to look at them and slumps back. "Absolutely perfect, Bea-dle-dy," Coward calls out. One by one, her suitors present their gifts and Lillie comments on them as she seizes them avidly: rubies—"such *cru*-el stones, aren't they?"—diamonds—"lovely, so cold"—pearls, that belonged to the man's mother—"and did they make her happy?"—biting the pearls as she takes them. "Splendid!" They build up the scene as they go along, Coward making this point, Lillie that. When Lillie dismisses her beaux with the announcement that she is "utterly and completely exhausted," her head slumps forward and she barely has the energy to snap it back. It is "life" that has done this to her; *"life!"*

She raises her hand limply above the table. One of the men kisses it. Another comes up. "Wait," Miss Lillie says. "We'll try it another way." She holds her arm out, the wrist arched up. The man kisses her hand, and she lets her whole arm fall with a thud onto the table. "Marvelous," Coward calls out as he runs up to play the man's part opposite Miss Lillie and to time all his movements and gestures carefully. "He mustn't seem to notice that she has done anything queer. *Right!"* He watches them go through it again. This time, as she drops her arm, the fall makes her body jerk in the opposite direction so that she almost slips off the chair. She holds up her hand for the next man to kiss, lets it fall again. "No, that's not good. Let me try it over." Out goes her hand; the man kisses it. This time she leaves her arm suspended for a fraction of a second, then slowly and gracefully lets it float down to the table. This gets an instantaneous laugh from the company and a warm note of approval from Coward. "I'm *afraid* this scene's going to be funny, Bea. . . . *Look,* I've thought of something. When you put out your hand the second time, shift the pearls you're holding, then make a quick grab for them so that he won't get them. You'll vary all these bits, of course, once you get an audience reaction; but let's get as many of them set now as possible. Right!"

When Miss Lillie—alone at last—begins her song: "Weary of it all," Coward dances it out beside her, beating the tempo for the piano player with his hands. She comes to the lines: "Caviar and grouse in an overheated house" and her whole body seems to crumple with world weariness, then, suddenly, completely unexpectedly, and out of time with the music, she galvanizes herself into a mine of energy and sweeps forward to sing her next lines in a throaty hot-cha voice, her body swaying in swing rhythm. The whole cast, including Coward, break into peals of laughter. Lillie, as swiftly as she has cast it off, replaces the mantle of jaded sophisticated weariness and walks, with her back to the audience, towards the exit singing: "I'm so weary"—pause, a droop of her head—"weary"—she picks up her evening cloak in pantomime—"weary"—she is at the door now, she wiggles her hips faintly—"of it"—she starts to go out, then just when you expect the "all" to come out, she suddenly turns so that her profile faces the audience, bursts into harsh, maniacal laughter and exits. The shock of the laugh—no one has heard it before—renders the cast almost speechless, then the whole company breaks down completely. "That pulled it up, Noel, didn't it?" Lillie says. She cocks one finger in the air, screws her mouth a little, then she, too, starts to laugh.

As you watch Miss Lillie in one incredible absurdity after another, keeping the company convulsed in rehearsals, even when she does the same scene over and over, you begin to realize how much the projection of comedy depends on timing, on the physical line of the body in gesture and movement, and on the sound pattern of a performance. You see, also, how much these elements spring from "the infinite capacity for taking pains," rather than from divine comic inspiration.

"The simple movements on the stage," as Coward explains to an actor in relation to a dance step, "only look spontaneous if they are studied over, and over, and over. You must know exactly how many steps to take to reach your partner and you must take the same number of steps each time you do it. Otherwise it will look sloppy. Spontaneity on the stage is only possible in movements and nuances which are superimposed after you've got a rigid pattern."

To say that Miss Lillie is funny only because she has a superlative comedian's technique is, of course, foolish. The light of real comic genius sparkles from beneath her dark eyelashes, radiates from each of the unexpected angles of her countenance, and illumines every motion and gesture she makes. But she would never be the Mistress of the Absurd if her technique were less sure. Her most inspired moments of spontaneous comic combustion would only pop and fizzle if they were not executed with perfect timing and the use of every trick in the comedian's bag.

Miss Lillie never delivers the comic thrust of a speech without reacting to it by some movement, however imperceptible; she never makes a gesture with her hand which is not reflected in a twist of her torso, a crook of her knee, a tightening, or a loosening, of her muscles. Let her toss her hand absurdly forward and her back will respond (when the laugh has subsided) by a sudden stiffening which throws her posterior into relief, gaining another laugh, which she will top by a slight, but surely a refined, wiggle. The "line" of her performance is always pliable and angular—always, that is, until she wants to get a comic effect by making it motionless and straight. It always has contrast. So it is with the "sound," which is measured to fit and to enrich this "line." It is, with the sound, a question of *crescendo* here and *piano* there; of suddenly beating a slow tempo (or an unresponsive audience) into quivering alertness by an unexpected increase in the volume of tone—one of Miss Lillie's favorite, and most favored, tricks.

There is something else, much harder to put your finger on, which illuminates Miss Lillie's playing—a quality which differentiates the great artist, in any field, from the merely competent one—the power to make some comment of her own on anything she essays. She sings a ditty about a party on the Riviera in which the denouement is, to say the least, unexpected. It always gets a laugh. But the laugh is twice as big when Miss Lillie, either before or after the climax (she varies this at rehearsals), looks at the audience with an expression of horrified amazement or of enraptured understanding, is if to say: "Have you ever *heard* of such a party?" taking them into her confidence. In another scene she stands angrily on stage as the chorus insists on singing "Ah! Ah! Ah!," preventing her from starting in on her next verse, and pushes one foot out in a petulant pose. That is the comic statement; the comment comes when, a moment later, drawing her shoulders together, she looks down over the peak of her nose and stares at her foot with mock incredulity.

"All right. Let's get on to the next scene," as Coward puts it. "And remember, boys," he is poised on the edge of the runway, "I want sharpness, vitality, brilliance, talent and charm!" He clicks his fingers and hurries into the orchestra. But the next scene has to wait until the evening session because a Mr. Winston, the stage manager announces, is here to measure the men for shirts and to get Mr. Coward's approval of the patterns. And the "fine patrician quartet of us" which sings of England's stately homes goes down to the men's room to be fitted instead of acquainting the company with the fact that:

Our duty to the nation,
It's only fair to state,
Lies not in procreation
But what we procreate.
And so we can cry
With Kindling eye,
As to married life we go,
What ho! for the stately homes of England!

February 1939

ADOLPHE APPIA

*

The Future of Production

[*Translated from the French by Ralph Roeder from the manuscript of an unpublished lecture delivered by Appia in December, 1921.*—THE EDITORS.]

WHEN A PLAYWRIGHT has completed his play, what is the element essential to its performance? The actor, unquestionably. Without the actor there can be no action, hence no performance, hence no play—except on our bookshelves. The first stage in externalization is the actor. In space—space "without form and void" —the actor represents three dimensions; he is plastic and occupies, accordingly, a fragment of space upon which he imposes his form.

But the actor is not a statue; being plastic, he is also alive, and his life is expressed by *movement;* he occupies space not only by his volume, but also by his movement. His body, isolated in an unlimited space, measures that space by its gestures and evolutions; or, more precisely, he appropriates a portion of that space, he limits and conditions it. Remove him, and space reverts to its infinity and eludes us. In this sense, the body creates space.

What we need is to master Time in a similar way. The evolutions of the body have a span of duration; we say X walks slowly or quickly. Space measurement involves time measurement, therefore, as well. . . . But all this is as yet purely arbitrary; the movements have not been regulated, and their duration remains uncertain; one directing mind must command and measure them. From our point of view this governing mind comes from the playwright; in his hands the actor is a compass for Space, a clock for Time. . . .

An organic hierarchy results from these facts, which we may name as follows: the Author, the Actor and (scenic) Space. You will observe that I have not mentioned Time. And indeed, if the presence of the actor affects Space, which the author can only measure through him, Time remains in the hands of the author, in other words, the author imposes directly on the actor the time duration of his role, but must act through the actor to realize that duration in Space. This would seem to be self-evident; we shall see, however, that our theatrical anarchy today is due to our ignorance in this respect.

Suppose we take our hierarchy at its base; that is, the author and his written text. This text is of a certain length and is divided into fragments which have, each, their respective length. The question arises: has the author any means of setting the *duration* of his text definitely enough to impose it on the actor? He has not. The duration of speech is indeterminate; speech may be uttered slowly or rapidly, it may be broken, and so forth, and these variations occur in a lapse of time difficult to span; too much slowness may destroy the connection of ideas; too much rapidity may make them unintelligible; but between these extremes there is a wide margin. The author may interline his text with directions for its delivery; he may even use a metronome for that purpose; but these notes would not be *contained* in his text proper, they are not an integral part of it, and the metronome would not appear, thank God, on the stage! Moreover, the actor, who should dominate Time, does not dominate it at all; the element of speech does not permit him to. . . .

The written word does not, then, contain the norm of Time needed to speak it; its duration is approximate, and is left to the discretion of the actor. From this it follows that the actor, responsible for a set of indeterminate durations, projects on the stage—what?—an indeterminate Space. This system of discretion is the estate of our modern Stage; the director, the decorator, the electrician, the stage-hands, and so forth, are all working in a loose approximation which would be intolerable in any other form of art. The will of the author should be law, but as we know, he does not control all the wires. Far from it! More often than not, he serves merely to prevent them from altogether entangling themselves.

It may be objected that theatrical art is complex. Undoubtedly. And, in this connection, let us draw a comparison. Suppose, for example, we take the musician who has composed a symphonic poem with *soli* and *choruses*. He is not hampered in its execution by the restrictions of the stage; but he is faced with the terrible complexity of the voices and the orchestra just the same. . . . His hierarchy never suffers from gaps or interferences. The tenors do not direct the orchestra or question the director, and the harpist does not meddle with the music of the soprano solo. The composer is sole master; if his will alone is not observed the composition is not performed; and if it is performed, it is because the author alone has decreed how it shall be rendered, and has seen to it that his will is obeyed; his tyranny is absolute; every player feels it; he must like it or leave it. Why? The score is set down on paper, just like the manuscripts of the dramatist; the conventional symbols of music are the equivalent of those other conventional symbols, the letters of the alphabet; and the presence of the composer is the same human presence as that of the dramatist. Where, then, lies the difference?

Let us go one step further and suppose that the composer is dead, and that the director has only the score with which to execute his will; what, then, distinguishes him from the theatrical director who produces a play by a dead author, since, after all, the script of a play and the score of a symphony are both a mere matter of conventional script?

Since we are dealing with conventional signs, we must conclude that those signs themselves are totally different. We have mentioned the approximate and often indeterminate nature of the duration of a script; the letters of the alphabet and the succession of words which ensue do no possess, in themselves, the power to establish definitely the duration of speech. The conventional signs of musical notation, on the other hand, do possess this power; it is, in fact, their *raison d'être;* if they lacked it, they would not represent music, music being an art of precision. The orchestral conductor possesses in the score, independently of his own will, whatever he needs to project those signs in the playing Time, in a duration or a success of durations, which have been finally and perfectly determined beforehand; and if the players do not obey it, they are no longer performing the score!

Where is the commanding baton of the dramatist? And if he had one, who or what would legalize its authority? His text? But is there anything in that text which presupposes the direction of a baton? And if the actors or the director are absent-minded or recalcitrant, can that text call them to order, and would the play be ruined by the maladroitness of the leading man or of the scene-painter? Alas, we are here in the domain of discretion! A false note or a missed cue, and the music ceases to be what it is. Can we say as much of the numberless slips of a theatrical rehearsal? What is it that gives to the score its despotic ascendancy—a kind of categorical imperative, that makes everyone feel its compulsion: *To be or not to be . . . ?*

Time, of course! Yes. In the score Time is determined; and in the play-script it is not. The baton transmits to the players the rhythm of Time; how could it do so for a spoken text? In the written score these rhythms are preserved past attainder. No one will deny that there is a great difference between the written composition of the dramatist and the written composition of the musician: a difference so great that they seem not to belong to the same order of facts. Yet both claim the dignity of works of art. Is that claim justified?

A work of art is the result of an ensemble of technical means commanded by one artist. The artist must grasp in his hand alone, and control by his will alone, the technical methods which he considers suitable for his purpose; the value of his work depends on it. To be an artist means, after all, to conceive and to execute a work of art. If this involves a division of labor, the division is only apparent, not real; the artist will and must be, always and in everything, the master; the work he offers the audience is his own work, otherwise it has no place in the realm of art. The musician dominates his work even in its performance. This essential right is denied the dramatist, and the work he offers the audience is not wholly his own; he does not dominate it and cannot, therefore, be an artist. Whatever his influence or his authority, they are not implicitly contained in his text. Let us repeat once more, and for the last time: the musician *dominates* Time, the dramatist merely *locates* his work in Time, and it is this which gives his work its arbitrary character. The stage gives him a space, which he has not measured; it remains alien to his manuscript. In the course of rehearsals, the author feels his impotence; he appreciates it even more painfully if he talks to a painter or a musician in the intermission.

We have now reached, not the crux of the problem, but its true beginning. It would be a waste of time to discuss staging if it were not to produce a work of art. Its fascination lies, in fact, in that aim. . . . The problem of staging presents itself, categorically, as follows: how can the dramatist become an artist, and who can furnish him the means to become one, since he has not been able to himself.

We can answer this problem only if we cease to consider the dramatist's work as divided into two parts: on the one hand, the manuscript, on the other, the stage. This requires an effort; but we can accomplish it, if we remember the work of the musician and its concert performance. The same *concerted* performance should be possible for the dramatist.

What is the relation of music to staging? Movement. But do its durations and proportions correspond to the habitual movements of the actor? *In no wise, and that is precisely our problem!* A convention, reciprocally accepted, must unite them. The movements of the actor *indicate* the movements of his spirit; they do not *express* them. The actor's forefinger raised in an imperative gesture does not in itself express a consuming ambition, nor a frown his mute, patient suffering. The actor notes, in himself or in others, these indications and applies them as best he can to his role; that is what is called composing a part. Words also are indications—symptoms; but the word *Love* has never expressed what we feel—when we love. We may love all our life without breathing a word of it; we may be loved, even, and never suspect it (at least, so Arvers says!) Such is the duration of words!—without relation to the duration of our feelings. Our gestures go deeper but, like words, their duration is not that of our feelings: a dagger thrust does not *express* the long hatred that culminates in that act; it merely indicates it. With our external life we have no means of *direct* communication and expression, and it is by a detour that we *infer* the feelings of which it is only the indication. The actor without music is a mere index-bearer, nothing more. . . .

If music controls Time, it must have good reasons and a sufficient justification for so doing; for, otherwise, how could it presume to violate an element which penetrates us, as Time does? Well, the justification lies in *ourselves!* How can we accuse an art, which we have ourselves invented and developed, of violence? We are ourselves the authors of the violence of music, and we are irresistibly impelled to that violence by our indestructible desire to express ourselves *to* ourselves. We gladly admit that music expresses what our gestures and words can not; and we concede it beforehand, for that purpose, every liberty. What use—relatively to us—does music make of Time? The dramatist enlarges its durations, in order to situate the indications he needs for his communication. Music on the other hand, has nothing to enlarge or prolong: it merely *expresses,* and its expression will assume, without any preliminary design, the form and the duration it requires. The spirit of the musician flows through it and directs it; *but, so soon as this secret is transcribed on paper, it is the music which assumes the direction:* the musician has unburdened himself. The music reveals to the listener the form and intensity of his inner life, in proportions which he accepts because he knows their origin (and we all know the deadly boredom we feel, when we do *not* accept them!) It would be a remarkable medium between the manuscript of the dramatist and the stage. Furthermore: in establishing the succession of duration, it would also establish their relative intensities, in other words, their dramatic value. The actor who sings his role no longer needs to interpret it; the music does that for him, it imposes its own eloquence upon him; the actor need not grope for his intonation, the music supplies it; he need not "bring out," on his own initiative, a particular passage, the music has already underlined it. The pauses of the actor are marked by the music and, what is more, they are filled by it. In a word, music takes command of the whole drama and projects only so much of it as is necessary to motivate and sustain its expression. Thus, it becomes the supreme regulator of the complete and integral dramatic composition; it dictates its balance.

The hierarchy with which we began contained only three levels: the author, the actor and the scenic space. Music adds a fourth. In fact, by taking over Time, music takes its rank in the hierarchy *between the author and the actor. . . .*

The literary play attempts to substitute what music alone could provide for it, and with a sure instinct it gives the actor supreme sway. Painted scenery has had its day; all our decoration has at last been sacrificed to the living body. It was high time! Then a remarkable thing occurred; music made its entrance into the spoken drama. In making the plastic presence of the actor supreme, we stripped and reduced the setting. A lacuna was the result, and we have filled it with music. Music returns to the actor by a side-door. Neither the author nor the director can longer be blind to their close technical kinship; but they upset the hierarchy by taking speech as their point of departure. Thus, music plays a secondary role; it supports or rounds out the action. Who has not felt the shock, unique of its kind, when, in the course of a play, the strains of music suddenly rise? Truth seems then gently to appear, pure and unveiled, to strip the actor of the tinseled rags that mask him, of all the contingencies which stifle him.

It is as if Music said to us: "You allow me this brief revelation; so be it; but I could say more, much more. . . ." And when words are superimposed upon it, we feel at once how impotent they are. Music tells the truth, always; if it lies, it tells us it lies; whereas words—! A scene into which music enters, no matter what it may be, is immediately ennobled, and fortunately we have the decency to use it with discretion; such indiscreet melodramas as *Manfred* or *L'Arlésienne* annoy us. A deity is not to be introduced with impunity into any company. This somewhat underhand and covert use of music is significant, because of the need it reveals; weary of the unbroken music of the lyric drama, we still long for its accompaniment; we feel how much closer its power of expression brings the spirit of the actor to our own. As yet we do not realize its stylizing power in Space, but we have felt a first intimation; and so has the actor; in the brief moments of musical accompaniment, he modifies his gestures, he feels the divine element penetrating his body, and he would be crude indeed if he did not recognize it. It is a step in the right direction; music has found a footing in the fortress. If, for instance, a scene in which music plays its invisible role has been rehearsed without music, at the first rehearsal with it the whole scene will have to be corrected and re-set; the arbitrary character of the previous rehearsals will have found its master.

The play without music will yet survive a long time, maybe forever, and its staging, tainted with dead tradition, will find new life at the touch of a less specialized art; it will adopt and distort these new elements. But the art of staging can be an art only if it derives from music. This does not mean that a spoken play may not be excellently performed at times; but this measure of excellence will always be fortuitous.

We have now reached two conclusions: the first affects the source of the play, that is, the author, the second, the form of the performance, that is, the actor. If the author is to master his art, as any artist must, he should be a musician. If the actor is to dominate Space and make it pliable to his mobile and plastic body, he must first receive music from the author. We may add that the forms of Space (including Light) will become expressive—i.e. living—only when they are subordinated to the actor (not directly to the author, as we already know). On these principles everyone may ponder, according to his own fancy. It is no longer a matter of taste, it is a statement of fact. Those to whom music is a concert art will perhaps be displeased; the others, those who know that music is an art of eurhythmics, an expression of the order and general harmony of the Universe, will find in these technical facts the confirmation of their expectations. Technic can not err, its laws and their connections exceed our understanding; if we despise those laws, it is we who err. In the art of the drama we have gone wrong for a very long time; we have split it, and have clung to the part which can, if necessary, exist without the stage. And, indeed, for many, dramatic art is contained on a shelf of their bookcases. Need I add that it is superfluous in that case to build theatres and to fill the columns of our newspapers and to paper our newsstands with matter concerning the stage? Let us read plays, close the book, and change the subject. . . .

To derive a play from music does not mean that musical sounds must themselves be the source of a dramatic idea, but merely that the object of music should also be the object of that idea. It is an *interiorisation* of the dramatic emotion, prompted by the assurance that music will furnish the means of *expressing* all that hidden life, unhampered. Certainty must underlie and inform an integral dramatic action. Before the most beautiful block of marble a sculptor will be at a loss, if he has no hammer and chisel to carve it. In art the process is the artist's primary inspiration. If he lack the means of expressing his vision in three dimensions, he will become a painter or an engraver, and his inspiration will not be three-dimensional form. If the dramatic artist knows that he can express unimpaired the conflicts of our nature (I say, *express,* not merely *indicate*), that knowledge will inspire an action very different from one which words alone would suggest. And if, moreover, he can rely, as we have seen, on its exteriorisation in a corresponding space, his whole dramatic vision will be transformed.

Let us pass, now, to the actor. We have seen that musical expression modifies profoundly the external form of our gestures, that is, their successive durations, and that the actor has no need any longer to interpret his role but merely to render it clearly, as it has been entrusted to him; the actor's value will be his docility; the music transfigures him; . . . he first submits to and then accepts the modifications which are the condition of art, and in so doing discovers the secret of his own beauty. Convinced of his admirable metamorphosis, he will seek in space whatever can support this superior mode of existence and heighten its value; *thus the actor will control the design*. At this point we come to the decorative technique itself. . . . Our last problem is the animation of Space by music, through the actor, transformed by musical proportions.

A clean sweep, a fresh start—that is what we began with. Now we shall take the reverse course and begin with the stage, as it exists today in the ordinary repertory theatre.

The floor of the stage resembles a transformable and removable bookshelf; the stage-opening, turned toward the spectator, is approximately half the total height of the whole scenic structure, with the result that the stage-floor is a flat surface suspended between two more or less empty spaces. It is a common expression to say that "the boards (i.e. the boards of the stage) are a world"; it would be more correct to apply that expression to the stage as a whole, from the flies to the cellar; the stage which the spectator sees is a mere fragment of the whole. The essential factor of our setting, as everyone knows, is the painted scene, cut out and propped in a series of slices which form a perspective; and as these parts of the picture are continually replaced by others, the drops are suspended in the flies, or stowed away in the cellar, so as to be easily hoisted or let down onto the stage. The floor is divided latitudinally into segments of a fixed size, which can be opened to allow of the passage of the scenery to and from the stage. The mobility of the stage-floor is proportionate to its intermediate position. Many stages, however, still have a rigid framework, its only flexibility lying in the traps and the openings for the scenery which are frequently very large. But the tendency of recent construction has been to give this floor the least possible fixity, with a view to lowering it either entirely or in part. Some stages have, flush with the floor, a revolving platform, the diameter of which extends slightly beyond the stage-frame; upon this the sets are placed, filling the stage aperture in rotation; they are so built as to fit into each other. In this way, a play with several shifts may be completely set up before the performance and unfolded to the audience like a picture book. Under our prevailing system of painted scenery, the maximum flexibility of the stage-floor is a highly desirable thing. The background of the set is enclosed by a single painted drop; the overhead can be shut down by a canvas ceiling, hung at more or less of a right angle to the vertical backings of the wings; the sides and the back of the stage may also be shut in; so that the stage, when set, resembles a sort of fly-cage. The *practicables* are all three-dimensional constructions, which are set between and before the vertical drops for the use of the actors; and the word is extended to apply to whatever is plastic and corresponds, therefore, to the plasticity of the human body. What, alas, remains impracticable in these *practicables* is the fact that it is impossible to reconcile them with the flat fictitious painting of the scenery; no ingenuity can disguise this incongruity.

Now for the lighting. The stage space being dark, it is necessary to light, and light effectively, the painting of the drops. This painting contains light and shadows which simulate a relief, or modeling, of some sort; the shadows, no less than the lights, must be visible; hence they must be illuminated! There are, then, two kinds of light for painted scenery: one painted on the canvas, the other thrown on it to make it visible. The painted light can, of course, not strike the actor, though it concerns him; the actual light does strike the actor, though it concerns only the scenery. Such is the environment in which we place the living plastic and mobile body of the player; he is bathed in a light which is not directed on him and moves before painted lights and shadows. He is visible; but that is all. The floor must also be illuminated, or the painting would be unevenly visible: this necessitates footlights; and the footlights also catch the actor. This fine lighting system corresponds to the mechanism of an organ or a keyboard, being controlled and varied as a whole or in part by the switchboard. Sometimes the painting is lit by transparencies; the canvas must then be prepared and painted expressly for that purpose. At Bayreuth, in the first scene of the third act of *Siegfried* the fire which flames down from the rock of the Valkyrie, growing steadily more menacing, is represented by gradually revealing from behind the parts of the mountain which depict the areas of flame; and these parts are painted in transparency. So much for lighting; now comes the question of color. The painter can use whatever pigments he likes; but even the best equipped theatres have only three or four tones on tinted gelatine for lighting; the rest is haphazard.

Such is the decorative material of our repertory theatres. It would be difficult to conceive an ensemble more utterly inconsistent, and it is miraculous that we obtain even the fictive semblances to which we are accustomed. Still, when the curtain rises on a stage picture in which there are no actors, or if the stage remains empty for a moment, the effect is passable, as a rule; the painting, properly lighted, makes its effect, its fictitious perspectives and reliefs create an illusion, and with a little skillful manipulation the canvas cut-outs combine to some effect; and, as it is the actor who draws our attention to the bottom of the picture, in his absence we are indulgent and do not criticize the crude, unavoidable contact of a perpendicular painting with a horizontal floor; we look elsewhere. If, after admiring some beautiful frescoes or wonderful tapestries, a group of people were to come and talk and sing and move before us, and we were asked to consider the subjects represented in those decorations as forming part of the group, we should question the common sense of our guide; but who would dare say as much of our stage directors?

Such is the incurable inconsistency against which we directed our first attempts at reform; and we soon perceived that in tampering with one element of the *mise-en-scène,* we put all the others out of joint. If we directed the lighting on the actor alone, the painting suffered, it was better to abolish it; and the same thing was true of the floor and the *practicables*. The slightest effort in favor of the actor tended, at every point, to eliminate the painter. Now, the actor can not be eliminated! How are we to escape this dilemma? The whole problem comes down to this: *either the actor or the painter;* and our present reform is essentially concerned with the degree of environment and the number of objects which the setting can represent, without too much detriment to the actor; for, after all, we must represent something, a place of some sort. . . .

This may astonish those whose memories of the theatre are confined to realistic plays. With few exceptions, the rooms they saw harmonized with their furnishings and the presence of the actor; and as facial play is of primary importance in this type of piece, they were not annoyed by the footlights. Very well. But is all dramatic action to be restricted to an enclosed space, pierced by doors and windows? And suppose the play called for a garden? Well, you may say, we all know that trees can not be transplanted to the boards; and anyway, the actor is the main thing. True enough. The theatre is a place for conversation, and it matters little where the people who make it are supposed to be, provided we can see and hear them clearly. But then why have the stage and its artifices at all, or separate the auditorium from it? Why not have merely a hall, well-lit with good acoustics? It would be so much cheaper that we could open theatres in every other street. The theatre would be the last salon, the last asylum of conversation. To this there can be possible objection; for this is deliberately to choose one of the forms of dramatic art and to adhere to it, to the exclusion of every other. That may perhaps come to pass in the future, and a sharp division would be justified, I admit. Rightly or wrongly, however, the majority—like all majorities—would not be satisfied with so little. Like all majorities, it would think that the sum of our passions is too complex to find its outlet and expression in mere conversations; it would consider Space as a *thing-in-itself,* the influence of which is not to be denied, and much less despised; it would feel, too, that we have, for the expression of our inner life, other and more powerful means than words; for the manifestations of life are not all contained in speech; and, lastly, it would insist that dramatic art should represent life as a whole. Let us admit, then, that the realistic play offers no scenic problems, and consider the question from a higher angle.

Modern reform has begun with lighting, but it has preserved all the rest, and the footlights are the lead in our innovations. The footlights affect the base of the picture, the space occupied by the actors; they make the players perfectly visible; we miss none of their facial play! We are satisfied: *we can see!* But facial play is not isolated; on the contrary it is related to the carriage of the head and to each of our gestures and attitudes. This general mobility must be not merely visible but expressive, and to be highly expressive it must have relief. Relief results, everywhere and always, from our opposition of light and shadow (except, of course, for the sense of touch, but unfortunately we do not touch the actors!) The actor, bathed in a general illumination which suppresses shadows, is struck by a light which comes from below and which kills the last vestige of shadow he can cast. We see a salon studded with brackets and chandeliers, the floor of which is violently luminous. In such surroundings a group of people would cut a very poor figure; they would seem to be suspended between earth and heaven. This is what happens to the actor with the footlights. Since his whole body is deprived of relief, he gives, roughly, the effect of a painting; we have done our best, in fact, to bring him down to two dimensions! Now, the mobility of his features is also three-dimensional; if you suppress its relief, you must substitute something else; just as the photographer, who focuses his lens on the eyes, is forced to correct and re-touch the exaggerated detail of the face. The actor paints his face, according to the requirements of his part; and it is this *make-up* that *moves!* The eyes, however, can not be painted. What we have then is a painted face in which the eyes preserve their natural expression, though, to be sure, they are blinded by a too bright light.

This is what is meant by *seeing!* And we have the audacity to advance, as an excuse for this crime of *lèse-humanity,* the laws of theatrical perspective! We are so anxious to lose nothing of the actor that we leave little of him. The example of the footlights proves that what we call *seeing* is an infantile fancy; like children, we wish to grasp the object instead of looking at it; and when we hold it tight, we no longer see it. Gradually the use of footlights has been restricted; the public protested; its dearest habits were being infringed, and it fought for them. "We do not see very well" was the usual complaint; but the monkey in this case was not the chap with the lantern. The scene-painter saw, then, that he could easily slack his work without being detected; his traditional virtuosity had, indeed, plenty of tricks. Today his only resource is color, unless we except line, wherever line can blend with a stage-floor, which we can at last completely manipulate. The scene-painter, in the original sense of the word, is the master of an instrument which has been relegated to the junk heap; he will survive himself for some time to come, thanks to the force of inert routine, and will then disappear like the historical or narrative painter.

Lighting, let me repeat, has determined all our scenic reform, and it has done so in the actor's favor; so that, after all, we have been forced to consider him as the first factor in the . . . hierarchy.

The responsibility of the actor has founded the era of a normal hierarchy. We are still groping, no doubt, but we are on firm ground; we still lack a technique, but not its principle. We see the proof of it in the heroic efforts of a Pitoëff, a Gordon Craig, a Stanislavski, a Copeau. For each of these, in his own medium and manner, the living being takes the leading rank.

But if the ground is firm, it is also vast, and that is where our stage-directors often show their shortcomings. They have "emptied the baby with the bath," as the Germans say; and often enough little is left. . . . But that is, perhaps, not a bad thing. It is better to build slowly and cautiously than to stifle ourselves with superfluities. It is a remarkable fact that the new movement started with the speaking stage and the dancers and pantomimic artists. In the one, the human body is used as a means of expression, without words, and with music; in the other, as the medium of an action without music, and with words. In the former, music is supreme, in the latter, the visual dramatic action on an equal footing with speech. These two extremes have adopted the hierarchy. On the other hand, all that has remained between them rambles on, more or less in the old, traditional manner. If we go from a performance by Pitoëff to one of the *Valkyrie,* we step, or rather we plunge, from the most extreme modernity into the most abject routine. In the very medium in which the coordinating element should dominate, we deny it authority, except where the dramatic action is subordinated to physical expression (i.e. pantomime and dance). Nothing is more instructive. The conclusion to be drawn is this—allow me to underline it—: music has not yet been recognized as what it is, the basic governing element, unique of its kind, and peerless in its power. The actor has won a power which speech alone does not justify, since it can not regulate it. If, then, instinctively, we normally apply the hierarchy we have re-discovered to *physical* expression, it follows that this hierarchy must probably be derived directly from our body—in order to be formulated into a final law. In short, despite Wagner and his imitators, lyric drama does not furnish us with the basis we expected, and music will triumph in the theatre only through the medium of our physical feeling, without combining with it, at least for the present, the dramatic element which we began by taking as the indispensable source of its inspiration.

Physical feeling alone means gymnastics and sport; to give it a character of art, we must *modify* it; we know that this can be done only through music; so that we are once more face to face with music and the living body, but this time with a full and enlightened appreciation of their possibilities and connections, and with only one preoccupation: to unite them indissolubly in a harmony, whose lofty import and happy future we begin to discern.

August 1932

* *

JOHN GIELGUD

*

Granville-Barker's Shakespeare

TWO VOLUMES of Harley Granville-Barker's prefaces to Shakespeare are now published in America by the Princeton University Press. It would be an impertinence on my part to add to the praises already lavished upon these famous essays by scholars, men of letters and experts of the theatre in England and in America. They originally appeared in England in two volumes of three plays each and a third entirely devoted to *Hamlet*. This was in the late twenties, just at the time I was first engaged to play in Shakespeare at the Old Vic Theatre, and rereading the prefaces today recalls that time vividly. The director for the Old Vic productions in that period was F. Harcourt Williams, an admirable actor and a Shakespearean student of great integrity. He had been trained under Ellen Terry, Frank Benson and William Poel, and had worked with Granville-Barker as a fellow-actor as well as having been directed by him.

At the first rehearsal Harcourt Williams told us to read the Barker prefaces, and four of the productions of those two seasons (1929-30) were planned as far as possible on the lines laid down by Barker: *Romeo and Juliet, Antony and Cleopatra, King Lear* and *The Merchant of Venice*.

In his book, *Four Years at the Old Vic,* Williams has told how our efforts to speak the text at a great pace and to rush the action nearly made a shambles of the first night of the season when we opened with *Romeo and Juliet;* how the Old Vic audience, resenting the apparently revolutionary methods of the new director and his inexpert company, expressed its disapproval in no uncertain terms; and how much perseverance was needed on the part of all of us (and tolerance on the part of the directress of the theatre's policy, Miss

Lilian Baylis, whose shrewd sense of box-office economics was only matched by a God-fearing integrity of spirit worthy of Saint Joan herself) before we emerged from the failures of the first two or three productions to a period of success.

Ten years passed before I returned to the Vic again, and Granville-Barker was once more to figure in the event. In the years between, I had been directing some Shakespearean plays myself and had corresponded with him on several occasions, when he had been good enough to write me critical and encouraging letters about my work. He even came to a rehearsal of *Hamlet* when I was preparing to play it at Elsinore in 1939 and spent several hours giving me notes and advice about the production.

Now, with the war in its first year, and during those terrible weeks before Dunkirk and the fall of France, I was asked to reopen the Old Vic with a production of *King Lear.* We had something of an all-star company, and Lewis Casson (who was to direct the play) and I decided to wire to Granville-Barker and ask him to give us his advice and, if possible, more practical help. To our delight he accepted, and came to his home in London from Paris and conducted rehearsals for ten days, working with a sureness and magically inspired ability which none of us has ever forgotten. He refused to accept any public or critical recognition and left after the final dress rehearsal without ever seeing the play acted before an audience.

After this episode I met him only once or twice in London again, shortly before his death in Paris in 1946.

In the few conversations I had with him, when we were not speaking of our work, I was always urging him to work in the theatre again. I argued that he himself admitted to finding many things during actual rehearsals which led him to change or modify statements and treatments of the text which he had written of in the prefaces. His reply was always the same. He felt that the written word was something that would stand for many years to give inspiration and guidance to actors, students, scholars and directors, whereas the practice of a few short weeks, carried out in inevitable imperfection by a group of players, could only be tenuous and ephemeral and would be quickly broken up and lost.

Now that he is dead, I cannot help being glad that the writer in him triumphed over the actor-director, for his prefaces give a wonderfully composite picture of his many brilliant gifts. There are pages for everyone—the ordinary reader, the theatre expert, the actor, the scholar. Everyone will have his favorite among the prefaces, and if I myself find the *Antony and Cleopatra* essay the most brilliant and rewarding it may be because I first read it at a time when I did not know the play at all and found that I was studying the part of Antony at very short notice.

The last two prefaces, those to *Othello* and *Coriolanus,* seem to be written with a certain distant attitude. The perception and sensibility are undiminished but there seems to be a greater mass of detailed observation and a less broad comprehensive sweep than in the earlier essays. One English critic has said that in the *Othello* preface Barker seemed to be "nibbing one's nose" in the play and there is some truth in that criticism. But when one has known a man personally and seen him actually at work one cannot help a feeling of dramatic fatalism in reading the final pages of his work, though it may be merely my actor's imagination that endows the later prefaces with a slight air of distant melancholy, as if, like Shakespeare himself writing his *Coriolanus* in retirement during those last years at Stratford, Granville-Barker seems to be aware that his great days as a comrade and worker in the theatre are gone forever, and that the light which shone so brightly the moment he set foot inside the doors of a playhouse must now burn only in the memories of those who saw him work there. How fortunate I am to have been among their number! And for those who were never privileged to know him there will always be his books, so full of his wit, his wisdom, his tireless searching for beauty and integrity and truth.

October 1947

* *

JOHN VAN DRUTEN

*

The Job of Directing

WHEN I WAS about to start directing a professional play for the first time in my life, three years ago, I was overtaken by a fit of panic. Suddenly I realized that I knew nothing about the job, apart from having watched it done on my own plays over a period of years, almost entirely by one director, recently dead. I tried to remember how Auriol Lee used to work, and could recall little except a vocabulary that was vivid and completely individual to her, and a highly fastidious standard of acting, based on long experience. She had once told me that she thought no one could direct who could not act, and that if I ever wanted to be a director myself, I should begin by getting a job as an actor. It was too late to do that now.

I turned to books on directing, and they frightened me still more. The day before my first rehearsal I went to two directors, both young men whom I admired, and asked them for their help. The first proceeded to draw diagrams illustrating the various playing areas on a stage, and indicating what kind of scene should be played in each. He told me to plan every move and position in advance, and to have an answer ready for everything; he talked about dynamics, fusion, levels, mood and integration; he covered his diagrams with dotted lines and arrows, and left me in a worse state of jitters than before.

From him, I went on to cocktails with the other, who had once been a stage manager for me, telling him how badly I was feeling. His answer was "Don't be so silly. All you have to do is use your common sense, and see that it *looks* well. You have seen enough plays and have good enough taste to be able to do that. And don't ever be afraid of telling your actors that you don't know something. You don't have to be infallible to keep their respect." This comforted me. It did not sound like classical advice, nor conform with the things I had found in the books, but at least it made it possible for me to start directing, equipped with no more than my own common sense, theatrical taste, and what experience of the theatre I had picked up in seeing my own plays produced over a period of fifteen years. It seemed to turn out all right.

I did not think I knew very much about directing then. In the three productions which I have directed since, I have learned a little more, although the same panic assails me every time I am about to start. The diagrams; the books on theory, full of abstract nouns; the reputations of great Continental directors, all return to haunt and frighten me. I have to remind myself that books on playwriting affect me in the same way; that I have never been able to construct a scenario in accordance with their rules, nor analyze the mechanics of a scene or situation as they do, and that I have gotten along fairly well as a playwright, all the same. What skill I have acquired has come from doing the job as best I could, aiming only at satisfying my own sense of what a play ought to be. What skill I have acquired or may acquire as a director must come in the same way.

There are hints, of course, that can be given, pointers to save time and trouble. There are few books, as far as I know, in which they are to be found. The most useful of all is a tiny pamphlet, written by Bernard Shaw and issued by Samuel French, entitled *The Art of Rehearsal*. The name itself is significant, with its use of the word "rehearsal," practical and workmanlike, rather than "direction," with its overtones of mystery and esotericism. It is a simple, factual and down-to-earth little manual on how to conduct rehearsals so as to get the best out of the actors. It is full of excellent suggestions, even more excellent "don't's," and one brief passage of what seems to me real wisdom:

> Only geniuses can tell you exactly what is wrong with a scene, though plenty of people can tell you that there is something wrong with it. So make a note of their dissatisfaction; but be very careful how you adopt their cure if they prescribe one.

Not long ago in New York, I saw a production of a play which I had greatly admired in manuscript, but which on the opening night fell very flat, boring the audience a good deal. Most of them told me that it was too slow, and the critics the next morning complained, almost without exception, about the slowness of direction. I remembered how the Shaw passage went on:

> For instance, if they say a scene is too slow (meaning that it bores them), the remedy in nine cases out of ten is for the actors to go slower and bring out the meaning better by contrasts of tone and speed.

The New York play in question has not been played too slowly, but too fast. The dialogue was of considerable delicacy, needing a close attention from the audience, which they had not been able to give because the actors never stopped to think or listen before they spoke. The cues were stepped on, the speeches rattled at lightning speed, and the result was boredom and a sense of slowness.

In this case it was my foreknowledge of the script that enabled me to spot where the direction was at fault. Had I been unfamiliar with the play, it would probably have bored and seemed slow to me, too. Without a knowledge of the manuscript, it seems to me almost impossible to gauge the values or demerits of a director's work. There are certain signs, of course (largely depending, like everything else in direction, upon one's personal tastes), by which one can judge a director. Broad overacting, hamming and mugging, especially if early in the run, are usually his fault; so is "playing front." These are things which, except in the case of immutable, old-fashioned stars, a director can and should change. When the stage pictures are attractive, the compositions well balanced, it is the director who can be praised for it. But for the most part, his work is or should be unobtrusive; his job is to bring out the value of his author's manuscript, and without acquaintance with it, no one can say whether or not he has succeeded. It seems to me that too much blame and too much praise are thrown around for direction on very insufficient evidence these days.

This is not to underrate the work of the director or his contribution to the show, but to try and estimate what these are. He has often been compared to the conductor of an orchestra, an analogy which seems to me a completely false one, since he can take no part in the performance. When the final dress rehearsal is over, his job is done, and he spends the opening night impotently watching, like a coach on the sidelines. Which, indeed, is far more what he is. It is only in recent years that he has been elevated to the dignity, even, of his name. Through the first decade of the present century he was still known as the stage manager; even the theatrical czar, David Belasco, was so described. The reviews of plays nowadays almost always comment on the direction, as they do on the acting and the scene designs; in the earlier notices it was taken for granted, except for an occasional tribute to a sunset, a forest fire or an especially effective mob scene. These were, and still are, the director's great opportunities for personal recognition, although they are apt to occur less frequently in modern scripts than in the more full-blooded days of the theatre before the movies had shown how much better they could do those things. Sometimes in Shaw's dramatic criticisms you will find exception taken to the way in which a scene was stage managed, meaning that the business was inexpertly handled or devised, but apart from such examples, the direction was seldom mentioned, which is,

I cannot help feeling, the way in which it should be treated. As I have said before, the best direction is unnoticeable, being merely a successful evocation of the values of the author's manuscript.

It may be that as a playwright I am prejudiced in so regarding it. Yet, so long as we are dealing with the theatre of the spoken word, I cannot see it otherwise. How is it achieved? What are the methods and the equipment of the stage director? The former will vary with each individual. Most will work out on paper the positions and the moves for each scene before rehearsal. In his pamphlet, Shaw recommends this, if only to save time. If I myself seldom do so, it is mainly because my visual imagination is poor and I need to see a group or a picture on the stage before I can know what it looks like. Many directors will not give the actors intonations or inflections, preferring to explain the meaning of a sentence, sometimes for ten minutes, rather than speak it for the actor to copy. Here, for the most part, I would adopt Shaw's argument of time-saving, although the decision must vary with the actor in each case, since many are incapable of taking an intonation, or become mechanical and parrot-like if they do. There are directors who resent any suggestions or contributions from the actor as to his part, and I have been amazed by the timidity with which players have ventured to ask if it would be all right for them to do this, that or the other in a scene, and by their surprise when I gratefully accepted the suggestion and encouraged them to others. A series of dictator-directors had terrified them in the past. Another director will sit back, doing nothing and saying nothing, letting the actors find their own way and often flounder for long stretches, before he will intervene. Some directors like to get up on the stage and show the actor what they want, playing the scene for him themselves; others will never leave their seat in the orchestra or at the director's table.

The methods, then, are individual, varying from director to director. The equipment, however, it seems to me, is standard. A knowledge of acting is important; perhaps essential. In her dictum that every director must be able to act, it is possible that Auriol Lee was going a little far. Actually, and probably not surprisingly, most directors are bad actors; but they must, I think, know something of the rudiments of acting, and of how effects *should* be produced, even if they cannot produce them, themselves. It is not enough to know what you want done; you have to know how it *should* be done. The same applies, it seems to me, to writing. The director, though he need not be able to write a play, must have some knowledge of theatrical construction. He must be able to tell the author what is wrong with his script, and indicate, at least, how it could be altered in a way that can fire the author's own imagination. If he can do that, both as regards author and actors, he has made his greatest contribution. At his top, he can be an inspirer; at his lowest he should be an elicitor, if such a word exists, of the best that his author and his actors have to give.

For the rest, his function seems to me to be mainly that of critic. Sitting in front at rehearsal, he watches the play, trying always to see it as a member of the audience, to gauge its effect on them, and to bring it to life upon the stage, so that they will see it there as he has seen it in his imagination. The knowledge of acting and of playwriting are among his technical qualifications; the remainder of his equipment lies in himself, in his good taste, judgment and experience, and is largely coincident with his equipment as a human being. High among its items ranks a sense of psychology. The handling of actors is perhaps the most ticklish of a director's problems. It is his job to know, or to sense, as speedily as possible, how each actor must be approached; which need encouraging and which restraining; which can take direct criticism without offense, and which need it wrapped in flattery. He must sense, too, just how much can be got from each, and be prepared to modify his conception of a part if it does not suit the actor, rather than try to impose it on him, making the best of the material to his hand, remembering that it is human, fallable and limited. All this seems elementary, and indeed, perhaps it is, resolving itself ultimately to little more than that household, though too infrequently encountered, commodity of common sense, which my kindly director friend listed so highly as an ingredient the day that he encouraged me to try my first job as a director.

November 1945

HERMINE RICH ISAACS

*

First Rehearsals

ELIA KAZAN DIRECTS A MODERN LEGEND

THE REHEARSAL ROOM is a chill rectangle on the top floor of the Theatre Guild building. In spite of assorted files and trunks, ladders and chairs, ranged round the room, there is a sense of monotone about the place which is enhanced by the grey day that simmers gloomily through small windows set high in the walls. In this unlikely setting an illusion must be born, a piece of theatre must start its journey from script to stage, growing as it moves until finally it has become a little larger, more intense, than life itself.

There is nothing quite like this sense of being in on the beginnings of a thing that may touch stars before it has run its course; it may head straightway for Cain's warehouse, too, but today, at any rate, it is the aura of endless possibilities that fills the minds of the men and women who have foregathered here for a first rehearsal. The actors, usually an exuberant lot, sit quiet and a little formal, ranged in an orderly circle around the director's desk. Stage manager, producers and press agent, even they are still; only one creature, an anonymous grey poodle, wanders freely and indifferently about the room, proving that in the world of artistic creation, at least, man's pleasures are exclusively his own.

The play that goes into rehearsal today is Franz Werfel's fantasy, *Jacobowsky and the Colonel.* This "comedy of a tragic episode" had a first-draft adaptation by Clifford Odets, and now, as rehearsals progress, is being drastically revamped by S. N. Behrman to make it gayer and more nimble, and to bring it closer to American tastes. Elia Kazan is in the director's chair, and in the circle around him sit such familiar actors as Oscar Karlweis (Jacobowsky), Louis Calhern (the Colonel), Annabella, J. Edward Bromberg, Herbert Yost and others, as well as Theresa Helburn, Lawrence Langner and Armina Marshall for the Theatre Guild. Although the actors already have their "sides" and some of them have read an early version of the script, today is for them in a real sense the start. To Elia Kazan, however, *Jacobowsky and the Colonel* is an old, familiar friend. He has lived with it for weeks, thinking it through, talking it through, filling a stenographic notebook with random thoughts about the play and its production. As far as he is concerned, the show is well along toward realization when first rehearsals roll around.

A graduate of the Group Theatre, Kazan has carried many of its methods along with him, revising them, however, in the light of his ebullient sense of humor, his experience as an actor and the exigencies of workaday Broadway production. Like such Group directors as Harold Clurman, he is not one to take a play at its face value, letting words and actions fall where they will. Instead he will try, first of all, with each new script, to ferret out the essential qualities of the play and catch them in a phrase. This may seem trivial or mystical, but it is neither; it is a highly practical scheme to find an idea keynote to which his whole production will be tuned. In the light of it he casts his play, works with his designer, stages his production, in this case even aids in the rewriting of the script. In the last analysis, a show may stand or fall on the appositeness of these preliminary bouts with the abstract; in the past year, for instance, *Harriet, The Skin of Our Teeth, One Touch of Venus,* all directed by Kazan, stood.

To characterize *Jacobowsky and the Colonel,* Kazan has settled on the phrase, "A Modern Legend"—"a legend is fantastic, its essence is romance. Its comicality, though abundant, is wise; its figures, though human and essentially comic, are still both representative and universal." Both of the play's heroes are legendary figures, although the legend is no older than the Fall of France. Jacobowsky is the wandering Jew, the cosmopolitan, living entirely by his charm, his wit, his cultivation. The Colonel is the man of force, strong, humorless, uncompromising. Each has his virtues, but for each his virtue will not be sufficient for survival; so the play becomes the story of how, out of these two relics of the old, something new is born. Though the subject and the scene are grim, the tale is gaily told, "the production must dance," its style be "light and charged with wit"; "every single person in the play must be a subtly comic figure"—in summary, it will be "a modern legend of rebirth from death, told in comic grotesques."

Although such thoughts as these fill many pages in Kazan's preliminary notebook and are useful in his talks with the playwright and the scene designer (Stewart Chaney), he is much too much a practical man of the theatre to burden and confuse his actors with such abstractions; in fact, he vows, "I will say nothing to an actor that cannot be translated directly into action." As if to prove his point there are no "speeches" before the first rehearsal. Promptly at two o'clock the work begins. Kazan, still decorously dressed—soon coat and tie and sweater will be stripped for action—starts off by reading the first three scenes of Behrman's newest version of the play. He reads with pace and meaning but still careful not to give an actor's reading of the lines. During rehearsal he assiduously avoids imposing his own interpretation on an actor, using the right sense but the wrong words if he finds himself compelled to say a speech to indicate an action or a mood.

After a ten-minute break it is the actors' turn. Kazan tells them what he wants: "Read with good normal speaking energy. Take it very easy—don't try to give a performance. But talk to each other, find out whom you're talking to and, especially, listen to what they're saying to you. Remember that the play takes place in France—therefore English is French. From the Polish characters (Jacobowsky and the Colonel are both Polish, as are several others of the dramatis personae) I want the flavor to come from a certain largeness of speech, a melody, rather than from actual pronunciation. This is all I want from your first reading, but I want it right."

The actors take over, but they don't get far before Kazan begins to interrupt. The scene is an air-raid shelter in Paris and Reynaud's voice, heard over the radio, places the time as the eve of the fall of France. An Old Lady from Arras is complaining about the present state of affairs. "How long will it last?" she says, querulously, a little tearfully. Kazan stops her to explain: "The stage directions are misleading there. Cross them out. You do not whine; you ask the question as if you wanted to get an answer, although you realize that none will be forthcoming. It's as if you were asking, 'Will Roosevelt be re-elected?' " . . . A Tragic Gentleman serves as a sort of chorus throughout the first scene of the play, making editorial comments from the sidelines. Kazan reminds the actor, who is speaking his lines in the highly cultivated tones of a British gentleman, "Remember you are Gallic, not English—your speech must be light and witty; you are not delivering yourself of wise remarks." . . . A comic character actor plays the Colonel's servant. He is a trouble-maker—"like a jackal," Kazan suggests; "the jackal always wants to egg the lion and the tiger on to fight, because he knows that one will be killed and he will get something to eat." . . . There is a scene of parting between the Colonel and a young girl, Cosette. The actress is playing her sweetly, tenderly. Kazan corrects her: "Cosette is not shy, modest, inhibited, remember she is a Frenchwoman, direct, a realist. She is an extrovert, and you must play her for that to contrast with the Colonel who is all introvert." . . . To another minor actor, "You are making trouble for yourself by trying to observe the punctuation of your speeches which is *literary*. You as *actors* cannot break up your speech at every comma or the effect will be ponderous and halting. Almost every speech is a single thought; say it straight through." . . . Once he reminds the cast "this is not a tragedy. We have to make choices in all these characters that are comic and colorful—not heavy and sententious."

So the first day passes while Kazan points up the active, Gallic, humorous qualities of the play and sketches rough relationships between the characters. Once a point is made, he does not go back but asks the actor to "think about it and bring it in the next time." By the following afternoon, readings begin to take new shape in the light of Kazan's suggestions. A few of the actors will have to be replaced during the flexible five days that Equity allows, but on the whole the cast is moving easily along with the director. The role of Jacobowsky is too diffusely written for our impatient theatre, and so Kazan, with the unprecedented encouragement of Oscar Karlweis (an actor who agrees to have a phrase cut from his part is something like a general who admits that his shoulder would look neater with one less star), goes surely and decisively about cutting it, working with a keen sense for a line's apt length, the timing of a scene. Sometimes it is a new line that must be written in, and then he will provide a makeshift, waiting for Behrman to supply the finished article. During these preliminary days, he leaves the readings of the principals more or less alone, and wisely so, since both Karlweis and Calhern have from the beginning a sure sense of their roles that needs no major psychological adjustments.

With the fourth day things begin to happen. The rehearsal room is modestly transformed, the floor marked off by chalk to indicate the outlines of a stage, as well as doors and platforms; trunks and chairs are set in place to represent the major properties. A blueprint of the floor-plan for scene I is on the wall for reference and next to it a paper with phonetic spellings of the Polish names. The actors are beginning to learn their roles; a few already falter bravely on without their sides. Along the margins of the room, players who are not onstage walk up and down, mumbling their lines, testing out abortive gestures, smoking innumerable cigarettes. It is a moment to be severely shunned by anyone with less than an unconquerable faith in the ultimate sanity of the theatrical trade.

Onstage, or rather in that section of the room marked off by chalk, Kazan is in action. His chief preoccupation at the moment is with the question of logistics, theatre fashion: getting the right actors to the right places with the right props at the right time. At this point in the progress of the play, Kazan is still the only person who has in his own mind a clear conception not only of the shape of each particular passage but of the larger outlines of the play itself. He has worked out the high spots of each scene, the passages which must be gotten through as fast as possible, the ones to be drawn out for emphasis. He knows the full importance of establishing certain relationships in the first act so that certain passages in the second act will make sound theatre sense. He is the momentary star; his players, now at least, seem more like talking pawns as he pushes them about the stage at will, suggesting a piece of business here, a gesture there, shouting, cajoling, kidding as the occasion requires. No one knows better than the director that this is only a temporary stage, a necessary pause in the show's progress. In a while, he promises, the actors will begin to argue back, to resist suggestions and contribute ones of their own. Then he will know that the actors' steam is up and the play is on its own. But today is his day and he is one to make the most of it.

A problem comes up at the outset of Act I. Reynaud's last speech is coming over the radio: "The situation is serious but not desperate. On the Somme our valiant troops are defending every inch of their native soil with the greatest bravery. However, the superiority of the enemy in men and material is so great that we must be prepared to expect . . ." Kazan intends to start the scene on a high note. He has the actor read the words with urgency and volume. Oscar Karlweis, who heard the actual speech, points out, however, that the French premier spoke his valedictory flatly, almost in a monotone. It is the eternal conflict between realism and dramatic effectiveness. Kazan tries out the speech both ways and reserves decision.

The "top" of the first scene comes when the apparently innocuous Old Lady drops a bombshell: "My daughter is right," the Old Lady announces, "she always says what France needs is a Hitler!" There is a shocked silence, then Jacobowsky terminates the conversation: "Don't worry, madame, your daughter will probably get her wish, moustache, forelock and all." It is his first serious moment. The letdown must be immediate and emphatic. Kazan has Karlweis speak the sentence quickly, pick up his stool and move away from the Old Lady. Director and actor rework the scene many times; timing and distances here must be precise.

Once Kazan suggests a piece of business to Calhern, "but," he adds, "don't do it unless it feels right to you." Another time, when Karlweis has leaned forward in a characteristic gesture from the waist to hear the answer to a question, Kazan picks it up. "That's good, Oscar; keep that in." For the Old Lady from Arras he prescribes a property, a pillow she can carry with her, sit on, fluff up, arrange and rearrange. "That's a wonderful piece of business," he says, "you'll thank me for that!" Here he works out an intricate problem of timing with Joe Bromberg, playing it out himself; there he suggests a capering step for Karlweis, dancing a gay and cocky turn of his own. Once in a while he moves over to the sidelines to watch the players in action or to make a note in his script. But it is only a moment's pause. Although the show begins to take on theatre shape, the director's volatile figure still holds center-stage.

Twenty-eight days to convert a show from script to theatre piece—no wonder things move fast on the commercial boards of Broadway! Only six days after rehearsals began, the scene of action on the *Jacobowsky* set has shifted to a nearby theatre. The director is abandoning his stellar role and sits quiet and attentive on the sidelines, while the actors are in the process of taking over. It is a painful process still, as all transitions must be. There is a feeling of sudden insecurity, and more than once a player can be heard predicting dolefully, "We'll never open on the 27th!"

Kazan has been through all of this before. He does not seem inordinately worried.

March 1944

* *

OSCAR SERLIN

*

Every Day Is Christmas

DON'T CALL IT THEATRE when you're parked in Sardi's. If you're talking about Broadway, don't call it theatre. Call it show business, entertainment, medicine show, fabrication, hippodrome, carny con, midway or grab-bag distraction, but don't call it theatre.

When the chefs of the true theatre serve you, yours is a bountiful portion of an emotional and intellectual feast. The memory becomes a part of your bloodstream for you don't forget experiences that wrap you in poetry, music, beauty, vitality and the eternal verities; that arouse your imagination, compassion, mobility, hope, love or exuberant humor. *That's* the theatre. Every day is Christmas.

You won't find much of it around just now, for as matters stand today the doughboys of Broadway don't want to lose any more time "producing" than it takes to reach into the wagon and whip out their pedler's pack of shimmer, dazzle, aphrodisiac and gunshots —hot, mind you, overlooking the embellishment of low lights, schmaltzy lullabies and a soupçon of grind.

Do you wonder how it is that these Times Square Wallingfords keep open for business? Well, there's a war on, there's too much money floating around. Values are cockeyed. A lot of people are going to the theatre today for the same reason they're going to antique shows at the Waldorf, buying caviar at Gristede's, or walking into Hattie Carnegie's in their overalls, with that moola smoking in their jeans.

The couple that used to scratch to extract $1.50 from the weekly budget for a neighborhood movie and for entertainment is becoming acquainted now with the plushy superiority of the Broadway bazaars dealing in corporeal actors. True, they still don't demand much more than the movie type of story and the movie thrill, uncensored, but they don't mind paying more for it.

When I started on Broadway in 1928, a one-set play could be done for a borrowing. My first show represented a cash outlay of $2100. The same debut-opus today would cost many times that much—and you can use the approximation as a barometer of audiences as well. Money's no object today, if you don't complicate production with the exercise of taste or discrimination. And, indeed, why bother? How many producers are going to wear themselves out with dramatic imagination or gropings for sincere delineation of humor and character, of the revelation of human beings, when all they need to start lines forming at the box-offices are rewrites of last season's hits, or those of two seasons ago, or five—complete with ballet and "names"? The average audience today isn't expected to sit through anything as prosaic as Ibsen, O'Neill, Shaw, Chekhov, Molnar, Shakespeare or O'Casey unless it first has been given "action," "timing," "pace" or "streamlining" by some of our better experts in the manufacture of firecrackers.

There is not one noteworthy experimental theatre in all of Manhattan that can legitimately be called active and professional. The realtors and the racketeers see no profit in arty stuff. The 15% shysters are "again" it, the 10% absentee agents too busy, the cafe gangsters too wise, the cigar store adventurers foresee insufficient personal aggrandizement, the movie moguls won't wait, the Dramatists Guild can't get a quorum, and the unions just plain goddamit won't.

Meanwhile, the moment any potentially gifted writer bobs his head above water he is rushed out to Hollywood, where in no time at all he is protesting that he needs "a hundred thousand a year just to pay the income tax." The writer who has learned how to say it hasn't anything to say. The writer with magic vitality and an awareness of his time hasn't any place to learn his complicated draft.

George Freedley, a critic and historian of integrity, did a careful job of diagnosing the disease in his now famous article, "The Theatre Has Swallowed a Tapeworm." In similar vein, some years ago, Joseph Verner Reed, the producer, enumerated the ills that beset him on Broadway. He needed a book to tell his full story. But neither Mr. Freedley nor Mr. Reed offered any hope. Unlike these gentlemen, I cannot get myself to believe that the militant young will give up so easily. I have become father confessor to dozens of young hopefuls—writers, directors, actors, designers, yes, and even press agents—who recognize, as I have, that for years the theatre, as we laughingly call it, has ostriched so pathetically that it has not gone beyond the corner grocery stage. We recognize, too, that the older producers—those who once had ideals—have either been killed by too much "21" or have cynically sold out to sets of dishes and marriages on the stage.

There's a long, tough job ahead if we're going to do anything to correct all this. It's an educational job, and it's going to require real skill, plus professional leadership, sweat and drive. Going to the theatre is a habit. It's not something you decide to do because you have an evening free. I don't think that we should try to compete with the Broadway trifles or explosions. Symphony doesn't have to compete with jive, nor Picasso with a poster.

We must woo the type of audience that wants good theatre and, when afforded the opportunity, will make a habit of it. The educational strategy and tactics will be laborious, and the results will be discouragingly meager at the outset. The ancient Broadway policy of "If you don't want it, the hell with you" is going to require some drastic revision before the better type of prospect can be persuaded to believe that real theatregoing is a habit suffused with compulsion, excitement and glowing rewards. Splenetic box-office men, draughty, decaying theatre, careless ushers and rapacious concessionaires must be liquidated or exported to the boardwalks. We won't be able to afford them any more. Adult human beings—the kind with more self-respect than resignation—don't thrive on that sort of sadism.

The theatre in a more genteel era—when what we called "the carriage trade" inspired a more conscientious effort at amenity—was on the right path, I believe. We must try to reinculcate the zest and spirit, the thoughtfulness, of that approach. The theatre must remain theatre. If we of the theatre don't take the trouble, the theatre will pass completely into the hands of the moneyed monsters who have about as much interest in theatres as a rattlesnake has in Renoir.

The ranks are woefully thin, but we are by no means lacking in men and women of real stature and vigorous talent to lead the crusade for inspiring contemporary expression behind the footlights.

One creative force that has come to its finest fruition within the past two years is that of Oscar Hammerstein II. Mature, warm-hearted, imaginative and brilliantly gifted, Hammerstein is attaining his rightful place as an American theatre poet of almost heroic proportion. His influence in *Carmen Jones* and, with Richard Rodgers, in *Oklahoma!* has been tremendous. In their subsequent function as producers of *I Remember Mama* they have again brought their consummate skills into gratifying focus.

There is boundless hope for the future in the quality, love and wisdom of such veterans. Being true to their own affections and writing and producing from the heart instead of from formula, these men are showing the way to achievement that enriches our theatre not only today, but tomorrow and always.

From *The Last Mile* to *The Searching Wind,* a period covering nearly fifteen years, Herman Shumlin has been a producer who has maintained a consistently high standard. He has been fortunate, of course, in developing and working with the fine dramatist, Lillian Hellman. But the Hammersteins and the Rodgers, the Shumlins and the Hellmans, can be multiplied by dozens if we stop thinking in terms of smash hits and movie rights. This can only be accomplished by doing plays of quality; by the establishment, fostering and provisioning of experimental theatres throughout the country; by the encouragement, guidance and economic support of young writers, and by the breaking down of union mistrusts founded largely on bona fide suspicions bred through the years by irresponsible adventurers in the producers' saddles.

And for a starter, we have an imperative need of as many permanent repertory companies as are feasible, with the cooperation of the various creators to play as many of the standard classics as they can handle. These theatres would be the tryout laboratories for new writers, directors, actors and designers concerned with an intelligent reflection of our world.

Which comes first, the chicken or the egg? Personally, I belong to the chicken school. First, we must attract back from Hollywood as many writers as we can, before they drift too far into their beach-combing decline. Second, we must meet at the boat every returning soldier who has a contribution to make to society through the medium of the theatre. Third, we must educate our backers, benefactors and stage-struck brothers to a realization that the theatre can be made into a profitable business if we stick to an ideal and stop comparing it to the buzzer in the window that inveigles the carnival crowd.

Fourth, we must have deep respect for our audiences and not patronize them. They're much smarter than you think. Give them courageous, rewarding emotional experiences and Selznick-Sinatra will get only the overflow. Stay with your audiences by giving them something they can't get anywhere else. Propel them to heaven with enchantment and truth. Leave the false notes, the counterfeit cracks, to the Broadway picture panderers.

We had the beginnings of a healthy theatre audience among the people who went to see the Provincetown Players, the Neighborhood Playhouse, the early Theatre Guild productions, Eva Le Gallienne's Civic Repertory Company, the Group Theatre, Labor Stage and, above all, the very exciting, warm-hearted, wonderful audiences that started going to the Federal Theatre.

Fifth, remember that this is 1945 and that we are living in an age of propaganda. American advertising is a highly developed art. Herr Schickelgruber and Dr. Goebbels learned too much from it and utilized it for evil. We can adapt it for good by telling people about the wonderment of the theatre. We must do the job well, for we are competing with electronics, radio, motion pictures, television, Hollywood cheesecake, glamour names and luxury products.

We also are competing with a type of audience that has been conditioned to believe in getting a lot for a little, which believes in 25-cent all-silk neckties, 10-cent sterling costume jewelry, 50-cent gold-filled fountain pens, Borax period furniture, coupons and trading stamps. They must be inculcated with a sense of the joyous values to be discovered in the theatre. If we make it attractive enough for them, they will remember what they saw and heard instead of trying to forget on escapist treadmills. And if we are successful, we will have a contemporary theatre not only in New York but all over America.

The spirited young need the nutrition of the theatre. We can aid them in the acquisition of joy, hope and belief in the future, and of the cultural habit of going to the theatre, where every day is Christmas. When that new day comes, the Broadway baboons will disappear with the trampled snow, the Lindy landsleit be swept back to their bagels and racing forms, and the young, with dynamite in their souls, courage in their hearts and juice in their veins, will reflect their world in their theatre!

January 1945

XII · THE FILMS IN REVIEW

* * *

OTIS FERGUSON

*

Hollywood's Gift to Broadway

THE MOVIES have a hard time in the court of criticism, finding themselves generally in the position of being guilty until they prove themselves innocent. (This is particularly true of American as opposed to foreign productions, for are not the former in a language we use daily and a tradition so familiar as to seem no tradition at all? Quite common indeed.) The prosecution can always cite ten bad pictures to the one good picture found by the defense. And sometimes twenty-five. Hence, triumph. Hence pictures as art are simply not, not nearly; and there is nothing left for the defense to say except possibly that art shall not live by its bad works alone, and that anyone in the more established fields who squinted down the tradition and saw only the fertilizer and not the flower would be punished horribly.

Such abc matters would certainly be unnecessary in a field where abc's had been spoken long enough and with enough pomp to make people like it. But at present those who know how a picture is made keep their mouths shut and continue to make pictures; and those who officially review the finished product have either learned the business from the press-agent angle, or are too choleric with art and stern with prophecy to go seriously to school in any institution so complicated, vast, popular and amorphous. So that when a picture like *Mutiny on the Bounty* comes along, how is it to be placed?

The picture takes a large and partly incredible theme from history, a series of episodes extending over years in time and half way around the world. It would ordinarily be ticketed as an adventure story, but

Hollywood carries it well beyond any such easy category. The picture has excitements and binds them together with good dramatic amalgam; but it also has its truth and beauty—the ship is lovely under canvas, as a ship should be, and a madhouse below with maggoty beef and overworked men, as a ship should never be but infallibly is. The life of the "Bounty," its death on the rocks off Pitcairn, are the foundation of the story, which is about the officers and men in it—how they were a normal collection of stout hearts and bad hats and simpletons, working their way into the Cape storms and making their landfalls of enchanted islands; thrown finally by an abnormal sequence of events into mutiny, and sooner or later dying of it.

The main strength of the story and of this picture is the captain of the ship, a mean, hard, competent master, despicable and grand. This part, played by Charles Laughton, was never realized in the book from which the film is taken. For that matter, I do not know that a character so supreme and admirable in villainy has been realized anywhere since Iago. And for another matter, it is one thing to play Iago, as already laid down, and quite another to conceive and make plausible Captain Bligh, a great seaman full of jealousy and striving, brewing his own ruin—a character about whom we know nothing but the bones of fact, about whom there are few lines to spout, and to recreate whom therefore requires not only dignity of person but power and subtlety of mind.

But the part of Bligh alone does not make the show. *Mutiny* is a good film because its details are worked out with the highest skill—from violent action to how sweetly the ship lies in the ground-swell off Tahiti—because it works these details of a cumbrous story into a whole that is massive rather than heavy, that carries along rather than weighs down. There seems to have been some feeling that governed everything in it, so that even the most incidental of bit-parts are likely and done with spirit. I am by profession the sworn enemy of long pictures, but I sat through this double-length picture twice and I can remember very clearly that I have pulled every oar, and hated every oppressor, and ducked every blow in that story.

For anyone who is looking for vivid action without the tragic overtones of the life of Captain Bligh, I should recommend a transcript of the drama of our own times: *Show Them No Mercy*. This film shows four kidnappers holing up until the furor blows over and the money cools, safe so long as they hold tight but carrying their own destruction within them. Under the unnatural strain they are not unnaturally prone to suspicion, jealousy, claustrophobia and what not; three of them defy the leader and strike out, two of them to their present death. The third comes back wounded, betrays the leader and is shot himself. All this is done with a rare sense of suspense, a fine command of the illusion of strong action and violent death. Death on the stage is in itself very little: what the movies have learned better than anyone else is the trick of fattening personality before killing it, of mixing bacon-and-eggs and wisecracks and petty bickerings with the desire for escape, life, until the fear in which these men stand and the desperation with which they scramble through the brush at night becomes a personal matter; until the end of a character becomes the end of a man and leaving the theatre, in a certain sense, an awakening from bad dreams. This picture is really outside the G-Men cycle. Order and decency are there, but as dim perfunctory shapes, the stage being consistently held by the figures of Cesar Romero, Bruce Cabot, Warren Hymer and Edward Brophy, good men for the job. Except for a weak tag ending and several flaws in procedure, *Show Them No Mercy,* with its nicely calculated pace and tension, is an exciting story, a document behind the headlines.

Another action picture, somewhat like but basically in contrast to this, was recently sent over from England and may still be seen here: *The 39 Steps.* Its story is on the Oppenheim side, with the young man dashing in and out of railway stations and danger to save the nation from a ring of international plotters. One of these stories where the turn of almost every supposition is made-up and false, but in an open, good-humored sort of way—the audience sees that it is plot for plot's sake, and goes on from there. The picture has charm, nice photography, plenty of drive and action (never at the expense of any needed restraint). It has humor as well, but not to the detriment of the plot—as witness the scene where the hard-pressed young man harangues the political meeting, one of the finest tempered bits of dramatic hokum I can remember. And its Robert Donat plays well.

Nothing that is wholly false is worth anything, and perhaps we may explain the merits of such a film by drawing a distinction between philosophic truth and dramatic truth. There is, for example, little logic and less reason to the scene where the girl gives up her message, but at the start a note is struck in the audience by curtains blowing wild in the opened window, and it increases in intensity as the girl comes in, walking queerly, crumpling slowly, the knife in her back coming in view with an unobtrusiveness that is more violent than if you had seen it planted; and the note keeps rising, tapering off finally into the strident insistence of the telephone bell in the death room. It is all unlikely, but it has been made to happen on the screen, no one can doubt it. The dramatic truth achieved in this picture lies sometimes in the conception of sequences, sometimes in the way action is put on an impressive background—as in the case over the Scotch moors, with one very pretty shot of Donat climbing a rock, outlined against heavy clouds; as in the picture of the railroad bridge looming above where he climbs from the river; as in the contrast of the dying memory-man with the line of girls kicking out their dull routine, seen on the stage through the wings just behind him. *The 39 Steps* starts with nothing but thrills, most of these unnecessary, but by the end it proves itself a notable exercise in the best methods of the screen.

There are pictures of much stouter stuff than these last two—most of them, curiously, dominated by one central figure. The French version of *Crime and Punishment* is the best of these and quite a good picture. It is arranged and put together so that its characters have a natural life; its settings (particularly interiors—some exteriors here are stiff and cardboardy) are appropriate and often beautiful; its approach to the story is intelligent. But the story still seems too vast and subtle to be anything but confused on the screen. Outside the occasional heaviness of Pierre Blanchar, the milk-and-wateriness of Madeleine Ozeray as Sonia, its principal flaw lies in an indecisiveness that is only underlined more strongly by some very dim camera work. What with poor focus, jerky trucking shots and several bad lighting effects, there is frequently the impression that some of the sequences were taken with a pocket kodak, and on a rainy day at that.

But the farther I get from it, the more *Crime and Punishment* becomes an indistinct but appropriately somber frame for the part of Porphyre as played by Harry Baur, subtle of mind and immense in guile, a pleasant, strange and terrible man, using legitimately every means to express what it would be impossible to say. He is fine on details and surrounds the part with business—his fascinating operations with a cigarette, the smoke twisting up and smarting his eye, his leafing through a dossier, his solemn hat on, off, his fingers at his face. But this is not a circus: Baur's restless motion focuses rather than diverts the attention, confirming and illuminating a presence that can be felt from his first ten feet in the film. His method of emphasis is one particularly adapted to pictures, where varying camera perspectives and planes and the many possibilities of cutting (full, immediate entrances and exits; the effect of words on their object without the distraction of watching the speaker) expand the range of effects and in their turn demand a rangy, mobile style.

I can remember very little about Hollywood's *Crime and Punishment* except that it has Peter Lorre, another actor who lasts after the show is over. His Raskolnikoff was much more interesting to me than that of the French film, more complex, more suggestive of inner turmoil. Lorre is above all the actors I can think of in using the best resources of the screen. His emotion is indicated more by the whole body than by any separate members—something hits him and he is instantly in motion, walking deliberately or freezing in a sort of special immobility. In an art where cameras can follow a man up a winding stairs or halfway across the city, this dynamic inertia can become a very powerful force, and deserves better materials to work with than it has been given in English-speaking pictures so far.

For laughs, the best thing on the screen so far this winter has been *A Night at the Opera,* which contains the Marx Brothers, whose antic, like the work of other good comics in the medium (Chaplin, Clair, Capra, Willie Howard, W. C. Fields), is pretty largely visual. There still remains more than a trace of the vaudeville blackout and the radio gag in their horseplay, but their best sequences are so all-over-the-place that nothing short of a double-jointed camera could cover them—take the stateroom business, or the opening night at the Metropolitan. They travel best at high and erratic speeds—and as for what they pass through the screen to us, I haven't thought of anything in addition to what I said in originally reviewing the picture: "They are very like someone exploding a blown-up paper bag —all bang and no taste; but they are also irrepressible clowns with a great sense of the ridiculous. They tear into it by guess and by god, they rush through it as though it were meat and they starving; their assurance, appetite and vitality are supreme; they are both great and awful." . . .

Coming to the point of *Ah, Wilderness!* I can't help taking up the banner of Hollywood and carrying it forward to the extent of saying that in this instance the movies have used their own genius to make quite a lot out of very little. And that when you wish to point out the immaturity of Hollywood, as illustrated by any given joke about Sam Goldwyn or the Warner Brothers, I give you for keeps Mr. Eugene O'Neill, who has become so overweening on the strength of good work well done in the early years that he can speak with the postures of a major dramatist and in the actual words of Gene Stratton Porter, and get completely away with it. The MGM cast does nothing to hide this play's weakness—false idealization, a lusterless eye for truth but a rare memory for all stereotypes in the way of generalities and situations. It reads ham lines and makes them seem even more so, meaning no offense but ameliorating none, hammering literally away at every nail, bent or straight.

Where Hollywood really goes to work here is in the background O'Neill suggested—small-town New England in the year 1906, a background that is so far removed from mere drops and properties as to become an active part of the picture. They went on location in North Grafton, Mass., to get the lawns and overloaded parlors and decent streets and all. But they went farther, they went somehow back to books and old natives and the lord knows what, and reconstructed a frame of the locale, the life of the town within it—all things as strong and irretrievable as Mrs. Hixon's preserved ginger in the sitting room, as taffy pulls, sleigh rides, town-hall meetings, cantatas, fairs. In the end, the production goes beyond the meaning of the play, immersing all the business good or bad in a mood that it is difficult to quarrel with. It is blurred with illusion yet inexorable in its details, tugging at silly heartstrings yet common enough; it seems projected on a screen purely in order that these dead times shall be remembered again, with amusement, exasperation and fondness.

February 1936

MORTON EUSTIS

*

Hollywood Comes of Age

TO SUGGEST that any two films epitomize the coming of age of a prodigy which has been nibbling at maturity with increasing vigor and success for over twenty-five years would be an assumption both brazen and hifalutin. Let the simple statement be made, therefore, that *Mr. Smith Goes to Washington* and *Ninotchka* reveal a degree of maturity in spirit, form and content which is seen but rarely in the product ground out of Hollywood's mill. Neither film is "epic" or "world-shaking" in the vocabulary of Sunset Boulevard, if we except that historic moment when Greta Garbo first laughs aloud, but each has an adult point of view, each is conscious of it, and each projects it in the best possible cinematographic way. . . .

Although the Garbo ("Don't Pronounce it—SEE IT!") picture is comedy of manners, light, gay, sophisticated, while *Mr. Smith* is comedy-drama, brash, explosive, sentimental and melodramatic, the photoplays have several denominators in common which are fairly uncommon in the everyday picture world. And the things they have in common are what give them their importance: the level on which their material is handled, the contemporaneity of the material itself, the excellence of all the techniques employed—from acting and dialogue to photography and direction—and the precision with which the basic plan is adhered to throughout the production. . . .

Mr. Smith Goes to Washington tells the story of a Middle Western youth, idolized as the head of a chain of boys' clubs, who attempts to pit his naive but idealistic concept of honor among politicians against a corrupt political machine at home and in the nation's capital. Appointed to fill a Senate vacancy, and with no qualification for the job beyond the expectation that he will vote as the machine dictates, he goes to Washington full of patriotic fervor. He makes a laughing stock of himself before a cynical press and Congress. But his faith in the integrity of his colleagues in the Senate chamber remains undimmed until he introduces a bill which threatens (though he is unaware of it) to expose a grafting piece of legislation endorsed by his fellow Senator and the state machine. One rude awakening after another follows for the young Senator, culminating in the attempt by the colleague, whom he deeply reveres, to oust him from the Senate on framed charges of dishonesty. His spirit broken by this assault, he determines to go back to his boys' clubs. But his hard-boiled secretary, who, needless to say, has fallen under the spell of his simple sincerity, urges him not to run away. As they stand in the moonlight on the steps of the Lincoln Memorial, she exhorts him to do what Lincoln would have done, to go in and fight for decent government, no matter how overwhelming the odds against him. When the Senate meets to vote on his expulsion, Mr. Smith, to everyone's surprise, takes the floor in his own defense and stages a one-man filibuster for twenty-three consecutive hours, hoping to gain time to expose the corruption of the machine to the voters in his state. His cause seems lost when he discovers that not a word of what he has said has been printed in the state's controlled press. But he fights on courageously, with the galleries behind him and the Senators taking notice for the first time, until he faints from exhaustion. His crooked colleague, overcome by the strain, tries to shoot himself and then confesses to his guilt. Mr. Smith is exonerated. The Vice-President grins in sardonic delight; the galleries and the audience cheer.

It is all just as simple as that—a kind of patriotic debauch, unashamedly sentimental, jingoistic and improbable, if you attempt to subject it to much critical analysis. But critical analysis is the last emotion that you feel as you follow Mr. Smith on his way to fame in the national capital. You accept the photoplay immediately on its own terms, swept forward by its emotional appeal, its humor and its sincerity. Once the spell has worn off, you realize that it was not the story itself but the skill with which the story was enacted that held you glued to your seat for over two hours. But what of that? *Mr. Smith* makes its appeal, as it should do, in the theatre. If, by means of honest and straightforward "ham," it can move its enormous potential audience to thought and feeling about a subject that is of vital importance today, the more power to it. That it can do so is already indicated by the opposition it has aroused in certain political circles.

Chief credit for the success of this *comédie humaine* must go to Frank Capra, the director, who is responsible for the sweep, the unflagging pace and so many of the shrewd, satiric bits and humorously human touches that enliven the film. But it is Capra's Mr. Smith, in the person of James Stewart, who endows the film with its richly appealing quality and gives it emotional punch. Played by any of the screen's Robert Taylors, Mr. Smith would have been an unbearably priggish Boy Scout. But in Stewart's brilliantly modulated performance he emerges as one of the most engaging characters of screen history.

Without Stewart to give conviction to the role of the young man who gasps with callow excitement at his first glimpse of the capitol dome and Claude Rains to make a splendidly three-dimensional character of the dishonest Senator, without Frank Walker to focus his camera so that it becomes a living character in the drama and without a host of other fine actors and technicians, Frank Capra would have been hard put to it to turn *Mr. Smith* into a persuasive document, the most vivid example yet seen of the use of the screen as a medium to inform and arouse public opinion. One scene, in this connection, stands out sharply as a triumph of technical artistry, a montage, executed by the Russian technician, Slavko Vorkapich, in which the camera and the special-effects department take the audience and Mr. Smith on a sight-seeing tour of Washington. No actors are visible, only the government buildings, the inscriptions on their walls and superimposed shots of the Liberty Bell and the American flag. Yet the scene projects as pure motion-picture dynamics—more exciting, by far, than any real-life tour of the capital. And the montage never obtrudes itself—as most montages do—upon the audience consciousness.

If the Capra touch, already famous in such comedies as *It Happened One Night* and *Mr. Deeds Goes to Town,* individualizes every sequence of *Mr. Smith,* Ernst Lubitsch's special style permeates the film *Ninotchka* in just as vivid a fashion. *Mr. Smith* makes its point through action rather than words (though one must not forget its feat of making the audience laugh at one instant, and applaud the next, by a reading of the United States Constitution). *Ninotchka's* primary appeal, *as a dramatic script,* is through dialogue and situation. (We italicize this point about the script lest any reader be tempted to exclaim, with ample justification: "The primary appeal of *any* Garbo picture, if you please, is Greta Garbo.")

The plot of *Ninotchka*—only a springboard for gay, pertinent and irreverent social comment—deals with the attempt of a Soviet Government, starved for cash, to sell to a Parisian bidder certain jewels seized from a Grand Duchess. The Grand Duchess, of course, is in Paris; so is her lover, Leon, suave and sophisticated, more than a match for Stalin's bearded emissaries. Leon ties up the sale of the jewels by a law suit and proceeds to corrupt the three bewildered Russians by feeding them champagne and introducing them to three cigarette girls. Another emissary is dispatched from Moscow, a cold, practical, efficient and unfeminine creature called Ninotchka, who believes that love is nothing more than a solemn method of procreating the Communist credo and who never, on any occasion, laughs—never, that is, until the redoubtable Leon falls off his chair in a restaurant. From then on, under the warming influence of Paris and of Leon, she too forgets the sacred purpose of her mission and becomes a woman in love with life and love. Her first taste of champagne goes so charmingly to her head that she calls all the ultra-capitalistic guests at a night club her "comrades" and then goes to sleep in all her finery at her hotel, leaving the safe, in which the jewels are kept, unlocked. The Grand Duchess secures the jewels through a White Russian who is working in the hotel as a waiter and returns them to Ninotchka on condition that she leave Leon and take the next plane back to Russia. Leon tries to follow her and is denied a visa. But they are reunited once again, thanks to a diabolical trick of Leon's, this time in Constantinople and, this time, for good.

What gives *Ninotchka* its distinction as a comedy is not its fairly cut-and-dried sequence of events, but the gaiety and impishness of its social satire, the delightfully carefree manner in which it pokes fun at communism, capitalism and other accepted "isms." Nothing is sacred to Lubitsch, except the importance of turning out a film that ripples with merriment. The consequence is, looking back at *Ninotchka* (and forgetting again Miss Garbo, for the moment), that it is an incident here, a snatch of dialogue there, a bit of photography or of direction that, added together, make the general impression so captivating.

The outraged snort of the Parisian headwaiter: "This is a restaurant, not a meadow!" after Ninotchka has ordered a luncheon of raw vegetables. . . . The banquet Leon gives to undermine the social consciousness of the Russian emissaries, where Lubitsch trains his camera, not on the banquet table but on the door outside the Royal Suite, letting the audience hear the steadily mounting roars of acclaim with which the food and drink is received, culminating in a bellow of delight as three cigarette girls go in. . . . The bearded stranger at the station whom the Russians take to be the new emissary, until he raises his hand in the Nazi salute and greets his wife with a "Heil Hitler!" . . . Ninotchka's coldly matter-of-fact statement to her terrified colleagues: "The last mass trials were a great success. There are going to be fewer but better Russians." . . . The scene on the traffic island of the Place de la Concorde—where Ninotchka and Leon first meet—and Leon informs her that he has been "interested in the five-year plan for the past fifteen years." . . . The photograph of Lenin which obligingly smiles when the tipsy Ninotchka asks it to. . . . The excited comment of one of the bearded men to Ninotchka's request for a cigarette: "You just telephone and you get what you want. That is the capitalistic system." . . . The opening subtitle, which informs us—to the tune of a jazzed "Internationale"—that the events to come transpire in those wonderful days when, among other things, "if a Frenchman turned out the lights, it was not on account of an air raid." . . . The obsequious Russian Consul who tells a society matron not to worry about her comforts in Moscow, as they change the towels once a week at all the best hotels. . . . The burlesque of a Russian May Day parade, with hundreds of faintly satirical pictures of Stalin on placards. . . . These bits and others like them maintain throughout the steady crackle of good comedy.

If none of this, however, gives evidence that *Ninotchka* is anything more than an entertaining piece of fluff, it is because no mention has been made, except in passing, of the performance of Miss Garbo in the title role. Any good actress could play Ninotchka—it is not a particularly exacting part—and make the film amusing. Miss Garbo not only makes it amusing, confounding the critics who thought she could never adapt her peculiar magic to the exigencies of comedy by showing herself to be as deft a comedienne as she is a tragic actress. She also endows it with overtones of glamour and distinction that never detract from the froth of the comedy but add immeasurably to its style. Her Ninotchka is an enchanting creature, both as "a tiny cog in the great wheel of evolution" and, later, as a woman. And Miss Garbo effects the transition between the two basically different characters with great subtlety and technical skill—not only by a change of expression, of gesture and of tone of voice, but in the whole line of her body. Although Miss Garbo—thank God—is always Miss Garbo, you have only to see her in such contrasting roles as Camille and Ninotchka to realize that she is an actress of radiant quality and ability.

Ina Claire gives a glittering performance as the Grand Duchess—her technique just as sure in the film medium as on the stage; Melvyn Douglas is more than adequate in that most difficult of all roles—leading man to Miss Garbo; and Sig Rumann, Felix Bressart and Alexander Granach acquit themselves honorably, and most amusingly, as the Russian emissaries. But *Ninotchka* is, first, last and foremost, Miss Garbo's film—a Lubitsch comedy which has been lent the aura of greatness by the light of a Nordic star.

February 1940

* *

C. A. LEJEUNE

*

Two English Films

IT IS TO BE hoped that nobody will be beguiled into seeking an association between Laurence Olivier's film production of *Henry V* and the present war, on the grounds that the heroic actions of last summer and fall were fought so closely along the route that Henry Plantagenet followed. Such an association would be unfortunate; it would inevitably reveal in *Henry V* a touch of brassy romanticism; diminishing, by unnatural contrast with a very different sort of greatness, the stature of the play.

Henry V is not a great war play. The Elizabethans were too much in love with beauty and splendor and the heady draft of words to write great war plays; and Laurence Olivier, who produced, directed and starred in the screen version of *Henry V,* was too much in love with Shakespeare to make a great war film. The stuff of war is patience and endurance, courage in cold blood, and a kind of long, hard, impersonal anonymity. These are not qualities for the playhouse, still less for the movie theatre. What Shakespeare wrote in *Henry V,* and what the film has splendidly caught in its own fashion, is a fanfare; a flourish; a salute to high adventure; a kind of golden and perennially youthful exaltation of man's grim work.

The picture runs for two hours and a half, and retains about two-thirds of the original text. The only interpolations are a borrowed speech from *Henry IV, Part II,* used to explain the references to Falstaff, and superimposed over a silent scene of the Fat Knight's deathbed; and a couple of lines from Marlowe's *Tamburlaine,* given Pistol when he goes off to the wars. Mr. Olivier and his colleagues have taken one daring license with their material. They have presented *Henry V* as a play within a play. The opening and closing scenes are represented as taking place during the first performance of the piece at the old Globe Theatre, and are played deliberately broad for comedy. Speech, gestures and make-up are formally exaggerated; players and audience mingle in a kind of stylized puppet play. As a device for emphasizing "this wooden O" the conceit is ingenious; as a theory of presentation it is entirely legitimate; but in practice it works out a little self-consciously tiresome, a rather redundant addition to a film that is handsomely intelligible on its own account.

With the gathering of the English fleet at Southampton, however, the film breaks loose. The background opens out, the action is filled with a wide bustle, the poetry takes charge, and the audience is clearly no longer watching a stylized piece taking place on the stage of a theatre. From that moment onwards, the picture is a beauty. It moves with a flowing line, a rhythmic pattern of mass and color, that has only been equalled on the screen in the best of the Disney fantasies. One rich composition after another fills the eye; the light, airy tracery of the French court scenes; the blazing canvas of the battlefield; the deep, whispering quiet of a darkened camp waiting for the morning; bold massed groups, single heroic figures; a quaint formal flower-garden for a fairy-tale princess; a rearing and curvetting of caparisoned chargers for a couple of kings at war.

The producers have gone to the Italian painters, and particularly to Uccello's "Rout of San Romano," for their battlescapes, and to Holbein and Brueghel for their colors. For the superb charge of the French cavalry at Agincourt, they have relied on the tempo of a musician. Before a foot of this scene was shot, the composer William Walton worked out an exact musical score, to be used as a guide-track for timing. The result is a classic sequence, in which, as in the unforgettable scene on the Odessa steps in *Potemkin,* the poetry of pure mathematics is applied to the practice of drama. Music and movement gather impetus together; pulsing, pounding, quickening, loudening, until they break over you thunderously like the mountain of a wave.

It takes powerful acting to match this splendor of production, and fortunately *Henry V* has it. Mr. Olivier has collected a cast of some of the finest Shakespearean actors on the English stage, so that every speech gets its due, every lightest word its measure. Leslie Banks, as Chorus, flings the gateway to romance wide open with a flourish. Robert Newton plays the Ancient Pistol with a huge Elizabethan gusto. The scenes in the French camp, always a little dull in the reading, are quickened by the beautiful performances of Leo Genn as the sober Constable, Ralph Truman as the joyous herald Mountjoy, and Max Adrian as the sleek Dauphin. Renée Asherson plays Katharine with a demure coquetry and a kind of school-girl secrecy that is altogether winning.

Laurence Olivier's own Henry is a development of the performance he gave some years ago at the Old Vic, adapted very shrewdly to the enlargement of the scene beyond the four walls of a theatre. As the central figure of a huge crowd in a vast campaign, he strikes a high heroic note, and uses the full leather of his lungs. "Once more unto the breach, dear friends" is a war-cry; the Crispin's Day speech ends on something that is almost a brazen scream. Mr. Olivier is not afraid to hint that Henry Plantagenet was unafraid of showmanship But that is only half the portrait. He has another sort of King for another sort of occasion: a shy and tender wooer; a lonely man, watchful over his camp in the darkness. Above all, he suggests a Henry who is under all circumstances a leader; the sort of man honest men will follow till they drop.

One can pick out actor after actor for note, and still not catch the film's especial quality; which is that everyone in it, and concerned with it, from Mr. Olivier onwards, seems to be in love and tune with Shakespeare. That is as it should be in a Shakespearean performance; behind the footlights and in front of them; on the screen and in the lodges. For too long Shakespeare has suffered from being a compulsory subject in our education. Because he has been presented to us from infancy as a classic, the Immortal Bard, a writer of set books for examinations, an author of plays to be pulled to pieces with the help of annotations and a glossary, the most exciting of our playwrights has become a bore. What we need is a little healthy hunger for Shakespeare; an absence from felicity awhile; and then a zest to make us rediscover him as something of our own, as we might discover Donne, or Vaughan, or Belloc. I think the Olivier *Henry V* has this special relish, and even if it were not such an eye-ful, *that* would be good enough for me.

Henry V is, without a doubt, the most glowing film enterprise of the year in England. But if I were asked to name the film that seemed to me our best all-around job of work, I should unhesitatingly pick *The Way Ahead,* that study of the evolution of a civilian into an invasion soldier.

The Way Ahead follows the fortunes of seven civilians who are drafted into an infantry platoon. They represent the usual "slice of life." One of them is a farmer; another a floor-walker in a multiple store; another a boiler-worker in the House of Commons; and so it goes on. They are handed over to the tender charge of a young Lieutenant, a garage mechanic who has joined the Territorials before the war; and a rather less tender Sergeant, with seven years' experience as a professional soldier. The film studies the training of this one platoon; shows how they gain toughness and stature; how they orient themselves to their officers and to each other; how they grow fighting fit; how the qualities that earn a man a stripe become discernible without any fuss or fanfare; how they learn that in modern warfare every man's first job is not to let the other fellows down; how they are sent abroad raring for action, torpedoed and sent back again; how in the end they find themselves in the big show with bayonets fixed and morale unwavering.

Nothing very new in the story, is there? Sounds dull, doesn't it? And yet the extraordinary fact remains that this dull-sounding, not-very-new subject, without the benefit of glamour, romance or leg-art, has been an instant hit wherever it has been shown to British soldiers. I have a great clip of letters on my desk testifying to its popularity, not only at home but in camp cinemas in Italy, in the Middle East, in India. Soldiers notoriously dislike war-films. What makes this particular war-film succeed where so many others have failed? Three things, I suggest: an idea, a script and a director.

First, the idea. It is by no means customary, although it would seem profitable, for a film to start with an idea. Most films start as a "vehicle" for a contract star. Some start as radio acts or vaudeville turns. One or two start as nothing more substantial than a popular song. A few, it is true, based on successful novels or plays, may start with a plot, but in such a case the people involved are usually at great pains to change it.

The Way Ahead started with an idea in the heads of the War Office Department of Army Psychiatry. In the early years of the war, during the big turnover of manpower to the Services, the Department recommended that a training film should be made dealing with the orientation of various types of civilian to Army life: showing how, in time of war, an individual becomes part of a corporate body; how a civilian may gain stature and comradeship as he develops into a soldier.

Three bright young men from the Army Film Unit—director Carol Reed, thriller-novelist Eric Ambler, and playwright Peter Ustinov—promptly got to work. They called their little film *The New Lot.* It was approved by Army psychiatrists both here and in the United States. It was so persuasive and sensible along its own specialized lines that the authorities suggested a commercial film should be made by the same men on the same theme. *The Way Ahead* grew out of *The New Lot.* A few of the original actors were carried over, including Peter Ustinov, who appears in a small but brilliant sketch in the film of his own writing. In deference to the exigence of nervous moviegoers, David Niven was borrowed from the Army to lend a touch of star appeal.

Second, the script. It has long been apparent to the critical mind that screen writing is the weakest part of our film effort in this country. Our scripts are seldom inspired, hardly ever witty, and often just plain bad. Dialogue in British films seems to vary between the cross-talk of small-time vaudeville, and something picked up casually in a West-End restaurant over luncheon. But *The Way Ahead* has a real script and dialogue that every British soldier recognizes as his own currency. Except for *The New Lot,* and a few Army instructional films, Messrs. Ambler and Ustinov have never, I understand, tried their hand at film writing. The result is startling. *The Way Ahead* actually plays and talks life.

Third, the director. Since Alfred Hitchcock deserted the British studios for Hollywood, Carol Reed has generally been regarded, both here and in the United States, as our Number One director. He is certainly our most talented all-round craftsman. He relishes making films as films, and isn't choosey about his subjects. If you ask him what sort of film he would like to make, he answers frankly: "Well, I don't think it matters much, do you?"

Nor does it, since every film he tackles, whether it be costume piece or thriller, romance or comedy, is reduced in the end to the human element. Mr. Reed has made many good films, notably *Three on a Week-End, The Stars Look Down, Kipps, Night Train* and *The Young Mr. Pitt,* but *The Way Ahead* is by far his most mature and successful effort. It is a lesson in movie-making to observe how diligently the casual effects of his scenes are contrived; how patiently the characters are allowed to develop in their own time and through their own idiom. There is nothing spectacular about *The Way Ahead.* In spite of its subject, it is mainly a quiet film; often a very funny film. It has not the "big" feel of Noel Coward's *In Which We Serve.* But in their own way, Mr. Reed and his colleagues have turned out an Army picture that is a counterpart to Mr. Coward's Navy picture; something of which they and their countrymen can be quietly proud; something that brings the audience on close human terms with the people on the screen, and does the official job with as much heart as authority.

June 1945

* *

HERMINE RICH ISAACS

*

A Sight of Paradise

IN *LES ENFANTS DU PARADIS* Marcel Carné has created no ordinary drama on film but rather an extraordinary tapestry spread out in time. In spite of its backstage theme this picture owes more to the artisans of Gobelin than it does to Molière and Corneille. Many things contribute to this effect.

The picture opens on a street scene during the reign of Louis Philippe. It is carnival time and the Boulevard du Temple, street of theatres, is filled with a gaudy, surging mass of humanity bent on every form of amusement from flirtation to violence. Out of the crowd emerge the chief characters in the story: the young actor, Frédéric Lemaître, and the mime Baptiste Deburau; Garance, the lady of their love; Jericho, the fortune-teller, a kind of early-day newscaster; and Pierre Lacenaire, the dapper scoundrel who runs like a thread of evil through all their lives. Their encounter is casual at first, then slowly the fabric tightens. Together they travel for a while along the line of their mutual destiny and then, once again, it is carnival time and the crowd which brought them together now buffets them apart. In the final fadeout, Baptiste is entangled in the mob in hopeless pursuit of Garance. Frédéric, Jericho are not far away. It is like the repeating pattern with which the tapestry-maker frames his work.

Within the frame the camera shifts over the face of the tapestry with only the barest propulsion from dramatic necessity. In *Les Enfants du Paradis* nothing ever changes. True there is a sequence in time; the young people, poor and unsuccessful at the start, grow rich and famous in the end. Yet their loves and hates, their susceptibilities and their dreams go on unabated, and their mutual relationships remain unaltered. They saunter across the scene unimpelled by the changing impact of events which is the dynamic element of formal drama.

Even in appearance *Les Enfants du Paradis* has the lively surface of a tapestry. The background is an alluring display of colorful detail spread out to the very edges of the screen. There is no satiety for the eyes. This is the Paris of Balzac and Daumier come to life. Their names are written by indirection on the credits alongside those of Marcel Carné the director, Jacques Prevert the writer, Lucien Barsacq and Raymond Gabutti who are responsible for the decor and Antoine Mayo who designed the costumes. It is not accidental that the mime, Baptiste Deburau, bears the same surname as the great Pierrot of the Funambules whose visage Daumier recorded for posterity; nor that Frédéric Lemaître is the name of the actor who was ruling the legimate scene when Deburau reigned over pantomime.

The Deburau of the film, Jean-Louis Barrault, is endowed by nature for the role. With the sculptured cheekbones and deepset eyes of the tragic mask, he requires only an application of rice-flour for the sweet, sad countenance of the clown. Beneath the limp outlines of the traditional Pierrot costume, he fuses a dancer's grace and an actor's emotional tension. His portrait of the pure young man who swoons for the love his purity denies is a thing both fragile and compelling, both tragic and absurd. By contrast, Pierre Brasseur as Frédéric Lemaître is the complete extrovert, brash, irresponsible, talented. Arletty, whose rare beauty stems from heavy-lidded eyes, is Garance, the femme fatale beloved of both. Supported by a rich duke, sleeping with Frédéric and assorted gentry, she loves Baptiste with a fine pure flame which only the French would see fit to plant in so unseemly a brazier.

On the scene of *Les Enfants du Paradis* no line of cleavage marks where theatre leaves off and life begins. Each interprets and informs the other. Scenes from theatrical performances are woven right into the fabric of the plot as a comment, a reflection on the action itself. For these are the days of the theatre's ascendancy. To everyone, from the wealthy box-patrons to the "enfants du Paradis"—the tumultuous gallery gods who load the air with their taunts and praises—the theatre is a section of life at least as real as the fantastic pageant that eddies along the boulevards outside.

December 1946

*

A Picture of Our Lives

THIS UNNATURAL peace that rushed into the vacuum left by war has caught our poets and prophets unawares. It is a curious fact that with the exception of Norman Corwin's *On a Note of Triumph* no novelist, no poet and no playwright has yet emerged with an adequate expression of the spirit and problems of our day. It appears that peace, too, must be recollected in tranquillity. In view of this default in the other arts it seems more than a minor miracle that Samuel Goldwyn, Robert Sherwood and William Wyler have succeeded in building a platform of tranquillity above the press of the times and in crystallizing the sum of their vision in a superlative motion picture, *The Best Years of Our Lives.*

That the two creative members of the triumvirate succeed where so many others have failed (not for lack of trying) may be laid to the unusual circumstances that found them both involved in the war when most men of their years and experience were left behind on the home front. Though neither was actively in combat, both shared in the stirring and sometimes shattering experience of separation from home and each was constrained to contemplate and interpret events as they occurred. Unlike many of the war's most sensitive reporters, young men whose baptism by fire coincided with their emotional coming of age, both Wyler and Sherwood had attained maturity, not only physically but emotionally and with respect to their crafts. When peace came they were possessed of both the emotion and the tranquillity, as well as the skill to express what they saw.

And so in this story (built on the raw materials of MacKinlay Kantor's *Glory for Me*) of three veterans' return to their homes, they have captured in brilliant flashes of detail and in the steady illumination of compassion the turmoil, the misery and the profound necessity for reevaluation that faces reunited families all over the world. They have noted shrewdly the warrior's homesickness for war, the officious, the blundering, the helpful civilians, the shortages, the petty irritations and the changing values, the phony dreams and the phonier realities. They have captured, too, the humorous aspects of the scene; the wartime habits unconsciously remembered, the peacetime habits forgotten over the years. Sherwood and Wyler are not orators; it is a film they have made, not a diatribe. Their observations are revealed in terms of dramatic give-and-take, of visual intimation. The simplicity with which they have interwoven three stories into a single revelation of humor and humanity is a work of artful deception.

Fredric March is the sergeant, Al Stephenson, who returns to a loving wife (Myrna Loy), two grown children (Teresa Wright and Michael Hall) and a nice fat job as vice-president in charge of small loans at the local bank. His problem, once he has overcome the initial strangeness of homecoming, revolves around the conflict in his job between human and commercial values. On occasion he is not averse to the bottle and this predilection provides Fredric March with more than one opportunity to explore the rigors of drunkenness in hilarious and intimate detail.

Captain Derry (Dana Andrews) was a soda-jerker before the war, married to the brassy blonde Marie (Virginia Mayo) twenty days before he shipped overseas. He returns with his bomber-bred dreams of a home of his own and a job that is worthy of his war-born mettle, only to meet with disillusion as his marriage breaks up and the new job that he so hoped for is not forthcoming.

Homer Parrish (Harold Russell) is a sailor who lost both hands in the South Pacific. Though the Navy has trained him proficiently in the use of prosthetic "hooks," they could not train him to put his arms around his girl or to deal with the painful solicitude of his family. He must work that out for himself.

As these episodes progress, sometimes separately, sometimes together, each story moves inevitably toward its climax. Al Stephenson confounds his bank president with a witty and incisive parable delivered at a dinner in honor of his homecoming. Fred Derry has it out with his wartime illusions alone in the nose of an abandoned bomber. Homer Parrish tests his girl and himself by revealing his helplessness in an episode of affecting solemnity.

That all of the players, from the most experienced down to Harold Russell—whose only equipment for the part was the fact that he, like Homer, had lost his hands in the war—perform with variety, skill and profound integrity reflects credit beyond the limits of the actors themselves. It means that Robert Sherwood has given them people to image and lines to speak that lend focus and meaning to their performance, and that William Wyler has guided them through the maze of the story with extraordinary sensitivity. He has set them a leisurely pace and proved endlessly resourceful with business to bring them along through a difficult speech or a moment of silence. On the visual side he has urged Gregg Toland, the cameraman, and George Jenkins and Perry Ferguson, the art directors, to eschew the beautiful or striking in favor of a kind of uncluttered realism. Only at a time when the event dictates the technique, as it does during Derry's visit to the bomber graveyard, does Wyler resort to pure cinema artifice. By composing a symphony for this episode out of visual and orchestral effects, he has achieved a disturbing expression of Derry's emotional crisis.

Hugo Friedhofer's score provides sturdy support both here and elsewhere throughout the film, where his musical motif grows frequently out of the scene itself—be it Hoagy Carmichael's piano jingles, Marie's strident radio or the jungle-rhythms of a night-club band.

It may seem paradoxical to report that a motion picture which lasts nearly three hours is a paragon of economy. And yet it is the strength of *The Best Years of Our Lives* that almost no line is wasted, no action irrelevant, no episode pushed beyond the limit of necessity.

January 1947

*

When Is a Fiction a Fact?

WHOEVER sets out to delimit the boundary between fact films and fiction films is doomed to defend his views against dissidents for the rest of his natural life. Even if he succeeds in silencing all other opposition, he can never shout down the realist who declares that every person—even an actor—is a fact; every idea—even a bad one—is a fact; and therefore every film—even a shoddy fabrication—is a film of fact.

You may say that the fiction film selects and heightens and rearranges persons and events to suit its purposes, but so does the fact film. You may point out that the former makes use of professional actors and constructed sets whereas the latter favors actuality, but the reverse is frequently the case. It is true that the fact film cherishes the semblance of authenticity, but this gives it no monopoly in the service of truth. The most imaginative work of drama may be profoundly truthful in its revelation of the human spirit. The most impressive array of on-the-spot photographs is often intensely deceptive. It is only by assigning qualities in terms of the broadest purposes that you can hope to emerge with your argument whole.

The theme is timely because of the presence on the scene of no less than four films which undertake to mix elements of fact and fiction in a single unit. All four pictures employ a fictional form to tell more or less factual stories. *The Beginning or the End,* MGM's saga of the atom bomb, casts professional actors in the roles of living men and women and reenacts the entire story on the studio lot. *13 Rue Madeleine,* the second in Louis de Rochemont's series (the first was *The House on Ninety-second Street*), intermingles a more aggressive fictional line with its documentary material and shoots considerable portions of the film on location (though not on the spot). *Boomerang* (also a de Rochemont production) is shot entirely on location, near the actual scene, and mingles non-professionals with professionals in the cast. *Man's Hope* is a reenactment on the spot and at the time (1938) and with the actual men and women who played in the real-life drama of the Spanish Civil War.

Here, then, is the progression from almost complete fiction to almost complete actuality. No one picture represents anything radically new on the film horizon; but taken together they indicate a trend worth considering, and provide a basis for measuring how much fiction films stand to profit from being injected with persons, scenes and events from reality.

The answer is not clear-cut. It varies from film to film and from one moment to the next within a film. But in each case it is dominated by one criterion: the nature of the reality, its interest and its significance.

A scene of the Spanish war which shows the look of the land, the distinctive faces of the peasants and the manner of civil warfare is a rich and revealing document because the reality was rich and revealing. The same could be said for the scenes that made up *Fighting Lady,* which forecast Mr. de Rochemont's feature productions in the current vein. That story of an aircraft carrier in the Pacific gained an increment of power from the fact that the pictures were shot in the midst of the battle. Actions and emotions came direct from life, without suffering the interference of reenactment.

A camera which turns its sights on a human being caught up in the toils of a great event is likely to capture a revelation of the human spirit which no actor's rendition, no matter how masterly, can simulate. The middle-aged Frenchman weeping at his country's defeat, the Chinese baby burned and frightened and alone in the middle of a bombed-out railroad siding, gave moments to film without parallel. What happens, however, when such "natural" players are set to remembering and recreating an event in front of the camera? By and large they communicate little beyond the appearance of extreme discomfort. The shapes of their faces or the drape of their dress may have certain documentary interest; occasional flashes of characteristic gesture may survive the ordeal; but insofar as they succeed in the act of recreation, they are succeeding as *actors,* not as naturals.

Evidence to the contrary can be found all the way from the early works of Flaherty down to moments in the current films. One thinks of the befuddled peasant in *Man's Hope* admitting sheepishly that he cannot read a map; of the back-porch grandmother in *Boomerang,* smoking a cigarette, pushing a baby carriage and listening to a radio all at once. But these incidentals prove more about the quick eye, the good fortune and the extraordinary patience of the film-makers than they do about the art of film.

So much for natural actors. Natural settings are subject to similar considerations. If the actual scene is interesting or beautiful or intensely characteristic, there is value in going to it and taking pictures. But to shoot for the sake of sweet reality in a place which is none of these but simply outside the studio walls is to sacrifice motion-picture values to an illusory objective.

When it comes to reenacting real events on the screen, old standards of story-telling set in. There are times when actual occurrences arrange themselves into sprightly narrative form; but more often the truth is too flat for fiction, or too strange. Then it has to be tampered with. The moviemaker who tries to fit a documentary story into a dramatic mold is on shifty ground, for he is always in danger of losing the casual patterns of authenticity without acquiring the focus and emotional precision of a well-made tale.

Although these are abstract considerations, they all have pertinence here. They do not explain why *The Beginning or the End* is so monumental a frost, for that is simply a matter of inept moviemaking despite the best of intentions. But they do suggest why that form of complete reenactment of events on the whole undramatic (despite their world-shaking significance) could never have succeeded entirely. They explain why *13 Rue Madeleine* is most absorbing in the early scenes that reveal our techniques for training spies in the fine arts of deception, jiu jitsu and such, and least successful in the latter half when it casts off its documentary garb without donning the fictional garment with grace. They explain the extraordinary impact of André Malraux's *Man's Hope* despite the authentic gaucherie of his cast. And, finally, they explain why *Boomerang* has succeeded signally in certain ways, and why it has not quite come off in others.

In the latter film, the director Elia Kazan is telling a first-class mystery tale informed with nice political comment. Anthony Abbott's story, from which Richard Murphy has fashioned his screenplay, was taken from the record of Homer Cummings when he was a young state's attorney for Connecticut. By setting up shop in

Stamford (the original incident took place in nearby Bridgeport), and by making use of local landmarks and local people, Kazan has sought to imbue his film with the air of natural occurrences. Since he is dealing, however, with facts which are nowise sacred, he has the necessary sanction to alter history in favor of a dramatic unity of both vigor and wit. Casting such actors as Lee Cobb, Sam Levene, Dana Andrews, Jane Wyatt and Taylor Holmes in the leads—all excellent players who are at the same time familiar types—Kazan has merged the professionals and the non-professionals in his cast with a minimum of friction. In other words, he has surmounted the difficulties to which he was committed with the use of nautral actors and natural settings (which frequently photograph poorly and in several instances actually hamper the action).

However transitory may be the values of such a style, there is much to be gained from it at the moment. Hollywood pictures have turned their backs more and more on the characteristic line and curve of American life. Drastic measures are needed to restore them face to face with reality. One way is to provide them, in the manner of Mr. de Rochemont's films, with internal comparisons—injections of realistic detail, of scenes and characters from actual life—that will serve as a constant pressure to thrust the whole motion-picture pattern back into line.

April 1947

*

On with the New

UNTIL RECENTLY, the history of film has been written largely in terms of its innovators—such men as Eisenstein, Griffith, Disney, Hitchcock. These men belonged to the generation that forged their tools as they used them, creating, often simultaneously, the film and its technique. Their high points have never been equaled, not even by themselves. Herein lies the innovator's tragedy: that once he has blazed the trail and mounted the heights he seldom goes forward from there or even stands still but rather, by slow irrevocable steps, retires from his topmost point of conquest. Committed to a kind of artistic special pleading, he loses something of the very quality that first sent him surging ahead of the crowd, the fine free impulse of creative excitement.

With Disney and Hitchcock still in active production, with Eisenstein once more represented on the screen and the airwaves still carrying rumors of Griffith's return from retirement, it can be hoped that these generalizations will prove as false as most, but the signs in the past few years have been marked too clearly to be easily misinterpreted.

It is partly for this reason that Carol Reed's *Odd Man Out* becomes the most significant picture to reach these shores in many months, for it marks a milestone in the development of one of the screen's most authentic younger talents.

Carol Reed is no innovator. He shows no inclination to develop new forms, to invent new techniques or otherwise to press out the boundaries of film. Rather he is the cultivated heir to the riches of the older generation. He has learned from the masters and assimilated their lessons. He knows them so well that he has them almost as second nature, to use when he wants, to refrain from using when he chooses. Uncommitted to a particular form of montage, of camera usage for expressive or decorative effect, of tricks of timing and dramatic irony, he can use them brilliantly or he can leave them alone, an act of renunciation of which their originators have proved generally incapable.

It is hardly surprising to learn that his favorite director is William Wyler, for he shares with the American certain basic convictions, including a fervent respect for the story and a disinclination to obtrude his technique on the scene. He starts, however, with the great advantage that geography gives him. Working out of London, his environment is more of the world than is the cloud-cuckoo-land of our own film capital. His sources are living people and lively places. Wyler has lately shown what he could do when he formed his impressions away from Hollywood. It is to be hoped that Reed—even if he takes advantage of the organization and resources of Hollywood to make occasional pictures within its confines—will never commit himself so to retire from the world as to take up permanent residence there.

Odd Man Out is set in Belfast. Johnny McQueen, the leader of a revolutionary organization, kills a man in the robbery of a flax mill and himself is wounded in the fray. During the escape he slips from the getaway car and is lost among the alleys of the city. The weather closes in, a heavy afternoon rain followed by snow in the evening. Weak and only half-conscious, Johnny is chased by the police, sought by his friends and pursued by his own inexorable fate. The element of Wagnerian despair is strong in the treatment of the central character, and the denouement of the picture, in which he is "saved" in death by a woman who loves him, makes the parallel with *The Flying Dutchman* compelling.

Another parallel, so obvious that it cannot be disregarded, is with *The Informer*. Yet though the locale and the skeleton of the plot are similar in the Hollywood classic, the contours bear little resemblance. The line of the earlier film showed a straight, rapid rise from beginning to end; in *Odd Man Out* frequent jogs interrupt the forward thrust of the story. And whereas the earlier film kept its sights intently on the chase and the victim of the chase, *Odd Man Out* has turned the bulk of its attention to the people who shiver in the sudden breath of its tragic events.

These include Johnny's comrades in the organization, especially Kathleen who loves him (played by the Irish beauty, Kathleen Ryan); the Head Constable (a figure of quiet power in the hands of Dennis O'Dea), who pursues him doggedly but without hate; Father Tom, the elderly priest on whom all parties converge for comfort and advice; and finally the various men and women of Belfast whom Johnny passes on his way to death, ranging out from a commonplace core of children, young lovers and housewives to an eccentric periphery that includes a shady underworld character named Shell and the mad painter Lukey.

The camera lingers affectionately on these people and well it might, for between them they mount an intimate and engaging gallery of Irish genre portraits. From the Abbey Theatre, Carol Reed has borrowed one of the founders, W. G. Fay, for the role of Father Tom and—for Shell—the veteran player, F. J. McCormick, whose detailed revelations of petty knavery are so richly displayed that they tempt the director to tarry in their presence after the story would well be on its way. Fay Compton and Beryl Measor provide a hearteningly normal interlude as the housewives Rosie and Maudie, while, at the other end of the scale, Robert Newton—as the artist Lukey who longs to paint the portrait of death that he sees in Johnny's eyes—performs with a florid style that emphasizes how far Johnny's flight has taken him out of the workaday world.

As Johnny, James Mason is pitted against actors of considerable skill in a role that permits him comparatively little defense through the ordinary channels of action or speech. Nonetheless with the aid of shrewd photography and direction he has succeeded in bulking a larger-than-life-sized effigy of mystery and doom.

With the aid of the director of photography, Robert Krasker, Carol Reed has merged location scenes with studio sequences so that it is virtually impossible to tell where one leaves off and the other begins. The alleys of the dour town of Belfast and the cluttered yards that surround its wharves seem the natural habitat of fugitives. There the lonely maze of the streets, the sounds of the city and the very shadows conspire to hound and bemuse their victim. Mr. Reed is especially wise in the ways of contrasting extraordinary events with ordinary backgrounds. He is, on the other hand, least successful when it comes to portraying the fitful processes in the half-conscious mind of his protagonist. But here the director is not alone, for he shares his defect with nearly everyone who has sought to convey the subjective element on the screen.

Odd Man Out has been extracted by Robert Sherriff and F. L. Green from the latter's novel with an admirable combination of fidelity and compliance with film necessity. Few books come along in the ordinary course of events which are such natural sources for film, not in the derogatory sense of pat types and formula plot lines but rather in the sense of characters dramatically visualized and relationships charged with the current of dramatic interplay. It is as if the author had held a camera instead of a mirror up to nature. In one way, however, the picture suffers from the quality of the original. There comes a time when the Irish penchant for searching the mystical recesses of the soul slows matters to a discursive pace that works insidiously against the rising flood of tension. This is the ebb before the action climbs once more to a tremendous climax, but it seems for a while as if the tide had pulled out so far it might never find its way to shore.

May 1947

ARTHUR KNIGHT

*

The Small Screen

[*From a monthly column on 16mm. films*—THE EDITORS.]

INTERNATIONAL FILM FOUNDATION, a non-profit film-producing organization, has just released a new animated picture on race relations called *Boundary Lines*. It is an extremely interesting production, and not only for the very worthy things it has to say about its central problem. Its technique, indeed its very conception, is a new approach to animation and sound synchronization.

What is a line? the film asks. A line is a concept. It can be anything we choose to make it. A line can be a mountain, a river, a man—or the barrier between men. These boundary lines are man-made, created by men as they note differences in color, in nationality, in language, in religion. But while they exist in the mind they are strong enough to lead to war. If we are agreed that war is undesirable, the film says, then we must realize that since these boundary lines are of our own making we can make of them what we will. We can even make of them neighborly fences with which the whole world could become one large, friendly community freed from the threat of war by mutual understanding and respect.

To artist Phillip Stapp goes credit for both the original conception of *Boundary Lines* and its artistic execution. Equal credit, however, is due Gene Forell who composed the score that is such an integral part of the film. Actually, the music was written first, based on the idea that *Boundary Lines* was to convey, but before the action had been laid out. Action was then matched to the music, and so closely that one is often reminded of those abstract films that interpret music in terms of visual movement. Forell's music is modern in idiom, and so too is Stapp's art work. His method is better described as animation rather than cartooning, with the drawings themselves often static and the impression of action being derived through camera movement—panning, tracking, tilting. His cards, however, are designed specifically to accept that movement. There is never a sense of forced or superimposed motion. *Boundary Lines* is successful not only as an artistic experience but as an intellectual one as well.

The picture has already been shown to good effect in clubs, churches, schools and adult forums. In the schools it was discovered with some surprise that the younger children, unspoiled by any traditional approach to art, proved to be among its most enthusiastic audiences. Its modern designing was perfectly acceptable to them, and its message, apparently, perfectly clear. *Boundary Lines* is one reel, color, and available in 16mm. only.

International Film Foundation, Inc. was founded late in 1945 by Julien Bryan, the noted camera explorer, on a grant from the Davella Mills Foundation, its purpose being "to promote better understanding between peoples of different nations, races and religions . . . to present and interpret other nations and people to the American people and to present and interpret the American people to other nations and peoples . . . through the production and distribution of motion pictures. . . ."

August 1947

* *

SIEGFRIED KRACAUER

*

Filming the Subconscious

THESE NOTES on several recent experimental films are inspired by the growing response to this genre. When Cinema 16, an organization specializing in the distribution of avant-garde films of all kinds, presented its first program in New York last fall, most of its performances were sold out in advance. The same interest stirs in Los Angeles, Chicago and Minneapolis. And Amos Vogel, the young director of Cinema 16, tells me of unknown amateurs whose film experiments are so promising that he plans to show them in future programs. There seems to be a new avant-garde movement in the making. In all likelihood, it owes something to the widespread discontent with the current Hollywood output.

Maya Deren, who received a Guggenheim fellowship and whose work is perhaps the most familiar of the group, has made four experimental films, of which all but one externalize psychological reality in the material of outer reality. This has been done before, in particular by Germaine Dulac in her *The Seashell and the Clergyman* (1928). But Miss Deren carries on with such vitality that she instills new life into the old patterns.

Meshes of the Afternoon (1943), which she made in collaboration with her husband, Alexander Hammid, one of our best cameramen, sets forth the state of mind of a frustrated girl. The girl returns home from a walk and finds her house deserted, with everything upside down, as if her husband or lover had run away on the spur of the moment. She falls asleep in a chair and in her subsequent dream elaborates with morbid insistence upon her experiences in the deserted house. This incident, as the dream reveals, touches off in her the sensation of being forever rejected by the world. In picturing the girl's moods, Miss Deren combines psychological insight with a film sense which enables her to draw on the expressive functions of various cinematic devices. The afternoon spectre of a black-clad woman with a mirror instead of a face intimates that the dreaming girl cannot break through the crust that separates her from others. The deliberate reiterations, only slightly varying in detail, of whole sequences and occurrences symbolize her complete stagnation. And the scene in which she, or one of her incarnations, hurries after the slowly pacing black woman and yet does not succeed in catching up with her illustrates the girl's vain effort to overcome her inhibitions.

At Land (1944) treats the same theme, with special emphasis on distortions of time and space provoked by frustration. A nymph-like girl, thrust ashore by the waves, feels at sea on terra firma. Whatever she pursues evades her in an endless flight of objects, persons and situations. She crawls over the table of a room in which a banquet is held, without being noticed by anyone; she sneaks into a log cabin and, frightened by a stranger in the bed, escapes through one door after another; she joins two girls on the beach who continue to play chess as if unaware of her presence; finally she runs back to the sea. To a soul lacking an exit, the world thus turns into a succession of fleeting phenomena. And so does time waver: memories and current events fuse with each other.

Miss Deren's subsequent experiment, the three-minute short, *A Study in Choreography for Camera* (1945), seems to have sprung from her increasing interest in purely formal problems. Her concern with psychological borderline cases is now superseded by her desire to establish, with the aid of the moving camera, artistic time-space relations. A dancer begins a leap in the woods and ends it in a room. In this way he circles and swirls from one setting to another, until he finally takes off to fly in slow motion toward a landscape, his ultimate goal. It is, as Miss Deren puts it, "a duet between space and a dancer."

Her last film, *Ritual in Transfigured Time* (1945-1946), resumes the leitmotif of the frustrated girl on a more sophisticated level. This time the girl's inner life materializes in the figure of a Negro woman who embodies the desires and griefs of the soul from which she emanates. Like her predecessors, the woman attempts to escape from the prison of her self; but, unlike them, she is not doomed until she has experienced love. Artistically, this complex film indicates progress in that it aims at a synthesis of form and content, dance and psychology. The scene of a social gathering, with the Negro woman ignored by the crowd, is shot and cut in such a way that it becomes a dance involving everybody and everything. Miss Deren has arrived at the expression of meaning through rhythm; the problem is only what the meaning itself amounts to.

In *The Potted Psalm,* shot in San Francisco during the summer of 1946, Sidney Peterson and James Broughton mingle fragments of reality with unreal elements after the manner of Miss Deren. But here the similarity ends. Faintly reminiscent of certain surrealistic experiments of the Twenties, this film is a sequence of loosely knit associations, ranging from a man without a head to two feet rubbing their toes together and a human leg which turns into a piano leg. The program note maintains that *The Potted Psalm* deals with "the chaotic inner complexities of our post-war society." This interpretation is rather generous, for the film-makers fail to substantiate their aspirations cinematically. The camera does not contribute much, nor is the "montage" rhythmically structured. Thus the meanings remain inchoate.

A few recent experimental films featuring non-objective patterns yield interesting results. *Glen Falls Sequence* by Douglass Crockwell —an animation of pictures painted on several movable layers of glass —combine unknown shapes and vaguely familiar elements into a universe which is as impossible as it is funny. Micro-organisms congregate for no imaginable purpose; mushrooms stroll through a Tanguy landscape; flourishes, never finished, cover a sort of sheet that grows out of an inkblot-like cloud; compact masses let something drop or are pregnant with minuscule crystals which emerge from sudden fissures in them; a chimney turns into a saw which tries to cut through its own smoke. Modern science defies the law of causality and considers mass a manifestation of energy. Matter is in constant flux, all substances are in principle interchangeable. Crockwell takes science at its word by transforming geometric and organic forms into one another. He is a wit who plays Providence. His abstract compositions either originate in cactuses and the like or breed themselves new creatures with a semblance of life. Now and then cultural reminiscences interfere. A death's head comes out of an urn, and a white cross is perched on what may be a mountain range, a heap of yeast or a concurrence of rolling waves.

Aided by a Guggenheim fellowship, John and James Whitney have produced a series of shorts, *Abstract Film Exercises* (1943-1945), in which they try to establish aesthetically valid relations between form, color and sound. The forms are derived from paper cut-outs; the sound effects are produced by a machine which regulates the shape of a light ray thrown directly on the sound track. Such experiments are not new, but the Whitney brothers, though not particularly inventive in rhythm and imagery, nevertheless leave all past attempts behind. Theirs is a vision of what people have come to call our atomic age. And guided by it they go to the limit in creating a cosmos filled with nothing but swirling corpuscles all aglow with reds and greens that quiver and flicker in unlimited space. Tiny balls rush to the foreground, develop into radiant suns and vanish again. Atoms thus play about aimlessly, and their games are accompanied by a music strongly reminiscent of jungle noises, as we know them from war films about Burma and Guadalcanal. It seems extremely difficult for humanity to assert itself at this juncture of cosmic and animal life.

Hans Richter's full-length color film, *Dreams That Money Can Buy,* which received an award as "the best original contribution to the progress of cinematography" at the Venice film festival, is a mosaic of isolated episodes, each based upon the work or an idea of a contemporary artist.

The Max Ernst sequence, "Desire," inspired by six drawings of

La Semaine de Bonté, features the voluptuous dream of a sleeping girl. Her vagabond unconscious materializes in an enraptured soliloquy through images in which fragments of conventional reality help build up a more real dream world. Shipwrecked bodies are dragged from under the girl's bed, and her bedroom itself floats through a jungle of threatening corridors and dungeons. When her lover finally joins her, the girl's solitary dream is superseded by their common dream—a succession of exuberant visions which symbolize the ecstasy of love fulfillment and its vibrant afterglow. A figure enacted by Ernst himself follows the lovers as a sort of superego, silently witnessing, and thus counterbalancing, their revel in emotional irresponsibility.

In contrast with this glowing display of passion, the Fernand Léger episode is a playful satire on mechanical love-making. Mannequins of a type common in Grand Street shop windows embark on a sentimental affair which so badly ruins the bride's beautiful wedding gown that her amorous feelings are also spoiled. Libby Holman and Josh White accompany this ill-fated flirtation with a song by John Latouche which comments ironically in ballad fashion on "The Girl with the Pre-fabricated Heart." The whole has the character of a *ballet mécanique* unfolding in the atmosphere of American folklore.

Compared to these two sequences, the Man Ray episode, drawn from his own script, is an anticlimax. Entitled "Ruth, Roses, Revolvers," it indulges in dialogue and pretends to deeper meaning. The fogs disperse only in one single passage in which fun is poked at movie audiences eager for identification with some screen character. But the fun is too obvious to be amusing. Fortunately, it is possible to identify oneself with Darius Milhaud's music.

Two other artists emerge in full splendor. The evolutions of Marcel Duchamp's moving discs are interspersed with a procession of female nudes reminiscent of his painting, "Nude Descending a Staircase"—a fascinating combination of cobweb-like spirals and luxuriant bodies. Their interplay is followed by an impressive rephrasing of Alexander Calder's creations. His mobiles turn into a pageant of form and colors; and his circus figures, delightful products of an atavistic imagination, parade to a score by Paul Bowles which enhances their eerie non-existence.

In an attempt to unify these disparate elements, Richter has devised a framing story, with music by Louis Applebaum, and Jack Bittner as the protagonist. Bittner's Joe, a poor young poet, determines to capitalize on his unique gift for resuscitating slumbering dreams: he settles down in a fancy office, selling to his clients whatever he molds in the material of their unconscious. There is, of course, a well-defined relationship between dreams and dreamers: the Max Ernst orgy externalizes the longings of a pale husband, while the Léger satire enables a high-strung girl to relax. In shaping these dreams, Joe proves himself an artist rather than a psychiatrist. He comforts those in distress by transforming their inmost desires into tangible works of art. The realm of art is thus presented as a refuge from the world in which we actually live.

Out of the framing story grows Richter's own episode, "Narcissus," the last of the film. It is a dream of Joe's own, rendering his inner experiences in drastic symbols. His face turns blue when he discovers his identity; and as he climbs up a ladder, intent on following his destiny, one rung after another vanishes under his feet. Thus in pictures conspicuous for their fervor, the genesis of any creator is made manifest—his insistence on self-realization, his fight against indifference and his inexorable loneliness. At the end, a bust of Zeus, suggestive of Joe's dearest memories, shatters to bits, and Joe as a person dissolves. All that remains of him are his works, bright color compositions flowing through space.

Small wonder that so ambitious a film does not fulfill all its promises. The principle, sound in itself, of featuring the "voice of the unconscious" has been exaggerated. There is also a tendency throughout the film to misuse literary metaphors as visual symbols. But these imperfections should blind no one to the film's great merits. Richter is an innovator. For the first time he transfers the essential content of modern art to the screen.

Modern art, as it appears in this film, intertwines the region of pure forms with the virgin forest of the human soul. What lies between—the vast middle sphere of conventional life—is tacitly omitted or overtly attacked. Both the Léger and Richter episodes are very explicit in defiance of our mechanical civilization. They mock at it or present the seeming normality as a distortion of the really normal. Contemporary art, the film suggests, opposes a world which smothers the expression of love and creative spontaneity—hence the sustained concern of modern artists with unconscious urges and abstract structures. Richter makes it unmistakably clear that the latter would not come into their own without the steady influx of the former. To point out their interdependence he not only superimposes the female nudes and Duchamp's rarefied movements, but lets a primitive mask and a sort of ram's horn join company with Calder's mobiles. And in the Max Ernst sequence the turmoil of sex so radically upsets the nineteenth-century interiors that they seem on the point of disintegrating—scattered elements predestined to be reborn within non-objective textures. The inherent moods of the whole film bear out its main concepts. Melancholia, our lot as creatures, alternates with the gaiety which is inseparable from artistic fulfillment; and all the foggy sentiments characteristic of the middle sphere are suppressed mercilessly.

Richter's film is of consequence for yet another reason: it demonstrates conclusively that certain works of art have much to gain by a proper cinematic rendering. For instance, the Calder constructions yield quite unsuspected effects on the screen—effects produced by the incorporation of their shadows, artful close-ups, surprising color schemes, and not least by Edgar Varese's magnificent score. Sparkling, dangling and jingling in a universe composed of nothing but light and hue, these mobiles which we thought we knew now seethe with strange revelations. Like his Joe, Richter brings out what, all unknown to us, was latent in them.

By conjuring up the secret dream life of drawings, paintings and plastic forms, *Dreams That Money Can Buy* sets a propitious pattern for the future cooperation of art and cinema.

February 1948

XIII · BROADWAY IN REVIEW

* * *

KENNETH MACGOWAN

*

The Jest; John Ferguson

THE JEST is one of those vigorous dramas in which Italian poets of today reconstruct with all modern psychological—even pathological—niceness the cruel, bloody and very beautiful times of Latin greatness. The plays of D'Annunzio are fairly common on American bookshelves. The work of Sem Benelli, who wrote *The Jest,* is known to us only by the opera, *The Love of the Three Kings,* which Mr. Montemezzi made upon the basis of his play. *The Jest* has all the movement of Broadway melodrama, and a lot of its slangy humor, too. Through four acts a young painter of Leonardo's court matches his wits against the brawn of a hulking mercenary. The painter is a jelly of cowardly nerves, who has been put upon since youth by this wine-swilling soldier, "full of quaint oaths" and quainter devilries. One of these was to buy the boy's sweetheart and turn her into a callous little pampered drab. Another was to catch the painter upon a bridge in Florence, to prick with daggers emblems of love and derision upon various portions of his body, and to fling him, sacked, into the river for the town to mock at. This last set young Giannetto actively plotting the destruction of the soldier Neri. The first act shows Neri marching off, roaring drunk, to fulfill a wager cleverly conceived to bring him to the madhouse.

In the second act Neri, escaped, comes upon Giannetto and the girl in her apartments, only to suffer recapture, while the boy toys with her. The third is a mingling of physical and psychological horrors in the underground prison of the Medici. The fourth brings

Neri back to the girl's house in time to murder a dearly loved brother and go truly mad.

The players add considerably to the surface qualities of this keen and cruel Punch and Judy show. John Barrymore plays the painter with the most delicate shadings of tortured beauty. (In the original the painter was a hunchback.) He makes no attempt, as one might imagine Moissi doing, to picture a creature of almost uncontrollable nerves, with a strange moral courage flashing up through physical cowardice. The part is therefore limited by the actor's definition, but sharply and truly done within these limits. Lionel Barrymore plays Neri in the simple vein of a roaring, cursing, swaggering giant—all on one note of physical strength. With the face largely hidden by matted hair, the body lumbering about in the conventional poses of brute strength, and the voice ever steeped in the gutter, the impersonation, while effective, leans towards the conventional, the histrionic. But though it has none of that spiritual brutishness which Lynn Harding might give (recall his Bill Sykes), its forceful, vigorous humor does a great deal towards spicing the play with something as far from the usual romantic type as its sadistic cruelty and its neuropathic precision. So far, *The Jest* might be merely an interesting but disquieting "sport" of modernity. The quality of the production—devised by Robert Edmond Jones and Arthur Hopkins—lifts the thing whole planes higher. In settings, lights and costumes there has been no such beautiful, effective, expressive and heightening spectacle on our dramatic stage.

The play has three simple sets. One is a large hall, one a small dungeon and one a medium-sized boudoir. Each is well designed, though none is unusual or strikingly distinguished in shape or ornament. I doubt if the raw color on the canvas is particularly beautiful. But by the handling of light, the spreading of a glow of amber upon a dining table, a flood of moon-blue through a window, a shaft of cold white down the side of a prison pillar, the rich and pregnant atmosphere of the renaissance fills these rooms with beauty and with cruelty. And in these pools of light, catching a color here and a glow there, move costumings that have all the imagination and precision which Mr. Jones has shown himself to be so successful in wedding ever since his *Man Who Married a Dumb Wife* was first seen.

The Jest without Jones would be a bare and ugly thing. Perhaps that is what it should be. With Jones *The Jest* is a sensation. Added to the other colorful and picturesque plays of the season, it makes a very good case for a romantic revival. War unquestionably gave us too much reality. We sought "surcease from sorrow." It also cultivated a taste for violence, for madder music and redder wine, for "sensation." It set the stage for revulsion from Ibsenic realism, from "problems" and social evils, towards irresponsible and seductive and stirring romance. Some of us, feeling the too-terrible realities of life in 1914-19, foreswore the once-loved reality of social drama for the anaesthesia of the aesthetic; that should account for the fame of Dunsany. And soon the rest, who had faced the jazz music of busy Berthas and scare-head casualty lists, were back in the theatre with what seemed likely to be a callousness toward anything but color and vigor and excitement equal to the fury of Europe. Upon such a basis, it was easy to see in *The Jest* and in other plays, and even moving pictures of the same sort, a romantic revival which would sweep reality clear out of the playhouse.

It was easy until the Theatre Guild put on a dour little play of Ireland called *John Ferguson*. St. John Ervine's drama is nothing, if not utter naturalism. Its story is simple and bare: a hard, lustful land-grabber forecloses a mortgage and assaults the daughter of the house. Her other admirer, a cowardly little victim of the same man, tries to kill him—and hasn't the courage. Instead, the deed is done by her brother, a boy who has had to give up the ministry to work the farm while his sick old father reads of Christian humility in the Book of Books. The physical violence is done off-stage. There is no more color and romance than can be furnished by a half-wit, dreaming and chortling in the inglenook. Yet *John Ferguson* stirred its audience and won the critics hardly less than *The Jest*. There is no resisting the deep humanity of its characters, the full and touching understanding that they win. Mr. Ervine and the actors have simply done what playwrights and players in sundry Continental theatres have been doing for twenty or thirty years—picturing truthfully our own times and our own peoples.

America has shown no particular fondness for this sort of thing in the past—not, at least, for ultimate and complete naturalism. When it has encountered a play of the perfection of *John Ferguson* it has usually passed by on the other side. Now, however, it accepts, and accepts enthusiastically.

Partly, this may be accounted for by the extraordinarily good production of the Theatre Guild: Dudley Digges, Augustin Duncan, Helen Westley, Helen Freeman, Henry Herbert and Rollo Peters gave almost perfect performances. Yet, you cannot help feeling that in the reaction of the New York public to realistic *John Ferguson* as in its reaction to romantic *Jest* there is a certain quality wrought out by the war. Perhaps it is a somewhat different public; perhaps only a different angle of the same public. At any rate, New York seems eager for pungent theatrical fare, entertainment with fullness and vigor in it. It may be the fullness and vigor of rich colors and violent romantic action. It may be the fullness and vigor of true humanity truly seen and fully bodied forth. But at least this acceptance of both *The Jest* and *John Ferguson* is a sign of one excellent thing—impatience with anaemia and indolence and compromise. The end of the season leaves good hope that America in its new days of peace will ask more from the theatre than it has ever asked before.

July 1919

*

The Emperor Jones

IN *THE EMPEROR JONES* that remarkable organization, the Provincetown Players, which shows no fear whatever of producing ten very ordinary and ineffective plays for every single contribution to the advancement of American playwriting, has opened up a new reach in American drama and in the talents of that fine young playwright of its discovery, Eugene O'Neill. The play itself is printed in this issue of THEATRE ARTS MAGAZINE. There in its lines you will find the same strong and natural speech that has always set Mr. O'Neill apart from all of our playwrights except Edward Sheldon. There you will also find two qualities that Mr. Sheldon notably lacks. You will find in the denouement, with its off-stage death, a true and untheatrical power; and you will find a new strain of rhythmed beauty in his long monologs. Here, as in no other American play except that "sport," *The Yellow Jacket,* there is genuine imagination both in the material and in the structure of the drama. These eight short scenes shake free from the traditional forms of our drama; they carry forward easily and honestly upon the track of discovery. We follow a path that gathers bit by bit the progressive steps in a study of personal and racial psychology of real imaginative truth.

Considering the record of the Provincetown Players for producing their real discoveries, such as the plays of Mr. O'Neill, Susan Glaspell and Edna St. Vincent Millay, with little more adequacy than they give to their experimental commonplaces, their production of *The Emperor Jones* is a surprise as well as a sensation. During the summer the Provincetown Players installed on the tiny stage of their makeshift theatre near Washington Square one of these plaster sky-domes or *Kuppelhorizonte* with which so many German theatres have replaced the flat canvas of the cyclorama. It is a property of this curving plaster to catch and mix light so deftly that, in the diffused glow that reaches the spectator, it is impossible to focus the eye with any degree of assurance upon the actual surface of the dome. Well lighted as to color and intensity, the *Kuppelhorizont* can counterfeit the beauty and almost the reality of the sky. Again and again in the seven jungle scenes, which follow the flight of the Pullman porter from his brief but prosperous rule as emperor of "bush niggers," Director George Cram Cook and his scenic artist, Cleon Throckmorton, have used this sky with such inspiring effect as has never been achieved in New York before. For the first scenes of the Emperor's flight, there is hardly more than a dark suggestion of the shadowy night-sky behind the gaunt trees. It blazes out into beauty when we reach the edge of a clearing and see the magnificent naked body of the Emperor silhouetted against it. The concluding scenes of darker and darker terrors call less upon the sky, but in them all—particularly in the vision of the old chain gang from which Jones escaped by murder—the director and the artist have handled the lighting of the stage and its people quite as well as the lighting of the *Kuppelhorizont.*

To the skill of its producers and the lesson of the sky-dome, the Provincetown Players have added in this production a magnificent piece of acting. From Harlem they brought a colored player, Charles Gilpin, to impersonate the emperor. Mr. Gilpin had played a wise old Negro in one of Ridgeley Torrence's plays produced some years ago by Robert E. Jones, and last season he was the humble Negro Custis in *Abraham Lincoln*. In *The Emperor Jones* he shows not only a great power and a great imagination, in addition to his fine voice, but he displays an extraordinary versatility. It is a genuine impersonation, a being of flesh and blood and brain utterly different from the actor's other work. He carries the long soliloquy of the six scenes in the forest with extraordinary ease, building up steadily from his fright at the first Little Formless Fears, through his terror at the recurring visions of his crimes, to the horror that overwhelms him as the dim, buried, racial fears rise to carry him back to the auction block, the slave ship and the voodoo gods of the Congo. Mr. Gilpin's performance is the crown to a play that opens up the imagination of the American theatre and builds beauty and emotion out of the spiritual realities of one corner of our life.

January 1921

*

The Moscow Art Theatre; Barrymore's Hamlet

THE HEART of the Moscow Art Theatre is the actor. It has presented plays of the greatest distinction in Russia, and, though the short repertory shown New York is sadly lacking in variety, it is undeniably sound. But, in almost every way, the work that Stanislavski and his collaborator, Nemirovitch-Dantchenko, have done in the past twenty years has looked to the perfection of an acting machine. Now ensemble is not the only lack upon the American stage. We have certain actors who can outdo in some single performance any player of the Moscow Art Theatre except perhaps Katchaloff; but their number is very few indeed, their range is unbelievably limited, and the great bulk of our players hardly know the art of acting—in the sense that these Russians know it.

The visit of the Moscow Art Theatre is, therefore, uncommonly significant as a lesson in the most essential part of the art of the theatre. It shows us sharply individualized characterizations, a virtuosity of impersonation on the part of each player, the highest proficiency and the most sincere and sustained spiritual effort, and the welding of all the various performers of a play into an ensemble of fluid, varied, yet concerted and pointed quality. But the lesson for America that is quite as important lies in the means by which this acting-machine has been built up. We may not care to imitate such highly detailed and naturalistic playing, but we must learn how to train and develop our actors—whatever their style—or we may as well close up our theatres.

And the lesson of the Moscow Art Theatre is the very simple lesson of the repertory theatre. Here we see demonstrated before us the theory which some of us have diligently preached, which is that until you have a permanent company, a permanent direction, a permanent policy as to plays, and a more or less permanent audience, both economic and artistic progress in the theatre is extremely difficult. On the side of acting, it is well-nigh impossible. Stanislavski did not, of course, create the first repertory theatre in Russia or the only one on the Continent; he merely added to this type of organization an ideal and a theory and, above all, a personality, which swung the players violently into line behind a spiritualized realism exceptionally welcome in its time. But I am ready to assert that any Russian company of the first quality, any German company of the same grade, even the Comédie Française, could show us fundamentally the same lesson in proficient acting which the Moscow Art Theatre company displays, and which almost none of our own actors can possibly learn until we have such a training school for them as the repertory theatre.

Our actors are picked up piecemeal for each play. They are chosen not so much for their acting ability as for their resemblance physically and temperamentally to the parts to be cast. They come to work with other actors whom they know only slightly. They work under a director relatively unfamiliar with them and therefore unable to inspire or draw them out. They end by repeating their familiar self-impersonations with, you might say, the shadows of little clouds of fresh meaning racing fitfully across the familiar scene. Perhaps they are playing the same part in the same play for months on end—learning nothing, forgetting everything. At the best they are playing the same part in two or three different plays, and getting a certain kind of ineffectual practice at rehearsals.

The Russians—or any repertory company—live together, artistically speaking, like a family. They know one another's possibilities; their directors know them. They read their new plays over time after time, and rehearse for months if necessary. They achieve ensemble readily because of their familiarity and practice together, and they achieve it as brilliantly as the limits of the director's intuitions and ingenuity permit. Far more important in developing proficiency in the individual actor, these players are given five to fifteen different parts to play each season, and these cannot all be parts to which their personalities are closely fitted. This might seem the great drawback of a repertory company. Actually, it is its greatest virtue. Because the actor is given a part not precisely the same as his part in the comedy called life, he must become an artist. He must learn to state one thing in terms of another. He must learn the technical means for impersonation, and then he must find the deeper, emotional individuality of the characters created by another artist, the playwright. The fact that repertory theatres are in the habit—for some curious reason—of giving good plays instead of crassly popular ones seems to have something to do with the matter also.

At any rate, here we find a company of actors who are physically almost unrecognizable—the men at least—in their different parts. Realism and the art of make-up work together here. They are also differentiated spiritually to almost as great an extent. We see, in *The Cherry Orchard,* the gigantic Stanislavski playing a very casual and helpless aristocrat with gray hair and an engaging manner, and a shorter actor named Luzsky playing the man's old, incredibly infirm, and doglike servant. These impersonations are not only brilliantly exact and meaningful; they contrast quite amazingly with the fact that, a week before, we saw these two men playing the same part in *Tzar Fyodor* on different evenings—the part of Prince Ivan, the noble, doomed opponent of Boris Godunoff. Each of these Princes was essentially Ivan, yet they were different and pungent with their own flavors. Extend this principle to the whole company and add the nervous genius of Katchaloff—the greatest of the troupe—the rich comedy of Moskvin, the simplicity and power of Mme. Knipper-Tchekhova, and talents running down the line to the agile sensitive young clown, Bulgakoff, and you have the Moscow Art Theatre—a thing founded in repertory and raised to dominance by the genius of Stanislavski and Dantchenko.

From the Moscow Art Theatre it is an easy and a very far step to John Barrymore's *Hamlet.* There is no body of acting here to compare with the work of the Russians. Barrymore himself gives the most brilliant Prince of this generation of English speaking actors—sensitive, gracious, intellectual, lovely of voice, and poignant with emotion—but he is not yet the responsible and self-dominating artist who can hold his work to a single steady impression. Upon the opening night he played too carefully, too quietly. On another night he was unhappy over something—a taxi, his food, a cold perhaps—and he slouched through the part. When the Russian players sat in the audience at a matinee during a week when he was playing nine performances in order to better Booth's record of a hundred, and race off on a steamer to Europe, Barrymore played with a hot-spirited vigor which recognized and exploited to the fullest the mad quality of Hamlet's speech in the first half of the drama. It was wild and beautiful. But toward the end this fervor had grown monotonous and weak, and he played the graveyard scene as tamely as ever, and only summoned up strength to keep his magnificent murder of the king upon the plane it had reached on the first night. I stress the uncertainty of Barrymore's art only because his performance was so fine in different moments and on different occasions. Finer for one brief moment—and always fine—was Rosalind Fuller's Ophelia, mad, indecently mad, in the way Shakespeare intended.

The Russians sat before this *Hamlet* visibly perplexed and perhaps a little contemptuous. Here there was no richness of detail and nothing at all approaching an active ensemble. The players supporting Barrymore, excellent men and women by our standards, did little to make their parts constantly alive. And in the whole picture there was almost no variety or movement. The court must have seemed a court in wax works. Posed in lovely groups up and down those steps of Robert Edmond Jones which so annoyed John Corbin, these actors showed by their movements no perturbation at the course of events in Elsinore.

Now I should be the first to grant that our actors are very badly trained for their work, but I must maintain that here in *Hamlet* is an ideal of the art of performance—call it acting or not, as you will—which is deliberately at variance with the practice of the Russians. I must also maintain that it may be a very fine thing, and a thing far more in the modern mood. This is acting stylized. Like expressionism, it is almost the poster. For this kind of production the essential thing is a mood created by the color of voice and light and costume, an emotional relationship expressed in the contrast or harmony of tone and position. Taking each individual actor, you could find in the "modern" player no such pattern of almost infinite detail as in every member of the Russian company. One big outline only, and on the edges of it a fringe of definitive but very reticent detail. Our actors, I say, cannot achieve this fully or skillfully because they are untrained—no twenty-five years of acting together have given them proficiency and *rapport*. But I say equally that this aim of theirs, as Arthur Hopkins haltingly holds them to it, is a legitimate aim and more important for the moment as a channel of new effort than the aim of the Moscow Art Theatre. The acting of the Russians is more than realism, but the art which this *Hamlet* aims at is never less in intent than a poetic expressionism.

The physical production of *Hamlet* carries us over into another comparison with the Russians. They brought us only one set of scenes of any pretensions, those for *Tzar Fyodor,* and they were, like most Muscovite art, built and composed in color. The other settings were almost all of them old-fashioned or even shoddy. There was nothing here to hint at the *Hamlet* that Craig made for this theatre. The lighting is hardly more than passable. On only one point can it claim value. It is at least bright enough and well-directed enough for us to see the faces of the actors. Our own producers and their artists have gone in too much for overhead lighting; the hats of the actresses rejoice in the brilliant illumination that used to shine upon the underside of the jaw in the days of the refulgent footlights. Light from in front—as David Belasco throws it—is essential. Jones is putting it into Hopkins' productions. No new theatre should be equipped without some variety of light sockets in the balcony. There is no proper place for the discussion of the details of lighting technique, so there must be a word here for the ingenuity of George Schaff, the Hopkins-Jones electrician, and for the Pevear system of color-mixing borders which Lee Simonson installed for the Theatre Guild for *Peer Gynt.*

When we pass from the Russian settings to the setting for *Hamlet* we pass from a curious combination of peephole realism and old-fashioned false perspective to a new—almost a very old—theatrical conception. Jones built a single background—half symbolic, half actual—a towering old hall combined with a simple decorated front curtain and a forestage. This was always frankly artificial and theatrical. It was never reality, but always a place where players acted a play. Much can be arbitrary in such a place, if only it is expressive of the poet.

April 1923

Duse in Repertory

BEFORE THE fifty-two weeks of 1923 are passed New York will have seen the art of the three most powerful figures of the European stage—Stanislavski, Duse and Reinhardt. Two other men and one more woman share with them the crown of the modern theatre; Chaliapin and Isadora Duncan have been frequent visitors to the United States, while no stage has seen more of the Achillesian Craig than the American. Six great artists of the theatre leaving their impress upon our stage, and, of them all, none so impressive as the frail lady with the dun cheeks and the corded neck who makes us live with beauty.

Arthur Symons once spoke of Duse as "a chalice for the wine of imagination." I doubt if that perfect phrase ever fitted more perfectly than it did in the sixty-fourth year of her life when she came out, a very remote figure, upon the yawning stage of the Metropolitan. Then she was doubly the chalice. To the mystery and exaltation of her art was added a strange element of aloofness which made her, not the hybrid of actress and dramatic character to which this curious art of the theatre accustoms us, but a great person in the cast of another drama, which we call Life. Our imagination rose to the art of voice and hands and body, but it rose, too, to an art of living which brought this extraordinary woman before us. It rose higher, I think, to the woman Duse than to the actress; for not only an alien tongue, but the vasty gulf of the Metropolitan intervened between our emotions and Ibsen's *Lady from the Sea*. Duse's art is more than realism, but it is founded, nevertheless, upon the intimacy of the realistic theatre, and neither at the Metropolitan nor at the Century, where she played the remainder of her brief engagement, can the living word of the playwright and the living presence of the player fuse with the soul of the spectator. In both houses Duse was not so much an actress ministering to emotion as an extraordinary person, a legendary heroine, perhaps a goddess, come before us. And it was not as though she were a great woman appearing in our midst as Wilson appeared in Paris. Behind the footlights, and across the gulf of these abominable theatres, Duse became a kind of story. She seemed to be a legend of herself.

All of which is a very murky effort to say how strangely the figure of Duse moved many of us on this epochal occasion, and how oddly the art of Duse left our playgoing emotions cold. Concede this anaesthesia, admit that we did not suffer with the women of *Ghosts* and *The Lady from the Sea*; then let us look more closely at the art which, under happier circumstances, might have left us wrung with the emotion of Ibsen.

Duse has reached an age at which actors retain none too much of their vigor, and actresses are so sapped that only the greatest—Bernhardt and this Italian—can keep a grip on their art. Duse has lived more truly and more fully than Bernhardt, and given more of herself to life. Duse is weak; she can play only twice a week, and two hours on the stage leave their mark upon her as she takes her final curtain. Duse never tolerated make-up or any artifice of wig or clothing to imitate vanishing youth. So today her Ellida Wangel would be aged, and her fascination for the young sailor a disgusting absurdity, if it were not for the soul and the art that still animate her so fully. The voice is endlessly musical and shadowed with infinite expression; it runs light as a bird's for the most part, singing note after note of beauty colored by hope, doubt, fear, love, exaltation; it plunges suddenly into deeper tones that carry suffering upon their dark, slow wings. Occasionally the voice breaks or goes dull, but these weakenings are very few. Duse's body, Duse's hands above all—for D'Annunzio was the true-seeing poet when he called her Duse of the Beautiful Hands—play a symphony of movement. There seems nothing studied in her actions, nothing deliberate; sometimes her hands flash nervously across her face when we are most anxious to see her expression. Her movements are not an artifice but an inevitable outcome of emotion felt in the very soul and irresistibly commanding a body fashioned consummately to obey. It is here in the soul of Duse and in the mystery of the body made one with it that we sense the ultimate of her art. And we cannot tag and label it.

We can be downright and documentary, however, on one aspect of Duse. It is the relation of her acting to current modes. We have had roughly three kinds of playing in this first generation of the twentieth century. We have had the exploitation of personality colored by artifice, a thing that begins with any one of our agreeable women stars and rises to the brittle pinnacles of Bernhardt. We have had the exploitation of personality fitted to type parts, a cast of characters by mail-order, a kind of stock-room realism. And we have had —most notably in the Moscow Art Theatre—true impersonation, made up of the surface art of wig and grease paint, and of the deeps of emotional identification. Duse gives us a fourth art, an art unique in its combination of qualities. She is unforgettably a person; she is Duse. She is skillful with voice and body, but by inner emotion, not by artifice. The bare, clean skin of her cheeks speaks both sincerity and a kind of realism that stands against the theatrical even at its best. She turns her back on all the deliberate maskings of face and body which make so much of the art of the Russians, and which they make so much of. Duse dresses her hair differently for the Lady from the Sea and the mother in *Ghosts,* and she wears appropriately different garments; yet it is essentially by the movement of hands, face and voice that she defines the gulf between the two characters. Through the hands, the face and the voice, Duse remains Duse. It is only that an inner spirit has changed, and emanations appear before us in wrist or smile or intonation. Duse understands more completely than any actress I have ever seen the mysteries by which the inner spirit is kindled and the emanations arise.

January 1924

*

The Miracle

THE ARRIVAL of Max Reinhardt upon the American stage has proved a far more astounding and staggering business than any of his admirers could have imagined. Perhaps it was the cooping up of his great spectacle *The Miracle* in an ordinary theatre; perhaps it was the association with Norman Bel Geddes, most titanic of designers, and with Morris Gest, most luxuriant of managers; at any rate, Karl Vollmoeller's elaboration of the Sister Beatrice legend has come through as three hours of beauty and torture almost indescribable in the demands that they make upon the attention, the emotions and the endurance of an audience.

The key to the impression which the whole spectacle achieves is the place in which it is played. Obviously *The Miracle* should have been given in Madison Square Garden, a parallel to the London Olympia and the Circus Busch, where it was shown in Berlin. At the least it should have had the broad spaces of the Hippodrome. To make the best of the Century Theatre Geddes has simply obliterated it. Not a square inch of gawdy gilt remains. The place is a cathedral. Real walls and balcony rails are hidden by cloths and banners. Cloisters and carven doors hide the boxes. Walls of masonry broken by sixty-foot towers and high pulpits sweep in towards tripartite arches which fill the proscenium. Beyond we see the choir and apse of a Gothic cathedral rise in pillared strength and lose themselves in glowing glass of a clerestory almost a hundred feet in air. High above the auditorium are rose windows and a vault of dim lights which hardly need carved pew-ends on the rows of seats to set upon the spectator a mood of awesome, even oppressive, reverence. The spell of old cathedrals descends upon you; but it is not quite the spell in which the naiver peoples of the dark ages found drama leaping from mass and sacred legend. Your spirit is dazed and mystified by beauty, and bound down to the kind of ceremonial which the modern imagination ever associates with religion.

For one hour the life of this great cathedral ministers to this imagination. The lights dim down upon the shirt fronts of elegance, but not before sacristans and worshippers have begun to wander through the pillared choir. Far voices chant. Nuns appear in the cloisters. A taper-bearer lights high candles. The verger tolls a bell. The life of the cathedral begins. Soon the women of the nunnery are gathered in hundreds to see the investiture of the new Sister Sacristan who is to guard the miraculous statue of the Madonna. Down the stone aisles of the auditorium pour villagers to worship. Last come the lame and the halt to pray for health before the Virgin. Suddenly an old piper, borne in on a cot, moans and struggles to his knees. He raises an amazed and stricken face as he turns to the statue. Power comes to his limbs again. He staggers up. The mob cries out, shouts, screams. Men and women rush to see. The piper struggles through them, over their bodies, over their heads, convulsed and twitching in every limb, till he stands before the Virgin. Bells ring out the miracle, the mob shouts and sings. May branches shake in the air like the quivering arms of multitudes.

With Werner Krauss playing the piper—Werner Krauss, better known to America for his Caligari than for the distinguished work he has done in Reinhardt's theatres in Berlin—this scene is the most exciting in the whole *Miracle*. The hour of worship wanes as the villagers depart, the piper tempts the young nun with the love of an earthly knight, the girl deserts the altar to follow her lover, the Madonna comes down from her pedestal to take up the service and the nuns sweep in in terror to find the Virgin gone and the Sister Sacristan suffused with a miraculous beneficence. It is all a spell; but nothing that follows quite touches the miracle of the piper.

You would imagine that the episodes of the nun's adventures in the world outside, which make the middle of the spectacle, would be far more exciting than any scene in the cathedral. They are nothing of the kind. Three of them, at least, are downright dull. The synopsis betrays the fact that the good nuns have never been quite able to decide whether these adventures actually happened to the Sacristan in the world outside or whether she imagined them all out of the desires of the flesh, and told them when the Virgin had returned to her pedestal. As a matter of fact, I fear that the producer and his assistants have been just as unable to make up their minds, and confusion has hampered them. These scenes do not live with the tremendous vitality that murder, rape, mock marriage, and mad imperial ambitions displayed in the Middle Ages quite as much as any other time. Perhaps the fault is a little Geddes'. His great pile of cathedral pillars, filling the whole stage and spacing across the proscenium opening, serve the church scenes as no other structure could. But those pillars, particularly the two in front, tie down the acting space for the middle scenes to much too small an area. Then, too, these scenes are stylized in varying molds which dispel the passions and terrors of the story. Or, at least, they place a task before the actors which they cannot meet. On the opening night the episode of the count, set and costumed as if in figures from a mediaeval window, struck the kind of stained glass attitudes that you associate with Bunthorne or *Alice in Wonderland*. A comic card game out of Lewis Carroll does not seem the way of settling the fate of a nun. The mock wedding with the prince fares much better in its bizarre costumes of oilcloth; for it is itself a mockery. The madness of the emperor who takes the nun to wife excuses a court made up of golden vessels and candelabra come to life, yet the method obscures the sufferings of the victim. Other short scenes will doubtless go better after more performances. They can hardly equal, however, the best moment in the latter half of the play, the scene of the inquisition, in which another of Reinhardt's extraordinary mobs sweeps everything before it.

The return of the nun to the cathedral, which concludes *The Miracle,* is essentially a repetition in mood and action of the beginning of the spectacle. This leaves you with the impression of a tremendous start, an overpowering lunge into a mystic beauty, then an unconvincing interlude of grotesquerie, and finally a brief and weaker repetition of the first impression. And out of it all you come with the feeling that never have eyes and ears been assailed with so much in three hours' entertainment.

Of the acting there is very little to say, far too little. Certain of the players are obviously excellent—Krauss, much of the time; Lady Diana Manners always when she plays the Virgin; Rudolph Schildkraut to a degree; Rosamond Pinchot no more perhaps than a number of our young movie actresses might be, though she brings a clear spontaneity to the nun. This gargantuan sort of pantomime cannot, of course, provide the acting values of drama; nor even those values which the intimate dumb-show *Sumurun* had in so much larger a degree. Reinhardt's work in *The Miracle* is the crowd and the great conception of the whole. Here he is magnificent. His other virtues he cannot display. His debut would have been happier if he had had a gigantic auditorium in which to animate the whole tale—cathedral, love story and all—with the vitality which he gave the thing in London. Yet it is impossible to deny that he has accomplished a task unprecedented in America, and achieved an hour of such vivid, communicating beauty as we have not known here. And not the least part of his triumph is that he has liberated Geddes' remarkable talents and given them a scope which no American producer dared to conceive.

March 1924

* *

JOHN MASON BROWN

*

The Dybbuk

ANSKY'S *THE DYBBUK,* which opened the season of the Neighborhood Playhouse, presents exceptional challenges to the director.

The play is steeped in the ecstatic spirituality of Chassidism, an extreme mystic cult of the Hebraic faith. Its three acts are equally concerned with the world of the living and the world of the dead. It is, in fact, what the program calls it, a "mystic melodrama," in which the spirit of a dead lover enters and takes possession of the body of his sweetheart on her marriage day. Ansky himself describes it as "a realistic play about mystic people." But both Ansky and the director are faced with the problem of making the mysticism and the reality of this special cult real to an audience in the theatre which might scoff at the one and be ignorant of the other.

The play that Ansky provides is a mere scenario from which the director may work. Its three acts are devoted to three separate folk ceremonies of the Chassidic Jews. The first is laid in a synagogue, the second at a wedding feast and the third in the Prayer Room of the Tsadik, the holy man of Chassidism, who alone can cast out an evil spirit which has seized upon a member of the sect. In each of these scenes there must be the reality of the facts they represent, yet in them and above them the hush of the supernatural must be felt. The beggars who dance at the wedding feast cannot dance as beggars alone. Though they must suggest beggars rioting and snatching at the food of the contented rich, they must serve, too, as ominous symbols of the evil spirit which is about to enter Leah. In the same way, the Professional Prayer Men in the Synagogue cannot drone their chants merely for the sake of lending reality to the scene. The haunting minor of their song must establish the desired mood, and evoke in the audience the willingness to believe in the destruction which may overtake anyone except the Tsadik who pries into the secrets of the mystic book, the Kabala.

Throughout the play the details of realism take on a supernatural significance. Quite obviously this intertwining of the two worlds does not facilitate the work of the producer. Instead it complicates his task, presenting him with problems which would prove insurmountable in an ordinary production. The production at the Neighborhood, however, is by no means ordinary. It has a beauty and unity of playing rarely seen. Its interest does not center on any particular actor or actress. It arises from the extraordinary cohesion and fluidity of the playing of the entire cast. Its actors have brought to their work a reverence for the theatre which is plain in any moment of the performance. Though there are weaknesses in some of the individual characterizations they are lost sight of in the excitements of the production as a whole.

As an example of creative direction *The Dybbuk* has had no equal in our native theatre in several seasons. Much of the credit for this must be given to David Vardi, who assisted with the original performance of the play in Moscow and who directed it at the Neighborhood Playhouse in association with Alice Lewisohn. He has so saturated his players with the details and ecstasy of Chassidism that in each act he can set a mood by the use of a group and sustain it after that by the acting of his principals. Working with a superstition alien to his actors, he has made them exalt in it to such an extent that it becomes comprehensible and terrifying to their audiences.

The Dybbuk as it is performed in Grand Street belongs to no creed or folk. It stimulates, excites and awes an audience regardless of faith by virtue of its vibrant theatricality. It is not, on the other hand, the result of an imported director driving a company of New York players into a perfected ensemble. It is the inevitable outcome of the hard work and the high ideals of the Neighborhood Playhouse, where a permanent company has been working patiently and well for ten years, and has slowly come into its own.

February 1926

*

Escape; Coquette

THOUGH WILLIAM SHAKESPEARE has walked away with the largest number of openings, he has by no means had a corner on the interest of this month, during which Broadway has momentarily forgotten its predilection for melodrama and turned hungrily to more serious business. In *Escape,* for example, it sits spellbound before one of those taut and compassionate chronicles in which John Galsworthy excels. This time, however, it finds him attacking no alterable evils. He is not trying to reform the statute book, or masking the horrors of face prejudice beneath the cloak of melodrama. He is not even passing judgment on a futile warfare waged between the leaders of opposing social forces. Instead, he is concerned with the agony of the pursued, the torture of the hunted who finds the whole pack yapping at his heels. He dismisses a specific problem and enlarges his tragedy by having his hero merely the victim of bad luck. Matt Denant is only a nice young Englishman of moderate means who is tripped up by uncontrollable misfortune. Sitting in Hyde Park he enters into conversation with a prostitute who happens to be sitting next to him. When he starts to leave, a detective threatens her with arrest for plying her trade in public. As a gentleman, Matt Denant can do nothing but protest. Angry words ensue, followed by an exchange of blows during which the detective is felled and killed by hitting his head against a railing. By one of those curiously illogical tricks of fortune, Denant discovers that his chivalry has made a murderer of him.

When Mr. Galsworthy has stated his premise in this gripping prologue, he devotes his nine succeeding scenes to studying a short forty hours of his hero's life after he has escaped from jail. In each new scene Mr. Galsworthy shows him getting a different reaction from each group with which he comes in contact. Meanwhile the hopelessness of his plight, which is clear from the first, mounts during these uneven, moving, but always intelligent scenes, into a gnawing crescendo. When, at the very end, Matt surrenders to the police rather than have the minister, with whom he has taken refuge, tell a lie, he utters one of those grand and all too specific beatitudes that are always on tap at Mr. Galsworthy's curtains. "It's one's decent self one can't escape," he cries, and satisfied that his play has its "spire of meaning," Mr. Galsworthy drops the curtain.

Winthrop Ames has given *Escape* a smooth production that is as successful in its understatement as it is sure in its characterization and swift in its onward march. Rising above both the play and the production, however, is Leslie Howard's superlatively fine playing of Matt Denant. Mr. Howard is a familiar and welcome figure in the polite comedies that are a part of each season's crop. In them he has played himself pleasantly and well, but as Denant he emerges as an actor of a new stature. Without losing his sense of comedy he makes it a tool for his tragic equipment. He knows what is said more strongly when it is never said at all. And he merges his own personality with such an uncanny completeness into the tortured, harried figure he is projecting that the memory of his acting will outlast many seasons.

So, too, the memory of Helen Hayes' performance of that charming and indirect little Southern girl in *Coquette* will survive when all the shots and chivalry of this tragi-comedy by George Abbott and Ann Preston Bridgers have been forgotten. Though you are not given the chance to guess it until the third act is under way, because of the verisimilitude of the production, *Coquette* as a play must be made of very different stuff from *Coquette* as a performance. If suddenly its tricks and even the stability of its tragic plotting seem debatable, it is the more disillusioning because what has gone before is more tremulous and tender than the theatre customarily affords.

Its story of Norma Besant, the belle of a small Southern town, who has fallen in love with Michael, a boy of no social background and few worldly hopes, laughs its way into tragic complications. There are threatening moments, of course, when Norma's father insults Michael and orders him out of the house. But the tragedy of this misalliance is established so cunningly, while drawling young things discourse on love and a younger brother worries about basketball, that its final unleashing has the full terror of reality. The verbal pleasantries of Norma Besant, the pretty, fluffy overstatements and well-meant insincerities which decorate her daily speech and are not important enough to pass as lies, have won her everything she wants and made her think that life is just as simple as manufacturing compliments. Then she is brought face to face with facts, but she cannot live down her habit of evasion. When her father asks Norma if what her lover has said about *having* to let him marry her is true, she lies, thinking that by postponing the truth she can make it bearable. What follows is what any full-fledged Southern gentleman, who knows his juleps, is honor-bound to do—on the stage. The father reaches for his nearest pistol and shoots Michael.

It is in the last act, when her father faces execution and Norma's purity is a matter of legal importance, that she admits to a former lover she is carrying Michael's child. It is in this same act, too, that the play, which has really ended with the second act, runs thin and turns improbable. In particular, it never quite explains why Norma should have to do a Paula Tanqueray offstage. Supposedly, her suicide is planned to save her father, but how it will help is never made quite clear, unless we are presumed to believe that in this chivalrous Southland, where honor is a shooting matter, jurors are too well-bred to insist upon autopsies. In any event, it is in this last act, when reality burns low, that the playwrights are caught red-handed in the heartless procedure of wringing tears for the sheer delight of torture without regard for either necessity or logic.

That they have succeeded, even when the play has lost its witchery, is only an added tribute to the performance *Coquette* is given. George Abbott, as director, has turned from the night club of *Broadway* and the gangster warfare of *Four Walls,* and shown an equal skill in making the prattle of a Southern family throb with theatre values, even while it has a reality that seems to annihilate the proscenium arch. He has been aided by an unusually suitable cast that, from Andrew Lawlor, Jr.'s unctuous playing of Norma's "kid" brother to Albert Smith's touching reserve as the rejected suitor, obscures the basic triteness of the play's materials. As Michael Jeffrey, Elliot Cabot adds immeasurably to the sorcery of the production. Charging his outbursts with a sullen, sweeping passion that is as shrewd as a weapon of climax as it is true to the character he creates, he also solves the difficult problem of making Michael's attraction for Norma as understandable as are his objections from her father's viewpoint.

In Helen Hayes' Norma *Coquette* takes on a real importance. It is by far the best performance of her career, lacking in all the kittenish mannerisms that managers have tried to force on her and possessing a burnished authenticity. In the course of a single evening, and with a sincerity that almost hurts, Miss Hayes changes from the silly, light-headed and warm-hearted little heroine of the first act into a woman whose whole being has been subdued and broken by tragedy.

January 1928

*

Danton's Tod; The Irish Players

THERE IS a scene in *Danton's Tod* when, for once, the gods and mankind seem to be laughing at the same thing and at the same time. A mob that soars out of sight on the bleachers in the background, packs the tiers of seats on either side, and spills over to fill the vast depths of the Century Theatre's auditorium, pushes hungrily against the little pen in the middle of the stage. In that pen Camille Desmoulins, the friend of Danton, huddles in the corner, broken by the Revolution and fearful in the face of the Tribunal. It is not he, however, who catches the eye and holds it. He offers no sport; he has been crushed too easily. The rabble waits for the man who can thrill it by a spirited defiance, to break the monotony of the day's long list of passive butcheries. This it finds in Danton, more particularly in the Danton of Paul Hartmann, who stands there a giant in size and calm, pleading his own case so well that Robespierre and St. Just, who have slated him for the guillotine, are forced to call a halt to his rhetoric. It is Danton, composed in the face of death, who makes the mob look small beside him. He has been one with these people who are accusing him. It is his strong hands which are supposed to have held the bleeding head of Louis aloft when it rolled from under the knife, and now these people have turned on him as he has turned from them. He has outgrown his belief that liberty can be bought by blood alone, just as he has grown to hate the men who prosper by roaring its cant without sincerity. Confronted by this mob and with his executioners before him, this Danton laughs. At first, it is a low and single chuckle that resounds in that breathless Tribunal. It begins to grow and fills out into a long laugh—a solitary comment on man's dreams and ambitions. Suddenly someone else is carried away by the daring and contagion of its comment. The laugh swells slowly but perceptibly, from the rabble onstage to the mob in the auditorium, enlarging, including more and more people, until the theatre rocks with a Gargantuan roar, and everyone laughs, at first without knowing why, but continues nonetheless heartily on discovering that this derision is aimed at the whole futility of life, laughs hoarsely, madly, for what seems an age of disillusionment, and keeps on laughing until the stiff backs of the enclosing soldiery remind the crowd all too harshly of the world they live in.

This scene comes as the supreme moment that the Reinhardt season in New York has so far revealed, and as one of those experiences in the theatre that burns its way into the memory of those who have been a part of it. A part of it—because it is preeminently successful in wiping out all barriers between actors and audiences, and in establishing between them that dynamic kinship which is the final tribute to this kind of showmanship. The device of stationing crowds in the audience as a connecting link between the stage and the auditorium may seem somewhat battered to those sophisticates who have learned about crowds from *The Spider* and other such recent offerings. But, though it has lost its novelty by wide appropriation since Reinhardt first stumbled on it as a means of granting intimacy to his "circus" productions, it has not lost its effectiveness. At its best (and Reinhardt's best is its best) it is one of the surest and most breath-taking of Reinhardt's tricks, but one that pales in subtlety when compared with the magic of his handling of crowds. He is without a peer in managing his supernumeraries so that they are no haphazard stragglers, but a living entity with real emotions and an aggregate will. In the present production his results are the more remarkable when one remembers that his squalling rabble is an American mob, with only a week or so of rehearsals behind it and having little idea of the German in which it is harangued. Except in its tribunal scenes *Danton's Tod* follows a tame and frequently dull course, because George Buchner's play is a sprawling and profuse affair that is as hospitable to all warring factions of the French Revolution (both in their public and domestic life) as it is awkward in dealing with them. It is whipped into some kind of coherency by the sheer vitality of Paul Hartmann's Danton, and focused by the interestingly mannered Robespierre of Vladimir Sokolov. Over the howling of the mobs, the insidious conversational quietness of Arnold Korff's St. Just dominates in superb contrast. Oddly enough—and to the evident confusion of the audience, which refuses to take the last act of the present version as a real climax—Reinhardt has closed his production with a woeful anticlimax in which Lili Darvas is given the impossible task of building a finale out of a super-romantic Ophelia act, with its stock-in-trade fennel and mad song. Following fast upon mob scenes of unparalleled vigor, this comes as a depressant which, while it momentarily obscures what has gone before, cannot efface the memory of its drive.

With the Irish Players opening their season with *The Plough and the Stars* and following it with *Juno and the Paycock*, New York has had its first real chance to judge the full stature of Sean O'Casey. It is true that, two seasons ago, this same *Juno* was brought to the dwarfish stage of the Mayfair Theatre, but in spite of the several virtues this rambling, ill-assorted production had, it was no more than a letter of introduction to O'Casey, and the real meeting had still to take place. Now, however, it has been brought about in such a way that it cannot soon be forgotten, because these two plays have been carried to New York by actors who belong to Sean O'Casey's Dublin, just as they seem to belong to him and to his dramas. The merits and the excesses of their acting are the merits and excesses of his plays, and, in the case of each, the merits more than redeem the excesses.

Both *Juno* and *The Plough* are bitter, brutal ironies, so strongly felt and so passionately stated that, in spite of their broad comedy and their gorgeous wit, they scorch and bruise the spectator. In both of them the sorry story of the waste of revolution is told, and innocent bystanders suffer most cruelly from its havoc. In *Juno* revolution creeps up those sinister backstairs, which lead from the streets of Dublin that are blood-stained from the battles of the Free Staters and the Die Hards, fairly bursting in upon what might otherwise have been a droll little character comedy about a legacy which never materialized. In *The Plough* it is the story that is forced to climb the stairs of the tenement house to escape the woes of a ravaged city. In both of them, the comment on Irish character is as good-natured as it is relentless, and in each, before the final curtain, O'Casey's puppets can be taken as symbols of Ireland and Irish virtues and faults.

In *Juno,* where the trite little plot is more self-reliant, the course of the playwright is always clear, but in *The Plough* he seems lost in a pleasing labyrinth of mixed modes until suddenly, in the last act, all of his by-paths converge and his meaning rings out with a deafening clarity. He is without a rival in snatching people of the backstairs out of their pubs and tenements, and transferring them to the stage in such a way that they remain people seen in the round instead of dwindling into types observed from only one convenient angle. His plots are minor, almost incidental, and he interrupts them at will to dally with protracted interludes of character comedy, or terrifying moments of anguish. He is not above using some tricks again and again as the standard of his comic currency, repeating a word like "darling" or "derogatory," or a phrase like "God give me patience," until he fairly flagellates his comic point. In the same way he doubles on his tragic ingredients, piling his catastrophes one above the other, introducing them at such a swift rate in the last act of *Juno* that they strain the credulity, or turning from such a really fine moment as the death of Bessie Burgess in *The Plough* to let loose another one of those mawkish Ophelia scenes—nightgown, broken songs, madness and all—to weaken his ending and blur his final curtain.

The performances the Irish Players give *The Plough* and *Juno* have that same lack of restraint which marks the texts. In moments of fisticuffs (and there are many), their own exuberance makes them overstep the bounds of comedy and leap into farce. In the lulls in action and the preparatory stretches, their methods demand a readjustment from playgoers accustomed to the insistent drive of American productions. These actors have a deliberateness of attack that is, at first, as disconcerting as the shuffling gait of O'Casey's plots. Both their slowness and their expansiveness prove, before the evening is over however, to be the proper—almost the inevitable—manner of giving the plays their final authenticity.

It is, of course, Arthur Sinclair who plays the Paycock in *Juno,* and Fluther Good in *The Plough*. In each he shows an amazing shrewdness in making and holding his points and in managing, though using the same wallop in both parts, to create two radically different characters. Miss O'Neill, whether as the pugnacious sentimentalist in *The Plough* or the cheery Maisie Madigan in *Juno,* sweeps each of her tirades from a climax of rhetoric, which seems the very summit of human eloquence, to another and yet another, until she appears the epitome of the wit and passion of phrase-loving Ireland. Sara Allgood, who vocalizes her innocent bystander in *The Plough* with a relish that is more obvious than forgivable, gives a memorable performance as *Juno*—quiet, moving and tender beyond the ordinary scope of acting, and heroic with simplicity.

February 1928

* * *

JOHN HUTCHENS

*

The Green Pastures

IN THE PLAY the matter of emphasis—themes and characters and events, the speed, the vocal tone—rest all fundamentally and essentially on a base of music"—Stark Young set that down some years ago in his essay on "The Art of Directing," aware certainly that one searches a long time for a play to which this pure theatre ideal applies recognizably. But into the last months of a season which at its best had done the old things well, Marc Connelly's *The Green Pastures* brought, besides the glow of a quiet beauty and a self-sustaining form, something closely akin to the melodic and harmonious lines of fine musical composition.

Its source material, Roark Bradford's *Ol' Man Adam an' His Chillun,* balanced on the edge of the theatre, awaiting the imaginative transcription that Mr. Connelly—as playwright and director—has brought to it. The Bradford sketches were instinct with the poetry and feeling of the Negro, his old yearning and child-like intimacy with and love for a personal God. What Mr. Connelly grasped with dramatic and creative intuition was that here was material which in the theatre, and by the theatre's essential mediums, was to be enlarged into an all-enveloping emotional experience. Through his skillful selection and arrangement, his reach below the surface of the situations and events of the stories, he has made *The Green Pastures* express the relationship, in simple terms, of anyone and his God. As folk fantasy, the play is a visualization in eighteen scenes of the Negro of the Deep South: of his rich, humble conception of heaven as a site of eternal fish-fries, of the Lord as a beneficent old gentleman, kindly but firm, who deals with his children directly. From its prologue the play makes its own version of Old Testament events—the dawn of man in the Garden of Eden; the Lord in his heavenly office—a tired ruler to whom "being God is no bed of roses"; the Lord in conference with Noah over the flood; Moses and his brother at the court of the Pharaoh; Moses halting at the Jordan as the Children of Israel go on to conquer Jericho; Babylon's sin seen as a Harlem night club; the final divination of the Christ. . . .

Neither this conception nor the actual writing of it is imaginative work of the very first order. *The Green Pastures,* while it is often finely creative, is still chiefly a derivation, and late in its course it falls away from its own expression to a form of objective comment. But Mr. Connelly's direction puts the theatre as a medium to uses seldom approached in Broadway practice. It is theatrically important that the play has the essential quality of the spirituals which are its tonal background and its recurrent motif; that it has primal rhythms, sonorous and indicated, and a pulse that is close to the edge of song.

Mr. Connelly has achieved a complete simplicity in the arrangement and movement of the large cast of Negro players—sometimes there are scores upon the stage, and then you see, or rather feel, the lights and shadows of changing emphasis played across a group performance. The scenes vary in tone, in speed and in length, each held to its importance as part of an episodic sequence. The chorus chants, in unison or antiphonally, and new and deeper emotions and meanings well up suddenly as they do in spirituals. There are no crowds, no confusion; and details—small, unextravagant humors—are subjected to the thread of a simple narrative that Robert Edmond Jones has dramatized for the eye in lucid, fanciful lines. And through the pageantry, the Lord, in the person of Richard B. Harrison, moves with a lonely benignity that Mr. Harrison has captured by one does not know what deep, natural sincerity divorced from artifice. He has never acted before.

May 1930

*

Romeo and Juliet

EVA LE GALLIENNE, as her last Civic Repertory production of the season, gave a brilliantly paced *Romeo and Juliet,* played as a play rather than the starring vehicle that has been made of it here in recent years. Miss Le Gallienne has rearranged accepted acting versions to strike a staccato order of scenes; has, by means of Aline Bernstein's severe, simple and adaptable settings, left the play open to spirited movement that quickens the glamour and tragedy. Scenes that ordinarily are omitted from the play are brought back to round out the dramatic narrative; repetitious plot factors, previously retained as precious starring material, are deleted in the interest of a swift continuity. Opening to a key-note of drum beats and a tune of swords clashing up and down long flights of stairs, Miss Le Gallienne's production hurries the play without loss of time into the atmosphere of its story. Stairs leading out of the orchestra pit furnish additional exits and entrances and an extended platform serves to carry on the action of the play during important scene changes. . . . In its script and mechanics, *Romeo and Juliet* awaited a fast, thorough and non-starring performance on the Civic Repertory stage.

But what principally gives luminous life to this latest and best of recent Shakespearean productions is Miss Le Gallienne's Juliet, one of the few outstanding roles she has taken since the adventure in Fourteenth Street began. However, completely as she has fitted every part, including her own, into the pattern of the play, her performance is a striking reminder of how fine and compelling an actress she is. For this Juliet, beautiful and young and warm, blends softness and power, humor and tragic despair in a character done with sentiment as well as a constantly intelligent emotion. Her supporting company, though it lacks her own quality, is satisfactory and gives further evidence of the excellence of its repertory training. Donald Cameron's Romeo is at least balanced and competent; J. Edward Bromberg, as Mercutio, works steadily into the character following an unsuccessful encounter with the Queen Mab speech; and minor roles—particularly that of the Nurse, as played by Leona Roberts—have decisive individuality. But because the play is given for its own sake, according to Miss Le Gallienne's general policy, it is certain to improve and ripen with repetition, as most Civic Repertory productions have done. This *Romeo and Juliet,* worked out according to Miss Le Gallienne's finest production ideals, suggests the quite definite coming of age of her organization.

June 1930

*

The House of Connelly

WHY THE THEATRE GUILD did not present Paul Green's *The House of Connelly* during the years in which it held the rights to the play is a question better saved for some future summary of the caprices of that producing organization. At the moment, certainly, it is hardly more than a sidelight to what seems one of the more important events native to the American theatre since the stirrings of the Provincetown in Macdougal Street or the Guild's own first manifestoes. *The House of Connelly,* held on a tentative list from season to season, has come to the stage as the first offering of the new Group Theatre. And, on its arrival, it is seen to be a play that could afford—a play, indeed, that demanded—to await the scrupulous attention that the Group Theatre was equipped to give it. For the company assembled by Cheryl Crawford, Harold Clurman and Lee

Strasberg, while it is generally experienced, is notably young. In its first work as a unit it has achieved beauty and significance as only a company can do when it is finely enthusiastic, patient and explorative.

By now it is history of a sort that the Group Theatre had been working for about three years toward the finish and perception that it disclosed in *The House of Connelly*. There were months of eager planning, but no chance of action until, armed with the Guild's permission to rehearse the play, the company went to Brookfield Center for ten weeks last summer. That period, in which they worked also with another play, has meant the difference between a competent production and a luminous one. In the weeks in which *The House of Connelly* was given over to the discipline of developing an acting ensemble, of working and re-working the interpretation of a play whose conception is in poetry, there flowered a wholeness and soundness for which Broadway's fevered offices have generally no time. In molding its performance to a play as elusive but exacting in form as this one, the Group Theatre's triumph is greater by proportion. For Mr. Green is still as rebellious against the conventions of the commercial theatre as when he wrote in a preface to his published plays that "the American professional stage is an industry and not an art . . . a business run to the pattern of supply and demand." *The House of Connelly* continues on a plane with his other work in refusing to sacrifice probity to the bright lights.

In the six scenes of the slow death and flaming re-birth of the Connelly family, the many-sided truth, force and quiescence of Paul Green's writing are unrolled in a scheme as secure as Chekhov's. Like the Chekhov plays—above all like *The Cherry Orchard* which it frequently suggests—its larger background is nature moving now objectively, remotely, more often directly entwined in the destiny of its people, swaying all of them with different meanings. Directly from that soil the conflict in *The House of Connelly* stems in the heat of possessive forces at war; an old, poverty-wrenched Southern family watching its dreams and pride against the fresh, positive blood of a new, incoming civilization. Mr. Green has stated a good deal of his theme in flat key speeches. He has realized more of it in rounded, dramatic symbols of character—an old uncle, lecherous, decadent, aristocratic; Will Connelly's two sisters and his mother, proud, very proud, until their pride, being their life, is an intensely dramatic factor. More precisely, the play is a duel between Will, son of the house, surrounded by the remnants and characters of his tradition, and Patsy Tate, the tenant's daughter who loves and seeks the land, plays upon his passion to attain it, and falls in love with him as she does so. What happens has about it the force of inevitable change. The uncle commits suicide, the mother dies, the sisters retreat in the face of the new order established by the marriage of Will Connelly and Patsy Tate—this is the movement of the play. How much was to be said by its performance is scarcely evident in a flat statement of its theme.

"Bring into harmony all . . . creative elements . . ." Stanislavski told his players as they prepared to act *The Bluebird*. The dictum holds for every company that sets before itself the ideal of an ensemble, and the direction of this one by Miss Crawford and Mr. Strasberg has maintained the universal quality of the play even while its actors have approached their roles from different points of view. Franchot Tone's insight into the strength and weakness of Will Connelly is invariably right in its sweep, full of an intensity caught and sustained by Margaret Barker, as the girl; Stella Adler, the older of the two sisters; Morris Carnovsky, the uncle. The variations from the universal quality of the play, a quality that would assure its meaning for audiences having not even a general knowledge of its background, are for the most part enriching. Mr. Tone, for instance, has attempted a Southern accent and succeeded. Miss Barker and Miss Adler, without incorporating such localized values, have followed a simpler acting design which fits no less exactly into the pattern of the play. Mr. Carnovsky's creation of the old uncle alone is so thoroughly rounded and developed as a piece of individual work that it wanders from the ensemble idea; and, being neither local as Mr. Tone's performance nor severe and general as Miss Barker's, wanders so far back into its Russian theatrical background as to be discordant though excellent of its kind.

Mr. Green has written other roles less well and fitted them less carefully into his plan. The invalid-mother, played by Mary Morris with a sense of weakness rather than gentility, is trundled out upon the stage rather too often, to the detriment of fluent action; and the two old Negro women servants, who are a chorus to the action, are rather too cryptically sketched into a play whose surface of scene and character is realistic. The effect of such minor faults of characterization is to retard the flow of the poetry of the play, but no more than slightly. As dramatic and as harmonious as the performance is the best of Cleon Throckmorton's recent settings: the large dining room of the Connelly house, the fine, gracious, simple line still on it, with a story told mutely and a mood visualized in its haze of discolor, its uncertain streaks of age.

December 1931

*

Mourning Becomes Electra

OF *MOURNING BECOMES ELECTRA* it is first to be said that Eugene O'Neill's sense of the theatre—of deep emotion evoked sharply and sustained by extraordinary narrative skill—has never fulfilled itself more completely than in this trilogy as the Theatre Guild has presented it. We have seen him fumble over his analysis of the spiritual ills of the time; brood in the terms of advanced psychology and the asides of the Victorian theatre, as he probed the thoughts and more often the nightmares at the heart of a complex humanity; and no matter what eloquence and persuasion he has sometimes achieved in the grim pursuit of various pseudo-philosophies, there had been of late this uneasy sensation: that he was too often sacrificing his greatest gift as an emotional writer, the power to tell a tale superbly. Here now, in the three plays of this trilogy—*Homecoming, The Hunted* and *The Haunted*—he has gone back to one of the world's greatest stories, the *Electra,* not reinterpreting it exactly in terms of the America of 1865-6, not reproducing consistently the Greek mood and imagery, but choosing from the various Greek versions such points of analogy and departure as serve best a horrific murder story. Mr. O'Neill was never more fully an artist than in filling out this pattern to the limit of its possibilities as melodrama. That it has neither the exaltation of poetic drama nor the "final radiantly sad contentment" of great tragedy will be of concern only to those who claim too much for him. They are absent qualities having little to do with the fact that the great story is for the most part finely rendered in this, its latest telling.

The skill with which he has adapted from the Greek pattern, redirecting its suspense to that of the inner movement of the trilogy, is apparent in a quick synopsis. The House of Atreus is the House of Mannon, the time is April, 1865, when Lee's surrender is as yet an unconfirmed rumor. The first scene of the first play is the exterior of the Mannon house, its Doric columns rising in reminiscent austerity. The family awaits the return from the war of Brigadier-General Ezra Mannon, the Agamemnon of the play, who had won fame in the Mexican War, become rich in the shipping trade, been the mayor of the small New England town in which he lived, and won further glory in the Civil War. The return of his son, Orin (the Orestes), is also imminent. The first scene is compact in exposition. Christine Mannon (Clytemnestra), wife of Ezra, and their daughter Lavinia (Electra) are at swords' points of mutual hatred and suspicion. Lavinia is in love with a sea captain, Adam Brant (the Aegisthus), an illegitimate son of her great-uncle by a French servant girl. She discovers that her mother has been having an affair with Brant, has been seeing him at intervals in New York, whither she has been going on some pretext. She acquaints her mother with her knowledge of the affair, makes her promise to see no more of Brant, and together the two women await the return of Ezra. In a hurried interview with the captain, Christine has plotted the murder of Mannon, which takes place on the night of his homecoming a week later. By telling him of her affair with Brant she brings on one of the heart attacks to which he is subject, then gives him poison instead of medicine, a fact which Lavinia ascertains as she breaks into the room and hears her father accuse her mother.

With the return of Orin two days later, there begins a struggle between the two women to dominate him, ending in victory for Lavinia when she takes him to Brant's ship at a Boston wharf and, from the deck above, they look down into the cabin and see Christine with her lover. When she has left him, Orin murders Brant, the brother and sister return to their home and confront their mother with the fact of Brant's death, upon which she commits suicide and brings the trilogy to its climax at the end of the second play. Thereafter Mr. O'Neill's invention is more or less free of its Greek background. The furies that haunt Orin consist not only of an active madness of blood-guilt for the death of his mother, but also the transition of his fixation for her into an incestuous passion for Lavinia, of which his sudden awareness is provocation for his suicide. She, who had "tried to become the wife of her father and the mother of Orin," has grown recognizably into a likeness of her mother; Orin's and her own knowledge of this, their mutual guilt and twisted relationship are the culmination of the theme which has flared fitfully throughout the play: that the dead shall come back to haunt and pillory the living; that heredity and crime shall be expiated only as Lavinia expiates them when she forsakes her own future, bars the house and retires into it forever.

In spinning his selective way in and out among the sources of the story, Mr. O'Neill has evolved a structure whose five hours of playing time are not free from prolixity, particularly in the third play which is raised to the artistic level of the first two only by the final portrait, complete in picture, mood and feeling. In other words, it is in the first two-thirds of the trilogy, or in the crescendo of its action, that his skill for sustaining a narrative is at its exciting best, the third play and its interpretation of the action falling into old faults of wordiness and repetition. In perspective the great effective moments of *Mourning Becomes Electra* are those of melodramatic situation carefully prepared and caught at the crest of their suspense, suffering no anticlimax; the sinister plotting of Ezra Mannon's murder in the shadows of his study; the murder itself, and Mannon gasping out an accusation as his daughter breaks into the room; the scene in which Lavinia, in the presence of her brother, places the poison on the corpse of her father and admits their mother into the room of wavering candlelight to test her weakening nerves; the scene on the boat, with Brant and Christine in a cross-section of his cabin giving away their secret while Lavinia and Orin stand concealed on the deck above them; the wracking half minute while Brant is returning to his certain death in the cabin at the hands of Orin; the suicide of Christine.

There is no implication here of inadmissible stage trickery or of insincerity. Mr. O'Neill's writing in this trilogy is admirably straightforward and full of fine splendor, particularly in the soliloquies, which are beautifully written and, by no accident, shrewdly expository. And to the vibrant needs of the play the Guild gives bountiful aid. Philip Moeller's direction is scarcely less distinguished than in *Strange Interlude,* a more difficult technical task, three years ago. He gives to the performance as a whole a background of slowly increasing force and deliberate quietude from which it draws an additional starkness of outline (the sluggishness of the last play could hardly be lessened without cutting the text severely). There are in the trilogy three individual performances of genuine stature, finely wrought in the face of different problems, and in particular of the one which stands between Mr. O'Neill's work and real tragedy —the fact that not a character in the trilogy is of heroic mold, that whatever happens to any of them is not conceivably a fall from greatness. They are small people. Alla Nazimova's Christine is a sinister and deeply realized creation, all her fine technical resourcefulness responding flawlessly to the role through which the themes of the trilogy run most fiercely during the first two plays. More stringent in the demands upon its continuity, the task of Alice Brady, the Lavinia, has been differently conceived. Through the entire action and its final interpretation she moves now as a participant, now as a passive figure in whom the doom is foreshadowed and finally symbolized, and always with a mask-like rigidity which in formalized style is set apart from the rest of the performance. The slow pace which the part has been given by Mr. Moeller is open to question, an unnecessary connection between slowness and impressiveness being suggested, but within its deliberate repression it is a performance almost perfectly sustained, never blurred and triumphant in its pictorial values. Earle Larrimore reaches the highest point in his career in the acting of Orin, a constantly emotional role in which he is entirely free from the falsity of average theatrical neuroticism and alert in conveying the tortured relationships which swirl around him.

The settings of Robert Edmond Jones are never inadequate, and in two instances—the pillared front of the House of Mannon and the deck of the clipper ship by night—they are intensely dramatic. The former is entirely complementary to the action, entering into the changing moods of the play and closing it exactly on the note it has sought and gained by turns. In the moment when Lavinia, in black, stands framed between the white pillars of the House of Mannon, the sunset dying at her feet, the course of passion run—in that moment, playwright, performer and artist come together in a superb conclusion that belongs as completely and solely to the theatre as Mr. O'Neill himself.

January 1932

EDITH J. R. ISAACS

*

Tobacco Road

THERE IS one play that dared to open during the tricky holiday month that followed the autumn's harvest of successes which will, it seems safe to say, be remembered and spoken of—with admiration or with sharp distaste—long after the last curtain has fallen upon its sordid scene. It is *Tobacco Road,* a story of the Georgia "crackers," which Jack Kirkland fashioned out of a novel of the same name by Erskine Caldwell. It is one of the few dramatizations which emerges as a play in its own right, and is probably one of the bitterest plays ever produced in New York, but one of the most compelling. . . .

The scene is set before the dilapidated cottage which has been the home of generations of Lesters, tenant farmers living on the edge of a great plantation, some miles out of Augusta. Perhaps the Lesters had always been a weak lot, as so many of the tenant farmers were who were content to take their land and their homes, their seed and their orders, from the plantation masters. Perhaps they had been for so long close to the land itself as to become a part of it, to share in its gradual impoverishment and neglect until Jeeter Lester and those that were left here of his family (there were seventeen children in all, were there not, most of whom had died or run away or found some other escape) had sunk to a level that was barely human, but not kind or alive or faithful enough to be called animal.

The old master is dead—the young master has mortgaged the land, stopped the small allowance, and even the rations of his tenants, and gone off to Augusta. For years now old Jeeter, lazy, slow-witted, lecherous, dishonest, has been sitting on the back stoop, waiting for his decrepit old mother to bring in branches from the woods for the fire, waiting for his shabby wife, whose one ambition is to have a stylish dress to be buried in, or for his harelipped daughter to find him roots to feed on, or, when that does not come, sneaking off to the house of some slightly less shiftless neighbor to steal a little flour or a few turnips to make a meal.

This joyless picture does not change throughout the play, all of whose events center around this terrible family. The father gives the youngest daughter as wife to a neighbor for seven dollars and she will not share his bed; Grandma Lester dies in the woods and nobody bothers to search for her body—although they mean to do it some day; the worthless son marries a traveling woman preacher twice his age on her promise to buy him a new Ford car; the car runs over and kills the mother; the fair daughter escapes to Augusta; the master's son comes with the Augusta banker, who has foreclosed the mortgage on the land, to tell Jeeter he must go.

That is about what happens, but out of the narrow circle of events there rises a picture, not only of a family, but of a people, as real, true and terrible, as far out of key with our American ideal of living, as the dwellers in the slums of our big cities. In fact there is nothing about the picture of Jeeter Lester or about the quality of the human decay in *Tobacco Road* that makes it especially a play of the South except the feeling the play creates that it is the sun and not the cold that has sapped the strength of this particular family's life.

Henry Hull as Jeeter Lester is the protagonist, not only of the play but all of these people. If *Tobacco Road* has done nothing else, it would have been worth the theatre's attention to give him a part so apt for his creation. It remains one of the miracles of the art of acting that a man who has so long been cast to the type of his own pleasant presence can pick up a part as difficult as that of Jeeter Lester and make it live. Somewhere in the memory of his early Kentucky days Henry Hull must have kept a thousand details of the character of a man like Jeeter Lester, and of how it expresses itself in the way he sits and walks and talks. He has remembered the way Jeeter can do nothing for a stretch of time, walk half a dozen steps with one shoe on and one off before his mind picks up the idea that one shoe is off and he sits down in the road to put it on; just how he would look at the bag of turnips when he was hungry or at the golden hair of his wife's daughter (that was not his); how his eyes would light up at the sound of the horn on the new Ford car, or dim down at the sight of his wife lying dying before him, or how he would let the grains of earth—his land—run through his fingers lovingly, and flame up with terror and anger at the thought of leaving the farm to work in a factory.

This old man, as Erskine Caldwell drew him, may be a fat morsel for a player, full of opportunity for theatre device. Perhaps it was easy for Mr. Hull to make him as bad and rotten as he was, but that was only the outer edge of his achievement. The important thing he did was to re-create in Lester the shadow of those qualities which had once made him, or his father, a man and a farmer—the love of the land and the love of a woman's beauty.

Erskine Caldwell knows very well all of this black part of the South and of Southern living. He knows also all the outer aspects of the country and of the people, he has caught the rhythm and richness of their speech, which turns easily into theatre speech. He never shirks the last unpleasant accent on any situation, such, for example, as the harelipped sister's sex hunger. Nevertheless, he gives you always the feeling of having created something and not merely reported on it, of making it worth his players' while to follow him the full way along the road he chooses for them. Besides Henry Hull the play has good support in Margaret Wycherly as Lester's wife, Sam Byrd as Dude Lester, his worthless son, and Ruth Hunter as Ellie May, his pathetic daughter.

Almost unanimously the dramatic critics of the daily papers agreed that Henry Hull had done the best piece of acting of his career, but that *Tobacco Road* was too brutal for the theatre. They resented especially the emphasis on the distorted sex aspects of the play as being almost unbearable to watch, and their opinion has been supported by the greater part of those who have seen the play. Which seems strange in a theatre that can gaily take to its heart almost the same distortion treated as farce in *The Pursuit of Happiness,* that accepts with pleasure the nakedness of *Murder at the Vanities,* and for which no burlesque joke is too free to be funny. The only thing that makes this comment pertinent to dramatic criticism is the query whether the difference in the reaction to like situations by people who take their theatre seriously is not in itself a comment on what the theatre can do when it exerts its power, making an audience unconsciously share vicariously, or consciously refuse to share, in the play's experience.

February 1934

Four Saints in Three Acts

THE PLEASANTEST event of the month, and the most harmonious, was undoubtedly *Four Saints in Three Acts,* called "an opera to be sung," with words by Gertrude Stein and music by Virgil Thomson. If, after saying that, you add that the words were only partially successful, judging them by their own intention, and that the music was at best happily reminiscent and well-adapted to the form of the performance, and if you go on to say that *Four Saints* is not, as the authors call it, an opera to be sung, but a sung dance, you may lay yourself open to the charge of straining as violently for effect as this violently artificial production itself did; and you are bound to defend such a judgment.

The words, as anyone knows who knows Gertrude Stein, intentionally make no sense. They are supposed to be rhythmic, evocative, and by their sound lend themselves easily to song. Since the words are the basis of the whole production, they must be credited with having evoked in the collaborating artists the working ideas for the delightful scheme, but to a listener they seemed, after the first few moments, and except for a few shining phrases, dully repetitive in their suggestion and often ugly and unsingable.

By pounding out—and over and over again—the names and the qualities of the saints, they evidently evoked in Mr. Virgil Thomson, who was once a church organist, a memory of church music and operatic, churchlike music—reminiscent of Handel, Mendelssohn, Sullivan. With real skill and invention Thomson strung the tunes together on a highly effective melodic and dramatic line. By a masterly stroke, too, he chose for his entire cast Negroes who could be made good singing actors, who took over easily the pace of the music in its pseudo-serious moments, the dancing line in its lighter aspects, and who maintained the mood of solemn nonsense with a balanced freedom and restraint. The beautiful singing of Edward Matthews as St. Ignatius, and his steady adherence to the solemnity of his part, set the tone for unity. The scenery and costumes by Florine Stettheimer were neatly suited to the character of the action and freshly and gaily beautiful in their own right. They may cause an invasion of cellophane cycloramas and scrim palm trees, but they are so entirely right for *Four Saints* that they are altogether wrong for anything else and the impression of Christmas-tree sainthood which they made can never be duplicated.

This then was the background of words, music, light, color, singing and acting that was presented to Frederick Ashton for his dance design, and a considerable share of the success of *Four Saints in Three Acts,* the quality in the performance that made of the large first-night audience a laughing, singing, applauding host, surely belongs to Mr. Ashton, who was responsible not only for the slight dances but for the lovely patterned movement of the rhythm that fused the music and the action and gave life to the designs. There was no external evidence of Mr. Ashton's labors, only the achieved style of the thing itself; and of that style, if you have seen the work of the Ballet Club in London, you recognize the hall-mark. In this lovely theatre prank you see an example of the kind of theatre that Marie Rambert, who has been Frederick Ashton's teacher, has been working towards, that Ashley Dukes is forever talking about, that Copeau and Alice and Irene Lewisohn and the Habima Players understood, that Martha Graham aims at, that Norman Geddes experimented with in *Arabesques,* that Leopold Stokowski plans for, that Robert Edmond Jones has written about. This is theatre that begins with the director and not a kingdom of argument. The pleasanter day will undoubtedly come when we have the same sort of unified production that will be based on beautiful words that mean something and do not deny us altogether the use of our wits, and with music more original, more modern, more theatrical. But it is doubtful whether a more compelling score or a libretto that imposed the interpretation of ideas would (at this moment in theatre history) have left the director and his singing actors free enough of all the traditions to have made so fresh an approach.

April 1934

*

Roll, Sweet Chariot

HENRY JAMES once said that no man loves a woman enough who does not love her more than enough. He might have written the same thing about the theatre. He felt that way about it in spite of the bitterness of his theatrical experience. And surely anyone who does not enter the theatre and sit before the great dropped lids of the curtain eager and enthralled, even while he remembers how often they have opened on infidelity and greed, does not love the theatre enough. He should never be allowed to enter the theatre as a critic. It is the mark of the real theatre passion that should be an essential part of every critic's equipment, that he does not go to the theatre bored, that no matter how bad the last dozen plays have been, he still expects every curtain to rise on some new glory. Usually something does shine for him; if not great glory, at least a little one; the play's theme, if not its writing; if not the leading actor, then someone doing a lesser role; the build-up of a scene or a passage of dialogue; the magic of a setting or direction. Every critic worth his salt goes to the theatre that way, expecting good of it, being neither cynical nor self-centered in his approach. And as long as he does he can never harm the theatre or the theatre's people, no matter how bitter or angry, disappointed or defrauded, he may feel when he leaves. He may be difficult to please, determined in his standard, uncompromising, outspoken, rigorous, but he will never be a toady, he will never be indifferent, and, if he can write at all, his reviews will be more discerning, open-minded and critically generous, even when they are unfavorable, than those of a man who goes gaily but without caring, who is ready to write that everything is "swell," not because he thinks so or thinks at all, but because somebody's money, or somebody's pleasure, or his own pay, is involved. The critic who loves the theatre has had a mighty good time in New York this month. He has seen more fine acting than is usually provided in a year—some of it by players of fame and distinction but much of it by young people in small parts. He has seen expert playwriting and imaginative direction. He has heard lovely music, beautifully sung and heartily applauded.

If he happened to see the first night of Paul Green's *Roll, Sweet Chariot,* he had the thrilling experience of coming unexpectedly upon a great production. The clear, high talent expressed in Paul Green's earlier work, and the advance news of the unusual quality of this "symphonic play of the Negro people" (coming in from a road tryout that was probably not completely in hand) gave no hint of the actual achievement. *Roll, Sweet Chariot* is a great new thing *done,* not worthily *tried,* but beautifully *done.* For years there has been talking and writing of the possibility of modern plays that should use their people and themes as the Elizabethans did, not singly but together, weaving the individual stories into a pattern of character and action, adding to all the strength of each. For years there has been a looking forward to the time when someone would make a play of words and music, not separately but jointly, so that the music should be as integral a part of the play's sound and meaning as the words. *Roll, Sweet Chariot* achieves all this. It is a melodrama about a heterogeneous group of Negroes that live and hang around a boarding house in a run-down settlement that is invaded by a steam roller, building a new road that threatens the isolation of the wretched, inchoate community. *Roll, Sweet Chariot* uses every well-tried element of theatrical emotion—love and crime, jealousy and fear, the presence of poverty and the hope of wealth, pistols, the police, the chain gang. It blends them all through music and the poetry of words, action and fine acting, so that they become humanly exciting and dramatically satisfying and stimulating. The beat of the play goes on within you long after you leave the playhouse. Dolphe Martin's dramatic music, skilfully handled by orchestra and actors, makes him a figure to be reckoned with in any future discussion of music for the theatre.

As one of the singing actors, Frank Wilson, who has played well every part he attempted—*Porgy, The Emperor Jones, In Abraham's Bosom,* and many other plays—gains a new flexibility and eloquence in his role of the laborer Levin Farrow. Lloyd Horton as Doodle Wilson the boy preacher, Philip Carter as Bad Eye Smith, Luoneal Mason as Bantam Wilson, Eleanor Wallace as Quiviene Lockley, and many others of the large group give performances finely characterized, powerful, genuine. What Warren Coleman, playing the taxing role of the false "John Henry," lacks during the play in outline and emphasis, he makes up for in the Epilogue—in which he leads the procession of the chain gang singing and digging the long road through Potter's Field.

Roll, Sweet Chariot is melodrama in the grand manner of the theatre. It is far ahead of anything Paul Green has done—of *In Abraham's Bosom,* that won the Pulitzer Prize, of *Field God* and *The House of Connelly*. But it is not Paul Green's play alone, and he would be the first person to say so. It belongs to the new theatre that uses imaginatively all the means at its command.

November 1934

*

Within the Gates

AS IT IS PRODUCED in the New York theatre, with the lavish talents of an unusually fine company devoted to its performance, *Within the Gates* comes out as a moving drama, with "simple austerity, swinging merriment, beauty in music of word and color of scene, and [almost, but not quite] with a tragedy too deep for tears." Those are the qualities that Mr. O'Casey desires to bring back to the theatre, according to his own words in an interview he gave to *The New York Times* before the play opened. Those are, indeed, the qualities inherent in the best lines and scenes of *Within the Gates*. Seeing it performed is a rich theatre experience, after which it is difficult to say that *Within the Gates* seemed, in the writing, for long stretches at a time, only sentimental and banal for all the earnest simplicity of its intention.

Mr. O'Casey complains of the critics in London that "the play was over their heads, and so they began to trample it under their feet." They were perplexed by it, he says; yet it is an obvious play, the elaborate symbolism quite elementary, and even old-fashioned, if such a word can ever be fairly applied to any statement of man's relationship to man and woman and nature and religion. *Within the Gates* has none of the high perplexity of the author's beautiful, tormenting *Silver Tassie,* which went down to critic's damnation a few years ago, as Paul Green's *Roll, Sweet Chariot* went a few weeks ago, to the theatre's great loss. Perhaps the playing and direction, the costumes and design in London were less lovely and creative than they were in New York. One does not know, of course; but it is certain that there has seldom been a script to which the director, Melvyn Douglas, the designer, James Reynolds, the composers, Milton Lusk and A. Lehman Engel, and especially the actors have contributed so much as to this production of *Within the Gates*. They have lifted every part of the play to the level of the author's best work; singly and together they have achieved to the full every opportunity the play presented or suggested for freedom, richness and harmony. If *Within the Gates* is poetry's gift to the theatre, Mr. O'Casey is not the only poet to be credited with the offering, although he wrote all the words and some of them are as golden as The Dreamer's song and the Chorus of Down-and-Outs, and other lines like these:

> Through the lovely confusion of singing of
> birds and of blossom and bud.

or

> Till the wide ear of the wide world is deafen'd
> with wisdom!

Within the Gates is a panoramic play about life as it might appear to those who come and go through Hyde Park in the four seasons of life's year. The Church, the State, the Salvation Army, youth and old age, wisdom and folly, poetry, music, dance, creation and death are all there, meeting life half-way or fighting it off, or meeting it full-face and going out with it gaily on the road to death, as The Young Whore goes, who is in a way the protagonist of the play. When you read *Within the Gates* it is easy to imagine Lillian Gish in this part, to see her as you have always seen her in the movies and on the stage, with that filmy, floating, slightly supernal quality which is at once the essence of her strength and her peculiar weakness. She might reasonably have played The Young Whore in that key, with little effort to herself. Instead, she raised the part to a new thing, bigger than what she found on the page—to a frail, hard, living, dying, bold, sensitive, suffering, dancing creature, who knew better than any of the others what O'Casey meant in the first line of the Spring Chorus:

> Our mother, the earth is a maiden again,
> young, fair, and a maiden again.

The vigor and sound and clear definition of Miss Gish's playing ran like a line of light through the performance. Perhaps some of the other actors might not have clarified their parts so well if Miss Gish had not given them the key. Perhaps, on the other hand, she might not have been able to hold her line so steadily and forcefully if they had done a little less well. Moffat Johnston played the hypocritical Bishop (an obsolescent character for the theatre although there may well be Bishops like that), and he is always a bulwark for the players around him. Barry Macollum and John Daly Murphy were both good as a sort of two-part chorus—"symbols of life's wreckage." Mr. Murphy has forgotten more about fine acting (and remembered more, especially about ensemble playing) than most people ever learn. Bramwell Fletcher as The Dreamer, Morris Ankrum as The Atheist, Byron McGrath as The Young Salvation Army Officer, Ralph Cullinan as The Foreman, Stanley Wood as the disputatious Man in the Bowler Hat—altogether they and their forty fellows made a fine company. Altogether they made you grateful to Bushar and Tuerk, the producers of the play, for the wisely generous casting, the obviously generous rehearsal, the vividly generous line and color and scale of the production.

December 1934

*

Winterset

WINTERSET, Maxwell Anderson's newest play, presented by Guthrie McClintic with settings by Jo Mielziner, is a companion-piece to *Paths of Glory,* telling of the depths to which life can sink in a world at peace, if you can call a world at peace in which men are continually battling with one another against lust and power, fear and hunger. For setting, the play builds one of the great towers of approach to a Manhattan bridge under which, early one December morning, the day begins for a small world of men and women without a home, some without a name, who hide from the cold, or from the law, or from revenge. Before night falls on *Winterset,* even this bitter life has ended for many of them, the young and the old. How it happens is told in one of the most exciting gangster melodramas, one of the noblest poetic plays, one of the hardest-hitting, straightest-fighting, crusading dramas against the fruits of injustice ever presented on the American stage.

It is a commonplace in writing about Maxwell Anderson to say that his plays run a dual course—the work of a poet (*Elizabeth the Queen, Night Over Taos* and *Valley Forge*) on one hand, and of a journalist with a conscience (*What Price Glory?* and *Both Your Houses*) on the other. In *Winterset* the two ways meet.

Just after the execution of Sacco and Vanzetti, Maxwell Anderson (with Harold Hickerson) wrote *Gods of the Lightning,* an angry, deeply offended, excited journalist-playwright's protest against what he considered a miscarriage of justice. *Gods of the Lightning* was a noble-hearted venture, but not a good enough play to do the job it set out to do. It was a propagandist's play, an attempt to use the theatre to make men *see* and believe facts they would not *read* and believe, or believe enough to fight for. But facts and anger, even in a noble cause, do not make good plays. Men and women who cared about what happened to Sacco and Vanzetti, or about abstract justice, cared about *Gods of the Lightning*. The others said, "Too bad, but what's done cannot be undone. They were anarchists, anyway. Not a very good play. They're dead; to whom can it matter now?" *Winterset* is the artist's answer to that final question.

It mattered so much to Maxwell Anderson that for years the "why" and "upon whom" social injustice wreaks its final vengeance has burned in the crucible of his imagination. The answer comes in the form of this poetic play, this exciting human story of how such a wrong festers in society until it destroys the mind of the judge who fears that he may have made an error in convicting an innocent man; wrecks the victim's son, who wanders through his whole life in search of evidence to prove his father's innocence, alone except for a great hate for society; adds the last measure of brutality to the leader of the gang who ordered the murder, and to his henchman who fired the gun; involves a boy who was a witness to the shooting but kept his mouth shut to save his own skin, and the boy's old father who has no place in any world that is newer than the Talmud, and the boy's young sister who, by an accident of fate (*Winterset* is a story of fate), is the final link in the chain between innocence and crime, love and hate, life and death.

It takes a little time to make your adjustment, watching the play, to the manner in which Maxwell Anderson has put—intentionally, of course—the years that have passed, the age of the characters, the places in which things happened or are happening, somewhat out of focus, distorting the actuality to give the play greater perspective. The adjustment once made, however, you realize how the contrivance adds to the power of the performance, heightening much of the sordid detail at the same time that it relieves the emphasis on the personal and the accidental.

If *Winterset,* as play material, is a companion-piece to *Paths of Glory,* so it is on the level of the acting. Richard Bennett is the judge gone mad with worry; he plays the distraught and broken mind with a discernment that is not only the fruit of long human and theatrical experience but an actor's inspiration. Eduardo Ciannelli as Trock, the leader of the gang, and Harold Johnsrud as the gunman, Shadow, manage somehow to add to the realistic portrayal just the right shade of unreality which attaches to the gangster as he lives and acts among us in our own day. Theodore Hecht is Garth, the boy who wants to live and play the violin more than he wants to tell the truth, and his sister, Miriamne, is Margo, a young actor-dancer brought on from Hollywood, who in face and form, voice and gesture, and quality of emotion, fits so smoothly into the part and is carried up so easily and entirely by its mystery and poetry that it is difficult to tell how much of what she does is acting; all that you can say is that she does the difficult role a beautiful justice.

And then there is Burgess Meredith, who came to Broadway only four years ago, and who is already remembered for such varied characterizations as Red Barry in *Little Ol' Boy,* Buz Jones, the wild collegian, in *She Loves Me Not,* and the young, sick genius, Leonard Dobie, in *Flowers of the Forest.* What Meredith does with the part of Mio, the son of the law's victim, will be remembered when he is old as one of the finest, freest and yet most completely balanced of poetic theatre portraits. It is an extraordinary piece of work for a young man to do. He seems to have all the actor's tools at his command—voice, gesture, body and mind, clear, resonant speech, the power of long steady tension and quick release, an instinctive rightness of tempo for each scene and an unusual range of emotional quality. He takes the double realistic, poetic characterization and fuses it into one, takes the short speeches in a rhythm that sharpens them to a point, and holds out the longer ones (sometimes too long for the action)—giving the phrases back to the audience in the full measure that the poet-playwright has given them, even when the playwright seems wrong. It is a grand job, and if Burgess Meredith is fortunate to find so fat a part, Maxwell Anderson is fortunate to have found an actor who can handle so complex a part so valiantly.

November 1935

Paradise Lost; Nazimova in Ghosts

WHEN CLIFFORD ODETS, the author of *Paradise Lost,* came onto the stage to take a curtain-call at the end of the play's first night, it was not only the audience that applauded his entrance, it was the actors too; in fact, theirs was the more vociferous response. And when in the morning papers a day later an advertisement signed "The Group Theatre" appeared, saying "We believe Clifford Odets' *Paradise Lost* is a great and important play. We are proud to present it," the words in print were an echo of the players' applause. The Group Theatre believes in its playwright, which is a matter of first importance to many others besides themselves. For one of the chief values that a complete and permanent organization set down in the center of an inchoate theatre world can contribute to that world comes through having at least one playwright, and preferably more, steadily at work with the other artists of the group in solving the problems whose answers are the expression of their common faith. In such a scheme, the best equipped playwright may stumble along the way and cause his companions to stumble, but the Group cannot complain of that embarrassment. Odets is the outstanding talent among them; he has moved steadily and rapidly forward. He has given the group not only release but success with more than the usual measure of critical acclaim. He has earned their faith.

Paradise Lost is not a great play, as the Group thinks it is. But it is without doubt an important play because in material and method it marks the fresh, swift advance of a young dramatist who not only thinks and feels deeply but whose writing talents are essentially and in an unusual degree theatre talents: the power to state a situation in terms of its most dramatic elements, to observe and define character, to write active dialogue, to conquer attention.

Paradise Lost, so far as one can interpret Mr. Odets through the play and through what he has said about it in print, aims to be the story of the disintegration of the middle-class liberals in America under the capitalist system and their hope of redemption through a new social system. This is almost exactly the theme of *Awake and Sing,* except that in the earlier play Mr. Odets chose a family in the Bronx as his protagonist, and tried to prove his thesis from his type. In *Paradise Lost* he has broadened his canvas "to find a theatrical form with which to express the mass as herd." That is a master playwright's task, and you will judge Mr. Odets' zeal in attempting it according to whether you admire his courage more than you deplore his complacency. *Paradise Lost* cannot be said to have set a new goal for the mass-as-hero plays; even Hauptmann and Toller did the job better, but only because they were wiser, not because they were braver.

Leo Gordon is a gentle, honest, pocket-book designer with a bright philosophic vision but little insight into the characters or the events around him, little understanding even of the lives of his own wife or children, not to mention the dishonest partner with whom he has been associated for more than twenty years. The Gordons appear at first to be simply "the family" again. But if, as audience, you use your own imagination you soon realize that Mr. Odets seems to mean that Gordon, his crude wife and maladjusted children, their hangers-on, and the politicians and bums used to heighten the scene of the play here and there, together represent the whole round circle of the "middle class" that is doomed to destruction. The home (whose slightly frayed prosperity is still represented at the play's opening by fruit on the table, a son's dinner clothes, the mother's fur-trimmed coat) gradually breaks under the strain of financial and social disaster. Sickness, dishonesty, cruelty, adultery, crime and violent death crawl out of the walls and, before the play's end, overwhelm the occupants of the house, all except Leo Gordon himself, who just at the final moment suddenly sees the light that can come through a changed order.

It is good, in these cowardly days when old men are afraid to think freely, to see a young man boldly hitting out for a new paradise, convinced not only that he knows what is wrong and why, but that he can, quite surely, put us all on the real right road out of a world's unrighteousness that tortures him. "Take it from me," he seems to say; and whether you take it or not, you must be impressed by his earnestness and his ideals.

Such a subjective method applied to playwriting has, of course, its obvious penalties. As you watch the play, you find the playwright himself recurrently, and insistently, showing through his characters, and pretty soon you find yourself judging not the play but the playwright, saying to yourself, "This boy thinks the Bronx is the world. He is not only cock-sure, but naively inexperienced." Someone should tell him that the Gordons, and Gus Michaels (the not too full-witted family friend), his unclean daughter, her gangster lover, and Mr. Pike (the aristocratic furnace man), Phil Foley (the crooked ward politician), the insurance man who suggests arson, and the homeless philosophers, while they may be American citizens, are not in any sense representative of the middle-class, nor is there anything in their thinking or acting to indicate that they are liberal. They are the dregs of the social system, money-loving, money-starved capitalists who have gone rotten through spinelessness and the frustration of their own golden longings. No revolution would help them. They are too old—every one of them, but especially the young ones.

All of this only means that Mr. Odets has not made you accept either his first premise or his conclusion. But between the two there still stands a play of more than usual power, observation, tension.

It may be remembered that Harold Clurman, who directed *Paradise Lost,* in some notes from the diary of a Russian visit printed last November, quoted Stanislavski as saying, "Tell Mr. Odets for me not to give up acting. It will always help him in his playwriting. When he needs time off to write a play, give him the time, but let him continue to act." The special quality in Odets' playwriting that the actors of the Group applaud and that is the most developed facet of his talent is related to his own acting experience—although it is by no means accounted for by that alone. His plays are made to the measure of his actors; there is nothing he demands of them, no characterization, no action, no conflict, that is beyond the reach of a fairly competent player. He knows how and why and when actors should speak, when the emphasis should be on the character who is speaking, on the immediate situation, on the play's theme. Not all of the players in *Paradise Lost* realize the whole of Mr. Odets' intention for them. But where they do not it is their fault rather than his. Where a player is able to take Mr. Odets' sharp outline and fill it in, and make it grow as Roman Bohnen does with Gus Michaels or Elia Kazan with Kewpie, the young gangster, you get a figure that is alive and personal. Even when he takes only what Odets gives him, as Sanford Meisner does with Julie, the younger son afflicted with sleeping-sickness, or Morris Carnovsky with Leo Gordon or Grover Burgess with Mr. Pike, the furnace man, you still get more than the average of character portrayal.

Odets' speech, moreover, when it is not affected, or perhaps it is more generous to say when it is not affected by his desire to try the higher flights of poetry, almost speaks itself, it is so exactly and seems so instinctively right for the stage—even if it is not always rightly adjusted to the individual character. Half of the strength of *Waiting for Lefty* was the strength of speech, clear, simple, expressive, every word doing its work singly and as a part of a phrase, a speech, a scene. In *Paradise Lost* Odets has carried both of these marked talents—the talent for the word and for writing an actors' play—far ahead of what he did in *Awake and Sing*.

Nazimova's performance of Mrs. Alving in Ibsen's *Ghosts* is something to remember. Having watched her with mounting interest and sympathy and admiration during the course of the bitter drama which stirred the world of the theatre so deeply years ago, and almost challenging her to stir us with it today, the whole great audience in the old Empire Theatre sat breathless at the end of the play, when Mrs. Alving stands before her only son, stricken by his father's sin, and hesitates for a full half minute, wondering whether she dares to give him the poison he has begged of her. That moment of silent tension bespoke more appreciation than applause would have done. Nazimova had made *Ghosts* live and walk again.

Nazimova plays Mrs. Alving quietly, intensely, far less vigorously than Mary Shaw did, and Mary Shaw's was perhaps more the way that Ibsen meant, more the northern and less the introspective Russian way. For if Mrs. Alving did not make the sacrifice of a strong personal power and a fullness of desire in order—for her son's sake—to live under the rod of a horrible duty to her husband, the sacrifice might not in its day, when the woman's problem was immediate and potent, have seemed quite great enough. But the special social silence that made Mrs. Alving's tragedy inevitable in Ibsen's day is neither true enough today, on the one hand, nor remote enough, on the other, to seem inevitable to us a single generation later. The details of *Ghosts* are, it must be said, a little old-fashioned in 1935. What Nazimova does to the play—not only to her part in it—is to separate the temporary argument from the eternal, to take from the situation all of its elemental values and give us not so much Ibsen's Mrs. Alving as the woman of any age who finds her motherhood betrayed, and who comes before us at the moment when nature interferes to settle the account. Taken on that basis, Nazimova's performance is very nearly perfect, full of variety, showing a hundred angles of her character, fluid and steadily mounting in strength and in suffering. It is a performance to be grateful for.

McKay Morris playing Pastor Manders, and Raymond O'Brien as Jacob Engstrand, give her sufficient, if not distinguished, support. Ona Munson was cast out of her range as Regina; but, on the other hand, Harry Ellerbe as Oswald Alving widened his range distinctly to meet a part larger and more difficult than any he has played before.

February 1936

*

Saint Joan

ONE OF THE essential differences between a saint and a lawmaker is that a saint, for whom there is no might but righteousness, beyond and apart from self, attains his ends by faith in a superior spirit that works through him, and not through a power delegated to him by his inferiors. The saints are closer to the arts than the lawmakers; their aloofness seems to forbid the average painter, sculptor, playwright—especially the playwright—from trying to do a part of their job for them, perhaps because the average man is willing to grant the saints their privilege of martyrdom, but the humblest sees himself a potential improvement on any lawmaker.

Even Saint Joan and Thomas à Becket, two very argumentative martyrs in the hands of two very argumentative dramatists, G. B. Shaw and T. S. Eliot, manage to keep their sainthood—and their theatricality—in command over their interpreters, at a time when dictators, economists, politicians and the lesser household tyrants are failing ignobly to assert themselves. . . .

Saint Joan believed in the Voices that spoke through her, that were not the peasant girl of Domremy but Saint Catherine, Saint Margaret and Saint Michael. Except for the short months of her defeat, imprisonment and death, she made others believe in those Voices for the length of her young life and for centuries after her death. Such a saint, such an historic figure, such a dramatic personality, is a "natural" on any stage that has faith in its rightness for the task, and that can make an audience believe in Joan and fight her battles by her side. . . .

An actress-manager who trusted the theatre less than Katharine Cornell does, and who still wanted to produce *Saint Joan,* might easily have focused her faith on her own undoubted talents, have chosen a designer and a director who would point up the values in Shaw's play as a star vehicle for an actress, and have surrounded herself with players little enough to make her seem big by contrast. But the theatre has now come to know that that is not the way Katharine Cornell works. If the play is too long for ordinary attention, the individual speeches too big for the average actor to handle, the play's theme too magnificent for our own mental habit, she will, with Guthrie McClintic's cooperation and his skill as director, not scale it down, but scale it up still more. She will choose a designer—Jo Mielziner—who instead of detracting from the vibrant color and pattern of the period will add a slight, very slight, edge of elegance to the setting, the costumes, the light, which will remove the play at once from hurried, immediate reality, and take it up into the world of poetry and painting where we have become accustomed to sit and look and listen.

She will engage actors like Arthur Byron who, by the range and mellowness of their voices and the sustained continuity of their projection, can compel attention for even such a long, difficult, philosophical speech as that of the Inquisitor, Brother John Lemaître, at Joan's trial, one of the finest theatre speeches in all modern drama, without the fullness of which the play would never make explicit the death of the conflict between the Maid and the established order represented by the Church and the Feudal System. She will give time and point to scenes in which she has no part, like the religious-political discussion between Peter Cauchon, the Bishop of Beauvais; Richard de Beauchamp, Earl of Warwick; and Master John de Stogumber—and put actors like Eduardo Ciannelli and George Coulouris so on their mettle that they play better than they have ever played before. She will give Maurice Evans, playing the Dauphin, such scope in the creation of the strange and difficult role that you will accept his unaccounted Cockney accent without objection, because it belongs to a characterization that is free and creative, and that expresses so well the weak and muddled spirit of the king and the temporal kingdom for which Joan fought, thinking she was fighting heaven's fight. At the moment of Joan's triumph, pushing forward to the ramparts of Orléans, and at the moment of her greatest tribulation, when the tide of the trial is finally overwhelming her, instead of turning the scenes inward upon herself in a star's way, she will open them up widely enough to include young players like Kent Smith (as Dunois, the Bastard of Orléans) and John Cromwell (as Martin Ladvenu), so that they spontaneously turn back to her an enriched opportunity.

In *Saint Joan* Shaw has aimed to retrieve both a martyr and her judges from the legends in which their humanity was interred. The play is a study of a girl who sees clearly because she is never blinded by fear or prejudice, who becomes a prey to society because "fear will drive men to any extreme: and the fear inspired by a superior being is a mystery which cannot be reasoned away."

The qualities that mark Katharine Cornell's conception of the part of Saint Joan are all in Shaw's portrait: the joyous, simple faith in the Voices and her humble dedication to their service; her blatant pride before men, the vanity that makes her love her youth's clothes and her uniform, the boyishness that demands an equal association with soldiers and their commanders. Out of these elements Katharine Cornell builds up her Joan from the inspired village girl who comes to the castle at Vaucouleurs, asking for a guard to take her to the King, through the leadership of the King's forces and the hour of triumph, to the tragic final day as a sorcerer and heretic. Through the scene of the trial—one of the season's memorable hours—she weaves all these elements of character like counterpoint against the fears, the bitterness, the narrowness of her opponents, lifting the scene up so that when she is finally led forth to the burning in the public square you are there with her, and at the same time she is still there with you in the hall of the castle, the scene of the trial, where Joan remains alive in spirit to this day.

May 1936

Hamlet

THERE HAS probably been no production in years more eagerly awaited than that of John Gielgud's *Hamlet,* produced by Guthrie McClintic, with Lillian Gish as Ophelia, Judith Anderson as the Queen, Arthur Byron as Polonius, and Jo Mielziner setting the stage. Gielgud first played Hamlet at the Old Vic in London in the season of 1929-30 and made his own London production of the play in 1934 with extraordinary success. At that time Ashley Dukes wrote of him: "Speaking always to himself as Hamlet must, whether in soliloquy or otherwise, he so beautifully conveys the conversation of mind with mind that the most familiar line comes with an element of surprise, fresh-wrought although inevitable." Charles Morgan said, "If I see a better performance of the play than this before I die, it will be a miracle." And a few weeks ago, when the new American production of the play with Gielgud as Hamlet opened in Toronto, a critic there said that if Gielgud had ever seen anyone else play the part, he must have forgotten it, his own performance was so fresh, strong and inevitable.

Not a word of this is a word too much of praise when applied to Gielgud's performance. The thing that immediately distinguishes him from other great players of the role is that he—the Gielgud-Hamlet and the Hamlet-Gielgud—is such a young man, a young prince, good, noble, affectionate, desolated by the loss of his honored and beloved father and by his mother's too-quick marriage with his uncle, and tortured by his own inexperience of life, by lack of all the impulse to direct action of which a happy life in a pleasant royal home has deprived him. Most actors wait until they have reached maturity—in technique as well as in person—before essaying (or at least before mastering) the part of Hamlet. Gielgud has the rare advantage of having maturity and youth together; a native skill and craftsmanship added to an innate understanding; a mind and a body both perfectly tuned—as well as trained—to performance. He knows —each moment—exactly how Hamlet feels. He has forgotten nothing. And with his rare gift of projection, he flings that feeling across the footlights, stirring the emotion of the audience, establishing and maintaining a tension—in them—that leaves him free to go on building to superb, and superbly simple, climaxes.

Gielgud is quoted as saying that he will not play Hamlet after he is thirty-five. You see why at once, when you see him in the part; but he can safely play it at fifty—the young man's spirit will not fail him simply because the clock of time has ticked off a few more years. John Gielgud is every inch an actor, but he is more than an actor, he is an actor-poet. And this Shakespeare at the grand old Empire Theatre that houses it so well is all a poet's play, a poet's words spoken with a poet's ringing voice that never fails to give a syllable its best advantage.

There have been many notable performances of *Hamlet,* even in the limited theatre of our time, but none of them has achieved, so completely as this, the triumph of Shakespeare's poetry—of the words themselves, the richness and clarity of their tone, the philosophy and humanity of the story they tell, the grand procession of their lines, their essential theatric value. This *Hamlet* is not always "blank verse"; it is poetic drama, every inch of it. The great speeches are not set apart; the lesser passages flow into them with an unaltered strength and security. You hope that they will have this added power the moment you hear Hamlet begin:

> A little more than kin, and less than kind.

You believe it when he says:

> But I have that within, which passeth show;

and again:

> How weary, stale, flat, and unprofitable
> Seem to me all the uses of this world!
> Fie on't! O fie! 'tis an unweeded garden,
> That grows to seed; things rank, and gross in nature,
> Possess it merely.

You know it beyond question, when he cries:

> Mother, for love of grace,
> Lay not that flattering unction to your soul,
> That not your trespass, but my madness speaks.

You marvel at it afresh as the grand lines in the Fortinbras scene (usually omitted) come rolling out in their unfamiliar majesty.

Besides youth and verbal beauty, there is another feature that sets off this presentation: the aspiration behind it, the obvious will of everybody concerned in the making of the show to add to its sum the best of what he has to give. To Guthrie McClintic, of course, must go, graciously and appreciatively, the credit for the company he has assembled, as well as for the unity and quality he has contributed to the direction of the performance. Jo Mielziner's settings are not only nobly conceived and designed, but they seem to be more beautifully painted than theatre settings usually are. The costumes are a satisfaction to the eye. The lighting follows always the exact mood of the scene. And all of this enveloping material advantage seems to be there on the stage to give the players bounds and liberty for their accomplishment. It might have been expected that Arthur Byron would make Polonius count in this ensemble, both as father and as politician; that Lillian Gish would have the perfect accent and the line of gentle grace for Ophelia's madness; that Judith Anderson would equip the Queen with a majestic terror; and that Malcolm Keen would give a good account of the trying role of the ignoble King. But there was in each performance something better than the actor's natural best, something taken from the store of their joint desire to make this *Hamlet* a memorable performance.

November 1936

*

Of Mice and Men

OF MICE AND MEN, John Steinbeck's dramatization of his own story, never fails, never even falters for a moment in its achievement. It is a perfect piece of dramatic writing in a small frame. It is simple, rich and authentic, with a foundation set strongly in a social situation that has within it every element of drama, and with a structure built as strongly on the characters and the human relationships that arise inevitably out of the situation. The dialogue is perfect—direct, revealing, brutally true, so uninhibited as to leave no place for implication, expressive of the ranch life it represents and of the natures of the men who speak it. The drama is the perfect example of what a social play can be, without a line or a word of preachment, with only an artist's creative presentation of his theme and his characters. There is no personal resentment showing through Steinbeck's work, but only pity, deep pity, for the men to whom such things happen in our day, and for the men that let them happen. To the author's accomplishment George S. Kaufman has added a perfect piece of direction with exactly the pace, the movement, the emotional crescendo and the pauses that enrich the action. Donald Oenslager's setting is a perfect piece of stage design that acts like an echo of the story and never insists upon itself. And *Of Mice and Men* is as nearly perfect an acted work as any play with ten characters can be. This is extravagant praise, and *Of Mice and Men* offers extravagant enjoyment of all the arts of the theatre, an enjoyment complete within the range the drama sets for itself.

The burden of acting falls on Broderick Crawford as Lennie—the great, powerful man with the mind of a child and hands so strong that they crush the living things he touches most lovingly—and Wallace Ford as George—the intelligent, lonely, itinerant rancher, who has made the defense of Lennie his life work, who could have kept his jobs and lived so easily if he could have gone his way alone, unburdened by the need to have some human soul that needed him. It would be difficult to recall in our theatre—where actors have so little opportunity to learn each other's methods and to embellish each other's playing—two men who have played so harmoniously and creatively together, complementing, clarifying, enriching, constantly heightening each other's stature. From the moment that the curtain rises on the little opening in the woods, down the road from the ranch where they are headed, George and Lennie become a part of your own living experience, and you share with George the knowledge that is so much surer than foreboding, that here in this quiet spot where the little river flows under the broad-branched trees, Lennie will pay the price of death which our society so often demands for misfortunes like Lennie's.

Among the men crowded together in the bunkhouse, each dreaming of having his own bit of land to work some day, the acting is on almost the same high level. John F. Hamilton as Candy, the old man with the crippled arm and the half-blind, wretched dog; Thomas Findlay as the boss; Sam Byrd as Curley, his braggart son; Will Geer as Slim, the team driver; Charles Slattery as Carlson and Walter Baldwin as Whit, add their share to the canvas. And out in the barn, in the room with a manure pile under the window, a room which he has to himself because he is a black man and cannot go into the white man's bunkhouse, Leigh Whipper as Crooks makes the pitiful picture complete. Complete so far as the men go; but there is also Claire Luce, Curley's vain and lonely wife, with her showy legs, who cannot stay away from the men, and who offers her golden hair to Lennie to stroke because she wants somebody else to notice how soft it is. The way in which John Steinbeck has joined, inseparably, the portraits of George and Lennie and then fused them into the larger picture is only surpassed in dramatic execution by the scene in the barn between Lennie and Curley's wife, sitting so close, thinking so separately each of himself, so fatally united.

January 1938

* *

ROSAMOND GILDER

*

Leave It to Me!

. . . THE INCREDIBLE INEPTITUDES, the waste of money and talent, the stupidities, commercial and artistic, of nearly half the winter's offerings can almost be forgotten, if not forgiven, in rejoicing over the restoration of song and dance to the bosom of a doting public.

Victor Moore leads the way, his body borne precariously ahead of his unwilling legs, his moon face riding high over a wrack of packages, his smile tentative, ingratiating. He is, as always, in a tough spot. Through the machinations of Bella and Samuel Spewack who evolved *Leave It to Me!* from their own comedy, *Clear All Wires,* and Vinton Freedley who produced it, Victor Moore, in the guise of Alonzo P. Goodhue, a mild middle-western business man, finds himself heading for Moscow where he is to take up his duties as American Ambassador. This in itself is bad enough, for Alonzo is a home-body who cares nothing for foreign affairs, but the plot is seriously complicated by the fact that one J. H. Brody covets the honor Goodhue despises, and is determined to do him in. He is aided and abetted in this intention by Buckley Joyce Thomas (alias William Gaxton), an enterprising newspaperman who blithely undertakes to ruin Goodhue and get him recalled. The resulting international imbroglio brings Victor Moore and William Gaxton together again in a riotous evening of unalloyed delights for which Cole Porter has written some of his gayest tunes and lyrics, Albert Johnson has designed two memorable railroad stations and some acceptable interiors and Raoul Pène du Bois has whipped together a frothy collection of colorful costumes.

"For God's sake, can't you do the *wrong* thing?" Gaxton asks Moore in a sudden fury of despair when his efforts to get the Ambassador into hot water have all failed. As far as the audience is concerned the answer is *no*. Whether he is Vice-President or Public Enemy Number 13, whether he is Throttlebottom, Goodhue or just plain Stinky-to-his-friends, Victor Moore can do no wrong. His attack on that section of the human anatomy which harbors idiot laughter is infallible. The mirth he provokes is unorthodox, as far as the philosophers are concerned, for it is not thoughtful as Meredith would have it, nor does it spring from any desire to instruct or correct as the learned doctors insist it should. It is a laughter born of sympathy, compounded of smiles and chuckles. Victor Moore is the Timid Soul in person, terrified by a bustling, competent world, browbeaten by his womenfolk. He is friendly among the ruthless, trusting among the predatory—eager for simple joys. "I want to go back to old Topeka" is a plaintive wail, a parody of all home and mammy songs, an exquisite caricature, which has yet a spark of eternal truth.

Like all great comedians, Victor Moore has the gift of projecting without words a sequence of thought and mood. In the scene with the Nazi emissary his face is a comic battleground. On it are registered in lightning succession a series of conflicting emotions: his dislike of the paunchy bully who stands at attention before him; his desire to give him a swift kick in the belly; his terror at the mere thought of such an action; his growing excitement as he glances from Gaxton who is silently urging him on, to the tempting, khaki-clad midriff before him; his despairing appraisal of his own weakness, in contrast with the other's rigid strength; his mischievous appreciation of the ludicrous effect of making that complacent balloon collapse and his sudden resolution. The black-out comes before Moore moves, but the projected action and its ridiculous consequences have already been seen by the audience, mirrored in his expressive face.

The genius of comic acting lies largely in the skill with which such moments are elaborated. Sometimes it is a matter of business: packages that fall to the ground and have to be picked up, mechanisms that refuse to work, the malice of inanimate objects. Moore's performance abounds in these bits of completely lunatic entertainment, comic cadenzas embroidered on a simple theme. In the scene following that with the Nazi envoy he has received a cable from Washington which he blissfully hopes will contain his recall. Aided by Gaxton, he proceeds to decode the telegram, looking each phrase up in his book and writing the message syllable by syllable on a large blackboard. The code is made up of the first lines of familiar songs and as he turns the pages of his little book he bellows out the line again and again until he has found the right place and written the decoded word on the blackboard. All the elements of masterly clowning are used in this brief scene—perfect timing, exactly the right amount of reiteration, concentration, contrast and frustration. He plays the whole scene with consummate skill, sensing to a nicety just what volume of voice, what amount of repetition, will land his laughs. His many years in vaudeville have given him a sixth sense with which to gauge his audience and carry it with him through these moon-struck moments.

Sophie Tucker also has the sure vaudevillian touch. One line, one simple musical phrase, is enough for her. Before she has finished with that little lyric beginning, "Most gentlemen don't like love," every possible (and impossible) variation on the theme has been juggled in the air and tossed across the footlights. Rubicund and hearty in her robust maturity, her very presence is a guarantee against gloom. She is the perfect foil for Moore, and their rendering of a travel ditty entitled "From the USA to the USSR" provides the happiest combination of two expert talents. Gaxton brings his familiar cheerleader drive to enliven the proceedings, and Mary Martin, on this her first appearance in New York, hits the bull's-eye with an edifying strip-tease executed on the Russian Steppes, during which she explains, quite clearly, that her "heart belongs to Daddy." With plenty of plot involving "Buck" Thomas and Collette (sung by Tamara), Dolly and her Daddy, Mrs. Goodhue and her five daughters, and some unusually good dancing on the part of the

Buccaneers and Les Girls, the new Cole Porter ticket, carrying those old Presidential team-mates Gaxton and Moore, is already running up a heavy vote.

January 1939

*

War Plays; There Shall Be No Night; Watch on the Rhine

TWO YEARS of war have had very little effect on the New York theatre, but they have produced a few outstanding plays dealing directly with the subject. If the Spanish War plays, *Key Largo* and *The Fifth Column,* are included, the total for the past two seasons is five—with *The Wookey,* six. The attack in all these plays, except the last, has been profoundly serious. The authors have attempted in each case to show war with all the horror and stupidity that it presents to any rational mind, yet to distil from that horror and that stupidity some constructive meaning. Maxwell Anderson crystallized his belief in the last moments of *Key Largo* when his protagonist who by running away and saving his skin in the Spanish War had, in a sense, lost his soul—wins through to a new perception of the meaning of life:

> It doesn't come to us all. It comes to many in certain generations, comes to only a few in others; and it says, if you want to live you must die now . . .
>
> A man must die for what he believes—if he's unfortunate enough to have to face it in his time—and if he won't then he'll end up believing in nothing at all —and that's death, too.

In *The Fifth Column* Ernest Hemingway's hard-bitten journalist acts in the end on the same impulse. Tempted to leave Spain when all hope of winning the fight is over, he sticks it out, determined to die a futile and grubby death rather than turn his back on comrades who must remain to the end in a losing fight. The whole action of these two earlier plays evolves around the hero's struggle to remain steadfast when defeat, discouragement and above all the searing light of common sense show another way out.

In the current war plays the forces are more closely engaged. The protagonists of *There Shall Be No Night* which has recently reopened on the road, and *Watch on the Rhine,* still running in New York, have each locked horns with the adversary. There is no question here of evading the issue; there is only the inevitability of death which must somehow be accepted and justified. It is interesting to see how the two authors, both expert craftsmen of the theatre, present on the stage the material with which they are so deeply concerned. Mr. Sherwood sets before his audience immediately the type of man, the type of aspiration, of thinking and living that seem to him the most important product of civilization. Dr. Valkonen, a role which Alfred Lunt has made his own, is a scientist, an intellectual. He is engaged in important research; he has made radical discoveries for the benefit and amelioration of all mankind. His sympathies, his friendships, his vision are international; his private life is honorable. He is a kindly, gentle, humane man—a non-political animal, desiring only to be left in peace so that he may devote himself wholly to his complex and far-reaching inquiries and to the simple pleasures of his hearth and home. All this Mr. Sherwood conveys within five minutes of the rising of the curtain. At the same time he introduces the antagonist—the threat against all intellectual and spiritual growth which the present mad outbreak of violence and obscurantism has released.

The struggle in the play is the struggle in Valkonen's mind to understand the reason for and accept the necessity of undeserved suffering—the old tragic issue. The answer is forecast in Valkonen's first speech, when he quotes Jung as saying, "There is no coming to consciousness without pain." Finally, after the battle has been lost, Valkonen's son killed, his own death imminent, he formulates his belief that this suffering and death is a symbol—"a little symbol, to be sure, but a clear one—of man's unconquerable aspiration to dignity and freedom and purity in the sight of God." Throughout the play, which deals with the poignant moments of parting and grief as the happy family of the first scene is torn apart by one catastrophe after another, Mr. Sherwood has exercised a rigid self-control and reticence in the verbal expression of emotion. The situations are allowed to speak for themselves with a minimum of words. But in the matter of defining philosophic ideas, the author has permitted himself unusual leeway. By the device of a radio speech in the first scene, an impromptu lecture in the sixth and the reading of a letter in the last, he has given his spokesman, Valkonen, ample opportunity to round out his belief in the ultimate perfectibility of mankind.

Lillian Hellman has also a fighting message to deliver, but she is content to give it by implication and by emotional impact rather than by argument. She takes for granted that it is sufficient to state, as indeed it is, that her hero, Kurt Mueller (so admirably interpreted by Paul Lukas), is an anti-fascist, for the justice of his cause and the heroism of his action to be thoroughly understood. "We are all anti-fascist," Kurt's American hostess remarks. But Kurt's wife is quick to point out the difference. "Kurt *works* at it," she exclaims, with a sort of anguished pride, for "working at it" in and near Germany during the Hitler regime had meant persecution, torture, flight, misery, the constant threat of death and worse.

Miss Hellman has concentrated her efforts on the character of Kurt, treating the structure of her play casually up to the moment when her hero gets into action. In her desire to make her audiences understand the full horror of a world which forces such sensitive and highly strung beings as Kurt into bitter action and even bloodshed, she presents him in the moments of his extreme agony, allowing no detail of his Gethsemane, no private anguish, no syllable of his parting with his wife and children to go unexpressed. Nor does she spare the audience the shock of actual violence. Miss Hellman has the courage to point out quite ruthlessly and logically that it is sometimes necessary to kill, even when that killing is the personal, individualistic kind called murder and not the abstract, mass type called war. Her gentle and kindly hero exclaims in agony, "I hate the violent—They are the sick of the world—and perhaps I am sick too!" But when he has to kill, he kills—with repugnance, with deep-seated disgust, but without illusion. He does it for the ultimate good of mankind—just as King McCloud found himself ready to kill and be killed for his soul's sake; just as Valkonen strips off his Red Cross bandeau and takes up his pistol to fight for "man's aspiration." All of these playwrights seem to say, as Kurt Mueller says to his children, that men will steal and lie and kill, yes, even kill for a good cause. "But don't forget—it is bad—it is still bad."

November 1941

Broadway Blackout

THE LIGHTS are darkened along Broadway. The Brobdignagian goldfish made of a million gleaming, multicolored bulbs is gone; the cheerful nonsense of its rippling tail and ever-mounting bubbles has been wiped out by the grim non-sense of war. With all the waving, dancing, gyrating lights and colors that nightly turned the drab streets and highways of mid-town into a giant fair-ground, it is no more. Even the Times Building, where once the writing on the wall warned hurrying theatregoers of doom to come, is stark and silent.

> The Moving Finger writes; and having writ,
> Moves on; nor all your Piety nor Wit
> Shall lure it back to cancel half a line
> Nor all your Tears wash out a Word of it.

In the streets below, the lava-flow of humanity is thicker than ever, but it is plunged in penumbra; it moves slowly; it is feverish but subdued. The sprinkling of men in uniform that marked the first months of last season has turned into a strong current. They are mostly young, these men and boys, these soldiers, sailors, marines, coast-guardsmen, workers, citizens of all the allied nations, young and supremely restless, eager, seeking. What has the theatre to offer? Will it lead or follow? How will it welcome, entertain, delight, inspire these citizens of a world torn loose from its moorings?

November 1942

*

The Skin of Our Teeth

WHEN THE BREATH of creative imagination blows through the theatre, what exhilaration to the lungs, what refreshment to the spirit! Doors may bang and scenery fly about; audiences may be outraged, infuriated, delighted, but the theatre is once more alive. Thornton Wilder's *The Skin of Our Teeth* is not only a tribute to the indestructibility of the human race as its author indicates; it is also a giddy proof of the theatre's own imperishable vitality. After months of mediocrity and of a "fair to good" rating at best, Mr. Wilder's cosmic fooleries came flapping and rocketing into town, setting a new high in theatre unconfined. For Mr. Wilder has been as unconventional in his stage technique as in his subject matter. Just as he skips lightly to and fro through the adventures of mankind during some five thousand odd years, so he juggles with theatre conventions, laughingly exhibiting the wrong side of canvas walls, actors behind characters—the reality beyond the appearance of things. And from the welter of anachronisms with which he litters his stage, from the theatrical highjinks and intellectual handstands and flip-flops with which he spices his comedy, there emerges not only laughter and good will but that note of certitude and hope, that lift of the heart, which is the theatre's chiefest gift to mankind.

The step from the sublime to the ridiculous is notoriously narrow. Even more exiguous is the distance that separates the fantastic from the fatuous. *The Skin of Our Teeth* achieves the impossible by being sublimely ridiculous and by keeping its fantasy pure and undefiled. Mr. Wilder's plot, if any, is lunatic. It seems to concern events in the lives of Mr. and Mrs. Antrobus of Excelsior, New Jersey, their children, Henry and Gladys, their maid, Sabina. Actually it ranges over the entire experience of the human race from the ice age to the present (or the future) war. The Antrobus family goes through many adventures and trials. Pestilences, famines, floods and wars threaten it with annihilation at every turn, but through all its calamities it manages to survive and to move forward. Mr. Antrobus builds the alphabet, apprehends numbers, invents the wheel. Mrs. Antrobus, chiefly concerned with the preservation and protection of her family, her race, her species, does her share by transmuting the necessities of living into a better way of life. Even Sabina, effervescent and unstable—menace, delight and slave in one—struggles intermittently and hysterically to understand and help. The children are, of course, the ultimate focus of the adventure. In them is the hope and terror of the future: hope, because to them can be handed on the gains and conquests of man's mind; terror because on Henry's forehead is an ineradicable mark, the deep—and today how deeply branded—mark of Cain.

All this Mr. Wilder presents with the deftest and most engaging gaiety. His concern with the human race is second only to his delight in the nonsense and the magic of theatre. His play is as much theatre burlesque as it is satire on some of the foibles of the human race. In the opening scene, for instance, when the curtain goes up on a small town "interior," a typical, perky, parlor-maid soubrette of a venerable theatre tradition is "discovered" whisking about with her feather duster and propounding in rattling soliloquy all about the author's exposition: The Antrobus family is described, their anxieties about food, clothing and the weather discussed, the last subject being a poignant one, for though it is mid-August, it is the coldest day of the year and "the dogs are sticking to the pavements." All this runs along smoothly, except that there seems to be something wrong about the mechanism of the show: there are no masking pieces and no ceiling so that the set stands out precariously on a bare stage; everything seems slightly off center; some of the flats fly up in the air just as the parlor maid is about to dust them. Then suddenly a cue is missed. Sabina repeats the line, flounders, ad libs, finally gives up and comes down to the footlights to express her frank opinion of the whole situation: "I hate this play, every word of it. I don't understand a single word of it anyway," and proceeds to confide her own personal woes to the audience until the frantic stage-manager calls her to order and starts the ball rolling again. This is but one of any number of absurd and gaily erratic tricks by which Mr. Wilder points his moral while he keeps his audience laughingly alert.

Its strongly theatrical quality, its use of presentational techniques, its variety and color make *The Skin of Our Teeth* a director's holiday of which Elia Kazan has taken spirited advantage. Produced by Michael Myerberg, the play boasts a cast which with few exceptions could not be bettered. Tallulah Bankhead as Sabina, Miss Atlantic City, Lilith or what you will flaunts her bright plumage through three acts of make-believe in which she is alternately pert and seductive, brash and touching, comic and pathetic. Her personal qualities of vitality and variety, her bold theatricalism, her zest and drive are given ample scope in this role which demands fluidity and fire rather than interpretive concentration. After the solid achievement of her portrait of Regina Giddens in *The Little Foxes* and her tense, if somewhat uneven, study of Mae Wilenski in *Clash by Night,* Sabina is a field-day for Miss Bankhead, allowing her to play with a variety of comedy situations and techniques as well as to touch, on one or two occasions, that vibrant chord of tenderness and emotion of which she is possessed.

Fredric March as Mr. Antrobus storms boldly through the play with just that touch of the noble and the absurd the text requires. He presents him as the typical pater familias, huffing and sometimes bluffing his way through the mazes of life—but with a saving grace of imagination and faith that makes him take up the burden of continuance just where it seems too heavy to bear. In outlining the values of Mrs. Antrobus, Florence Eldridge has perhaps erred on the side of the shrewish. A warmer, richer, somewhat phlegmatic approach might have counteracted the stridency of certain scenes where the pitch seems too high for comfort. In Mrs. Antrobus, Miss Eldridge has the least happily realized role among the three, or, if Henry is included, the four principal figures. Montgomery Clift gives an excellent performance as Henry who is Cain—the self-tormented, murderous, unresolved element in the racial mind. This young actor has built steadily since his first appearance as the boy-father in *Dame Nature* through the role of Dr. Valkonen's son in *There Shall Be No Night* to the violent, explosive statement of this Cain. He succeeds in conveying the tension and anguish of evil and frustration and in making understandable Father Antrobus' cry of despair when he comes home after seven years of war to find his son who is the Enemy once more installed at his hearth: "The sight of you drives out all my hopes and plans. It is easier to fight you than to live with you."

January 1943

*

Oklahoma!

WHILE NATURE indulged in unseasonable April snow showers, the Theatre Guild ushered in the spring with one of the sunniest events of recent years.

> "Oh, what a beautiful mornin',
> Oh, what a beautiful day,
> I got a beautiful feelin'
> Everything's goin' my way,"

sings Curly, the dapper cowboy of *Oklahoma!*, and his song is an appropriate introduction to the musical play which Richard Rodgers and Oscar Hammerstein II have fashioned from Lynn Riggs' memorable *Green Grow the Lilacs.* It is a pellucid show, full of bright light and lilting songs, with dances, designed by Agnes de Mille, which epitomize the gaiety and graciousness of a lively occasion. The show has all the polish and precision of Broadway at its best, but it has escaped the dull devil of formula that so often haunts the musical comedy stage. Rouben Mamoulian's direction, Lemuel Ayers' crisp landscapes, Miles White's costumes with their forceful display of color and their exaggeration of line emphasize a theatric "climate" which, while very different from that of Lynn Riggs' play, has its own special charms. *Green Grow the Lilacs* was an excursion into American backgrounds that had the lusty flavor of the plains. It was sweet and bitter, tender and violent, gay and raucous. Its speech had a poetry of its own which was both authentic and revelatory. There was primitive violence, even brutality, in the "shivoree" and a melting sadness in the lonely cowboy songs which the new version does not attempt to exploit.

The musical, however, has availed itself of the plot and of a great deal of the dialogue of the play up to the "shivoree" scene where it breaks away from the original to wind up in a sunny finale appropriate to the gayer and more superficial mood of the occasion. *Oklahoma!* is laid in a thoroughly theatrical West where some of Richard Rodgers' most enchanting melodies reaffirm the spirit of American folk music without making use of its content, just as Oscar Hammerstein's lyrics catch up and embroider a phrase or two from Lynn Riggs' dialogue to make such songs as the one already quoted or "The Surrey with the Fringe on the Top" or "Pore Jud."

Agnes de Mille has designed the pattern of the dances in the same mood of re-creation rather than repetition. Her contribution to the effectiveness of the show as a whole is outstanding, winning instant recognition from theatre audiences that suddenly realized a dance can be comic, gaily satiric, as well as lyric and robust. Miss de Mille's dances do not interrupt the action with an arbitrary restatement of a lyric theme in terms of movement, but on the contrary they move the plot forward, enlarging its scope, enriching it with their own special contribution, as do Mr. Rodgers' songs. Both are part of the fabric of the play in a way quite different from the effect achieved in the original production, in which genuine cowboy songs and folk dances were used, but they are entirely appropriate to the new form. The Hammerstein book, for instance, provides a dream sequence for Laurey which is a ballet in itself. Danced by Marc Platt and Katharine Sergava as the dream versions of the cowboy and the maiden, it is at once humorous, touching, gallant and sentimental. Its bevies of awkward farm girls and long-limbed horsemen astride imaginary broncos sweep the stage with gusts of merriment; they are the essence, the embodied spirit of the hearty girls and boys whose vigorous measures enliven the other scenes of the play. Most of the dances are based on folk forms but all have a fluency and wit peculiar to Miss de Mille's choreography.

The Theatre Guild and Mr. Mamoulian made a happy choice in casting Alfred Drake in the leading role. As Curly, Mr. Drake is pleasantly unaffected and direct, his voice nicely fitted to the occasion, his acting more than adequate to the modest demands made upon it. Joan Roberts brings an agreeable voice, youth and pulchritude to the simplified Laurey of the musical version while Betty Garde plays Aunt Eller with hearty good humor though without the bite and sting that Helen Westley imparted to the role in the play version. Mr. Hammerstein has converted Ado Annie Carnes into a cartoon character to which Celeste Holm brings an unexpected comic punch, sketching in the outlines of the girl who "Cain't Say No" with large abandon. Her foil is the pedlar man, developed from a single incident in the original into a shrewd, gay punchinello played by Joseph Buloff with his customary relish and resourcefulness. Lee Dixon as the stalwart, nimble-footed Will Parker (whose matrimonial complications involving Ado Annie are new to the plot), Howard da Silva as the sinister Jud Fry and those giddy little dancers, Joan McCracken, Kate Friedlich, Margit DeKova and Bambi Linn, give sharply individual performances that linger in the mind's eye.

June 1943

*

The Glass Menagerie; Carousel

JUST AS THE 1944-45 season, pushed into the wings by mighty public events, was about to subside into featureless anonymity, a minor miracle took place. In the middle of routine productions that were only remarkable for their ability to restate platitudes in outworn forms, and to make money in the process, the theatre suddenly asserted itself in its own best terms. Tennessee Williams' *The Glass Menagerie* proved once again what magic can be wrought when playwright, actor and artist meet on common ground. The play as performed by Laurette Taylor in Jo Mielziner's sets, under Eddie Dowling's direction (assisted by Margo Jones), is something more than the sum of all its parts; it has a significance and abundance of life, a variety and complexity, that is the hallmark of creative achievement. When the New York critics gave it their annual award, it was in recognition of this total effect. Not since Saroyan's *My Heart's in the Highlands* dropped into town one day in the spring of 1939 has there been a production as encouraging to those who believe in the theatre as a form of significant expression and not exclusively as an entertainment racket.

Not that *The Glass Menagerie* is not good entertainment. The queue at the box-office; the applause of the critics in Chicago, where it opened, as well as in New York; the laughter that ripples through the audience as the inter-relationships between four people—mother, son, crippled daughter and "gentleman caller"—unfold on a mist-shrouded stage, all bear witness to the fact that "what the public wants" is a valid work of art no matter how unexpected its form or tragic its content. For Mr. Williams' play is steeped in tears; the pathos of remembered things, the longings, the futilities, the frustration at the heart of life. He has used the device of a narrator, The Son who remembers his past youth, to achieve a sense of perspective. These are not people in the harsh reality of the present, but obscured by time and distance and the intolerable burden of pity. The device is pertinent to the play and Jo Mielziner's set with its transparent gauzes which veil the past until The Son himself moves onto the scene are a harmonious realization of the playwright's intention. Light and music, the latter written by Paul Bowles, weave a continuous, iridescent pattern around the succession of remembered moments which form the body of the play.

The Son has wandered away from home and gone to sea. But no matter how far away he is, or in what exotic seaport he may find himself, the memory of a drab flat in a dark alley in St. Louis and of his mother and his crippled sister haunts him. He looks back through grey layers of memory and there they are; he finds himself once more listening to his mother's nagging tongue, his sister's playing of worn-out records on a broken victrola, the music of the dance hall next door. The daily grind of dull labor in a warehouse claims him. "Arise and shine," his mother calls and he grits his teeth. "I'll arise, all right, but I won't shine." The day has begun, dominated by The Mother's anxious fussing, her stories of past splendors as a much sought-after southern belle who married the wrong man, her futile efforts to keep up appearances, her constant worry about her daughter's fate and the necessity for "gentlemen callers" if the girl is ever to be taken care of after her mother's death.

As The Mother, Laurette Taylor gives an electric performance. Mr. Williams has provided her with a script that she turns to pure gold; its delicate and varied shadings are exactly captured in the subtle coloration of her readings. A simple phrase is packed with multiple meaning by an unexpected breath withheld, a pause so delicate as to seem unconscious, yet so timed that every shade of emotion, every latent implication is suddenly made clear. The Mother is vain and pitiful, a victim of circumstances, simultaneously infuriating and pathetic. Miss Taylor turns these facets in her hand, presenting the thing itself and her comment on the thing. Her every hesitant gesture, her waverings and dartings, her movements at once purposeful and blurred, all build an unforgettable image of a complex human being.

In the role of The Son, Mr. Dowling is more staid than the lines indicate; he seems a man already resigned to frustration rather than a youth chafing at chains. It is difficult to believe that he would write poetry or that his revolt is anything more than a desire to escape responsibility. But Mr. Dowling's performance is deeply felt on its human side and, on the whole, simple and straightforward. As the crippled daughter who collects the translucent animals that give *The Glass Menagerie* its title, Julie Haydon has a role suited to her wan, emaciated beauty. Her awkward, angular movements fit the part and, in the scene with The Gentleman Caller, when that cheerful extrovert, forcefully played by Anthony Ross, makes love to her and finally makes her dance, she melts for a space into the theatrical picture. But the play is pre-eminently Miss Taylor's. She has given Tennessee Williams' revealing and sensitive script the illuminating interpretation it deserves. The combination of a new writing talent and of a seasoned, subtle and infinitely varied acting gift is indeed cause for rejoicing and for gratitude to Mr. Dowling (and his co-producer, Louis J. Singer) for bringing this event about.

By way of closing their twenty-seventh season with an appropriate flourish, the Theatre Guild whirled into town on its new *Carousel.* The success with which a former Guild play, *Green Grow the Lilacs,* was transmogrified into the musical "smash hit," *Oklahoma!,* inspired the same group of alchemists to try their hands on Ferenc Molnar's *Liliom.* The results make for an evening of delightful music, of fresh engaging songs and dances and eye-filling scenes. The challenge involved in setting Molnar's fantasy to music has been somewhat evaded by transplanting the locale and characters from Hungary to New England. Richard Rodgers and Oscar Hammerstein II, though willing to go as far afield as Budapest for their inspiration, evidently felt compelled to bring their trophy home and clothe it in Americana. In the process the play loses its continental patina, its elements of vulgarity and cynicism which were sharply contrasted, in the original, with the innocent obstinacy of Julie's love. Liliom becomes Billy Bigelow, barker in a traveling fair. He is no less brash and boastful than the original "tough," but he is singularly lacking in villainy, while the meek, rather drab little servant girl of Molnar's play becomes a bright-haired factory worker in the translated scene.

Under the baton of the scene designer, the grubby purlieu of Budapest with its frowsy carnival blossoms into an arresting gaiety and color. Jo Mielziner's carousel might have come from the World's Fair; his fishing village with its painted backdrop of ships at anchor suggests grand opera. He is happiest in the brief moment when Billy finds himself in the backyard of Heaven, where the janitor hangs out stars on a celestial clothesline. Miles White's costumes—though expressed in musical comedy, not in realistic, terms—have a pleasing variety. He has thought of them as clothes for people, not as mass effects on a stage. The actors and dancers wear them easily and they add their share of accent to the scene. Once again Agnes de Mille is called on to interpret American backgrounds in dances that are partly pure ornament and partly a development of the story. Her hornpipe between the sailors and their girls in the first part is as gay and whirling a dance as could be desired, while in the second part she is assigned the task of telling the brief life-story of Billy's daughter in a play within the play that is dramatic and touching, imaginatively conceived and full of variety. Bambi Linn dances the wild youngster with gaiety and abandon in a stark setting of sea and cloud. She is a pupil of Miss de Mille's and a graduate, like Joan McCracken in *Bloomer Girl,* of the *Okla-homa!* dancing forces.

Rouben Mamoulian and The Guild have once more rounded up a group of talented young people for a far from easy assignment. John Raitt, Jan Clayton, Jean Darling and Christine Johnson as Billy, Julie, Julie's friend and Julie's kindly Aunt have the requisite voices and appearance, though it must be admitted that they do more credit to Mr. Rodgers' music than to Mr. Hammerstein's plot. Murvyn Vye as Jigger contributed some of the comedy which mainly hinges around Julie's friend Carrie and her "Mr. Snow," played by Eric Mattson. On the whole, Mr. Mamoulian has failed to direct the dramatic scenes effectively. The actors speak their lines with a certain feeling for character and situation, but where any emotion other than gaiety and playfulness is required they are unable to surmount their difficulties.

June 1945

*

V-J Day

THE POST-WAR SEASON opened on Broadway not with the first night of some tight little drama run off demurely in a side-street playhouse, but with a roar and a howl of exultation, with dancing in the streets and the blaze of lights, with flags waving, ticker-tape streaming, confetti raining from high-flung windows and a blare of noise dinning the ears. This was the people's festival, a Dionysian revel, unstaged and unrehearsed, expressing a nation's blind joy that the killing was over, that Tom, Dick and Harry would come safely home, that it was good to be alive. A great human cyclone struck the theatre section and turned it into a giant fair-ground. But by midweek the pace had slowed. The crowds strolled more quietly down the middle of the streets and avenues, or sat, country fashion, on the curbs. Faces grew thoughtful; the inward eye contemplated the future.

What did it all mean? Why had the war been, and where was the "peace" leading to? These are the questions everyone asks today, and for the theatre-minded they become specific. Will the stage, which during the war has served well enough as a place of refuge from the crowding terrors of this most brutal of conflicts, take up the task of helping to build the peace? Will it at last allow itself to grow to its own full stature, repudiate its inferiority complex and step out into the light as a mature and dynamic art? Obviously it is too soon to tell, but there are hopeful signs and portents.

October 1945

*

The Iceman Cometh

EUGENE O'NEILL'S RETURN after twelve years of absence has done more than give the new season a fillip of interest: it has restored to the theatre something of its intrinsic stature. O'Neill's gift for puzzling, infuriating and delighting his audiences makes everything he writes important even to those whom it exasperates. *The Iceman Cometh* presented by the House of O'Neill, the Theatre Guild, in an admirable production directed by Eddie Dowling has stirred Broadway from its daydreaming even as his hero Hickey stirs the bums in the backroom of Harry Hope's dump from their alcohol-ridden fancies. Sardi's and Twenty-One, Walgreen's and El Morocco seethed with indignant argument after an opening "night" that began at 4:30 in the afternoon and continued until 10—an opening for which the theatrically knowing and those who like to be seen at important events turned out in force. Though baseball and the movies may draw greater crowds, the theatre can console itself with the fact that in the end playwrights last longer in man's recollection. And certainly Eugene O'Neill will, because his plays, and this one in particular, exist on more than one plane. *The Iceman Cometh* is made of good theatre substance—meaty material for actors, racy dialogue, variety of character, suspense and passion—all within the strait-jacket of a rigid pattern. It is also primarily an allegory of man's pitiful estate, a parable of his search for redemption.

O'Neill has gone back to the saloons and gin-mills of his early days—and plays—for the setting of *The Iceman,* which he wrote in 1939. Harry Hope's bar and the backroom behind it is a composite of the dives he himself used to frequent in his restless youth. Hope's place is, according to one of its "inmates," the No Chance Saloon, Bedrock Bar, the End of the Line Café where five-cent whiskey—"cyanide cut with carbolic acid to give it a mellow flavor"—is sold to a motley collection of down-and-outers by an amiably boozy proprietor. The whole action of the play, such as it is, swings between the bar itself with its half-door on the street and the dingy backroom where, as the curtain rises, a dozen assorted drunks sit at round tables drinking and dreaming of that golden tomorrow which will see them restored once more to a living world. They are waiting for Hickey, a traveling salesman, who comes to them from time to time to live out a "periodical," a fabulous bender in which they share his whiskey and listen to his jokes, particularly that one about his loving wife whom he has treated so badly but who is all right now because he left her safely at home in bed—"with the iceman." While waiting for Hickey, Larry, the philosophic ex-anarchist, tells the newly-arrived Parritt (who is the son of a famous woman anarchist now under arrest for participating in a bombing episode on the West Coast) all about the other members of this dead-end club. Each has a story of fraud or failure behind him; each lives in an alcoholic "pipe dream" of future hope—till Hickey arrives.

Then the trouble starts. Hickey has reformed. He is off the booze; he has found salvation and he intends to make all his friends follow his path to peace and happiness. They are to face their dream tomorrows in actual fact. But the results of his proselytizing are disastrous. Hate, fear, anguish and despair descend on the inhabitants of the erstwhile fools' paradise. Hickey finds to his horror that his gospel of disillusionment does not work. He is forced to explain the cause of his own reform in order to prove he is right. He pours out the story of his life, of his relations with his wife whom he loved and who loved him too well—and whom he killed to save her from the suffering he was forever inflicting. He had left her that very morning safe in bed—"with the iceman," Death. And then as Hickey tells the story of the woman he murdered for love he realizes with a sudden blinding flash that this too was illusion, that he had killed her because he hated her; he killed her and cursed her for her intolerable, overwhelming love. This last confession brings a final reversal. The murder and the cursing were madness. "I must have been crazy," Hickey cries out in despair. The bums who had been listening to his story in a sort of horrified stupor stir at the words. Hickey was crazy all the time! His reform was a pipe dream too. They can go back to their old illusions, their whiskey, their dreams; they reach thirstily for their bottles. Only the boy Parritt, Larry and Hickey himself are changed. Hickey gives himself up to the police for murder, Parritt commits suicide realizing he is as guilty of mother-murder as Hickey of wife-murder and Larry the philosopher faces the fact that for him too death is the only answer. The cycle is complete. If this is life then indeed "The best of all were never to be born."

Like Peer Gynt's onion, the story of *The Iceman* has its layers and layers of meaning. It touches on a dozen different themes and relationships. While the subsidiary characters are separate microcosms of despair, the three chief figures, Hickey, Larry and Parritt, are three aspects of man—each element loving and loathing the other.

The play is in a very special sense a summary of much of O'Neill's past writing. Superficially it goes back as far as the vigorous sea plays with which he made his debut. Its frank barroom talk, its conventional tarts, its amiable drunks, its passion and violence are reminders of the impact of his first writing. Don Parritt, the boy rejected by his mother, haunted by the guilt of his betrayal of her, which is nothing less than matricide, recalls O'Neill's days of absorption in psychoanalysis, while Larry the philosopher is the O'Neill who attempted a detachment and objectivity never native to him.

But it is through Hickey who has known the love that passeth understanding and rejected it that we glimpse O'Neill's ultimate meaning. Blind, besotted and misguided, man haunted by death lives by lies. "The lie of a pipe dream is what gives life to the whole misbegotten mad lot of us, drunk or sober," Larry says at the opening of the play. But there is truth which is not the truth of alcohol or political shibboleths, or psychology or philosophy, or even the truth of "facing the truth" which Hickey preaches. The greatest illusion of all is to believe that disillusionment—the unaided processes of the intellect—can solve man's dilemma. There is a force that, like the love that Hickey's wife bore him, is made of understanding and forgiveness. Man finds such love intolerable. "I couldn't forgive her for forgiving me," Hickey explains. "I caught myself hating her for making me hate myself so much. There is a limit to the guilt you can feel and the forgiveness and pity you can take." And so man denies, destroys and blasphemes such love, only in the end to find that this too will be forgiven. The denizens of Hickey's world and of the world at large find a simple answer to Hickey's final revelation. The man is mad! Hamlet to the contrary notwithstanding, there is nothing more in heaven and earth than can be compassed in any current philosophy. Pass the bottle. Drink up. What the hell! It's a good play, brother, why bother.

And it is a good play, excellently acted and directed, full of substance. It would seem that it could readily be compressed into a more reasonable running time, but O'Neill has a tendency to shirk the task of selection and condensation. He has so much to say that even this four-and-a-half-hour play must seem short to a man who thinks in terms of trilogies and nine-play cycles. For the onlooker, however, a shorter play would have brought into sharper focus the conflicting and merging elements of the three chief figures of the fable. The subsidiary characters are not sufficiently important or rounded to demand the time and attention they absorb. They are each set in their groove in the first half hour. They never emerge from the pattern to take on human proportions. The reiterated pattern of their false redemption and its death-dealing effect becomes tedious. Mr. O'Neill seems to underestimate the ability of the audience to grasp his idea, or perhaps more truly he has so fond a remembrance softened by time and distance of these denizens of his kingdom of despair that he cannot bear to tear up the sketches he has made in his mind's eye as he sat with them at marble-topped tables or leaned against mahogany bars in a hundred saloons the world over.

December 1946

*

The Importance of Being Earnest; Love for Love; Sweethearts

IT IS A STRANGE BUSINESS, this business of making gentlefolk laugh," Molière remarked several hundred years ago. A strange business and a difficult one—but highly rewarding. Molière himself knew very well how to do it, for he was master of the two chief elements of comedy—the word and the deed; wit and the prat-fall. The New York stage presents two brilliant examples of these opposite extremes: Oscar Wilde as interpreted by John Gielgud, Bobby Clark as interpreted by Bobby Clark. . . .

The return of John Gielgud, after ten years' absence, in two comedies, *The Importance of Being Earnest* and *Love for Love,* is a pleasant if somewhat surprising event. His *Hamlet* is not forgotten by those who care about the fine art of acting. He gave his sensitive and revealing interpretation of the role with such poetry and power that his position as one of the few great Shakespearean tragic actors of the day was firmly established even though New York has not yet seen him as Richard II, Lear, Macbeth, Shylock or any of the other major roles which he has played with outstanding success in London.

The ten years which have elapsed since Mr. Gieglud's long run in *Hamlet* in New York have been strenuous for an actor who is also a director and from time to time a producer. During the war he ran a repertory company at the Haymarket where *The Importance* and *Love for Love* as well as *Hamlet, King Lear, The Duchess of Malfi* and other plays were given. The present company is somewhat different in make-up from the one which played with him through the war years, but its members perform with the homogeneity and easy give-and-take of experienced actors thoroughly accustomed to ensemble.

It is a truism that comedy dates more quickly than tragedy. Aristophanes is more remote than Sophocles or Euripides, Shakespeare's clowns more dated than Shakespeare's kings. Wit, being a matter of words and their implications, depends on the "climate" of currently accepted ideas for its effect. But in the theatre still another element comes into play. Oscar Wilde's words on the lips of one set of actors will fail dismally to make the smallest effect; the same words handled by adepts such as the Gielgud company gleam and dart with their original sparkle. There is a gusto about their performance, a kind of joy in the game, that carries the audience irresistibly into the mood of absurdity and fun. Wilde's paradoxes are batted to and fro with the agility of championship tennis. The neat balance of players, the superbly absurd counterpoint of the whole procedure, is carried out in the details of Mr. Gielgud's direction and the buoyant precision of his company's performance.

Margaret Rutherford, as Lady Bracknell dripping in feather boas and cascades of lace and frills, is a Victorian gorgon of awesome dignity. She is perhaps not as incisively elegant as was Edith Evans in the part, but she presents an overpowering example of frumpish aristocracy as amusing as her hearty spiritualist, the unforgettable Madame Arcati, in the film version of *Blithe Spirit*. The interview between Lady Bracknell and John Worthing when that unfortunate young man asks for the hand of her daughter Gwendolen, "a girl brought up with the utmost care," is a high-water mark in comedy writing and is given superb gravity and finesse by the two protagonists in this production.

Algernon, the amiable and vacuous young man whose bachelor flat—filled with tasteless furniture and an assortment of knick-knacks and what-nots—provides the setting for the first act, is pleasantly portrayed by Robert Flemyng. He was last seen in New York in Cornell's production of *No Time for Comedy.* The two girls who partner the young men in this suave game of mixed doubles, Pamela Brown and Jane Baxter, pirouette through their parts, following Hamlet's advice to speak the speech "trippingly." Miss Brown, who has recently been playing Goneril with considerable success in Oliver's *King Lear,* proves a piquant comedienne, with her curious, pointed face and ornamental gestures. Her attack on the part has the brio of an accomplished technician enjoying the sheer fun of his expertness. Miss Baxter plays, as she should, in a more subdued key but with an equal relish, while Jean Cadell has packed into the role of Miss Prism a wealth of experience and a note of human understanding for the mincing little old maid which enlarges the scope of an all-too-brief part.

Mr. Gielgud's Jack Worthing is happily set off against this background of excellent performances. As a first-rate artist he knows that the better his supporting cast, the more effectively he can build his own role. He has played Jack Worthing for many years—a pleasant diversion from the exhausting demands of Hamlet, Lear or Raskolnikoff—and he plays him with relish and appreciation. His comedy timing is as exact as his tragic readings, for they are the product of an understanding of the actor's art which is both intellectual and emotional. He knows to a hair's breadth every gesture of the role. He presents this absurd, serious and vacuous young man in all his inanity, yet he makes you feel for him. As he delivers them, the Wildean epigrams seem simple expressions of sincerity and truth until their two-edged meaning emanates as a sort of afterglow from his unaccented delivery.

Gielgud's comedy is implicit; the distortion in the mirror he holds up to nature is never crude. For instance, when he makes his famous entrance in the second act, clothed in funeral black for the death of a brother who never existed, the solemnity of his face, the dignity of his carriage are so nearly the real thing that one wonders how he conveys so instantaneously the whole ridiculous impact of the situation. Yet the audience roars with laughter before he is half-way downstage, for he can project the comic content of the moment with as great a force as he projected Hamlet's tragic mood.

Bobby Clark's methods are simpler but no less effective. He plays entirely with action, having the least possible truck with words. His jokes, mostly antiquated and always obvious, are only a negligible accompaniment to the virtuosity of his person, the absurdity of his appearance, the complications of his costumes. It is the beguiling inanity of those painted spectacles, that whirling cane, that animated cigar that sets the risibles vibrating. But Gielgud and Bobby Clark have one thing in common—a zest for their "difficult business of making gentlefolk laugh."

Part of the fun of watching Bobby Clark race around the stage in his inimitable crouching run is that he seems to be enjoying himself so thoroughly—even though he may be causing the other actors and even the scenery some inconvenience. The current excuse for his gyrations is a revival by Paula Stone and Michael Sloane of Victor Herbert's *Sweethearts* but the whole Zilanian business is cheerfully forgotten in memories of Bobby scuttling about in a succession of insane get-ups: as a washerwoman committing mayhem on defenseless shirts; in a Dutch costume clattering about in sabots; as a courtier in astounding splendor waving an elegant lace handkerchief. "Never" he remarks at one point, addressing the audience in his usual nonchalant fashion, "never was a thin plot so complicated." But it serves its purpose of providing Bobby with a stage big enough to romp about on and gives him the necessary stooges—five of them at one point all dressed as monks with Bobby leading the singing in his fortunately inimitable style. The evening would have been ill-spent if he did not also from time to time paw the earth with his foot and let out his peculiar wolf-cry, a cross between an anguished yelp and the tuneful bay of a hound-dog barking at the moon, or if his eternal pursuit of the female of the species had not been provided for by an appropriately opulent leading lady and a half-a-dozen soubrettes.

April 1947

*

Medea

SHE IS the panther of the stage. With a panther's terrible beauty and undulating grace she moves and stands and glares and springs. Scorn, triumph, rage, lust and merciless malignity she represents in symbols of irresistible power." The words describe Judith Anderson's Medea so vividly that it is difficult to believe they could be applied to anyone else. Yet, actually, they were written by that discerning critic George Henry Lewes about the great French tragedienne Rachel some hundred years ago. As Rachel left an unforgettable image of her Phèdre on the minds even of generations that have not seen her, so Judith Anderson's Medea will remain—a symbol of power. For Miss Anderson has made this poet's version of a poet's masterpiece her own. Her performance is an event in our theatre, a work combining superb craftsmanship with intense emotional drive.

In his *Medea* "freely adapted from the *Medea* of Euripides" Robinson Jeffers has created a terrifying image of evil. It is the apotheosis of the religion of hate—the ultimate, fiery end of the doctrine of an eye for an eye. Medea has been wronged, she calls for justice, but the chorus reminds her that actually she seeks

> Not justice: vengeance.
> You have suffered evil, you wish to inflict
> evil.

And to make quite clear just what this terrible play means to our world today, the Chorus continues:

> I have heard evil
> Answering evil as thunder answers lightning,
> A great waste voice in the hollow sky
> And all that they say is death . . .
> The sword speaks
> And the spear answers: the city is desolate.
> The nations remember old wrongs and destroy each
> other,
> And no man binds up their wounds.

The nations destroy each other, as Medea destroys her enemies. But she destroys herself as well, the self that lives on in her own offspring. In her horrible ecstasy of love-turned-hate she speaks the word that haunts the world today: "Annihilation." She would annihilate the past; she would, with awful logic, also annihilate the future. Jeffers made a powerful rendering of this song of hate and by the force of Miss Anderson's playing and the effectiveness of the stage presentation we are provided with an unusual example of that process of purgation through pity and fear of which Aristotle spoke.

Miss Anderson's interpretation does, indeed, evoke more terror than pity. Her Medea is pure evil, dark, dangerous, cruel, raging, ruthless. From beginning to end she maintains an almost incredible intensity, yet she varies her moods so constantly, she moves with such skill through unexplored regions of pain and despair, that she can hold her audience in suspense throughout the evening. From the first sound of her voice, heard back of the grim doors of Medea's palace, to her last proud words, "not me they scorn," as she goes out "under the cold eyes of weakness-despising stars," she mounts to what seems to be an ever-ascending spiral of passion and fury, from raging despair to a raging triumph of revenge.

Miss Anderson's use of a voice of great range and vibrancy is no less remarkable than the use of her body. Speech and movement are one. Her hands and arms are as expressive as the high carriage of her head or the skillful sweep of drapery that marks her progress—a dark wave streaked with red. Again and again she and her director find the unforgettable gesture, the climactic pose: her entrance through the great doors of the palace, for instance, or the moment when she makes Aegeus swear he will protect her—the two arms crossed in a pact that is suddenly ominous, doom-fraught—above all, the awful physical joy and terror of her body as it lives, through her imagination, the fiery agony of the death she has inflicted on her enemy. Through this whole scene, blood lust, sexual jealousy and ruthless vengeance rise to a paroxysm of barbaric joy which is almost unendurable. Miss Anderson expresses Medea's state in every inch of her writhing body, finally thrusting herself between the pillars of the house as though ecstasy could not be contained but needed the stone walls to hold it in.

The play of passion on Miss Anderson's mobile face—dark, hawklike, with black, burnt-out eyes, like a mask of despair—her variations of mood, her moments of control when she attempts to curb her rage but can do so only for a short space, her sudden outbursts—all these details of a masterly performance should be studied by anyone who wishes to understand the art of acting in the great tradition, the tradition that has made the names of Kean and Rachel, Salvini and Bernhardt words to conjure with.

The production which Robert Whitehead and Oliver Rea, a new firm of young producers, have provided is one that does justice to the occasion. John Gielgud turns for the first time to the direction of a Greek play and has handled what is always a difficult assignment with success. Taking his lead from Jeffers' free treatment of the Greek form, he has given variety and fluidity to his over-all pattern. He has selected three women of different ages and contrasting voices and personalities to play chorus to the high and terrible events, bringing gentleness, wisdom and the commonplace into a scene that has little relief from violence.

The setting by Ben Edwards is conceived in terms of realism; a huge doorway flanked by columns and heavy stonework fills most of the stage, a glimpse of the Bay of Corinth and the wooded hills is seen on one side with a suggestion of ancient gnarled trees nearby. The steps to the palace provide varied acting levels which are effectively used to mark Medea's passionate progress and her diverse relations to the men who come to her—Creon to pronounce her banishment, Aegeus to offer her asylum and Jason to reason with her.

Mr. Gielgud himself plays Jason. It is an ungrateful part and not at all in what might be considered Mr. Gielgud's territory. Yet being an accomplished technician as well as one of the few great actors of our day, he successfully conveys exactly what he intends to: the quality in Jason that made him a hero "beloved of women" but also made him obtuse, rather pompous, indifferent to anything but his own advancement, in fact something of a Greek stuffed shirt. The very slight shadow of humor that this laughless play affords is his specious argument that he is marrying "the little Creûsa" for Medea's sake—for her protection and the advancement of their children. Only in the last moments of the play does Jason's role offer Mr. Gielgud the kind of material that he can handle so brilliantly. Then, after the murder of the children, when he says very quietly and in a curious, flat, toneless voice "It is no matter now who lives or dies," he touches the height of tragic despair by a route exactly opposite of that followed by Miss Anderson.

There is, in fact, very little for a cast to do except to "support" Miss Anderson's electric performance. Florence Reed achieves her best effect in her recounting of the horrible death agonies of Creûsa and Creon—a description strangely foreshadowing John Hersey's report of the effect of nuclear fission on the human body. Grace Mills, Kathryn Grill and Leone Wilson, who are the chorus, and Don McHenry, who gives the tutor's part a gentle credibility, play in a more realistic style than Miss Anderson's heroic vein but remain within the framework of the play. The children—as is almost inevitable—break out of the "mystic circle" and threaten the headlong pace of the play. Jeffers has made more of their part in the proceedings than Euripides suggests, but in any case their long-legged, towheaded presence on the stage does not add to the poignancy of the situation but rather serves to remind us that we are seeing actors on a stage and not actually taking part in the terrible and exalting experience into which Miss Anderson's performance had transported us.

December 1947

NOTES ON CONTRIBUTORS

APPIA, ADOLPHE. Artist-philosopher and scene designer, whose space sets and writings created a revolution in 20th Century staging, he died in 1928 in his native Switzerland at the age of 62.

ARGENTINA. The greatest of modern Spanish dancers, she took her name from the country of her birth. At nine she made her debut at the Royal Theatre in Madrid, and in 1911 she made her first phenomenally successful tour of Europe. She toured America first in 1916 and many times before her death in 1936.

AUSTIN, MARY. American writer celebrated for her novels and short stories of Indian life in the Southwest, such as *The Land of Little Rain,* and for such plays as *The Arrowmaker*.

BEISWANGER, GEORGE. Assistant editor and dance critic of *Theatre Arts* between 1935 and 1939, he subsequently returned to the teaching profession, as professor of philosophy at Georgia State College for Women.

BERNSTEIN, ALINE. Leading American woman scene and costume designer, she began working with the Neighborhood Playhouse and has had a long career on Broadway. A novelist of distinction, she has taught at Vassar and was co-founder of the American Costume Institute.

BESSIE, ALVAH. Novelist (*Dwell in the Wilderness, Bread and Stone*), critic and film writer (*Hotel Berlin, Objective Burma,* etc.), he was indicted in 1947 for contempt of Congress for refusal to reveal his political affiliations to the Thomas Committee.

BOLGER, RAY. One of "A Pair of Nifties" in vaudeville in 1925, he has continued to be a nifty in musical comedies and films ever since, as a "round" actor as well as expert dancer.

BROWN, IVOR. British author and drama critic, of the Manchester *Guardian* and the *Illustrated London News,* he is the editor of *The Observer,* London weekly.

BROWN, JOHN MASON. Critic, essayist and lecturer, he joined the staff of *Theatre Arts* a year after his graduation from Harvard, was subsequently drama critic of the New York *Evening Post* and since 1944 columnist for *The Saturday Review of Literature*. He is the author of numerous scholarly and popular books.

BRUGUIÈRE, FRANCIS. One of the first artist-photographers of the theatre, he left on his death a remarkable collection of pictures recording the renascent American theatre following World War I.

CARMER, CARL. Writer and lecturer, he was a college professor before he became a newspaper columnist and, between 1929 and 1933, assistant editor of *Theatre Arts*. The author of *Stars Fell on Alabama* and *Listen for a Lonesome Drum,* he is the editor of the *Rivers of America* Series.

CHENEY, SHELDON. Founder and first editor of *Theatre Arts,* he is the author of many invaluable books on the theatre, including *The Theatre —Two Thousand Years,* and more recently several histories of painting and modern art.

CLARK, BARRETT H. Starting out as an actor, he became editor for Samuel French, Ltd., then of *Drama Magazine* and of the Dramatists' Play Service, which he helped organize for the Dramatists Guild. A prolific writer, he has published important books of theatre history and criticism.

COLUM, PADRAIC. Irish poet, critic and dramatist, one of the founders of the Irish National Theatre, he came to the United States in 1914. Among other activities he has taught at Columbia.

COOK, WILL MARION. Trained under Joachim in Europe, he became, with *Clorindy, The Origin of the Cakewalk,* the first Negro composer to achieve a Broadway success. He married its leading lady, Abbie Mitchell, and wrote other popular musicals, such as *Abyssinia* and *Bandana Land.*

CORWIN, NORMAN. Perhaps the most highly regarded of American radio writers, he was the first to receive a grant from the American Academy of Arts and Letters (1942). Beginning in 1949 he has been chief of special projects, United Nations Radio.

COVARRUBIAS, MIGUEL. Mexican painter and anthropologist, who began his career as a caricaturist for Mexican papers and later for *Vanity Fair,* he is the author of *Island of Bali, Mexico South* and several books of original drawings.

DE MILLE, AGNES. American dancer and choreographer, she has contributed new forms to the repertory of Ballet Theatre and has arranged the dancing for such Broadway shows as *Oklahoma!, One Touch of Venus* and *Gentlemen Prefer Blondes.*

DUERR, EDWIN. Formerly assistant professor of theatre at Western Reserve University, he is director of radio and television for Young and Rubicam and author of *Radio and Television Acting* (1950).

DUKES, ASHLEY. British dramatist, producer and critic, he was for many years English editor of *Theatre Arts.* Since 1933 he has managed the Mercury Theatre in London and more recently was advisor on entertainment to British Military Government in Germany. His plays include *The Man With a Load of Mischief* and *The Dumb Wife of Cheapside.*

EATON, WALTER PRICHARD. Drama critic and historian, playwright and teacher, he is also the author of books on gardening and the "Boy Scouts" series for teen-agers. In 1947 he retired as professor of playwriting at the Yale School of the Drama.

EISENSTEIN, SERGEI. One of the great directors and theorists of cinema, he was trained as an engineer in Russia and came to films there via the theatre. He is best known for *Potemkin* (1925), *Ten Days That Shook the World* (1927) and *Alexander Nevsky* (1938).

ENGEL, LEHMAN. Composer, conductor and arranger, he has been responsible, in one or more of these capacities, for the music of nearly 80 Broadway shows. A choral group which he led has done extensive recordings of little-known classics.

EUSTIS, MORTON. A former newspaperman, he was an editor of *Theatre Arts* from 1933 until 1942, and was the author of *B'way, Inc.* and *Players at Work.* He was killed in 1945 commanding a tank in the Colmar Pocket in France, and his war letters were privately printed.

FERGUSON, OTIS. Killed in action as a merchant seaman in World War II, he was film critic for the *New Republic.*

FLANAGAN (DAVIS), HALLIE. National Director of the Federal Theatre during its entire life (1935-1939), she was a pioneer in college theatre work, head of the Vassar Experimental Theatre, and later served as dean of Smith College and director of its drama department.

FREEMAN, JOSEPH. Author of *An American Testament* and *The Long Pursuit,* he has had a diversified career as a poet, critic, foreign correspondent, lecturer, novelist and magazine editor.

FUCHS, THEODORE. Teacher and lighting specialist, he was for many years connected with the General Electric Company, and later director of the college theatre and professor at Northwestern University.

GEDDES, NORMAN BEL. American painter, scene and industrial designer, famed for his reconversion of the Century Theatre into a Gothic cathedral for Max Reinhardt's *The Miracle* and for the "Futurama" of the New York World's Fair.

GIELGUD, JOHN. British actor and director, who has appeared with outstanding success on both sides of the Atlantic, he made theatre history with his versions of *Hamlet, King Lear, The Importance of Being Ernest.*

GIELGUD, VAL. British playwright, producer, novelist and radio writer, a brother of John Gielgud, he is co-director, in charge of radio drama, of the Third Program of the British Broadcasting Corporation.

GILDER, ROSAMOND. Associated with *Theatre Arts* since 1925, she became its Broadway critic in 1938 and was its editor from 1945-48. She has been editorial secretary of the National Theatre Conference, secretary, since 1945, of the American National Theatre and Academy and director of the International Theatre Institute (UNESCO). The author of various books on the theatre, she was awarded a Guggenheim Fellowship in 1950 and is a staff lecturer at Barnard College.

GREEN, PAUL. While teaching at the University of North Carolina, he has written a long series of distinguished short stories, novels and plays, which include *In Abraham's Bosom* (Pulitizer Prize, 1927), *The House of Connelly* and *The Lost Colony.*

GRANVILLE-BARKER, HARLEY. British producer, director, playwright and actor who introduced many of Ibsen's and Shaw's plays to England, he instituted radical changes in direction, and his prefaces to Shakespeare's plays, in two volumes, are considered definitive.

HAMILTON, EDITH. A classics scholar at Bryn Mawr, she was the first woman admitted to the University of Munich, where she received a doctorate in Latin literature. Her first and perhaps most celebrated book, *The Greek Way,* published in 1930, was made up largely of articles she had written for *Theatre Arts.*

HARDWICKE, SIR CEDRIC. An actor in London since he was nineteen, he gained prominence with the Birmingham Repertory Theatre. Since then he has had a distinguished career as an actor for the stage and screen.

HOPKINS, ARTHUR. American producer, director and dramatist, he was particularly noted for his productions of *The Jest,* Barrymore's *Hamlet, The Hairy Ape* and *What Price Glory?*

HOUGHTON, NORRIS. Starting out as a scene designer with the University Players, he wrote *Moscow Rehearsals* and *Advance from Broadway,* was on the staff of *Theatre Arts* and has directed plays in London and New York.

HUTCHENS, JOHN K. Literary and drama critic, he was associate editor for *Theatre Arts* from 1928 to 1932, and has since been drama editor of the New York *Times,* editor of the *Times Weekly Book Review,* columnist and assistant editor of the *Herald Tribune Book Review Supplement.*

ISAACS, EDITH J. R. As editor of *Theatre Arts* for most of its life, she was an important force in the American theatre. The author of *The Negro in the American Theatre,* she edited many other volumes, including *Architecture for the New Theatre, Plays of American Life and Fantasy* and *Theatre.*

ISAACS, HERMINE RICH. Film critic for *Theatre Arts,* she was a member of its editorial staff from 1936 to 1948.

JONES, ROBERT EDMOND. One of the great artists to become scene designers in the World War I period, he is noted for his sets for *The Jest,* Barrymore's *Hamlet, Mourning Becomes Electra;* was director of several O'Neill plays as well as of *Holiday* and *Serena Blandish;* and is the author of the inspiring book, *The Dramatic Imagination.*

JOUVET, LOUIS. One of France's outstanding theatrical figures—actor, producer, designer and director—he has also supervised and acted in many films.

KIRSTEIN, LINCOLN. Authority on ballet and the dance, patron and art critic, he founded and still directs the first ballet school in America, has founded various American ballet companies of distinction. Onetime editor of *Hound and Horn* and *Dance Index,* he has written many books on ballet and the visual arts.

KNIGHT, ARTHUR. Film critic and educator, he has been assistant curator of the Museum of Modern Art film library and chairman of the film department of the Dramatic Workshop and Technical Institute.

KOLODIN, IRVING. Writer on musical subjects, he has been critic for the New York *Sun* and for the *Saturday Review of Literature* and is the author of *The Metropolitan Opera*—1883-1935 and *The Critical Composer.*

KRACAUER, SIEGFRIED. Formerly an editor of the *Frankfurter Zeitung,* he is the author of an analysis of films and poliltical events, *From Caligari to Hitler.* For UNESCO he has made a study of national stereotypes as projected in films.

LA FARGE, CHRISTOPHER. American poet and novelist, author of *Each to the Other, The Sudden Guest,* etc., he has been a practicing architect and has exhibited his paintings at leading galleries.

LEJEUNE, C. A. British film critic since the days of the silents, for many years contributing regularly to *The Observer* (London), she has twice published collections of her criticisms, *Cinema* (1931) and *Chestnuts in Her Lap* (1947).

LESSER, SOL. Veteran Hollywood producer, he started his career as a projector operator in Fox theatres. His name has been carried around the world on the magic carpet of the Tarzan series.

LEVINSON, ANDRÉ. Ballet critic and historian, he left his native Russia in 1918, and up to his death in 1936 lived in France where he published many books and hundreds of articles on all phases of the dance.

LINDSAY, HOWARD. Leading American actor, producer and playwright, he was for long identified in the public mind with Clarence Day, Sr., the part he played in *Life with Father* and *Life with Mother,* both of which he wrote with Russel Crouse.

LOCKE, ALAIN. The first Negro to receive a Rhodes Scholarship, he is professor of philosophy at Howard University and the New School for Social Research and the author of numerous books on Negro culture and race relations.

MAYER, ARTHUR L. Motion picture importer, exhibitor and distributor, he was chief of the Motion Picture Branch of the American Military Government in Germany after World War II.

MACGOWAN, KENNETH. An editor of *Theatre Arts* from 1919 to 1925, he became a director and producer in the theatre, went on to serve in both capacities in Hollywood. After retiring from the movies, he organized and became chairman of the department of theatre arts at the University of California at Los Angeles, and has pursued his studies in American anthropology.

MIELZINER, JO. Although he came late in the artists' renaissance in the American theatre, he has designed with ingenuity and flare a long succession of New York productions, from *The Guardsman* (1924) to *The Innocents* (1950).

NICHOLS, DUDLEY. Former motion-picture critic who went to Hollywood to become one of its top script-writers, he was responsible for such movies as *The Informer* and *The Long Voyage Home.*

OENSLAGER, DONALD. One of the busiest and most creative Broadway scene designers, he has also found time to do off-Broadway productions, teach at the Yale School of the Drama, and produce a body of paintings recently exhibited in New York.

PETERS, ROLLO. One of the group of scene designers who revolutionized American staging following World War I, he was the first director of the Theatre Guild, and has since acted in many plays and films.

PILCHER, VELONA. Manager of the famed Gate Theatre in London, she wrote frequently for *Theatre Arts* throughout its history.

REED, EDWARD. An assistant editor of *Theatre Arts* in the 1930's, he returned to the magazine as managing editor after serving with the Office of War Information and the Army during World War II.

RICH, MARIAN. Voice teacher long associated with the Neighborhood Playhouse School of the Theatre, the New School for Social Research, and the American Theatre Wing School.

RIGGS, LYNN. Poet and dramatist, he is a native of the Southwest, the locale of his *Russet Mantle* and *Green Grow the Lilacs,* which formed the basis for the musical, *Oklahoma!*

RODGERS, RICHARD. Composer, he wrote the music to the lyrics of Lorenz Hart and Oscar Hammerstein II to make some of the outstanding musicals of modern times. With the latter he has also been producer of serious plays as well as musical comedies.

ROTHA, PAUL. One of the pioneers of the documentary film in England, he is the author of *The Film Till Now.*

SAROYAN, WILLIAM. Short-story writer, novelist and playwright, he wrote *My Heart's in the Highlands* and the Pulitzer Prize-winning *The Time of Your Life,* as well as the motion picture *The Human Comedy.*

SARTRE, JEAN-PAUL. A professor of philosophy, he emerged in France during and after World War II as a novelist, playwright and leader of the Existentialist movement. His plays produced in New York include *No Exit, The Respectful Prostitute* and *Red Gloves.*

SERLIN, OSCAR. Producer of many Broadway plays, his most notable success has been *Life with Father.*

SEYLER, ATHENE. One of England's great comediennes, the list of whose roles takes four columns in *Who's Who in the Theatre,* she is the author, with the late Stephen Haggard, of *The Craft of Comedy.*

SHAW, GEORGE BERNARD. Irish dramatist.

SHERWOOD, ROBERT E. Dramatist, who started out as a humorist and critic for *Vanity Fair* and the old *Life,* he has three times been awarded the Pulitzer Prize, for *Abe Lincoln in Illinois, Idiot's Delight* and *There Shall Be No Night.* During World War II he was an advisor in the White House, and later wrote the best-selling *Roosevelt and Hopkins.*

SIMONSON, LEE. Scene designer and painter, he was a founder and director of the Theatre Guild, for which he was chief designer for many years. He is author of *The Stage Is Set, Part of a Lifetime* and *The Art of Scenic Design.*

SKINNER, CORNELIA OTIS. For many years a successful monologist, she has starred in plays with large casts and continued the distinguished record of her father. At the same time she has maintained a second career as author of hilarious short stories and books of reminiscence.

SKINNER, OTIS. Celebrated American actor, best remembered perhaps for *Kismet* and his many Shakespearean roles, he also wrote several books on the theatre.

SMITH, CECIL. Editor of *Musical America* and music critic for the *New Republic,* he also writes the program notes on all new music for the New York Philharmonic. Formerly lyric theatre critic for *Theatre Arts,* he was before that drama, dance and music critic for the Chicago *Tribune* and chairman of the music department of the University of Chicago. He is the author of *Musical Comedy in America* (1950).

STOKES, SEWELL. British journalist, novelist and playwright, he was author, with his brother Leslie, of *Oscar Wilde.*

TAYLOR, DAVIDSON. Radio director and executive, he was connected with the Columbia Broadcasting System from 1933 to 1949 as director of programs, director of public affairs and vice president. He is now with the Voice of America.

THORNDIKE, DAME SYBIL. British actress famed for her Shakespearean and Shavian roles, she has also appeared in many films and been a producer-manager.

URBAN, JOSEPH. Theatre architect and scene designer, he came to New York from Vienna before World War I and introduced and devised many new techniques of stage presentation. Through the 1920's he designed lavish productions for the *Ziegfeld Follies* and was architect for the Ziegfeld Theatre.

VAN DRUTEN, JOHN. British-born dramatist, now a resident of California, he is perhaps best known for *Young Woodley, The Damask Cheek* and *The Voice of the Turtle.*

WEBSTER, MARGARET. Descendant of a famous English theatrical family, daughter of Dame May Whitty, she was a star actress before she came to the United States where she is best known as director of Shakespearean plays.

WADE, ROBERT J. Director of the technical facilities division of NBC Television, he has solved many of the scene designing problems of television, has designed sets of distinction and written extensively about television.

WILDER, THORNTON. Outstanding man of letters, he did drama criticism for *Theatre Arts* early in his career, abandoned it to write novels and, later, plays. His novel, *The Bridge of San Luis Rey,* won the Pulitzer Prize, while two of his plays, *Our Town* and *The Skin of Our Teeth,* received drama Pulitzer Prizes.

YOUNG, STARK. Originally a professor of literature at Amherst, he came to Broadway as dramatist, director and critic. He was for many years (1921-40) associate editor of *Theatre Arts,* and he was drama critic for the New York *Times* (1924-25) and the *New Republic* (1925-47). Author of many books on the theatre and aesthetics, he wrote several novels, including *So Red the Rose,* and is also a painter of distinction.

SELECTIVE INDEX